2014

CHILDREN'S WRITER'S & ILLUSTRATOR'S MARKET

Chuck Sambuchino, Editor

GLEN COVE PUBLIC LIBRARY
4 GLEN COVE AVENUE
GLEN COVE, NEW YORK 11542-2885

WD
WRITER'S DIGEST
BOOKS
WritersDigest.com
Cincinnati, Ohio

3 1571 00316 2750

2014 CHILDREN'S WRITER'S & ILLUSTRATOR'S MARKET. Copyright © 2013 by F+W Media Inc. Published by Writer's Digest Books, an imprint of F+W Media Inc., 10151 Carver Road, Suite 200, Cincinnati, Ohio 45242. Printed and bound in the United States of America. All rights reserved. No part of this book may be reproduced in any form or by any electronic or mechanical means including information storage and retrieval systems without permission in writing from the publisher, except by a reviewer, who may quote brief passages in a review.

Publisher & Editorial Director, Writing Community: Phil Sexton

Writer's Market website: www.writersmarket.com
Writer's Digest website: www.writersdigest.com
Writer's Digest Bookstore: www.writersdigestshop.com
Guide to Literary Agents Blog: www.guidetoliteraryagents.com/blog

Distributed in Canada by Fraser Direct
100 Armstrong Avenue
Georgetown, Ontario, Canada L7G 5S4
Tel: (905) 877-4411

Distributed in the U.K. and Europe by F+W Media International
Brunel House, Newton Abbot, Devon, TQ12 4PU, England
Tel: (+44) 1626-323200, Fax: (+44) 1626-323319
E-mail: postmaster@davidandcharles.co.uk

Distributed in Australia by Capricorn Link
P.O. Box 704, Windsor, NSW 2756 Australia
Tel: (02) 4577-3555

ISSN: 0897-9790
ISBN-13: 978-1-59963-726-6

Attention Booksellers: This is an annual directory of F+W Media, Inc. Return deadline for this edition is December 31, 2014.

Edited by: Chuck Sambuchino
Cover designed by: Claudean Wheeler
Interior designed by: Geoff Raker
Production coordinated by: Greg Nock

CONTENTS

RESOURCES

MARKETS AND MORE

INDEXES

FROM
THE
EDITOR

PHOTO: Al Parrish

Over the years, the *Children's Writer's & Illustrator's Market* has featured interviews with some amazingly prolific authors. We've showcased huge names like Meg Cabot, Tamora Pierce, and more. But who bigger to anchor this year's author features than the kidlit horror master himself: R.L. Stine. When I got confirmation we would be including him in this edition, I got chills. (You thought I would say *goosebumps*, didn't you?)

Beyond the interviews, you need to check out the updated market listings in this edition of *CWIM*. We spent time beefing up the art reps section, and made sure we included several new book publisher imprints, as well—so you can have more markets to target. And just like last year, we've spotlighted new/newer literary agents who are actively building their roster of clients. These reps are smart targets for unpublished writers seeking agents. So delve into the markets at any time so you can start highlighting text and dog-earing pages!

Something else giving me chills besides the Stine interview is a recent personal success in the children's book realm. A few weeks ago, I sent out queries for a picture book I'd co-written and recently finished. Within days, I got two offers of representation from agents (*wow*). It just goes to show that if you always keep moving forward and continue writing, good things will indeed happen.

Please stay in touch with me at guidetoliteraryagents.com/blog and on Twitter (@chucksambuchino). I love hearing feedback and success stories. Until we next meet, good luck on your writing journey!

Chuck Sambuchino
literaryagent@fwmedia.com; chucksambuchino.com
Editor, *Guide to Literary Agents / Children's Writer's & Illustrator's Market*
Author, *How to Survive a Garden Gnome Attack* (2010); *Red Dog / Blue Dog* (2012); *Create Your Writer Platform* (2012)

HOW TO USE
CWIM

As a writer, illustrator or photographer first picking up *Children's Writer's & Illustrator's Market*, you may not know quite how to start using the book. Your impulse may be to flip through the book and quickly make a mailing list, then submit to everyone in hopes that someone will take interest in your work. Well, there's more to it. Finding the right market takes time and research. The more you know about a market that interests you, the better chance you have of getting work accepted. We've made your job a little easier by putting a wealth of information at your fingertips. Besides providing listings, this directory includes a number of tools to help you determine which markets are the best ones for your work. By using these tools, as well as researching on your own, you raise your odds of being published.

USING THE INDEXES

This book lists hundreds of potential buyers of freelance material. To learn which companies want the type of material you're interested in submitting, start with the indexes.

Editor and Agent Names Index

This index lists book and magazine editors and art directors as well as agents and art reps, indicating the companies they work for. Use this index to find company and contact information for individual publishing professionals.

Age-Level Index

Age groups are broken down into these categories in the Age-Level Index:

- **PICTURE BOOKS OR PICTURE-ORIENTED MATERIAL** are written and illustrated for preschoolers to 8-year-olds.

- **YOUNG READERS** are for 5- to 8-year-olds.
- **MIDDLE READERS** are for 9- to 11-year-olds.
- **YOUNG ADULT** is for ages 12 and up.

Age breakdowns may vary slightly from publisher to publisher, but using them as general guidelines will help you target appropriate markets. For example, if you've written an article about trends in teen fashion, check the Magazines Age-Level Index under the Young Adult subheading. Using this list, you'll quickly find the listings for young adult magazines.

Subject Index

But let's narrow the search further. Take your list of young adult magazines, turn to the Subject Index, and find the Fashion subheading. Then highlight the names that appear on both lists (Young Adult and Fashion). Now you have a smaller list of all the magazines that would be interested in your teen fashion article. Read through those listings and decide which ones sound best for your work.

Illustrators and photographers can use the Subject Index as well. If you specialize in painting animals, for instance, consider sending samples to book and magazine publishers listed under Animals and, perhaps, Nature/Environment. Because illustrators can simply send general examples of their style to art directors to keep on file, the indexes may be more helpful to artists sending manuscript/illustration packages who need to search for a specific subject. Always read the listings for the potential markets to see the type of work art directors prefer and what type of samples they'll keep on file, and obtain art or photo guidelines if they're available online.

Photography Index

In this index, you'll find lists of book and magazine publishers that buy photos from freelancers. Refer to the list and read the listings for companies' specific photography needs. Obtain photo guidelines if they're offered online.

USING THE LISTINGS

Many listings begin with symbols. Refer to the pull-out bookmark (shown later in this article).

Many listings indicate whether submission guidelines are indeed available. If a publisher you're interested in offers guidelines, get them and read them. The same is true with catalogs. Sending for and reading catalogs or browsing them online gives you a better idea of whether your work would fit in with the books a publisher produces. (You should also look at a few of the books in the catalog at a library or bookstore to get a feel for the publisher's material.)

⊕ market new to this edition

Ⓐ market accepts agented submissions only

◔ award-winning market

◔ Canadian market

◔ market located outside of the U.S. and Canada

◔ online opportunity

◔ comment from the editor of *Children's Writer's & Illustrator's Market*

◔ publisher producing educational material

◔ book packager/producer

ms, mss manuscript(s)

SCBWI Society of Children's Book Writers and Illustrators

SASE self-addressed, stamped envelope

IRC International Reply Coupon, for use in countries other than your own

b&w black & white (photo)

(For definitions of unfamiliar words and expressions relating to writing, illustration and publishing, see the Glossary.)

Especially for artists & photographers

Along with information for writers, listings provide information for illustrators and photographers. Illustrators will find numerous markets that maintain files of samples for possible future assignments. If you're both a writer and an illustrator, look for markets that accept manuscript/illustration packages and read the information offered under the **Illustration** subhead within the listings.

If you're a photographer, after consulting the Photography Index, read the information under the **Photography** subhead within listings to see what format buyers prefer. For example, some want the highest resolution .jpg available of an image. Note the type of photos a buyer wants to purchase and the procedures for submitting. It's not uncommon for a market to want a résumé and promotional literature, as well as sample URLS linking to previous work. Listings also note whether model releases and/or captions are required.

⊕ MERIT PRESS

A DIVISION OF ADAMS MEDIA (PART OF F+W MEDIA), 57 LITTLEFIELD ST, AVON, MA 02322. (508)427-7100. **E-MAIL:** MERITPRESS@FWMEDIA.COM. **WEBSITE:** WWW.AD AMSMEDIA.COM/MERIT-PRESS-BOOKS. **CONTACT:** JACQUELYN MITCHARD, EDITOR-IN-CHIEF.

Focuses on contemporary YA, usually based in reality.

FICTION "Natural is good; a little bit of supernatural (as in, perhaps foreseeing the future) is okay, too. Normal is great (at least until something happens) but not paranormal. What we are not seeking right now is tryphids, blood drinkers, flesh eaters and even yetis (much though we love them)."

HOW TO CONTACT "We do accept direct submissions as well as submissions from literary agents. We don't accept submissions in hard copy. Send full or partial manuscripts and queries to meritpress@fwmedia.com."

TIPS "I want to publish the next *Carrie, The Book Thief, National Velvet, Tuck Everlasting, Mr. and Mrs. Bo Jo Jones,* and *The Outsiders.* These will be the classics for a new generation, and they're being written right now. Since suspense (noir or pastel, comic or macabre) is my love, I hope I have a sense for finding those stories. As it turns out, a big part of my vocation, at this point in my career, is the desire to discover and nurture great new writers, and to put great books in the hands of great readers."

ADDRESSES AND WEBSITES

SPECIFIC CONTACT NAMES

INFO ON WHAT A PUBLISHER HANDLES

SUBMISSION TIPS

QUICK TIPS FOR WRITERS & ILLUSTRATORS

//

If you're new to the world of children's publishing, buying *Children's Writer's & Illustrator's Market* may have been one of the first steps in your journey to publication. What follows is a list of suggestions and resources that can help make that journey a smooth and swift one:

1. MAKE THE MOST OF *CHILDREN'S WRITER'S & ILLUSTRATOR'S MARKET*. Be sure to read "How to Use This Book" for tips on reading the listings and using the indexes. Also be sure to take advantage of the articles and interviews in the book. The insights of the authors, illustrators, editors and agents we've interviewed will inform and inspire you.

2. JOIN THE SOCIETY OF CHILDREN'S BOOK WRITERS AND ILLUSTRATORS. SCBWI, more than 22,000 members strong, is an organization for both beginners and professionals interested in writing and illustrating for children. It offers members a slew of information and support through publications, a website, and a host of Regional Advisors overseeing chapters in almost every state in the U.S. and a growing number of locations around the globe (including France, Canada, Japan and Australia). SCBWI puts on a number of conferences, workshops, and events on the regional and national levels (many listed in the Conferences & Workshops section of this book). For more information, contact SCBWI, 8271 Beverly Blvd., Los Angeles CA 90048, (323)782-1010, or visit their website: scbwi.org.

3. READ NEWSLETTERS. Newsletters, such as *Children's Book Insider*, *Children's Writer* and the *SCBWI Bulletin*, offer updates and new information about publishers on a timely basis and are relatively inexpensive. Many local chapters of SCBWI offer regional newsletters as well. (See "Helpful Books & Publications later in this book for contact information on the newsletters listed above and others.) For information on regional SCBWI newsletters, visit scbwi.org.

4. READ TRADE AND REVIEW PUBLICATIONS. Magazines like *Publishers Weekly* (which offers two special issues each year devoted to children's publishing and is available on newsstands as well as through a digital subscription), *The Horn Book* and *Book-links* offer news, articles, reviews of newly published titles and ads featuring upcoming and current releases. Referring to them will help you get a feel for what's happening in children's publishing.

5. READ GUIDELINES. Most publishers and magazines offer writer's and artist's guidelines that provide detailed information on needs and submission requirements, and some magazines offer theme lists for upcoming issues. Many publishers and magazines state the availability of guidelines within their listings. Send a self-addressed, stamped envelope (SASE) to publishers who offer guidelines through the mail. You'll often find submission information on publishers' and magazines' websites.

6. LOOK AT PUBLISHERS' CATALOGS. Perusing publishers' catalogs can give you a feel for their line of books and help you decide where your work might fit in. If catalogs are available (often stated within listings), send for them with a SASE. Visit publishers' websites, which often contain their full catalogs. You can also ask librarians to look at catalogs they have on hand. You can even search Amazon.com by publisher and year. (Click on "book search" then "publisher, date" and plug in, for example, "Lee & Low" under "publisher" and "2013" under year. You'll get a list of Lee & Low titles published in 2013, which you can peruse.)

7. VISIT BOOKSTORES. It's not only informative to spend time in bookstores—it's fun, too! Frequently visit the children's section of your local bookstore (whether a chain or an independent) to see the latest from a variety of publishers and the most current issues of children's magazines. Look for books in the genre you're writing or with illustrations similar in style to yours, and spend some time studying them. It's also wise to get to know your local booksellers; they can tell you what's new in the store and provide insight into what kids and adults are buying.

8. READ, READ, READ! While you're at that bookstore, pick up a few things, or keep a list of the books that interest you and check them out of your library. Read and study the latest releases, the award winners and the classics. You'll learn from other writers, get ideas and get a feel for what's being published. Think about what works and doesn't work in a story. Pay attention to how plots are constructed and how characters are developed, or the rhythm and pacing of picture book text. It's certainly enjoyable research!

9. TAKE ADVANTAGE OF INTERNET RESOURCES. There are innumerable sources of information available online about writing for children (and anything else you could possibly think of). It's also a great resource for getting (and staying) in touch with other writers and illustrators through listservs, blogs, social networking sites and e-mail, and it can serve as a vehicle for self-promotion. (Visit some authors' and illustrators' sites for ideas. See "Useful Online Resources" in this book for a list of websites.)

10. CONSIDER ATTENDING A CONFERENCE. If time and finances allow, attending a conference is a great way to meet peers and network with professionals in the field of children's publishing. As mentioned earlier, SCBWI offers conferences in various locations year round. (See scbwi.org and click on "Events" for a full conference calendar.) General writers' conferences often offer specialized sessions just for those interested in children's writing. Many conferences offer optional manuscript and portfolio critiques as well, giving you a chance for feedback from seasoned professionals. See the Conferences & Awards section of this book for information on conferences. The section features a Conferences & Workshops Calendar to help you plan your travel.

11. NETWORK, NETWORK, NETWORK! Don't work in a vacuum. You can meet other writers and illustrators through a number of the things listed earlier—SCBWI, conferences, online. Attend local meetings for writers and illustrators whenever you can. Befriend other writers in your area (SCBWI offers members a roster broken down by state)—share guidelines, share subscriptions, be conference buddies and roommates, join a critique group or writing group, exchange information and offer support. Get online—sign on to listservs, post on message boards and blogs, visit social networking sites and chatrooms. Exchange addresses, phone numbers and e-mail addresses with writers or illustrators you meet at events. And at conferences, don't be afraid to talk to people, ask strangers to join you for lunch, approach speakers and introduce yourself, or chat in elevators and hallways.

12. PERFECT YOUR CRAFT AND DON'T SUBMIT UNTIL YOUR WORK IS ITS BEST. It's often been said that a writer should try to write every day. Great manuscripts don't happen overnight; there's time, research and revision involved. As you visit bookstores and study what others have written and illustrated, really step back and look at your own work and ask yourself—honestly—*How does my work measure up? Is it ready for editors or art directors to see?* If it's not, keep working. Join a critique group or get a professional manuscript or portfolio critique.

13. BE PATIENT, LEARN FROM REJECTION, AND DON'T GIVE UP! Thousands of manuscripts land on editors' desks; thousands of illustration samples line art directors' file drawers. There are so many factors that come into play when evaluating submissions. Keep in mind that you might not hear back from publishers promptly. Persistence and patience are important qualities in writers and illustrators working toward publication. Keep at it—it will come. It can take a while, but when you get that first book contract or first assignment, you'll know it was worth the wait. (For proof, read the "First Books" article later in this book!)

BEFORE YOUR FIRST SALE

If you're just beginning to pursue your career as a children's book writer or illustrator, it's important to learn the proper procedures, formats and protocol for the publishing industry. This article outlines the basics you need to know before you submit your work to a market.

FINDING THE BEST MARKETS FOR YOUR WORK

Researching publishers thoroughly is a basic element of submitting your work successfully. Editors and art directors hate to receive inappropriate submissions; handling them wastes a lot of their time, not to mention your time and money, and they are the main reason some publishers have chosen not to accept material over the transom. By randomly sending out material without knowing a company's needs, you're sure to meet with rejection.

If you're interested in submitting to a particular magazine, see if it's available in your local library or bookstore, or read past articles online. For a book publisher, obtain a book catalog and check a library or bookstore for titles produced by that publisher. Most publishers and magazines have websites that include catalogs or sample articles (websites are given within the listings). Studying such materials carefully will better acquaint you with a publisher's or magazine's writing, illustration and photography styles and formats.

Many of the book publishers and magazines listed in this book offer some sort of writer's, artist's or photographer's guidelines for a self-addressed, stamped envelope (SASE). Guidelines are also almost always found on publishers' websites. It's important to read and study guidelines before submitting work. You'll get a better understanding of what a particular publisher wants. You may even decide, after reading the submission guidelines, that your work isn't right for a company you considered.

SUBMITTING YOUR WORK

Throughout the listings, you'll read requests for particular elements to include when contacting markets. Here are explanations of some of these important submission components.

Queries, cover letters & proposals

A query is a no-more-than-one-page, well-written letter meant to arouse an editor's interest in your work. Query letters briefly outline the work you're proposing and include facts, anecdotes, interviews or other pertinent information that give the editor a feel for the manuscript's premise—enticing her to want to know more. End your letter with a straightforward request to submit the work, and include information on its approximate length, date it could be completed, and whether accompanying photos or artwork are available.

In a query letter, think about presenting your book as a publisher's catalog would present it. Read through a good catalog and examine how the publishers give enticing summaries of their books in a spare amount of words. It's also important that query letters give editors a taste of your writing style. For good advice and samples of queries, cover letters and other correspondence, consult the article "Crafting a Query" in this book, as well as *Formatting & Submitting Your Manuscript, 3rd Ed.* and *The Writer's Digest Guide to Query Letters* (both Writer's Digest Books).

- **QUERY LETTERS FOR NONFICTION.** Queries are usually required when submitting nonfiction material to a publisher. The goal of a nonfiction query is to convince the editor your idea is perfect for her readership and that you're qualified to do the job. Note any previous writing experience and include published samples to prove your credentials, especially samples related to the subject matter you're querying about.
- **QUERY LETTERS FOR FICTION.** For a fiction query, explain the story's plot, main characters, conflict and resolution. Just as in nonfiction queries, make the editor eager to see more.
- **COVER LETTERS FOR WRITERS.** Some editors prefer to review complete manuscripts, especially for picture books or fiction. In such cases, the cover letter (which should be no longer than one page) serves as your introduction, establishes your credentials as a writer, and gives the editor an overview of the manuscript. If the editor asked for the manuscript because of a query, note this in your cover letter.
- **COVER LETTERS FOR ILLUSTRATORS AND PHOTOGRAPHERS.** For an illustrator or photographer, the cover letter serves as an introduction to the art director and establishes professional credentials when submitting samples. Explain what services you can provide as well as what type of follow-up contact you plan to make, if any. Be sure to include the URL of your online portfolio if you have one.

- **RÉSUMÉS.** Often writers, illustrators and photographers are asked to submit résumés with cover letters and samples. They can be created in a variety of formats, from a single-page listing information to color brochures featuring your work. Keep your résumé brief, and focus on your achievements, including your clients and the work you've done for them, as well as your educational background and any awards you've received. Do not use the same résumé you'd use for a typical job application.
- **BOOK PROPOSALS.** Throughout the listings in the Book Publishers section, publishers refer to submitting a synopsis, outline and sample chapters. Depending on an editor's preference, some or all of these components, along with a cover letter, make up a book proposal.

A *synopsis* summarizes the book, covering the basic plot (including the ending). It should be easy to read and flow well.

An *outline* covers your book chapter by chapter and provides highlights of each. If you're developing an outline for fiction, include major characters, plots and subplots, and book length. Requesting an outline is uncommon, and the word is somewhat interchangeable with "synopsis."

Sample chapters give a more comprehensive idea of your writing skill. Some editors may request the first two or three chapters to determine if they're interested in seeing the whole book. Some may request a set number of pages.

Manuscript formats

When submitting a complete manuscript, follow some basic guidelines. In the upper-left corner of your title page, type your legal name (not pseudonym), address and phone number. In the upper-right corner, type the approximate word count. All material in the upper corners should be single spaced. Then type the title (centered) almost halfway down that page, the word "by" two spaces under that, and your name or pseudonym two spaces under "by."

The first page should also include the title (centered) one-third of the way down. Two spaces under that, type "by" and your name or pseudonym. To begin the body of your manuscript, drop down two double spaces and indent five spaces for each new paragraph. There should be one-inch margins around all sides of a full typewritten page. (Manuscripts with wide margins are more readable and easier to edit.)

Set your computer to double-space the manuscript body. From page two to the end of the manuscript, include your last name followed by a comma and the title (or key words of the title) in the upper-left corner. The page number should go in the top right corner. Drop down two double spaces to begin the body of each page. If you're submitting a novel, type each chapter title one-third of the way down the page. For more information on manuscript formats, read *Formatting & Submitting Your Manuscript, 3rd Ed.* (Writer's Digest Books).

Picture book formats

The majority of editors prefer to see complete manuscripts for picture books. When typing the text of a picture book, don't indicate page breaks and don't type each page of text on a new sheet of paper. And unless you are an illustrator, don't worry about supplying art. Editors will find their own illustrators for picture books. Most of the time, a writer and an illustrator who work on the same book never meet or interact. The editor acts as a go-between and works with the writer and illustrator throughout the publishing process. *How to Write and Sell Children's Picture Books*, by Jean E. Karl (Writer's Digest Books), offers advice on preparing text and marketing your work.

If you're an illustrator who has written your own book, consider creating a dummy or storyboard containing both art and text, and then submit it along with your complete manuscript and sample pieces of final art (hi-res PDFs or .jpgs—never originals). Publishers interested in picture books specify in their listings what should be submitted. For tips on creating a dummy, refer to *How to Write and Illustrate Children's Books and Get Them Published*, edited by Treld Pelkey Bicknell and Felicity Trotman (North Light Books), or Frieda Gates' book, *How to Write, Illustrate, and Design Children's Books* (Lloyd-Simone Publishing Company).

Writers may also want to learn the art of dummy-making to help them through their writing process with things like pacing, rhythm and length. For a great explanation and helpful hints, see *You Can Write Children's Books*, by Tracey E. Dils (Writer's Digest Books).

Mailing submissions

Your main concern when packaging material is to be sure it arrives undamaged. If your manuscript is fewer than six pages, simply fold it in thirds and send it in a #10 (business-size) envelope. For a SASE, either fold another #10 envelope in thirds or insert a #9 (reply) envelope, which fits in a #10 neatly without folding.

Another option is folding your manuscript in half in a 6x9 envelope, with a #9 or #10 SASE enclosed. For larger manuscripts, use a 9x12 envelope both for mailing the submission and as a SASE (which can be folded in half). Book manuscripts require sturdy packaging for mailing. Include a self-addressed mailing label and return postage. If asked to send artwork and photographs, remember they require a bit more care in packaging to guarantee they arrive in good condition. Sandwich illustrations and photos between heavy cardboard that is slightly larger than the work. The cardboard can be secured by rubber bands or with tape. If you tape the cardboard together, check that the artwork doesn't stick to the tape. Be sure your name and address appear on the back of each piece of art or each photo in case the material becomes separated. For the packaging, use either a manila envelope, a foam-padded envelope, or a mailer lined with plastic air bubbles. Bind nonjoined edges with reinforced mailing tape and affix a typed mailing label or clearly write your address.

Mailing material first class ensures quick delivery. Also, first-class mail is forwarded for one year if the addressee has moved, and it can be returned if undeliverable. If you're concerned about your original material safely reaching its destination, consider other mailing options such as UPS. No matter which way you send material, never send it where it requires a signature. Agents and editors are too busy to sign for packages.

Remember, companies outside your own country can't use your country's postage when returning a manuscript to you. When mailing a submission to another country, include a self-addressed envelope and International Reply Coupons, or IRCs. (You'll see this term in many listings in the Canadian & International Book Publishers section.) Your postmaster can tell you, based on a package's weight, the correct number of IRCs to include to ensure its return. If it's not necessary for an editor to return your work (such as with photocopies), don't include return postage.

Unless requested, it's never a good idea to use a company's fax number to send manuscript submissions. This can disrupt a company's internal business. Study the listings for specifics and visit publishers' and market websites for more information.

E-Mailing submissions

Most correspondence with editors today is handled over e-mail. This type of communication is usually preferred by publishing professionals because it is easier to deal with as well as free. When sending an e-mailed submission, make sure to follow submission guidelines. Double-check the recipient's e-mail address. Make sure your subject line has the proper wording, if specific wording was asked for. Keep your introduction letter short and sweet. Also, editors and agents usually do not like opening unsolicited attachments, which makes for an awkward situation for illustrators who want to attach .jpgs. One easy way around this is to post some sample illustrations on your website. That way, you can simply paste URL hyperlinks to your work. Editors can click through to look over your illustration samples, and there is no way your submission will get accidentally deleted because of attachments. That said, if editors are asking for illustration samples, they are most likely used to receiving unsolicited attachments.

Keeping submission records

It's important to keep track of the material you submit. When recording each submission, include the date it was sent, the business and contact name, and any enclosures (such as samples of writing, artwork or photography). You can create a record-keeping system of your own or look for record-keeping software in your area computer store.

Keep copies of articles or manuscripts you send together with related correspondence to make follow-up easier. When you sell rights to a manuscript, artwork or photos, you can "close" your file on a particular submission by noting the date the material was accepted, what rights were purchased, the publication date and payment.

Often writers, illustrators and photographers fail to follow up on overdue responses. If you don't hear from a publisher within their stated response time, wait another month or so and follow up with an e-mail asking about the status of your submission. Include the title or description, date sent and a SASE (if applicable) for response. Ask the contact person when she anticipates making a decision. You may refresh the memory of a buyer who temporarily forgot about your submission. At the very least, you'll receive a definite "no" and free yourself to send the material to another publisher.

Simultaneous submissions

Writers and illustrators are encouraged to simultaneously submit—sending the same material to several markets at the same time. Almost all markets are open to this type of communication; those that do not take simultaneous submissions will directly say so in their submission guidelines.

It's especially important to keep track of simultaneous submissions, so if you get an offer on a manuscript sent to more than one publisher, you can instruct other publishers to withdraw your work from consideration. (Or, you can always use the initial offer as a way to ignite interest from other agents and editors. It's very possible to procure multiple offers on your book using this technique.)

AGENTS & ART REPS

Most children's writers, illustrators and photographers, especially those just beginning, are confused about whether to enlist the services of an agent or representative. The decision is strictly one that each writer, illustrator or photographer must make for herself. Some are confident with their own negotiation skills and believe acquiring an agent or rep is not in their best interest. Others feel uncomfortable in the business arena or are not willing to sacrifice valuable creative time for marketing.

About half of children's publishers accept unagented work, so it's possible to break into children's publishing without an agent. Writers targeting magazine markets don't need the services of an agent. In fact, it's practically impossible to find an agent interested in marketing articles and short stories—there simply isn't enough financial incentive.

One benefit of having an agent, though, is it may speed up the process of getting your work reviewed, especially by publishers who don't accept unagented submissions. If an agent has a good reputation and submits your manuscript to an editor, that manuscript will likely bypass the first-read stage (which is generally done by editorial assistants and junior editors) and end up on the editor's desk sooner.

When agreeing to have a reputable agent represent you, remember that she should be familiar with the needs of the current market and evaluate your manuscript/artwork/photos accordingly. She should also determine the quality of your piece and whether it is saleable. When your manuscript sells, your agent should negotiate a favorable contract and clear up any questions you have about payments.

Keep in mind that however reputable the agent or rep is, she has limitations.

Representation does not guarantee sale of your work. It just means an agent or rep sees potential in your writing, art or photos. Though an agent or rep may offer criticism or advice on how to improve your work, she cannot make you a better writer, artist or photographer.

Literary agents typically charge a 15 percent commission from the sale of writing; art and photo representatives usually charge a 25–30 percent commission. Such fees are taken from advances and royalty earnings. If your agent sells foreign rights or film rights to your work, she will deduct a higher percentage because she will most likely be dealing with an overseas agent with whom she must split the fee.

Be advised that not every agent is open to representing a writer, artist or photographer who lacks an established track record. Just as when approaching a publisher, the manuscript, artwork or photos, and query or cover letter you submit to a potential agent must be attractive and professional looking. Your first impression must be as an organized, articulate person. For listings of agents and reps, turn to the Agents & Art Reps section.

For additional listings of art reps, consult *Artist's & Graphic Designer's Market*; for photo reps, see *Photographer's Market*; for more information and additional listings of literary agents, see *Guide to Literary Agents* (all Writer's Digest Books).

RUNNING YOUR BUSINESS

The basics for writers & illustrators.

A career in children's publishing involves more than just writing skills or artistic talent. Successful authors and illustrators must be able to hold their own in negotiations, keep records, understand contract language, grasp copyright law, pay taxes and take care of a number of other business concerns. Although agents and reps, accountants and lawyers, and writers' organizations offer help in sorting out such business issues, it's wise to have a basic understanding of them going in. This article offers just that—basic information. For a more in-depth look at the subjects covered here, check your library or bookstore for books and magazines to help you. We also tell you how to get information on issues like taxes and copyright from the federal government.

CONTRACTS & NEGOTIATION

Before you see your work in print or begin working with an editor or art director on a project, there is negotiation. And whether negotiating a book contract, a magazine article assignment, or an illustration or photo assignment, there are a few things to keep in mind. First, if you find any clauses vague or confusing in a contract, get legal advice. The time and money invested in counseling up front could protect you from problems later. If you have an agent or rep, she will review any contract.

A contract is an agreement between two or more parties that specifies the fees to be paid, services rendered, deadlines, rights purchased and, for artists and photographers, whether original work is returned. Most companies have standard contracts for writers, illustrators and photographers. The specifics (such as royalty rates, advances, delivery dates, etc.) are typed in after negotiations.

Though it's OK to conduct negotiations over the phone or via e-mail, get a written contract once both parties have agreed on terms. Never depend on oral stipulations; written contracts protect both parties from misunderstandings. Watch for clauses that may not be in your best interest, such as "work-for-hire." When you do work-for-hire, you give up all rights to your creations.

When negotiating a book deal, find out whether your contract contains an option clause. This clause requires the author to give the publisher a first look at her next work before offering it to other publishers. Though it's editorial etiquette to give the publisher the first chance at publishing your next work, be wary of statements in the contract that could trap you. Don't allow the publisher to consider the next project for more than 30 days and be specific about what type of work should actually be considered "next work." (For example, if the book under contract is a young adult novel, specify that the publisher will receive an exclusive look at *only* your next young adult novel.)

Book publishers' payment methods

Book publishers pay authors and artists in royalties, a percentage of either the wholesale or retail price of each book sold. From large publishing houses, the author usually receives an advance issued against future royalties before the book is published.

After your book has sold enough copies to earn back your advance, you'll start to get royalty checks. Some publishers hold a reserve against returns, which means a percentage of royalties is held back in case books are returned from bookstores. If you have a reserve clause in your contract, find out the exact percentage of total sales that will be withheld and the time period the publisher will hold this money. You should be reimbursed this amount after a reasonable time period, such as a year. Royalty percentages vary with each publisher, but there are standard ranges.

Book publishers' rates

First-time picture book authors can expect advances of $500–20,000; first-time picture book illustrators' advances range from $2,000–15,000. Rates go up for subsequent books. Experienced authors can expect higher advances. Royalties for picture books are generally about five percent (split between the author and illustrator) but can go as high as 10 percent. Those who both write and illustrate a book, of course, receive the full royalty. Advances for novels can fetch advances of $1,000–100,000 and 10 percent royalties.

As you might expect, advance and royalty figures vary from house to house and are affected by the time of year, the state of the economy and other factors. Some smaller houses may not even pay royalties, just flat fees. Educational houses may not offer advances or may offer smaller amounts. Religious publishers tend to offer smaller advances than trade publishers. First-time writers and illustrators generally start on the low end of the scale, while established and high-profile writers are paid more. For more information, SCBWI members can request or download SCBWI publication "Answer to Some Questions About Contracts." (Visit scbwi.org.)

Pay rates for magazines

For writers, fee structures for magazines are based on a per-word rate or range for a specific article length. Artists and photographers have a few more variables to contend with before contracting their services.

Payment for illustrations and photos can be set by such factors as whether the piece(s) will be black and white or four-color, how many are to be purchased, where the work appears (cover or inside), circulation, and the artist's or photographer's prior experience.

Remaindering

When a book goes out of print, a publisher will sell any existing copies to a wholesaler who, in turn, sells the copies to stores at a discount. When the books are "remaindered" to a wholesaler, they are usually sold at a price just above the cost of printing. When negotiating a contract with a publisher, you may want to discuss the possibility of purchasing the remaindered copies before they are sold to a wholesaler, then you can market the copies you purchased and still make a profit.

KNOW YOUR RIGHTS

A copyright is a form of protection provided to creators of original works, published or unpublished. In general, copyright protection ensures the writer, illustrator or photographer the power to decide how her work is used and allows her to receive payment for each use.

Essentially, copyright also encourages the creation of new works by guaranteeing the creator power to sell rights to the work in the marketplace. The copyright holder can print, reprint or copy her work; sell or distribute copies of her work; post her work online; or prepare derivative works such as plays, collages or recordings. The Copyright Law is designed to protect work (created on or after January 1, 1978) for her lifetime plus 70 years. If you collaborate with someone else on a written or artistic project, the copyright will last for the lifetime of the last survivor plus 70 years. The creators' heirs may hold a copyright for an additional 70 years. After that, the work becomes public domain. Works created anonymously or under a pseudonym are protected for 120 years, or 95 years after publication. Under work-for-hire agreements, you relinquish your copyright to your employer.

Copyright notice & registration

Although it's not necessary to include a copyright notice on unregistered work, if you don't feel your work is safe without the notice (especially if posting work online), it is your right to include one. Including a copyright notice—(©) (year of work, your name)—should help safeguard against plagiarism.

Registration is a legal formality intended to make copyright public record, and it can help you win more money in a court case. By registering work within three months of publication or before an infringement occurs, you are eligible to collect statutory damages and attorney's fees. If you register later than three months after publication, you will qualify only for actual damages and profits.

Ideas and concepts are not copyrightable, only expressions of those ideas and concepts can be protected. A character type or basic plot outline, for example, is not subject to a copyright infringement lawsuit. Also, titles, names, short phrases or slogans, and lists of contents are not subject to copyright protection, though titles and names may be protected through the Trademark Office.

You can register a group of articles, illustrations or photos if it meets these criteria:

- the group is assembled in order, such as in a notebook
- the works bear a single title, such as "Works by (your name)"
- it is the work of one writer, artist or photographer
- the material is the subject of a single claim to copyright

It's a publisher's responsibility to register your book for copyright. If you've previously registered the same material, you must inform your editor and supply the previous copyright information; otherwise, the publisher can't register the book in its published form.

For more information about the proper way to register works and to order the correct forms, contact the U.S. Copyright Office, (202)707-3000. For information about how to use the copyright forms, request a copy of Circular 1 on Copyright Basics. All of the forms and circulars are free. Send the completed registration form along with the stated fee and a copy of the work to the Copyright Office.

For specific answers to questions about copyright (but not legal advice), call the Copyright Public Information Office at (202)707-3000 weekdays between 8:30 a.m. and 5 p.m. EST. Forms can also be downloaded from the Library of Congress website: copyright. gov. The site also includes a list of frequently asked questions, tips on filling out forms, general copyright information, and links to other sites related to copyright issues.

The rights publishers buy

The copyright law specifies that a writer, illustrator or photographer generally sells one-time rights to her work unless she and the buyer agree otherwise in writing. Many publications will want more exclusive rights to your work than just one-time usage; some will even require you to sell all rights. Be sure you are monetarily compensated for the additional rights you relinquish. If you must give up all rights to a work, carefully consider the price you're being offered to determine whether you'll be compensated for the loss of other potential sales.

Writers who only give up limited rights to their work can then sell reprint rights to other publications, foreign rights to international publications, or even movie rights, should the opportunity arise. Artists and photographers can sell their work to other markets such as paper product companies who may use an image on a calendar, greeting card or mug. Illustrators and photographers may even sell original work after it has been published. There are a number of galleries throughout the U.S. that display and sell the original work of children's illustrators.

Rights acquired through the sale of a book manuscript are explained in each publisher's contract. Take time to read relevant clauses to be sure you understand what rights each contract is specifying before signing. Be sure your contract contains a clause allowing all rights to revert back to you in the event the publisher goes out of business. (You may even want to have the contract reviewed by an agent or an attorney specializing in publishing law.)

The following are the rights you'll most often sell to publishers, periodicals and producers in the marketplace:

FIRST RIGHTS. The buyer purchases the rights to use the work for the first time in any medium. All other rights remain with the creator. When material is excerpted in this way (from a soon-to-be-published book in this manner) for use in a newspaper or periodical, first serial rights are also purchased.

ONE-TIME RIGHTS. The buyer has no guarantee that she is the first to use a piece. One-time permission to run written work, illustrations or photos is acquired, and then the rights revert back to the creator.

FIRST NORTH AMERICAN SERIAL RIGHTS. This is similar to first rights, except that companies who distribute both in the U.S. and Canada will stipulate these rights to ensure that another North American company won't come out with simultaneous usage of the same work.

SECOND SERIAL (REPRINT) RIGHTS. In this case, newspapers and magazines are granted the right to reproduce a work that has already appeared in another publication. These rights are also purchased by a newspaper or magazine editor who wants to publish part of a book after the book has been published. The proceeds from reprint rights for a book are often split evenly between the author and his publishing company.

SIMULTANEOUS RIGHTS. More than one publication buys one-time rights to the same work at the same time. Use of such rights occurs among magazines with circulations that don't overlap, such as many religious publications.

ALL RIGHTS. Just as it sounds, the writer, illustrator or photographer relinquishes all rights to a piece—she no longer has any say in who acquires rights to use it. All rights are purchased by publishers who pay premium usage fees, have an exclusive format, or have other book or magazine interests from which the purchased work can generate more mileage. If a company insists on acquiring all rights to your work, see if you can negotiate for the rights to revert back to you after a reasonable period of time. If they agree to such a proposal, get it in writing. Note: Writers, illustrators and photographers should be wary of "work-for-hire" arrangements. If you sign an agreement stipulating that your work will be done as work-for-hire, you will not control the copyrights of the completed work—the company that hired you will be the copyright owner.

FOREIGN SERIAL RIGHTS. Be sure before you market to foreign publications that you have sold only North American—not worldwide—serial rights to previous markets. If so, you are free to market to publications that may be interested in material that's appeared in a North American-based periodical.

SYNDICATION RIGHTS. This is a division of serial rights. For example, if a syndicate prints portions of a book in installments in its newspapers, it would be syndicating second serial rights. The syndicate would receive a commission and leave the remainder to be split between the author and publisher.

SUBSIDIARY RIGHTS. These include serial rights, dramatic rights, book club rights or translation rights. The contract should specify what percentage of profits from sales of these rights go to the author and publisher.

DRAMATIC, TELEVISION AND MOTION PICTURE RIGHTS. During a specified time, the interested party tries to sell a story to a producer or director. Many times options are renewed because the selling process can be lengthy.

DISPLAY RIGHTS OR ELECTRONIC PUBLISHING RIGHTS. They're also known as "Data, Storage and Retrieval." Usually listed under subsidiary rights, the marketing of electronic rights in this era of rapidly expanding capabilities and markets for electronic material can be tricky. Display rights can cover text or images to be used in a CD or online, or they may cover use of material in formats not even fully developed yet. If a display rights clause is listed in your contract, try to negotiate its elimination. Otherwise, be sure to pin down which electronic rights are being purchased. Demand the clause be restricted to things designed to be read only. By doing this, you maintain your rights to use your work for things such as games and interactive software.

SOURCES FOR CONTRACT HELP

Writers' organizations offer a wealth of information to members, including contract advice:

SOCIETY OF CHILDREN'S BOOK WRITERS AND ILLUSTRATORS members can find information in the SCBWI publication "Answers to Some Questions About Contracts." Contact SCBWI at 8271 Beverly Blvd., Los Angeles CA 90048, (323)782-1010, or visit their website: scbwi.org.

THE AUTHORS GUILD also offers contract tips. Visit their website: authorsguild.org. (Members of the guild can receive a 75-point contract review from the guild's legal staff.) See the website for membership information and application form, or contact The Authors Guild at 31 E. 28th St., 10th Floor, New York NY 10016, (212)563-5904. Fax: (212)564-5363. E-mail: staff@authorsguild.org.

STRICTLY BUSINESS

An essential part of being a freelance writer, illustrator or photographer is running your freelance business. It's imperative to maintain accurate business records to determine if you're making a profit as a freelancer. Keeping correct, organized records will also make your life easier as you approach tax time.

When setting up your system, begin by keeping a bank account and ledger for your business finances apart from your personal finances. Also, if writing, illustration or photography is secondary to another freelance career, keep separate business records for each.

You will likely accumulate some business expenses before showing any profit when you start out as a freelancer. To substantiate your income and expenses to the IRS, keep all invoices, cash receipts, sales slips, bank statements, canceled checks and receipts related to travel expenses and entertaining clients. For entertainment expenditures, record the date, place and purpose of the business meeting, as well as gas mileage. Keep records for all purchases, big and small. Don't take the small purchases for granted; they can add up to a substantial amount. File all receipts in chronological order. Maintaining a separate file for each month simplifies retrieving records at the end of the year.

Record keeping

When setting up a single-entry bookkeeping system, record income and expenses separately. Use some of the subheads that appear on Schedule C (the form used for recording income from a business) of the 1040 tax form so you can easily transfer information onto the tax form when filing your return. In your ledger, include a description of each transaction—the date, source of income (or debts from business purchases), description of what was purchased or sold, the amount of the transaction, and whether payment was by cash, check or credit card.

Don't wait until January 1 to start keeping records. The moment you first make a business-related purchase or sell an article, book manuscript, illustration or photo, begin tracking your profits and losses. If you keep records from January 1 to December 31, you're using a calendar-year accounting period. Any other accounting period is called a fiscal year.

There are two types of accounting methods you can choose from—the cash method and the accrual method. The cash method is used more often: You record income when it is received and expenses when they're disbursed.

Using the accrual method, you report income at the time you earn it rather than when it's actually received. Similarly, expenses are recorded at the time they're incurred rather than when you actually pay them. If you choose this method, keep separate records for "accounts receivable" and "accounts payable."

Satisfying the IRS

To successfully—and legally—work as a freelancer, you must know what income you should report and what deductions you can claim. But before you can do that, you must prove to the IRS you're in business to make a profit, that your writing, illustration or photography is not merely a hobby. The Tax Reform Act of 1986 says you should show a profit for three years out of a five-year period to attain professional status. The IRS considers these factors as proof of your professionalism:

- accurate financial records
- a business bank account separate from your personal account
- proven time devoted to your profession
- whether it's your main or secondary source of income
- your history of profits and losses
- the amount of training you have invested in your field
- your expertise

If your business is unincorporated, you'll fill out tax information on Schedule C of Form 1040. If you're unsure of what deductions you can take, request the IRS publication containing this information. Under the Tax Reform Act, only 30 percent of business meals, entertainment and related tips, and parking charges are deductible. Other deductible expenses allowed on Schedule C include: car expenses for business-related trips; professional courses and seminars; depreciation of office equipment, such as a computer; dues and publication subscriptions; and miscellaneous expenses, such as postage used for business needs.

If you're working out of a home office, a portion of your mortgage interest (or rent), related utilities, property taxes, repair costs and depreciation may be deducted as business expenses—under special circumstances. To learn more about the possibility of home office deductions, consult IRS Publication 587, Business Use of Your Home.

The method of paying taxes on income not subject to withholding is called "estimated tax" for individuals. If you expect to owe more than $500 at year's end and if the total amount of income tax that will be withheld during the year will be less than 90 percent of the tax shown on the current year's return, you'll generally make estimated tax payments. Estimated tax payments are made in four equal installments due on April 15, June 15, September 15, and January 15 (assuming you're a calendar-year taxpayer). For more information, request Publication 533, Self-Employment Tax.

The Internal Revenue Service's website (irs.gov) offers tips and instant access to IRS forms and publications.

Social Security tax

Depending on your net income as a freelancer, you may be liable for a Social Security tax. This is a tax designed for those who don't have Social Security withheld from their paychecks. You're liable if your net income is $400 or more per year. Net income is the difference between your income and allowable business deductions. Request Schedule SE, Computation of Social Security Self-Employment Tax, if you qualify.

If completing your income tax return proves to be too complex, consider hiring an accountant (the fee is a deductible business expense) or contact the IRS for assistance. (Check their website, irs.gov.) In addition to offering numerous publications to instruct you in various facets of preparing a tax return, the IRS also has walk-in centers in some cities.

Insurance

As a self-employed professional, be aware of what health and business insurance coverage is available to you. Unless you're a Canadian who is covered by national health insurance or a full-time freelancer covered by your spouse's policy, health insurance will no doubt be one of your biggest expenses. Under the terms of a 1985 government act (COBRA), if you leave a job with health benefits, you're entitled to continue that coverage for up to 18 months; you pay 100 percent of the premium and sometimes a small administration fee. Eventually, you must search for your own health plan. You may also choose to purchase disability and life insurance. Disability insurance is offered through many private insurance companies and state governments. This insurance pays a monthly fee that covers living and business expenses during periods of long-term recuperation from a health problem. The amount of money paid is based on the recipient's annual earnings.

Before contacting any insurance representative, talk to other writers, illustrators or photographers to learn which insurance companies they recommend. If you belong to a writers' or artists' organization, ask the organization if it offers insurance coverage for professionals. (SCBWI has a plan available to members in certain states. Look through the Clubs & Organizations section for other groups that may offer coverage.) Group coverage may be more affordable and provide more comprehensive coverage than an individual policy.

VOICE IN FICTION

*Bring your prose to life and hook
readers immediately.*

....

by Diana Lopez

Teen fads last about as long as it takes to type "lol" or "omg." No wonder YA writers often struggle to sound young. After all, many of us were 15 long before cell phones and iPads. So how can you sound like a teen when you're one (or four) decades older?

Here are six tips for creating an authentic teen voice.

1. DON'T SOUND GROOVY

"Big banking" means earning lots of money. A "snap-back" is a baseball cap with snaps instead of Velcro or elastic. Teens used to say "my bad" when they made mistakes or "wolfing it" when they needed haircuts. They used to say "groovy" and "far out" too. Popular slang is constantly changing, so any book that features a lot of it is going to sound outdated by the time it hits the shelves—not good for establishing a plausible teen voice with readers for years to come.

YA writers are often encouraged to spend time with teens. This can be a great strategy for character development, but it doesn't mean you should just jot down what they say. Instead, focus on where their words *really* come from.

"What doesn't work? A hypothetical, generic teen using (quickly outdated) slang," says Cynthia Leitich Smith, bestselling author of the Tantalize series and forthcoming Feral series. "Choose a language that reflects your character's personality. Think about his 'go-to' words."

I had the characters in my YA novel *Choke* create "word-morphs" by blending familiar terms—"boycentric," "meanormous," or "magtastic"—each in response to an emotion or event. Letting the slang emerge organically from the teens' situations and surroundings added personality to my characters, avoided putting a time stamp on my book, and tapped into a timeless quality of teen speech: word play.

So when it comes to slang, don't borrow. Invent!

2. DON'T FORGET THE POWER OF PROPS

When the school district I once worked for decided to require uniforms, my eighth graders couldn't stop complaining. "How can we be unique when all of us are wearing khaki pants and white shirts?" They quickly found a loophole in the dress code, and soon the girls were sporting wacky socks, while the boys wore brightly colored shoelaces.

Their small act of rebellion points to an important teen characteristic: They love to express themselves in concrete, visual ways. After all, they are trying to establish their individuality, and one of the first steps is inventing a unique style.

I followed my students' example when I wrote *Confetti Girl*. My protagonist, Lina, is a "sockiophile" and chooses her socks according to her mood. But she takes this prop one step further by using socks for potholders, puppets and "sockerchiefs," her version of a handkerchief. The socks not only reflect her emotions but her creativity too, and they become a memorable detail in the story. In fact, Lina frequently talks about socks as well as other props such as *cascarones* (confetti eggs), *Watership Down*, whooping cranes and potato babies.

So don't forget the power of props. Harry Potter has his glasses and magic wand. Katniss of *The Hunger Games* hunts with a bow and arrow and wears a mockingjay pin. Melinda in *Speak* hangs a Maya Angelou poster in a janitor's closet. Characters are often defined by what they cherish, and though props may not seem related to voice, they *are* because these special items are what teens think and talk about.

3. DON'T USE COOKIE CUTTERS

Jocks, nerds, cheerleaders, slackers—every high school has its cliques. The jocks wear letter jackets, while the slackers hide behind long bangs and large T-shirts. And who can picture a cheerleader without also seeing the way she flips back her hair or a nerd without a row of pencils in his shirt pocket? They're stereotypes, and like all stereotypes, they come preprogrammed in appearance, action and voice.

But stories that rely too heavily on these cookie-cutter characters are predictable. The star football player bullies the skinny guy at the party, while the math geek stands on the sidelines at the prom. Big deal! We've seen this hundreds of times. Once these characters enter the scene, your readers know what they're going to say and *how* they're going to say it. So how can we blame them if they tune out, or worse, close the book?

Cliques are an important part of high school. You *should* have characters in band, football or the chess club, but throw out the cookie cutter and throw in a twist. Maybe the jock writes poetry. Maybe the cheerleader is too shy to attend her best friend's party even though she has no problem doing cartwheels in a packed stadium. Maybe the slacker is a workaholic at home as he helps his parents with their catering business. Throw a wrinkle into their starched personalities and listen. There's a good chance their voices will be more interesting, more surprising and more *teen*.

Avoiding cookie-cutter characters is good advice for all writers, but YA authors are often dealing with *two* layers of stereotype. Not only must we avoid the high school clichés, but we must also avoid our own biases about teens in general, especially the trap of underestimating how smart and resourceful they can be.

4. DON'T DUMB DOWN

I teach freshman composition, and sometimes my students try to elevate their language with a thesaurus. The result is "meteorological phenomenon" instead of "weather." YA writers, conversely, are tempted to oversimplify. Nothing is more condescending than writing as if teens are not smart enough for sophisticated language, or, perhaps more important, sophisticated themes. Always remember this: Teens aren't dumb—they're *inexperienced*.

When Kristen-Paige Madonia wrote *Fingerprints of You*, she imagined an adult audience. After selling it as a YA book, she worried about changing it for teens, but her agent warned, "Don't dumb it down."

"Our job is to write the truth—no sugar coating," Madonia says. "Teens face complex issues, and it's the author's responsibility to provide smart honest literature, so they have access to stories that empower them and affirm that they aren't alone as they confront the challenges of the teen years."

So how can you avoid dumbing down your fiction? Try smarting it up! To challenge young readers with your material is to help them grow.

First, don't run from big words (or bad language) when they're consistent with character and not over the top, and don't be afraid to acknowledge the darkness when it comes to plot or theme. Our young people don't live in a perfect world; they live in the *real* world where bad things sometimes happen. Jay Asher's *Thirteen Reasons Why*, for example, deals with teen suicide, and Patricia McCormick's acclaimed *Cut* features self-mutilation. I'm not suggesting you deliberately use dark themes, but don't deliberately avoid them either. It may appear at first glance tangential, but it ties directly into voice—your characters will not have authentic voices unless they're put in honest and real situations and act accordingly.

Second, let your characters fix their problems. Too often, aspiring YA writers face the teen-in-distress scenario as Mom, Dad or Favorite Teacher comes to the rescue. This form of dumbing down is a missed opportunity because it robs teens of the independence they are working so hard to earn. Instead, remove the grown-ups, let your characters handle the tough situations, and remember that they are *trying out* coping tools, not *relying* on them.

Their true voices will pop. They won't be able to come out if you stifle them by having adults do the heavy lifting.

5. DON'T LOOK BACK

Because YA writers are inspired by their own history, they sometimes write with the benefit of hindsight. The voice, then, is calmer and wiser as the narrator looks back at himself, maybe even judging his foolish past.

The trouble with looking back is that you risk patronizing your readers. You also lower the stakes for your character because if he is telling a story that happened five or 10 years ago, and everything has worked out, then his dire situation obviously wasn't so dangerous after all.

Perhaps the best way to avoid a retrospective tone is to dump the map. In other words, forget the experiences you've collected over the years by throwing aside that been-there-done-that attitude. Seeing like a teen means seeing for the first time so that the ordinary—bagels, traffic jams, kisses—is extraordinary again.

Work to capture the overwhelming awe, confusion or joy teens feel. If you can't remember that sense of newness, live without your map for a while. Learn a new dance, for example. Go somewhere you know you'll feel out of place. Wear an outfit that is the complete opposite of your normal style. Do these activities make you feel self-conscious? Good! That's how teens often feel.

Before the new experience becomes a distant memory, write down your emotions, impressions and surprises, rediscovering what it feels like to be a novice, to be awkward, to be a teen.

6. DO LISTEN TO YOUR INNER TEEN

At the Montgomery County Book Festival, I had the pleasure of speaking on a panel with Jill Alexander, author of YA novels *Paradise* and *The Sweetheart of Prosper County*. During the Q&A session, an aspiring writer asked Alexander why she decided to write for young people.

"I didn't decide," she answered. "When I sit down to write, I hear a teenager. It's my natural storytelling voice."

People often ask, "Where do your stories begin?" I have to agree with Alexander. My stories begin with voice. I have to hear my characters before I write. When my protagonist is sitting in a busy food court, what does she see, and more important, what does she notice? What words does she use to describe the scene? How does she *sound*? A popular maxim is "write what you know," but I propose that you write what you *hear*.

Young adult fiction is a hot market right now with bestselling books and blockbuster movies. No wonder authors are drawn to this genre, but too often, beginning writers chase trends. Desperate to get published, they look for what's selling, and then try to write about that topic even when their hearts are somewhere else. So before writing a YA book, visit your old high school, dance to hit songs from your homecoming, read the autographs in your yearbook. Then listen to your inner teen. Let your younger self be your guide to an authentic teenage voice.

Wendy Mass, author of YA novel *A Mango-Shaped Space*, has this to say, "Every writer has a voice in their head that stops at a certain age. For me, it's between 12 and 16."

How old is *your* voice? If it's one (or four) decades older than 15, don't fret. Some people get facelifts to look younger. So how about getting a "voice-lift"? Play with language, use props, throw out the cookie cutter, "smart-up" your story, dump the map, and above all, hear your inner teen. Remember that sounding like a teen is not related to your age but to your state of mind.

DIANA LÓPEZ is the author of *Confetti Girl, Choke* and *Ask My Mood Ring How I Feel*. Her short fiction has appeared in various journals and anthologies. She teaches composition and creative writing at the University of Houston-Victoria, and is the editor of the literary journal *Huizache*.

PICTURE BOOK STRUCTURE & PLOT

How to utilize a picture book's three acts.

....

by Ann Whitford Paul

Are you like me when it comes to plotting?

I have a great idea for an opening. It's catchy, the character is appealing, and the problem involving. I've cut away the setup and started smack in the middle of the action. Often I know how the book is going to end. And that ending is tight and satisfying.

The problem is I don't know how to get to my ending in a way that isn't:

1. too thin to fill up the middle of my book.

2. predictable and obvious from the get-go.

3. boring, oh so boring, even I yawn while I'm writing it.

4. lacking in tension and incentives for the reader to turn the page.

When books fail, the author is usually driving along a word highway without a map to show the way to the destination.

This article is about how to drive your story forward. But a word of caution: No one map can get *every* story to its destination. Much as we'd love a simple formula to plug every story into, it makes writing much more challenging not to have one. It also makes every working day a challenge and, therefore, stimulating.

THREE-ACT STRUCTURE

Three-act structure simply means having a beginning, middle and end. John Gardner states it this way: "In nearly all good fiction, the basic—all but inescapable—plot form is: A central character wants something, goes after it despite opposition (perhaps including his own doubts), and so arrives at a win, lose or draw."

The opening is the first act. The characters and problem are introduced, along with an inciting incident, or turning point, that moves the reader from Act I to Act II. This first act in picture books needs to come smack at the beginning—certainly within the first half-page of your typed manuscript. It's a brief act that forces you quickly into Act II.

In Act II, the main character takes action, and more action, and even more action to solve his problem. The act most often culminates in a low moment when all feels lost.

The last act contains the resolution of the problem, or the ending. Once the problem set out in the beginning of the picture book is solved, the story is over, finished—except perhaps for quickly tying up any loose ends. The solution of the problem usually occurs on pages 30 and 31 of a published picture book. The tying together of any dangling threads falls on page 32.

This three-act structure is just as valid for nonfiction and concept books as for fiction. In nonfiction, the first act is where the subject is introduced. In the second act, the subject is explored and expanded upon. In the final third act, the writer comes to a conclusion.

Concept books are the same. The first act introduces an idea, then expands on that in the second act and wraps everything up in the third act.

The second act most often needs work. Many manuscripts fail in the middle of the book.

So you can see how this three-act structure works, let's make up a story about a boy named Steve.

> Act I: Steve lives in a small town where everyone knows everyone and it's safe for him to walk to the store by himself. Today he wants to buy a comic book.
> Act II: He takes the money he's saved out of his piggy bank and goes to the store.
> Act III. He buys his comic book.

That's the end.

There's no tension. The only action consists of walking to the store and choosing a comic. Nothing stops him. Nothing interferes with his goal. This story is seriously missing a second act. But it's also missing something else.

Suppose instead of going to buy a comic book, today is his mother's birthday and he wants to get her a present. Now we've put added weight onto his purchase. It's not for him. It's for his mom's special day.

But if Steve opens the piggy bank, gets the money, goes to the store and buys a bar of her favorite soap, the story is still too easy. There's no problem and ... *no problem means no tension.*

No tension means bored readers and, worse yet, a rejection from an editor.

Suppose Steve opens his piggy bank and finds it empty. Now we have a real problem. Steve knew he had money. Where is it? How can he buy something for his mom without money? Steve looks under his bed and *Wow* There's his five-dollar bill. He's saved.

Is this a good story?

Not yet. It's over way too quickly.

THE RHYTHM OF THREES

Let's revise by adding three attempts of Steve to solve the problem.

> *Steve opens his piggy bank and it's empty!*
> *First Steve looks under his bed.*
> *No money there.*
> *Next he looks in his desk.*
> *No money there.*
> *The third place he looks is in the cushions of his chair.*
> *Still no money.*
> *Steve plops down on the chair. He's sure he's never going to find the money to buy a present for his mother.*

What happened here?

We gave the reader more time to get to know Steve and to feel his increasing tension. The reader is more connected to him and his problem. Now we worry for Steve.

This rhythm of threes is all around us.

Three strikes and you're out.

Father, Son and Holy Ghost.

Goldilocks and the Three Bears.

The Three Little Pigs.

It's part of our history and our culture.

Why?

Because it's satisfying.

Three failures up the stakes so the reader worries more for the main character.

But Steve's story still lacks *interesting action*. All Steve does is look and look and look. Boring words and pictures! There's more to action than threes.

VARIED ACTION

Sticking with Steve, let's suppose he finds the money in his piggy bank and starts off to the store.

> *At the park, he stops to join his friends for a game of softball. In his first at bat, he hits a home run! Wow! Is he happy! But he remembers his mom's birthday present, waves good-bye to his friends, and goes on toward the store.*
> *On the way he offers to help his mother's friend, Mrs. Binder, weed her garden.*
> *When that's finished, he pauses to chat with police officer Hurley, who afterward blows her whistle, holds up her hand, and stops the traffic so Steve can safely cross the street.*
> *Then Steve walks on to the store where he buys the soap. Then he goes back home to give his mother the present.*

More action?

Of course.

Varied action?

Absolutely.

Steve plays softball and scores a run.
He helps Mrs. Binder in her garden.
Then he talks to the police officer.

We have action here, but it's not the right kind of action.

The actions in this series are *incidental*. These things could happen in any order. Steve could garden with Mrs. Binder before he plays softball. Officer Hurley could stop traffic for him on the way home from the store.

The action we want in our stories is action that leads directly to a reaction, that leads to another action.

CAUSE-AND-EFFECT ACTION

Because this is where many manuscripts fall flat, let's go back to Steve's story to understand the difference between incidental action and cause-and-effect action.

Steve gets his money out of his piggy bank. He has just enough to buy his mom her favorite bar of soap. He leaves the house and passes the park where his friends yell, "Come on Steve! We need another player." He stops to join them in a game of softball.

But this time, instead of scoring a run, Steve slams the ball through Mrs. Binder's window. CRASH!

Everybody races away.

Everyone but Steve. He's stunned. He can't move. Needless to say, Mrs. Binder finds him. Tears fill her eyes. She struggles to make do on her monthly social security check and replacing a broken window is not in her budget.

Help!

Steve shifts from one foot to the other. "I'm sorry," he says. But he can tell by her tears an apology won't be enough. "I'll pay for the window," he adds, and reaches deep into his pocket. He hands Mrs. Binder the six quarters, ten dimes, five nickels, and seventeen pennies he's saved for his mother's present.

Mrs. Binder counts the change. "Thank you, Steve," she says. "Two dollars and ninety-seven cents is a sweet gesture, but not nearly enough for my new window."

Thinking quickly, Steve offers to work for her. She accepts and together they sweep up the broken glass. Then he helps her weed her flower garden.

However, Steve is distracted the whole time, trying to figure out what he can do now for his mother's birthday present.

When they finish, since he has no money, Steve doesn't even bother going to the store. What's the point?

Dejectedly he starts home.

Poor Steve!

He's crying now. His eyes are so filled with tears and his mind so concerned about what to give his mother that he steps into the street without looking.

Uh-oh!

A car's coming down the road.

Double uh-oh!

The car is speeding!

Triple uh-oh!

The car is a police car!

Quadruple uh-oh!

SCREEEEEEEE-EEEEEECH!

Yikes! This is big trouble.

This is your classic page turn. Don't you have to find out whether Steve gets hit by the police car?

The police car stops just before it hits Steve. Thank heavens! BUT ...

Officer Hurley is both furious and frightened over what might have happened if she hadn't stopped in time. She gives Steve a talking to and then takes him home in the police car to tell his mother.

Now Steve has no present for his mother and, to make matters worse, he's going to be in trouble with her.

This is Steve's darkest moment.

Look closely at the cause-and-effect pattern of these actions. Steve is walking to the store to buy his mother a present. On his way he passes the park, his friends call to him, and he joins them. If he weren't going to the store, he wouldn't have been tempted to play softball. If he hadn't been playing softball, he wouldn't have broken Mrs. Binder's window. If he hadn't broken the window, he wouldn't have had to give her his money and work for her. If he hadn't been so upset by his new poverty, he wouldn't have crossed the street without looking and he wouldn't have almost gotten run over by Officer Hurley who now, at Steve's worst moment, is going to tell his mom how she almost hit him. Steve has no money, no present, and to make matters worse, everything he's done has led to the possibility of getting in huge trouble with his mom ... on her BIRTHDAY!

I hope you noticed that using **cause-and-effect action**, we've still kept our **rhythm of threes**. *One*, playing baseball, leads to *two*, breaking a window, leads to *three*, almost getting killed. We've also made sure of something else here.

ESCALATING ACTION

Notice that I didn't write the biggest, most exciting action first. In a humorous book, don't place your funniest incident first, either. Stories need to build from smaller to larger, as I did in Steve's story, or from slightly laughable to ridiculous in a humorous story.

Suppose Steve had almost gotten hit by the police car first and joined the baseball game at the end. The story wouldn't have been nearly as satisfying.

The three-act structure is critical to everything you write. Also important are *the rhythm of threes* to increase your tension, just as *cause-and-effect* and *escalating action* build toward your end.

For a classic example of this in a published book, look at *Ming Lo Moves the Mountain* by Arnold Lobel.

> *In the first two sentences, we learn that Ming Lo and his wife love their house at the bottom of a mountain, but they don't love the mountain. They decide to move the mountain. But how?*
>
> *They resolve to ask the village wise man. We have the problem and the turning point, and that is the end of Act I.*
>
> *In Act II, the first action suggested by the wise man is to cut down a large tree and push it against the mountain.*
>
> *When that doesn't move the mountain, Ming Lo goes back to the wise man for another (his second) suggestion. This time the wise man says, "Take some pots and pans from your kitchen and pound them with spoons. Yell as loud as you can and frighten the mountain into moving." Notice how this suggestion is more ridiculous than the first.*
>
> *Ming Lo and his wife try this approach and fail, too. Their frustration mounts and Ming Lo returns to the wise man whose third suggestion is to take cakes and breads to the spirit who lives at the top of the mountain. Because the spirit is always hungry, he will grant whatever they wish. Ming Lo and his wife do what they are told. You can probably guess the outcome: Ming Lo rushes back to the wise man.*

Notice how one event causes another. Ming Lo and his wife want to move the mountain. Because they don't know how, they go to the wise man. He makes a suggestion. It doesn't work, so they go back again. This suggestion doesn't work, so they go back again. And his new suggestion doesn't work either.

We're up to three different tries to move the mountain. Now we think Ming Lo and his wife will have to endure the mountain's falling rocks and stones, and the holes caused by them in their home, forever.

This is the story's darkest point. And here we are propelled into Act III, where Ming Lo and his wife follow another suggestion from the wise man. They bundle up everything in their house and then bundle up the sticks the house was made out of. They carry some of the bundles on the tops of their heads. Others they carry in their arms. Then they face the mountain, close their eyes, and dance the dance the wise man taught Ming Lo.

Because the dance involves putting one foot behind the other, over and over again, when they open their eyes several hours later, the mountain is far away. Problem solved. In a short pulling together of loose ends, Ming Lo and his wife rebuild their house and put their belongings away. They live happily ever after. And that's the end of Act III.

In this story we have three acts, the rhythm of threes, one event leads to another, and each attempt to solve the problem becomes increasingly ridiculous. Arnold Lobel, who also did the illustrations, shows the wise man smoking a pipe. Each time Ming Lo returns, the puff of smoke around the wise man grows bigger and bigger to show his increased pondering before each new suggestion.

TESTING A MANUSCRIPT

How do we determine whether a story has three acts?

First of all, I print out a hard copy of my manuscript. Then I mark where the story problem catapults the reader into the second act. Afterwards I look for the place where the character solves the problem that was set up in the beginning. The in-between part is the second act.

On separate sticky notes, I write each time the character takes an action toward solving the problem. Are there at least three? If not, I must add more. If I have more than three, perhaps some can be deleted.

Then I spread the action notes on my desk or table to make sure each action leads directly to another. If they don't lead directly, I know I must rewrite so they do, or shift around the order of my actions.

Last of all, I consider whether my sticky notes build to an exciting climax. If the most dramatic action comes first, I need to rework and reshuffle.

This test shows me exactly where my plotting is strong and where it needs extra work.

Once in a while after testing the manuscript I'll discover that something is still missing. Raymond Chandler said, "When the plot flags, bring in a man with a gun."

Fortunately, we writers for children have several less violent methods to up the ante in our books.

WORKING TOWARD A GOAL OR EVENT

A goal or an event ups the stakes and sets a time limit for how long the main character has to solve his problem. Perhaps a child is going to compete in a spelling bee and is studying hard to memorize the words. Or perhaps a baseball game is coming up and a girl needs to improve her hitting.

Our Steve has always worked toward the event of his mother's birthday and the goal of finding her a present.

In *How to Make an Apple Pie and See the World* by Marjorie Priceman, the main character wants to make an apple pie but doesn't have the ingredients. She travels the world to collect them and finally bakes her pie. She achieves her goal.

SUSPENSE

Of course, every picture book needs suspense. The reader wants to worry if the main character can solve the problem. Without worry, the story is too predictable.

I tried to increase the suspense by putting Steve into deeper and deeper trouble until he's in a police car being driven home.

Play around with your story to see how you might increase the suspense so neither the reader nor the listener knows what the outcome will be until the very end. Keeping the three-act structure and basic plotting concepts in mind will help you arrive at the end of each new story.

ANN WHITFORD PAUL graduated from the University of Wisconsin and Columbia University School of Social Work. She's published 19 different award-winning books. For 10 years, she taught picture book writing through UCLA Extension. You can learn more about her, download writing tips and classroom activities, and contact her through her website, www.annwhitfordpaul.net.

CRAFTING A QUERY

How to write a great letter.

....

by Kara Gebhart Uhl

//

So you've written a book. And now you want an agent. If you're new to publishing, you probably assume that the next step is to send your finished, fabulous book out to agents, right? Wrong. Agents don't want your finished, fabulous book. In fact, they probably don't even want *part* of your finished, fabulous book—at least, not yet. First, they want your query.

A query is a short, professional way of introducing yourself to an agent. If you're frustrated by the idea of this step, imagine yourself at a cocktail party. Upon meeting someone new, you don't greet them with a boisterous hug and kiss and, in three minutes, reveal your entire life story including the fact that you were late to the party because of some gastrointestinal problems. Rather, you extend your hand. You state your name. You comment on the hors d'oeuvres, the weather, the lovely shade of someone's dress. Perhaps, after this introduction, the person you're talking to politely excuses himself. Or, perhaps, you begin to forge a friendship. It's basic etiquette, formality, professionalism—it's simply how it's done.

Agents receive hundreds of submissions every month. Often they read these submissions on their own time—evenings, weekends, on their lunch break. Given the number of writers submitting, and the number of agents reading, it would simply be impossible for agents to ask for and read entire book manuscripts off the bat. Instead, a query is a quick way for you to, first and foremost, pitch your book. But it's also a way to pitch yourself. If an agent is intrigued by your query, she may ask for a partial (say, the first three chapters of your book). Or she may ask for your entire manuscript. And only then may you be signed.

As troublesome as it may first seem, try not to be frustrated by this process. Because, honestly, a query is a really great way to help speed up what is already a monumentally slow-paced industry. Have you ever seen pictures of slush piles—those piles of unread queries on many well-known agents' desk? Imagine the size of those slush piles if they held full manuscripts instead of one-page query letters. Thinking of it this way, query letters begin to make more sense.

Here we share with you the basics of a query, including its three parts and a detailed list of dos and don'ts.

PART I: THE INTRODUCTION

Whether you're submitting a 100-word picture book or a 90,000-word novel, you must be able to sum up the most basic aspects of it in one sentence. Agents are busy. And they constantly receive submissions for types of work they don't represent. So upfront they need to know that, after reading your first paragraph, the rest of your query is going to be worth their time.

An opening sentence designed to "hook" an agent is fine—if it's good and if it works. But this is the time to tune your right brain down and your left brain up—agents desire professionalism and queries that are short and to the point. Remember the cocktail party. Always err on the side of formality. Tell the agent, in as few words as possible, what you've written, including the title, genre and length.

Within the intro you also must try to connect with the agent. Simply sending 100 identical query letters out to "Dear Agent" won't get you published. Instead, your letter should be addressed not only to a specific agency but a specific agent within that agency. (And double, triple, quadruple check that the agent's name is spelled correctly.) In addition, you need to let the agent know why you chose her specifically. A good author-agent relationship is like a good marriage. It's important that both sides invest the time to find a good fit that meets their needs. So how do you connect with an agent you don't know personally? Research.

1. Make a connection based on an author or book the agent already represents.

Most agencies have websites that list who and what they represent. Research those sites. Find a book similar to yours and explain that, because such-and-such book has a similar theme or tone or whatever, you think your book would be a great fit. In addition, many agents will list specific topics they're looking for, either on their websites or in interviews. If your book is a match, state that.

2. Make a connection based on an interview you read.

Search by agents' names online and read any and all interviews they've participated in. Perhaps they mentioned a love for X and your book is all about X. Or, perhaps they mentioned that they're looking for Y and your book is all about Y. Mention the specific interview. Prove that you've invested as much time researching them as they're about to spend researching you.

3. Make a connection based on a conference you both attended.
Was the agent you're querying the keynote speaker at a writing conference you were recently at? Mention it, specifically commenting on an aspect of his speech you liked. Even better, did you meet the agent in person? Mention it, and if there's something you can say to jog her memory about the meeting, say it. And better yet, did the agent specifically ask you to send your manuscript? Mention it.

Finally, if you're being referred to a particular agent by an author who that agent already represents—that's your opening sentence. That referral is guaranteed to get your query placed on the top of the stack.

PART II: THE PITCH

Here's where you really get to sell your book—but in only three to 10 sentences. Consider the jacket flap and its role in convincing readers to plunk down $24.95 to buy what's in between those flaps. Like a jacket flap, you need to hook an agent in the confines of very limited space. What makes your story interesting and unique? Is your story about a woman going through a midlife crisis? Fine, but there are hundreds of stories about women going through midlife crises. Is your story about a woman who, because of a midlife crisis, leaves her life and family behind to spend three months in India? Again, fine, but this story, too, already exists—in many forms. Is your story about a woman who, because of a midlife crisis, leaves her life and family behind to spend three months in India, falls in love with someone new while there and starts a new life—and family?—and then has to deal with everything she left behind upon her return? *Now* you have a hook.

Practice your pitch. Read it out loud, not only to family and friends, but to people willing to give you honest, intelligent criticism. If you belong to a writing group, workshop your pitch. Share it with members of an online writing forum. Know anyone in the publishing industry? Share it with them. Many writers spend years writing their books. We're not talking about querying magazines here, we're talking about querying an agent who could become a lifelong partner. Spend time on your pitch. Perfect it. Turn it into jacket-flap material so detailed, exciting and clear that it would be near impossible to read your pitch and not want to read more. Use active verbs. Write your pitch, put it aside for a week, then look at it again. Don't send a query simply because you finished a book. Send a query because you finished your pitch and are ready to take the next steps.

DOS AND DON'TS FOR QUERYING AGENTS

DO:

- Keep the tone professional.
- Query a specific agent at a specific agency.
- Proofread. Double-check the spelling of the agency and the agent's name.
- Keep the query concise, limiting the overall length to one page (single space, 12-point type in a commonly used font).
- Focus on the plot, not your bio, when pitching fiction.
- Pitch agents who represent the type of material you write.
- Check an agency's submission guidelines to see how it would like to be queried—for example, via e-mail or mail—and whether or not to include a SASE.
- Keep pitching, despite rejections.

DON'T:

- Include personal info not directly related to the book. For example, stating that you're a parent to three children doesn't make you more qualified than someone else to write a children's book.
- Say how long it took you to write your manuscript. Some bestselling books took 10 years to write—others, six weeks. An agent doesn't care how long it took—an agent only cares if it's good. Same thing goes with drafts—an agent doesn't care how many drafts it took you to reach the final product.
- Mention that this is your first novel or, worse, the first thing you've ever written aside from grocery lists. If you have no other publishing credits, don't advertise that fact. Don't mention it at all.
- State that your book has been edited by peers or professionals. Agents expect manuscripts to be edited, no matter how the editing was done.
- Bring up screenplays or film adaptations; you're querying an agent about publishing a book, not making a movie.
- Mention any previous rejections.
- State that the story is copyrighted with the U.S. Copyright Office or that you own all rights. Of course you own all rights. You wrote it.
- Rave about how much your family and friends loved it. What matters is that the agent loves it.
- Send flowers, baked goods or anything else except a self-addressed stamped envelope (and only if the SASE is required).
- Follow up with a phone call. After the appropriate time has passed (many agencies say how long it will take to receive a response) follow up in the manner you queried—via e-mail or mail.

PART III: THE BIO

If you write fiction, unless you're a household name, an agent is much more interested in your pitch than in who you are. If you write nonfiction, who you are—more specifically, your platform and publicity—is much more important. Regardless, these are key elements that must be present in every bio:

1. Publishing credits

If you're submitting fiction, focus on your fiction credits—previously published works and short stories. That said, if you're submitting fiction and all your previously published work is nonfiction—magazine articles, essays, etc.—that's still fine and good to mention. Just don't be overly long about it. Mention your publications in bigger magazines or well-known literary journals. If you've never had anything published, don't say you lack official credits. Simply skip this altogether and thank the agent for his time.

2. Contests and awards

If you've won many, focus on the most impressive ones and the ones that most directly relate to your work. Don't mention contests you entered and weren't named in. Also, feel free to leave titles and years out of it. If you took first place at the Delaware Writers Conference for your fiction manuscript, that's good enough. Mentioning details isn't necessary.

3. MFAs

If you've earned or are working toward a Master of Fine Arts in writing, say so and state the program. Don't mention English degrees or online writing courses.

4. Large, recognized writing organizations

Agents don't want to hear about your book club and the fact that there's always great food, or the small critique group you meet with once a week. And they really don't want to hear about the online writing forum you belong to. But if you're a member of something like the Romance Writers of America (RWA), the Mystery Writers of America (MWA), the Society of Children's Book Writers and Illustrators (SCBWI), the Society of Professional Journalists (SPJ), etc., say so. This shows you're serious about what you do and you're involved in groups that can aid with publicity and networking.

5. Platform and publicity

If you write nonfiction, who you are and how you're going to help sell the book once it's published becomes very important. Why are you the best person to write it and what do you have now—public speaking engagements, an active website or blog, substantial cred in your industry—that will help you sell this book?

Finally, be cordial. Thank the agent for taking the time to read your query and consider your manuscript. Ask if you may send more, in the format she desires (partial, full, etc.).

Think of the time you spent writing your book. Unfortunately, you can't send your book to an agent for a first impression. Your query *is* that first impression. Give it the time it deserves. Keep it professional. Keep it formal. Let it be a firm handshake—not a sloppy kiss. Let it be a first meeting that evolves into a lifetime relationship—not a rejection slip. But expect those slips. Just like you don't become lifelong friends with everyone you meet at a cocktail party, you can't expect every agent you pitch to sign you. Be patient. Keep pitching. And in the meantime, start writing that next book.

KARA GEBHART UHL, formerly a managing editor at *Writer's Digest* magazine, now freelance writers and edits in Fort Thomas, KY. She also blogs about parenting at pleiadesbee.com. Her essays have appeared on The Huffington Post, *The New York Times'* Motherlode and *TIME: Healthland*. Her parenting essay, "Apologies to the Parents I Judged Four Years Ago" was named one of *TIME*'s "Top 10 Opinions of 2012."

Dear Ms. MacLeod,

I am seeking literary representation and hope you will consider my tween novel, REAL MERMAIDS DON'T WEAR TOE RINGS.

First zit. First crush. First ... mermaid's tail?

1 Jade feels like enough of a freak-of-nature when she gets her first period at almost fifteen. She doesn't need to have it happen at the mall while trying on that XL tankini she never wanted to buy in the first place. And she really doesn't need to run into Luke Martin in the Feminine Hygiene Products **2** aisle while her dad Googles "menstruation" on his Blackberry **4** .

3 But "freak-of-nature" takes on a whole new meaning when raging hormones and bath salts bring on another metamorphosis— complete with scales and a tail. And when Jade learns she's inherited her mermaid tendencies from her late mother's side of the family, it raises the question: if Mom was once a mermaid, did she really drown that day last summer?

Jade is determined to find out. Though, how does a plus-sized, aqua-phobic mer-girl go about doing that, exactly ... especially when Luke from aisle six seems to be the only person who might be able to help?

5 REAL MERMAIDS DON'T WEAR TOE RINGS is a lighthearted fantasy novel for tweens (10-14). It is complete at 44,500 words and available at your request. The first ten pages and a synopsis are included below my signature. I also have a completed chapter book for boys (MASON AND THE MEGANAUTS), should that be of interest to you.

My middle grade novel, ACADIAN STAR, was released last fall by Nimbus Publishing and has been nominated for the 2009/2010 Hackmatack Children's Choice Book Award. I have three nonfiction children's books with Crabtree Publishing to my credit (one forthcoming) as well as an upcoming early chapter book series. Thank you for taking the time to consider this project.

Kind regards,
Hélène Boudreau
www.heleneboudreau.com

1 One of the things that can really make a query letter stand out is a strong voice, and it seems that is one of the things writers struggle with the most. Hélène, however, knocked it out of the park with her query letter. I find young readers are very sensitive to inauthentic voices, but you can tell by just the first few paragraphs that she is going to absolutely nail the tween voice in the manuscript—you can see this even by the way she capitalized Feminine Hygiene Products **2**.

3 The first time I read this query, I actually did laugh out loud. Instead of merely promising me RMDWTR was funny (which it absolutely is), Hélène showed me how funny she can be, which made me want to request the manuscript even before I got to her sample pages.

I also loved how clearly and with just a few words she could invoke an entire scene. Hélène doesn't tell us Jade gets embarrassed in front of a local hunk, she plops us right down in the middle of the pink aisle with the well-intentioned but hopelessly nerdy Dad **4** . I felt this really spoke to her talents— if she could bring bits of a query to life, I couldn't wait to see what she could do with a whole manuscript. **5** And on top of all of this, she had a phenomenal title, a bio that made it very clear she was ready to break out, and a hook so strong it even made it onto the cover!

SAMPLE QUERY NO. 2: YOUNG ADULT
AGENT'S COMMENTS: MICHELLE HUMPHREY (MARTHA KAPLAN LITERARY)

Dear Ms. Humphrey,

I'm contacting you because I've read on various writing websites that you are expanding your young adult client list.

In LOSING FAITH, fifteen-year-old Brie Jenkins discovers her sister's death may not have been an accident ❶. At the funeral, an uncorroborated story surfaces about Faith's whereabouts the night of her tragic fall from a cliff. When Brie encounters a strange, evasive boy ❸ at Faith's gravesite, she tries to confront him, but he disappears into a nearby forest.

Brie searches out and questions the mysterious boy, finding more information than she bargained for: Faith belonged to a secret ritualistic group, which regularly held meetings at the cliff where she died. Brie suspects foul play, but the only way to find out for sure is to risk her own life and join the secret cult. ❷

LOSING FAITH (76k/YA) will appeal to readers of ❹ John Green's LOOKING FOR ALASKA and Laurie Halse Anderson's CATALYST. My published stories have won an editor's choice award in *The Greensilk Journal* and appeared in *Mississippi Crow* magazine. I'm a member of Romance Writers of America, where my manuscript is a finalist in the Florida chapter's Launching a Star Contest. For your convenience, I've pasted the first chapter at the bottom of this e-mail. Thank you for your time and consideration.

Sincerely,
Denise Jaden
www.denisejaden.com ❺

Everything about Denise's query appealed to me. She gave me a quick sentence about why she chose to query me, and then went right into the gist of her novel. ❶ Her "gist" is very much a teaser, or like the back blurb of a book. She gives plot clues without revealing too much of the plot. She keeps the plot points brief and keeps the teaser moving; most important is where she ends—on a note that makes the agent curious to know more. ❷ Denise also gives us vivid characters ❸ in this teaser: the smart, investigative protagonist, Brie; the mysterious boy at the gravesite; the sister, Faith, who's not what she seems. By creating hints of vivid characters and quick engaging plot points in a paragraph, Denise demonstrates her storytelling ability in the query—and I suspected it would carry through to her novel. ❹ Denise includes some other elements that I like to see in queries: comparisons to other well-known books (two or three is enough) and credentials that show her ability to write fiction. ❺ I like, too, that she included her website—I often visit websites when considering queries.

Dear Ms. Roth,

A boy with a hidden power and the girl who was sent to stop him have 24 hours to win a pickle contest.

1 12-year-old Pierre La Bouche is a *cornichon*. That's French for "pickle," but it also means "good-for-nothing." A middle child who gets straight C's, he's never been No. 1 at anything. When the family farm goes broke, grandfather Henri gives Pierre a mission: to save the farm by winning an international pickle contest.

2 En route to the contest, Pierre meets Aurore, the charming but less-than-truthful granddaughter of a rival farmer. She's been sent to ensnare Pierre, but after a wake up call from her conscience, she rescues him. Together, they navigate the ghostly Paris catacombs, figure out how to crash-land a plane, and duel with a black-hearted villain who will stop at nothing to capture their pickles. In their most desperate hour, it is Pierre's incredible simplicity that saves the day. Always bickering but becoming friends, Pierre and Aurore discover that anything is possible, no matter how hard it may seem.

3 *Pickle Impossible* is complete at 32,500 words. I'm a technical writer by day, optimistic novelist by night. Recently, I've interviewed a host of pickle makers and French natives. My own pickles are fermenting in the kitchen. I grew up in Toronto and live with my wife and children in Israel.

Thank you for your consideration. I hope to hear from you.

Kind Regards,

Eli Stutz

1 The first paragraph introduces the main character and the set-up. He uses concrete things to describe Pierre. He throws in the French flair of the book right away. And he doesn't beat around the bush to tell me what Pierre has to accomplish. **2** The second delves a little deeper into the plot. It gives me the complication that will drive the story forward—someone is out to stop Pierre. And then Eli accomplishes the most important trick here: He gives me some fun examples of what will happen in the book without summarizing the entire plot. That is key because I don't want to read the whole book in the query letter. But he gives me flavor. **3** The bio paragraph is straight to the point, not overcrowded with his whole life history, and also ties light-heartedly right back to the subject of the book. I loved that he tried fermenting his own pickles. (He later told me they weren't very good.) Here's the kicker. The total word count on this letter is 242 words. 242! Look how much he fits into 242 words. There's plot, character, personality and quirk. From this tightly written letter I know I'm going to get a fun, zany story. Those of you who wanted 250 words just to pitch your book, take heed! Shorter is better.

SOCIAL MEDIA ROUNDUP

The value of blogging, Twitter, and more.

....

by Kristen Grace

Writer and illustrators are now expected to be the masters of their own publicity. But with round-the-clock Twitter updates, Google+ hangouts, Facebook fan pages, and what seems like an endless supply of reading material dished out on author's blogs, it's hard to know where yet another aspiring author fits into the vast online landscape. How much time do you need to spend cultivating your online prescience? Do you need an account on every site? How much exposure is too much? We've invited four online writer/illustrator personalities to share their thoughts and personal guidelines for making the online community work for you.

SARAH OCKLER is the bestselling author of young adult novels *Twenty Boy Summer, Fixing Delilah*, and *Bittersweet*. Her books have been translated into several languages and have received numerous accolades, including ALA's Best Fiction for Young Adults, Girls' Life Top 100 Must Reads, ABA's Indie Next and more. When she's not writing or reading, Sarah enjoys taking pictures, hugging trees and road-tripping through the country with her husband, Alex. Visit her website at sarahockler.com or find her on Twitter or Facebook.

LINDSAY WARD has a BFA in Illustration from Syracuse University. She has illustrated a handful of children's picture books including *The Yellow Butterfly* (Bright Sky Press) by Mehrnaz S. Gill, *A Garden for Pig* (Kane/Miller) by Kathryn Thurman, and the covers of both STAR Academy books by Edward Kay (Random House Canada). Lindsay's most recent books *Pelly and Mr. Harrison Visit the Moon* (Kane/Miller) and *When Blue Met Egg* (Dial Books for Young Readers) were both written and illustrated by her. Her upcoming book with Dial Books for Young Readers will be released in 2013. You can visit her on the web at lindsaymward.com or see her blog at respectthecupcake.blogspot.com.

 **RAYMOND BEAN** is a father, teacher and the Amazon best-selling author of the Sweet Farts Series. His books have ranked #1 in children's humor, humorous series, and fantasy and adventure. The Sweet Farts series is consistently in Amazon's top 100 books for children. Foreign editions of his books have been released in Germany and Korea. Editions for Italy, Brazil and Turkey will be released soon. His School Is a Nightmare digital series launched in November of 2011. He writes for kids who claim they don't like reading. You can e-mail him at raymondbeanbooks@gmail.com.

 **KATE MESSNER** is the award-winning author of more than a dozen current and forthcoming books for children and teens. Her titles include E.B. White Read Aloud award-winner *The Brilliant Fall of Gianna Z.*, *Sugar and Ice*, and *Eye of the Storm* with Walker-Bloomsbury; the popular Marty McGuire chapter book series and *Capture the Flag* with Scholastic; and picture books like *Sea Monster's First Day* and *Over and Under the Snow*, an ALSC and *NY Times* Notable Children's Book and 2012 SCBWI Golden Kite Award winner with Chronicle Books. A TED 2012 speaker and former middle school English teacher, Kate is a frequent presenter at writing and education conferences. She also loves visiting classrooms and libraries in person and via Skype to talk about reading and writing with kids. You can follow her on Twitter (@katemessner) and learn more at her website: katemessner.com.

What social media outlets are you currently using? Which is your favorite? Which do you think is the most effective outlet to reach readers and buyers? Why?

OCKLER: I use Twitter, a Wordpress blog, Goodreads, YouTube and a limited Facebook fan page with no connected profile. My favorites—and consequently the most successful for me—are Twitter and the blog.

Now, here's a secret every aspiring and published author should know: The reason for their effectiveness has little to do with Twitter or Wordpress as media platforms and everything to do with authenticity and effort. Readers (especially teens) can spot insincerity a mile away, and if an author is using social media merely out of an obligation to pedal books, she's going to fail. Similarly, if authors don't actively cultivate their social sites, readers will stop showing up. There are lots of ways to reach readers and buyers, but the bottomline best strategy is pretty simple, online and off: Show up. Be yourself.

WARD: Currently I use Facebook, Twitter and my blog as my social media outlets. I have two Facebook profiles, one as an author/illustrator and one for my personal life. Although I am on Facebook from time to time I prefer Twitter as a way to reach the public in terms of upcoming events, new books and other book-related news. My blog enables me to expand on the promotion of my books, events, and everyday thoughts on writing and illustrating that Twitter would not allow because of the character limit.

BEAN: I have accounts with Facebook, Twitter and Skype. I also have a website and in my view, Amazon.com is also a form of social media. It's a hub where my readers can write reviews, read about my books and find links to my other social media sites.

Since my audience is generally reluctant readers between the ages of eight and 12, the goal of my social media efforts is to reach parents, teachers and librarians trying to find books that will motivate those reluctant readers.

MESSNER: I have a blog that's connected to my website, as well as Facebook, Twitter, Goodreads and Pinterest accounts. I'd have a tough time choosing a favorite of those because they all connect me with different kinds of readers and gatekeepers, and in different ways. I love my blog because it's a place to share the stories behind books—the research tidbits and photographs that may not make it into a book, even though I love them. And I think it's also a place where readers can see "Author= Kate" as a real person, too.

Tell us a little about how you came to this point. How did you get into social media in the first place? How did your use of it evolve to promote your books and make connections?

OCKLER: My use of the sites evolved along with my publication journey—once I had a book deal, I started meeting other authors online, and once that book hit the shelves, I was connecting more with actual teen readers, book bloggers, librarians and booksellers. Connecting is the key word—I try not to look at social media strictly as a promotional tool. Sure, promotion happens and it's important, and I definitely share links about new books and reviews and other related news, but I also chat about other authors' books, writing advice, food, television and the random stuff of life.

WARD: Up until recently I was a bit of a hermit when it came to promotion and social media. There are times when I am on Twitter and I see people who spend all day on there and I wonder how they get any work done. It takes a lot of self-discipline to write and/or illustrate from home because you have to step away from the TV or Internet and actually get work done. For this reason I stayed away from social media in the beginning of my career, until I realized how incredibly powerful and helpful it could be. I generally use my social media outlets as ways to discuss what is going on with me as an author/illustrator.

BEAN: When I first self-published in 2008 I used very little social media. I had a basic website with a contact link and that was about it. I didn't even have a Facebook account until fairly recently.

My experience was unique in that I wrote my first book, *Sweet Farts,* under a pen name. I didn't tell friends, family or colleagues about the book for over a year. My hunch was that if I wrote a book that young readers really enjoyed, they would promote it through word of mouth. I was very fortunate that my hunch paid off. My approach was unconventional, and I was fortunate that the book found an audience.

MESSNER: I was never involved in social media sites before I had books to promote, and really, that's why I started exploring territory like Facebook and Twitter. But once I started my blog and later on, joined Facebook, Twitter, GoodReads and Pinterest, I found that I really loved being part of those communities of teachers, librarians, parents and book lovers.

How much time each day (or week) do you dedicate to tweeting, blogging, updating, etc? How do you make sure you limit your time so you can actually write?

OCKLER: I don't have a set number of hours dedicated to social media—I just pop on when I feel like saying hello or when I have something interesting to share. For me, catching up with the Twitter stream often feels like grabbing a cup of coffee with friends—and then suddenly you look out the coffee shop window and it's dark, and they're about to close, and you realize you didn't get any work done, and now your latte's cold.

WARD: I generally don't really dedicate a specific amount of time to social media. I tweet when I have something to announce or share, which I usually do in the morning when I am spending time on e-mails and such. As for my blog, I try to post an entry every Wednesday if possible. The key to having a blog is maintaining it, which can be very difficult when work is busy. However, no one will read your blog if you only post twice a year. I think the best way to approach social media without it taking over your life is to give yourself a certain amount of time each day to do it and try to stick to that schedule.

BEAN: I try to limit how much and how often I post to Facebook, Twitter, etc. I have lesson plans to write and papers to grade! If I have a new cover to share or a new book coming out, I'll share it. If I hit a bestseller list somewhere, I'll post it and thank my readers.

MESSNER: I try to blog at least once a week, but it's often more than that if I'm doing a lot of book events or research trips and I'm excited to share photos. Aside from those blog entries, which may take anywhere from 10 minutes to an hour to write, I probably spend about an hour a day on social media, answering Tweets and Facebook messages, and posting updates and links. Writing always comes first, though.

What kinds of content are you offering readers that's making your efforts a success? How has your content and social media outreach changed or become better over time?

OCKLER: Before I was published, my blog was just a place to chat about my day or share the challenges of writing a YA novel while working a corporate gig. But now, I have a much wider audience that includes not only people I know in real life, but teen readers, librarians, book bloggers, booksellers, publishers, other published authors and aspiring writers seeking advice or anecdotes about the journey.

I try to blog about things that will appeal to these different audiences—maybe an article on finding an agent for the aspiring writers, followed by a review or giveaway of a YA book I loved for my teen readers, or a personal anecdote about something funny that happened that day just because. Twitter is more of a constant stream of chatter, like an ongoing conversation that can shift gears at any moment, and it's fun to jump in on other people's threads or retweet an interesting article, or comment on the latest episode of "The Walking Dead."

WARD: I try to offer my followers my perspective on things. Write what you know, which I know sounds like a cliché but it's true. I would never post a blog entry on tips for writing a YA novel because I don't know the first thing about it. Generally I try to offer my input on writing picture books and illustration, because that is what I feel comfortable with. My blog also tends to be more about what is going on in my life as an author/illustrator, which I think makes me seem more real and accessible to my readers.

BEAN: I try to always write my books with the reluctant reader in mind. I try to write content they'll talk about, and their parents and teachers will recommend.

MESSNER: I assume the people who are following me are interested in the kinds of books I write, so I try to ask myself, "What would be of interest to readers who like my books?" As someone who taught middle school for 15 years, I work especially hard to make teachers' and librarians' lives easier, sharing book recommendations, links and resources that they can use with students in the classroom.

What opportunities or connections have befallen you that you can directly attribute to your work through social media and blogging?

OCKLER: One experience that really stands out is the Speak Loudly campaign. In September 2010, Laurie Halse Anderson's incredible novel, *Speak*, was challenged in the Republic, Missouri school district along with Kurt Vonnegut's *Slaughterhouse-Five* and my novel, *Twenty Boy Summer*. Teacher Paul Hankins started the #SpeakLoudly hashtag on Twitter to spread the word about the challenges and encourage people to speak out against them. Through the Twitter conversation and all the ensuing blog posts, I "met" tons of readers, teachers, librarians and parents in the district. A year later, after the challenge was fully investigated by the school board, *Speak* was finally reinstated, but *Twenty Boy Summer* and *Slaughterhouse-Five* were both banned. The Springfield-Greene County Library that serves Republic invited me to visit during Banned Books Week in 2011, as did the Kurt Vonnegut Memorial Library in Indianapolis.

WARD: I have had conversations with editors and art directors that I don't think I would have had, had we not started chatting via social media. It's amazing what you can connect with another person about. And who knows what will come of those conversations.

BEAN: I've made connections with other writers in my genre. It's amazing how easily you can connect with others using social media. I've heard from teachers and readers all over the world thanks to Facebook, Twitter and my website. The first Sweet Farts book was released in Germany under the title *Stinker*. The illustrator of the German version found me on Facebook. I don't think he and I would have ever connected before social media.

MESSNER: I actually got a book deal thanks to my blog. I like to share my writing process, especially when it comes to revision, because I know how helpful it can be for a teacher to have examples of real authors revising to show students who are reluctant writers. So whenever I can, I post revision stories and photos of my marked-up manuscripts, with tips for student writers. One day, I got an e-mail from the acquisitions editor at Stenhouse, asking if I'd be interested in writing a book to demystify the revision process.

My Twitter feed and blog have also led to school visits and other speaking invitations. I've also presented on using social media to connect readers and authors at a number of national conferences for teachers, librarians and writers.

Let's say you're addressing a group of new writers. How should budding authors and illustrators be using social media to further their career? What would

you tell them? (In other words, what did you wish you knew at the beginning of your journey?)

OCKLER: Social media is a great way to connect with readers and colleagues, but if you're not writing anything for us to read, all the "follows" and "likes" in the world aren't going to further your career. Only your books can do that.

WARD: Go on the Internet and see what is out there, spend time reading some blogs, tweeting, and see what people are discussing in the industry. And then close your computer and do what you do. Write. Illustrate. Focus. Because you are never going to write your book if you are tweeting all day. Pull what you can from social media but don't let it run your life.

MESSNER: Be interesting, friendly and helpful—and social media will work for you. Share a variety of ideas, news, links and photos. When you have good news about your books, share that, too. Celebrate other writers' good news at least as often as you celebrate your own, and share book recommendations for lots of titles that you didn't write.

Do you set any rules for yourself when interacting online? If so, what are they?

OCKLER: I try to follow the rule of common sense, which means I don't share overly personal information or air my dirty laundry (and that's not a pun on my work pajamas). It's one thing to be authentic and honest, but it's another thing entirely to report every single opinion, thought, location, desire, fear, mother's maiden name, meal, doctor visit, relationship details, scars … you get the idea! Social networking is a great way to connect with other book lovers, but no matter how chummy and informal it feels, it's not a venue for opening up every aspect of our lives to outside observation, commentary and icky corporate data mining.

WARD: The only rule I really have for myself when it comes to social media is how much I share, especially when it comes to my personal life. I would never tweet or post something on Facebook that I wouldn't want anyone in the world to be able to read. I am a firm believer in keeping your private life separate from your professional life. Also, when it comes to tweeting, I don't force conversations with editors just because I really admire them and I want to talk to them. There is a fine line between polite conversation and being intrusive or pushy.

MESSNER: In everything I do online, I remember that I write books for kids. You'll read about a huge variety of things on my social media feeds—how I write, what I'm reading, trips I'm taking and what I'm learning about—everything from tornadoes to airport security to venomous snakes. But you'll never read anything on my blog or any of my social media feeds that a teacher couldn't share with a class full of fifth graders.

How do you approach other writers and illustrators to develop online connections? How do others approach you?

OCKLER: For the most part, young adult authors and illustrators are really friendly and open online, so it's pretty easy to connect. I might read and comment on another author's blog, post a review of his work on mine, or just start following him on Twitter. Authors find me in much the same way. From there, it's easy to build a rapport because we're all chatting about similar writerly interests: books, authors, movies, chocolate, coffee—stuff like that.

WARD: Generally, if I want to tell someone how great I think their work is or something along those lines I will say it, even if I don't know them. At the end of the day, we as writers and illustrators want to know that people are appreciating and enjoying our work and what better way to do that than connecting with each other about it. Most of my online connections have developed through other people. Either we share the same agent, participate in a book club together, have met in passing at a conference or something along those lines. And from there I meet their connections. The circle keeps on growing.

MESSNER: Authors and illustrators who maintain blogs and Twitter feeds are pretty much universally delighted to be followed, so there's no reason you can't follow and interact with anyone you admire online. Facebook can be a little trickier because people set up accounts there with different expectations. Some authors share photos of their kids with family members via Facebook and may feel strange about having many "friends" they've never met in real life. But many—most, I'd guess—are happy to have readers, teachers, librarians, booksellers and fellow writers as friends. When you add someone you don't know personally on Facebook, it's not a bad idea to send a message along with the request. Just a quick note saying "I love your books" or "I heard you speak at such-and-such a conference …" to let the person know that you're already a friend in the literary world.

When you're viewing other people's blogs and Twitter accounts and Facebook profiles, where are other writers going wrong in their outreach, in your opinion?

OCKLER: The first mistake is when writers commandeer social media strictly for the hard sell. It's great to share news about a new book, retweet a glowing review, chat about a work in progress or answer reader questions—after all, readers and fans connect online because they *want* to hear about an author and her books. But if a Twitter stream is full of "buy my book, buy my book, buy my book" with no genuine personality or real reciprocity in the conversation, that's a huge turnoff and the quickest way to alienate readers and lose fans.

The second mistake is when writers set up dozens of different social media accounts just because they feel they have to, and then struggle with updating or participating in any meaningful way. When authors abandon their social media accounts, or they just post the same few links to every single media outlet, it becomes a waste of everyone's time and after awhile, readers will venture elsewhere.

WARD: I definitely think that when people are inappropriate about other writers' work or have a bad experience with someone in the industry and talk about it on a public forum, such as Facebook or Twitter, that reflects badly. Obviously there are going to be reviews and blog posts that tear apart your work. If you publish something, that means everyone is allowed to have an opinion on it unfortunately. But keep in mind that you never know who is reading your posts or tweets about said agent/writer/illustrator/editor. You don't want to be known for bad-mouthing peers in the industry.

MESSNER: I know people approach social media with different expectations, but I have to be honest—I cringe when I see someone who writes books for children or teens tweeting a string of expletives or blogging about how they were drunk the night before. It makes it difficult for teachers and librarians to share your online links with students.

The other mistake I see enthusiastic new writers making is tweeting only about their books. I've heard people compare social media outlets to cocktail parties, and I think that's a good metaphor. When you're at a social gathering, you want to hang out with people who are interesting—who talk about lots of different things and share neat ideas. If some of them wrote books, you'd be interested in hearing about those, for sure. But you probably wouldn't spend very long talking with someone who blabbed on about his or her book and nothing else all night long. Social gatherings online are no different.

KRISTEN GRACE is an Ohio-based writer and contributor to *Writer's Digest*. She recently earned her Master's Degree in English from Miami University of Ohio. Her favorite time of the day is mid-morning when she can sit on the porch, sip coffee and read a good book. You can check out her blog at kegrace.wordpress.com or follow her on twitter (@kayeeegee).

WRITING CONVINCING CHARACTERS IN YA

Compose characters that pop off the page.

....

by K.L. Going

Whether you're writing for teens, kids or adults, creating memorable characters is what elevates an idea from a novelty to a story with substance that will draw us in and make us care about the outcome. If your audience invests in your characters, whether that investment comes in the form of love, hate or morbid fascination, they'll keep turning the pages and following the story until the bitter end.

So what makes a good character? Why do some characters live while others fall flat? How can you create teen characters who are both believable and sympathetic? In this article we'll take a look at creating the characters who will bring your stories to life.

WHAT MAKES A CHARACTER?

Every human being has certain attributes, but those attributes are always in flux. We have physical attributes such as eye color, hair color, age, weight and height, as well as myriad other features that make us unique—large ears, a small nose or exceptionally big feet. Many of these physical traits will change as we grow and mature, and teen characters, especially, are in transition.

For example, physical changes such as puberty often lead to changes in personality, and personality traits are a big part of defining a character. Teens can be irritable, kind, stingy, open, rude, false, generous, conniving, hyper, morose or curious, just to name a few. They are often many of these things simultaneously, and over the course of a lifetime each person will embody almost every personality trait there is.

Our personalities reveal themselves through our speech, actions and body language. Every person has a unique way of talking, walking, sitting, eating, sleeping and doing just about any activity you can think of. We all have habits and idiosyncrasies, but again, these habits don't stay the same forever. Teens are often purposefully trying to shape their habits, looking to mold themselves into the people they'd like to become, and those imagined future selves might be rich and famous, or they might be saving the world. Or both!

Watching what a character does or does not do can reveal what she wants and help create a fuller sense of who she is both physically and emotionally. This is especially true when we reveal the reasons behind her actions. Although different people may appear to make similar decisions, our choices are based on our varied life experiences. When we reveal a character's history and inner life, in addition to showing his actions, we shed light on his motivations, attitudes, desires and struggles, and this adds depth to our portrayal.

MAKING CHOICES

Each character we create is a totally distinct person, and it's our job to reveal them to the world. But there's a wealth of information that can be conveyed about any human being, and teens are especially complex because they are still figuring out who they are and what roles they want to take in life. So how do we give the reader an accurate portrait?

Part of what it means to be an author is deciding which information to convey to your reader and how to convey it. Writing isn't just about putting words on a page; it's about artistry. Like any artist, you'll need to make decisions about what to include or exclude in order to produce the most impact or the greatest beauty.

When it comes to character development, choices are essential. Obviously you can't describe every character trait—if you did, you'd fill entire volumes with description and there'd be no room for anything to actually happen in the story, nor would there be any artistry. Instead, choose which features best define your character; this description can be a mix of physical traits, personality, backstory and character choices.

What we most need to know about a character is what makes him who he is and what will drive his actions. Many times, especially for teens, physical appearance plays a large part in this. An awkward teen will behave very differently from an effortlessly beautiful one. Not only will she make different choices, she will move differently through space.

Think about the characters you create. What will your reader need to know to make them real? Do you allow for complexity? How does a character's physical appearance affect his mental state? Instead of falling back on the tried-and-true descriptions of hair color, eye color, and one or two dominant personality traits, consider what truly defines each of your characters. Choose the information—whether it comes in the form of physical appearance, body language or backstory—that will best reveal your character to your reader, and you'll find that your story will come to life.

PASSIVE VS. ACTIVE CHARACTERS

While it's true that we all know people in real life who seem to drift along on the tide, never taking much initiative to affect their circumstances, we don't necessarily want to read about them. We're all familiar with the stereotype of the antisocial teen who hides out in her bedroom, but would you want to read a book about that person? Not only is it hard for the audience to figure out who she is, it's tough to invest in her journey because there's nothing she's looking to learn or accomplish.

Active characters, on the other hand, are endlessly fascinating because we're always wondering what they'll do next. It's easy to feel as if we know them well, and when a reader feels like they know a character in the same way they know a real person, they'll invest in loving him, hating him, rooting for him or laughing with him. Active characters shape the plot through the choices they make, and their desires create mirrored desires in the audience.

As a writer, you have two very powerful tools for creating active characters: actions and dialogue. Active characters use plenty of both. They make choices, doing and saying things that lead to new choices and new actions, advancing the plot. Give your characters plenty to say and do. Make them leap, make them dance, make them cry and make them laugh. In short, make them live.

USING ACTION TO DEFINE CHARACTER

Contrary to what many people think, action isn't just about plot. Actions also reveal character. What a person does shows us who he is—not just who he says he is. We all know how this works in real life. How many of us had a classmate who was saccharine sweet on the outside but talked with an acid tongue as soon as someone else's back was turned? Do you remember the shy girl who never said a word, but when courage was needed she was the first one who stepped up? Or how about the popular guy who acted conceited until he was alone, then he couldn't stop talking about his little brothers and sisters?

The revelatory power of our actions is no less true in fiction. In fact, it's probably even more necessary on the page, where a story exists for only one reader at a time and there's no one to ask for a second opinion. The best example of this power is the use of the unreliable narrator. When an author uses this technique, the character is telling the audience one thing, but the audience is expected to come to a different conclusion based on the character's actions.

If you are using the unreliable narrator technique, make sure your character's actions are not interpreted for the reader by the narrator. The most important element in creating this kind of character is trusting your reader to reach her own conclusions. Let your character's actions become the palette through which you, as the author, influence your audience.

Show the reader what the character does and he will see your character's true nature. Remember that a reader brings with him all of his own life experiences and most of us, by the time we reach our teenage years, have developed a good sense of human nature. We're capable of seeing what people do and, based on that, discerning a piece of who they are. No matter what, don't be afraid to let your reader use his judgment.

DIALOGUE

Dialogue is another important tool for defining character. Teenagers don't act in a vacuum. They talk about their lives with their friends, family, teachers and significant others. These conversations both shape and reveal who a person is. Like action, dialogue is a way for a character's true personality to show without you, as the author, having to explicitly state the message you're trying to get across. And unlike a deliberately stated explanation, dialogue draws a reader in.

Imagine a teacher standing at the front of a packed classroom lecturing. After a while, the students start shifting in their seats and sneaking glances at their watches. Straight exposition can only hold our attention for so long. In a teen novel, that time period is mercilessly short.

Dialogue, however, works in an entirely different manner. Imagine that same teacher standing in the hallway whispering to another teacher. Now they truly have your attention and they can hold it for a lot longer because of the "What ifs" created by the format. In dialogue we are constantly wondering what someone will say and how the other person will respond.

By using dialogue, you can create an intimate tone, letting your audience feel as if they're overhearing something interesting, even while the main character withholds information that isn't revealed until the end of the book. Remember to use both the positive (what is said) and the negative (what isn't said) as you craft your conversations on the page. Read them aloud to make sure they sound natural.

BODY LANGUAGE

Body language is a combination of action and dialogue, and it can be a very powerful tool. When done well, body language can add a subtle layer underneath the overt action, enhancing what your characters are saying and doing, and giving your audience additional insight into the scene you're creating.

We all read each other's body language in real life, so why not let it work for you in your fiction? That scowl you've seen flitting across your mother-in-law's face? The tension that creeps into your friend's shoulders every time she talks about her past? Study the way she reacts and use it to paint a picture for your readers that hints at something your character isn't revealing. Don't be afraid to let your characters itch, twitch, squirm and squint.

WORDS OF CAUTION

Body language and dialogue are two of the best ways to bring characters to life, but I would offer a few words of caution, especially regarding dialogue. Characters in books do not speak the same way people in real life speak. Most of us ramble, cutting off sentences in the middle and never getting back to them. We allow our train of thought to take us off the topic of conversation. Some of us might repeat the same actions, like twitching or blinking or scratching, far more than we're aware. We say "um," "like," and "you know" so often that we cease to hear them.

If you've ever had to take dictation you understand what I mean. When you read through an actual transcript of a conversation it's nearly impossible to follow. While writers strive for realism, this is not something we want to emulate. Remember that dialogue is meant to reveal character, not writing prowess. In the best scenes the writer fades into the background so much so that the reader forgets the writer exists. The reader has suspended his disbelief to the point where he feels as if he is listening to a conversation between two real people.

Dialogue, as well as first-person narrative, is all about weighing what sounds real against what makes for clean reading. A good rule of thumb is that a little goes a long way. Do you feel your teen character would say "like" a lot? Well, one strategically placed "like" can have more impact than the more realistic dozens of uses because the flow of the text is not interrupted. The same can be applied to accents and regional words. Dialogue is a powerful tool, but choose your characters' words wisely. Remember, writing is not about capturing speech verbatim—it's about using rhythm and word choice to capture the truth of what your characters say. How the words translate to the reader is more important than how they would sound in real life.

TYPES OF CHARACTERS

When you begin a story, it's important to be very clear about whose story you're telling. Many writers relate experiences where characters they intended to keep in the background gain prominence as the story progresses. Characters can take on lives of their own, which is great because it allows for spontaneity as we create our novels, but when push comes to shove, it's still our job to make sure the right story gets told. Sometimes, that story might truly belong to a character other than the one we thought was the main character. If so, this will involve going back to square one to start over again. But more often than not, what needs to happen is for you to be clear in your own mind about who the main character is and what that character's story arc should be.

Remember this: The main character is the one the story is about. She is the one whose actions should most affect the plot. This is not to say there won't be other major characters with story arcs of their own. A secondary character can even end up being a reader's favorite character, but in the end, the story is not his, and if it was, it would be told very differently.

Secondary characters exist to interact with the main character. They might be fabulous, interesting, hilarious or brilliant, but if they didn't relate to the main character's story, we wouldn't know about them. Consider comic books as an example. Every hero has a sidekick, and while he is central to the story, he never takes over the main character's role.

In addition to the main character and major secondary characters, there are also minor characters who play smaller roles in your main character's life. I've often heard these characters likened to extras on a movie set. Some extras have speaking roles and they might reappear during the course of the movie, but others will only be seen in the background, never being named or clearly defined.

With every character you create, be sure the amount of time you spend developing them is proportional to their importance. Let your reader know right from the start who your main character is and be consistent throughout. The most action and dialogue should go to your main character and the major secondary characters she interacts with.

STEREOTYPES

When dealing with your main character and your major secondary characters, stereotypes should either be avoided or given a surprise twist so your reader doesn't feel like he is reading a cliché. When a major character relies too heavily on stereotypes, your reader will feel like he's read your story before and it will be difficult for him to suspend his disbelief. However, if you take a conventional character type, such as the popular cheerleader, and give her companion traits the reader isn't expecting—a MENSA IQ perhaps, or maybe a rebellious streak and a penchant for tattoos—this will wake the reader up again. We're interested in what's unfamiliar. That's why characters with interesting quirks are so attractive.

The times you can use stereotypes without subverting them are when you're developing minor background characters you want your reader to be able to recognize without taking the time to tell that character's entire story, or when you're using parody or humor and want to poke fun at the stereotype itself.

Stereotypes can be a tool, allowing the reader to feel like he knows a minor, insignificant character, or they can be a launching pad for creating an against-type character, but either way they must be used judiciously. When you choose to use a stereotype, you not only risk boring your readers, you risk offending them. Choose your risks wisely.

YOUR MOST VALUABLE PLAYERS

No matter what type of characters you decide to create, remember that, when done well, characterization can be your most valuable tool. It's the characters your readers must root for, sympathize with or despise, and the more real your characters seem, the more real the story will become to your audience.

Take time to study the teens you interact with in your daily life. See if they have traits you can use. Human beings are complex, and this complexity makes us endlessly fascinating. Characters you vividly portray, exploring their nuances and delving into their motivations, contradictions and emotions, will draw your teen readers in and allow them to gain insight into themselves as they recognize pieces of who they are in what your characters do and say.

Our teenage years are characterized by exploration of the world as we transition from childhood to adulthood. Experiences are new and intense, and our passage to self-discovery is at a critical juncture. As teens recognize the places of darkness and light within the characters we create, they will also begin to recognize those places within themselves. We owe it to them to dig deeply, offering more than what is on the surface of human nature.

As an author for young adults, you have the opportunity to bring to life characters that will stick with your readers long after they have closed your book, illuminating aspects of human nature that might otherwise have remained in the dark. You have the chance to influence your readers at a time when they are still forming their worldviews and discovering themselves. This is both the solemn responsibility and the great joy of writing YA novels.

K.L. GOING's first novel, *Fat Kid Rules the World*, was a Michael Printz Honor Book, listed with YALSA's Best Books for Young Adults and their Best Books for the Past Decade. Her books have been Booksense picks, Scholastic Book Club choices, Junior Library Guild selections, NY Public Library Best Books for the Teenage, and winners of state book awards. Her work has been published in Korea, Italy, Japan, Germany, and the UK, and *Fat Kid Rules the World* is now a major motion picture. To visit KL online, go to klgoing.com or find her on Twitter.

CREATE YOUR WRITER PLATFORM

How novelists can get noticed.

....

by Chuck Sambuchino

The chatter about the importance of a writer platform builds each year. Having an effective platform has never been more important than right now. With so many books available and few publicists left to help promote, the burden now lies upon the author to make sure copies of their book fly off bookshelves. In other words, the pressure is on for writers to act as their own publicist and chief marketer, and very few can do this successfully.

Know that if you're writing nonfiction, a damn good idea won't cut it. You need to prove that people will buy your book by showing a comprehensive ability to market yourself through different channels such as social networking sites and traditional media. If you can't do that, a publisher won't even consider your idea.

WHAT IS PLATFORM?

Platform, simply put, is your visibility as an author. In other words, platform is your personal ability to sell books right this instant. Better yet, I've always thought of platform like this: When you speak, who listens? In other words, when you have a something to say, what legitimate channels exist for you to release your message to audiences who will consider buying your books/services?

Platform will be your key to finding success as an author, especially if you're writing nonfiction. Breaking the definition down, realize that platform is your personal ability to sell books through:

1. Who you are
2. Personal and professional connections you have
3. Any media outlets (including personal blogs and social networks) that you can utilize to sell books

In my opinion, the following are the most frequent building blocks of a platform:

1. A blog of impressive size
2. A newsletter of impressive size
3. Article/column writing (or correspondent involvement) for the media—preferably for larger publications, radio and TV shows
4. Contributions to successful websites, blogs and periodicals helmed by others
5. A track record of strong past book sales that ensures past readers will buy your future titles
6. Networking, and your ability to meet power players in your community and subject area
7. Public speaking appearances—especially national ones; the bigger the better
8. An impressive social media presence (such as on Twitter or Facebook)
9. Membership in organizations that support the successes of their own
10. Recurring media appearances and interviews—in print, on the radio, on TV or online
11. Personal contacts (organizational, media, celebrity, relatives) who can help you market at no cost to yourself, whether through blurbs, promotion or other means.

Not all of these methods will be of interest/relevance to you. As you learn more about to how to find success in each one, some will jump out at you as practical and feasible, while others will not.

"PLATFORM" VS. "PUBLICITY"

Platform and publicity are interconnected yet very different. Platform is what you do before a book comes out to make sure that when it hits shelves, it doesn't stay there long. Publicity is an active effort to acquire media attention for a book that already exists. In other words, platform falls upon the author, whereas (hopefully) publicity will be handled by a publicist, either in-house or contracted for money.

Do something right now: Go to Amazon.com and find a book for sale that promises to teach you how to sell more books. Look at the comparable titles below it and start scrolling left to right using the arrows. (Do it now. I'll wait.) Tons of them, aren't there? It's because so many authors are looking for any way possible to promote their work, especially the many self-published writers out there. They've got a book out—and now they realize copies aren't selling. Apparently having your work online to buy at places like Amazon isn't enough to have success as a writer. That's why we must take the reins on our own platform and marketing.

As a last thought, perhaps consider it like this: Publicity is about asking and wanting—*gimme gimme gimme*. Platform is about giving first, then receiving because of what you've given and the goodwill it's earned you.

THE FUNDAMENTAL PRINCIPLES OF PLATFORM

1. It is in giving that we receive.

In my experience, this concept—*it is in giving that we receive*—is the fundamental rule of platform, and it will rear its head in every chapter of this book, over and over again. Building a platform means that people follow your updates, listen to your words, respect and trust you, and, yes, will consider buying whatever it is you're selling. But they will only do that if they like you—and the way you get readers to like you is by legitimately helping them. Answer their questions. Give them stuff for free. Share sources of good, helpful information. Make them laugh and smile. Inform them and make their lives easier and/or better. Do what they cannot: cull together information or entertainment of value. Access people and places they want to learn more about. Help them achieve their goals. Enrich their lives. After they have seen the value you provide, they will want to stay in contact with you for more information. They begin to like you, and become a follower. And the more followers you have, the bigger your platform becomes.

2. You don't have to go it alone.

Creating a large and effective platform from scratch is, to say the least, a daunting task. But you don't have to swim out in the ocean alone; you can—and are encouraged to—work with others. There are many opportunities to latch on to bigger publications and groups in getting your words out. And when your own platform outlets—such as a blog—get large enough, they will be a popular source for others seeking to contribute guest content. You will find yourself constantly teaming with others on your way up, and even after you've found some success.

3. Platform is what you are *able* to do, not what you are *willing* to do.

I review nonfiction book proposals for writers, and in each of these proposals there is a marketing section. Whenever I start to read a marketing section and see bullet points such as "I am happy to go on a book tour" or "I believe that Fox News and MSNBC will be interested in this book because it is controversial," then I stop reading—because the proposal has a big problem. Understand this immediately: Your platform is not pie-in-the-sky thinking. It is not what you hope will happen or maybe could possibly hopefully happen sometime if you're lucky and all the stars align when your publicist works really hard. It's also not what you are willing to do, such as "be interviewed by the media" or "sign books at trade events." (Everyone is willing to do these things, so by mentioning them, you are making no case for your book because you're demonstrating no value.) The true distinction for writer platform is that it must be absolutely what you can make happen right now.

4. You can only learn so much about writer platform by instruction, which is why you should study what others do well and learn by example.

I don't know about you, but, personally, I learn from watching and doing better than I learn from reading. On that note, don't be afraid to study and mimic what others are doing. If you are looking for totally original ideas on how to blog and build your platform, I'll just tell you right now there likely are few or none left. So if you want to see what's working, go to the blogs and websites and Twitter feeds and newspaper columns of those you admire—then take a page from what they're doing. If you start to notice your favorite large blogs include all their social networking links at the top ("Find me on Twitter," "Find me on Facebook"), then guess what? Do the same. If people are getting large followings doing book reviews of young adult fantasy novels, why not do the same?

WHAT CONSTITUTES A FICTION NICHE?

Nonfiction writers have a relatively clear route with platform. But what's a novelist's specialty? In my opinion, writers of fiction have three different platform journeys they can take:

1. THE "LOOSE SUBJECT CONNECTION" NICHE

This approach means focusing on a major theme in your book and making that your focus. Perhaps your books always feature detectives of Native-American descent—most of the time solving cases on reservations. You obviously have a great interest in Native-American culture, so how can that translate into a blog? Perhaps you can write about news involving First Peoples communities, or inspiring stories of what's going on in the West today. Or perhaps you can do some research and share interesting stories from the past that many people don't know. You're creating content that has a major relation to what you're writing, so those who come to your site and also read fiction would be target readers for you.

2. THE "ALTOGETHER DIFFERENT" NICHE

This approach is when you simply try to build a blog and platform of some size while acknowledging that it has little or no connection to your novels and memoir. For example, let's say you're writing literary fiction and are now sitting around brainstorming what to blog about—asking yourself, "What do I love to discuss in life?" Perhaps the number one answer you keep coming back to is, of all things, mountain biking. OK. If this is your true passion in life, and you won't easily get bored writing about it, then I say go for it. Create content with passion and gusto, and build a community around yourself. The goal is simply to create a huge readership, and hope some of that visibility translates to book sales—which it no doubt will, though exact numbers will be difficult to come by.

3. THE "WRITING FOCUS" NICHE

This approach is where the primary content focus of the blog is your own writing journey, along with your own personal successes and challenges along the way. The immediate good news is that there are plenty of up-and-coming writers who will immediately identify with your subject matter. The bad news is that there must be more than 10,000 of these "new writer" blogs out there. And that means you are immediately facing stiff competition everywhere in every direction. Try to have different dimensions and elements to your brand other than "writer trying to make it who wants to update you about their writing journey."

5. You must make yourself easy to contact.

I have no idea why people make themselves difficult to contact without a website and/or e-mail listed online. Besides "visibility," another way to think about platform is to examine your reach. And if your goal is reach, you do not want to limit people's abilities to find and contact you much if at all. You want people to contact you. You want other writers to e-mail from out of the blue. I love it when a member of the media finds my info online and writes me. I don't even mind it when a writer sends me an e-mail with a random question. I've made long-term friends that way—friends who have bought my book and sung my praises to others. It's called networking—and networking starts by simply making yourself available, and taking the next step to encourage people with similar interests or questions to contact you.

6. Start small and start early.

A true writer platform is something that's built before your book comes out, so that when the book hits your hands, you will be above the masses for all to see. I won't lie—the beginning is hard. It's full of a lot of effort and not a whole lot of return. Fear not; this will pass. Building a platform is like building a structure—every brick helps. Every brick counts. Small steps are not bad. You must always be considering what an action has to offer and if it can lead to bigger and better things. "What frustrates most people is that they want to have platform now," says literary agent Roseanne Wells of the Marianne Strong Literary Agency. "It takes time and a lot of effort, and it builds on itself. You can always have more platform, but trying to sell a book before you have it will not help you."

7. Have a plan, but feel free to make tweaks.

At first, uncertainty will overwhelm you. What are you going to blog about? How should you present yourself when networking? Should your Twitter handle be your name or the title of your book/brand? All these important questions deserve careful thought early on. The earlier you have a plan, the better off you will be in the long run—so don't just jump in blind. The more you can diagram and strategize at the beginning, the clearer your road will be.

As you step out and begin creating a writer platform, make sure to analyze how you're doing, then slowly transition so you're playing to your strengths and eliminating your weakest elements. No matter what you want to write about, no matter what platform elements you hone in on, don't ignore the importance of analysis and evolution in your journey. Take a look at what you're doing right and wrong to make sure you're not throwing good money after bad. And feel free to make all kinds of necessary tweaks and changes along the way to better your route.

8. Numbers matter—so quantify your platform

Always be looking to quantify your platform. If you don't include specific numbers or details, editors and agents will be forced to assume the element of platform is unimpressive, which is why you left out the crucial detail of its size/reach. Details are sexy; don't tease us. Try these right and wrong approaches below:

WRONG: "I am on Twitter and just love it."
CORRECT: "I have more than 10,000 followers on Twitter."

WRONG: "I do public speaking on this subject."
CORRECT: "I present to at least 10 events a year—sometimes as a keynote. The largest events have up to 1,200 attendees."

WRONG: "I run a blog that has won awards from other friendly bloggers."
CORRECT: "My blog averages 75,000 page views each month and is growing at a rate of 8 percent each month over the past year."

Also, analyzing numbers will help you see what's working and not working in your platform plan—allowing you to make healthy changes and let the strategy evolve (see Fundamental Principle No. 7). Numbers reflect the success you're having, and it's up to you to figure out why you're having that success.

CHUCK SAMBUCHINO (chucksambuchino.com, @chucksambuchino on Twitter) edits the *Guide to Literary Agents* (guidetoliteraryagents.com/blog) as well as the *Children's Writer's & Illustrator's Market*. His pop humor books include *How to Survive a Garden Gnome Attack* (film rights optioned by Sony) and *Red Dog / Blue Dog: When Pooches Get Political* (reddog-bluedog.com). Chuck's other writing books include *Formatting & Submitting Your Manuscript, 3rd. Ed.*, and *Create Your Writer Platform* (fall 2012). Besides that, he is a husband, guitarist, dog owner, and cookie addict. He loves meeting new writers at conferences and events all across the country.

"PLATFORM" VS. "CREDENTIALS"

Like we discussed, the most important question you will be asked as you try to get your nonfiction book published is: "Why are you the best person to write this book?" This question is two-fold, as it inquires into both your credentials and your platform. To be a successful author, you will need both, not just the former.

Your credentials encompass your education and experience to be considered as an expert in your category. For example, if you want to write a book called *How to Lose 10 Pounds in 10 Weeks*, then my first thought would be to wonder if you are a doctor or a dietician. If not, what position do you hold that would give you solid authority to speak on your subject and have others not question the advice you're presenting? Or maybe you want to write a book on how to sell real estate in a challenging market. To have the necessary gravitas to compose such a book, you would likely have to have worked as an agent for decades and excelled in your field—likely winning awards over the years and acting in leadership roles within the real estate agent community.

Would you buy a book on how to train a puppy from someone whose only credential was that they owned a dog? I wouldn't. I want to see accolades, leadership positions, endorsements, educational notes and more. I need to make sure I'm learning from an expert before I stop questioning the text and take it as helpful fact.

All this—all your authority—comes from your credentials. That's why they're so necessary. But believe it or not, credentials are often easier to come by than platform.

Platform, as we now know, is your ability to sell books and market yourself to target audience(s). There are likely many dieticians out there who can teach people interesting ways to lower their weight. But a publishing company is not interested in the 90 percent of them who lack any platform. They want the 10 percent of experts who have the ability to reach readers. Publishing houses seek experts who possess websites, mailing lists, media contacts, a healthy number of Twitter followers and a plan for how to grow their visibility.

It's where credentials meet platform—*that's* where book authors are born.

WRITING NONFICTION

The essentials of writing true-life books for kids.

....

by Audrey Vernick

Today's nonfiction for kids bears little similarity to the nonfiction books I had to read in grade school. I vividly, palpably remember the anguish caused by having to get through a yellowy library book about Florence Nightingale. An avid reader of *good* books, I found that biography to be torture. I shouted out updates on my halting progress from the bedroom: "Seventy-four more pages!"

Today's nonfiction pops. It rocks. It makes me want to read everything. Who knew there could be books for kids about the history of the hot dog and spies and Barbie and sugar and Superman and ice cream? Nonfiction is reaching a wider audience, a trade audience, because the books are finally, well, interesting. And well written.

"Children deserve our absolute best work," says Tami Lewis Brown, author of the non-fiction picture book *Soar Elinor*. "They deserve to know the truth as best as we can tell it."

So where's an author to begin? The straight-up answer: with a rock-solid idea, and a lot of thoughtful consideration.

THE IDEA

Some people are idea hunters. Others are like me: good ideas have been kind enough to seek us out. We just had to pay attention (see this article's sidebar).

However the idea finds you, or you it, the next steps usually go like this: research/think/write, repeat. Mixed in there are the following questions to continuously ask yourself: Is this idea good enough? Can it sustain a book? Has it been done before? Can I develop something new and unique? Does it have an audience?

"Have a killer idea," suggests Erin Murphy of the Erin Murphy Literary Agency. "Easy, right? Something relatable to kids that hasn't been done to death, preferably with some universal curriculum tie-ins. Something fresh!"

It's a heady, think-heavy time when you're all excited about a new idea. Some writers let their idea marinate for a while. Others dive right into research on their subject. Some might do a broad market search to see what, if anything, has been published on the same or similar topics.

Thorough research, with proper citations, is essential. Murphy suggests that writers "prove yourself to be respectful of the nonfiction genre—do your research, cite it, have as many primary sources as possible, and include an author's note fleshing out the information as needed."

"I tend to think about projects a lot before I actually start doing any work on them—or rather, I let them sit, and if I find myself thinking about one a lot, then I know that it's a project that would sustain my interest for a good long while," says Chris Barton, author of *The Day-Glo Brothers* and *Can I See Your I.D.?*

The thinking a writer does at this stage can go a long way toward preventing all kinds of rookie mistakes—from insufficient or undocumented research to incorrectly identifying who your readers will be.

WHO'S THE AUDIENCE?

This usually gets folded into the research/think/write mix, but it's worthy of its own heading because it's so important. For some projects, the intended audience is clear at the outset. Some books, for example, are only suitable for a middle grade or teen audience because the subject matter would be inappropriate for picture book readers. But other times, determining the proper audience—and thus the appropriate format for the book—can be murky business.

"The intended age of my audience evolves as I get to know the story," says Tanya Lee Stone, author of award-winning nonfiction books including *Almost Astronauts* and *The Good, the Bad, and the Barbie*. "I have started several picture books that have turned into long-form nonfiction for older readers. The structure can only really come after I know what the story is I need to tell."

Remaining open to that kind of change is difficult, but it's essential. You don't only need to be a master of the subject matter—you need to know who needs to know that story, and what would be the best way to tell it.

"I knew that *The Day-Glo Brothers* had to be a picture book—the whole point was to show the colors—but that (unfortunately) didn't stop me from initially shopping around a 6,200-word draft," Barton says. "The stories in *Can I See Your I.D.?* contain elements best suited for older readers, but whether that older-than-a-picture-book format would be geared toward middle grades or YA became clearer only as I decided which of those elements truly needed to be included."

KNOW AND RESPECT THE CATEGORY

Readers count on the author to present an authentic representation of the truth. And writers often feel a tremendous responsibility to tell their subject's story in a way that would do the subject proud. "As a pilot, a writer and a woman, I felt a big responsibility to get Elinor's story right and tell it well," Brown says.

Telling a compelling story while providing enough context for young readers without being didactic is an extremely delicate balancing act. "Writing for kids doesn't mean writing down, which is a frequent mistake even experienced writers make," says Jennifer Greene, senior editor at Clarion Books. "At the same time, one can't assume kids have the same knowledge base as educated adults."

Getting all your nonfiction ducks in a row—that's the easy way to show an agent or an editor that you know what you're doing.

PROPOSAL OR FULL MANUSCRIPT?

As with most things in publishing, there's no set-in-stone answer to whether you need to submit a completed manuscript or a thorough proposal when seeking publication. Generally, though not always, first-time authors will need to complete the work before submitting. "From first-time nonfiction writers, I have only acquired projects that were complete," Greene says. Nonfiction writing, especially for kids, is just as much of a craft as fiction writing, and even with a great topic and hook and previous writing experience, there's no guarantee a writer will be able to do it well, or have an understanding of the level of research and work that is entailed."

There are occasional exceptions. Cynthia Levinson, author of the 2012 release *We Have A Job: The 1963 Birmingham Children's March*, was a first-timer when Peachtree acquired her project based upon a proposal. According to Levinson, it was "a very detailed and solid proposal, which consisted of five sample chapters; a narrative outline with several paragraphs on each of the remaining chapters; an extensive bibliography that included background reading, personal interviews and other primary-source research, and a trip to Birmingham; and a list of ancillary materials and back matter."

It's more common for seasoned authors than first-timers to sell their books based on a proposal. According to Stone, "I have been able to sell a new book based on an idea, an outline and a sample. But I'm not sure I prefer it. There are upsides and downsides to selling something before having figured it out completely."

MY OWN STORY

I never imagined I'd be an author of nonfiction picture books. Even after I wrote one.

The first picture book I published, *Bark and Tim: A True Story of Friendship,* co-written with my sister Ellen Glassman Gidaro, was supposed to be a one-shot deal. I didn't seek out a nonfiction book project; it was more like Bark sat on my lap.

I saw a painting by outsider artist Tim Brown and fell in love. I showed the picture to my sister who said, "That would be such a good illustration in a children's book." One thing led to another. We were given permission to interview Tim (through an intermediary—Tim lives alone in a home without electricity) and to use his paintings to illustrate our book.

It wasn't easy to find a publisher for that project, but that's when I learned the tremendous role small regional publishers can play in publishing quirky children's nonfiction. Overmountain Press is a family-owned publisher, with a primary focus on Southern history and nonfiction. Working with them was a fabulous introduction to the world of children's nonfiction.

I returned to writing fiction after the publication of *Bark and Tim* until another nonfiction subject started calling.

A short piece about Effa Manley in a children's news magazine caught my attention. As an avid baseball fan, I could not believe that a woman—a woman I had never heard of—was about to be inducted into the National Baseball Hall of Fame.

I researched her story (which included an awesome road trip to the Hall of Fame in Cooperstown, N.Y.), and my agent sent out my picture book manuscript. Two editors requested a revision, both looking for the same kind of changes. Upon reading the revision, one editor said, "Wow, this is kind of all over the place, huh?" And the other said, "Wow, you really hit it out of the park." (I offer this as a reminder of what a subjective business publishing is.)

Thankfully, it only takes one.

She Loved Baseball: The Effa Manley Story was published by HarperCollins in 2010, a Junior Library Guild selection.

Even before Effa's official publication date, one more story started calling me. This one had local roots. I knew a man, a friend of my husband, whose father was one of 12 baseball-playing brothers. The family team had been honored by the Hall of Fame as the longest-playing all-brother baseball team.

Hello? Audrey Vernick? this story said. I'm your next book.

I invited myself to the home of one of the three surviving brothers. I was told to come on Tuesday, as that was spaghetti night. It was a remarkable, memorable experience—

listening to the stories, food forced upon me for hours, laughing, friends new and old joining us at the table.

The resulting book, *Brothers at Bat: The True Story of an Amazing All-Brother Team*, was published in March 2012.

Jennifer Greene, senior editor at Clarion, who published the book, says, "With *Brothers at Bat*, at first glance this might seem like a project not well suited for me. I like the energy and atmosphere of a good baseball game as well as anyone else, but I don't consider myself a real fan. But I loved this manuscript for the *story*—a family with 12 boys who loved baseball and had their own team! It's a slice of Americana, and it has so many moving moments throughout as we watch this family grow."

As for what's ahead … there's one story—yet another baseball story. Right now, it's calling quietly. We shall see.

You can visit Audrey Vernick online at audreyvernick.com and read her blog posts at shelovedbaseball.wordpress.com.

MAKING THAT FIRST SALE

It's the perpetual frustration of the not-yet-published writer: Having something published gets you noticed by agents and editors. Ahem. *How do you get something published without having that first credit?*

"Develop your writing chops and your contacts," Murphy advises. "Get paid to do interesting research that could lead to viable book projects by writing for kids' magazines and websites. Much more so with nonfiction than fiction, when an author queries me, I find a list of published magazine credits to be persuasive."

"Present your project in the most professional way possible," Greene suggests. "Try to offer the publisher the best possible picture of your vision for the book. Comparing it to successful books on the market in terms of feel, length and audience doesn't hurt, either, if your comparison is fair."

Of course, all the typical publishing advice also applies. Write well. Revise vigorously. Attend conferences. Network. Listen. Brown heard her future editor, Melanie Kroupa, speak at Vermont College. "She spoke about books she'd edited and I knew right away she was 'the one' for me and for *Elinor*."

PLATFORMS

Writers of adult nonfiction are advised that it's all about the *platform*; no publisher will take a chance on a writer who's not an expert in her field or who doesn't have an army of book-buying supporters already lined up. While a platform can only help you, it doesn't seem to be a deal-breaker when looking for that first children's nonfiction sale.

"The author's credentials, experience in the field and track record as a nonfiction writer all come into consideration when I look at a manuscript or proposal," Scott says. "It's always nice when someone is an expert in the field about which they are writing, but it's not essential. More important is the author's writing ability—that indefinable skill at making words on paper exciting and accessible to children."

STAY THE COURSE

Take your pick of all the publishing clichés—most have to do with persistence. My first nonfiction picture book was rejected 27 times before it was accepted.

It's a good idea to remain mindful that the writing, and what you get out of the writing, counts too. It's not all about publication. Listen to Tanya Lee Stone—she knows of what she speaks: "Embrace change; everything you write, whether you end up using it or not, takes you to the next place in your writing. It is all valuable to the process."

Scott adds, "Keep up the faith! I think there are a lot more opportunities in nonfiction, for newcomers and established authors alike, than in traditional picture book fiction."

It's a long road from idea to published book, and it's usually riddled with detours and potholes and accidental side trips. But it's a great time to be writing nonfiction for kids. Children have a plethora of fantastic, exciting nonfiction books at their disposal. Instead of counting down the pages until finally, finally reaching the end, today's nonfiction reader is working to make it last, turning the last few pages slowly and calling out a different refrain: "I don't want it to end!"

AUDREY VERNICK (audreyvernick.com) is the author of three nonfiction books: *Bark and Tim: A True Story of Friendship*; *She Loved Baseball: The Effa Manley Story*; and *Brothers at Bat: The True Story of an Amazing All-Brother Team*. Audrey also wrote *Is Your Buffalo Ready for Kindergarten?*; *Teach Your Buffalo to Play Drums*; and *Edgar's Second Word*. Her debut upper middle grade novel, *Water Balloon*, was published last year. Audrey lives near the ocean with one of each of the following: husband, son, daughter, dog.

You can visit Audrey's website at audreyvernick.com and her blog at shelovedbaseball. wordpress.com.

CONFERENCES

Get the most out of a writing event.

....

by Mary Kole

You've finally taken the plunge and decided to invest in a writers' conference. Or perhaps you're planning this year's conference schedule and hitting all your favorite events. Great! There's no better way to network with publishing professionals, meet fellow writers, learn about the current marketplace and get a jolt of inspiration for your craft.

When you're choosing your next conference, keep in mind that there are two major types: big group and small group. The big group conferences feature breakout speaker sessions, panels and other information-packed classes for large audiences of writers. Small group conferences, like workshops or retreats, often break attendees into smaller classes and focus directly on participants' writing samples.

I go to dozens of events every year as a faculty member and can share a few tips to help you get the most from your experience at both types of events. Read below for hints on big conferences, small workshops, pitching and aligning your expectations.

BIG CONFERENCES

At a big group conference, you'll be going to sessions with dozens or hundreds of your writing peers. This was the case at the DFW Writers' Conference (dfwwritersconference. org), the Society of Children's Book Writers and Illustrators (scbwi.org) New York and Los Angeles national conferences, the Florida Writers Association Conference (floridawriters.net), the San Diego Writers' Conference (writersconferences.com), the Writer's Digest Conference (writersdigestconference.com), and many more. Independent regional conferences and big writing groups like the Romance Writers of America (rwa.org) often host these types of events, too.

Sessions at big conferences range from the general—perhaps "Trends in the Children's Marketplace"—to the specific—"Humor for Picture Book Illustrators." You'll also get informational sessions from agents and editors about their agencies, tastes and houses. Big conferences can be overwhelming, and the issue is often too many great sessions to choose from!

Here's how you make the most of a big conference:

- **MIX UP YOUR SCHEDULE:** Check the schedule with an eye toward variety. Mix craft seminars with talks by publishing bigwigs. If a session isn't satisfying you, it's perfectly OK to get up and visit a concurrent one. Make sure you go to all of the panels, too.

- **MINGLE:** Even if you're naturally shy, you'll get more out of a big event by meeting other writers, talking to the professionals, asking questions during sessions (we love getting smart questions!) and otherwise putting yourself out there. Writing is a solitary pursuit, but this isn't the time to hold back on the socializing!

- **PRINT BUSINESS CARDS.** Whether you get a set designed or use free services like VistaPrint (vistaprint.com) you'll want something with your name and e-mail to give out. Staying in touch with people is Networking 101, and if you don't have them, you'll end up regretting it.

- **MEET YOUR NEW CRITIQUE GROUP.** Connect with other writers at the event so you can exchange pages after you go home and the conference buzz wears off.

I urge every writer to go to a big conference at least once. You'll get relevant information, meet other writers and rub elbows with agents and editors. Such a massive event is also a jolt of creative inspiration, which is worth the price of admission every time.

SMALL CONFERENCES, WORKSHOPS AND RETREATS

Smaller conferences and workshops focus on an attendee's work in a hands-on environment. Here, you'll be in small groups with a writing teacher or publishing professional and you'll work on your writing sample in a critique setting.

Workshops and retreats are great because you're getting personalized advice on your writing. You're also working in small groups. These events are intense—lots of information to soak up, lots of critique to give, lots of interactions with writers and faculty—but totally worth it. The Andrea Brown Literary Agency hosts the Big Sur Writing Workshop twice a year (December and March, henrymiller.org) on the beautiful Northern California Coast, and I am always amazed by how much writers evolve from Friday to Sunday. There's nothing quite like a focused workshop to really take craft to the next level.

I've seen the same happen at other workshops I've attended, like the SCBWI LA Retreat, the SCBWI New York Writers Intensive, and the workshops put on by the Highlights Foundation (highlightsfoundation.org) on their secluded property in Pennsylvania. That's the other benefit of small conferences: They're often held in scenic locations that are perfect for courting your muse.

Here are my tips for taking advantage of a small group workshop or retreat:

- **COME READY TO WORK.** A retreat should be relaxing, right? Wrong! While you'll benefit from a gorgeous setting or a lot of personal attention, you should also come with a notepad, a laptop and your regular writing tools. Attendees are often inspired to make changes to their writing sample mid-workshop, so make sure you're equipped to do so.

- **ADJUST YOUR CRITIQUE ATTITUDE.** Writers learn to revise—the biggest skill in a working author's toolbox—by first looking constructively at the work of others. Don't just sit in workshop waiting for them to talk about your work. Actively critique, participate, examine and analyze the work of your fellow writers. They'll return the favor, and your editorial eye will be that much sharper as a result, which you'll need to finesse your own work.

- **USE THE FACULTY.** We show up to a retreat weekend knowing that our time belongs to the attendees. You'll have access to authors, agents and editors. Ask questions, really drill into craft topics and take full advantage of the faculty's knowledge base.

Whether it's your first retreat or your tenth, you'll leave the weekend with new connections and a deeper understanding of your work and the bigger writing craft.

PITCHING

You'll most likely have the opportunity to pitch the faculty at both kinds of conferences. My biggest piece of advice on this fraught writing topic is: relax. Seriously. I've had people burst out crying during a pitch. I've had people mumble their memorized monologue into their laps. People read off of cue cards. People shake. People forget their words.

Don't do any of the above. Just talk to me. Tell me about your book. Pique my curiosity. Have a conversation and make a personal connection … *that's* what I'll remember as I head off to the airport. I have experienced thousands of pitches. Don't put undue pressure on yourself to knock my socks off or get an offer of representation right off the bat. Just being casual and interesting is enough. And for goodness sake, don't worry about memorizing your lines or fret if you misremember them. Only you know how it's supposed to go, so don't put so much emphasis on getting every word right.

Once you loosen up and talk to me, you'll be ahead of the pack.

KNOW BEFORE YOU GO

As an agent, I wish more writers went into conferences with the right attitude. You should be prepared to have fun, make new friends, network with the pros, pitch casually and leave with new ideas to take your work to the next level. You shouldn't go in expecting a contract or a big break. You shouldn't pack your suitcase with 20 copies of your full manuscript and spend all weekend trying to slip them to faculty. That's unrealistic. If you ever leave a conference feeling *crushed* and unable to go on, you need to revise your expectations. You don't have to be a "conference success story" in order to have a successful conference.

The benefits of a conference are inspiration and knowledge. You may see the positive effects immediately, or you may wake up with a brainstorm months after the event. Either way, a conference is something every writer should invest in at least once in their career.

See you on the conference circuit!

MARY KOLE is a literary agent for Movable Type Management (mtmgmt.net). Formerly, she was an agent at the Andrea Brown Literary Agency. Mary runs Kidlit.com, a website for writers of children's books, and is the author of *Writing Irresistible Kidlit: The Ultimate Guide to Crafting Fiction for Young Adult and Middle Grade* (Writer's Digest Books). As an agent, Mary represents outstanding young adult works, middle grade novels, and picture books. She accepts freelance editing clients at marykole.com.

SELF-PUBLISHING BASICS

Resources for brave souls.

....

by Darcy Pattison

To self-publish a book is a lengthy process. It means taking on the role of a publisher, which means deciding what book to publish in what format, content editing, art design, copyediting, managing production, distributing, selling, promoting and accounting. If you have skills in some of these areas and not others, you can hire help, but that adds to the bottom line. For most self-publishers, it's a balancing act to control costs, while creating a quality finished product.

LEGAL ISSUES.

The first hurdle is to create your own publishing company and decide up front how you want to handle various financial and legal issues. You'll want to look at tax issues and decide if you want to incorporate or just be a sole proprietorship, or other business structure. You can always research what the IRS has to say: irs.gov.

In your home state, there may be issues of sales tax, registering your business in your state or city, and other issues. Consult a local office of the Small Business Administration for information particular to your area (sba.gov).

The name of your publishing company is also important, because it will represent your brand name. Experts recommend against using your name in the company, against too "cutsey" names and against regional names. Instead, decide on something that says "business" and has a national reach.

Joni Sensel is the author of the Farwalker's Trilogy, a fantasy series for middle grade readers. The first two books of the trilogy were published by Bloomsbury Press. The first book, *The Farwalker's Quest* was named a Bank Street Best Book for 2010. But Bloomsbury declined the third book in the trilogy. Sensel self-published it to complete the trilogy—

and please her fans. *The Skeleton's Knife* is published by Dream Factory Books. Sensel says, "When we started our publishing company, we had a long brainstorming session for a name, and that was the winner, in part because the illustrator had ideas right off for logo and letterhead. No reason other than that we were manifesting the dream of producing some books together and I've always had a soft spot for factories."

BUSINESS PLAN

Next, you need to decide on a business plan. Will you produce books by printing and warehousing in quantity, make them available through a print-on-demand service, or publish as e-books, PDFs or other formats sold from your website, or a combination of these.

JoAnn Kairys, author of *Sunbelievable* (storyquestbooks.com), decided to print 3,000 copies and has sold 1,500 in the first year, a successful year by self-publishing standards. This route means ongoing costs for warehousing and fulfillment costs, but the hardcover allowed her to go through Barnes and Noble's process for Small Press Department approval for distribution (tinyurl.com/d362oxv). After approval, her book can be ordered and stocked by any B&N store. She also sells her book from her website, at independent bookstores and novelty stores.

Some self-publishers prefer the option of printing in quantity and warehousing because the per-book-cost is much lower, the quality of printing can be excellent and if you special printing needs or require special formats, it can only be done this way. For example, board books, books with accompanying CDs or lift-the-flap books will require special printing, packaging and distribution. If you choose this business plan, be sure to factor in the costs of warehousing and fulfillment (shipping the books when ordered).

Chris Eboch's first novel, *The Well of Sacrifice*, was published by Clarion in 1999 to good reviews and sales. When Clarion didn't buy her second historical novel, *Eye of the Pharoah*, she decided to self-publish it. She chose to make it available through print on demand (POD) and e-books. POD services maintain digital files of a book and when a book is ordered, they custom print the book and ship it to the customer. POD services such as Amazon's Create Space (createspace.com) or Lightning Source International (lightningsource.com) require a high quality PDF for both interior and cover. Read their specs carefully and make sure you can comply, or the files will be rejected as unprintable.

Once the book files were ready, Eboch followed directions on CreateSpace to upload and set up distribution. One advantage of CreateSpace is instant distribution through Amazon. The other major POD company, Lightning Source, is a sister company to Ingrams, one of the largest book wholesalers in the U.S.; if you POD your book with Lightning Source, it will automatically be listed in Ingram's catalog, which means distribution with Amazon, but also with BN.com and other locations. If you give a 40 percent or larger discount to retailers, bookstores can also order the book from Ingrams.

"Some people like to go through [Lightning Source] for print publication, because it's supposed to be better for bookstore distribution," Eboch says. "I go directly through Amazon's CreateSpace. I figure most print orders will be through Amazon, so I cut out the middleman. They have clear step-by-step instructions. CreateSpace also offers various services, from cover design to publicity, but I expect you can find better, cheaper people on your own."

For more on the difference between these POD options, read Aaron Shepard's book, *POD for Profit: More on the NEW Business of Self Publishing, or How to Publish Your Books With Online Book Marketing and Print on Demand.*

Eboch also took the next step and turned the print book into an e-book for Amazon's Kindle (kdp.amazon.com), Barnes and Noble's Nook (PubIt.barnesandnoble.com) and Smashword.com for other e-book distribution. Each platform requires a slightly different file and Eboch used Liberwriter.com for conversions. Others recommend a combination of two programs, Calibre and Sigil, to convert and tweak files for each platform. Others use the Jutoh program (jutoh.com) successfully. Still others find freelancers to do the conversion at sites such as elance.com, odesk.com or 99designs.com. For Apple's iTunes store or iBookstore, you can use an ePub format and then tweak, or use Apple's new iCreator software program. All of Apple's formats require a Mac to upload.

Finally, I offer some e-books through my website (darcypattison) as PDFs only, or as an alternate to the print or e-book versions. Ejunkie.com allows me to upload a PDF file, then handles the transaction. At $5/month, it's simple and cost-effective.

Depending on the business plan you choose, you may need to register your publishing company with Bowker and purchase ISBNs. Even for CreateSpace, which offers an option to use their ISBN numbers, most experts recommend that you purchase your own. For some formats, ISBN numbers for e-books are optional and for others it is required. Refer to the specs for each service to decide if you'll purchase ISBNs or not.

PRODUCING THE FILES

Once you have decided on book format and distribution, you need to set up accounts with the services you will use, then read specs. Each service operates slightly different and you'll want to know exactly what those requirements are. Here's where attention to detail is essential, because you will lose time and money if you don't follow specs exactly.

The book must be written, edited, illustrated, designed, copyedited and proofread before you export it in the approved format for a particular service. The most common advice given to self-publishers and the most common advice ignored is to get professional help.

Kairys spent three frustrating years trying to produce a high-quality book. Finally, she attended the Independent Book Publisher Association national conference and their Publishing U program (ibpa-online.org). Every professional said her art was great but the book design needed work.

She says, "I knew something was missing but I didn't know how to get from what I had done to get to that level. I worked with a graphic designer who had never done books. It really cost me a lot of time and investment to not find a professional book designer. It would have saved me at least two years. And now, of course, I see a lot of information on how to avoid all the pitfalls. I totally agree, make the investment—it's really critical."

Eboch and Sensel, who were both traditionally published first, already had a working knowledge of the professional demands of self-publishing. Eboch, who has an art and graphic design background, designed the interior of her book and the book cover. However, she bartered for the actual cover art with illustrator Lois Bradley.

She says that finding good help for art, design and conversions is partly trial and error. "But networking helps. I'm on a listserv for mystery writers who share publicity tips, so people recommend cover designers and so forth."

Sensel hired professional illustrators and book designers. "And I hired my New York editor to edit my novel because it helped give me confidence in the work," she says. "For me, the decision process balances what I know I can do a truly professional job of; an assessment of what someone else can do better (and why); what I like to do; what is a good use of my time; and where I want some input or control to ensure a professional product—and by that, I mean it looks like it came from a traditional publisher, not like it was laid out in Microsoft Word. Knowing what each element costs is part of my decision to self-publish in the first place. I'm a believer in 'do it right or don't do it at all.'"

Before uploading the book files, decide on all the meta-data for your book: title, subtitle, book description, categories for the listing, properly formatted thumbnails of the cover, etc. These are important so that the search engines for the online bookstores can find your books. You want to get this right, but after publication, you can always tweak Amazon settings at authorcentral.com. For more on the importance of meta-tags, read *Amazon Categories Create Best Sellers* by Aggie Vallanueva.

Finally, it's a simple process to upload files to the service you've chosen, order proof copies and set up the distribution channels. Just follow directions.

PROMOTION AND SELLING

If quality matters in the book production, it also matters in the marketing. Here, you'll make decisions about a website, social media, press releases, promotional materials such as postcards and book marks, attending conferences, speaking at schools, and much more. When you self-publish, all the marketing falls on your shoulders.

Kairys says that one of the best ways to sell her books is to cold call 10 Barnes and Noble stores, ask if they stock her book, and when they say no, ask them to short-list it (order a small number for a short time). She tries to call 10 at a time and repeat as often as possible.

For my picture book, *Wisdom, The Midway Albatross*, here are some of the promotional activities I've done:

- created a website (albatross.darcypattison.com)
- postcards
- free coloring pages
- contacted conference organizers for scientific organizations for book sales
- Facebook promotions
- "Draw a Bird," April 8 promotion each year (tinyurl.com/brr2zbf)
- teacher resources (tinyurl.com/cfdbmmg)
- press releases
- book contests such as the Writer's Digest Self-Published awards.

Your book will also need extensive and ongoing promotion, publicity and marketing to reach its readers. Plan for this before you jump in.

Self-publishing is a long, complicated process because you must take on every single role. There are many resources, such as software programs, tutorials and freelancers for every stage, but you accept full responsibility for each step. Your book sells or doesn't sell depending on how well you can fulfill each and every role. Don't be afraid to get help with some of the tasks, to study tutorials to improve your own skills or even to risk failure. When a self-published work succeeds, it is indeed a big thrill. Take courage: You'll need it.

....

DARCY PATTISON (darcypattison.com) is the poster child for authors who are straddlers, those with traditionally published books and self-published books. In 2013 her picture book, Widsom, *The Midway Albatross: Surviving the Japanese Tsunami and Other Disasters For Over 60 Years* (Mims House), was named the Writer's Digest Self-Publishing Books Award winner for the children's picture book category, a $1,000 cash prize; the book also received a starred review in *Publishers Weekly*. At the same time, her traditionally published book, *Desert Baths* (Sylvan Dell), was named a 2013 Outstanding Science Trade Book.

....

SELF-PUBLISHING RESOURCES ////////////////////////////////////

POD PRINTERS

CreateSpace.com is Amazon's POD service, with national and international distribution.

LightningSource.com is Ingram Wholesaler's POD sister company; if you POD with LSI, your books are automatically listed in Ingram's catalog.

E-BOOKS

Smashwords.com is the independent e-book publisher that distributes e-books to all major ebook retailers.

KDP.Amazon.com: Amazon's Kindle self-publishing program.

Publt.barnesandnoble.com – B&N's Nook self-publishing program.

Itunesconnect.apple.com – Apple's iBook program

FREELANCE EDITORS

rachellegardner.com/2009/03/freelance-editors/

henandinkbytes.com/2013/01/17/first-aid-for-floundering-kidlit-novel-manuscripts-part-2-10-freelance-whole-novel-editors-for-hire/

PUBLICITY

Dana Lynn Smith's "Book Maven Marketing" newsletter for children's authors (free): bit.ly/KidLitEzine

AuthorCentral.Amazon.com allows you to control your author page on Amazon.com, make corrections to listings and monitor sales figures.

FREELANCE ILLUSTRATORS

Odesk.com; Elance.com; 99Designs.com.

FIRST BOOKS

Hear from debut authors of picture books, middle grade and young adult.

by Chuck Sambuchino

There's something fresh and amazing about debut novels that's inspiring to other writers. It's with that in mind that we collected eight successful debuts from the past year and sat down to ask the authors questions about how they broke in, what they did right and what advice they have for scribes who are trying to follow in their footsteps. These are writers of picture books, middle grade stories and young adult novels—same as you—who saw their work come to life through hard work and determination. Read on to learn more about their individual journeys.

PICTURE BOOKS

① TARA LAZAR (TARALAZAR.COM)

The Monstore (**ALADDIN BOOKS**)

QUICK TAKE: "Zack wants to return the monsters he bought because they don't spook his pesky little sister—but there are no returns or exchanges at The Monstore."

WRITES FROM: New Jersey

PRE-BOOK: I always knew I wanted to write for children, but I broke into publishing by writing flash fiction for adults. I'm very comfortable with the short form. That experience translated well when I switched over to picture books.

TIME FRAME: The title *The Monstore* was something I had in my head for months, but I had no premise. After a conference, I was encouraged to create a storyline and show it to an agent. She thought the idea was a winner, but it still took me months to sit down and write it. But once I did, it spilled out in an afternoon. Of course, it then went through umpteen revisions.

ENTER THE AGENT: I met my agent through a series of social media connections. Ammi-Joan Paquette of the Erin Murphy Literary Agency saw [my friend's] tweet about my book and asked what she was reading. I then got a referral to Joan (as she prefers to be called) and we clicked.

BIGGEST THRILL: When I was asked my opinion about the illustrator choice, James Burks. Not all authors get that opportunity. I reviewed his portfolio and said "Yes! Yes! A thousand times, yes!" He interpreted the characters and the scenes better than I ever could have imagined.

WHAT YOU DID RIGHT: I kept writing new stories. *The Monstore* was probably the 20th picture book I wrote.

DO DIFFERENT NEXT TIME: I would have started years earlier! I finally realized I had to make the time. I basically stopped watching TV.

PLATFORM: I began my taralazar.com blog in 2007 and launched Picture Book Idea Month (PiBoIdMo) in 2009, which has gained a tremendous following.

ADVICE FOR WRITERS: Read, read, read. Write, write, write. There's really no other way.

NEXT UP: A second book called *I Thought This Was a Bear Book*, about an alien who crash-lands into the story of the three bears.

② JESSE KLAUSMEIER (JESSEKLAUSMEIER.COM)

Open This Little Book (CHRONICLE, JAN. 2013)

QUICK TAKE: *Open This Little Book* is my love letter to books; a conceptual and interactive book that takes readers on an unexpected journey of friendship and celebrates the love of reading.

WRITES FROM: Los Angeles, Calif.

PRE-BOOK: I worked for a small independent production studio and wrote and/or edited TV series treatments for network pitches, and copy for commercials, infomercials and instructional/corporate videos. Later, at Nickelodeon, I worked on promos and series launches for their animated shows. I've always loved children's literature, so I joined the Society of Children's Book Authors and Illustrators (SCBWI) and that group played an instrumental role in me finding my publisher and my agent.

TIME FRAME: I first had the idea of a book about books-inside-of-books when I was five years old. About 4 pages in, I got distracted and quit. The idea of books within books stuck with me though, and I wrote the first draft of *Open This Little Book* 20 years later. Now, I'm so happy to be able to show young readers that their ideas are important, and their books could get published, too.

ENTER THE AGENT: I met my agent, Steve Fraser (Jennifer De Chiara Literary) at a SCBWI writing retreat in Encino. A year later, at that very same SCBWI writing retreat, I shared *Open This Little Book* with editor Victoria Rock from Chronicle, who ended up acquiring it. When Victoria expressed interest, I got back in touch with Steve and he signed me on.

WHAT YOU LEARNED: I had no concept of the amount of time it took from acquisition to publication for a picture book. I sold the manuscript at the end of 2008 and it came out in January 2013.

WHAT YOU DID RIGHT: I think the best things I did were becoming an active member of SCBWI, getting the annual *Children's Writer's & Illustrator's Market* books, and really committing to learning the craft of writing for children. I read and studied hundreds of picture books.

PLATFORM: I'm on Facebook, Twitter (@jesseklausmeier), Pinterest and try to interact with people on all platforms.

③ THYRA HEDER (THYRAHEDER.COM)

Fraidyzoo (**ABRAMS**)

QUICK TAKE: "Little T is afraid of the zoo but can't remember why, so her family spends the day building hilarious homemade animal costumes until she finds the confidence to not only face her fear, but to make something fun out of it, too."

WRITES FROM: Brooklyn, N.Y.

TIME FRAME: I think of images before words, so it's hard to pinpoint the beginning of this book. However, once I landed on basing the story within a version of my own family I wrote the text of the whole book on a napkin sitting at the bar of my favorite restaurant in about 45 minutes. I'd say about 95 percent of what made it into the final book was on that napkin but figuring out the images ended up taking the rest of the year. After I sold the book to Abrams, with the text and sketches finalized, the paintings took about 4 months.

ENTER THE AGENT: Peter Brown, a wonderful author/illustrator who just won a Caldecott Honor, gave me the great advice of seeking out a young agent who could rally behind me and my project and passed along Stephen Barr at Writers House as an example. Luckily, my website intrigued him enough for a meeting. I showed up with several handmade books in attempt to convince him and it became clear we had very similar instincts when it came to telling stories. He actually did not agree to represent me until a couple weeks had passed, after he had perused the presents I left him.

WHAT YOU LEARNED: The most important thing I learned was that I should always try a note before rejecting it. It's easy to feel defensive when receiving revisions, but just because something wasn't my first instinct doesn't mean it won't work, or even be better than my original idea. Staying open and game throughout the process also gave me a better leg to stand on when I wanted to fight for something.

WHAT YOU DID RIGHT: For one, I did a lot of work before I attempted to contact an agent and publishers. Once I was in the process of pitching, I stayed adaptable through critiques and revisions and didn't assume "No" was the end. I definitely had really down moments, but tried to keep moving forward rather than dwelling on insecurities or rejections.

NEXT UP: Another picture book and a very slow moving graphic/comic novel.

④ KENNETH KRAEGEL (KENNETHKRAEGEL.COM)

King Arthur's Very Great Grandson (CANDLEWICK)

QUICK TAKE: "Henry Alfred Grummorson, the great, great, great, great, great, great, great grandson of King Arthur, goes out looking for adventure and encounters a Dragon, a Cyclops and a Griffin, but none of them want to fight, so he goes down to the sea and challenges the Leviathan."

WRITES FROM: Grand Rapids, Mich.

PRE-BOOK: I was writing and illustrating other picture book stories that generated some interest, but never quite enough.

ENTER THE AGENT: Ronnie Ann Herman of the Herman Agency is my agent. I had sent her a story a couple of years earlier that she was interested in, but declined. Later on, I sent her one or two new stories that she didn't like. I wrote her to tell her about an illustration award I had won and she was excited about that, so I sent her the dummy of my book and she signed me almost immediately.

BIGGEST SURPRISES: 1) I was surprised at how slowly the publishing world moves. I thought that once you had a contract things moved along at a nice pace. That hasn't been the case, things still move slowly. 2) I have been amazed at how kind and helpful everyone I have worked with has been. It has been a pleasure working with all of them.

WHAT YOU DID RIGHT: Eventually I figured out that my illustrations did not make sense to people without my words and my words didn't make sense without my pictures. Once I had a dummy with illustrations and words together, I began to get real traction. Also, maintaining a relationship with an agent post-rejection proved very fruitful.

DO DIFFERENT NEXT TIME: I probably would have started going to conferences earlier.

PLATFORM: I had a portfolio website then, and now I have the website and blog, as well as a Facebook page. I speak at schools and give readings when I am invited. The best events are the ones that I am invited to, rather than the ones I initiate.

NEXT UP: I am in the beginning stages of working on a brand new picture book with Candlewick Press.

MIDDLE GRADE

⑤ FLEUR BRADLEY (FTBRADLEY.COM)

Double Vision (**HARPER CHILDREN'S**)

QUICK TAKE: "When 12-year-old Linc Baker replaces a junior secret agent for a mission in Paris, he has only his quick wits to crack secret codes and find a dangerous painting—before the bad guys do."

WRITES FROM: Biloxi, Miss.

PRE-BOOK: I wrote short crime fiction for years, getting published in small press magazines and e-zines. I still write shorts when I can—it's the best way to stay sharp craft-wise. I also wrote freelance articles to pay the bills.

TIME FRAME: I'm one of those freak success stories: the Double Vision series (three books) sold on proposal. I had only written 75-odd pages, and about half didn't even make it into the first draft. From first draft to copyedited manuscript took about eight months.

ENTER THE AGENT: I had pitched Stephen Barbara at Foundry Literary & Media two different YA manuscripts, but no luck. We spoke on the phone, and he suggested, based on my writing, that I try middle grade. Long story short: We worked on the sample pages and proposal for about six months before he sold *Double Vision*.

WHAT YOU LEARNED: I'm still amazed by how great editors are at what they do. If I'm ever stuck creatively, they always have the key to unlock the story and make it better.

WHAT YOU DID RIGHT: I kept writing something new. I'm not afraid to throw stuff out—I'll cut chapters, passages or plot lines that don't work. I even have six manuscripts in the drawer that'll never see print.

DO DIFFERENT NEXT TIME: Start writing middle grade sooner! It's such fun.

PLATFORM: I have a blog (YA Sleuth) and am active on Facebook as well as Twitter. I'm on Goodreads and Skype now, and attending conventions to connect with librarians and booksellers.

NEXT UP: Edits on the second book in the series.

⑥ TAMERA WILL WISSENGER (TAMERAWILLWISSINGER.COM)

Gone Fishing: A Novel in Verse **(HOUGHTON MIFFLIN)**

QUICK TAKE: Gone Fishing is a humorous fishing adventure and sibling rivalry novel in verse for children ages six and up that includes poetry writing information.

WRITES FROM: Florida and Chicago.

PRE-BOOK: I had been writing poetry and picture books and had published single poems in the children's magazine market. After trying to publish my picture books for a number of years, I was receiving good feedback but no offers for publication. At that point I enrolled in Hamline University's MFA program in writing for Children and Young Adults.

WHAT YOU LEARNED: There is an amazing and rich network of fellow authors, illustrators, educators, librarians, booksellers and industry professionals, all of whom are committed to excellence in writing for children, and helping place great stories in the hands of kids.

BIGGEST SURPRISE: A polished manuscript plus a book contract is not an ending, it's the ending of one thing and the beginning of something else. Experiencing the revision process has increased my admiration for what a good and kind editor and her publishing team bring to the table.

WHAT YOU DID RIGHT: Two things: First, I was willing to evolve as a writer. I recognized that there were things about writing for children and the publishing industry that I needed to learn. I was fortunate to be able to return to school to develop my writing and critical thinking skills, and I began studying the industry on my own. Second, I continued writing and trying to make my story better. When it was as polished as I could make it, I kept submitting with the goal of finding it a good home.

NEXT UP: Currently I'm writing more poetry and fine-tuning a couple of quirky picture books and a traditional middle grade historical fiction novel.

⑦ MELANIE CROWDER (MELANIECROWDER.NET)

Parched **(HARCOURT CHILDREN'S BOOKS)**

QUICK TAKE: "Told in three voices and set in a near future scarred by drought and devastation, *Parched* is a story of survival and of hope."

WRITES FROM: The Colorado front range.

PRE-BOOK: I published a couple of curriculum activity guides for teachers while I worked on my fiction. It was a long process, but I'm glad I had time to learn and experiment and grow as a writer before putting myself out there.

ENTER THE AGENT: After graduation and a thorough round of revisions, I began (somewhat belatedly) to search for an agent who would fit with the vision I have for my career. Lucky for me, I found Ammi-Joan Paquette at Erin Murphy Literary Agency, and *Parched* sold shortly thereafter!

WHAT YOU LEARNED: I never realized what a team effort publishing a book can be. So many people at [a publishing house] are invested in this project, and every tiny detail is thoughtfully attended to. It's really amazing, and I am grateful for the work they have all put in!

WHAT YOU DID RIGHT: The best thing I did was to get my MFA at Vermont College. It was a time for me to forget about the pressures of the industry and just focus on the craft of writing. Those two years were truly invaluable—the academic rigor, the collegiality, the connections—I wouldn't be where I am today without it.

ADVICE FOR WRITERS: Don't expect success on the first try (or even the fifth!) Find readers who you trust to be kind, insightful and brutally honest. Listen to them. Be authentic, take risks and keep writing.

NEXT UP: Right now, I'm working on a YA historical verse novel. It's very different from my debut, and a real challenge, which I love!

⑧ TIM FEDERLE (TIMFEDERLE.COM)

Better Nate Than Ever (**SIMON & SCHUSTER**)

QUICK TAKE: "A small-town eighth grader runs way from home to crash an audition for *E.T.: The Broadway Musical*."

WRITES FROM: Manhattan.

PRE-BOOK: I moved to New York City when I was a teenager to dance on Broadway. After 10 years and 5 shows—yes, I understudied the seagull in *The Little Mermaid*—I felt eager to tell a different kind of story than I could as a performer. *Better Nate Than Ever* was ultimately inspired by my time coaching the child stars of *Billy Elliot*. (But no child actors were harmed in the making of this book.)

TIME FRAME: I don't have an MFA. I don't even have a BFA, or any degree at all. And so I didn't want to approach writing like a "writer"—outlines and critique groups would have been too much pressure for me. Instead, I kept the writing process to myself, and approached

Better Nate Than Ever like an actor does an improv, which is to always say "Yes" to any impulse that leapt out. I didn't allow myself to edit at all until I'd typed "The End."

ENTER THE AGENT: I shared my book with a mentor—a theatrical producer—who, without my knowing it, passed it along to a publishing colleague, who passed it along to an agent friend of his. A week later, Brenda Bowen of {XYZ Agency] e-mailed to say she'd read chapter one of my book and could we talk about working together? It was a dream.

WHAT YOU LEARNED: 1) A lot of people in publishing love theater just as much as I do! 2) It›s important to celebrate the milestones along the way -- to not put all your hopes on "the launch." Make sure to stop and smile and drink a little champagne when you type "The End"; when you get an agent; when you sell the book; when your galleys arrive. It's all part of the story—your story.

WHAT YOU DID RIGHT: I tried to be very specific when I'd reach out to somebody: "Can you read these two paragraphs and tell me if the joke is working about the tap shoes?" as opposed to "Can you read my whole book and tell me how to get published?"

NEXT UP: My first novelty cocktail recipe book for English majors, *Tequila Mockingbird* (Running Press), is out now, and the sequel to *Better Nate Than Ever: Five, Six, Seven, Nate!* (yes, really), is due out Spring 2014. Did I mention I'm lucky?

YOUNG ADULT

⑨ AMANDA SUN (AMANDASUNBOOKS.COM)

Ink: The Paper Gods Series **(HARLEQUIN TEEN)**

QUICK TAKE: "After her mother's death, 16-year-old Katie moves to Japan, where she crosses paths with her new school's kendo star, whose drawings come to life in dangerous ways."

WRITES FROM: Toronto

PRE-NOVEL: I had a few short stories published in anthologies—one literary fiction set in Japan, and two YA Fantasy stories—but I really wanted to write something that combined my interests. The Paper Gods series is inspired by my own time living in Japan, and is a way to write both what I love and what I know.

TIME FRAME: The first half was written in the fall of 2009 and the second half in the spring of 2010. I posted an excerpt of *Ink* in an online blog contest, where it was spotted by an agent who asked me to query her as soon as the project was ready. I didn't end up signing with that agent, but her belief in the project helped give me the courage to keep going.

ENTER THE AGENT: I queried Melissa Jeglinski of The Knight Agency through the recommendation of a mutual friend. Melissa was a dream agent to me, and I'd queried her before with earlier projects.

BIGGEST SURPRISE: The glowing rejections I received. Who knew agents and editors could praise your work and still turn you down? It turns out rejections aren't so much about "no" as about finding the right person for your work. You need an agent and editor who get your vision and can push you. It takes time for the stars to align.

WHAT YOU DID RIGHT: I was aware of the market. I started following 50 YA blogs and reading every novel I could get my hands on. Then I wrote *Ink*, and it sold quickly.

DO DIFFERENT NEXT TIME: I think it's easy to get hung up on querying a novel and forget to keep writing new ones. The second novel I wrote is the one that sold, and I held back that success by focusing too much on the first project. Even if a book doesn't sell, it teaches you something important about craft.

PLATFORM: I spend a healthy dose of time on social media every day. My book is set in Japan, so I also like to go to anime conventions and chat with readers there.

NEXT UP: Book Two of The Paper Gods series, out in 2014.

10 COREY HAYDU (COREYANNHAYDU.COM)

OCD Love Story (SIMON PULSE)

QUICK TAKE: "When Bea and Beck meet, they find common ground, and even a romantic connection, through their obsessions and compulsions, but Bea is hiding infatuations and behaviors from Beck, from her therapist, and from herself."

WRITES FROM: Brooklyn, N.Y.

PRE-BOOK: Before writing *OCD Love Story*, I published a few short stories (for adults, not teens!) in some small literary journals, and I was working on an ill-fated adult literary novel. I started working in children's publishing, randomly happening upon a job with a literary agent who focused on YA literature, and I fell in love with it. I decided to pursue my MFA in Writing for Children when I realized what an exciting, diverse and inspiring genre YA literature is.

TIME FRAME: I wrote the first draft in about five months.

ENTER THE AGENT: I'm represented my Victoria Marini of Gelfman Schneider Literary. I queried Victoria in March of 2011 with another project, a different YA novel. She wasn't ready to sign me, but gave me a lot of helpful notes to consider, and said she'd love to see a revision, or to hear about what other projects I might be working on. I think we both knew we had similar tastes, interests and a really easy communication.

WHAT YOU LEARNED: I think my process finding my agent and in finding the right publisher taught me a lot about patience. I learned that if you're trying to have a long career, those short-term disappointments or setbacks often lead to later, future victories.

WHAT YOU DID RIGHT: That one's easy. I kept writing. While I was querying my first, unpublished novel, I wrote *OCD Love Story*. Querying can be a long process, and I didn't simply sit around waiting to hear back from agents (even though I did refresh my e-mail quite a bit!)

ADVICE FOR WRITERS: Do your research. Knowing what kinds of books specific agents and editors like is incredibly helpful. Stay informed. Know what books everyone is talking about. Know what books you yourself love.

NEXT UP: I'm currently working on a new young adult novel, and am trying my hand at writing a middle-grade novel as well!

⑪ STEFAN BACHMANN (STEFANBACHMANN.COM)

The Peculiar **(GREENWILLOW BOOKS)**

QUICK TAKE: "In an alternate-history 19th century England, faeries and Victorians live together in a fragile peace, which is shattered when changelings, the children of faeries and humans, are found murdered, floating in the Thames and covered in mysterious red markings."

WRITES FROM: Zurich, Switzerland

PRE-BOOK: I wrote about four complete manuscripts before this one, and dozens of short stories. Two or three of those stories were published in various e-zines, and the four manuscripts will hopefully never be seen again.

TIME FRAME: I wrote the first draft in about six months and then spent at least a year polishing the manuscript. I was sending out queries at the same I was polishing, so after every rejection, I would go back to the manuscript and work on it. I think the rejections were really great in that sense, because it made me work on the book that much more.

ENTER THE AGENT: I wrote a query, sent it out, got a few rejections, re-wrote the query, got some bites, and about a year later two agents wanted to represent it and I went with Sara Megibow of Nelson Literary Agency.

WHAT YOU LEARNED: When I got my revision letter for *The Peculiar* I stressed myself completely out, because I thought once I sent off this revision that was the last time I would be able to work on it and the book had to be perfect. Of course, that's not the way it works, but I had no clue that writers usually go through round after round of revisions with their editors, and stressing out is never a good thing.

WHAT YOU DID RIGHT: I practiced a lot, wrote a lot of junk, read a lot of books, wrote some more junk, and eventually I wrote a book I liked and tried to make it the best it could be.

DO DIFFERENT NEXT TIME: I wouldn't have put my age in my query letter. An agent won't rep your book because of how old you are, they'll rep it if they love the first 10 pages, and then the next hundred pages, and then the entire manuscript.

NEXT UP: Greenwillow/HarperCollins bought *The Peculiar* in a two-book deal, and I'm revising the second one right now. *The Whatnot* hit shelves in Fall 2013.

12 T.L. COSTA (TLCOSTA.COM)

Playing Tyler (**STRANGE CHEMISTRY**)

QUICK TAKE: "A boy with ADHD discovers that his favorite video game may be more than just a game."

WRITES FROM: Connecticut

PRE-BOOK: I was pitching a YA horror at the time, convinced of its stellar market appeal, and getting a lot of the dreaded "it's great but I can't sell it" responses from agents. Frustrated, I decided to stop caring about the market trends, and write a book about who and what I wanted. I had no idea if the book would even work, let alone sell, but from the moment I pitched it the response has been overwhelming.

TIME FRAME: I began the book as an attempt at National Novel Writing Month. I think I wrote all of maybe 20 or 20,000 words in November. But the practice of getting in front of the computer and writing every day helped me realize that I could comfortably write a thousand words a day. All told, the rough draft of the book took about seven months.

ENTER THE AGENT: I met my agent, Jenny Bent of Bent Literary, at CT Fiction Fest.

WHAT YOU LEARNED: I think the biggest thing for me is to keep writing. It is so easy to get completely obsessed refreshing my inbox for updates from my editor or my agent or whomever, but the only thing that is going to keep me employed as a writer is to keep working on the next project.

ADVICE FOR WRITERS: Write what you want to write and write it well. What's on the shelf now reflects what publishers were buying last year, if not earlier. Write the book you need to write, and hope that when you are ready to sell, the market will want it.

NEXT UP: I'm working on the edits of my next book.

⑬ BRITTANY GERAGOTELIS (BRITTANYGERAGOTELIS.COM)

What the Spell? (SIMON & SCHUSTER)

QUICK TAKE. "A teenage girl who's sick of being invisible among her peers and decides to use her newfound witchy powers to rise up the social ranks at her school."

WRITES FROM: New York City

PRE-BOOK: I tried my best to get published the traditional route for over eight years to no avail. Finally, I decided to write and post (for free) an original book on the online writing community site, Wattpad. The novel was called *Life's a Witch* and people fell in love with it! After a year of having it up on the site, I had over 18 million reads of it and decided to self-publish. About a month after I self-published, the traditional publishing world came calling and the series went into auction between four different houses, before I decided to go with Simon & Schuster Books for Young Readers. *What the Spell?* is the prequel/spin-off to *Life's a Witch*.

ENTER THE AGENT: I was actually contacted by my foreign rights agent, Taryn Fagerness (Taryn Fagerness Agency) first, after she'd read about me in *Publishers Weekly*. After signing with her, I asked if she worked with any literary agents who might be interested in taking me on as a client. A week or so later, she introduced me to the lovely Kevan Lyon of the Marsal/Lyon Literary Agency and I really connected with her.

WHAT YOU DID RIGHT: The minute I stopped telling myself that in order to become a successful author I had to get an agent who would sell my book to a publisher and only then will I have made it, everything started to happen for me. I think it's really short-sighted to think there's only one path to success. Times are changing and we have a lot of opportunities available to us today ... people just have to find what works for them and remain open-minded.

DO DIFFERENT NEXT TIME: I wouldn't have let the rejection of others hold so much weight on my dreams. After so many years of rejection, I almost stopped writing. If I had, none of this would've happened. And like I said before, I wish I'd been more open-minded in terms of how I was going to get to the title of "published author."

NEXT UP: World domination. Kidding. Kind of. The true beginning to the Life's a Witch series (by the same title) came out in July 2013, and then the sequel, *The Witch is Back* will be out Jan 2014! I'll be doing a lot of panels, signings and appearances hopefully, and we're exploring our movie/TV options.

CHUCK SAMBUCHINO (chucksambuchino.com, @chucksambuchino on Twitter) edits the *Guide to Literary Agents* (guidetoliteraryagents.com/blog) as well as the *Children's Writer's & Illustrator's Market*. His pop humor books include *How to Survive a Garden Gnome Attack* (film rights optioned by Sony) and *Red Dog / Blue Dog: When Pooches Get Political* (reddog-bluedog.com). Chuck's other writing books include *Formatting & Submitting Your Manuscript, 3rd. Ed.*, and *Create Your Writer Platform*. Besides that, he is a husband, sleep-deprived new father, guitarist, dog owner, r and cookie addict. He loves meeting new writers at conferences and events all across the country.

AGENTS TELL ALL

Literary agents answer some common (and not-so-common) questions.

by Chuck Sambuchino, Ricki Schultz and Donna Gambale

Whether during their travels to conferences or on their personal blogs, literary agents get a lot of questions from writers—some over and over. Below is a roundup of such questions answered by some of the top children's agents in the business.

ON STARTING STRONG

When you're reviewing a partial fiction manuscript, what do you hate to see in Chapter 1?

I hate to see a whiny character who's in the middle of a fight with one of their parents, slamming doors, rolling eyes and displaying all sorts of other stereotypical behavior. I hate seeing character "stats" ("Hi, I'm Brian. I'm 10 years and 35 days old with brown hair and green eyes."). I also tend to have a hard time bonding with characters who talk to the reader ("Let me tell you about the summer when I ...").

> **KELLY SONNACK** *is a literary agent with the Andrea Brown Literary Agency*

In YA and teen, what are some page 1 clichés you come across?

The most common problem I see is a story that's been told a million times before, without any new twists to make it unique enough to stand out. Same plot, same situations, same set up = the same ol' story. For example: abusive parents/kid's a rebel; family member(s) killed tragically/kid's a loner; divorced parents/kid acts out. Another problem I often see is when the protagonist/main characters don't have an age-appropriate voice. For example: If your main character is 14, let him talk like a 14-year-old. And lastly, being unable to "connect" with the main character(s). For example: Characters are too whiny or bratty, or a character shows no emotion/angst.

—**Christine Witthohn** *is the founder of Book Cents Literary*

What are some Chapter 1 clichés you often come across when reading a partial manuscript?

One of my biggest pet peeves is when writers try to stuff too much exposition into dialogue rather than trusting their abilities as storytellers to get information across. I'm talking stuff like the mom saying, "Listen, Jimmy, I know you've missed your father ever since he died in that mysterious boating accident last year, but I'm telling you, you'll love this summer camp!" So often writers feel like they have to hook the reader right away. In some ways that's true, but in others you can hook a reader with things other than explosions and big secrets being revealed. Good, strong writing and voice can do it, too.

—**Chris Richman** *is a literary agent with Upstart Crow Literary*

Tell me about some Chapter 1 clichés that you come across from time to time that immediately make you stop reading.

The "information dump" is one—paragraphs of information about the protagonist, the protagonist's parents, background information about the protagonist's situation. Often, this information is unnecessary, and if it is necessary, a blend of telling and showing, along with a measured unfolding of information, is a stronger approach. Another is starting the first chapter with the wrong action. Writers are often instructed to start a story in the middle of the action, but it's important that it be the right action. For example, I recently read a manuscript in which the protagonists embark on a dangerous outing in the first chapter. But since I didn't have a clear sense yet for the significance of this outing, the action was undermined and I wasn't invested in the outcome. It was a crucial scene, but the author needed to back up and start with completely different action that placed me more firmly in the world of the story. Finally, I stop reading when the first chapter starts with the protagonist saying something like, "Hi, my name is (fill in the blank)."

—**Jen Rofe** *is an agent with Andrea Brown Literary Agency*

What are some reasons you stop reading a YA manuscript?

Once I've determined that the writing is strong enough, it's usually a question of plot (we receive many works that are derivative or otherwise unoriginal) or voice. As we know from the young adults in our lives, anything that sounds even vaguely parental will not be well received. And there's nothing worse than narration that reads like a text message from a grandmother. In the past month, I've received 29 YA partials. Looking back on my notes, I see that I rejected eight for writing, seven for voice, six for derivative or unoriginal plots, four because they were inappropriate for the age group, and two that simply weren't a good fit for the agency but may find a home elsewhere. Then there were two I liked and passed them on to others in my office. Also, I think a lot of writers, seeing the success of *Twilight*, have tried to force their manuscripts into this genre. I know you've heard it before, but it's so true: Write what you are meant to write—don't write what you think will sell.

—**JESSICA SINSHEIMER** *is a literary agent with the*
Sarah Jane Freymann Literary Agency

ON VOICE, CONCEPT AND SUBJECT MATTER

I've heard that nothing is taboo anymore in young adult books and you can write about topics such as sex and drugs. Is this true?

I would say this: Nothing is taboo if it's done well. Each scene needs to matter in a novel. I've read a number of "edgy" young adult books where writers seem to add in scenes just for shock value and it doesn't work with the flow of the rest of the novel. "Taboo" subjects need to have a purpose in the progression of the novel—and of course, need to be well written! If it does, then yes, I would say nothing is taboo. Taboo topics do, however, affect whether the school and library market will pick up the book—and this can have an effect on whether a publisher feels they can sell enough copies.

—**JESSICA REGEL** *is a literary agent with the Jean V. Naggar Literary Agency*

What are three of the biggest mistakes you see writers make when writing for kids/teens?

I find being very preachy is a big turnoff for me. Nine and a half times out of ten, when a query letter for a YA or MG starts talking about all the lessons the novel will teach kids, I reject it. Literature can be very powerful and it can teach lessons, but I think it is most important to focus on writing something that kids will want to read first. I've also seen a lot of things lately set in the '80s or '90s that don't need to be; I think it is because this is when the writers remember being teenagers. However, it is important to remember that a 15-year-old now was born in 1997. The '90s are historical fiction to them, and if the story can work at all set in 2011, it probably should be. Finally—and this isn't a mistake, per se—but writing an authentic teenage voice is very difficult, and I see a lot of writers struggling with it. If there is one thing YA and MG writers should practice and work to perfect, it is writing a teenage voice.

—**LAUREN MACLEOD** *is an agent with The Strothman Agency*

What are some subjects or styles of writing that you rarely receive in a submission and wonder why more writers don't tackle such a subject/style?

In terms of style and execution, I'd love to see more MG and YA submissions use innovative narrative strategies deliberately and well. For example: alternating voices/points of view, or a structure that plays with narrative time. Kids are sophisticated readers.

Books that engage them on the level of storytelling, as well as story, could break out. In terms of subject matter, I don't see as many stories as you'd think about multicultural families and friendships. I'd also love to see more YA submissions depict awkward, funny and real—rather than flat and glossy—teen romance.

—**MICHELLE ANDELMAN** *is a literary agent with Regal Literary*

Regarding submissions, what do you see too much of? What do you see too little of?

I'm definitely looking for projects with something timeless at their core, whether it's the emotional connection a reader feels to the characters, or the universal humor, or issues that are relevant now and will still be relevant years from now. Can readers truly understand what it's like to be the prince of Denmark? Probably not, but they can identify with feeling disconnected from a dead loved one and the anger at watching him be replaced by a conniving uncle. I want stories that, no matter what the setting, feel true in some way to the reader. I definitely see too many people trying to be something else. I used to make the mistake of listing Roald Dahl as one of my favorite writers from my childhood, but I've found that just inspires a bunch of Dahl knockoffs. And trust me, it's tough to imitate the greats. I get far too much emulation of Dahl, Snicket, Rowling, and whatever else has worked in the past. It's one thing to aspire to greatness; it's another to imitate it. I want people who can appeal to me in the same way as successful writers of yore, with a style that's their own. I see too few writers willing to take chances. I just finished Markus Zusak's wonderful novel, *The Book Thief*. It breaks so many so-called rules for kids' books—there are tons of adult characters and points of view, it's a historical at heart, and it's narrated by Death for crying out loud. It's one of the best young adult novels I've read recently.

—**CHRIS RICHMAN** *is a literary agent at Upstart Crow Literary*

Are there any subjects you feel are untapped and would, therefore, be a refreshing change from the typical multicultural story?

When I was a [bookstore buyer], I was tired of certain subject matters only because those subjects have been explored so well, so often, that you really needed to bring something special to the page to make anyone take notice. Send me a story about some modern immigrant stories, some multi-generational stuff, like the YA novels of Carlos Ruiz Zafon. There are deeply rich stories about being an outsider, and yet how assimilation means a compromise and loss. I'd also love to see more issues of race discussed in modern terms, where there is the melting pot happening across the U.S., yet the tensions are still there, like the fear of the other. I think these stories, when done well, are universal stories, as we all feel that way at some point. Look at Junot Diaz's *The Brief Wondrous Life of Oscar Wao* as exhibit A.

—**JOE MONTI** *is a literary agent with Barry Goldblatt Literary*

ON PICTURE BOOKS & ILLUSTRATIONS

Do you often get queries from authors who have also illustrated their children's book? Are the illustrations usually of enough quality to include them with the submission to publishers?

I do receive many queries from author/illustrators, or from authors who aren't necessarily illustrators but fail to understand that they don't have to worry about submitting illustrations. But most often I find that most illustrators are not the best at coming up with compelling storylines or can't execute the words like a well-seasoned writer (or vice versa: The better writers usually are not the best illustrators).

—**REGINA BROOKS** *is the founder of Serendipity Literary*

With picture books, I suspect you get a lot of submissions and most of them get rejected. Where are writers going wrong?

Rhyming! So many writers think picture books need to rhyme. There are some editors who won't even look at books in rhyme, and a lot more who are extremely wary of them, so it limits an agent on where it can go and the likelihood of it selling. It's also particularly hard to execute perfectly. Aside from rhyming, I see way too many picture books about a family pet or bedtime.

—**KELLY SONNACK** *is a literary agent with the Andrea Brown Literary Agency*

Many people tend to try their hand at children's writing and picture books, but it's often said that writing such books is much more difficult than writers first consider. Why is this so?

I suspect the common thinking goes that if a writer "knows" children, she can write for them. But a successful children's author doesn't simply "know" children—what makes them tick, what their internal and emotional lives are like—she also knows children's literature. She's an avid reader, so she's familiar with what's age-appropriate and authentic to her category of the market. If she's writing a picture book, she's a skilled visual storyteller and can offer up a plot, character, relationship or emotional arc in miniature—but still, and this is the difficult part, in full.

—**MICHELLE ANDELMAN** *is a literary agent with Regal Literary*

What can writers do to increase their chances of getting a picture book published?

I know it sounds simplistic, but write the very best picture books you can. I think the market contraction has been a good thing, for the most part. I'm only selling the very best picture books my clients write—but I'm definitely selling them. Picture books are generally skewing young, and have been for some time, so focus on strong read-alouds and truly kid-friendly styles. I'm having a lot of luck with projects that have the feel of being created by an author-illustrator even if the author is not an artist, in that they're fairly simple, have all kinds of room for fun and interpretation in the illustrations, and have a lot of personality. I see a lot of picture book manuscripts that depend too heavily on dialogue, which tends to give them the feel of a chapter book or middle grade novel. The style isn't a picture book style.

—**ERIN MURPHY** *is the founder of the Erin Murphy Literary Agency*

ON CHILDREN'S NONFICTION

Can you give us some 101 tips on writing nonfiction for kids?

You can write about almost anything when it comes to children's nonfiction, even if it's been done before. But you need to come at the subject from a different angle. If there is already a book on tomatoes and how they grow, then try writing about tomatoes from a cultural angle. There are a ton of books on slavery, but not many on slaves in Haiti during the Haitian Revolution. (Is there even one? There's an idea—someone take it and query me!) Another thing to always consider is your audience. Kids already have textbooks at school, so you shouldn't write your book like one. Come at the subject in a way that kids can relate to and find interesting. Humor is always a useful tool in nonfiction for kids. Adding to a series is a great way to get started as a writer of nonfiction. But it can't hurt to research the market and try to come up with an idea of your own.

—**JOANNA STAMPFEL-VOLPE** *is an agent with New Leaf Literary*

You're looking for nonfiction for young adults, such as picture book biographies. Can you give a few good examples of this for people to read and learn from?

The most important thing to me is that the nonfiction reads like fiction—that there is a "story behind the story." For example, Pamela S. Turner's *George Schaller: Life in the Wild*, from FSG/Kroupa (2008), is a biography of the great field biologist George Schaller. The book explores Dr. Schaller's career both as a scientist and as an advocate for vanishing wildlife. Appealing to children who are interested in animals, science, adventure and the outdoors, each chapter of the book will also be a "mini-biography" of the species being studied. Several of Pamela's other books study certain environments or animals and make science fun and interesting for kids.

—**CARYN WISEMAN** *is a literary agent with the Andrea Brown Literary Agency*

ON CHILDREN'S WRITING CATEGORIES

You seek books with dystopian themes. That seems to be a healthy area of market—particularly in YA. Why do you think this is so? As well, what do you see for the future? Will it always be so hot?

YA topics and trends are cyclical, but I think dystopian is always relevant and in-demand. It's funny that the term "science fiction" is still not "cool" or commercial, still relegated to genre fiction—but *dystopian*—suddenly that word is very cool. Do people not realize that most of it is science fiction? Or magical realism? In that sense, the theme has been hot forever.

It's fascinating to ponder the question "what if?" These books make us think about the world and humanity—how people act toward each other when pushed to the brink, when fighting for survival. It's so interesting to think how quickly these societies we've built could break down and we'd be left with the most basic human instincts.

—**MELISSA SARVER** *is an agent with Elizabeth Kaplan Literary*

If someone asked about the line between middle grade and young adult, how would you explain the difference?

Is there a line? It seems to me there is scale more than a line. An editor said to me recently that if the main character is 14, it automatically gets shelved in YA in the chain stores. There's a line. But I work with authors whose light and wholesome novels, with teen main characters, are read mostly by tweens; and others whose novels are populated by middle graders going through such intense experiences that the readership skews to the high end of MG/low end of YA. I try to focus on helping my clients make their stories the best stories they can be rather than fitting them into boxes. The line sometimes feels like a moving target, and the writer has little control over it; better to focus on what you can control, which is how good it is. That said, characters should feel as though they are truly the age they are supposed to be—and that age *today*. Kids are savvier than they used to be even five or 10 years ago. They are exposed to more and more at a younger age. Writers should respect their readership accordingly.

—**ERIN MURPHY** *is the founder of the Erin Murphy Literary Agency*

Can you explain exactly how chapter books differ from middle grade?

There is a lot of overlap between categories, so the difference between older chapter books and younger middle grade is often just a matter of marketing. Younger chapter books are for kids who have graduated from easy readers and are starting to read more fluently. They usually have 8–10 short chapters, each with a cliffhanger ending. They are often a series, like Captain Underpants or Magic Tree House, and can be lightly or heavily illustrated. Middle grade is for readers in the 8–12 age group. They can have a complex plot and subplot, and while often humorous, they can certainly be more serious. The vocabulary is more sophisticated than chapter books, and the emphasis is on character. *The Qwikpick Adventure Society* by Sam Riddleburger (Dial) is an example of a middle grade book in which the targeted reader is at the younger end of the spectrum. At the older end of the middle grade spectrum is "tween." It's realistic, often contemporary, often edgier than traditional middle-grade, and deals with identity issues, school-based situations, family vs. friends, and just how hard it is to be 12.

—**CARYN WISEMAN** *is a literary agent with the Andrea Brown Literary Agency*

Does "tween" exist as a category?

Tween *does* exist, and various publishers even have specific tween imprints in place. As for queries, the same standard holds true for me in terms of tween as it does with YA or MG: If the voice is authentic, then I'm probably interested. However, I do look more at plot with tween novels. Right now, it's not enough just to have a great tween voice—the storyline also needs to be unique enough to stand out in the marketplace.

—**MEREDITH KAFFEL** *is a literary agent at DeFiore and Company*

ON EVERYTHING ELSE

What's your best piece of advice for new writers who wish to submit their work to agents?

My best one word of advice: professionalize. A new writer who has done her homework on the children's market ahead of time, and submits to agents in a way that suggests a professional approach to a writing career, is going to stand out. Professionalizing may mean doing a few different things that make all the difference: joining a critique group that can help you polish your manuscript before you query, researching and approaching agents according to submission guidelines, crafting a query that aims to pique interest in—rather than fully explain—your project, and joining the Society of Children's Book Writers & Illustrators (SCBWI).

—**MICHELLE ANDELMAN** *is a literary agent with Regal Literary*

One of the areas you seek is young adult. That is a healthy market—and has been for quite some time. However, what do you see for the future? Will it always be so hot?

It's hot; it's just that the competition is huge. Especially in the paranormal romance genre. I think that the YA market will continue to grow in the future, and we will see more variety and dimension in the work that is offered to this market. Authors who are targeting this market really need to bring the groundbreaking stories in order to be competitive due to the saturation factor in the paranormal genre. The window is still open; it's just not open as wide.

—**JENNIFER SCHOBER** *is a literary agent with Spencerhill Associates*

What do you see for the future of young adult literature?

A shift to enhanced e-book domination. My older kids are 9 and 13, and while they love stories and enjoy reading, they also like the computer and the iPad and the television more—in spite of having parents and stepparents that are all voracious readers. Young adult authors are going to have to abandon the urge to be old-school about their writing, in most cases, if they want to find a healthy audience among tomorrow's kids. I've personally got little use for links to music and video and other material I consider extraneous, but the minds of kids today work completely differently than they did even just 10 years ago, for better or for worse. It's just a different, more fragmented requirement for all entertainment.

—**DAVID DUNTON** *is a literary agent at Harvey Klinger, Inc.*

Best piece of advice we haven't talked about yet?

Don't hold back from your passion. Too many folks get caught up in what the market-place is supposedly looking for, and they lose sight of what they're trying to write. That, and read your drafts (Note the plural usage!) aloud for imperfections of language and cadence. It's an old horse, but not done enough because it may take you days to finish—but the results are astounding.

—**JOE MONTI** *is a literary agent with Barry Goldblatt Literary*

Best piece of advice we haven't talked about yet?

Don't hold back from your passion. Too many folks get caught up in what the market-place is supposedly looking for, and they lose sight of what they're trying to write. That, and read your drafts (Note the plural usage!) aloud for imperfections of language and cadence. It's an old horse, but not done enough because it may take you days to finish—but the results are astounding.

—**JOE MONTI** *is u literary ugent with Barry Goldblatt Literary*

Best piece of advice we haven't talked about yet?

Don't hold back from your passion. Too many folks get caught up in what the market-place is supposedly looking for, and they lose sight of what they're trying to write. That, and read your drafts (Note the plural usage!) aloud for imperfections of language and cadence. It's an old horse, but not done enough because it may take you days to finish—but the results are astounding.

—**JOE MONTI** *is a literary agent with Barry Goldblatt Literary*

Best piece of advice we haven't talked about yet?

Don't hold back from your passion. Too many folks get caught up in what the market-place is supposedly looking for, and they lose sight of what they're trying to write. That, and read your drafts (Note the plural usage!) aloud for imperfections of language and cadence. It's an old horse, but not done enough because it may take you days to finish—but the results are astounding.

—**JOE MONTI** *is a literary agent with Barry Goldblatt Literary*

CHUCK SAMBUCHINO (chucksambuchino.com, @chucksambuchino on Twitter) edits the *Guide to Literary Agents* (guidetoliteraryagents.com/blog) as well as the *Children's Writer's & Illustrator's Market*. His pop-humor books include *How to Survive a Garden Gnome Attack* (film rights optioned by Sony) and *Red Dog / Blue Dog: When Pooches Get Political* (reddog-bluedog. com). Chuck's other writing books include *Formatting & Submitting Your Manuscript, 3rd. Ed.*, as well as *Create Your Writer Platform* (fall 2012). Besides that, he is a husband, guitarist, dog owner, and cookie addict.

RICKI SCHULTZ (rickischultz.com) is an Ohio-based freelance writer and recovering high school English teacher. She writes young adult fiction and, as coordinator of The Write-Brained Network (writebrainednetwork.com), she enjoys connecting with other writers.

DONNA GAMBALE works an office job by day, writes young adult novels by night, and travels when possible. She is a contributing editor for the Guide to Literary Agents Blog and freelances as a copyeditor and proofreader of both fiction and nonfiction. She is the author of a mini kit, *Magnetic Kama Sutra* (Running Press, 2009). You can find her online at firstnovelsclub.com, where she and her critique group blog about writing, reading, networking and the rest of life.

R.L. STINE

A conversation with the man who's successfully spooked kids for decades.

....

by Zachary Petit

It's not that he acts nothing like you might assume, though he is wearing all black. He's funny and charming, and his amiable character throws kids off on school visits: "They expect someone with fangs, wearing a cape," he says.

It's not that nobody calls him "R.L." except book jackets. (He goes by Bob.)

It's not even that he has written some 300–400 books (!), and has sold more than 350 million in his Goosebumps series alone, making him at one point the bestselling children's series author of all time. (He's now No. 2, right behind J.K. Rowling.)

No, it's how he writes the things that freaks me out: He begins with *the titles*.

"That's the inspiration!" he says with a laugh. "You want to know where ideas come from—for me, they come from the title."

For instance, he was walking his dog around New York City, and he thought, *Little Shop of Hamsters*. It just popped into his head. He liked it, so he came up with a story to bring it to life—*What can I do to make hamsters scary? OK, a boy goes into a strange pet shop. It's all hamsters, and there's something wrong with one of them …*

"Most authors I know work backwards," he says.

So I decide to conduct an experiment: I'm going to be like Stine. I'm going to work backward, and I'm not going to write a word of my article about him until I've got the perfect title, one I can build a story around. Simple enough for a little profile, right?

And without knowing it, I've fallen into the trap of R.L. Stine, the trap of writing for kids, maybe the trap of writing anything: It all looked so damn easy.

Which means it's time for some placeholder text:

Title TK.

THE FIRST SCREAM

Naturally, Stine's story started with fear.

When he was a kid growing up in suburban Columbus, Ohio, Stine's mom had an ominous rule: *Never go up to the attic.* He obeyed—but he'd lie in bed at night and wonder what horrifying things might be up there, and the monster in the attic found its way into the scary stories he and his brother had a habit of trading at night. (Of course, Stine would end his with a cliffhanger to torture his sibling—a technique patrons of Stine's fiction would recognize well, including grown magazine editors spotted researching at coffeehouses, unapologetically flipping Goosebumps pages wide-eyed.)

Eventually, he faced his fears and climbed the stairs. He was 9 years old, and although no monsters were lurking about—turns out his mom just didn't want him going up there because the floorboards were rotting—he found something else. Something that would eventually leave millions of kids addicted to nefarious ventriloquist dummies, demonic masks, deranged teachers, et al. . . .

And this is probably going to sound too good to be true, too convenient, but I'm really not making it up:

The young storyteller found a typewriter.

So he wrote—but his roots began in goofball humor, not horror. Comics ("Super Stooge"). Joke magazines ("*HAH, For Maniacs Only!!*"). On and on.

"My parents didn't understand it at all," he says. "You know, some guy staying in his room typing. And my mother would say, 'Go out and play, go outside—what's wrong with you?' I'd say, 'It's boring out there.'"

Thus, he'd stay in his room and create. And as the years went on, he never stopped.

"People say, 'What advice do you have for people who want to be writers?' I say, they don't really need advice, they know they want to be writers, and they're gonna do it," he says. "Those people who know that they really want to do this and are cut out for it, they know it."

After he graduated from Ohio State in 1965, he moved to New York City to fulfill his dreams of working for a magazine ... but the only gig he could rope was one in which he was told to *make up* interviews with celebrities for fan magazines. So he did—he (faux-)interviewed all the greats, from The Beatles to Diana Ross, and he sharpened both his speed and his imagination in the process.

Following a flat stint at *Soft Drink Industry* (no joke), he found his way to Scholastic, where he'd spend the next 16 years, mastering the art of writing at different grade levels, and presiding over his kids' humor magazine, *Bananas*.

His debut book, *How to Be Funny*, followed in 1978—under the name "Jovial Bob Stine." He wore bunny ears to his first signing.

In those days, Stine was in heaven: He'd always wanted his own humor magazine, and now he had it.

"I thought I would just coast for the rest of my life," he recalled at a recent appearance. "It didn't work out."

More specifically, his magazine folded—so Stine began freelancing full time, producing a boggling variety of material: bubblegum cards, Indiana Jones and G.I. Joe novels, coloring books, joke books, scripts for "Eureeka's Castle" on Nickelodeon (where he became head writer).

And then one day he sat down for a lunch that—forgive the cliché here, but it really is true—would change his life forever. And, naturally, it all started with a title. Which brings me back to my problem.

Title Update: Not going well. "It Came From Ohio!"? Perfect, but it's the title of his autobiography, and likely would come across as, well, lazy, given my extravagant setup. "The Monster in the Attic"? Very 400 words ago. "Title TK"—calling it that would be funny and clever, right? No. "In the Wake of Super Stooge"? Potentially offensive. Sigh.

Title TK.

GHOULS GONE WILD!

At that fateful lunch with Stine's Scholastic friend Jean Feiwel, she asked him a simple question: Have you ever thought about writing young adult horror? And she made an equally simple suggestion: Go home and write a book called *Blind Date*.

"I said, 'OK, sure, no problem,'" he recalls.

And the amazing thing is—and this is a hint at what makes Stine stand out from millions of other writers, a testament to how much of a born storyteller he truly is—*he actually did it*. He outlined for a month. He wrote for three. He spent a month revising. He sent it in. It came out in 1986, and became an instant bestseller.

During the writing process, he developed his trademark cliffhanger chapter structure—something he picked up in his humor career. In fact, Stine says the line between humor and horror isn't all that distinct—horror is like a rollercoaster in which the intention is to laugh and scream simultaneously. And a cliffhanger is a lot like a punch line.

"I think after I came up with that, it was easy," he says. "Then, it was storytelling."

More books followed—notably his breakout series, Fear Street (the title just popped into his head, so, of course, he wrote the books to accommodate it). Novels began pouring out of him at a monthly rate.

How'd he match the demand? "Writing is the only thing that ever came easily to me," he says. "It's the only thing I'm really competent at. And I never had trouble. I was always confident about it; I could always sit down and write 10 pages. In those days, I could write 20 pages a day."

Still, he didn't *feel* like a hit yet—at least nowhere near the caliber of a hit he'd become. But then he got a call from the book packaging company his wife founded, Parachute Press—they wanted to know if he'd like to try writing books for younger kids ... novels that married his horror skills *and* his humor abilities. R.L. meets Jovial Bob, if you will.

Naturally, he needed his title. One day, he was browsing *TV Guide*, and he saw an ad proclaiming that it was "Goosebumps" week on Channel 11. (In a delightfully corny joke he's fond of telling, he called his wife over and said he'd found the title—*Channel 11!*)

He wrote the first Goosebumps book, *Welcome to Dead House*, in just over a week. It was released in 1992. Two more books followed, to little fanfare.

And then everything exploded. Kids went nuts for it. Stine says there was no advertising, no hype, no bunny-eared signings. It was just readers telling readers—the best advertising an author can get. Oodles of books followed. T-shirts. TV shows. A Goosebumps attraction at Disney World. Overall, he attributes the series' mindblowing success to the fact that it was the first to nab equal amounts of female and male readers.

"It was unbelievable for me—you just never dream of having something like that," he says. "I don't know if it taught me any lesson; it was just lucky, I think. The only lesson is, you gotta keep at it."

Title Update: I am now at war with the title (not to mention the meta fits the article seems to have contracted). The story is too far gone to be written based on it anymore—but it still has to be good, Stine-ish. My designer has just inquired about the status of the piece. It's long overdue. "If you can just get me the hed and dek, I can start …" she says, mercifully. I flee the office. At home, a brilliant idea emerges: I'll call Stine, and ask him what he'd title the thing. Yes! He's the master, after all. So I do. But he's on vacation; the doctor is out. Uh-oh.

Title TK.

FIELD OF SCREAMS

First off, yes, Stine is still writing. A lot. And second—and this is something I bring up only because he laughingly notes it's one of his biggest pet peeves on Twitter or during a library visit—he's not "a blast from the past," and no, he is not dead.

Far from it: He's written about 100 Fear Street books and about 105 Goosebumps. He sits down at 10 a.m. and writes six days a week. He does six new Goosebumps a year, which he has described as "like a vacation," compared to his previous output. His method?

A Goosebumps manuscript is 120 pages. He has his title. He doesn't really do research, preferring to work off his imagination. He creates a character list and takes two to four days to outline—extensively (which he says also prevents him from getting writer's block). The outline has dialogue, every chapter ending, and so on, up to 20 pages. And then, when he returns to the book, all the work is done. He writes 10 pages a day, does a second draft for a couple days, and turns it in. Grand total: About three weeks.

How does he pull it off? He says you have to love it.

"I'm cut out for it," he says. "I'm cut out for working at home: I don't get distracted, I'm very disciplined…"

When asked if he's gotten tired from producing such a massive output for so many years, he laughs.

"Well, look at me! I'm a wreck!" he says. "No, I still enjoy it. I still look forward to it in the morning. It's gotten harder to come up with new ideas. It's more challenging: new kinds of scares, new chapter endings…"

And he's still garnering accolades. This past summer, Stine took home the top award of ThrillerMaster at the massive ThrillerFest genre conference. International Thriller Writers co-president Douglas Preston—co-author of *The Monster of Florence* and *Relic*—says many thriller writers love Stine, because he brought them their audience by hooking their future readers when they were kids.

"He's incredibly inventive," Preston says. "I don't know if I've ever met anyone who has just had so many fantastic ideas."

Waiting in line at Stine's ThrillerFest book signing, Sandra Brannan, author of *In the Belly of Jonah,* says she too loves his work—he scared her kids to death.

"His strength is he definitely knows his audience," she says. "He writes for that audience, and we're all those 7- to 12-year-olds that love to be scared."

Which brings us to something that may upset some writers on first read. It can be hard to hear. But hear him out. During our interview, I ask Stine what he thinks is the *worst* writing advice out there.

"Well, *I hate it* when authors come into a school and they say to kids, 'Write from your heart, write from your heart, only write what you know, and write from your heart.' I hate that because it's *useless*. I've written over 300 books—not one was written from my heart. Not one. They were all written for an audience, they were all written to entertain a certain audience."

The problem with such advice, Stine says, is that if you tell people to write from their hearts and to write only something they know, they get blocked totally. Instead, he says, it's all about the imagination. (Hey, it worked for him.)

As for the writing he does for those very kids, Stine does have rules he plays by in his books: Keep the language simple. Show kids that reading is fun and easy. Keep the parent characters out of the way, and let the kids find a way out of the trouble using their own wits. Don't cross the line of being too scary. Also, skip the references to things that happened before the audience was born.

Of course, while writing may seem like the only thing Stine does, he lives a normal life in his beloved New York City home, devoid of the capes and fangs some of his readers expect: He goes to the theater and opera, he walks his dog in the park, he takes vacations.

As for the future, he's 68 but has no plans of retirement, and is working on an adult novel right now because he wanted a challenge. Which brings me to ask him if he ever gets tired of being so closely associated with a single series, like Goosebumps.

His answer is immediate.

"No, I love it. It's a wonderful thing. I feel so lucky. I would never resent it in any way," he says. "I'll always be *Goosebumps Author R.L. Stine*. I'll always be called that. Always."

I mention that I was going to ask him what he wants his legacy to be.

"That's it," he says, laughing. "You can't escape it, right, so you might as well enjoy it, right?"

And then, on my desk, I see it. Finally. My title.

Indeed, I fell into the trap of Stine, the trap of any writing: It all looked so easy. But it's also monstrously easy to overcomplicate the craft for yourself (see: my fool's errand that became this narrative). Stine's ride wasn't an easy one, but if you think about it, his path to success wasn't all that complicated: He became so skilled because of years of practice, years of honing his craft, chiseling away at an inescapable urge.

Years of doing the only thing he was ever good at (his words, not mine).

Like, say, writing the series that is his legacy. And what you can expect from him in the future and beyond:

More & More & More Tales to Give You Goosebumps

... The name of one of his books piled high atop my desk. Which is another thing that freaks me out about R.L. Stine: Turns out he gave me some help with my title long ago without even knowing it—not to mention all my subheadings.

Damn, he's good.

ZACHARY PETIT (zacharypetit.com) is an award-winning journalist, the senior managing editor of *Writer's Digest* magazine, and the executive editor of *Writer's Workbook*. Alongside the hundreds of articles he has penned as a staff writer and editor, covering everything from the secret lives of mall Santas to literary legends, his words have appeared in National Geographic magazine, National Geographic Kids, Melissa Rossi's What Every American Should Know book series, McSweeney's Internet Tendency and many other outlets..

BETH REVIS

How she kept writing through 10 unpublished novels and found success.

....

by Frankie Diane Mallis

Beth Revis was a school teacher and had been writing novels for a decade before she finally wrote what would become her debut published novel, a young adult, science-fiction, mystery. *Across The Universe* was published by Penguin Razorbill in January 2011. The novel, which takes place out of this world, literally took Beth away from her own. She quickly went from being a full-time teacher to a full-time *New York Times* bestselling author.

Here Beth recounts her journey into publishing, shares her experiences writing *A Million Suns* and *Shades Of Earth*, gives advice to writers and also gives hints about where she's planning to go next. To learn more about Beth and her books visit her website: bethrevis.com.

Across the Universe was your first published novel, but it wasn't the first novel you wrote. Can you tell us about some of the novels that you shelved before writing *Across the Universe*? How many did you write?

I wrote 10 novels over the course of 10 years, and none of them were published. The eleventh novel was *Across the Universe*, and it was the one that changed everything. But honestly? I almost didn't write that one. The tenth novel I wrote, I wrote "for the market." I did everything that I thought the market wanted ... and nothing that *I* wanted. It's the only book I regret, and it's the one that almost made me quit.

Across the Universe was a departure for me. Before that, I'd always written fantasy—*Across the Universe* is science fiction. I'd always written third person, past tense—*Across*

the Universe is first person, present tense. I'd never written in dual point of views, or in a boy's voice before *Across the Universe*.

I don't regret any of the other nine unpublished novels, because each one was a learning experience. Those words aren't publishable, but that doesn't mean they're worthless. And from them, there's one—maybe two—books that I might be able to go back to and publish in the future.

Did your find your writing process changing throughout the course of writing those 11 novels? And what does your writing process look like now?

I wrote *Across the Universe* in a whirlwind with a single-minded focus that I'd not felt in years. I was working as a teacher at the time, so I'd think about the story on the drive to and from work and jot notes, but I would write the bulk of the chapters on weekends and during holidays.

A well-worn piece of writing advice is to "write every day." Which is bull. When I was a teacher, I could *not* write every day. Being a teacher is exhausting! So is being a nurse, or a mom, or a factory worker, or a waiter, or any other job, and frankly, most of us have to have another job before we break into publishing (and often after, too). I *hate* that line, "write every day." It's a lie, and it's often discouraging. I wrote on the weekends, and not every weekend at that. Sometimes, the writing went well, and I'd get down ten thousand words in a weekend. During spring break, I think I wrote about a quarter of the whole novel. But I didn't write again for the rest of that month.

My writing process now still reflects the way I had to write as a teacher—I tend to *not* write every day, instead doing big chunks at a time.

Did you have an idea when writing *Across the Universe* that it would be the one? And did you have any idea of the success that would come with it, or that it would hit the *New York Times* bestseller list?

When I wrote the final scene of *Across the Universe*, there was a moment that I remember very distinctly. I leaned back in my desk chair, and thought very consciously, "This is the best thing I'd ever written." Because it was. I had a very deep conviction that if this book didn't make it, then I might as well give up, which made me terrified to query!

Once I did decide to query, one of the first things I did was go to my local bookstore. "I need to see all the YA science fiction you have," I said. The bookstore clerk handed me *Ender's Game*. "That's nice," I said. "Can I see something published this decade, though?" She handed me *The Host* by Stephanie Meyers. "Anything set in space?" I asked. Nope. Nothing. She literally had nothing on her shelves in the YA section, aside from Orson Scott Card, that had a story set in space.

This meant one of two things: either I would stand out as a unique title ... or I would be too risky to publish. Which terrified me. And when I started querying, I definitely felt that "too risky" vibe. Some agents who'd specifically asked for sci-fi in their descriptions rejected me out of hand. One agent offered—if I was willing to rewrite the book for an adult audience.

But then I found the right agent—the perfect agent. Merrilee Heifetz at Writers House was a dream agent, one who represented some of my favorite authors, who has a stellar reputation, who knew exactly where to place my strange novel. And it worked. And even though my publisher, Razorbill/Penguin, promised big things, I'd been burned by 10 years of querying and being unpublished. I had super-low expectations. I was so shocked when I hit the *NY Times* bestseller's list!

And just to keep my ego in check, the same week that I found out I hit the list, I got a late rejection from an agent telling me space sci-fi would never sell in the YA market.

What sparked the idea for *Across the Universe*? And did you know then it would become a series?

I wrote *Across the Universe* based on a lifetime of reading. I've always wanted to do a mystery like Agatha Christie's *Mousetrap*, where all the characters are trapped in snowbound inn. I wanted to write an unreliable narrator after reading Megan Whalen Turner's *The Thief*. Those were my biggest influences, and my original idea was to have the characters stuck on a cruise ship. But cruise ships are boring, and spaceships are exciting, so the story quickly became a sci-fi set amidst the stars.

Originally, though, the story was only one book. I was tired of writing books that required sequels and never having any of them sell. I intended *Across the Universe* to be a stand-alone from the start. When I signed with my agent, though, we started talking about how we wanted to present the novel to publishers. And in talking with her, I got the idea for the second and third books. But it literally wasn't until a few days before we sent it to publishers that I came up with a synopsis for the next book.

As you wrote the sequels *A Million Suns* and *Shades of Earth* did you have a plan in advance for them? Did they end up becoming the stories you thought they would? Or were you surprised along the way?

I *never* plan. Never. I wrote *Across the Universe* without any sort of outline at all. And while I gave my publisher synopses for *A Million Suns* and *Shades of Earth*, I did not follow those synopses *at all*. I cannot emphasize that enough. And obviously when you have this intricate of a plot paired with this disorganized of a writer, you have a *lot* of re-writes in your future.

Fortunately, I was working with an amazing editor who made sure the books were all they should be—actually better than I'd ever hoped. But when I say "re-writes" I mean drastically different re-writes. In *A Million Suns*, the original villain of the story in the synopsis was written out before the first draft. In the first draft, I had an entirely different villain than in the final draft. And the method of the mystery was entirely different as well. And don't even get me started on *Shades of Earth*. There are four entirely different books for that one: the synopsis (which has little in common with the final), the first draft (which has a different villain, different world, and different mystery), the second draft (which finally has the right world, but not the right villain or mystery), and the third version, which has all the same elements as the final book. One major character of *Shades of Earth*, though, wasn't introduced until about a month before the final book was turned in, though.

Were you always a huge fan of science fiction? What were some of your biggest influences?

While I loved *Ender's Game* since I first read it as a kid, I was never really a fan of science fiction in books. I blame my husband: he is a huge sci-fi reader, and he loves all the really big, thick, hard sci-fi books that had me screaming in the other direction.

Where I found my love of sci-fi was in television and movies. I am a hardcore fan of Joss Whedon's *Firefly* and *Serenity*, as well as *Star Trek, Star Wars, Doctor Who, Battlestar Gallactica*, and more. One day I really started to pay attention to *why* I loved these shows and movies but not the books. And for me, it was the emphasis over character instead of science. In hard sci-fi, the science is practically another character. Which is fine. But that's not for me, that's not what I wanted to do. I don't want to explain why the cool tech works, I just wanted the cool tech. And the television and movies I loved did that. All I did, then, was try to translate what I loved about sci-fi on the screen into a book.

What was it like on the day you learned that you would become a published writer? How did you find out?

I can remember the day very vividly. I had a relatively short time period on submission, and I wasn't expecting to hear from my agent yet. But she asked via e-mail if she could call me at work, and I walked right out of my classroom full of students, I was so nervous. She told me she was in negotiations—I couldn't believe it was happening so fast! After so many years of rejection, I'd expected to be on submission for a year or more. After school was over, my agent called me back. I sat in my car in the school's parking lot and heard all of the details, but I still couldn't quite believe that I was actually going to be published. I went home and then had a fancy celebratory dinner with my husband. Sometime that night, it really started to sink in that my life was going to change, that my dreams were coming true. At which point in time ... I threw up the entire fancy dinner. How graceful!

Was becoming a published author everything you dreamed it would be? What surprised you the most?

It absolutely was. I'm fully aware that I've been very lucky in this aspect—I adore my agent and my publisher and editor and wouldn't change a single thing. In fact, being published has been better than my dream, because I never expected to be able to be a full-time writer with my first book, or to hit the *NY Times* bestselling list, or any of that.

But I think what's surprised me the most was how now, so many of the authors that I'd idolized are now people who I consider to be friends. It's so strange! I'm still very much a fangirl, and sometimes I sit in awe of the fact that my favorite authors are not just my colleagues, but also my friends.

Since being published, how has your life changed?

In a million little ways—being my own boss, setting my own schedule, etc. But in one very significant way: Publication gave me the validation I never knew I needed so much. It's given me hope and happiness. There's something immensely powerful in knowing that dreams can come true, something life-changing and soul-affirming.

What has been your craziest moment as a published author?

Recently, I was at Y'all Fest in Charleston, S.C., and a girl comes up to me and asks, breathlessly, "Are you Beth Revis?" I nodded my head. "That is so cool!" she said, and ran back to her friends. That was such a funny experience, I don't think I'll ever forget it.

There was also a time I was at a writing conference and an agent I'd queried before pulled me aside after her workshop. She told me all about how I was "the one that got away" and how she regretted rejecting me. That was definitely surreal—it's the sort of thing I used to dream would happen back in my querying days!

What do you feel is your greatest strength as a writer and how have you cultivated that strength?

Before publication, I would have said that my greatest strength was my first drafts. I rarely did in-depth revisions and rewrites, believing in the strength of those early drafts (which definitely explains why it took me so long to get published). I mean, I *thought* I was editing and rewriting, but I didn't take it as far as I should have. But since working with an editor, I've come to realize that my greatest strength is really in my rewriting and revising skills. All I needed was the *right* direction ([provided] through my wise editor), and I was able to really make the book much better. Now, I approach first drafts as that—truly first drafts, knowing that the vast majority of the story can and probably will change.

Which part of the writing process do you find the most challenging? And how do you go about conquering it?

It's all challenging. Whatever step I'm on now is the hardest part. It's all a matter of doing it any way.

Growing up which books were your favorite to read? Which writers did you admire? Which writers do you most admire now?

My favorite books of all time were C.S. Lewis's Chronicles of Narnia. It's obviously a story that has symbolism in it, but when I read it as a kid, it was a great revelation to discover that symbolism on my own. It was the first experience I ever had with the idea that a story is more than just the words on the page, that there are layers of meaning. It set me on a path of loving books, which shaped my whole life.

And, as much as a cliché that it may be, I also have deep love for J.K. Rowling. I got into her works when I was in college. At the time, I was rather a literary snob. I'd been cramming my brain full of the works of dead European men, and I felt like, to be a True Lover of Literature, I couldn't read fun books. But my college roomie, also an English major, went with me to a bookstore and whispered, in reference to the teen section, "I sometimes like the books *over there.*" I realized it was really stupid of me to not read books just because they were fun, and I dove into YA lit, never looking back. When I read the Harry Potter books, I really began to understand that a book can be both entertaining and insightful, and that's the model I use for my own books.

What are some other influences on your writing outside of other novelists and books?

Two very different sources. The first is Pre-Raphaelite art. I've always loved the way Pre-Raphaelite art uses symbolism to add a much deeper meaning to the actual painting. A flower is just a flower in any other painting, but in Pre-Raphaelite works, a rose may mean death, a daffodil, life. I don't think every little thing in a book needs symbolism, but I do believe that if you have a few consistent symbols in your work, you're giving your reader a little something extra to uncover. For example, in *Across the Universe*, none of my characters have access to windows to the outside, so none of them have seen the stars, despite the fact that they live on a spaceship. This was a nod to Dante's *Inferno*, where stars are symbolic of hope. My characters don't see stars; they don't have hope until they do. It's not something that's very obvious, and only a handful of readers have caught it, but it's an integral part of the story.

My second influence would be the work of Joss Whedon. He's a master of storytelling, and I've learned so much from him. And I must admit that it's a great thing that watching his television shows and movies counts as research for me!

Can you describe in your gut the moment you knew you wanted to be a writer?

I honestly cannot remember a time when I didn't want to be a writer. This is so trite to say, but also true. It was always my deepest and dearest wish to write—and I did. I have "novels" from when I was in elementary school, notebooks full of story ideas that I jotted down rather than taking notes in class. Writing is as much a part of my life as breathing.

What was the best piece of writing advice you ever got, and what advice would you give to writers?

I can't remember who said it, but the best piece of advice I ever got was something along the lines of "whenever you have the choice to write or go out and experience something new, do the new thing." A life lived well is the best resource for a writer to ever have.

But my most common piece of writing advice is, "don't take any writing advice you hear as an absolute truth—even this." Some advice, such as "write every day," is well-meaning but can be very harmful to a writer. There is no single right path, no correct way. Do what works for you.

And when in doubt, blow something up or kill off a character.

What are some of your future writing plans? Do you think you'll ever write in another genre or for another age group?

I hope to continue writing (and publishing!) a book a year. I would love to have a huge bibliography, and to always have something I'm working on.

That said, I do think I'll probably always write YA, perhaps some MG. I doubt I'll stray much from those groups—it's what I like to read, and therefore what I like to write. And I don't think I'll do anything outside of science fiction or fantasy. I prefer my novels to have a definite chance of things blowing up.

Do you ever see yourself pursuing another form of art outside of writing?

I wish I could—I'd love to be able to paint, or sing, or something else—but my talent is very limited. I do other things for fun, like drawing or playing the piano, but it's never, ever, ever something that would be suitable for the public.

If you could redo one moment in your writing career, what would it be?

Not a thing. All of it, even the mistakes, were worthwhile and made me who I am today.

FRANKIE DIANE MALLIS is a young adult and children's fantasy writer and is represented by Laura Rennert of the Andrea Brown Literary Agency. She is a professor of composition and creative writing at Arcadia University. Frankie also runs a small children's library. When not writing, she can be found belly dancing and baking vegan food. Learn more by visiting her website: frankiediane.blogspot.com.

MARIE LU

On developing your craft and how life influences fiction.

by Donna Gambale

Marie Lu's debut young adult novel, *Legend* (Putnam Juvenile), released in November 2011 amid much buzz and an almost unparalleled marketing campaign from Penguin.

Such high expectations would make even a seasoned author nervous, but the *New York Times* review proclaimed, "*Legend* doesn't merely survive the hype, it deserves it." Lu's dystopian debut also garnered starred reviews from *Publishers Weekly*, Kirkus Reviews, VOYA, Library Media Connection and *Booklist*. The *Legend* juggernaut continued when CBS Films acquired the film rights in February 2011.

After its release, the book gained momentum with readers, reaching the *New York Times* bestseller list the month before publication of the much-anticipated sequel, *Prodigy* (Jan. 2013). *Prodigy* debuted at No. 2 on the list, with sales of both novels maintaining their bestseller status for weeks after publication. Lu is now hard at work on *Champion*, the final book in the trilogy.

Before becoming a full-time writer, Lu worked as an art director in the video game industry, a career that has inspired highly visual scenes in her books. Here, she talks about tackling lengthy revisions; why she doesn't believe in the term "boy reader"; how politics influenced her world-building; and what she learned from her unpublished novels. For more on Lu, check out her website at marielu.org.

Tell us about your first "author moment," when the reality of being published really hit you.

My first "author moment" didn't hit until the night before my first book (*Legend*) was to come out. I remember sitting in the dark, typing up a blog post about how happy I was that my book would launch the next morning, and then suddenly realizing that I'd been dreaming about writing this blog post since I was little. I put my head down on my desk and just cried. That moment stands out very vividly in my memory.

The middle book in a trilogy is notoriously difficult to write. What challenges did *Prodigy* present that weren't there while writing *Legend*?

Before *Prodigy*, I'd never written a book on deadline. *Legend* flowed organically because of that freedom. With *Prodigy*, I suddenly had a deadline to meet, a contract to fulfill, a publisher and readers and fans to please, and a first book to top. I don't think anyone is ever quite ready for that pressure. I ate a lot of chocolates.

When did you decide that the best way to write *Legend* would be through alternating first-person points of view? How did you differentiate June and Day's narrations?

I've written in alternating first-person points of view since I was in high school—my unpublished fantasy manuscript from my teen years was told in the same format. I learned it from Barbara Kingsolver's *The Poisonwood Bible*, one of my favorite books. I really love the intimacy of first-person, but I also want the advantage of hopping from head to head. The challenge, of course, is to make sure the characters sound distinct, and to do that, I tried to develop two characters with opposing personalities and who came from opposite worlds—traits that would affect their style of speech. As a result,

Day has a rough-and-tumble, hot-headed street personality, while June has a refined, upper-class, level-headed demeanor to complement.

Authors often receive lengthy revision notes from agents and editors, as well as from critique partners. How do you tackle an extensive, multi-part revision? (And how long was your longest revision letter?)

I think my longest revision letter was 12 pages. I like the revision process, oddly enough! It's much easier for me to work with something rather than create something from nothing. I tend to group a multi-part revision letter into related points (plot logistic problems in one pile, character development issues in another pile, and so on). Then I tackle it one pile at a time.

Before *Legend*, you wrote four unpublished novels that I like to call "training novels." What did you learn from them?

"Training novels" is a good term for them! I learned so much about character development from those early novels, as well as how to string together all of the moving threads of a decent plot. I also discovered my voice, strengths and weaknesses. The learning process continues today—it never ends.

There were many fuzzy gray areas of good and evil in *Legend*, but in *Prodigy*, I was truly impressed by your ability to create such multilayered characters. Good intentions and noble goals become twisted, and no one side is "right." Can you talk about why this complex morality was important to you to portray?

Thank you! I've always believed that dystopias are relative. One man's dystopia is another man's norm, and most dystopias emerge from "good" (if twisted) intentions. Everyone thinks he's right. Therefore, I wanted to portray the people of *Legend* and *Prodigy* the way real people are—a patchwork of shifting grays, where right and wrong depend largely on what society you grew up in and what values you were taught.

How does your background in the video game industry help your writing?

Because I used to draw for a living in the game industry, I tend to aim for very "visual" scenes. I never see words; I see a 3D map or a movie scene. One sequence in *Legend* involves a street duel between two characters, and I definitely imagined a round of Mortal Kombat while writing it.

John Barth said, "Everyone is necessarily the hero of his own life story." Who was your favorite secondary character to write, and how does his/her self-concept differ from how the reader sees this character?

My favorite secondary character, by far, is Kaede. She's essentially who I wish I could be: a brash, fearless, sharp-tongued fighter pilot. She doesn't always have a heart of gold, but she's practical, and I hope readers admire that about her.

What do you see as your greatest weakness as a writer, and how have you been working to improve that skill?

I think my greatest weakness is romance. I'm like my character June in this sense—we're both rather awkward in dealing with romance, and we tend to say the wrong things at the wrong times. I usually have to plan out romantic scenes far in advance, read a couple of romance books, and give myself months to hone my scenes. They take me forever!

It's a common struggle in YA to appeal to and reach a male audience, yet *Legend* has managed to do so. Tell us about these "elusive" boy readers, and how they've discovered your books.

I'm personally not a big fan of the concept that boy readers are somehow harder to reach than girl readers. I feel like this is a product of how things are marketed to them, and a result of gender history in general. When a parent asks me something like, "Do you think my 12-year-old son will like this?", I don't know how to respond, because I don't know the boy. Is he interested in military worlds? Does he prefer romance? Does he like comedy? What are his hobbies? I have no idea. This is where the term "boy reader" breaks down. To me, it helps more to cater to specific genre interests (i.e. this book is an action/thriller/sci-fi, not a "boy book" or "girl book") rather than gender interests. I believe in catering to "boy readers" the same way I would cater to any reader: strive to write a story with strong characters, addictive plot and high stakes. The more we treat boy—and girl—readers like people with varying interests instead of a category, the more I think they'll open up to what we can offer them.

What are your favorite and least-favorite parts of being a published author that have nothing to do with writing?

Other than sitting in your jammies all day, the best part of being a published author |is hearing from fans. Nothing makes me happier than to read a story about how a young reluctant reader has discovered the joy of reading after checking out one of my books. It's the best feeling! My least-favorite part is figuring out taxes. Does anybody enjoy taxes?

In the Legend trilogy, the Republic and the Colonies are the warring halves of the former United States. What was your inspiration for the world-building of these two distinct countries?

When I first began writing *Legend*, it was early 2009 and both of our political parties in the U.S. had split off into rather nasty exaggerations of themselves. I found it pretty disturbing to see. That division inspired the nature of the Republic and the Colonies, each of which represents an ideology twisted to extremes. Everything in moderation, I say!

You joked on Twitter that you were stuck in a "Valley of Hate" for the final book in the Legend trilogy, and in the *Prodigy* acknowledgments, you mentioned bouts of "panic attacks" and "desperate sobbing" during the writing process. Every writer experiences those impossible, discouraging days. How do you get through them?

So many panic attacks! I've learned to let them run their course. It's healthy to shake those nerves out, I think, by stepping away from the writing for a while. I tend to lose myself in sketching something or playing video games, which allows me to stay creative but in a different medium. After a couple of days, I usually calm down and get back into the nitty gritty of writing.

What's the best writing advice you've ever been given? What's your favorite advice to give writers?

My favorite bit of advice came from a writers' conference, where an established author reminded me that no one's first draft looks perfect. In that vein, my advice to writers is similar: Don't be afraid to write something bad. You have to get the bad words out of your system before you can get to the good stuff.

....

DONNA GAMBALE (firstnovelsclub.com, @donnagambale) works an office job by day, writes young adult novels by night, and travels when possible. She is a contributing editor for the Guide to Literary Agents Blog and freelances as a copyeditor and proofreader of both fiction and nonfiction. She is the author of a humorous mini kit, *Magnetic Kama Sutra* (Running Press, 2009).

....

DEBBIE RIDPATH OHI

The (Naked!) tuth about how this author/illustrator gets ink on her elbows.

....

by Ricki Schultz

Having been on the Internet longer than most of us have known about its existence, Debbie Ridpath Ohi has helped aspiring authors and illustrators hone their skills and build their writer platforms since she traded the corporate life for a career in the arts. Not only did the Toronto-based Ohi publish one of the first books dealing with online markets for writers, but her illustrations were one-half of *I'm Bored* (Simon & Schuster)—a collaboration with author and actor/comedian Michael Ian Black that ended up as one of *New York Times'* Notable Children's Books of 2012.

Hard at work on her second project with Black, *Naked!* (Simon & Schuster), Ohi's schedule is jam-packed with speaking engagements, interviews, conferences, freelance work, social media and her own writing projects.

So, just how does one maintain such a schedule? According to Ohi, a genuine love for her work and realistic expectations help her accomplish all she does in a given week. Always giving back to the writing community, she was kind enough to make time to share her story and offer no-nonsense tips on how to get started as a children's book author and illustrator.

Although you started out as a systems programmer/analyst, you "stepped off the corporate cliff" in lieu of a more creative path. Please talk to us about what led to the publication of your nonfiction book, *The Writer's Online Marketplace* (F+W Media), in 2001.

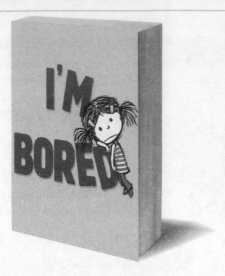

After stepping off that cliff, I took on part-time work in a public library and a children's bookstore as I pursued a freelance career. As I honed my craft, I began to get short nonfiction published plus a few poems and short stories.

I also created Inkspot, one of the first websites for writers on the Web. It began as a site for children's book writers but as it grew in popularity, I decided to expand it to include other genres. At its peak, my e-mail newsletter had nearly 50,000 subscribers and the site had over 200,000 unique visitors; as my readership grew, so did my site's appeal to potential advertisers. *Writer's Digest* was one of my advertising clients back then, and they also approached me about the book.

I still remember when Jack Heffron from F+W contacted me. For the first few moments, I thought it was a prank call. I mean, how often do newbie writers get approached by editors rather than the other way around? Jack asked me to put together a proposal, and the book was approved by F+W. That was my very first book contract.

The phrase "author platform" wasn't in popular use back then, but that experience helped me understand the value of visibility as well as a proven audience and reach.

As well, how did you go from writing about writing/the publishing industry to writing and illustrating yourself? Have you always been an artist/cartoonist? And what draws you to kids' lit?

I've always wanted to write for young people. My website began as a resource for children's book writers because that was my main career goal. I began writing nonfiction because it was a more reliable way to earn income while I worked on improving my writing for young people. I wrote and sold articles on pretty much any topic that publications would pay me for, from how to store your vegetables properly to how to choose a piano teacher to writing and publishing.

Meanwhile, I kept doodling, but mainly just for fun. I've always loved to draw. One of my earliest memories is getting in trouble for drawing faces in crayon on furniture. I've also enjoyed reading and creating comics for as long as I can remember. I was the self-declared editor of a family publication that I put together with the help of my siblings and parents every week, and I used to make comics for it. One of my first comic strips was about a somewhat demented baby called Boppy.

As for being drawn to kids' lit, I've enjoyed reading books for young people since ... well, since I was a kid. Even now, I'd say that 80 percent of the books I read are commercially classified as kidlit/YA. Why? Because I tend to enjoy the stories more than mainstream adult fiction, and they're more likely to have characters I like, and endings with hope.

How did you get your agent? Query, like the rest of us? Pitch at a conference? Something else?

A Santa Barbara children's book author named Lee Wardlaw was kind enough to look at my middle-grade manuscript. After helping me improve it, Lee passed the manuscript to her agent at Curtis Brown, Ginger Knowlton, and Ginger decided to take me on as a client. I love my agent, and I'll always be grateful to Lee for taking the time to help out a newbie.

You are one busy woman (an understatement!). With conferences, speaking engagements, interviews and multiple projects on the horizon, what does your typical writing week look like? A typical day?

This is a hard question to answer, because my work schedule changes from one week to another, depending on the stage of various projects.

My typical work day these days: I get up around 7 a.m., check my e-mail for anything that needs answering right away, browse publishing industry news while I'm having breakfast (yes, I tend to eat breakfast in front of my computer—bad, I know), do book contract work until around 2 or 3, go to the gym or out for errands.

If I get enough work done earlier in the day on contracted book projects, then I work on other book projects: brainstorming, outlining, writing and revising. If I don't get a chance to do the latter, then I make sure I carve out some time later in the week. If I have a really tight deadline, then I do more contracted book work for the rest of the afternoon.

For others who have many different types of projects on the go, what recommendations do you have for them?

1. Make a list of all your creative projects in progress.

2. Order the list according to importance to you.

3. Once you've finished your prioritized list, take a hard look and be realistic about how many of these projects you will actually be able to finish within a reasonable

amount of time. Consider taking the lower priority items off your list and putting them on the back burner for now, so you can focus on getting the higher-ranked projects finished.

Another useful piece of advice: Learn how to say no. I'm not talking about the requests that are easy to decline but rather the seemingly innocuous "it'll only take me a short time and anyway, it'll be fun" favors and tasks that end up accumulating and sucking up way more creative energy and time than you anticipated.

You also maintain, contribute to and participate in several blogs and online communities. You basically embody the very essence of writer platform. How do you do it all? Does it ever get overwhelming?

I'm still working on better managing my time. A few years ago, I was busy accumulating both print and digital rejection letters as I worked hard to get people in the industry to notice me. Now that I have their notice, I need to adjust how I use social media. I've had to force myself to pull back on blogging and social media somewhat to make more time for contracted books as well as new projects.

It's as if I was in a crowded room before, waving my arms and yelling, "I'm here! Look at me!" and now people are looking at me with, "Hey, we like what you've done. But now what else can you do?"

Right now, I'm experimenting with a new schedule, trying to stay off social media in the mornings and, um, that's not going so well. By the time people read this article, I should hopefully have settled into better habits. My biggest weakness is Twitter, so feel free to check on how I'm doing: @inkyelbows.

How did you get involved in so much in terms of social media? Would you send aspiring writers and illustrators down the same path?

The truth is that I've always loved online communities, long before the term became popular. I used to host an electronic bulletin board system back in the days before the Web. I love the idea of being able to interact with like-minded individuals, regardless of where they live.

As for whether aspiring writers and illustrators should embrace social media, it depends so much on the individual. I've heard some say that all writers and illustrators *have* to be on Twitter, on Facebook and so on. Social media can be a great benefit if someone is motivated, has taken the time to learn how to use it properly, and has realistic expectations. However, I've seen way too many writers and illustrators jump on the social media bandwagon without thinking it through.

My advice: If you're new to social media, pick one or two venues (Facebook and Twitter, for example) rather than trying to be everywhere. Before you create an account and start posting, do your research. Find writers or illustrators who are successful at social media and watch how they do it. Decide on some realistic goals. "Find someone who will give me a book contract" is not a realistic goal. "Find and follow children's book editors so I can find out more about what they're like and what they're looking for" is a realistic goal.

But be aware of how much time you spend on social media. It's way too easy to say, "I'll just check Facebook one more time" and then suddenly the smoke alarm upstairs is going off because an hour has gone by and you've forgotten something on the stove.

Not that this sort of thing has ever happened to me, of course. Ahem.

What should every aspiring author/illustrator have starting out? What is the most useful or appropriate social outlet to each of these types of artists?

My main piece of advice to both aspiring authors and illustrators is this: Persevere.

Persevere through rejections from agents, editors and art directors.

Persevere through bouts of soul-sucking insecurity. Most of us hit that black hole at some point or another. Sometimes more often than we can count (hand waving here).

Try not to compare yourself with other writers and illustrators. Focus on your own work. Everyone's journey is different. You will find your own way.

As for the most useful or appropriate social media, that depends on each individual's situation. My favorite social media venue is Twitter. I've made many mistakes while I was learning to use Twitter and have compiled a Writer's Guide To Twitter in case others find it useful: http://inkygirl.com/a-writers-guide-to-twitter.

You are currently working on illustrating a second book with actor/comedian/writer Michael Ian Black, *Naked!* (Simon & Schuster). How did you get paired with him on your first collaboration, *I'm Bored*?

My illustrator friend Beckett Gladney (artbeco.com) convinced me to enter the 2010 SCBWI Illustration Portfolio Showcase and helped me put together my very first portfolio. Up to that point, I had been focused entirely on writing for young people.

To my shock, I ended up winning two awards: a Mentorship program award (Penguin art director Cecilia Yung chose me) and one of two runners-up for the overall Showcase. One of the judges for the latter was Justin Chanda, publisher at Simon & Schuster Children's, and he asked me if I'd be interested in illustrating Michael Ian Black's newest picture book.

I laughed out loud when reading the manuscript for *I'm Bored* for the first time. I love illustrating Michael's work. Having so much fun illustrating *Naked!* right now.

Some people in the industry aren't crazy about so-called celebrity books, complaining about the injustice of famous people getting the book contracts with mediocre manuscripts while higher-quality content written by lower-profile authors gets rejected. Like other published books out there, the quality of celebrity books varies. I love

Michael's writing—not just his stories for young people, but books like his *You're Not Doing It Right* (Gallery Books).

As for celebrity books taking away opportunities from the aspiring masses, I want to say that it was the opposite in my case. There is no way that Simon & Schuster Books For Young Readers would have taken a chance on a totally inexperienced illustrator like me if they didn't have a well-known author who would bring in guaranteed sales.

I'm grateful to not only S&S but also Michael, who could have given me a pass and opted for a better-known illustrator instead. An aside: Michael may have a cynical and non-PG-rated public persona, but he has always been consistently professional, supportive and enthusiastic in private e-mail.

Young reviewers have given *I'm Bored* a thumbs up so far, and I'm delighted. In the end, after all, it doesn't matter how famous the author of a book might be. The most important thing is the story and its ability to connect with young readers.

What about the other series you're currently working on illustrating, the Ruby Rose series by Rob Sanders? How does that work?

HarperCollins sent me the manuscript for the first Ruby Rose book, asking if I'd be interested in illustrating two books in the series. I loved Rob's story, so I auditioned by sending in sample illustrations. I was delighted when they picked me; I'll start working on sketches for the first book in 2014.

And can you talk to us a little about the process of becoming a children's illustrator? You've blogged about the *I'm Bored* experience, but what immediate advice would you give to those who might see the process as a bit overwhelming? Where does one start?

Keep a sketchbook. Draw every day. Push yourself to draw subjects you don't normally draw. Experiment with different perspective, different styles. The more you practice, the better you'll get. Don't worry if you haven't yet found your own trademark style; that will come in time.

Learn how to tell a story sequence (maybe start with 3–4) with illustrations. Strive to keep your characters looking consistent throughout the sequence.

Go to your local library and children's bookstore, and read as many illustrated books for young people as you can. Ask for recommendations. Study how the illustrations and text work together. What do the illustrations tell the reader about the story that the text doesn't? How do the images affect pacing? What would you have done differently?

Join the SCBWI. Meet other illustrators, attend workshops, enter the Portfolio Showcase. Doing the latter got me my first book illustration contract as well as enabling me to become part of the SCBWI Illustration Mentorship Program (see KidLitArtists.com for our posts for aspiring children's book illustrators).

Harold Underdown has excellent advice for beginning children's book illustrators as well as writers on his website: underdown.org/.

I also recommend that aspiring children's illustrators read *Writing With Pictures: How To Write And Illustrate Children's Books* by Uri Shulevitz and *Show and Tell: Exploring The Fine Art Of Children's Book Illustration* by Dilys Evans.

According to your main site, you are working on a chapter book as well as a middle-grade novel. Are you working on these simultaneously, or do you typically finish one project like this before you start the other?

If I'm working on outlining or prepping for a revamp, I can work on multiple novel projects at the same time. Once I start serious writing, however, I'll usually focus on one project at a time.

It doesn't seem like it, but do you ever have writer's—or illustrator's—block? How do you maintain the energy and excitement you exude, and how do you stay fresh and prolific? Is it just part of your personality, or do you have some secrets?

I'm not sure if I ever get completely blocked, but I do find it harder for be creative on some days than others. When it's difficult, it's usually because I'm letting myself be distracted.

I liked Sean Tan's advice at a SCBWI conference, where he advised writers and illustrators to create a "bubble of delusion" in which they feel safe to create and tell themselves they will do great work. One way to do this is to surround yourself with encouraging people. Avoid negativity. Sean says he doesn't read reviews of his work.

Some things I do when my creative energy lags:

• Go out for a walk.

• Commiserate with my MiGWriters critique group (migwriters.blogspot.com), Illustrator Mentees (kidlitartists.com) and Pixel Shavings writer/illustrator group (pixelshavings.blogspot.com). We all take turns encouraging and supporting each other through rough spots.

• Meet up with other writers and illustrators in person. I do this through Torkidlit, the Toronto Area Middle Grade and Young Adult Author Group, as well as through SCBWI and CANSCAIP events.

• Work in a different environment than usual. I'll take my drawing or writing gear into a different room in the house, for instance, or go to a library or a coffee shop.

• Make sure I get enough sleep and regular exercise.

What would you say is a writing weakness of yours? How do you go about overcoming it?

I over-edit as I write. While some writers can edit well during their first draft, I find that it really bogs me down because I focus too much on perfecting details and voice too early. To help me get over this, I'm starting to focus on spending more time on the outline and then, when I'm happy with the overall plot, to write the first draft as quickly as possible so I can get the bare bones down before I start revising.

Like many artists, your work is pretty recognizable. Is this intentional? How did you develop your personal drawing style so that, when one sees a cartoon of yours, one knows it's an Ohi?

I have multiple illustration styles. I used to think I needed to settle on just one, but then my editor at Simon & Schuster told me that part of the reason he liked my portfolio was because I had more than one style.

I didn't consciously work at developing one personal drawing style; I think I'd be way too intimidated! Instead, I just draw *a lot*. I like experimenting, but I do find myself more comfortable with looser, more scraggly styles.

What's one thing you wish you'd known when you were starting out writing?

I wish I started going to SCBWI conferences (scbwi.org) regularly much earlier.

I used to think that if I worked very hard on my craft and wrote the best story I possibly could, that some editor would eventually want to publish me. While that still happens for some, I'm discovering that, these days, it's often more than just the work.

Suppose an agent or editor receives two manuscripts that are equally well written, but they only have the budget or list space for one of them. If the agent or editor has met and liked one of the authors, chances are good they will lean toward that person. It makes sense, really.

The conferences also offer insider information not easily available elsewhere. You can find out what particular agents, editors and publishing houses are looking for or *not* looking for.

But most of all, I find it inspiring to talk with other writers and illustrators at these conventions—not just published pros but also those in the early stages of their careers. Whatever angst I'm going through, it's encouraging to know that countless others have been through exactly the same thing.

As children's book author Nancy Parish says: Writing may be a solitary endeavor, but trying to get published doesn't have to be.

RICKI SCHULTZ (rickischultz.com) is an Ohio-based freelance writer and high school English teacher. She writes young adult fiction and, as coordinator of The Write-Brained Network (writebrainednetwork.com), she enjoys connecting with other writers.

KATHERINE APPLEGATE

The Newbery Medal winner talks with us.

by Jodell Sadler

The 2013 Newbery Medal was presented to *The One and Only Ivan* by Katherine Applegate (Anne Hoppe, editor), published by HarperCollins Children's Books on January 28. "Katherine Applegate gives readers a unique and unforgettable gorilla's-eye-view of the world that challenges the way we look at animals and at ourselves," says Newbery Medal Committee Chair Steven Engelfried.

The Association for Library Service to Children, ALSC, summarizes the story well: "Ivan's transformative emergence from the 'Ape at Exit 8' to 'The One and Only Ivan, Mighty Silverback,' comes to life through the gorilla's own distinct narrative voice, which is filled with wry humor, deep emotion and thought-provoking insights into the nature of friendship, hope and humanity."

Readers only need to open this book and step into the white space of the page with its spare and shiny text to be greeted by Applegate's unique narrative voice. Patricia Castelao's almost film-like illustrations help readers know they are experiencing a masterpiece. In *The One and Only Ivan*, readers step into that world that is keenly gorilla and really come to care deeply for his plight and his desire to free Ruby into that life of lavish wanderings. It's truly a "One and Only"—a memorable story so worthy of its Newbery.

There is something naturally enticing about a story based on real life. It has an unexplained depth, so it was exciting to ask Applegate about winning the award and about the story behind the story, her craft, as well as her insights for fellow writers.

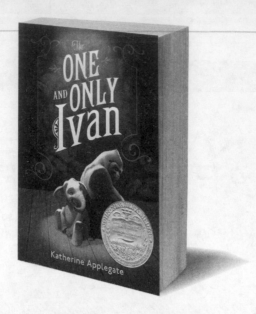

On receiving the Newbery Award news:

"Oh, pretty amazing—disbelief," says Applegate, who explained that she actually asked, "Are you sure?" and was stunned to silence. "It's humbling. I wish every writer could experience that moment. There are just so many deserving authors and books."

In a *Publishers Weekly* interview, Applegate called herself the "consummate hack," but said, "I've written so many books along the way"—more than 150, she guessed, including the bestselling Animorphs series, which she co-wrote with her husband. "I've worked in the trenches," she said. "I've reached the point where I really appreciate [the Newbery]. It's very gratifying."

On perseverance:

"As writers, there's always that question: Not, 'Can I write it?'—but 'Is it the right story?' It's mostly a matter of if a story will work and taking a real leap of faith," Applegate says. She actually found a scrap of paper on which she had written, "Should I give up on Ivan or not?" She remembers feeling stuck, having tried to write Ivan's story as a journal article. But it ran short and felt flat. She also tried to move on to other projects for her editor, Anne Hoppe, at HarperCollins, but Ivan's story simply kept calling out to her. She couldn't set it aside and focus on other things. Finally, Hoppe suggested that she fictionalize her journal article. "And this was a brilliant idea," says Applegate.

During this process, as she realized the need to flesh out and plot Ivan's story, the story became clearer. It was a challenge to write about a Mall gorilla that was so contained in this tiny and lonely prison, and have him tell his story. Realistically, Ivan lacked stimulation, social interactions and the connections we have come to discover are essential for gorillas to thrive in captivity. "I simply had to find a way to release Ivan in my fictional story," she says.

On blending fiction and nonfiction:

Following Ivan's story from the Tacoma Washington Mall and the controversy surrounding his captivity, Katherine found it heartbreaking. It took a long time to get the permissions needed to move Ivan to Zoo Atlanta. Litigation took forever. There was huge public outcry, but the details of Ivan's story and the depth of his plight kept her watching and exploring his experience.

Ivan's real-life story started with the gruesome death of his family. He was then captured and transported to the U.S. at a young age along with his twin sister, but she died en route.

Ivan's original owner and caretaker treated him like a human son until he became too unruly to handle and too destructive to keep inside the home. He then placed Ivan at the mall in a small cage (three walls with a glass front) as a roadside attraction where he remained for some 27 years. Alone.

Given all the scientific evidence that shares the importance of social interactions for gorillas in captivity, Applegate realized how important it was to share his story. His only connection to nature was a mural on the back wall of his domain. Grass, sticks, ponds and trees were all memories. He was a gorilla, who was alone.

When she went to write the story, she realized the challenges she faced in creating a story arc with the main character contained in such tight quarters. She needed to find a way for him to communicate. Writing his story as a fictional account solved this and other problems, and *The One and Only Ivan* grew from her research and work.

She also wanted to emphasize that there's not a perfect zoo. Zoos have resources, mandates and try to create natural areas, but the distinction between zoos and circuses is what struck her as even more important to discuss. Applegate says, "I wish children would never ask again to attend a circus," mainly because of the ill treatment of animals in those settings. She also knew she didn't want to be didactic. She wanted to directly share what she learned about how these animals were treated. The more she read about his struggle, the more it confirmed her resolve to base Ivan's story on his real life experience.

On adding additional characters:

"Sometimes we simply find what we need for our stories," Applegate says. Her research turned up novel hints that helped her through this process. When she read somewhere that there was an elephant at the Washington Mall at one time, this gave way to Stella, the elderly and injured former circus elephant featured in the story. When she needed motivation for Ivan's desire to change, she added Ruby, a baby elephant who suffers cruelty at the hands of her trainer, and who would become the impetus for Ivan's personal growth within the story.

When she learned a local businessman took a keen interest in Ivan's quality of life and often came with gifts to stimulate his environment, she was touched. But when she found that his gifts included paints that Ivan actually enjoyed using, this gave Ivan a way to communicate, and led to the secondary characters: the caretaker and daughter, who are a large part of this story.

On revision:

Applegate tried so many incarnations; she ultimately decided to celebrate the fact that writing is all about rewriting. "I was actually sitting in bed surrounded by crumpled paper as a reminder that writing is about making mistakes and finding a story," she says. "It's usually easy to find that good story that is so unbelievable and rare, but often times it doesn't transfer well to fiction."

In the end, she knew this piece would become an animal fantasy and she would give Ivan himself a story to tell. She tried to set it aside, but it kept distracting from other stories. "Finally Anne Hoppes, my editor at HarperCollins said, 'Why don't you go ahead and write the gorilla story?' So I did. Writing this story was a reminder that as writers have to expect a lot of u-turns along the way to a good story (and a GPS will not help)."

On free verse style:

"It helps me to think about the 'fact holding' of a story," says Applegate. Her husband, Michael Grant, author and writing partner for the Animorphs series urges her to think about plot first. "But," Applegate says, "I tend to think about what a story is it going to look like. The architecture of a story matters a great deal to me. It made sense to me that Ivan would be a gorilla of few words."

Katherine wanted there to be a lot of white space. This allowed the illustrations to enhance text and add depth. She had just finished a novel in free verse, *Home of the Brave* (Feiwel and Friends, 2007), which tells the story about a child learning a new language and is written from the point of view of a refugee of Sudan. She says, "This form felt right for a gorilla. I knew I needed to keeping writing small."

On writing small:

Applegate uses lists in her book in the "it," "romance" and "outside at last" chapters and it is a great example of what writers are often told: Do less to do more.

"This actually falls in line with my focus on brevity and writing small," says Applegate. "I watched a short video clip of Ivan's first encounter with two female gorillas at Zoo Atlanta and distilled it into few words. The 'it' chapter is really based off of the behaviors seen in this clip." Unlike wild male gorillas that would dominate and pound their chests, Ivan allowed the females to chase him. "He ran off as if he was playing tag, which he really would have done in his young gorilla life in the wild," she said. But the sad reality is that he didn't really know how to be a gorilla.

In the "romance" chapter that follows, Ivan shares fragmented thoughts about his integration process: "Make eye contact. / Show your form. / Strut. / Grunt. / Throw a stick. / Grunt some more. / Make some moves. / Romance is hard work…" One word sentences are used in the "outside at last" chapter, highlighting Ivan's emotional change. They are observations but also contrasts to what Ivan was lacking and had never experienced: "Sky. / Grass. / Tree. / Ant. / Stick … Mine. / Mine. / Mine." Applegate says, "Writing small really places readers in a scene—and is great for the most reluctant of readers."

On illustration:

"Writers are collaborating with an imaginary partner," Applegate says. "It's the ultimate challenge of writing small." She didn't see [illustrator's] Patricia Castelao's art until later on. "But what her art added to the text is truly unbelievable. I was amazed the first time I saw Patricia Castelao's art. It was perfect," Applegate says. "They do have a film-like quality to them. They feel real, and she did a wonderful job of showing Ivan's personality."

In *The Horn Book* article (2004), "Half the Story: Text and Illustrations in Picture Books," Hoppes says, "A well-placed word can leave you elated or break your heart. Pictures can evoke peals of laughter or cries of outrage." *The One and Only Ivan* benefits from both.

On voice:

In *The One and Only Ivan*, Applegate flawlessly gives readers a unique vision that is so gorilla while also sharing a universal truth through metaphor and simile—and it's simply spellbinding. When describing the baby elephant, Ruby, Ivan says, "Ruby turns her head. Her eyes are like Stella's, black and long-lashed, bottomless lakes fringed by tall grass." Writers are often told how important voice is to story, and Applegate manages to come up with lines that serve double duty.

"I'm flattered, but sometimes you don't think of those connections as you are writing them," Applegate says. "It was a fun book to write. It's a huge leap of faith to write animal fantasy. There is a challenge in presenting normal animal behaviors with just enough human character.

"In writing the Animorphs series, we faced this and lacked the Internet as a resource. There were 63 books in the series, so my husband and I were working on a book a month," Applegate says. She learned to study movements and behaviors, and came to understand how to hone them down to their essence and get them right. "Often times, we had to be careful, especially at an emotional plateau, not to pile it on. Not to write too much, but to write only what needed to be there, and just that."

Ivan's voice took a while, but came quite easily. In her *New York Times* interview, Applegate says, "Gorillas may seem terrifying because of their bodies, but they are really magnificent and very gentle. I wanted his voice to convey that calm dignity that I associate with gorillas. And I tend to write short, brief snippets—I lean toward the chamber music end as opposed to the symphony end of things. I realized that Ivan's voice was a good match for me. He is a gorilla of few words."

On theme:

Bob, the stray dog, reminds Ivan often that he is "The One and Only Ivan." There's a point in the story where it hits Ivan that Ruby will never leave Big Top Mall. Ivan watches her sleep and feels the need to protect her and says, "I can't let Ruby be another One and Only."

When those few words drop, it sinks in that Ivan—and Stella and Ruby and the dog— are clearly alone, lonely, and trapped. "The dog in this story really allowed me to continue the dialogue needed during those times Ivan would have normally been alone in his cage, says Applegate. Once she began to explore what each word and the architecture would add to the story, she really saw new ways to do more than she imagined.

A powerful scene in the story is when Ivan turns to stray dog just before he enters the crate to leave and tells Bob he is "The One and Only Bob." It's a satisfying full-circle moment in the story and another instance when theme comes out.

On the author-editor relationship:

"Having Anne as an editor has been a wonderful experience. We have the same sensibility. We share that love of spare writing," says Applegate. "A good editor is such a joy. Anne presents great ideas and suggestions that hone my craft. She's adorable and wonderful and genuinely dedicated to her authors and their stories."

In her *School Library Journal* interview, Applegate says, "Ivan would not be Ivan without Anne. Honestly, it was the most collaborative and fun adventure I've ever had with an editor."

On advice:

"Somewhere it was suggested that you take a story you love and read it 3-4 times, and then go back and type it out. As you type it, you begin to question and see more in the writing, and how the story is crafted," says Applegate. This is a great way to learn about the choices the author makes in regard to craft. "It's a way to climb inside a writer's head. It's important writers focus on craft and really learn to love to rewrite and be willing to go back and get rid of some of our favorites to get to the richness of our stories...

"Know yourself," says Applegate. "Don't worry so much about getting it right. I know I tend to want to feel a sentence is perfect before moving on, but I also know there's a lot of value in letting go and allowing yourself to simply write. I think it's important that writers write because they have to write. It's important to write those many drafts—all of them, however you must—knowing that among all the coal there is sure to be a diamond or two. Understand that writing is a process where joy and play figure in a great deal."

On surprise:

"One cool thing I found was all the connections to Ivan. I spoke in the Seattle, Wash. area and met so many people who genuinely cared about Ivan," says Applegate. "One parent mentioned visiting Ivan every Sunday afternoon." There were many stories that showed Applegate how very much people cared about Ivan. "I was surprised to learn Ivan, at one time, had a La-Z-Boy recliner in his cage. Another man showed me the actual court order the judge had signed for Ivan's release." At one point, she said, "I even met Jodi Carrigan, who was Ivan's caretaker at Zoo Atlanta for many years, and discovered that she saw Ivan as a buddy and very dear friend."

The same year his novel came out, Ivan died on August 21, 2012, while under general anesthesia to scan for what might have been causing his lack of appetite, weight loss and respiratory illness. According to the University of Georgia College of Veterinary Medicine Zoo and Exotic Animal Pathology Service, "[The] preliminary partial necropsy findings show[ed] that Ivan's immediate cause of death was likely associated with an invasive mass in the chest."

Applegate, while attending his funeral, learned even more about his behavior. In her *School Library* interview she said, "He was apparently quite a quirky guy. Ivan hated to get his feet wet. He did not like dampness, and when he went outside, one of his quirks was that he would take a burlap coffee bag, which were regularly supplied to the zoo by a local coffee supplier, and put it under his butt and under his hands. He would slide around on the ground and get around that way.

"It was just touching to learn so many people in various ways were working to change Ivan's situation and bring him a better life," says Applegate.

On the future:

"How do you follow a Newbery? It's still so unreal," Applegate says. "I am currently working on a new middle grade novel, which just might be another animal fantasy."

JODELL SADLER is the co-founder of Sadler-Caravette Children's Literary, which serves aspiring authors and illustrators in the field of children's literature. She also actively seeks speaking engagements to share her MFA thesis study on how 20 Tools Help KidLit to Wow!

RACHEL HARTMAN

On why revision may be the most important aspect of writing.

by Sara DeSabato

Rachel Hartman's debut novel *Seraphina* was published by Random House Books for Young Readers in July 2012. The book introduces us to Seraphina Dombegh, a court musician in the fantastical land of Goredd, where dragons and humans live with a tenuous peace between them. When the Crown Prince is murdered and a dragon is suspected, Seraphina finds herself in the center of everything, all while trying to keep her own terrible secret. *Seraphina* debuted on the *New York Times* bestseller list and went on to win the 2013 William C. Morris Award for best young adult work by a debut author. Rachel is now hard at work on a sequel, titled *Dracomachia*, due out in early 2014.

Rachel resides with her family in Vancouver, British Columbia, where she works double time as both a full-time writer and a full-time mom. Here, she talks about how she came up with the idea for *Seraphina*, her journey to publication, when she knew she wanted to be a writer, and how she conquers the self-doubting voice inside her head. To learn more about Rachel, visit rachelhartmanbooks.com.

Seraphina is quite a unique fantasy novel. Can you talk about how you came up with your original idea, and how that idea has evolved?

The first idea I had for *Seraphina* came to me in the form of a question: What if you married someone with a terrible secret, and you had no idea what it was until they were dead? Seraphina's father has that very problem, but over time it became much more of a background question. I rewrote the book completely three times, each with a differ-

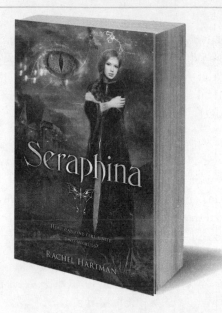

ent plot, and I had to keep finding new angles on things to keep myself interested. The book is now much more about finding your place in the world.

Can you walk us through your journey of writing *Seraphina* and becoming a published author?

Seraphina took nine years from my first inkling of an idea to publication. One of the reasons it took so long is that I was originally with a different publisher, but my editor left the publishing house, leaving me an orphan. Fortunately, I had an agent, and he was able to find a new home for the manuscript. My new editor had a very different vision than my first, however, so there was still a long way to go and some major rewrites.

Did you always know Seraphina's story would be told over more than one book? What are some of the challenges of continuing a story arc through more than one book?

I originally intended Seraphina's story to be one book, and I still think the first book wraps up most of the plot threads pretty well. Writing the second book is indeed harder, for a couple reasons. First, the expectations of readers weigh a lot, and the more they liked the first book, the scarier the idea of disappointing them becomes. Second, everything that happened in the first book is now set in stone. I can't contradict it, and that means there are a lot of wacky plot ideas I might have tried that are now off-limits.

Who is your own favorite character, and why?

The dragon-scholar Orma. The dragons in my world can take human form, but find it a baffling and sometimes overwhelming experience. It's great fun exploring humanity through Orma's non-human perceptions.

You were nominated for—and recently won—the William C. Morris award for outstanding debut novel. What has that experience been like?

It's such an honor and a bit overwhelming to receive so much attention after toiling in obscurity for so long. It takes some getting used to, but I realize how very lucky I am to have problems like this!

Are you a full-time writer? What does a day in the life of Rachel Hartman look like?

I'm a full-time writer and a full-time mom, so sometimes the two collide. Getting up early has been my salvation. I have an hour or two to myself, when it's just me and the work (and a cup of tea). By the time everyone else is up, I've already accomplished something. Then, even if the rest of the day gets derailed (as sometimes happens), at least I have that. It turns out my brain works better in the morning, too. My internal censor likes to sleep in.

Is *Seraphina* your first novel? If not, did you know while writing that this would be the book that would make you a published author?

Seraphina is my first, but as I mentioned, I rewrote it three times. So in a very real way, the novel as published is my fourth novel by the same name, featuring the same characters. The nice thing about it is that I got to know the characters really well. I feel like a director who's been privileged to work with the same actors for many years. The cast parties are a hoot.

What writing advice have you received and listened to? What advice have you received and ignored?

I'm so glad I listened to the people who advised me to get an agent (the ones I ignored were the ones who said I didn't need one! I heard both opinions a lot early on). My agent had been my staunchest ally on what turned out to be a very bumpy road. He has keen business instincts and good connections—two useful things that don't come naturally to me. I can talk to him when it would be impolitic to complain to anyone else. I'd be utterly at sea without him.

When did you know you wanted to be a writer? What was it like seeing your book in print for the first time?

My beloved sixth grade teacher once said I was "a real writer," so I have been a writer (in my mind, at least) ever since. I worked on *Seraphina* for so long, though, that I didn't quite believe I would ever be finished with it. An asteroid would hit Manhattan, or I'd wake up and discover it was 1992 and I'd dreamed the whole thing. Only when my editor sent me a finished copy and I couldn't put my hand through it, and I could swat flies with it, only then did it feel real. And then I cried a little.

How do you conquer the self-doubt so many writers face? What advice would you give to others for conquering it?

I'm not sure one ever really conquers it in the sense of "make it go away forever." It pops up again and again, like a whack-a-mole. For me, the key has been noticing that self-doubt is not the only voice in my head. Even when it's shouting really loudly (as it will), there's usually some other part of me, somewhere, that finds the self-doubt boring and is quietly pursuing other trains of thought. I go join that party instead. That's where all the humor and interest is. Self-doubt is a one-trick pony, and it gets old really fast.

Who inspires you as a writer?

Terry Pratchett. Not only is he one of my favourite fantasy writers, but he has been diagnosed with Alzheimer's disease and he's still writing. He has an assistant and uses voice recognition software, but by golly, he's working as hard as ever. How many people would have given in to despair, with that kind of thing hanging over their heads? If he can carry on, surely my little problems can't stop me either.

What part of the writing process feels easy for you? What part feels hard?

Ideas come easily to me. I have more ideas than I know what to do with. I could export ideas to idea-poor regions of the world and still have too many. The hardest part is completing the first draft. Filling a blank page is a terrible prospect for me, but I've learned to hold my nose and barge on through as fast as I can.

Revision is often just as important—and time consuming—as writing the first draft. What does your revision process look like?

In my case, revision is the most important and time consuming part of writing. My first drafts are invariably awful. It's much easier—and pleasanter—to look at a page of dreadful writing and figure out how to fix it. I think of myself as writing in layers, a bit like painting a picture. First you get the big composition, the darks and lights, the focal point. Then you go over it again and again, filling in a bit more detail each time, and only on the last pass is it finally as beautiful as you knew it could be all along.

What would you tell someone who wants to become a published author?

Be patient and persistent. Love what you do, because there are no guarantees in this business, and there will be times when writing has to be its own reward.

SARA DESABATO is a full time teacher and mom who saves up her spare time to work on her own young adult novel. She blogs with her critique group at FirstNovelsClub.com.

ELIZABETH WEIN

On how details can can yield unexpected results and bring a book to life.

....

by Kristen Grace

Elizabeth Wein is best known for her most recent novel, *Code Name Verity* (2012), which follows the friendship of two young girls during World War II, one a resistance spy and the other a transport pilot.

Though she was born in New York City, Wein has lived around the world, including England, Jamaica, and Scotland. During her time in England, Wein was surrounded by what she says was "an awareness" of war, something she relied upon when researching and writing *Code Name Verity*.

Wein studied at Yale University and received her Ph.D. in Folklore from the University of Pennsylvania in Philadelphia.

Her first novel, *The Winter Prince*, was published in 1993. Since then, she has published four more books in the Lion Hunters series. *The Lion Hunter* (2007) was short-listed for the Andre Norton Award for Best Young Adult Fantasy and Science Fiction in 2008. In addition to her novels, Wein has written a number of published short stories and essays.

Here she discusses how elements of her own life always seem to end up in her work, and how it was her own personal interest in flying that sparked the idea for *Code Name Verity*. She also explores her in-depth methods for research and how sometimes a unique narrative style can just sort of happen.

What do you suggest for writers struggling with how to open their novel? How do you decide where your story will begin?

I wish I knew a formula. I think it always helps to begin a scene in media res, in the middle of things. It doesn't have to be an action scene—it just has to be full of potential. If you're struggling, try writing a scene and then cutting out the first half. I sometimes find that acting out a scene (when there's no one watching) helps to crystallize it for me. Another thing I try is altering the viewpoint—writing the same scene from a different character's point of view, or in a different tense.

How much planning goes into your novels before you start writing?

I usually do the planning as I'm writing—I have a general idea of where I want to start and where I want to end up, and go from there. Usually the background reading gets me going. It gives me ideas and gets me in the mood for the book. Meanwhile, I'll take notes for scenes and action that I want to use later. The characters are the most important to me. I tend to make up a lot of backstory for them before I start to write.

How did you do your research for *Code Name Verity*?

I had a good base to build on. As recreational pilots, my husband and I go to a lot of air shows, and there are always wartime aircraft on display. My husband's parents were both teens during the war and have fascinating stories to tell about their experiences as evacuees and, later, young servicemen and women.

The one thing I really took in as an academic is how to do research, and for this project I started with basic background reading—finding out about the women of the Air Transport Auxiliary and the Special Operations Executive. From there, I moved on to museums and artifacts, the Internet of course, and finally to people. I attended a symposium where I got to meet four actual ATA pilots. I also find that period movies and fiction are a good way to pick up authentic details.

Sometimes checking up on details yields unexpected results. Some of Verity's confession is written on prescription forms, so I looked up some 1930s French prescription forms to get the right format. That is how I accidentally came across the prescription form described in the book, which states that a Jewish doctor named on the form can only legally prescribe medication to Jewish patients. Like Verity, I had not realized such things existed. This random discovery allowed me to add a layer of historic accuracy, mystery and even tragedy to an otherwise straightforward plot device, Verity's scavenging for paper.

What is your writing process like? How has it changed since your first book, *The Winter Prince*?

I usually work during the day when my kids are at school. I have a study, but I work at the dining room table anyway.

I write my first drafts longhand and then type them up as I go. I made the move from typewriter to computer about two-thirds of the way through writing *The Winter Prince* (in 1990), but I did the editing for *The Winter Prince* the old fashioned way— cutting and taping sentences and sheets of paper together! Now, I do all my editing on the computer. *Rose Under Fire* (2013) is the first book that I never printed out during the writing process.

What has been your most challenging book to write?

I think it must have been *A Coalition of Lions*, my second book. There is a 10-year publication gap between *The Winter Prince* and its sequel, *A Coalition of Lions*. The action is all set in Aksum, which is 6th century Ethiopia, and it actually took me years to get started because I was so overwhelmed by the amount of research I was going to have to do. When I finally buckled down to it, I was astonished at how quickly the plot came together.

But even after that, it was hard to write. I think by the time I'd finished I'd re-written it about 10 times. I wrote *The Sunbird*, my third book, before I'd even finished *Coalition*. And finally my husband took my two toddler kids away for a week so I could have some uninterrupted time to knock it on its head.

How do you handle the darker themes in your books, such as death and war, being that you are writing for young adults?

It honestly doesn't occur to me, as I'm writing, that I have to avoid facing up to evil just because I'm writing for young adults. I write character-driven adventure stories, and there's conflict in them. But I think that what redeems the darkness in my books is a sense of hope—my characters are always supported by people who love them. When all's said and done, they still have a hopeful future.

Yes, there are dark things going on in my books. That's because there are dark things going on in the world we live in. If in some small way I can help young readers to cope with fear and to meet it with love and hope for the future, then I'm doing my job the right way.

How much of your own life and experiences end up in your books?

I do draw on my own life to enhance the details of my books, and I think this is what makes them feel so real. *Code Name Verity* is full of my own experience beneath the surface. The bicycle adventure in the rain, with the flat tire and the farmer's wife coming to the girls' rescue was based on a trip I made with a friend; I once spent a backbreaking couple of afternoons clearing a grass airstrip of stones and rubble; I know what it's like to fly in a cockpit so cold that the air inside crystallizes into snow. And the character in *Code Name Verity* who can't keep his hands off pretty girls gets all his one-liners from what actual men have said to me. Over the years, I have become more shameless about using my own experiences in my books.

In *Code Name Verity*, you use an unusual style of narrative, with one of the characters talking about herself in the third person for a portion of the story. How did you handle writing this? Why did you choose this type of narrative?

It more or less came about accidentally. When I started writing, as Verity, I knew she'd be telling her friend Maddie's story from Maddie's point of view. But Verity herself doesn't come into the story until some time later. When it was time for her to make her appearance, I ran into a problem. If she talked about herself in the first person, the point of view was going to shift, and I didn't want to do that.

So I made the conscious decision to keep the story in Maddie's point of view and introduce Verity in the somewhat disguised role of Queenie.

There is one point in Verity's story where the Queenie mask slips, a violent moment when a German prisoner attempts to strangle her. Verity narrates this distressing past incident in the first person. Although the error is meant to be unconscious on Verity's part, it was very deliberate on mine.

What is the most useful advice you've ever received as a writer?

"Don't get it right, get it written." A friend of mine from college told me that, and I use it as a mantra.

What would you say is a writing weakness of yours? How do you go about overcoming it?

I think one of my great strengths is also a great weakness, and that is my attention to detail. I feel that specific, concrete details are the key to breathing life into fiction, but I have to guard against over-doing the detail.

I find that an easy way to overcome it is to do a word count and cut it down to some manageable number. There are 16 words in that description—ok, let's make it five. Which five can I keep and still have an evocative description?

What's next for you?

I've just finished the companion novel to *Code Name Verity*, called *Rose Under Fire*. It takes place a little later in World War II and finishes after the end of the war. The narrator is a new character whom readers haven't met before.

KRISTEN GRACE is an Ohio-based writer and contributor to *Writer's Digest*. She recently earned her Master's Degree in English from Miami University of Ohio. Her favorite time of the day is mid-morning when she can sit on the porch, sip coffee and read a good book. You can check out her blog at kegrace.wordpress.com or follow her on twitter (@kayeeegee).

GLOSSARY OF INDUSTRY TERMS

AAR. Association of Authors' Representatives.

ABA. American Booksellers Association.

ABC. Association of Booksellers for Children.

ADVANCE. A sum of money a publisher pays a writer or illustrator prior to the publication of a book. It is usually paid in installments, such as one half on signing the contract, one half on delivery of a complete and satisfactory manuscript. The advance is paid against the royalty money that will be earned by the book.

ALA. American Library Association.

ALL RIGHTS. The rights contracted to a publisher permitting the use of material anywhere and in any form, including movie and book club sales, without additional payment to the creator.

ANTHOLOGY. A collection of selected writings by various authors or gatherings of works by one author.

ANTHROPOMORPHIZATION. The act of attributing human form and personality to things not human (such as animals).

ASAP. As soon as possible.

ASSIGNMENT. An editor or art director asks a writer, illustrator or photographer to produce a specific piece for an agreed-upon fee.

B&W. Black and white.

BACKLIST. A publisher's list of books not published during the current season but still in print.

BEA. BookExpo America.

BIENNIALLY. Occurring once every 2 years.

BIMONTHLY. Occurring once every 2 months.

BIWEEKLY. Occurring once every 2 weeks.

BOOK PACKAGER. A company that draws all elements of a book together, from the initial concept to writing and marketing strategies, then sells the book package to a book publisher and/or movie producer. Also known as book producer or book developer.

BOOK PROPOSAL. Package submitted to a publisher for consideration usually consisting of a synopsis and outline as well as sample chapters.

BUSINESS-SIZE ENVELOPE. Also known as a #10 envelope. The standard size used in sending business correspondence.

CAMERA-READY. Refers to art that is completely prepared for copy camera platemaking.

CAPTION. A description of the subject matter of an illustration or photograph; photo captions include persons' names where appropriate. Also called cutline.

CBC. Children's Book Council.

CLEAN-COPY. A manuscript free of errors and needing no editing; it is ready for typesetting.

CLIPS. Samples, usually from newspapers or magazines, of a writer's published work.

CONCEPT BOOKS. Books that deal with ideas, concepts and large-scale problems, promoting an understanding of what's happening in a child's world. Most prevalent are alphabet and counting books, but also includes books dealing with specific concerns facing young people (such as divorce, birth of a sibling, friendship or moving).

CONTRACT. A written agreement stating the rights to be purchased by an editor, art director or producer and the amount of payment the writer, illustrator or photographer will receive for that sale. (See the article "Running Your Business.")

CONTRIBUTOR'S COPIES. The magazine issues sent to an author, illustrator or photographer in which her work appears.

CO-OP PUBLISHER. A publisher that shares production costs with an author but, unlike subsidy publishers, handles all marketing and distribution. An author receives a high percentage of royalties until her initial investment is recouped, then standard royalties. (*Children's Writer's & Illustrator's Market* does not include co-op publishers.)

COPY. The actual written material of a manuscript.

COPYEDITING. Editing a manuscript for grammar usage, spelling, punctuation and general style.

COPYRIGHT. A means to legally protect an author's/illustrator's/photographer's work. This can be shown by writing the creator's name and the year of the work's creation.

COVER LETTER. A brief letter, accompanying a complete manuscript, especially useful if responding to an editor's request for a manuscript. May also accompany a book proposal.

CUTLINE. See caption.

DIVISION. An unincorporated branch of a company.

DUMMY. A loose mock-up of a book showing placement of text and artwork.

ELECTRONIC SUBMISSION. A submission of material by e-mail or Web form.

FINAL DRAFT. The last version of a polished manuscript ready for submission to an editor.

FIRST NORTH AMERICAN SERIAL RIGHTS. The right to publish material in a periodical for the first time, in the U.S. or Canada. (See the article "Running Your Business.")

F&GS. Folded and gathered sheets. An early, not-yet-bound copy of a picture book.

FLAT FEE. A one-time payment.

GALLEYS. The first typeset version of a manuscript that has not yet been divided into pages.

GENRE. A formulaic type of fiction, such as horror, mystery, romance, fantasy, suspense, thriller, science fiction or Western.

GLOSSY. A photograph with a shiny surface as opposed to one with a non-shiny matte finish.

GOUACHE. Opaque watercolor with an appreciable film thickness and an actual paint layer.

HALFTONE. Reproduction of a continuous tone illustration with the image formed by dots produced by a camera lens screen.

HARD COPY. The printed copy of a computer's output.

HARDWARE. Refers to all the mechanically-integrated components of a computer that are not software—circuit boards, transistors and the machines that are the actual computer.

HI-LO. High interest, low reading level.

HOME PAGE. The first page of a website.

IBBY. International Board on Books for Young People.

IMPRINT. Name applied to a publisher's specific line of books.

INTERNET. A worldwide network of computers that offers access to a wide variety of electronic resources.

IRA. International Reading Association.

IRC. International Reply Coupon. Sold at the post office to enclose with text or artwork sent to a recipient outside your own country to cover postage costs when replying or returning work.

KEYLINE. Identification of the positions of illustrations and copy for the printer.

LAYOUT. Arrangement of illustrations, photographs, text and headlines for printed material.

LINE DRAWING. Illustration done with pencil or ink using no wash or other shading.

MASS MARKET BOOKS. Paperback books directed toward an extremely large audience sold in supermarkets, drugstores, airports, newsstands, online retailers and bookstores.

MECHANICALS. Paste-up or preparation of work for printing.

MIDDLE GRADE OR MID-GRADE. See middle reader.

MIDDLE READER. The general classification of books written for readers approximately ages 9–12. Often called middle grade or mid-grade.

MS (MSS). Manuscript(s).

MULTIPLE SUBMISSIONS. See simultaneous submissions.

NCTE. National Council of Teachers of English.

ONE-TIME RIGHTS. Permission to publish a story in periodical or book form one time only. (See the article "Running Your Business.")

OUTLINE. A summary of a book's contents; often in the form of chapter headings with a descriptive sentence or two under each heading to show the scope of the book.

PACKAGE SALE. The sale of a manuscript and illustrations/photos as a "package" paid for with one check.

PAYMENT ON ACCEPTANCE. The writer, artist or photographer is paid for her work at the time the editor or art director decides to buy it.

PAYMENT ON PUBLICATION. The writer, artist or photographer is paid for her work when it is published.

PICTURE BOOK. A type of book aimed at preschoolers to 8-year-olds that tells a story using a combination of text and artwork, or artwork only.

PRINT. An impression pulled from an original plate, stone, block, screen or negative; also a positive made from a photographic negative.

PROOFREADING. Reading text to correct typographical errors.

QUERY. A letter to an editor or agent designed to capture interest in an article or book you have written or propose to write. (See the article "Before Your First Sale.")

READING FEE. Money charged by some agents and publishers to read a submitted manuscript. (*Children's Writer's & Illustrator's Market* does not include agencies that charge reading fees.)

REPRINT RIGHTS. Permission to print an already published work whose first rights have been sold to another magazine or book publisher. (See the article "Running Your Business.")

RESPONSE TIME. The average length of time it takes an editor or art director to accept or reject a query or submission, and inform the creator of the decision.

RIGHTS. The bundle of permissions offered to an editor or art director in exchange for printing a manuscript, artwork or photographs. (See the article "Running Your Business.")

ROUGH DRAFT. A manuscript that has not been checked for errors in grammar, punctuation, spelling or content.

ROUGHS. Preliminary sketches or drawings.

ROYALTY. An agreed percentage paid by a publisher to a writer, illustrator or photographer for each copy of her work sold.

SAE. Self-addressed envelope.

SASE. Self-addressed, stamped envelope.

SCBWI. The Society of Children's Book Writers and Illustrators.

SECOND SERIAL RIGHTS. Permission for the reprinting of a work in another periodical after its first publication in book or magazine form. (See the article "Running Your Business.")

SEMIANNUAL. Occurring every 6 months or twice a year.

SEMIMONTHLY. Occurring twice a month.

SEMIWEEKLY. Occurring twice a week.

SERIAL RIGHTS. The rights given by an author to a publisher to print a piece in one or more periodicals. (See the article "Running Your Business.")

SIMULTANEOUS SUBMISSIONS. Queries or proposals sent to several publishers at the same time. Also called multiple submissions. (See the article "Before Your First Sale.")

SLANT. The approach to a story or piece of artwork that will appeal to readers of a particular publication.

SLUSH PILE. Editors' term for their collections of unsolicited manuscripts.

SOFTWARE. Programs and related documentation for use with a computer.

SOLICITED MANUSCRIPT. Material that an editor has asked for or agreed to consider before being sent by a writer.

SPAR. Society of Photographers and Artists Representatives.

SPECULATION (SPEC). Creating a piece with no assurance from an editor or art director that it will be purchased or any reimbursements for material or labor paid.

SUBSIDIARY RIGHTS. All rights other than book publishing rights included in a book contract, such as paperback, book club and movie rights. (See the article "Running Your Business.")

SUBSIDY PUBLISHER. A book publisher that charges the author for the cost of typesetting, printing and promoting a book. Also called a vanity publisher. (Note: *Children's Writer's & Illustrator's Market* does not include subsidy publishers.)

SYNOPSIS. A brief summary of a story or novel. Usually a page to a page and a half, singlespaced, if part of a book proposal.

TABLOID. Publication printed on an ordinary newspaper page turned sideways and folded in half.

TEARSHEET. Page from a magazine or newspaper containing your printed art, story, article, poem or photo.

THUMBNAIL. A rough layout in miniature.

TRADE BOOKS. Books sold in bookstores and through online retailers, aimed at a smaller audience than mass market books, and printed in smaller quantities by publishers.

TRANSPARENCIES. Positive color slides; not color prints.

UNSOLICITED MANUSCRIPT. Material sent without an editor's, art director's or agent's request.

VANITY PUBLISHER. See subsidy publisher.

WORK-FOR-HIRE. An arrangement between a writer, illustrator or photographer and a company under which the company retains complete control of the work's copyright. (See the article "Running Your Business.")

YA. See young adult.

YOUNG ADULT. The general classification of books written for readers approximately ages 12–16. Often referred to as YA.

YOUNG READER. The general classification of books written for readers approximately ages 5–8.

NEW AGENT SPOTLIGHTS

Learn about new reps seeking clients.

....

by Chuck Sambuchino

One of the most common recurring work blog items I get complimented on (besides my headshot, which my wife has called "semi-dashing … almost") is my "New Agent Alerts," a series where I spotlight new/newer literary reps who are open to queries and looking for clients right now.

This is due to the fact that newer agents are golden opportunities for aspiring authors because they are actively building their client list. They're hungry to sign new clients and start the ball rolling with submissions to editors and books sold. Whereas an established agent with 40 clients may have little to no time to consider new writers' work let alone help them shape it, a newer agent may be willing to sign a promising writer whose work is not a guaranteed huge payday.

THE CONS AND PROS OF NEWER AGENTS

At writing conferences, a frequent question I get is "Is it OK to sign with a new agent?" The question comes about because people value experience, and wonder about the skill of someone who's new to the scene. The concern is an interesting one, so let me try to list out the downsides and upsides to choosing a rep who's in her first few years agenting.

The cons
- They are likely less experienced in contract negotiations.
- They likely know fewer editors at this point than a rep who's been in business a while, meaning there is a less likely chance they can help you get published. This is a big, justified point—and writers' foremost concern.
- They are likely in a weaker position to demand a high advance for you.

- New agents come and some go. This means if your agent is in business for a year or two and doesn't find the success for which they hoped, they could bail on the biz altogether. That leaves you without a home. If you sign with an agent who's been in business for 14 years, however, chances are they won't quit tomorrow.

The pros

- They are actively building their client list—and that means they are anxious to sign new writers and lock in those first several sales.
- They are usually willing to give your work a longer look. They may be willing to work with you on a project to get it ready for submission, whereas a more established agent has lots of clients and no time—meaning they have no spare moments to help you with shaping your novel or proposal.
- With fewer clients under their wing, you should get more attention than you would with an established rep.
- If they've found their calling and don't seem like they're giving up any time soon (and keep in mind, most do continue on as agents), you could have a decades-long relationship that pays off with lots of books.
- Just as they may have little going for them, they also have little going against them. An established agent once told me that a new agent is in a unique position because they have no duds under their belt. Their slate is clean.

HOW CAN YOU DECIDE FOR YOURSELF?

1. FACTOR IN IF THEY'RE PART OF A LARGER AGENCY. Agents share contacts and resources. If your agent is the new girl at an agency with five people, those other four agents will help her (and you) with submissions. In other words, she's new, but not alone.

2. LEARN WHERE THE AGENT CAME FROM. Has she been an apprentice at the agency for two years? Was she an editor for seven years and just switched to agenting? If they already have a few years in publishing under their belt, they're not as green as you may think. Agents don't become agents overnight.

3. ASK WHERE SHE WILL SUBMIT THE WORK. This is a big one. If you fear the agent lacks proper contacts to move your work, ask straight out: "What editors do you see us submitting this book to, and have you sold to them before?" The question tests their plan for where to send the manuscript and get it in print.

4. ASK THEM "WHY SHOULD I SIGN WITH YOU?" This is another straight-up question that gets right to the point. If she's new and has little/no sales at that point, she can't respond with "I sell tons of books and I make it rain cash money!! Dolla dolla bills, y'all!!!" She can't rely on her track record to entice you. So what's her sales pitch? Weigh her enthusiasm, her plan for the book, her promises of hard work and anything else she tells you. In the publishing business, you want communication and enthusiasm from agents (and editors). Both are invaluable. What's the point of signing with a huge agent when they don't return your e-mails and consider your book last on their list of priorities for the day?

5. IF YOU'RE NOT SOLD, YOU CAN ALWAYS SAY NO. It's as simple as that. Always query new/ newer agents because, at the end of the day, just because they offer representation doesn't mean you have to accept.

NEW AGENT SPOTLIGHTS ("AGENTS & ART REPS" SECTION)

Peppered throughout this book's large number of agency listings (in the "Agents & Art Reps" listings section) are sporadic "New Agent Alert" sidebars. Look them over to see if these newer reps would be a good fit for your work. Always read personal information and submission guidelines carefully. Don't let an agent reject you because you submitted work incorrectly. Wherever possible, we have included a website address for their agency, as well as their Twitter handle for those reps that tweet.

Also please note that as of when this book went to press in 2013, all these agents were still active and looking for writers. That said, I cannot guarantee every one is still in their respective position when you read this, nor that they have kept their query inboxes open. I urge you to visit agency websites and double check before you query. (This is always a good idea in any case.) Good luck!

CHUCK SAMBUCHINO (chucksambuchino.com, @chucksambuchino on Twitter) edits the *Guide to Literary Agents* (guidetoliteraryagents.com/blog) as well as the *Children's Writer's & Illustrator's Market*. His pop-humor books include *How to Survive a Garden Gnome Attack* (film rights optioned by Sony) and *Red Dog / Blue Dog: When Pooches Get Political* (reddog-bluedog.com). Chuck's other writing books include *Formatting & Submitting Your Manuscript, 3rd. Ed.*, as well as *Create Your Writer Platform*. Besides that, he is a sleep-depreived new father, husband, guitarist, dog owner, and cookie addict.

YOUR 2013–2014 WRITING CALENDAR

The best way for writers to achieve success is by setting goals. Goals are usually met by writers who give themselves or are given deadlines. Something about having an actual date to hit helps create a sense of urgency in most writers (and editors for that matter). This writing calendar is a great place to keep your important deadlines.

Also, this writing calendar is a good tool for recording upcoming writing events you'd like to attend or contests you'd like to enter. Or use this calendar to block out valuable time for yourself—to just write.

Of course, you can use this calendar to record other special events, especially if you have a habit of remembering to write but of forgetting birthdays or anniversaries. After all, this calendar is now yours. Do with it what you will.

AUGUST 2013

SUN	MON	TUE	WED	THURS	FRI	SAT
				1	2	3
4	5	6	7	8	9	10
11	12	13	14	15	16	17
18	19	20	21	22	23	24
25	26	27	28	29	30	31

Think big. Establish large, long-term goals.

SEPTEMBER 2013

SUN	MON	TUE	WED	THU	FRI	SAT
1	2	3	4	5	6	7
8	9	10	11	12	13	14
15	16	17	18	19	20	21
22	23	24	25	26	27	28
29	30					

Break down what small steps you need to take to accomplish these long-term goals.

_____

_____

_____

_____

_____

OCTOBER 2013

SUN	MON	TUE	WED	THU	FRI	SAT
		1	2	3	4	5
6	7	8	9	10	11	12
13	14	15	16	17	18	19
20	21	22	23	24	25	26
27	28	29	30	31		

Set monthly writing goals for things such as word count or queries to submit.

_____

_____

_____

_____

_____

NOVEMBER 2013

SUN	MON	TUE	WED	THU	FRI	SAT
					1	2
3	4	5	6	7	8	9
10	11	12	13	14	15	16
17	18	19	20	21	22	23
24	25	26	27	28	29	30

Write a novel during November as part of NaNoWriMo!

DECEMBER 2013

SUN	MON	TUE	WED	THU	FRI	SAT
1	2	3	4	5	6	7
8	9	10	11	12	13	14
15	16	17	18	19	20	21
22	23	24	25	26	27	28
29	30	31				

Take the first steps to revise what you wrote during NaNoWriMo.

JANUARY 2014

SUN	MON	TUE	WED	THU	FRI	SAT
			1	2	3	4
5	6	7	8	9	10	11
12	13	14	15	16	17	18
19	20	21	22	23	24	25
26	27	28	29	30	31	

Evaluate your 2013 accomplishments and make 2014 goals.

_____

_____

_____

_____

_____

FEBRUARY 2014

SUN	MON	TUE	WED	THU	FRI	SAT
						1
2	3	4	5	6	7	8
9	10	11	12	13	14	15
16	17	18	19	20	21	22
23	24	25	26	27	28	

Make an effort to find writing friends and peers who can help you edit your work.

MARCH 2014

SUN	MON	TUE	WED	THU	FRI	SAT
						1
2	3	4	5	6	7	8
9	10	11	12	13	14	15
16	17	18	19	20	21	22
23	24	25	26	27	28	29
30	31					

Join a writing organization (perhaps a chapter of SCBWI) or small, local writers group.

APRIL 2014

SUN	MON	TUE	WED	THU	FRI	SAT
		1	2	3	4	5
6	7	8	9	10	11	12
13	14	15	16	17	18	19
20	21	22	23	24	25	26
27	28	29	30			

Try writing poetry for National Poetry Month.

MAY 2014

SUN	MON	TUE	WED	THU	FRI	SAT
				1	2	3
4	5	6	7	8	9	10
11	12	13	14	15	16	17
18	19	20	21	22	23	24
25	26	27	28	29	30	31

Plan to attend a writing conference this summer. Have work(s) ready to pitch.

_____

_____

_____

_____

_____

JUNE 2014

SUN	MON	TUE	WED	THU	FRI	SAT
1	2	3	4	5	6	7
8	9	10	11	12	13	14
15	16	17	18	19	20	21
22	23	24	25	26	27	28
29	30					

When your work is revised, start the query process. Query 6-10 markets at first.

JULY 2014

SUN	MON	TUE	WED	THU	FRI	SAT
		1	2	3	4	5
6	7	8	9	10	11	12
13	14	15	16	17	18	19
20	21	22	23	24	25	26
27	28	29	30	31		

Evaluate the submission process. If you're hitting a wall, tweak your query and first pages.

AUGUST 2014

SUN	MON	TUE	WED	THU	FRI	SAT
					1	2
3	4	5	6	7	8	9
10	11	12	13	14	15	16
17	18	19	20	21	22	23
24	25	26	27	28	29	30
31						

Get involved in social media. Set goals. Start a blog now, and join Twitter next month.

SEPTEMBER 2014

SUN	MON	TUE	WED	THU	FRI	SAT
	1	2	3	4	5	6
7	8	9	10	11	12	13
14	15	16	17	18	19	20
21	22	23	24	25	26	27
28	29	30				

Keep a comprehensive file of all your writing ideas, from book concepts to character quirks.

OCTOBER 2014

SUN	MON	TUE	WED	THU	FRI	SAT
			1	2	3	4
5	6	7	8	9	10	11
12	13	14	15	16	17	18
19	20	21	22	23	24	25
26	27	28	29	30	31	

Remember to back up all your writing on disc or through e-mail.

_____

_____

_____

_____

_____

NOVEMBER 2014

SUN	MON	TUE	WED	THU	FRI	SAT
						1
2	3	4	5	6	7	8
9	10	11	12	13	14	15
16	17	18	19	20	21	22
23	24	25	26	27	28	29
30						

Good writers read. Set a goal of reading at least two books a month.

DECEMBER 2014

SUN	MON	TUE	WED	THU	FRI	SAT
	1	2	3	4	5	6
7	8	9	10	11	12	13
14	15	16	17	18	19	20
21	22	23	24	25	26	27
28	29	30	31			

Reward yourself for good work. Celebrate successes, big and small.

BOOK PUBLISHERS

There's no magic formula for getting published. It's a matter of getting the right manuscript on the right editor's desk at the right time. Before you submit, it's important to learn publishers' needs, see what kind of books they're producing, and decide which publishers your work is best suited for. *Children's Writer's & Illustrator's Market* is but one tool in this process. (Those just starting out should turn to the Quick Tips for Writers & Illustrators article.)

To help you narrow down the list of possible publishers for your work, we've included several indexes at the back of this book. The **Subject Index** lists book and magazine publishers according to their fiction and nonfiction needs or interests. The **Age-Level Index** indicates which age groups publishers cater to. The **Photography Index** indicates which markets buy photography for children's publications. The **Poetry Index** lists publishers accepting poetry. The **Illustration Index** lists book publishers and magazines that accept illustrations for publication.

If you write contemporary fiction for young adults, for example, and you're trying to place a book manuscript, go first to the Subject Index. Locate the fiction categories under Book Publishers and copy the list under Contemporary. Then go to the Age-Level Index and highlight the publishers on the Contemporary list that are included under the Young Adults heading. Read the listings for the highlighted publishers to see if your work matches their needs.

Remember, *Children's Writer's & Illustrator's Market* should not be your only source for researching publishers. Here are a few other sources of information:

- The Society of Children's Book Writers and Illustrators (SCBWI) offers members an annual market survey of children's book publishers for the cost of postage or free online at scbwi.org (SCBWI membership information can also be found at scbwi.org)

- The Children's Book Council website (cbcbooks.org) gives information on member publishers.
- If a publisher interests you, send a SASE for submission guidelines or check publishers' websites for guidelines *before* submitting. To quickly find guidelines online, visit The Colossal Directory of Children's Publishers at signaleader.com.
- Check publishers' websites. Many include their complete catalogs that you can browse. Web addresses are included in many publishers' listings.
- Spend time at your local bookstore to see who's publishing what. While you're there, browse through *Publishers Weekly* and *The Horn Book*.

SUBSIDY & SELF-PUBLISHING

Some determined writers who receive rejections from royalty publishers may look to subsidy and co-op publishers as an option for getting their work into print. These publishers ask writers to pay all or part of the costs of producing a book. We strongly advise writers and illustrators to work only with publishers who pay them. For this reason, we've adopted a policy not to include any subsidy or co-op publishers in *Children's Writer's & Illustrator's Market* (or any other Writer's Digest Books market books).

If you're interested in publishing your book just to share it with friends and relatives, self-publishing is a viable option, but it involves time, energy, and money. You oversee all book production details. Check with a local printer for advice and information on cost or check online for print-on-demand publishing options (which are often more affordable).

WHICH PUBLISHERS ARE OPEN TO SUBMISSIONS?

Unfortunately, established, larger publishing houses are not open to direct submissions from writers. Houses like these, such as Random House, only want submissions from literary agents. We include these closed listings in editions of *CWIM* simply so that writers know not to send work to them. Otherwise, it may be unclear to writers if they are open to submissions or not. Keep in mind that you can submit your work to agents as well as publishers.

ABBEVILLE FAMILY

Abbeville Press, 137 Varick St., New York NY 10013. (212)366-5585. **Fax:** (212)366-6966. **E-mail:** abbeville@abbeville.com. **Website:** www.abbeville.com. "Our list is full for the next several seasons." Publishes 8 titles/year. 10% of books from first-time authors.

○ *Not accepting unsolicited book proposals at this time.*

FICTION Picture books: animal, anthology, concept, contemporary, fantasy, folktales, health, hi-lo, history, humor, multicultural, nature/environment, poetry, science fiction, special needs, sports, suspense. Average word length 300-1,000 words.

HOW TO CONTACT Please refer to website for submission policy.

ILLUSTRATION Works with approx 2-4 illustrators/year. Uses color artwork only.

PHOTOGRAPHY Buys stock and assigns work.

ABRAMS BOOKS FOR YOUNG READERS

115 W. 18th St., New York NY 10011. **Website:** www.abramsyoungreaders.com.

○ Abrams no longer accepts unsolicited manuscripts or queries. Abrams title *365 Penguins*, by Jean-Luc Fromental, illustrated by Joëlle Jolivet, won a Boston Globe-Horn Book Picture Book Honor Award in 2007. *Abrams also publishes Laurent De Brunhoff, Graeme Base, and Laura Numeroff, among others.*

ILLUSTRATION Illustrations only: Do not submit original material; copies only. Contact: Chad Beckerman, creative director.

ALADDIN

Simon & Schuster, 1230 Avenue of the Americas, 4th Floor, New York NY 10020. (212)698-7000. **Website:** www.simonsays.com. **Contact:** Acquisitions Editor. Aladdin publishes picture books, beginning readers, chapter books, middle grade and tween fiction and nonfiction, and graphic novels and nonfiction in hardcover and paperback, with an emphasis on commercial, kid-friendly titles. Publishes hardcover/paperback imprints of Simon & Schuster Children's Division.

HOW TO CONTACT Simon & Schuster does not review, retain or return unsolicited materials or artwork. "We suggest prospective authors and illustrators submit their mss through a professional literary agent."

AMERICAN PRESS

60 State St., Suite 700, Boston MA 02109. (617)247-0022. **E-mail:** americanpress@flash.net. **Website:** www.americanpresspublishers.com. Publishes college textbooks. Publishes 25 titles/year. 50% of books from first-time authors. 90% from unagented writers.

○ "Ms proposals are welcome in all subjects & disciplines."

NONFICTION "We prefer that our authors actually teach courses for which the manuscripts are designed."

HOW TO CONTACT Query, or submit outline with tentative TOC. *No complete mss.* 350 queries received/year. 100 mss received/year. Responds in 3 months to queries. Publishes book 9 months after acceptance.

TERMS Pays 5-15% royalty on wholesale price.

AMULET BOOKS

Abrams Books for Young Readers, 115 W. 18th St., 6th Floor, New York NY 10001. **E-mail:** abrams@abramsbooks.com. **Website:** www.amuletbooks.com. **Contact:** Susan Van Metre, vice president/publisher; Tamar Brazis, editorial director; Cecily Kaiser, publishing director. 10% of books from first-time authors.

○ *Does not accept unsolicited mss or queries.*

FICTION Middle readers: adventure, contemporary, fantasy, history, science fiction, sports. Young adults/teens: adventure, contemporary, fantasy, history, science fiction, sports, suspense. Recently published *Diary of a Wimpy Kid*, by Jeff Kinney; *The Sisters Grimm*, by Michael Buckley (mid-grade series); *ttyl*, by Lauren Miracle (YA novel); *Heart of a Samurai*, by Margi Preus (Newbery Honor Award winner).

ILLUSTRATION Works with 10-12 illustrators/year. Uses both color and b&w. Query with samples. Contact: Chad Beckerman, creative director. Samples filed.

PHOTOGRAPHY Buys stock images and assigns work.

⊕ AZRO PRESS

PMB 342, 1704 Llano St. B, Santa Fe NM 87505. (505)989-3272. **Fax:** (505)989-3832. **E-mail:** books@azropress.com. **Website:** www.azropress.com. **Contact:** Gae Eisenhardt.

○ "We like to publish illustrated children's books by Southwestern authors and illustrators. We are always looking for books with a Southwestern look or theme."

FICTION Picture books: animal, history, humor, nature/environment. Young readers: adventure, animal, hi-lo, history, humor. Average word length: picture books—1,200; young readers—2,000-2,500.

NONFICTION Picture books: animal, geography, history. Young readers: geography, history.

HOW TO CONTACT Query or submit complete ms. Responds to queries/mss in 3-4 months. Publishes book 1-2 years after acceptance.

ILLUSTRATION Accepts material from international illustrators. Works with 3 illustrators/year. Uses color and b&w artwork. Reviews ms/illustration packages. Reviews work for future assignments. Query with samples. Submit samples to illustrations editor. Responds in 3-4 months. Samples not returned. Samples are filed.

TERMS Pays authors royalty of 5-10% based on wholesale price. Pays illustrators by the project ($2,000) or royalty of 5%. Catalog available for #10 SASE and 3 first-class stamps or online.

TIPS "At the moment, we are focusing on books written and illustrated by residents of the Southwest."

BAILIWICK PRESS

309 East Mulberry St., Fort Collins CO 80524. (970) 672-4878. **Fax:** (970) 672-4731. **E-mail:** info@bailiwickpress.com. **Website:** www.bailiwickpress.com. "We're a micro-press that produces books and other products that inspire and tell great stories. Our motto is 'books with something to say.' We are now considering submissions, agented and unagented, for children's and young adult fiction. We're looking for smart, funny, and layered writing that kids will clamor for. Authors who already have a following have a leg up. We are only looking for humorous children's fiction. Please do not submit work for adults. Illustrated fiction is desired but not required. (Illustrators are also invited to send samples.) Make us laugh out loud, ooh and aah, and cry, 'Eureka!' Please read the Aldo Zelnick series to determine if we might be on the same page, then fill out our submission form. Please do not send submissions via snail mail or phone calls. **You must complete the online submission form to be considered.** If, after completing and submitting the form, you also need to send us an e-mail attachment (such as sample illustrations or excerpts of graphics), you may e-mail them to info@bailiwickpress.com."

HOW TO CONTACT "Please do not send submissions via snail mail or e-mail. We will reply to neither. Also, do not phone us.You must complete the online submission form to be considered. If, after completing and submitting the form, you also need to send us e-mail attachments (such as sample illustrations or excerpts of graphics), you may e-mail them to aldozelnick@gmail.com Responds in 6 months."

ILLUSTRATION Illustrated fiction desired but not required. Send samples.

Ⓐ BALZER & BRAY

HarperCollins Children's Books, 10 E. 53rd St., New York NY 10022. (212)207-7000. **Website:** www.harpercollinschildrens.com. Publishes 10 titles/year.

FICTION Picture Books, Young Readers: adventure, animal, anthology, concept, contemporary, fantasy, history, humor, multicultural, nature/environment, poetry, science fiction, special needs, sports, suspense. Middle Readers, Young Adults/Teens: adventure, animal, anthology, contemporary, fantasy, history, humor, multicultural, nature/environment, poetry, science fiction, special needs, sports, suspense.

NONFICTION "We will publish very few nonfiction titles, maybe 1-2 per year."

HOW TO CONTACT Agented submissions only. Publishes book 18 months after acceptance.

ILLUSTRATION Works with 10 illustrators/year. Uses both color and b&w. Illustrations only: send tearsheets to be kept on file. Contact: Editor. Responds only if interested. Samples are not returned.

PHOTOGRAPHY Works on assignment only.

TERMS Offers advances. Pays illustrators by the project.

Ⓐ BANTAM BOOKS

Imprint of Random House, Inc., 1745 Broadway, New York NY 10019. (212)782-9000. **Website:** www.randomhouse.com.

◯ *Not seeking mss at this time.*

BEHRMAN HOUSE INC.

11 Edison Place, Springfield NJ 07081. (973)379-7200. **Fax:** (973)379-7280. **Website:** www.behrmanhouse.com. Publishes books on all aspects of Judaism: history, cultural, textbooks, holidays. "Behrman House publishes quality books of Jewish content—history, Bible, philosophy, holidays, ethics—for children and adults." 12% of books from first-time authors.

NONFICTION All levels: Judaism, Jewish educational textbooks. Average word length: young reader—1,200; middle reader—2,000; young adult—4,000. Recently published *A Kid's Mensch Handbook*, by Scott E. Blumenthal; *Shalom Ivrit 3*, by Nili Ziv.

HOW TO CONTACT Submit outline/synopsis and sample chapters. Responds in 1 month to queries; 2 months to mss. Publishes book 18 months after acceptance.

ILLUSTRATION Works with 6 children's illustrators/year. Reviews ms/illustration packages from artists. "Query first." Illustrations only: Query with samples; send unsolicited art samples by mail. Responds to queries in 1 month; mss in 2 months.

PHOTOGRAPHY Purchases photos from freelancers. Buys stock and assigns work. Uses photos of families involved in Jewish activities. Uses color and b&w prints. Photographers should query with samples. Send unsolicited photos by mail. Submit portfolio for review.

TERMS Pays authors royalty of 3-10% based on retail price or buys ms outright for $1,000-5,000. Offers advance. Pays illustrators by the project (range: $500-5,000). Book catalog free on request.

TIPS Looking for "religious school texts" with Judaic themes or general trade Judaica.

Ⓐ BERKLEY BOOKS

Penguin Group (USA) Inc., 375 Hudson St., New York NY 10014. **Website:** us.penguingroup.com/. **Contact:** Leslie Gelbman, president and publisher. The Berkley Publishing Group publishes a variety of general nonfiction and fiction including the traditional categories of romance, mystery and science fiction. Publishes paperback and mass market originals and reprints. Publishes 500 titles/year.

〇 "Due to the high volume of manuscripts received, most Penguin Group (USA) Inc. imprints do not normally accept unsolicited manuscripts. The preferred and standard method for having manuscripts considered for publication by a major publisher is to submit them through an established literary agent."

FICTION No occult fiction.

NONFICTION No memoirs or personal stories.

HOW TO CONTACT *Prefers agented submissions.*

BETHANY HOUSE PUBLISHERS

Baker Publishing Group, 6030 E. Fulton Rd., Ada MI 49301. (616)676-9185. **Fax:** (616)676-9573. **Website:** www.bethanyhouse.com. Bethany House Publishers specializes in books that communicate Biblical truth and assist people in both spiritual and practical areas of life. While we do not accept unsolicited queries or proposals via telephone or e-mail, we will consider 1-page queries sent by fax and directed to adult nonfiction, adult fiction, or young adult/children. Publishes hardcover and trade paperback originals, mass market paperback reprints. Publishes 90-100 titles/year. 2% of books from first-time authors. 50% from unagented writers.

〇 *All unsolicited mss returned unopened.*

HOW TO CONTACT Responds in 3 months to queries. Publishes a book 1 year after acceptance.

TERMS Pays royalty on net price. Pays advance. Book catalog for 9 x 12 envelope and 5 first-class stamps. Guidelines available online.

TIPS Bethany House Publishers' publishing program relates Biblical truth to all areas of life—whether in the framework of a well-told story, of a challenging book for spiritual growth, or of a Bible reference work. We are seeking high-quality fiction and nonfiction that will inspire and challenge our audience.

◔ BIRDSONG BOOKS

1322 Bayview Rd., Middletown DE 19709. (302)378-7274. **E-mail:** birdsong@birdsongbooks.com. **Website:** www.birdsongbooks.com. **Contact:** Nancy Carol Willis, president. "Birdsong Books seeks to spark the delight of discovering our wild neighbors and natural habitats. We believe knowledge and understanding of nature fosters caring and a desire to protect the Earth and all living things. Our emphasis is on North American animals and habitats, rather than people."

NONFICTION Picture books, young readers: activity books, animal, nature/environment. Average word length: picture books—800-1,000 plus content for 2-4 pages of back matter. Recently published *The Animals' Winter Sleep*, by Lynda Graham-Barber (age 3-6, nonfiction picture book); *Red Knot: A Shorebird's Incredible Journey*, by Nancy Carol Willis (age 6-9, nonfiction picture book); *Raccoon Moon*, by Nancy Carol Willis (ages 5-8, natural science picture book); *The Robins In Your Backyard*, by Nancy Carol Willis (ages 4-7, nonfiction picture book).

HOW TO CONTACT Submit complete ms package with SASE. Responds to mss in 3 months. Publishes book 2-3 years after acceptance.

ILLUSTRATION Accepts material from residents of U.S. Works with 1 illustrator/year. Reviews ms/illustration packages from artists. Send ms with dummy (plus samples/tearsheets for style). Illustrations only: Query with brochure, résumé, samples, SASE, or tearsheets. Responds only if interested. Samples returned with SASE.

PHOTOGRAPHY Uses North American animals and habitats (currently wading birds—herons, egrets, and the like). Submit cover letter, résumé, promo piece, stock photo list.

TIPS "We are a small independent press actively seeking manuscripts that fit our narrowly defined niche. We are only interested in nonfiction, natural science picture books or educational activity books about North American animals and habitats. We are not interested in fiction stories based on actual events. Our books include several pages of back matter suitable for early elementary classrooms. Mailed submissions with SASE only. No e-mail submissions or phone calls, please. Cover letters should sell author/illustrator and book idea."

BLACK ROSE WRITING

E-mail: creator@blackrosewriting.com. **Website:** www.blackrosewriting.com. **Contact:** Reagan Rothe. "We publish only one genre—our genre. Black Rose Writing is an independent publishing house that believes in developing a personal relationship with our authors. We don't see them as clients or just another number on a page, but rather as people.. [and] we are willing to do whatever it takes to make them satisfied with their publishing choice. We are seeking growth in an array of different genres and searching for new publicity venues for our authors everyday. Black Rose Writing doesn't promise our authors the world, leading them to become overwhelmed by the competitive and difficult venture. We are honest with our authors, and we give them the insight to generate solid leads without wasting their time. Black Rose Writing works with our authors along many lines of promotion, (examples: showcasing your titles at festivals, scheduling book events, and sending out press releases and review copies) and provides a broad distribution that covers many book buyers and allows interested parties access to our titles easily. We want to make our authors' journeys into the publishing world a success and eliminate the fear of a toilsome and lengthy experience. Publishes majority trade paperback, occasional hard cover or children's book. Publishes 75+ titles/year.

HOW TO CONTACT Query via e-mail. Submit synopsis and author bio. Please allow 4-6 weeks for response. Responds in 2-3 months to mss.

TERMS Please check online submission guidelines before contacting by e-mail.

TIPS "Always spell-check, and try and send an edited manuscript. Do not forward your initial contact e-mails."

BLOOMSBURY CHILDREN'S BOOKS

Imprint of Bloomsbury USA, 1385 Broadway, 5th Floor, New York NY 10018. (212)419-5300. **E-mail:** bloomsbury.kids@bloomsburyusa.com. **Website:** www.bloomsburykids.com. Publishes 60 titles/year. 25% of books from first-time authors.

No phone calls or e-mails.

FICTION Picture books: adventure, animal, contemporary, fantasy, folktales, history, humor, multicultural, poetry, suspense/mystery. Young readers: adventure, animal, anthology, concept, contemporary, fantasy, folktales, history, humor, multicultural, suspense/mystery. Middle readers: adventure, animal, contemporary, fantasy, folktales, history, humor, multicultural, poetry, problem novels. Young adults: adventure, animal, anthology, contemporary, fantasy, folktales, history, humor, multicultural, problem novels, science fiction, sports, suspense/mystery.

HOW TO CONTACT Query with SASE. Submit clips, first 3 chapters with SASE. Responds in 6 months to queries; 6 months to mss.

TERMS Pays royalty. Pays advance. Book catalog available online. *Agented submissions only.* Guidelines available online.

TIPS "All Bloomsbury Children's Books submissions are considered on an individual basis. Bloomsbury Children's Books will no longer respond to unsolicited manuscripts or art submissions. Please include a telephone AND e-mail address where we may contact you if we are interested in your work. Do NOT send a self-addressed stamped envelope. We regret the inconvenience, but unfortunately, we are too understaffed to maintain a correspondence with authors. There is no need to send art with a picture book manuscript. Artists should submit art with a picture book manuscript. We do not return art samples. Please do not send us original art! Please note that we do accept simultaneous submissions but please be courteous and inform us if another house has made an offer on your work. Do not send originals or your only copy of anything. We are not liable for artwork or manuscript submissions. Please address all submissions to the attention of 'Manuscript Submissions.' Please make sure that everything is stapled, paper-clipped, or rubber-banded together. We do not accept e-mail or CD/DVD submissions. Be sure your work is appropriate for us. Familiarize yourself with our list by going to bookstores or libraries."

◎ BRIGHT RING PUBLISHING, INC.

P.O. Box 31338, Bellingham WA 98228. (800)480-4278. **Fax:** (360)592-4503. **E-mail:** maryann@brightring.com. **Website:** www.brightring.com. **Contact:** MaryAnn Kohl, editor.

◎ *Bright Ring is no longer accepting manuscript submissions.*

CALKINS CREEK

Boyds Mills Press, 815 Church St., Honesdale PA 18431. (570)253-1164. **E-mail:** contact@boydsmillspress.com. **Website:** www.calkinscreekbooks.com. We aim to publish books that are a well-written blend of creative writing and extensive research, which emphasize important events, people, and places in U.S. history."

FICTION All levels: history. Recently published *Healing Water*, by Joyce Moyer Hostetter (ages 10 and up, historical fiction); *The Shakeress*, by Kimberly Heuston (ages 12 and up, historical fiction).

NONFICTION All levels: history. Recently published *Farmer George Plants a Nation*, by Peggy Thomas (ages 8 and up, nonfiction picture book); *Robert H. Jackson*, by Gail Jarrow (ages 10 and up, historical fiction).

HOW TO CONTACT Submit outline/synopsis and 3 sample chapters.

ILLUSTRATION Accepts material from international illustrators. Works with 25 (for all Boyds Mills Press imprints) illustrators/year. Uses both color and b&w. Reviews ms/illustration packages. For ms/illustration packages: Submit ms with 2 pieces of final art. Submit ms/illustration packages to address above, label package "Manuscript Submission." Reviews work for future assignments. If interested in illustrating future titles, query with samples. Submit samples to address above. Label package "Art Sample Submission."

PHOTOGRAPHY Buys stock images and assigns work. Submit photos to: address above, label package "Art Sample Submission." Uses color or b&w 8×10

prints. For first contact, send promo piece (color or b&w).

TERMS Pays authors royalty or work purchased outright. Guidelines available on website.

TIPS "Read through our recently published titles and review our catalog. When selecting titles to publish, our emphasis will be on important events, people, and places in U.S. history. Writers are encouraged to submit a detailed bibliography, including secondary and primary sources, and expert reviews with their submissions."

CANDLEWICK PRESS

99 Dover St., Somerville MA 02144. (617)661-3330. **Fax:** (617)661-0565. **E-mail:** bigbear@candlewick.com. **Website:** www.candlewick.com. **Contact:** Deb Wayshak, executive editor (fiction); Joan Powers, editor-at-large (picture books); Liz Bicknell, editorial director/associate publisher (poetry, picture books, fiction); Mary Lee Donovan, executive editor (picture books, nonfiction/fiction); Hilary Van Dusen, senior editor (nonfiction/fiction). "Candlewick Press publishes high-quality, illustrated children's books for ages infant through young adult. We are a truly child-centered publisher." Candlewick title *Good Masters! Sweet Ladies! Voices from a Medieval Village*, by Amy Schlitz, won the John Newbery Medal in 2008. Their title *Twelve Rounds to Glory: The Story of Muhammad Ali*, by Charles R. Smith Jr., illustrated by Bryan Collier, won a Coretta Scott King Author Honor Award in 2008. Their title *The Astonishing Life of Octavian Nothing*, by M.T. Anderson, won the Boston Globe-Hornbook Award for Fiction and Poetry in 2007. Publishes hardcover and trade paperback originals, and reprints. Publishes 200 titles/year. 5% of books from first-time authors.

◎ *Candlewick Press is not accepting queries or unsolicited mss at this time.*

FICTION Picture books: animal, concept, contemporary, fantasy, history, humor, multicultural, nature/environment, poetry. Middle readers, young adults: contemporary, fantasy, history, humor, multicultural, poetry, science fiction, sports, suspense/mystery.

NONFICTION Picture books: concept, biography, geography, nature/environment. Young readers: biography, geography, nature/environment.

HOW TO CONTACT "We do not accept editorial queries or submissions online. If you are an author or illustrator and would like us to consider your work, please read our submissions policy (online) to learn more."

ILLUSTRATION Works with approx. 40 illustrators/year. "We prefer to see a range of styles from artists along with samples showing strong characters (human or animals) in various settings with various emotions." Candlewick accepts unsolicited art samples and dummies from illustrators and agents.

TERMS Pays authors royalty of 2½-10% based on retail price. Offers advance.

TIPS "See our website for further information about us."

CAPSTONE

1710 Roe Crest Rd., North Mankato MN 56003. **Website:** www.capstone.com. **Contact:** Heather Kindseth, creative director.

FICTION Young readers, middle readers, young adults: adventure, contemporary, fantasy, humor, light humor, mystery, science fiction, sports, suspense. Average word length: young readers—1,000-3,000; middle readers and early young adults—5,000-10,000.

HOW TO CONTACT Submit outline/synopsis and 3 sample chapters. Electronic submissions are preferred and should be sent to author.sub@capstone.com.

ILLUSTRATION Works with 35 illustrators/year. Uses both color and b&w.

TERMS Work purchased outright from authors. Catalog available on website.

TIPS "A high-interest topic or activity is one that a young person would spend their free time on without adult direction or suggestion."

⊕ CAPSTONE YOUNG READERS

1710 Roe Crest Drive, North Mankato, MN 56003. **E-mail:** author.sub@capstonepub.com. **Website:** www.capstonepub.com.

"Capstone is keenly interested in meeting authors and illustrators. In fact, they play an integral role, connecting with our young readers and often deepening the reading experience by interacting with them online. Most of our titles are conceptually developed in-house and written and illustrated by freelance writers and artists. However, we are interested in receiving authors' manuscripts and writing samples, and reviewing artists' portfolios."

FICTION "Authors should submit via e-mail: sample chapters, résumé, and list of previous publishing

credits, if applicable all in the body of the e-mail, not as attachments."

NONFICTION "Authors should mail résumé, cover letter, and up to three writing samples."

HOW TO CONTACT Fiction writers submit via e-mail to author.sub@capstonepub.com. Fiction illustrators submit via e-mail to il.sub@capstonepub.com. Nonfiction writers submit via U.S. mail to our address (c/o Capstone Nonfiction Editorial Director). Nonfiction illustrators submit via e-mail: to nf.il.sub@capstonepub.com. Will only respond if samples fit publishing needs

ILLUSTRATION Fiction illustrators should submit via e-mail: sample artwork, résumé, and list of previous publishing credits, if applicable all in the body of the e-mail, not as attachments. Nonfiction illustrators should submit via e-mail: sample artwork, résumé, and list of previous publishing credits, if applicable all in the body of the e-mail, not as attachments.

CAROLRHODA BOOKS, INC.

1251 Washington Ave. N., Minneapolis MN 55401. **Website:** www.lernerbooks.com. "We will continue to seek targeted solicitations at specific reading levels and in specific subject areas. The company will list these targeted solicitations on our website and in national newsletters, such as the SCBWI Bulletin."

Starting in 2007, Lerner Publishing Group no longer accepts submissions to any of their imprints except for Kar-Ben Publishing.

Ⓐ CARTWHEEL BOOKS

Imprint of Scholastic Trade Division, 557 Broadway, New York NY 10012. (212)343-6100. **Website:** www.scholastic.com. Cartwheel Books publishes innovative books for children, up to age 8. "We are looking for 'novelties' that are books first, play objects second. Even without its gimmick, a Cartwheel Book should stand alone as a valid piece of children's literature. Publishes novelty books, easy readers, board books, hardcover and trade paperback originals."

FICTION Again, the subject should have mass market appeal for very young children. Humor can be helpful, but not necessary. Mistakes writers make are a reading level that is too difficult, a topic of no interest or too narrow, or manuscripts that are too long.

NONFICTION Cartwheel Books publishes for the very young, therefore nonfiction should be written in a manner that is accessible to preschoolers through 2nd grade. Often writers choose topics that are too narrow or "special" and do not appeal to the mass market. Also, the text and vocabulary are frequently too difficult for our young audience.

HOW TO CONTACT *Accepts mss from agents, previously publishes authors only.*

TERMS Book catalog for 9 x 12 SASE. Guidelines available free.

TIPS "Audience is young children, ages 0-8. Know what types of books the publisher does. Some manuscripts that don't work for one house may be perfect for another. Check out bookstores or catalogs to see where your writing would 'fit' best."

MARSHALL CAVENDISH

99 White Plains Rd., Tarrytown NY 10591. (914)332-8888. **Fax:** (914)332-1082. **E-mail:** mcc@marshall cavendish.com; customerservice@marshellcavendish. com. **Website:** www.marshallcavendish.us. **Contact:** Margery Cuyler, publisher. "Marshall Cavendish is an international publisher that publishes books, directories, magazines and digital platforms. Our philosophy of enriching life through knowledge transcends boundaries of geography and culture. In line with this vision, our products reach across the globe in 13 languages, and our publishing network spans Asia and the USA. Our brands have garnered international awards for educational excellence, and they include Marshall Cavendish Reference, Marshall Cavendish Benchmark, Marshall Cavendish Children, Marshall Cavendish Education and Marshall Cavendish Editions. Several have also achieved household name status in the international market. We ceaselessly explore new avenues to convey our products to the world, with our extensive variety of genres, languages and formats. In addition, our strategy of business expansion has ensured that the reach and benefits of Marshall Cavendish's products extend across the globe, especially into previously uncharted markets in China and Eastern Europe. Our aspiration to further the desire for lifelong learning and self-development continues to guide our efforts." Publishes 60-70 titles/year.

○ *Marshall Cavendish is no longer accepting unsolicited mss. However, the company will continue to consider agented mss.*

ILLUSTRATION Contact: Anahid Hamparian, art director.

TERMS Pays authors/illustrators advance and royalties.

○ CHARLESBRIDGE PUBLISHING

85 Main St., Watertown MA 02472. (617)926-0329. **Fax:** (800)926-5775. **E-mail:** tradeart@charlesbridge. com; tradeeditorial@charlesbridge.com **Website:** www.charlesbridge.com. "Charlesbridge publishes high-quality books for children, with a goal of creating lifelong readers and lifelong learners. Our books encourage reading and discovery in the classroom, library, and home. We believe that books for children should offer accurate information, promote a positive worldview, and embrace a child's innate sense of wonder and fun. To this end, we continually strive to seek new voices, new visions, and new directions in children's literature." Publishes hardcover and trade paperback nonfiction and fiction, children's books for the trade and library markets. Publishes 30 titles/year. 10-20% of books from first-time authors. 80% from unagented writers.

○ "We're always interested in innovative approaches to a difficult genre, the nonfiction picture book."

FICTION Strong stories with enduring themes. Charlesbridge publishes both picture books and transitional bridge books (books ranging from early readers to middle grade chapter books). Our fiction titles include lively, plot-driven stories with strong, engaging characters. No alphabet books, board books, coloring books, activity books, or books with audiotapes or CD-ROMs.

NONFICTION Strong interest in nature, environment, social studies, and other topics for trade and library markets.

HOW TO CONTACT *Exclusive submissions only.* "Charlesbridge accepts unsolicited manuscripts submitted exclusively to us for a period of three months. 'Exclusive Submission' should be written on all envelopes and cover letters. Please submit only one or two manuscript(s) at a time.

FICTION For picture books and shorter bridge books, please send a complete manuscript. For fiction books longer than 30 manuscript pages, please send a detailed plot synopsis, a chapter outline, and three chapters of text. Manuscripts should be typed and double-spaced. Please do not submit material by e-mail, by fax, or on a computer disk. Illustrations are not necessary. Please make a copy of your manuscript, as we cannot be responsible for submissions lost in the mail. Include your name and address on the first page of your manuscript and in your cover letter. Be sure to list any previously published work or relevant writing experience."

NONFICTION For nonfiction books longer than 30 manuscript pages, send a detailed proposal, a chapter outline, and one to three chapters of text. Manuscripts should be typed and double-spaced. Please do not submit material by e-mail, by fax, or on a computer disk. Illustrations are not necessary. Please make a copy of your manuscript, as we cannot be responsible for submissions lost in the mail. Include your name and address on the first page of your manuscript and in your cover letter. Be sure to list any previously published work or relevant writing experience. Responds in 3 months. If you have not heard back from us after 3 months, you may assume we do not have a place for your project and submit it elsewhere. Publishes ms 2-4 years after acceptance.

TERMS Pays royalty. Pays advance. Guidelines available online.

TIPS "To become acquainted with our publishing program, we encourage you to review our books and visit our website (www.charlesbridge.com), where you will find our catalog. To request a printed catalog, please send a 9 x 12 SASE with $2.50 in postage."

○ CHICAGO REVIEW PRESS

814 N. Franklin St., Chicago IL 60610. (312)337-0747. **Fax:** (312)337-5110. **E-mail:** frontdesk@chicagoreviewpress.com. **Website:** www.chicagoreviewpress.com. **Contact:** Cynthia Sherry, publisher; Allison Felus, managing editor. "Chicago Review Press publishes high-quality, nonfiction, educational activity books that extend the learning process through hands-on projects and accurate and interesting text. We look for activity books that are as much fun as they are constructive and informative."

○ *Chicago Review Press does not publish fiction.*

NONFICTION Young readers, middle readers and young adults: activity books, arts/crafts, multicultural, history, nature/environment, science. "We're interested in hands-on, educational books; anything else probably will be rejected." Average length: young readers and young adults—144-160 pages. Recently published *Amazing Rubber Band Cars*, by Michael Rigsby (ages 9 and up); *Don't Touch That!*, by Jeff Day M.D. (ages 7 to 9); and *Abraham Lincoln for Kids*, by Janis Herbert (ages 9 and up).

HOW TO CONTACT Enclose cover letter and no more than a table of contents and 1-2 sample chapters; prefers not to receive e-mail queries. Responds to queries/mss in 2 months. Publishes a book 1-2 years after acceptance.

ILLUSTRATION Works with 6 illustrators/year. Uses primarily b&w artwork. Reviews ms/illustration packages from artists. Submit 1-2 chapters of ms with corresponding pieces of final art. Illustrations only: Query with samples, résumé. Responds only if interested. Samples returned with SASE.

PHOTOGRAPHY Buys photos from freelancers ("but not often"). Buys stock and assigns work. Wants "instructive photos. We consult our files when we know what we're looking for on a book-by-book basis." Uses b&w prints.

TERMS Pays authors royalty of 7.5-12.5% based on retail price. Offers advances of $3,000-6,000. Pays illustrators by the project (range varies considerably). Pays photographers by the project (range varies considerably). Book catalog available for $3. Ms guidelines available for $3.

TIPS "We're looking for original activity books for small children and the adults caring for them—new themes and enticing projects to occupy kids' imaginations and promote their sense of personal creativity. We like activity books that are as much fun as they are constructive. Please write for guidelines so you'll know what we're looking for." The detailed submission guidelines are available online.

CHILDREN'S BRAINS ARE YUMMY (CBAY) BOOKS

P.O. Box 92411, Austin TX 78709. (512)789-1004. **Fax:** (512)473-7710. **E-mail:** submissions@cbaybooks.com. **Website:** www.cbaybooks.com. **Contact:** Madeline Smoot, publisher. "Starting in 2011, CBAY Books will be accepting queries for teen books for original e-book publication. Books can be of any sub-genre including but not limited to mystery, fantasy, science fiction, historical, creative non-fiction, spiritual slant, etc. However, since this is for the e-book market, we are primarily interested in speculative fiction at this time. But we will consider anything." Publishes 8 titles/year. 30% of books from first-time authors.

HOW TO CONTACT Accepts international material. "All submissions must be electronic. Your query should include a cover letter and the first 3000 words of your manuscript in the body of the email. For security reasons, we will not open anything with an attachment."

ILLUSTRATION Accepts international material. Works with 0-1 illustrators/year. Uses color artwork only. Reviews artwork. Send manuscripts with dummy. Send resume and tearsheets. Send samples to Madeline Smoot. Responds to queries only if interested.

PHOTOGRAPHY Buy stock images.

TERMS Pays authors royalty 10%-15% based on wholesale price. Offers advances against royalties. Average amount $500. Brochure and guidelines available online at website.

TIPS "CBAY Books only accepts unsolicited submissions from authors at specific times for specific genres. Please check the website to see if we are accepting books at this time. Manuscripts received when submissions are closed are not read."

CHILDREN'S PRESS/FRANKLIN WATTS

Imprint of Scholastic, Inc., 90 Old Sherman Turnpike, Danbury CT 06816. **Website:** scholastic.com/library publishing. Publishes nonfiction hardcover originals.

○ "Children's Press publishes 90% nonfiction for the school and library market, and 10% early reader fiction and nonfiction. Our books support textbooks and closely relate to the elementary and middle-school curriculum. Franklin Watts publishes nonfiction for middle and high school curriculum."

NONFICTION "We publish nonfiction books that supplement the school curriculum. No fiction, poetry, folktales, cookbooks or novelty books."

HOW TO CONTACT Query with SASE.

TERMS Book catalog for #10 SASE.

TIPS Most of this publisher's books are developed in-house; less than 5% come from unsolicited submissions. However, they publish several series for which they always need new books. Study catalogs to discover possible needs.

CHILD WELFARE LEAGUE OF AMERICA

1726 M St. NW, Suite 500, Washington DC 20036. **E-mail:** books@cwla.org. **Website:** www.cwla.org/pubs. CWLA is a privately supported, nonprofit, membership-based organization committed to preserving, protecting, and promoting the well-being of all children and their families. Publishes hardcover and trade paperback originals.

HOW TO CONTACT Submit complete ms and proposal with outline, TOC, sample chapter, intended audience, and SASE.

TERMS Book catalog and ms guidelines online.

TIPS "We are looking for positive, kid-friendly books for ages 3-9. We are looking for books that have a positive message—a feel-good book."

CHRONICLE BOOKS FOR CHILDREN

680 Second St., San Francisco CA 94107. (415)537-4200. **Fax:** (415)537-4460. **E-mail:** frontdesk@chroniclebooks.com. **Website:** www.chroniclekids.com. "Chronicle Books for Children publishes an eclectic mixture of traditional and innovative children's books. Our aim is to publish books that inspire young readers to learn and grow creatively while helping them discover the joy of reading. We're looking for quirky, bold artwork and subject matter. Currently emphasizing picture books. De-emphasizing young adult." Publishes hardcover and trade paperback originals. Publishes 50-60 titles/year. 6% of books from first-time authors. 25% from unagented writers.

HOW TO CONTACT Books for younger children may be submitted in their entirety without querying first. Projects for older children should be submitted by query letter, synopsis, and three sample chapters. Does not accept proposals by fax, via e-mail, or on disk. When submitting artwork, either as a part of a project or as samples for review, do not send original art.. 30,000 queries received/year. Responds in 2-4 weeks to queries; 6 months to mss. Publishes a book 18-24 months after acceptance.

TERMS Pays 8% royalty. Pays variable advance. Book catalog for 9x12 envelope and 3 first-class stamps. Guidelines available online.

TIPS "We are interested in projects that have a unique bent to them—be it in subject matter, writing style, or illustrative technique. As a small list, we are looking for books that will lend our list a distinctive flavor. Primarily we are interested in fiction and nonfiction picture books for children ages up to eight years, and nonfiction books for children ages up to twelve years. We publish board, pop-up, and other novelty formats as well as picture books. We are also interested in early chapter books, middle grade fiction, and young adult projects."

CLARION BOOKS

Houghton Mifflin Co., 215 Park Ave. S., New York NY 10003. **Website:** www.houghtonmifflinbooks.

com; www.hmco.com. **Contact:** Dinah Stevenson, vice president and publisher; Jennifer B. Greene, senior editor (contemporary fiction, picture books for all ages, nonfiction); Jennifer Wingertzahn, editor (fiction, picture books); Christine Kettner, art director. "Clarion Books publishes picture books, nonfiction, and fiction for infants through grade 12. Avoid telling your stories in verse unless you are a professional poet." Publishes hardcover originals for children. Publishes 50 titles/year.

"We are no longer responding to your unsolicited submission unless we are interested in publishing it. Please do not include a SASE. Submissions will be recycled, and you will not hear from us regarding the status of your submission unless we are interested. We regret that we cannot respond personally to each submission, but we do consider each and every submission we receive."

FICTION "Clarion is highly selective in the areas of historical fiction, fantasy, and science fiction. A novel must be superlatively written in order to find a place on the list." For picture books and novels, send entire ms.

NONFICTION Submit synopsis and sample chapters.

HOW TO CONTACT "Your manuscript should be typed and submitted via mail. We do not accept submissions by e-mail or fax. Please do not send a SASE or postcard, as materials will not be returned." Responds in 12 weeks. Publishes a book 2 years after acceptance..

ILLUSTRATION For ms/illustration packages, submit to editorial department. Illustrations only. Submit to design department. "Send color copies or tear sheets; do not send original artwork or slides. Please show a limited selection of your strongest work. Illustrations that feature children or animals are helpful, but feel free to submit other subject matter."

TERMS Pays 5-10% royalty on retail price. Pays minimum of $4,000 advance. Guidelines for #10 SASE or online.

TIPS "Looks for freshness, enthusiasm—in short, life."

CLEAR LIGHT PUBLISHERS

823 Don Diego, Santa Fe NM 87505. (505)989-9590. **Fax:** (505)989-9519. **E-mail:** market@clearlightbooks.com. **Website:** http://clearlightbooks.com. **Contact:** Harmon Houghton, publisher. "Clear Light publishes books that accurately depict the positive side of human experience and inspire the spirit." Publishes hardcover and trade paperback originals. Publishes 20-24 titles/year. 10% of books from first-time authors. 50% from unagented writers.

NONFICTION Middle readers and young adults: multicultural, American Indian and Hispanic only.

HOW TO CONTACT Submit complete ms with SASE. "No e-mail submissions. Authors supply art. Manuscripts not considered without art or artist's renderings." 100 queries received/year. Responds in 3 months to queries. Publishes a book 1 year after acceptance.

ILLUSTRATION Reviews ms/illustration packages from artists. "No originals please." Submit ms with dummy and SASE.

TERMS Pays 10% royalty on wholesale price. Offers advance, a percent of gross potential. Book catalog free. Guidelines available online.

CONCORDIA PUBLISHING HOUSE

3558 S. Jefferson Ave., St. Louis MO 63118. (314)268-1108. **Fax:** (314)268-1329. **E-mail:** publicity@cph.org; sarah.steiner@cph.org. **Website:** www.cph.org. **Contact:** Sarah Steiner, editorial assistant. "Concordia Publishing House produces quality resources that communicate and nurture the Christian faith and ministry of people of all ages, lay and professional. These resources include curriculum, worship aids, books, and religious supplies. We publish approximately 30 quality children's books each year. We boldly provide Gospel resources that are Christ-centered, Bible-based and faithful to our Lutheran heritage." Publishes hardcover and trade paperback originals.

NONFICTION Picture books, young readers, young adults: Bible stories, activity books, arts/crafts, concept, contemporary, religion. "All books must contain explicit Christian content." Recently published *Three Wise Women of Christmas*, by Dandi Daley Mackall (picture book for ages 6-10); *The Town That Forgot About Christmas*, by Susan K. Leigh (ages 5-9, picture book); *Little Ones Talk With God* (prayer book compilation, ages 5 and up).

HOW TO CONTACT Submit complete ms (picture books); submit outline/synopsis and samples for longer mss. May also query. Responds in 1 month to queries; 3 months to mss.

ILLUSTRATION Works with 20 illustrators/year. Illustrations only: Query with samples. Contact: Norm Simon, art director. Responds only if interested. Samples filed.

TERMS Pays authors royalties based on retail price or work purchased outright ($750-2,000). Ms guidelines for 1 first-class stamp and a #10 envelope.

TIPS "Do not send finished artwork with the manuscript. If sketches will help in the presentation of the manuscript, they may be sent. If stories are taken from the Bible, they should follow the Biblical account closely. Liberties should not be taken in fantasizing Biblical stories."

CREATIVE COMPANY

P.O. Box 227, Manliato, MN 56022. (800)445-6209. **Fax:** (507)388-2746. **E-mail:** info@thecreativecompany.us. **Website:** www.thecreativecompany.us. **Contact:** Aaron Frisch. The Creative Company has two imprints: Creative Editions (picture books), and Creative Education (nonfiction series). Publishes 140 titles/year.

○ *"We are currently not accepting fiction submissions."*

NONFICTION Picture books, young readers, young adults: animal, arts/crafts, biography, careers, geography, health, history, hobbies, multicultural, music/dance, nature/environment, religion, science, social issues, special needs, sports. Average word length: young readers—500; young adults—6,000. Recently published *Empire State Building*, by Kate Riggs (age 7, young reader); *The Assassination of Archduke Ferdinand*, by Valerie Bodden (age 14, young adult/teen).

HOW TO CONTACT Submit outline/synopsis and 2 sample chapters, along with division of titles within the series. Responds in 3 months to queries/mss. Publishes a book 2 years after acceptance.

PHOTOGRAPHY Buys stock. Contact: Tricia Kleist, photo editor. Model/property releases not required; captions required. Uses b&w prints. Submit cover letter, promo piece. Ms and photographer guidelines available for SAE.

TERMS Guidelines available for SAE.

TIPS "We are accepting nonfiction, series submissions only. Fiction submissions will not be reviewed or returned. Nonfiction submissions should be presented in series (4, 6, or 8) rather than single."

● CRESTON BOOKS

PO Box 9369 Berkeley, CA 94709. **Website:** crestonbooks.co/books.html. **Contact:** Marissa Moss. Publishes a very small number of children's book each year.

○ "Creston Books is author/illustrator driven, with talented, award-winning creators given more editorial freedom and control than in a typical New York house."

FICTION Publishes picture books.

HOW TO CONTACT Send digital submissions via e-mail to submissions@crestonbooks.co. Multiple submissions are fine, but no more than one project per month from the same author.

TERMS "Authors will get smaller advances than at big houses, but still solid in terms of small press ranges. And of course, the royalties will be on a par if not better than New York, because I want an author-friendly contract. So the business model is different in that it's weighted toward the creators of the books."

CRICKET BOOKS

Imprint of Carus Publishing, 70 E. Lake St., Suite 300, Chicago IL 60601. (603)924-7209. **Fax:** (603)924-7380. **Website:** www.cricketmag.com. Cricket Books publishes picture books, chapter books, and middle grade novels. Publishes hardcover originals. Publishes 5 titles/year.

○ *Currently not accepting queries or mss. Check website for submissions details and updates.*

HOW TO CONTACT Publishes ms 18 months after acceptance.

ILLUSTRATION Works with 4 illustrators/year. Uses color and b&w. Illustration only: Please send artwork submissions via e-mail to: mail@cicadamag.com. Make sure "portfolio samples—cricket books" is the subject line of the e-mail. The file should be 72 dpi RGB jpg format. Responds only if interested.

TERMS Pays up to 10% royalty on retail price. Average advance: $1,500 and up.

TIPS "Take a look at the recent titles to see what sort of materials we're interested in, especially for nonfiction. Please note that we aren't doing the sort of strictly educational nonfiction that other publishers specialize in."

▲ DAVID R. GODINE, PUBLISHER

15 Court Square, Suite 320, Boston MA 02108. (617)451-9600. **Fax:** (617)350-0250. **E-mail:** info@godine.com. **Website:** www.godine.com. "We publish books that matter for people who care."

○ This publisher is no longer considering unsolicited mss of any type. Only interested in agented material.

ILLUSTRATION Only interested in agented material. Works with 1-3 illustrators/year. "Please do not send original artwork unless solicited. Almost all of the children's books we accept for publication come to us with the author and illustrator already paired up. Therefore, we rarely use freelance illustrators."

DELACORTE PRESS

1745 Broadway, 10th floor, New York NY 10019. (212)782-9000. **Website:** www.randomhouse.com/kids. Publishes middle grade and young adult fiction in hardcover, trade paperback, mass market, and digest formats. .

All other query letters or ms submissions must be submitted through an agent or at the request of an editor. No e-mail queries.

DIAL BOOKS FOR YOUNG READERS

Imprint of Penguin Group USA, 375 Hudson St., New York NY 10014. (212)366-2000. **Website:** www.penguin.com/youngreaders. **Contact:** Lauri Hornik, president/publisher; Kate Harrison, senior editor; Liz Waniewski, editor. "Dial Books for Young Readers publishes quality picture books for ages 18 months-6 years; lively, believable novels for middle readers and young adults; and occasional nonfiction for middle readers and young adults." Publishes hardcover originals. Publishes 50 titles/year. 20% of books from first-time authors.

FICTION Especially looking for lively and well-written novels for middle grade and young adult children involving a convincing plot and believable characters. The subject matter or theme should not already be overworked in previously published books. The approach must not be demeaning to any minority group, nor should the roles of female characters (or others) be stereotyped, though we don't think books should be didactic, or in any way message-y. No topics inappropriate for the juvenile, young adult, and middle grade audiences. No plays.

HOW TO CONTACT Accepts unsolicited queries and up to 10 pages for longer works and unsolicited mss for picture books. Please do not include SASE with your submission. You will not hear from Dial regarding the status of your submission unless we are interested, in which case you can expect a reply from us within four months. When submitting a portion of a longer work, please provide an accompanying cover letter that briefly describes your manuscript's plot, genre (i.e. easy-to-read, middle grade or YA novel),

the intended age group, and your publishing credits, if any." 5,000 queries received/year. Responds in 4-6 months to queries.

TERMS Pays royalty. Pays varied advance. Book catalog for 9 X12 envelope and 4 first-class stamps.

TIPS "Our readers are anywhere from preschool age to teenage. Picture books must have strong plots, lots of action, unusual premises, or universal themes treated with freshness and originality. Humor works well in these books. A very well-thought-out and intelligently presented book has the best chance of being taken on. Genre isn't as much of a factor as presentation."

DISKUS PUBLISHING

E-mail: editor@diskuspublishing.com. **Website:** www.diskuspublishing.com. **Contact:** Carol Davis, senior editor; Holly Janey, submissions editor. Publishes e-books and printed books. Publishes 50 titles/year.

"At this time DiskUs Publishing is closed for submissions. Keep checking our website for updates on the status of our submissions reopen date."

FICTION "We are actively seeking confessions for our DiskUs Confessions line, as well as short stories for our Quick Pick line. We only accept e-mailed submissions for these lines."

HOW TO CONTACT Send your submission to submissions@diskuspublishing.com with the word Diskus Submission in the subject line. Submit publishing history, bio, estimated word count and genre. Submit complete ms. Publishes ms 9-12 months after acceptance.

TERMS Pays 40% royalty. Book catalog is available online only. Guidelines for #10 SASE or online. "We prefer you get your guidelines online."

DK PUBLISHING

375 Hudson St., New York NY 10014. **Website:** www.dk.com. "DK publishes photographically illustrated nonfiction for children of all ages."

DK Publishing does not accept unagented mss or proposals.

DNA PRESS & NARTEA PUBLISHING

DNA Press, P.O. Box 9311, Glendale CA 91226. **E-mail:** editors@dnapress.com. **Website:** www.dna press.com. Book publisher for young adults, children, and adults. Publishes hardcover and trade paperback originals. Publishes 10 titles/year. 90% of books from first-time authors. 100% from unagented writers.

FICTION All books should be oriented to explaining science even if they do not fall 100% under the category of science fiction.

HOW TO CONTACT Query via e-mail. Detailed guidelines available online. 500 queries received/year. 400 mss received/year. Responds in 6 weeks to mss. Publishes book 8 months after acceptance.

TERMS Pays 10-15% royalty. Book catalog and ms guidelines free.

TIPS "Quick response, great relationships, high commission/royalty."

ⒶDOG-EARED PUBLICATIONS

P.O. Box 620863, Middletown WI 53562. (888) 364-3277. **Fax:** (608)831-1410. **E-mail:** field@dog-eared. com. **Website:** www.dog-eared.com. **Contact:** Nancy Field, publisher. "The home of Dog-Eared Publications is a perfect place to create children's nature books! Perched on a hilltop in Middleton, Wisconsin, we are surrounded by wild meadows and oak forests where deer, wild turkeys, and even bobcats leave their marks."

NONFICTION Middle readers: activity books, animal, nature/environment, science. Average word length: varies. Recently published *Discovering Black Bears*, by Margaret Anderson, Nancy Field and Karen Stephenson, illustrated by Michael Maydak (middle readers, activity book); *Leapfrogging Through Wetlands*, by Margaret Anderson, Nancy Field and Karen Stephenson, illustrated by Michael Maydak (middle readers, activity book).

HOW TO CONTACT *Currently not accepting unsolicited mss.*

ILLUSTRATION Works with 2-3 illustrators/year. Reviews ms/illustration packages from artists. Submit query and a few art samples. Illustrations only: Query with samples. Responds only if interested. Samples not returned; samples filed. "Interested in realistic, nature art!"

TERMS Pays author royalty based on wholesale price. Offers advance. Brochure available for SASE and 1 first-class stamp or on website.

DREAMLAND BOOKS INC.

P.O.Box 1714, Minnetonka MN 55345. (612)281-4704. **E-mail:** dreamlandbooks@inbox.com. **Website:** www.dreamlandbooksinc.com.

FICTION "We are not accepting children's story submissions at this time. However, if you have a master or doctoral degree in creative writing, literature, or like field AND already have at least one non-vanity book published, we welcome query letters."

DUTTON CHILDREN'S BOOKS

Penguin Group (USA), Inc., 375 Hudson St., New York NY 10014. **E-mail:** duttonpublicity@ us.penguingroup.com. **Fax:** (212)414-3397. **Website:** www.penquin.com/youngreaders. **Contact:** Lauri Hornik, president and publisher; Julie Strauss-Gabel, associate publisher (literary contemporary young adult fiction); Lucia Monfriend, senior editor (picture books and middle grade fiction);Sara Reynolds, art director. Estab. 1852. Dutton Children's Books publishes fiction and nonfiction for readers ranging from preschoolers to young adults on a variety of subjects. Publishes hardcover originals as well as novelty formats. Averages 50 titles/year. **Needs:** Dutton Children's Books has a diverse, general-interest list that includes picture books, and fiction for all ages and occasional retail-appropriate nonfiction. Currently emphasizing middle grade and young adult novels that offer a fresh perspective. De-emphasizing photographic nonfiction and picture books that teach a lesson. Approximately 80 new hardcover titles are published every year, fiction and nonfiction for babies through young adults. Publishes hardcover originals as well as novelty formats. Publishes 100 titles/year. 15% of books from first-time authors.

♀ "Cultivating the creative talents of authors and illustrators and publishing books with purpose and heart continue to be the mission and joy at Dutton."

FICTION Recently published *Skippyjon Jones Lost in Space*, by Judy Schachner (picture book); *Thirteen*, by Lauren Myracle (middle grade novel); *Paper Towns*, by John Green (young adult novel); and *If I Stay*, by Gayle Forman (young adult novel).

HOW TO CONTACT Query letter only; include SASE.

TERMS Pays royalty on retail price. Offers advance.

EAKIN PRESS

Wild Horse Media Group, P.O. Box 331779, Fort Worth, TX 76163. Phone/fax: (817)344-7036. **Website:** www.eakinpress.com. "Our top priority is to cover the history and culture of the Southwest, especially Texas and Oklahoma. We also have successfully published titles related to ethnic studies. We publish very little fiction, other than for children." Publishes hardcover and paperback originals and reprints.

○ No electronic submissions.

FICTION Juvenile fiction for grades K-12, preferably relating to Texas and the Southwest or contemporary. No adult fiction.

NONFICTION Juvenile nonfiction: includes biographies of historic personalities, prefer with Texas or regional interest, or nature studies; and easy-read illustrated books for grades 1-3.

HOW TO CONTACT In 2013, Wild Horse Media Group acquired Eakin Press and Nortex Press. The company has relocated from Waco, TX, to Fort Worth, TX. Check online for further news.

○ **EDCON PUBLISHING GROUP**

30 Montauk Blvd., Oakdale NY 11769. (631)567-7227. **Fax:** (631)567-8745. **E-mail:** dale@edconpublishing.com. **Website:** www.edconpublishing.com.

○ Looking for educational games and nonfiction work in the areas of math, science, reading and social studies.

NONFICTION Grades 1-12, though primarily 6-12 remedial.

HOW TO CONTACT Submit outline/synopsis and 1 sample chapter. Submission kept on file unless return is requested. Include SASE for return. Publishes book 6 months after acceptance.

ILLUSTRATION Buys b&w and color illustrations and currently seeking computerized graphic art. Send postcards, samples, links to edcon@EDCON-Publishing.com. Mailed submissions kept on file, not returned.

TERMS Pays illustrators by the project (range: $100-$500). Work purchased outright from authors for up to $1,000. Catalog available online.

○ **EDUPRESS, INC.**

P.O. Box 8610, Madison WI 53708. (800)694-5827. **Fax:** (800)835-2329. **E-mail:** edupress@highsmith.com; LBowie@highsmith.com. **Website:** www.edupressinc.com. **Contact:** Liz Bowie. Edupress, Inc., publishes supplemental curriculum resources for PK-6th grade. Currently emphasizing reading and math materials, as well as science and social studies.

○ "Our mission is to create products that make kids want to go to school!"

HOW TO CONTACT Submit complete ms via mail or e-mail with "Manuscript Submission" as the subject line. Responds in 2-4 months to queries and mss. Publishes ms 1-2 years after acceptance.

ILLUSTRATION Query with samples. Contact: Cathy Baker, graphic design manager. Responds only if interested. Samples returned with SASE.

PHOTOGRAPHY Buys stock.

TERMS Work purchased outright from authors. Catalog available on website.

TIPS "We are looking for unique, research-based, quality supplemental materials for Pre-K through eighth grade. We publish all subject areas in many different formats, including games. Our materials are intended for classroom and home schooling use."

○ **EERDMANS BOOKS FOR YOUNG READERS**

2140 Oak Industrial Dr. NE, Grand Rapids MI 49505. (616)459-4591. **E-mail:** youngreaders@eerdmans.com; info@eerdmans.com. **Website:** www.eerdmans.com/youngreaders. **Contact:** Jen Pott, editor-in-chief. "We are seeking books that encourage independent thinking, problem-solving, creativity, acceptance, kindness. Books that encourage moral values without being didactic or preachy. Board books, picture books, middle reader fiction, young adult fiction, nonfiction, illustrated storybooks. A submission stands out when it's obvious that someone put time into it—the publisher's name and address are spelled correctly, the package is neat, and all of our submission requirements have been followed precisely. We look for short, concise cover letters that explain why the ms fits with our list, and/or how the ms fills an important need in the world of children's literature. Send exclusive ms submissions to editor-in-cheif. We regret that due to the volume of material we receive, we cannot comment on ms we are unable to accept."

○ "We seek to engage young minds with words and pictures that inform and delight, inspire and entertain. From board books for babies to picture books, nonfiction, and novels for children and young adults, our goal is to produce quality literature for a new generation of readers. We believe in books!"

○ "Although Eerdmans publishes some regional books and other nonreligious titles, it is essentially a religious publisher whose titles range from the academic to the semi-popular. It is now publishing a growing number of books in the areas of spirituality and the Christian life."

FICTION Picture books: animal, contemporary, folktales, history, humor, multicultural, nature/environment, poetry, religion, special needs, social issues, sports, suspense. Young readers: animal, contemporary, fantasy, folktales, history, humor, multicultural, poetry, religion, special needs, social issues, sports, suspense. Middle readers: adventure, contemporary, fantasy, history, humor, multicultural, nature/environment, problem novels, religion, social issues, sports, suspense. Young adults/teens: adventure, contemporary, fantasy, folktales, history, humor, multicultural, nature/environment, problem novels, religion, sports, suspense. Average word length: picture books—1,000; middle readers—15,000; young adult—45,000. "Right now we are not acquiring books that revolve around a holiday. (No Christmas, Thanksgiving, Easter, Halloween, Fourth of July, Hanukkah books.) We do not publish retold or original fairy tales, nor do we publish books about witches or ghosts or vampires."

NONFICTION Middle readers: biography, history, multicultural, nature/environment, religion, social issues. Young adults/teens: biography, history, multicultural, nature/environment, religion, social issues. Average word length: middle readers—35,000; young adult books—35,000.

HOW TO CONTACT Send exclusive ms submissions (marked so on outside of envelope) to acquisitions editor. 6,000 mss received/year. Responds to mss in 3-4 months. Publishes middle reader and YA books 1 year after acceptance; publishes picture books in 2-3 years.

ILLUSTRATION Accepts material from international illustrators. Works with 10-12 illustrators/year. Uses color artwork primarily. Reviews work for future assignments. If interested in illustrating future titles, send promo sheet. Submit samples to Gayle Brown, Art Director. Samples not returned. Samples filed.

TERMS Pays 5-7% royalty on retail.

TIPS "Find out who Eerdmans is before submitting a manuscript. Look at our website, request a catalog, and check out our books."

EGMONT USA

443 Park Ave., Suite 806, New York NY 10016. (212)685-0102. **Website:** www.egmontusa.com. **Contact:** Elizabeth Law, vice president/publisher; Regina Griffin, executive editor; Alison Weiss, associate editor. Specializes in trade books. Publishes 1 picture book/year; 2 young readers/year; 20 middle readers/year; 20 young adult/year. "Egmont USA publishes quality commercial fiction. We are committed to editorial excellence and to providing first-rate care for our authors. Our motto is that we turn writers into authors and children into passionate readers." 25% of books from first-time authors.

○ *"Unfortunately, Egmont USA is not currently able to accept unsolicited submissions; we only accept submissions from literary agents."*

FICTION Young readers: adventure, animal, contemporary, humor, multicultural. Middle readers: adventure, animal, contemporary, fantasy, humor, multicultural, problem novels, science fiction, special needs. Young adults/teens: adventure, animal, contemporary, fantasy, humor, multicultural, paranormal, problem novels, religion, science fiction, special needs.

ILLUSTRATION Only interested in agented in material. Works with 5 illustrators/year. Uses both color and b&w. Illustrations only: Query with samples. Responds only if interested. Samples are not returned.

TERMS Pays authors royalties based on retail price.

FABER & FABER LTD

Bloomsbury House, 74-77 Great Russell St., London WC1B 3DA, United Kingdom. +44(0)20-7927-3800. **Fax:** +44(0)20-7927-3801. **Website:** www.faber.co.uk. **Contact:** Lee Brackstone, Hannah Griffiths, Angus Cargill, (fiction); Walter Donohue, (film); Julian Loose, Neil Belton, (nonfiction); Paul Keegan, (poetry); Belinda Matthews, (music). Faber & Faber have rejuvenated their nonfiction, music and children's titles in recent years and the film and drama lists remain market leaders. Publishes hardcover and paperback originals and reprints. Publishes 200 titles/year.

○ Faber & Faber will consider unsolicited proposals for poetry only.

HOW TO CONTACT *No unsolicited submissions.* Responds in 3 months to requested mss.

TERMS Pays royalty. Pays varying advances with each project. Book catalog available online.

TIPS Explore the website and downloadable book catalogues thoroughly to get a feel for the lists in all categories and genres.

FACTS ON FILE, INC.

Infobase Learning, 132 W. 31st St., 17th Floor, New York NY 10001. (800)322-8755. **Fax:** (800)678-3633. **E-mail:** llikoff@factsonfile.com; custserv@factson file.com. **Website:** www.factsonfile.com. **Contact:** Laurie Likoff, editorial director (science, fashion, natural history); Justine Ciovacco (science, nature, juvenile); James Chambers, trade editor (health, pop culture, true crime, sports); Jeff Soloway, executive editor (language/literature). Facts on File produces high-quality reference materials on a broad range of subjects for the school library market and the general nonfiction trade. Publishes hardcover originals and reprints. Publishes 135-150 titles/year. 25% from un-agented writers.

NONFICTION "We publish serious, informational books for a targeted audience. All our books must have strong library interest, but we also distribute books effectively to the trade. Our library books fit the junior and senior high school curriculum." No computer books, technical books, cookbooks, biographies (except YA), pop psychology, humor, fiction or poetry.

HOW TO CONTACT Submit outline and sample chapter with SASE. No submissions returned without SASE. Responds in 2 months to queries.

TERMS Pays 10% royalty on retail price. Pays $5,000-10,000 advance. Book catalog available free. Guidelines available online.

TIPS "Our audience is school and public libraries for our more reference-oriented books and libraries, schools and bookstores for our less reference-oriented informational titles."

FARRAR, STRAUS & GIROUX FOR YOUNG READERS

18 W. 18th St., New York NY 10011. (212)741-6900. **Fax:** (212)633-2427. **E-mail:** childrens-editorial@fsgbooks.com. **Website:** www.us.macmillan.com/FSGYoungReaders.aspx. **Contact:** Margaret Ferguson, Margaret Ferguson Books; Wesley Adams, executive editor; Janine O'Malley, creative director; Frances Foster, Frances Foster Books; Robbin Gourley, art director. Farrar title *How I Learned Geography*, by Uri Shulevitz, won a Caldecott Honor in 2009. Farrar/Frances Foster title *The Wall: Growing Up Behind the Iron Curtain*, by Peter Sís, won a Caldecott Honor Medal in 2008. Farrar/Melanie Kroupa title *Rex Zero and the End of the World* by Tim Wynne-Jones, won a Boston Globe-Horn Book Fiction and Poetry Honor Award in 2007. Farrar/Frances Foster title *Dreamquake: Book Two of the Dreamhunter Duet*, by Elizabeth Knox, won a Michael L. Printz Honor Award in 2008.

○ *As of January 2010, Farrar Straus & Giroux does not accept unsolicited manuscripts. "We recommend finding a literary agent to represent you and your work."*

FICTION All levels: all categories. "Original and well-written material for all ages." Recently published *The Cabinet of Wonders*, by Marie Rutkoski; *Last Night*, by Hyewon Yum.

NONFICTION All levels: all categories. "We publish only literary nonfiction."

ILLUSTRATION Works with 30-60 illustrators/year. Reviews ms/illustration packages from artists. Submit ms with 1 example of final art, remainder roughs. Do not send originals. Illustrations only: Query with tearsheets. Responds if interested in 3 months. Samples returned with SASE; samples sometimes filed.

TIPS "Study our catalog before submitting. We will see illustrators' portfolios by appointment. Don't ask for criticism and/or advice—due to the volume of submissions we receive, it's just not possible. Never send originals. Always enclose SASE."

FITZHENRY & WHITESIDE LTD.

195 Allstate Pkwy., Markham ON L3R 4T8, Canada. (905)477-9700; (800)387-9776. **Fax:** (905)477-9179. **E-mail:** fitzkids@fitzhenry.ca; godwit@fitzhenry.ca; charkin@fitzhenry.ca. **Website:** www.fitzhenry.ca/. **Contact:** Sharon Fitzhenry, president; Christie Harkin, children's publisher. Emphasis on Canadian authors and illustrators, subject or perspective. Publishes 15 titles/year. 10% of books from first-time authors.

HOW TO CONTACT Publishes book 1-2 years after acceptance.

ILLUSTRATION Works with approximately 10 illustrators/year. Reviews ms/illustration packages from artists. Submit outline and sample illustration (copy). Illustrations only: Query with samples and promo sheet. Samples not returned unless requested.

PHOTOGRAPHY Buys photos from freelancers. Buys stock and assigns work. Captions required. Uses b&w 8×10 prints; 35mm and 4×5 transparencies, 300+ dpi digital images. Submit stock photo list and promo piece.

TERMS Pays authors 8-10% royalty with escalations. Offers "respectable" advances for picture books, split 50/50 between author and illustrator. Pays illustrators by project and royalty. Pays photographers per photo.

TIPS "We respond to quality."

FIVE STAR PUBLICATIONS, INC.

P.O. Box 6698, Chandler AZ 85246. (480)940-8182. **Fax:** (480)940-8787. **E-mail:** info@fivestarpublications.com. **Website:** www.fivestarpublications.com.

Publishes 7 middle readers/year. **Contact:** Linda F. Radke, president. "Helps produce and market award-winning books."

◯ "Five Star Publications publishes and promotes award-winning fiction, nonfiction, cookbooks, children's literature and professional guides. More information about Five Star Publications, Inc., a 25-year leader in the book publishing/book marketing industry, is available online at our website." Other websites: www.LittleFivestar.com, www.FiveStarLegends.com; www.FiveStarSleuths.com; www.SixPointsPress.com.

ILLUSTRATION Works with 3 illustrators/year. Reviews ms/illustration packages from artists. Query. Illustrations only: Query with samples. Responds only if interested. Samples filed.

PHOTOGRAPHY Buys stock and assigns work. Works on assignment only. Submit letter.

TIPS Features the Purple Dragonfly Book Awards and Royal Dragonfly Book Awards, which were conceived and designed with children in mind. "Not only do we want to recognize and honor accomplished authors in the field of children's literature, but we also want to highlight and reward up-and-coming newly published authors, as well as younger published writers. In our efforts to include everyone, the awards are divided into distinct subject categories, ranging from books on the environment and cooking to books on sports and family issues. (Please see the complete categories list on the entry form on our website.)

FLUX

Llewellyn Worldwide, Ltd., 2143 Wooddale Dr., Woodbury, MN 55125. (877)639-9753. **Fax:** (651)291-1908. **Website:** www.fluxnow.com. **Contact:** Brian Farrey, acquisitions editor. "Flux seeks to publish authors who see YA as a point of view, not a reading level. We look for books that try to capture a slice of teenage experience, whether in real or imagined worlds." Publishes 21 titles/year. 50% of books from first-time authors.

◯ *Does not accept unsolicited mss.*

FICTION Young Adults: adventure, contemporary, fantasy, history, humor, problem novels, religion, science fiction, sports, suspense. Average word length: 50,000.

TERMS Pays royalties of 10-15% based on wholesale price. Book catalog and guidelines available on website.

TIPS "Read contemporary teen books. Be aware of what else is out there. If you don't read teen books, you probably shouldn't write them. Know your audience. Write incredibly well. Do not condescend."

FREE SPIRIT PUBLISHING, INC.

217 5th Ave. N, Suite 200, Minneapolis, MN 55401. (612)338-2068. **Fax:** (612)337-5050. **E-mail:** acquisitions@freespirit.com. **Website:** www.freespirit.com. "We believe passionately in empowering kids to learn to think for themselves and make their own good choices." Publishes trade paperback originals and reprints. Publishes 12-18 titles/year. 5% of books from first-time authors. 75% from unagented writers.

◯ Free Spirit does not accept fiction, poetry or storybook submissions.

NONFICTION "Many of our authors are educators, mental health professionals, and youth workers involved in helping kids and teens." No fiction or picture storybooks, poetry, single biographies or autobiographies, books with mythical or animal characters, or books with religious or New Age content. "We are not looking for academic or religious materials, or books that analyze problems with the nation's school systems."

HOW TO CONTACT "Please review catalog and author guidelines (both available online) before submitting proposal." Reponds to queries in 4-6 months. "If you'd like material returned, enclose a SASE with sufficient postage." Accepts queries only—not submissions—by e-mail. Query with cover letter stating qualifications, intent, and intended audience and market analysis (how your book stands out from the field), along with outline, 2 sample chapters, rèsumè, SASE. For early childhood submissions, the entire mss is required. Do not send original copies of work.

ILLUSTRATION Works with 5 illustrators/year. Submit samples to creative director for consideration. If appropriate, samples will be kept on file and artist will be contacted if a suitable project comes up. Enclose SASE if you'd like materials returned.

PHOTOGRAPHY Uses stock photos. Does not accept photography submissions.

TERMS Pays advance. Book catalog and ms guidelines online.

TIPS "Our books are issue-oriented, jargon-free, and solution-focused. Our audience is children, teens, teachers, parents and youth counselors. We are especially concerned with kids' social and emotional well-being and look for books with ready-to-use strategies for coping with today's issues at home or in school—written in everyday language. We are not looking for academic or religious materials, or books that analyze problems with the nation's school systems. Instead, we want books that offer practical, positive advice so kids can help themselves, and parents and teachers can help kids succeed."

FREESTONE/PEACHTREE, JR.

1700 Chattahoochee Ave., Atlanta GA 30318. (404)876-8761. **Fax:** (404)875-2578. **E-mail:** hello@peachtree-online.com. **Website:** www.peachtree-online.com. **Contact:** Helen Harriss, acquisitions; Loraine Joyner, art director; Melanie McMahon Ives, production manager. Publishes 4-8 titles/year.

○ Freestone and Peachtree, Jr. are imprints of Peachtree Publishers. No e-mail or fax queries or submissions, please.

FICTION Middle Readers: adventure, animal, history, nature/environment, sports. Young Adults: fiction, history, biography, mystery, adventure. Does not want to see science fiction, religion, or romance. Recent publications for comparison are: *This Girl is Different* by JJ Johnson (ages 12-16, young adult), *The Cheshire Cheese Cat* by Carmen Agra Deedy and Randall Wright, illustrated by Barry Moser (ages 8 and up, middle reader), and *Grow* by Juanita Havill, illustrated by Stanislawa Kodman (middle reader, ages 8-12).

NONFICTION Picture books, young readers, middle readers, young adults: history, sports. Picture books: animal, health, multicultural, nature/environment, science, social issues, special needs.

HOW TO CONTACT Submit 3 sample chapters by postal mail only. No query necessary. Responds in 6 months-1 year. Publishes book 1-2 years after acceptance.

ILLUSTRATION Works with 10-20 illustrators/year. Responds only if interested. Samples not returned; samples filed. Originals returned at job's completion.

TERMS Pays authors royalty. Pays illustrators by the project or royalty. Pays photographers by the project or per photo.

FRONT STREET

Boyds Mills Press, 815 Church St., Honesdale PA 18431. **Website:** www.frontstreetbooks.com. **Contact:** Acquisitions Editor. "We are an independent publisher of books for children and young adults." Publishes hardcover originals and trade paperback reprints. Publishes 10-15 titles/year. 30% of books from first-time authors. 60% from unagented writers.

FICTION "Front Street features children's and young adult fiction, in hardcover and paperback, and a unique line of art- and design-driven picture books."

HOW TO CONTACT Query with first 3 chapters and a plot summary and label the package "Manuscript Submission." 2,000 queries received/year. 5,000 mss received/year. Responds in 3 months. Publishes 1 year after acceptance.

TERMS Pays royalty on retail price. Pays advance. Book catalog available online. Guidelines available online.

TIPS "Read through our recently published titles and review our website. Check to see what's on the market and in our catalog before submitting your story. Feel free to query us if you're not sure."

GIBBS SMITH

P.O. Box 667, Layton UT 84041. (801)544-9800. **Fax:** (801)544-8853. **E-mail:** info@gibbs-smith.com. **Website:** www.gibbs-smith.com. **Contact:** Suzanne Taylor, associate publisher and creative director (children's activity books); Jennifer Grillone, senior editor. Publishes 3 titles/year. 50% of books from first-time authors. 50% from unagented writers.

○ Gibbs Smith is not accepting fiction at this time.

NONFICTION Middle readers: activity, arts/crafts, cooking, how-to, nature/environment, science. Average word length: picture books—under 1,000 words; activity books—under 15,000 words. Recently published *Hiding in a Fort*, by G. Lawson Drinkard, illustrated by Fran Lee (ages 7-12); *Sleeping in a Sack: Camping Activities for Kids*, by Linda White, illustrated by Fran Lee (ages 7-12).

HOW TO CONTACT Gibbs Smith is not accepting fiction at this time.

NONFICTION: Submit an outline and writing samples for activity books; query for other types of books. Responds to queries and mss in 2 months. Publishes ms 1-2 years after acceptance.

ILLUSTRATION Works with 2 illustrators/year. Reviews ms/illustration packages from artists. Query.

Submit ms with 3-5 pieces of final art. Illustrations only: Query with samples; provide résumé, promo sheet, slides (duplicate slides, not originals). Responds only if interested. Samples returned with SASE; samples filed.

TERMS Pays illustrators by the project or royalty of 2% based on retail price. Sends galleys to authors; color proofs to illustrators. Original artwork returned at job's completion. Pays authors royalty of 2% based on retail price or work purchased outright ($500 minimum). Offers advances (average amount: $2,000). Book catalog available for 9×12 SAE and $2.30 postage. Ms guidelines available online.

TIPS "We target ages 5-11. We do not publish young adult novels or chapter books."

GRAPHIA

222 Berkeley St., Boston MA 02116. (617)351-5000. **E-mail:** anna.meier@hmhpub.com. **Website:** www. graphiabooks.com. **Contact:** Anna Meier. "Graphia publishes quality paperbacks for today's teen readers, ages 14 and up. From fiction to nonfiction, poetry to graphic novels, Graphia runs the gamut, all unified by the quality of writing that is the hallmark of this imprint."

FICTION Young adults: adventure, contemporary, fantasy, history, humor, multicultural, poetry. Recently published: *The Off Season*, by Catherine Murdock; *Come in from the Cold*, by Marsha Qualey; *Breaking Up is Hard to Do*, with stories by Niki Burnham, Terri Clark, Ellen Hopkins, and Lynda Sandoval; *Zahrah the Windseeker,* by Nnedi Okorafor-Mbachu.

NONFICTION Young adults: biography, history, multicultural, nature/environment, science, social issues.

HOW TO CONTACT Query. Responds to queries in up to 3 months.

ILLUSTRATION Do not send original artwork or slides. Send color photocopies, tearsheets or photos to Art Dept. Include SASE if you would like your samples mailed back to you.

◯ GREAT SOURCE EDUCATION GROUP

Houghton Mifflin Harcourt, 181 Ballardvale St., Wilmington MA 01887. **Website:** www.greatsource. com. Great Source's main publishing efforts are instructional and focus on the school market. For all materials, the reading level must be appropriate to the skill level of the students and the nature of the materials.

NONFICTION Material must be appealing to students, proven classroom effective, and consistent with current research.

TERMS Guidelines available online.

GREENHAVEN PRESS

27500 Drake Rd., Farmington Hills MI 48331. **E-mail:** betz.deschenes@cengage.com. **Website:** www. gale.com/greenhaven. **Contact:** Betz Des Chenes. Publishes 220 young adult academic reference titles/year. 50% of books by first-time authors. Greenhaven continues to print quality nonfiction anthologies for libraries and classrooms. Our well-known Opposing Viewpoints series is highly respected by students and librarians in need of material on controversial social issues. Greenhaven accepts no unsolicited manuscripts. Send query, resume, and list of published works by e-mail. Work purchased outright from authors; write-for-hire, flat fee.

NONFICTION Young adults (high school): controversial issues, social issues, history, literature, science, environment, health. Recently published (series): Issues That Concern You; Writing the Critical Essay: An Opening Viewpoint Guide; Introducing Issues with Opposing Viewpoints; Social Issues in Literature; and Perspectives on Diseases and Disorders.

GREENWILLOW BOOKS

HarperCollins Publishers, 10 E. 53rd St., New York NY 10022. (212)207-7000. **Website:** www.greenwillowblog.com; www.harpercollins.com. **Contact:** Virginia Duncan, vice president/publisher; Paul Zakris, art director. Publishes hardcover originals, paperbacks, e-books, and reprints. Publishes 40-50 titles/year.

◯ Does not accept unsolicited mss. "Unsolicited mail will not be opened and will not be returned."

HOW TO CONTACT Publishes ms 2 years after acceptance.

TERMS Pays 10% royalty on wholesale price for first-time authors. Average advance: variable.

ⓐ GROSSET & DUNLAP PUBLISHERS

Penguin Putnam Inc., 375 Hudson St., New York NY 10014. **Website:** www.penguingroup.com. **Contact:** Francesco Sedita, president/publisher. Grosset & Dunlap publishes children's books that show children that reading is fun, with books that speak to their interests, and that are affordable so that children can build a home library of their own. "Grosset & Dunlap publishes high-interest, affordable books for children ages 0-10 years. We focus on original series, licensed properties, readers and novelty books." Publishes hardcover (few) and mass market paperback originals. Publishes 140 titles/year.

FICTION All book formats except for picture books. Submit a summary and the first chapter or two for longer works. Recently published series: Frankly Frannie; George Brown, Class Clown; Bedeviled; Hank Zipzer; Camp Confidential; Katie Kazoo, Switcheroo; Magic Kitten; Magic Puppy; The Hardy Boys; Nancy Drew; The Little Engine That Could. Upcoming series: Splurch Academy for Disruptive Boys; Gladiator Boy; Dinkin Dings; Hello, Gorgeous!. *Licensed Series:* Angelina Ballerina; Disney Club Penguin; Charlie & Lola; Star Wars: The Clone Wars; WWE; Disney's Classic Pooh; Max & Ruby; The Penguins of Madagascar; Batman: The Brave and the Bold; Strawberry Shortcake.

HOW TO CONTACT. "We do not accept e-mail submissions. Unsolicited manuscripts usually receive a response in 6-8 weeks."

TERMS Pays royalty. Pays advance.

⊙ GROUNDWOOD BOOKS

110 Spadina Ave. Suite 801, Toronto ON M5V 2K4, Canada. (416)363-4343. **Fax:** (416)363-1017. **E-mail:** ssutherland@groundwoodbooks.com. **Website:** www. houseofanansi.com. Publishes 13 picture books/year; 3 young readers/year; 5 middle readers/year; 5 young adult titles/year, approximately 2 nonfiction titles/year.

FICTION Does not accept unsolicited mss for picture books. Recently published: *One Year in Coal Harbour*, by Polly Horvath; *That Night's Train*, by Ahmad Akbarpour; *Nobody Knows*, by Shelley Tanaka; *My Name is Parvana*, by Deborah Ellis; *My Book of Life by Angel*, by Martine Leavitt.

NONFICTION Recently published: *La Malinche*, by Francisco Serrano, illustrated by Pablo Serrano.

HOW TO CONTACT Submit synopsis and sample chapters. Responds to mss in 4-6 months.

TERMS Offers advances. Visit website for guidelines: www.houseofanansi.com/Groundwoodsubmissions. aspx.

GRYPHON HOUSE, INC.

P.O. Box 10, 6848 Leon's Way, Lewisville NC 27023. **Website:** www.gryphonhouse.com. **Contact:** Kathy Charner, editor-in-chief. "Gryphon House publishes books that teachers and parents of young children (birth-age 8) consider essential to their daily lives." Publishes parent and teacher resource books, textbooks. Recently published *Reading Games*, by Jackie Silberg; *Primary Art*, by MaryAnn F. Kohl; *Teaching Young Children with Autism Spectrum Disorder*, by Clarissa Willis; *The Complete Resource Book for Infants*, by Pam Schiller. "At Gryphon House, our goal is to publish books that help teachers and parents enrich the lives of children from birth through age 8. We strive to make our books useful for teachers at all levels of experience, as well as for parents, caregivers, and anyone interested in working with children." Query. Submit outline/synopsis and 2 sample chapters. Responds to queries/mss in 6 months. Publishes a book 18 months after acceptance. Will consider simultaneous submissions, e-mail submissions. Book catalog and ms guidelines available via website or with SASE. "We are looking for books of creative, participatory learning experiences that have a common conceptual theme to tie them together. The books should be on subjects that parents or teachers want to do on a daily basis." Publishes trade paperback originals. Publishes 12-15 titles/year.

NONFICTION Currently emphasizing social-emotional intelligence and classroom management; de-emphasizing literacy after-school activities.

HOW TO CONTACT "We prefer to receive a letter of inquiry and/or a proposal, rather than the entire manuscript. Please include: the proposed title, the purpose of the book, table of contents, introductory material, 20-40 sample pages of the actual book. In addition, please describe the book, including the intended audience, why teachers will want to buy it, how it is different from other similar books already published, and what qualifications you possess that make you the appropriate person to write the book. If you have a writing sample that demonstrates that you write clear, compelling prose, please include it with your letter." Responds in 3-6 months to queries.

ILLUSTRATION Works with 4-5 illustrators/year. Uses b&w realistic artwork only. Query with samples, promo sheet. Responds in 2 months. Samples returned with SASE; samples filed. Pays illustrators by the project.

PHOTOGRAPHY Pays photographers by the project or per photo. Sends edited ms copy to authors. Original artwork returned at job's completion.

TERMS Pays royalty on wholesale price. Guidelines available online.

HARPERTEEN

10 E. 53rd St., New York NY 10022. (212)207-7000. **Fax:** (212)702-2583. **E-mail:** Jennifer.Deason@harpercollins.com. **Website:** www.harpercollins.com. HarperTeen is a teen imprint that publishes hardcovers, paperback reprints and paperback originals. Publishes 100 titles/year.

○ *HarperCollins Children's Books is not accepting unsolicited and/or unagented mss or queries. Unfortunately the volume of these submissions is so large that they cannot receive the attention they deserve. Such submissions will not be reviewed or returned.*

HAYES SCHOOL PUBLISHING CO. INC.

321 Pennwood Ave., Wilkinsburg PA 15221. (412)371-2373. **Fax:** (800)543-8771. **E-mail:** chayes@hayespub.com; info@hayespub.com. **Website:** www.hayespub.com. **Contact:** Clair N. Hayes. Produces folders, workbooks, stickers, certificates. Wants to see supplementary teaching aids for grades K-12. Interested in all subject areas. Will consider simultaneous and electronic submissions. Query with description or complete ms. Responds in 6 weeks. SASE for return of submissions.

ILLUSTRATION Works with 3-4 illustrators/year. Responds in 6 weeks. Samples returned with SASE; samples filed. Originals not returned at job's completion.

TERMS Work purchased outright. Purchases all rights.

HOLIDAY HOUSE, INC.

425 Madison Ave., New York NY 10017. (212)688-0085. **Fax:** (212)421-6134. **E-mail:** info@holidayhouse.com. **Website:** www.holidayhouse.com. **Contact:** Mary Cash, editor-in-chief. "Holiday House publishes children's and young adult books for the school and library markets. We have a commitment to publishing first-time authors and illustrators. We specialize in quality hardcovers from picture books to young adult, both fiction and nonfiction, primarily for the school and library market." Publishes hardcover originals and paperback reprints. Publishes 50 titles/year. 5% of books from first-time authors. 50% from unagented writers. "We do not publish mass-market books, including, but not limited to, board books, pop-ups,

activity books, sticker books, coloring books, series books, licensed books, or paperback originals."

FICTION Children's books only.

HOW TO CONTACT "Due to the volume of manuscripts we are receiving, Holiday House will no longer accept multiple submissions. Please send a query letter only, describing what the manuscript is about, for picture books as well as books for older readers. We do not accept certified or registered mail, nor do we consider submissions by e-mail or fax." A SASE or postcard must be included or there will be no reply. Responds in 2 months.

TERMS Pays royalty on list price, range varies. Agent's royalty. Guidelines for #10 SASE.

TIPS "We need manuscripts with strong stories and writing."

HOUGHTON MIFFLIN HARCOURT BOOKS FOR CHILDREN

Imprint of Houghton Mifflin Trade & Reference Division, 222 Berkeley St., Boston MA 02116. (617)351-5000; (800)225-3362. **Fax:** (617)351-1111. **E-mail:** children's_books@hmco.com. **Website:** www.houghtonmifflinbooks.com. **Contact:** Kate O'Sullivan, executive editor; Margaret Raymo, senior executive editor. Houghton Mifflin Harcourt gives shape to ideas that educate, inform, and above all, delight. Publishes hardcover originals and trade paperback originals and reprints. Publishes 100 titles/year. 10% of books from first-time authors. 60% from unagented writers.

○ Does not respond to or return mss unless interested.

NONFICTION Interested in innovative books and subjects about which the author is passionate.

HOW TO CONTACT Submit complete ms. Query with SASE. Submit sample chapters, synopsis. Does not accept submissions by fact or email. Complete guidelines available on website. 5,000 queries received/year. 14,000 mss received/year. Responds in 4-6 months to queries. Publishes ms 2 years after acceptance.

TERMS Pays 5-10% royalty on retail price. Pays variable advance. Guidelines available online.

IDEALS PUBLICATIONS INC.

39 Old Ridgebury Rd., Suite 2AB, Danbury, CT 06810.. (800)586-2572. **E-mail:** idealsinfo@guideposts.org. **Website:** www.idealsbooks.com. "Ideals Publications publishes 20-25 new children's titles a year, primarily for 2-8 year-olds. Our backlist includes more than 400

titles, and we publish picture books, activity books, board books, and novelty and sound books covering a wide array of topics, such as Bible stories, holidays, early learning, history, family relationships, and values. Our bestselling titles include *The Story of Christmas, The Story of Easter, Seaman's Journal, How Do I Love You?, God Made You Special,* and *A View at the Zoo.* Through our dedication to publishing high-quality and engaging books, we never forget our obligation to our littlest readers to help create those special moments with books."

FICTION Ideals Children's Books publishes fiction and nonfiction picture books for children ages 4 to 8. Subjects include holiday, inspirational, and patriotic themes; relationships and values; and general fiction. Mss should be no longer than 800 words. CandyCane Press publishes board books and novelty books for children ages 2 to 5. Subject matter is similar to Ideals Children's Books, with a focus on younger children. Mss should be no longer than 250 words.

ILLUMINATION ARTS

P.O. Box 1865, Bellevue WA 98009. (425)968-5097. **Website:** www.illumin.com. **Contact:** John M. Thompson, president.

○ "Note that our submission review process is on hold until notice on website so submissions are not currently being reviewed." Normal requirements include no electronic or CD submissions for text or art. Considers simultaneous submissions.

FICTION Word length: Prefers under 1,000, but will consider up to 1,500 words.

TERMS Pays authors and illustrators royalty based on wholesale price. Book fliers available for SASE.

TIPS "Read our books or visit website to see what our books are like. Follow submission guidelines found on website. Be patient. We are unable to track unsolicited submissions."

IMPACT PUBLISHERS, INC.

P.O. Box 6016, Atascadero CA 93423. (805)466-5917. **E-mail:** submissions@impactpublishers.com. **Website:** www.impact publishers.com. **Contact:** Freeman Porter, submissions editor. Imprints: Little Imp Books, Rebuilding Books, The Practical Therapist Series. "Our purpose is to make the best human services expertise available to the widest possible audience. We publish only popular psychology and self-help materials written in everyday language by professionals with advanced degrees and significant experience in the human services." Publishes 3-5 titles/year. 20% of books from first-time authors.

NONFICTION Young readers, middle readers, young adults: self-help. Recently published *Jigsaw Puzzle Family: The Stepkids' Guide to Fitting It Together,* by Cynthia MacGregor (ages 8-12, children's/divorce/emotions).

HOW TO CONTACT Query with samples, cover letter, résumé. Responds to queries/mss in 3 months.

ILLUSTRATION Works with 1 illustrator/year. Not accepting freelance illustrator queries.

TERMS Pays authors royalty of 10-12%. Offers advances. Book catalog for #10 SASE with 2 first-class stamps. Guidelines for SASE.

TIPS "Please do not submit fiction, poetry or narratives."

JEWISH LIGHTS PUBLISHING

LongHill Partners, Inc., Sunset Farm Offices, Rt. 4, P.O. Box 237, Woodstock VT 05091. (802)457-4000. **Fax:** (802)457-4004. **E-mail:** editorial@jewishlights.com. **Website:** www.jewishlights.com. **Contact:** Tim Holtz, art acquisitions. "Jewish Lights publishes books for people of all faiths and all backgrounds who yearn for books that attract, engage, educate and spiritually inspire. Our authors are at the forefront of spiritual thought and deal with the quest for the self and for meaning in life by drawing on the Jewish wisdom tradition. Our books cover topics including history, spirituality, life cycle, children, self-help, recovery, theology and philosophy. We do not publish autobiography, biography, fiction, haggadot, poetry or cookbooks. At this point we plan to do only two books for children annually, and one will be for younger children (ages 4-10)." Publishes hardcover and trade paperback originals, trade paperback reprints. Publishes 30 titles/year. 50% of books from first-time authors. 75% from unagented writers.

FICTION Picture books, young readers, middle readers: spirituality. "We are not interested in anything other than spirituality." Recently published *God's Paintbrush,* by Sandy Eisenberg Sasso, illustrated by Annette Compton (ages 4-9).

NONFICTION Picture book, young readers, middle readers: activity books, spirituality. Recently published *When a Grandparent Dies: A Kid's Own Workbook for Dealing with Shiva and the Year Beyond,* by

Nechama Liss-Levinson, Ph.D. (ages 7-11); *Tough Questions Jews Ask: A Young Adult's Guide to Building a Jewish Life*, by Rabbi Edward Feinstein (ages 12 and up).

HOW TO CONTACT Query with outline/synopsis and 2 sample chapters; submit complete ms for picture books. Include SASE. Responds to queries/mss in 4 months. Publishes ms 1 year after acceptance.

TERMS Pays authors royalty of 10% of revenue received; 15% royalty for subsequent printings. Book catalog and ms guidelines online.

TIPS "We publish books for all faiths and backgrounds that also reflect the Jewish wisdom tradition. Explain in your cover letter why you're submitting your project to us in particular. Make sure you know what we publish."

JOURNEYFORTH

Imprint of BJU Press, 1700 Wade Hampton Blvd., Greenville SC 29614. (864)242-5100, ext. 4350; (800) 845-5731. **Fax:** (864)298-0268. **E-mail:** jb@bju.edu. **Website:** www.journeyforth.com. **Contact:** Nancy Lohr, acquisitions editor. Specializes in trade books. Publishes 1 picture book/year; 2 young readers/year; 4 middle readers/year; 4 young adult titles/year. 10% of books by first-time authors. "We aim to produce well-written books for readers of varying abilities and interests and fully consistent with biblical worldview." "Review our backlist to be sure your work is a good fit." "Small independent publisher of trustworthy novels and biographies for readers pre-school through high school from a conservative Christian perspective, Christian living books, and Bible studies for adults." Publishes paperback originals. Publishes 25 titles/year. 10% of books from first-time authors. 8% from unagented writers.

FICTION Young readers, middle readers, young adults: adventure, animal, contemporary, fantasy, folktales, history, humor, multicultural, nature/environment, problem novels, suspense/mystery. Average word length: young readers—10,000-12,000; middle readers—10,000-40,000; young adult/teens—40,000-60,000. Our fiction is all based on a moral and Christian worldview. Does not want short stories.

NONFICTION Young readers, middle readers, young adult: biography. Average word length: young readers—10,000-12,000; middle readers—10,000-40,000; young adult/teens—40,000-60,000. Nonfiction Christian living, Bible studies, church and ministry, church history. We produce books from a conservative Christian worldview.

HOW TO CONTACT Fiction: Query or submit outline/synopsis and 5 sample chapters. "Do not send stories with magical elements. We are not currently accepting picture books. We do not publish: romance, science fiction, poetry and drama." Nonfiction: Query or submit outline/synopsis and 5 sample chapters. Responds to queries in 1 month; mss in 3 months. Publishes book 12-18 months after acceptance. Will consider previously published work.

ILLUSTRATION Works with 2-4 illustrators/year. Query with samples. Send promo sheet; will review website portfolio if applicable. Responds only if interested. Samples returned with SASE; samples filed.

TERMS Pays authors royalty based on wholesale price. Pays illustrators by the project. Originals returned to artist at job's completion. Pays royalty.

TIPS "Study the publisher's guidelines. No picture books and no submissions by e-mail." Book catalog available free. Guidelines available online.

◯ KAMEHAMEHA PUBLISHING

567 South King St., Suite 118, Honolulu HI 96813. (808)523-6200. **E-mail:** publishing@ksbe.edu. **Website:** www.kamehamehapublishing.org. "Kamehameha Schools Press publishes in the areas of Hawaiian history, Hawaiian culture, Hawaiian language and Hawaiian studies."

FICTION Young readers, middle readers, young adults: biography, history, multicultural, Hawaiian folklore.

NONFICTION Young reader, middle readers, young adults: biography, history, multicultural, Hawaiian folklore.

HOW TO CONTACT Responds in 3 months to queries and mss. Publishes ms 2 years after acceptance.

ILLUSTRATION Uses color and b&w artwork. Illustrations only: Query with samples. Responds only if interested. Samples not returned.

TERMS Work purchased outright from authors or by royalty agreement. Call or write for book catalog.

TIPS "Writers and illustrators must be knowledgeable in Hawaiian history/culture and be able to show credentials to validate their proficiency. Greatly prefer to work with writers/illustrators available in the Honolulu area."

A B KANE/MILLER BOOK PUBLISHERS

Kane/Miller: A Division of EDC Publishing, 4901 Morena Blvd., Suite 213, San Diego CA 92117. (858)456-0540. **Fax:** (858)456-9641. **E-mail:** info@kanemiller.com. **E-mail:** submissions@kanemiller.com. **Website:** www.kanemiller.com. **Contact:** Kira Lynn, editorial department. "Kane/Miller Book Publishers is a division of EDC Publishing, specializing in award-winning children's books from around the world. Our books bring the children of the world closer to each other, sharing stories and ideas, while exploring cultural differences and similarities. Although we continue to look for books from other countries, we are now actively seeking works that convey cultures and communities within the US. We are looking for picture book fiction and nonfiction on those subjects that may be defined as particularly American: sports such as baseball, historical events, American biographies, American folk tales, etc. We are committed to expanding our early and middlegrade fiction list. We're interested in great stories with engaging characters in all genres (mystery, fantasy, adventure, historical, etc.) and, as with picture books, especially those with particularly American subjects. All submissions sent via USPS should be sent to: Editorial Department. Please do not send anything requiring a signature. Work submitted for consideration may also be sent in the body of an e-mail. Please do not send attachments or links. Please send either the complete picture book ms, the published book (with a summary and outline in English, if that is not the language of origin) or a synopsis of the work and two sample chapters. Do not send originals. Illustrators may send color copies, tear sheets, or other non-returnable illustration samples. If you have a website with additional samples of your work, please include the web address. Please do not send original artwork, or samples on CD. A SASE must be included if you send your submission via USPS; otherwise you will not receive a reply. If we wish to follow up, we will notify you."

O   "We like to think that a child reading a Kane/Miller book will see parallels between his own life and what might be the unfamiliar setting and characters of the story. And that by seeing how a character who is somehow or in some way dissimilar—an outsider—finds a way to fit comfortably into a culture or community or situation while maintaining a healthy sense of self and self-dignity, she might be empowered to do the same."

FICTION Picture Books: concept, contemporary, health, humor, multicultural. Young Readers: contemporary, multicultural, suspense. Middle Readers: contemporary, humor, multicultural, suspense.

HOW TO CONTACT Responds in 90 days.

KAR-BEN PUBLISHING

Lerner Publishing Group, 1251 Washington Ave. N., Minneapolis MN 55401. (612)332-3344, ext. 229; (800)452-7736. **Fax:** 612-332-7615. **E-mail:** Editorial@Karben.com. **Website:** www.karben.com. Publishes hardcover, trade paperback and electronic originals. Publishes 10-15 titles/year. 20% of books from first-time authors. 70% from unagented writers.

FICTION "We seek picture book mss of about 1,000 words on Jewish-themed topics for children." Picture books: adventure, concept, folktales, history, humor, multicultural, religion, special needs; must be on a Jewish theme. Average word length: picture books 1,000. Recently published *Engineer Ari and the Rosh Hashanah Ride*, by Deborah Bodin Cohen, illustrated by Shahar Kober; and *The Wedding That Saved a Town*, by Yale Strom, illustrated by Jenya Prosmitsky.

NONFICTION "In addition to traditional Jewish-themed stories about Jewish holidays, history, folktales and other subjects, we especially seek stories that reflect the rich diversity of the contemporary Jewish community." Picture books, young readers: activity books, arts/crafts, biography, careers, concept, cooking, history, how-to, multicultural, religion, social issues, special needs; must be of Jewish interest. No textbooks, games, or educational materials.

HOW TO CONTACT Submit full ms. Picture books only. Submit completed ms. 800 mss received/year. Responds in 6 weeks. Most manuscripts published within 2 years.

TERMS Pays 3-5% royalty on NET price. Pays $500-2,500 advance. Book catalog available online; free upon request. Guidelines available online.

TIPS "Authors: Do a literature search to make sure similar title doesn't already exist. Illustrators: Look at our online catalog for a sense of what we like—bright colors and lively composition."

O KIDS CAN PRESS

25 Dockside Dr., Toronto, Ontario M5A 0B5, Canada. (416)479-7000. **Fax:** (416)960-5437. **E-mail:** webmas-

ter@kidscan.com; kkalmar@kidscan.com. **Website:** www.kidscanpress.com. U.S. address: 2250 Military Rd., Tonawanda, NY 14150. **Contact:** Corus Quay, acquisitions.

◌ *Kids Can Press is currently accepting unsolicited mss from Canadian adult authors only.*

FICTION Picture books, young readers: concepts. "We do not accept young adult fiction or fantasy novels for any age." Adventure, animal, contemporary, folktales, history, humor, multicultural, nature/environment, special needs, sports, suspense/mystery. Average word length: picture books—1,000-2,000; young readers—750-1,500; middle readers—0,000-15,000; young adults—over 15,000. Recently published *Rosie & Buttercup* by Chieri Ugaki, illustrated by Shephane Jorisch (picture book); *The Landing* by John Ibbitson (novel); *Scaredy Squirrel* by Melanie Watt, illustrated by Melanie Watt (picture book).

NONFICTION Picture books: activity books, animal, arts/crafts, biography, careers, concept, health, history, hobbies, how-to, multicultural, nature/environment, science, social issues, special needs, sports. Young readers: activity books, animal, arts/crafts, biography, careers, concept, history, hobbies, how-to, multicultural. Middle readers: cooking, music/dance. Average word length: picture books 500-1,250; young readers 750-2,000; middle readers 5,000-15,000. Recently published *The Kids' Book of Canadian Geography*, by Jane Drake and Ann Love, illustrated by Heather Collins (informational activity); *Science, Nature, Environment*; *It's Moving Day*, by Pamela Hickman, illustrated by Geraldo Valerio (animal/nature); *Everywear*, by Ellen Warwick, illustrated by Bernice Lum (craft book).

HOW TO CONTACT Submit outline/synopsis and 2-3 sample chapters. For picture books submit complete ms. Responds in 6 months only if interesed. Publishes book 18-24 months after acceptance.

ILLUSTRATION Works with 40 illustrators/year. Reviews ms/illustration packages from artists. Send color copies of illustration portfolio, cover letter outlining other experience. Contact: Art Director. Illustrations only: Send tearsheets, color photocopies. Responds only if interested.

KREGEL PUBLICATIONS

Kregel, Inc., P.O. Box 2607, Grand Rapids MI 49501. (616)451-4775. **Fax:** (616)451-9330. **E-mail:** kregel books@kregel.com. **Website:** www.kregelpublica

tions.com. **Contact:** Dennis R. Hillman, publisher. "Our mission as an evangelical Christian publisher is to provide—with integrity and excellence—trusted, Biblically based resources that challenge and encourage individuals in their Christian lives. Works in theology and Biblical studies should reflect the historic, orthodox Protestant tradition." Publishes hardcover and trade paperback originals and reprints. Publishes 90 titles/year. 20% of books from first-time authors. 35% from unagented writers.

FICTION Fiction should be geared toward the evangelical Christian market. Wants books with fast-paced, contemporary storylines presenting a strong Christian message in an engaging, entertaining style.

NONFICTION "We serve evangelical Christian readers and those in career Christian service."

HOW TO CONTACT Publishes ms 16 months after acceptance.

TERMS Pays royalty on wholesale price. Pays negotiable advance. Guidelines available online.

TIPS "Our audience consists of conservative, evangelical Christians, including pastors and ministry students."

WENDY LAMB BOOKS

Imprint of Random House Children's Books/Random House, Inc., 1745 Broadway, New York NY 10019. (212)782-9000. **Fax:** (212)782-9452. **E-mail:** wlamb@randomhouse.com; rhkidspublicity@randomhouse.com. **Website:** www.randomhouse.com. "Query letter with SASE for reply. A query letter should briefly describe the book you have written, the intended age group, and your brief biography and publishing credits, if any. Please send the first 10 pages (or to the end of the chapter) of your manuscript. Our turnaround time is approximately 4-8 weeks." Publishes hardcover originals.

◌ Literary fiction and nonfiction for readers 8-15.

FICTION Recently published *When You Reach Me*, by Rebecca Stead; *Love, Aubrey*, by Suzanne LaFleur; *Eyes of the Emperor*, by Graham Salisbury; *A Brief Chapter in My Impossible Life*, by Dana Reinhardt; *What They Found: Love on 145th Street*, by Walter Dean Myers; *Eleven*, by Patricia Reilly Giff. Other WLB authors include Christopher Paul Curtis, Gary Paulsen, Donna Jo Napoli, Peter Dickinson, Marthe Jocelyn, Graham McNamee.

TERMS Pays royalty. Guidelines for #10 SASE.

TIPS "Please note that we do not publish picture books. Before you submit, please take a look at some of our recent titles to get an idea of what we publish."

Ⓐ LAUREL-LEAF

Imprint of Random House Children's Books/Random House, Inc., 1745 Broadway, New York NY 10019. (212)782-9000. **Website:** www.randomhouse. com/teens.

Ⓠ   Quality reprint paperback imprint for young adult paperback books. *Does not accept unsolicited mss.*

⊕ LEDGE HILL PUBLISHING

P.O. Box 337, Alton NH 03809. (603)998-6801. **E-mail:** info@ledge hillpublishing.com. **Website:** www.ledgehillpublish ing.com. Publishes hardcover, trade paperback, and mass market paperback originals. Publishes 10-15 titles/year. 100% of books from first-time authors. 100% from unagented writers.

HOW TO CONTACT Submit proposal package, including syopsis and 4 sample chapters or submit complete ms. 20-40 queries received/year. 15-30 mss received/year. Responds in 1 month to queries and proposals, 2 months to mss. Publishes ms 3 months after acceptance.

TERMS Pays 2-15% royalty. Book catalog available online at website. Guidelines free on request by e-mail or online at website.

LEE & LOW BOOKS

95 Madison Ave., #1205, New York NY 10016. (212)779-4400. **E-mail:** general@leeandlow.com. **Website:** www.leeandlow.com. **Contact:** Louise May, vice president/editorial director. (multicultural children's fiction/nonfiction). "Our goals are to meet a growing need for books that address children of color, and to present literature that all children can identify with. We only consider multicultural children's books. Currently emphasizing material for 5-12 year olds. Sponsors a yearly New Voices Award for first-time picture book authors of color. Contest rules online at website or for SASE." Publishes hardcover originals and trade paperback reprints. Publishes 12-14 titles/year. 20% of books from first-time authors. 50% from unagented writers.

FICTION Picture books, young readers: anthology, contemporary, history, multicultural, poetry. Picture book, middle reader: contemporary, history, multicultural, nature/environment, poetry, sports. Average word length: picture books—1,000-1,500 words. Recently published *Gracias Thanks*, by Pat Mora; *Balarama*, by Ted and Betsy Lewin; *Yasmin's Hammer*, by Ann Malaspina; *Only One Year*, by Andrea Cheng (chapter book). "We do not publish folklore or animal stories."

NONFICTION Picture books: concept. Picture books, middle readers: biography, history, multicultural, science and sports. Average word length: picture books-1,500-3,000. Recently published *Seeds of Change*, by Jen Cullerton Johnson; *Sharing Our Homeland*, by Trish Marx.

HOW TO CONTACT Submit complete ms. Submit complete ms. Receives 100 queries/year; 1,200 mss/year. Responds in 6 months to mss if interested. Publishes book 2 years after acceptance.

ILLUSTRATION Works with 12-14 illustrators/year. Uses color artwork only. Reviews ms/illustration packages from artists. Contact: Louise May. Illustrations only: Query with samples, résumé, promo sheet and tearsheets. Responds only if interested. Samples returned with SASE; samples filed. Original artwork returned at job's completion.

PHOTOGRAPHY Buys photos from freelancers. Works on assignment only. Model/property releases required. Submit cover letter, résumé, promo piece and book dummy.

TERMS Pays net royalty. Pays authors advances against royalty. Pays illustrators advance against royalty. Photographers paid advance against royalty. Book catalog available online. Guidelines available online or by written request with SASE.

TIPS "Check our website to see the kinds of books we publish. Do not send mss that don't fit our mission."

LEGACY PRESS

P.O. Box 261129, San Diego CA 92196. (858)277-1167. **E-mail:** john.gregory@rainbowpublishers.com. **Website:** www.rainbowpublishers.com; www.leg acypresskids.com. Publishes 4 young readers/year; 4 middle readers/year; 4 young adult titles/year. 50% of books by first-time authors. "Our mission is to publish Bible-based teacher resource materials that contribute to and inspire spiritual growth and development in kids ages 2-12."

NONFICTION Young readers, middle readers, young adult/teens: activity books, arts/crafts, how-to, reference, religion.

HOW TO CONTACT Responds to queries in 6 weeks, mss in 3 months.

TERMS For authors work purchased outright (range: $500 and up). Pays illustrators by the project (range: $300 and up). Sends galleys to authors.

TIPS "Our Rainbow imprint publishes reproducible books for teachers of children in Christian ministries, including crafts, activities, games and puzzles. Our Legacy imprint publishes titles for children such as devotionals, fiction and Christian living. Please write for guidelines and study the market before submitting material."

LERNER PUBLISHING GROUP

1251 Washington Ave. N., Minneapolis MN 55401. (800)452-7236; (612)332-3344. **Fax:** (612)337-7615. **E-mail:** editorial@karben.com; photoresearch@lernerbooks.com. **Website:** www.karben.com; www.lernerbooks.com. Primarily publishes books for children ages 7-18. List includes titles in geography, natural and physical science, current events, ancient and modern history, high interest, sports, world cultures, and numerous biography series. **Contact:** director of photo research.

Starting in 2007, Lerner Publishing Group no longer accepts submission in any of their imprints except for Kar-Ben Publishing.

HOW TO CONTACT "We will continue to seek targeted solicitations at specific reading levels and in specific subject areas. The company will list these targeted solicitations on our website and in national newsletters, such as the SCBWI *Bulletin*."

ARTHUR A. LEVINE BOOKS

Scholastic, Inc., 557 Broadway, New York NY 10012. (212)343-4436. **Fax:** (212)343-6143. **E-mail:** arthuralevinebooks@scholastic.com. **Website:** www.arthuralevinebooks.com. **Contact:** Arthur A. Levine, vice president/publisher; Cheryl Klein, executive editor; Emily Clement, associate editor. Imprint of Scholastic, Inc. Publishes hardcover, paperback, and e-book editions.

FICTION "Arthur A. Levine is looking for distinctive literature, for children and young adults, for whatever's extraordinary." Averages 18-20 total titles/year.

HOW TO CONTACT Please follow submission guidelines at www.arthuralevinebooks.com/submission.asp. Responds in 1 month to queries; 5 months to mss. Publishes a book 18 months after acceptance.

LITTLE, BROWN AND CO. BOOKS FOR YOUNG READERS

Hachette Book Group USA, 237 Park Ave., New York NY 10017. (212)364-1100. **Fax:** (212)364-0925. **E-mail:** pamela.gruber@hbgusa.com. **Website:** www.lb-kids.com; www.lb-teens.com. "Little, Brown and Co. Children's Publishing publishes all formats including board books, picture books, middle grade fiction, and nonfiction YA titles. We are looking for strong writing and presentation, but no predetermined topics." *Only interested in solicited agented material.* Fiction: Submit complete ms. Nonfiction: Submit cover letter, previous publications, a proposal, outline and 3 sample chapters. Do not send originals. Publishes 100-150 titles/year.

FICTION Picture books: humor, adventure, animal, contemporary, history, multicultural, folktales. Young adults: contemporary, humor, multicultural, suspense/mystery, chick lit. Multicultural needs include "any material by, for and about minorities." Average word length: picture books—1,000; young readers—6,000; middle readers—15,000- 50,000; young adults—50,000 and up.

NONFICTION Writers should avoid looking for the 'issue' they think publishers want to see, choosing instead topics they know best and are most enthusiastic about/inspired by. Middle readers, young adults: arts/crafts, history, multicultural, nature, self help, social issues, sports, science. Average word length: middle readers—15,000-25,000; young adults—20,000-40,000. Recently published *American Dreaming*, by Laban Carrick Hill; *Exploratopia*, by the Exploratorium; *Yeah! Yeah! Yeah!: The Beatles, Beatlemania, and the Music that Changed the World*, by Bob Spitz.

HOW TO CONTACT *Agented submissions only.* Responds in 1 month to queries; 2 months to proposals and mss. Publishes ms 2 years after acceptance.

ILLUSTRATION Works with 40 illustrators/year. Illustrations only: Query art director with b&w and color samples; provide résumé, promo sheet or tearsheets to be kept on file. Does not respond to art samples. Do not send originals; copies only.

PHOTOGRAPHY Works on assignment only. Model/property releases required; captions required. Publishes photo essays and photo concept books. Uses 35mm transparencies. Photographers should provide résumé, promo sheets or tearsheets to be kept on file.

TERMS Pays authors royalties based on retail price. Pays illustrators and photographers by the project or royalty based on retail price. Sends galleys to authors; dummies to illustrators. Pays negotiable advance.

TIPS "In order to break into the field, authors and illustrators should research their competition and try to come up with something outstandingly different."

MAGINATION PRESS

American Psychological Association, 750 First St. NE, Washington DC 20002. (202)336-5618; (202)336-5500. **Fax:** (202)336-5624. **E-mail:** rteeter@apa.org. **Website:** www.apa.org. **Contact:** Kristine Enderle, managing editor. Magination Press is an imprint of the American Psychological Association. "We publish books dealing with the psycho/therapeutic resolution of children's problems and psychological issues with a strong self-help component." Submit complete ms. Materials returned only with SASE. Publishes 12 titles/year. 75% of books from first-time authors.

FICTION All levels: psychological and social issues, self help, health, parenting concerns and special needs. Picture books, middle school readers. Recently published *Nobody's Perfect: A Story for Children about Perfection*, by Ellen Flanagan Burns, illustrated by Erica Peltron (ages 8-12); *Murphy's Three Homes: A Story for Children in Foster Care*, by Jan Levinson Gilman, illustrated by Kathy O'Malley (ages 4-8).

NONFICTION All levels: psychological and social issues, self-help, health, multicultural, special needs. Recently published *Putting on the Brakes: Understanding and Controlling Your ADD or ADHD* (ages 8-13), by Patricia Quinn and Judith M. Stern, illustrated by Joe Lee.

HOW TO CONTACT Responds to queries in 1-2 months; mss in 2-6 months. Publishes a book 18-24 months after acceptance.

ILLUSTRATION Works with 10-15 illustrators/year. Reviews ms/illustration packages. Will review artwork for future assignments. Responds only if interested, or immediately if SASE or response card is included. "We keep samples on file."

MARTIN SISTERS PUBLISHING, LLC

E-mail: submissions@martinsisterspublishing.com. **Website:** www.martinsisterspublishing.com. **Contact:** Denise Melton, publisher/editor (fiction/nonfiction); Melissa Newman, publisher/editor (fiction/nonfiction). Firm/imprint publishes trade and mass market paperback originals; electronic originals. Publishes 12 titles/year. 75% of books from first-time authors. 100% from unagented writers.

HOW TO CONTACT Send query letter only to submissions@martinsisterspublishing.com. Responds in 1 month on queries, 2 months on proposals, 3-6 months on mss. Time between acceptance of ms and publication is 6 months.

TERMS Pays 7.5% royalty max on retail price. No advance offered. Catalog and guidelines available online.

MASKEW MILLER LONGMAN

P.O. Box 396, Cape Town, 8000, South Africa. (27) (21)531-8103. **E-mail:** mmlwCape@mml.co.za; customerservices@mml.co.za. **Website:** www.mml. co.za. "The Maskew Miller Longman Group has over 100 years of publishing experience in southern Africa, with staff and offices in countries throughout southern, central and east Africa. As partners to government in the educational arena, we develop local materials for local needs. We are one of the leading educational publishers in Africa. We tap into global expertise: whether it be in education, technology or customer services, we benefit from being part of Pearson Education, which is the largest educational publisher in the world and which produces the best and most up-to-date learning material available. We publish in more than 50 languages, including all of South Africa's official languages as well as French, Portuguese, and numerous African languages in each of the countries in which we operate." Publishes teacher references and dictionaries for educational markets. Interested in all genres (poetry/novels/short stories/plays) of African-language literature, as well as material for the Young Africa and They Fought for Freedom series in English."

MASTER BOOKS

P.O. Box 726, Green Forest AR 72638. (800)999-3777; (870)438-5288. **Fax:** (870)438-5120. **E-mail:** nlp@newleafpress.net; amanda@newleafpress.net. **Website:** www.masterbooks.net. **Contact:** Craig Froman, assistant editor. Publishes 3 middle readers/year; 2 young adult nonfiction titles/year; 15 adult trade books/year. 10% of books from first-time authors.

NONFICTION Picture books: activity books, animal, nature/environment, creation. Young readers, middle readers, young adults: activity books, animal, biography Christian, nature/environment, science, creation. Recently published *Passport to the World* (middle readers); *The Earth* (science book); *Demolishing Supposed Bible Contradictions*, compiled by Ken Ham (adult series).

HOW TO CONTACT Submission guidelines on website. Responds to queries and mss in 4 months. Publishes book 1 year after acceptance.

TERMS Pays authors royalty of 3-15% based on wholesale price. Book catalog available upon request. Guidelines available on website.

TIPS "All of our children's books are creation-based, including topics from the Book of Genesis. We look also for home school educational material that would be supplementary to a home school curriculum."

MARGARET K. MCELDERRY BOOKS

Imprint of Simon & Schuster Children's Publishing Division, Simon & Schuster, 1230 Sixth Ave., New York NY 10020. (212)698-7200. **Website:** www.simonsayskids.com. **Contact:** Justin Chanda, vice president; Karen Wojtyla, editorial director; Gretchen Hirsch, associate editor; Ann Bobco, executive art director. "Margaret K. McElderry Books publishes hardcover and paperback trade books for children from pre-school age through young adult. This list includes picture books, middle grade and teen fiction, poetry, and fantasy. The style and subject matter of the books we publish is almost unlimited. We do not publish textbooks, coloring and activity books, greeting cards, magazines, pamphlets, or religious publications." Publishes 30 titles/year. 15% of books from first-time authors. 50% from unagented writers.

FICTION "We will consider any category. Results depend on the quality of the imagination, the artwork, and the writing." Average word length: picture books—500; young readers—2,000; middle readers—10,000-20,000; young adults—45,000-50,000. Recently Published: *Monster Mess*, by Margery Cuyler, illustrated by S. D. Schindler (picture book); *The Joy of Spooking: Unearthly Asylum*, by P. J. Bracegirdle (middle grade); *Identical*, by Ellen Hopkins (teen); *Where is Home, Little Pip?*, by Karma Wilson, illustrated by Jane Chapman (picture book); *Dr. Ted*, by Andrea Beaty, illustrated by Pascal Lemaitre (picture book); *To Be Mona*, by Kelly Easton (teen).

HOW TO CONTACT Accept query letters with SASE only for picture books; query letter with first 3 chapters, SASE for middle grades and young adult novels..

TERMS Pays authors royalty based on retail price. Pays illustrator royalty of by the project. Pays pho-

tographers by the project. Original artwork returned at job's completion. Offers $5,000-8,000 advance for new authors. Guidelines for #10 SASE.

TIPS "Read! The children's book field is competitive. See what's been done and what's out there before submitting. We look for high quality: an originality of ideas, clarity and felicity of expression, a well organized plot, and strong character-driven stories. We're looking for strong, original fiction, especially mysteries and middle grade humor. We are always interested in picture books for the youngest age reader. Study our titles."

MERIT PRESS

A division of Adams Media (part of F+W Media), 57 Littlefield St, Avon, MA 02322. (508)427-7100. **E-mail:** meritpress@fwmedia.com. **Website:** www.adamsmedia.com/merit-press-books. **Contact:** Jacquelyn Mitchard, editor-in-chief.

Focuses on contemporary YA, usually based in reality.

FICTION "Natural is good; a little bit of supernatural (as in, perhaps foreseeing the future) is okay, too. Normal is great (at least until something happens) but not paranormal. What we are not seeking right now is tryphids, blood drinkers, flesh eaters and even yetis (much though we love them)."

HOW TO CONTACT "We do accept direct submissions as well as submissions from literary agents. We don't accept submissions in hard copy. Send full or partial manuscripts and queries to meritpress@fwmedia.com."

TIPS "I want to publish the next *Carrie*, *The Book Thief*, *National Velvet*, *Tuck Everlasting*, *Mr. and Mrs. Bo Jo Jones*, and *The Outsiders*. These will be the classics for a new generation, and they're being written right now. Since suspense (noir or pastel, comic or macabre) is my love, I hope I have a sense for finding those stories. As it turns out, a big part of my vocation, at this point in my career, is the desire to discover and nurture great new writers, and to put great books in the hands of great readers."

MERIWETHER PUBLISHING LTD.

885 Elkton Dr., Colorado Springs CO 80907. (719)594-4422. **Fax:** (719)594-9916. **E-mail:** editor@meriwether.com. **Website:** www.meriwether.com. **Contact:** Ted Zapel; Rhonda Wray. "Our niche is drama. Our books cover a wide variety of theatre subjects from play anthologies to theatrecraft. We publish books

of monologs, duologs, short one-act plays, scenes for students, acting textbooks, how-to speech and theatre textbooks, improvisation and theatre games. We also publish anthologies of Christian sketches. We do not publish works of fiction or devotionals." 75% of books from first-time authors.

FICTION Middle readers, young adults: anthology, contemporary, humor, religion. "We publish plays, not prose-fiction. Our emphasis is comedy plays instead of educational themes."

NONFICTION Middle readers: activity books, how-to, religion, textbooks. Young adults: activity books, drama/theater arts, how-to church activities, religion. Average length: 250 pages. Recently published *Acting for Life*, by Jack Frakes; *Scenes Keep Happening*, by Mary Krell-Oishi; *Service with a Smile*, by Daniel Wray.

HOW TO CONTACT Responds to queries in 3 weeks, mss in 2 months or less. Publishes book 6-12 months after acceptance.

ILLUSTRATION "We do our illustration in house."

TERMS Pays authors royalty of 10% based on retail or wholesale price.

TIPS "We are currently interested in finding unique treatments for theater arts subjects: scene books, how-to books, musical comedy scripts, monologs and short comedy plays for teens."

MILKWEED EDITIONS

1011 Washington Ave. S., Suite 300, Minneapolis MN 55415. (612)332-3192. **Fax:** (612)215-2550. **Website:** www.milkweed.org. Publishes 3-4 middle readers/year. 25% of books by first-time authors. "Milkweed Editions publishes with the intention of making a humane impact on society, in the belief that literature is a transformative art uniquely able to convey the essential experiences of the human heart and spirit. To that end, Milkweed Editions publishes distinctive voices of literary merit in handsomely designed, visually dynamic books, exploring the ethical, cultural, and esthetic issues that free societies need continually to address." Publishes hardcover, trade paperback, and electronic originals; trade paperback and electronic reprints. Publishes 15-20 titles/year. 25% of books from first-time authors. 75% from unagented writers.

FICTION Novels for adults and for readers 8-13. High literary quality. For adult readers: literary fiction, nonfiction, poetry, essays. Middle readers: adventure, contemporary, fantasy, multicultural, nature/environment, suspense/mystery. Does not want to see folktales, health, hi-lo, picture books, poetry, religion, romance, sports. Average length: middle readers—90-200 pages. Recently published *Perfect*, by Natasha Friend (contemporary); *The Linden Tree*, by Ellie Mathews (contemporary); *The Cat*, by Jutta Richter (contemporary/translation). No romance, mysteries, science fiction.

HOW TO CONTACT "Milkweed Editions is happy to accept unsolicited manuscripts from authors of all backgrounds (previously published or not), and our editorial staff reviews each submission during specified reading periods." Details are available online. "Though we strongly recommend that you use our online Submission Manager, we also accept printed submissions. Please enclose your submission and a SASE for response."

TERMS Pays authors variable royalty based on retail price. Offers advance against royalties. Pays varied advance from $500-10,000. Book catalog available online. Guidelines available online.

TIPS "We are looking for excellent writing with the intent of making a humane impact on society. Please read submission guidelines before submitting and acquaint yourself with our books in terms of style and quality before submitting. Many factors influence our selection process, so don't get discouraged. Nonfiction is focused on literary writing about the natural world, including living well in urban environments."

THE MILLBROOK PRESS

Website: www.lernerbooks.com. **Contact:** Carol Hinz, editorial director. "Millbrook Press publishes informative picture books, illustrated nonfiction titles, and inspiring photo-driven titles for grades K–5. Our authors approach curricular topics with a fresh point of view. Our fact-filled books engage readers with fun yet accessible writing, high-quality photographs, and a wide variety of illustration styles. We cover subjects ranging from the parts of speech and other language arts skills; to history, science, and math; to art, sports, crafts, and other interests. Millbrook Press is the home of the best-selling Words Are CATegorical® series and Bob Raczka's Art Adventures."

○ "Occasionally, we may put out a call for submissions, which will be announced on our website."

MITCHELL LANE PUBLISHERS INC.

P.O. Box 196, Hockessin DE 19707. (302)234-9426. **Fax:** (866)834-4164. **E-mail:** barbaramitchell@mitchelllane.com. **Website:** www.mitchelllane.com. **Contact:** Barbara Mitchell, publisher. Publishes hardcover and library bound originals. Publishes 80 titles/year. 0% of books from first-time authors. 90% from unagented writers.

NONFICTION Young readers, middle readers, young adults: biography, nonfiction, and curriculum-related subjects. Average word length: 4,000-50,000 words. Recently published *Katy Perry* and *Prince William* (both Blue Banner Biographies); *Justin Bieber* (A Robbie Reader); Earth Science Projects for Kids series; Your Land and My Land: Middle East series; and World Crafts and Recipes series.

HOW TO CONTACT Query with SASE. *All unsolicited mss discarded.* 100 queries received/year. 5 mss received/year. Responds only if interested to queries. Publishes ms 1 year after acceptance.

ILLUSTRATION Works with 2-3 illustrators/year. Reviews ms/illustration packages from artists. Query. Illustration only: Query with samples; send résumé, portfolio, slides, tearsheets. Responds only if interested. Samples not returned; samples filed.

PHOTOGRAPHY Buys stock images. Needs photos of famous and prominent minority figures. Captions required. Uses color prints or digital images. Submit cover letter, résumé, published samples, stock photo list.

TERMS Work purchased outright from authors (range: $350-2,000). Pays illustrators by the project (range: $40-400). Book catalog available free.

TIPS "We hire writers on a 'work-for-hire' basis to complete book projects we assign. Send résumé and writing samples that do not need to be returned."

MODERN PUBLISHING

155 E. 55th St., New York NY 10022. (212)826-0850. **Fax:** (212)759-9069. **Website:** www.modernpublishing.com. "Modern Publishing is a privately owned mass-market children's book publisher specializing in coloring and activity books, hardcover and paperback picture storybooks, puzzle and crossword collections, educational workbooks, board books, beginning readers, novelty and holiday books and other genres in various trim sizes and formats. Our titles feature both time-tested favorites and the hottest new licensed characters; generic characters; and characters from our Honey Bear imprint. Our titles are geared for children from infancy through ten years of age. Modern Publishing's history spans 40 years offering the highest quality book products at unbeatable prices. Our distribution includes chain drug stores, mass market, trade outlets, and educational and specialty stores in the U.S. and Canada, including book clubs and fairs, for all of the 250+ titles we publish yearly. We also offer full creative services to develop and print proprietary book products and premium promotional items."

○ "Modern Publishing is currently focusing on licensed properties and coloring and activity books. We are no longer considering submissions that don't fall within those categories."

Ⓐ MOODY PUBLISHERS

Moody Bible Institute, 820 N. LaSalle Blvd., Chicago IL 60610. (800)678-8812. **Fax:** (312)329-2019. **E-mail:** authors@moody.edu. **Website:** www.moodypublishers.org. "The mission of Moody Publishers is to educate and edify the Christian and to evangelize the non-Christian by ethically publishing conservative, evangelical Christian literature and other media for all ages around the world, and to help provide resources for Moody Bible Institute in its training of future Christian leaders." Publishes hardcover, trade, and mass market paperback originals. Publishes 60 titles/year. 1% of books from first-time authors. 80% from unagented writers.

FICTION "In our fiction list, we're looking for Christian storytellers rather than teachers trying to present a message. Your motivation should be to delight the reader. Using your skills to create beautiful works is glorifying to God."

NONFICTION Does not accept unsolicited nonfiction.

HOW TO CONTACT "We are no longer reviewing queries or unsolicited manuscripts unless they come to us through an agent. Unsolicited proposals will be returned only if proper postage is included. We are not able to acknowledge the receipt of your unsolicited proposal." 1,500 queries received/year. 2,000 mss received/year. Responds in 2-3 months to queries. Publishes book 1 year after acceptance.

TERMS Royalty varies. Book catalog for 9×12 envelope and 4 first-class stamps.

○ MOOSE ENTERPRISE BOOK & THEATRE PLAY PUBLISHING

684 Walls Rd., Prince Township, Ontario, P6A 6K4, Canada. (705) 779-3331. **Fax:** (705) 779-3331. **E-mail:** mooseenterprises@on.aibn.com. **Website:** www.moosehidebooks.com. **Contact:** Edmond Alcid. Editorial philosophy: "To assist the new writers of moral standards."

○ This publisher does not offer payment for stories published in its anthologies and/or book collections. Be sure to send a SASE for guidelines.

FICTION Middle readers, young adults: adventure, fantasy, humor, suspense/mystery, story poetry.

NONFICTION Middle readers, young adults: biography, history, multicultural.

HOW TO CONTACT Query. Responds to queries in 1 month; mss in 3 months. Publishes book 1 year after acceptance.

ILLUSTRATION Uses primarily b&w artwork for interiors, cover artwork in color. Illustrations only: Query with samples. Responds in 1 month, if interested. Samples returned with SASE; samples filed.

TERMS Pays royalties. Ms guidelines available for SASE.

TIPS "Do not copy trends; be yourself—give me something new, something different."

NOMAD PRESS

2456 Christian St., White River Junction VT 05001. (802)649-1995. **Fax:** (802)649-2667. **E-mail:** info@nomadpress.net. **Website:** www.nomadpress.net. **Contact:** Alex Kahan, publisher. "We produce nonfiction children's activity books that bring a particular science or cultural topic into sharp focus. Nomad Press does not accept unsolicited manuscripts. If authors are interested in contributing to our children's series, please send a writing resume that includes relevant experience/expertise and publishing credits."

○ Nomad Press does not accept picture books or fiction.

NONFICTION Middle readers: activity books, history, science. Average word length: middle readers—30,000. Recently published *Explore Transportation!*, by Marylou Moran Kjelle (ages 6-9); *Discover the Oceans*, by Lauri Berkenkamp (ages 8-12); *Amazing Biome Projects*, by Donna Latham (ages 9-12); *Explore Colonial America!*, by Verna Fisher (ages 6-9); *Discover the Desert*, by Kathy Ceceri (ages 8-12).

HOW TO CONTACT Responds to queries in 3-4 weeks. Publishes book 1 year after acceptance.

TERMS Pays authors royalty based on retail price or work purchased outright. Offers advance against royalties. Catalog available on website.

TIPS "We publish a very specific kind of nonfiction children's activity book. Please keep this in mind when querying or submitting."

NORTH ATLANTIC BOOKS

2526 MLK Jr. Way, Berkeley CA 94704. **Website:** www.northatlanticbooks.com. **Contact:** Douglas Reil, associate publisher; Erin Wiegand, senior acquisitions editor. Publishes hardcover, trade paperback, and electronic originals; trade paperback and electronic reprints. Publishes 60 titles/year. 50% of books from first-time authors. 75% from unagented writers.

FICTION Does not accept unsolicited fiction.

NONFICTION "See our submission guidelines on our website."

HOW TO CONTACT Submit proposal package including an outline, 3-4 sample chapters, and "a 75-word statement about the book, your qualifications as an author, marketing plan/audience, for the book, and comparable titles." Receives 200 mss/year. Responds in 3-6 months to queries, proposals, mss. Publishes ms 14 months after acceptance.

TERMS Pays royalty percentage on wholesale price. Book catalog free on request (if available). Guidelines online.

○ ONSTAGE PUBLISHING

190 Lime Quarry Rd., Suite 106-J, Madison AL 35758-8962. (256)461-0661. **E-mail:** submissions@onstagepublishing.com **Website:** www.onstagepublishing.com. **Contact:** Dianne Hamilton, senior editor. "At this time, we only produce fiction books for ages 8-18. We are adding an e-book only side of the house for mysteries for grades 6-12. See our website for more information. We will not do anthologies of any kind. Query first for nonfiction projects as nonfiction projects must spark our interest. Now accepting e-mail queries and submissions. For submissions: Put the first 3 chapters in the body of the e-mail. Do not use attachments! We will no longer return any mss. Only an SASE envelope is needed. Send complete ms if un-

der 20,000 words, otherwise send synopsis and first 3 chapters. 80% of books from first-time authors."

FICTION Middle readers: adventure, contemporary, fantasy, history, nature/environment, science fiction, suspense/mystery. Young adults: adventure, contemporary, fantasy, history, humor, science fiction, suspense/mystery. Average word length: chapter books—4,000-6,000 words; middle readers—5,000 words and up; young adults—25,000 and up. Recently published *China Clipper* by Jamie Dodson (an adventure for boys ages 12+); *Huntsville, 1892: Clara* (a chapter book for grades 3-5). "We do not produce picture books."

ILLUSTRATION Reviews ms/illustration packages from artists. Submit with 3 pieces of final art. **Contact:** Dianne Hamilton, senior editor. Illustrations only. Samples not returned.

TERMS Pays authors/illustrators/photographers advance plus royalties.

TIPS "Study our titles and get a sense of the kind of books we publish, so that you know whether your project is likely to be right for us."

ORCHARD BOOKS

557 Broadway, New York NY 10012. **E-mail:** mcroland@scholastic.com. **Website:** www.scholastic.com. **Contact:** Ken Geist, vice president/editorial director; David Saylor, vice president/creative director. Publishes 20 titles/year. 10% of books from first-time authors.

○ *Orchard is not accepting unsolicited submissions.*

FICTION Picture books, early readers, and novelty: animal, contemporary, history, humor, multicultural, poetry.

TERMS Most commonly offers an advance against list royalties.

TIPS "Read some of our books to determine first whether your manuscript is suited to our list."

OUR CHILD PRESS

P.O. Box 4379, Philadelphia PA 19118. Phone/fax: (610)308-8088. **E-mail:** info@ourchildpress.com. **Website:** www.ourchildpress.com. **Contact:** Carol Perrott, president. 90% of books from first-time authors.

FICTION All levels: adoption, multicultural, special needs. Published *Like Me*, written by Dawn Martelli, illustrated by Jennifer Heyd Wharton; *Is That Your Sister?*, by Catherine and Sherry Bunin; *Oliver: A Story About Adoption*, by Lois Wickstrom.

HOW TO CONTACT Responds to queries/mss in 6 months. Publishes a book 6-12 months after acceptance.

ILLUSTRATION Works with 1-5 illustrators/year. Reviews ms/illustration packages from artists. Manuscript/illustration packages and illustration only: Query first. Submit résumé, tearsheets and photocopies. Responds to art samples in 2 months. Samples returned with SASE; samples kept on file.

TERMS Pays authors royalty of 5-10% based on wholesale price. Pays illustrators royalty of 5-10% based on wholesale price. Book catalog for business-size SAE and 67 cents.

○ OUR SUNDAY VISITOR, INC.

200 Noll Plaza, Huntington IN 46750. **E-mail:** cmccauley@osv.com; oursunvis@osv.com. **Website:** www.osv.com. **Contact:** Jacquelyn Lindsey; David Dziena; Bert Ghezzi; Cindy Cavnar; Tyler Ottinger, art director. "We are a Catholic publishing company seeking to educate and deepen our readers in their faith. Currently emphasizing devotional, inspirational, Catholic identity, apologetics, and catechetics." Publishes paperback and hardbound originals. Publishes 40-50 titles/year.

○ Our Sunday Visitor, Inc. is publishing only those children's books that are specifically Catholic. See website for submission guidelines.

NONFICTION Prefers to see well-developed proposals as first submission with annotated outline and definition of intended market; Catholic viewpoints on family, prayer, and devotional books, and Catholic heritage books. Picture books, middle readers, young readers, young adults. Recently published *Little Acts of Grace*, by Rosemarie Gortler and Donna Piscitelli, illustrated by Mimi Sternhagen.

HOW TO CONTACT Submit proposals according to guidelines online. Responds in 2 months to queries/mss. Publishes ms 1-2 years after acceptance.

TERMS Pays authors royalty of 10-12% net. Pays illustrators by the project (range: $25-1,500). Book catalog for 9×12 envelope and first-class stamps; ms guidelines available online.

TIPS "Stay in accordance with our guidelines."

RICHARD C. OWEN PUBLISHERS, INC.

P.O. Box 585, Katonah NY 10536. (914)232-3903; (800)262-0787. **E-mail:** richardowen@rcowen.com. **Website:** www.rcowen.com. **Contact:** Richard Owen, publisher. "We publish child-focused books, with inherent instructional value, about characters and situations with which five-, six-, and seven-year-old children can identify—books that can be read for meaning, entertainment, enjoyment and information. We include multicultural stories that present minorities in a positive and natural way. Our stories show the diversity in America." Not interested in lesson plans, or books of activities for literature studies or other content areas. Submit complete ms and cover letter.

NONFICTION Our books are for kindergarten, first- and second-grade children to read on their own. The stories are very brief—under 1,000 words—yet well structured and crafted with memorable characters, language, and plots. Picture books, young readers: animals, careers, history, how-to, music/dance, geography, multicultural, nature/environment, science, sports. Multicultural needs include: "Good stories respectful of all heritages, races, cultural—African-American, Hispanic, American Indian." Wants lively stories. No "encyclopedic" type of information stories. Average word length: under 500 words. Recently published *The Coral Reef.*

HOW TO CONTACT Responds to mss in 1 year. Publishes a book 2-3 years after acceptance.

ILLUSTRATION Works with 20 illustrators/year. Uses color artwork only. Illustration only: Send color copies/reproductions or photos of art or provide tearsheets; do not send slides or originals. Include SASE and cover letter. Responds only if interested; samples filed.

TERMS Pays authors royalty of 5% based on net price or outright purchase (range: $25-500). Offers no advances. Pays illustrators by the project (range: $100-2,000) or per photo (range: $100-150). Book catalog available with SASE. Ms guidelines with SASE or online.

TIPS "Because our books are so brief, it is better to send an entire manuscript. We publish story books with inherent educational value for young readers—books they can read with enjoyment and success. We believe students become enthusiastic, independent, life-long learners when supported and guided by skillful teachers using good books. The professional development work we do and the books we publish support these beliefs."

⊕ PAGESPRING PUBLISHING

P.O. Box 21133, Columbus OH 43221. **E-mail:** ps@pagespringpublishing.com; yaeditor@pagespringpublishing.com. **Website:** www.pagespring-publishing.com. "PageSpring Publishing publishes young adult and middle grade titles under the Lucky Marble Books imprint and women's fiction under the Cup of Tea imprint. See imprint websites for submission details." Publishes trade paperback and electronic originals. Publishes 10-20 titles/year.

NONFICTION No nonfiction.

HOW TO CONTACT Submit proposal package including synopsis and first 30 pages. Responds to queries in 1 month. Publishes ms 6 months after acceptance.

TERMS Pays royalty on wholesale price. Guidelines available online at website.

PAUL DRY BOOKS

1700 Sansom St., Suite 700, Philadelphia PA 19103. (215)231-9939. **Fax:** (215)231-9942. **E-mail:** pdry@pauldrybooks.com; editor@pauldrybooks.com. **Website:** http://pauldrybooks.com. "We publish fiction, both novels and short stories, and nonfiction, biography, memoirs, history, and essays, covering subjects from Homer to Chekhov, bird watching to jazz music, New York City to shogunate Japan." Hardcover and trade paperback originals, trade paperback reprints.

💬 "Take a few minutes to familiarize yourself with the books we publish. Then if you think your book would be a good fit in our line, we invite you to submit the following: A one- or two-page summary of the work. Be sure to tell us how many pages or words the full book will be; a sample of 20 to 30 pages; your bio. A brief description of how you think the book (and you, the author) could be marketed."

HOW TO CONTACT Submit sample chapters, clips, bio.

TERMS Book catalog available online. Guidelines available online.

TIPS "Our aim is to publish lively books 'to awaken, delight, & educate'—to spark conversation."

PAULINE BOOKS & MEDIA

50 St. Paul's Ave., Boston MA 02130. (800)836-9723. **Fax:** (617)524-8034. **E-mail:** design@paulinemedia.com; editorial@paulinemedia.com. **Website:** www.

pauline.org. "Submissions are evaluated on adherence to Gospel values, harmony with the Catholic tradition, relevance of topic, and quality of writing." For board books and picture books, the entire manuscript should be submitted. For easy-to-read, young readers, and middle reader books and teen books, please send a cover letter accompanied by a synopsis and two sample chapters. "Electronic submissions are encouraged. We make every effort to respond to unsolicited submissions within 2 months." Publishes trade paperback originals and reprints. Publishes 40 titles/year. 15% of books from first-time authors. 5% from unagented writers.

FICTION "We would especially welcome well documented historical fiction and young adult novels in the middle grade and young adult categories. Although not our primary focus, we would also consider well written fantasy, fairy tales, science fiction, myths, or romance if approached from a Catholic perspective." Children's and teen fiction only. "We are now accepting submissions for easy-to-read and middle reader chapter books, and teen fiction. Please see our Writer's Guidelines."

NONFICTION Picture books, young readers, middle readers, teen: religion and fiction. Average word length: picture books—500-1,000; young readers—8,000-10,000; middle readers—15,000-25,000; teen—30,000-50,000. Recently published *Shine: Choices to Make God Smile*, the Christopher Award-winning picture book by Genny Monchamp; *Forever You: A Book About Your Soul and Body* by Nicole Lataif; *My First Book of Saints*; *The Mass Explained for Kids*; and *Teens Share the Word*. No biography/autobiography, poetry, or strictly nonreligious works considered.

HOW TO CONTACT "For picture books and board books, the entire manuscript should be submitted. For easy-to-read and middle reader books, please send a cover letter accompanied by a synopsis and two sample chapters." Responds in 2 months to queries, proposals, & mss. Publishes a book approximately 11-18 months after acceptance.

ILLUSTRATION Works with 10-15 illustrators/year. Uses color and b&w artwork. Illustrations only: Send résumé and 4-5 color samples. Samples and résumés will be kept on file unless return is requested and SASE provided.

TERMS Varies by project, but generally pays royalties with advance. Flat fees sometimes considered for smaller works. Book catalog available online. Guidelines available online and by e-mail.

TIPS "Manuscripts may or may not be explicitly catechetical, but we seek those that reflect a positive worldview, good moral values, awareness and appreciation of diversity, and respect for all people. All material must be relevant to the lives of readers and must conform to Catholic teaching and practice."

PAULIST PRESS

997 MacArthur Blvd., Mahwah NJ 07430. (201)825-7300. **Fax:** (800)836-3161. **Website:** www.paulist press.com. **Contact:** Donna Crilly, managing editor. "Paulist Press publishes ecumenical theology, Roman Catholic studies, and books on scripture, liturgy, spirituality, church history, and philosophy, as well as works on faith and culture. Our publishing is oriented toward adult-level nonfiction. We do not publish poetry or works of fiction, and we have scaled back our involvement in children's publishing."

HOW TO CONTACT Receives 250 submissions/year. Responds in 3 months to queries and proposals; 3-4 months on mss. Publishes a book 12-18 months after acceptance.

TERMS Royalties and advances are negotible. Illustrators sometimes receive a flat fee when all we need are spot illustrations. Book catalog available online. Guidelines available online and by e-mail.

PEACE HILL PRESS

Affiliate of W.W. Norton, 18021 The Glebe Ln., Charles City VA 23030. (804)829-5043. **Fax:** (804)829-5704. **E-mail:** info@peacehillpress.com. **Website:** www.peace hillpress.com. **Contact:** Peter Buffington, acquisitions editor. Publishes hardcover and trade paperback originals. Publishes 4-8 titles/year.

HOW TO CONTACT Submit proposal package, outline, 1 sample chapter. Publishes a book 18 months after acceptance.

TERMS Pays 6-10% royalty on retail price. Pays $500-1,000 advance.

PEACHTREE CHILDREN'S BOOKS

Peachtree Publishers, Ltd., 1700 Chattahoochee Ave., Atlanta GA 30318-2112. (404)876-8761. **Fax:** (404)875-2578. **E-mail:** hello@peachtree-online.com. **Website:** www.peachtree-online.com. **Contact:** Helen Harriss, submissions editor. "We publish a broad range of subjects and perspectives, with emphasis on innovative plots and strong writing." Publishes hardcover and trade paperback originals. Publishes 30 titles/year.

25% of books from first-time authors. 25% from un-agented writers.

FICTION Looking for very well-written middle grade and young adult novels. Juvenile, picture books, young adult. Looking for very well written middle grade and young adult novels. No adult fiction. No short stories. Published *Martina the Beautiful Cockroach, Night of the Spadefoot Toads, The Boy Who Was Raised by Librarians*. No collections of poetry or short stories; no romance or science fiction.

NONFICTION No e-mail or fax queries of mss.

HOW TO CONTACT Submit complete ms with SASE. Submit complete ms with SASE, or summary and 3 sample chapters with SASE. Responds in 6 months and mss. Publishes ms 1 year after acceptance.

ILLUSTRATION Works with 8-10 illustrators/year. Illustrations only: Query production manager or art director with samples, résumé, slides, color copies to keep on file. Responds only if interested. Samples returned with SASE; samples filed. "If possible, please provide samples which display your ability to depict subjects or characters in a consistent manner, which portray different kinds of subjects, and which display your abilities in various mediums, styles, or techniques."

TERMS Pays royalty on retail price. Book catalog for 6 first-class stamps. Guidelines available online.

PELICAN PUBLISHING COMPANY

1000 Burmaster St., Gretna LA 70053. (504)368-1175. **Fax:** (504)368-1195. **E-mail:** editorial@pelicanpub.com. **Website:** www.pelicanpub.com. **Contact:** Nina Kooij, editor-in-chief. "We believe ideas have consequences. One of the consequences is that they lead to a best-selling book. We publish books to improve and uplift the reader. Currently emphasizing business and history titles." Publishes 20 young readers/year; 1 middle reader/year. "Our children's books (illustrated and otherwise) include history, biography, holiday, and regional. Pelican's mission is to publish books of quality and permanence that enrich the lives of those who read them." Publishes hardcover, trade paperback and mass market paperback originals and reprints.

FICTION No adult fiction. Young readers: history, holiday, science, multicultural and regional. Middle readers: Louisiana history. Multicultural needs include stories about African-Americans, Irish-Americans, Jews, Asian-Americans, and Hispanics. Does not want animal stories, general Christmas stories, "day at school" or "accept yourself" stories. Maximum word length: young readers—1,100; middle readers—40,000. No young adult, romance, science fiction, fantasy, gothic, mystery, erotica, confession, horror, sex, or violence. Also no psychological novels.

NONFICTION Young readers: biography, history, holiday, multicultural. Middle readers: Louisiana history, holiday, regional. No multiple queries or submissions.

HOW TO CONTACT "We look for authors who can promote successfully. We require that a query be made first. This greatly expedites the review process and can save the writer additional postage expenses." Query with SASE. For brief books for ages 5-8, submit entire manuscript. Submit outline, clips, 2 sample chapters, SASE. Responds in 1 month to queries; 3 months to mss. Publishes a book 9-18 months after acceptance.

ILLUSTRATION Works with 20 illustrators/year. Reviews ms/illustration packages from artists. Query first. Illustrations only: Query with samples (no originals). Responds only if interested. Samples returned with SASE; samples kept on file.

TERMS Pays authors in royalties; buys ms outright "rarely." Illustrators paid by "various arrangements." Advance considered. Book catalog and ms guidelines online.

TIPS "We do extremely well with cookbooks, popular histories, and business. We will continue to build in these areas. The writer must have a clear sense of the market and knowledge of the competition. A query letter should describe the project briefly, give the author's writing and professional credentials, and promotional ideas."

PERSEA BOOKS

277 Broadway, Suite 708, New York NY 10007. (212)260-9256. **Fax:** (212)267-3165. **E-mail:** info@perseabooks.com. **Website:** www.perseabooks.com. "We are pleased to receive query letters from authors and literary agents for fiction and nonfiction manuscripts."

FICTION Seeking young adult books.

HOW TO CONTACT Send queries and manuscripts to info@perseabooks.com. Queries should include a cover letter, author background and publication history, a detailed synopsis of the proposed work, and a sample chapter. Please indicate if the work is simultaneously submitted. Responds in 8 weeks to proposals; 10 weeks to mss.

TERMS Guidelines online.

PHILOMEL BOOKS

Imprint of Penguin Group (USA), Inc., 375 Hudson St., New York NY 10014. (212)414-3610. **Website:** www.us.penguingroup.com. **Contact:** Michael Green, president/publisher; Annie Beth Ericsson, junior designer. "We look for beautifully written, engaging manuscripts for children and young adults." Publishes hardcover originals. Publishes 8-10 titles/year. 5% of books from first-time authors. 20% from unagented writers.

FICTION All levels: adventure, animal, boys, contemporary, fantasy, folktales, historical fiction, humor, sports, multicultural. Middle readers, young adults: problem novels, science fiction, suspense/mystery. No concept picture books, mass-market "character" books, or series. Average word length: picture books—1,000; young readers—1,500; middle readers—14,000; young adult—20,000. No series or activity books. No generic, mass-market oriented fiction.

NONFICTION Picture books.

HOW TO CONTACT For picture books, submit entire ms. For longer works, submit cover letter and ten pages maximum from the opening chapter(s).

ILLUSTRATION Works with 8-10 illustrators/year. Reviews ms/illustration packages from artists. Query with art sample first. Illustrations only: Query with samples. Send résumé and tearsheets. Responds to art samples in 1 month. Original artwork returned at job's completion. Samples returned with SASE or kept on file.

TERMS Pays authors in royalties. Average advance payment "varies." Illustrators paid by advance and in royalties. Pays negotiable advance. Book catalog for 9×12 envelope and 4 first-class stamps. Guidelines for #10 SASE.

TIPS Wants "unique fiction or nonfiction with a strong voice and lasting quality. Discover your own voice and own story and persevere." Looks for "something unusual, original, well written. Fine art or illustrative art that feels unique. The genre (fantasy, contemporary, or historical fiction) is not so important as the story itself and the spirited life the story allows its main character."

PIANO PRESS

P.O. Box 85, Del Mar CA 92014. (619)884-1401. **Fax:** (858)755-1104. **E-mail:** pianopress@pianopress.com. **Website:** www.pianopress.com. **Contact:** Elizabeth C. Axford, owner/editor. "We publish music-related books, either fiction or nonfiction, coloring books, songbooks, and poetry."

FICTION Picture books, young readers, middle readers, young adults: folktales, multicultural, poetry, music. Average word length: picture books—1,500-2,000. Recently published *Strum a Song of Angels*, by Linda Oatman High and Elizabeth C. Axford.

NONFICTION Picture books, young readers, middle readers, young adults: multicultural, music/dance. Average word length: picture books—1,500-2,000.

HOW TO CONTACT Responds to queries in 3 months; mss in 6 months. Publishes book 1 year after acceptance.

ILLUSTRATION Works with 1 or 2 illustrators/year. Reviews ms/illustration packages from artists. Query. Illustrations only: Query with samples. Responds in 3 months. Samples returned with SASE; samples filed.

PHOTOGRAPHY Buys stock and assigns work. Looking for music-related, multicultural. Model/property releases required. Uses glossy or flat, color or b&w prints. Submit cover letter, résumé, client list, published samples, stock photo list.

TERMS Pays authors, illustrators, and photographers royalty of 5-10% based on retail price. Book catalog available for #10 SASE and 2 first-class stamps.

TIPS "We are looking for music-related material only for any juvenile market. Please do not send non-music-related materials. Query first before submitting anything."

PINEAPPLE PRESS, INC.

P.O. Box 3889, Sarasota FL 34230. (941)706-2507. **Fax:** (941)739-2296. **E-mail:** info@pineapplepress.com. **Website:** www.pineapplepress.com. **Contact:** June Cussen, executive editor. "We are seeking quality nonfiction on diverse topics for the library and book trade markets. Our mission is to publish good books about Florida." Publishes hardcover and trade paperback originals. Publishes 25 titles/year. 50% of books from first-time authors. 95% from unagented writers.

FICTION Picture books, young readers, middle readers, young adults: animal, folktales, history, nature/environment. Recently published *The Treasure of Amelia Island*, by M.C. Finotti (ages 8-12).

NONFICTION Picture books: animal, history, nature/environmental, science. Young readers, middle readers, young adults: animal, biography, geography, history, nature/environment, science. Recently published *Those Magical Manatees*, by Jan Lee Wicker and *Those Beautiful Butterflies*, by Sarah Cussen. "We will consider most nonfiction topics when related to Florida."

HOW TO CONTACT Query or submit outline/synopsis and 3 sample chapters. 1,000 queries received/year. 500 mss received/year. Responds to queries/samples/mss in 2 months. Publishes a book 1 year after acceptance.

ILLUSTRATION Works with 2 illustrators/year. Reviews ms/illustration packages from artists. Query with nonreturnable samples. Contact: June Cussen, executive editor. Illustrations only: Query with brochure, nonreturnable samples, photocopies, résumé. Responds only if interested. Samples returned with SASE, but prefers nonreturnable; samples filed.

TERMS Pays authors royalty of 10-15%. Book catalog for 9×12 SAE with $1.25 postage. Guidelines available online.

TIPS "Quality first novels will be published, though we usually only do one or two novels per year and they must be set in Florida. We regard the author/editor relationship as a trusting relationship with communication open both ways. Learn all you can about the publishing process and about how to promote your book once it is published. A query on a novel without a brief sample seems useless."

PIÑATA BOOKS

Imprint of Arte Público Press, University of Houston, 4902 Gulf Fwy, Bldg 19, Rm 100, Houston TX 77204-2004. (713)743-2845. **Fax:** (713)743-2847. **E-mail:** submapp@mail.uh.edu. **Website:** www.latinoteca.com/arte-publico-press. **Contact:** Nicolas Kanellos, director. "Piñata Books is dedicated to the publication of children's and young adult literature focusing on U.S. Hispanic culture by U.S. Hispanic authors. Arte Público's mission is the publication, promotion and dissemination of Latino literature for a variety of national and regional audiences, from early childhood to adult, through the complete gamut of delivery systems, including personal performance as well as print and electronic media." Publishes hardcover and trade paperback originals. Publishes 10-15 titles/year. 80% of books from first-time authors.

Accepts material from U.S./Hispanic authors only (living abroad OK). Mss, queries, synopses, etc., are accepted in either English or Spanish.

FICTION Recently published *We Are Cousins/Somos primos*, by Diane Gonzales Betrand; *Butterflies on Carmen Street/ Mariposas en la calle Carmen*, by Monica Brown; and *Windows Into My World: Latino Youth Write Their Lives; Trino's Choice*, by Diane Gonzales Bertrand (ages 11-up).

NONFICTION Piñata Books specializes in publication of children's and young adult literature that authentically portrays themes, characters and customs unique to U.S. Hispanic culture. Recently published *Cesar Chavez: The Struggle for Justice/Cesar Chavez: La Lucha por la Justicia*, by Richard Griswold del Castillo, illustrated by Anthony Accardo (ages 3-7).

HOW TO CONTACT Submissions made through online submission form. Responds in 2-3 months to queries; 4-6 months to mss. Publishes book 2 years after acceptance.

ILLUSTRATION Works with 6 illustrators/year. Uses color artwork only. Reviews ms/illustration packages from artists. Query or send portfolio (slides, color copies). Illustrations only: Query with samples or send résumé, promo sheet, portfolio, slides, client list and tearsheets. Responds only if interested. Samples not returned; samples filed.

TERMS Pays 10% royalty on wholesale price. Pays $1,000-3,000 advance. Book catalog and ms guidelines available via website or with #10 SASE.

TIPS "Include cover letter with submission explaining why your manuscript is unique and important, why we should publish it, who will buy it, etc."

THE POISONED PENCIL

Poisoned Pen Press, 6962 E. 1st Ave., Suite 103, Scottsdale AZ 85251. (480)945-3375. **Fax:** (480)949-1707. **E-mail:** info@thepoisonedpencil.com. **Website:** www.thepoisonedpencil.com. **Contact:** Ellen Larson, editor. Publishes trade paperback and electronic originals.

Accepts young adult mysteries only.

FICTION "We publish only young adult mystery novels, 45,000 to 90,000 words in length. For our purposes, a young adult book is a book with a protagonist between the ages of 12 and 18. We are looking for both traditional and cross-genre young adult mysteries. We encourage off-beat approaches and narrative choices that reflect the complexity and ambiguity of today's world. Submissions from teens are very welcome. Avoid serial killers, excessive gore, and vampires (and other heavy supernatural themes). We only consider authors who live in the US or Canada, due to practicalities of marketing promotion. Avoid coincidence in plotting. Avoid having your sleuth leap to conclusions rather than discover and deduce. Pay attention to the resonance between character and plot; between plot and theme; between theme and character. We are looking for clean style, fluid storytelling, and solid structure. Unrealistic dialogue is a real turn-off."

NONFICTION No nonfiction.

HOW TO CONTACT "The Poisoned Pencil uses an online submissions manager to review materials from both authors and agents. Please do not query or submit your manuscript by email or snail mail. No simultaneous submissions." 250 submissions received/year. Responds in 6 weeks to mss. Publishes ms 15 months after acceptance.

TERMS Pays 9-15% for trade paperback; 25-35% for eBooks. Pays advance of $1,000. Guidelines available online at website.

TIPS "Our audience is young adults and adults who love YA mysteries."

PRICE STERN SLOAN, INC.

Penguin Group, 375 Hudson St., New York NY 10014. (212)366-2000. **Website:** http://us.penguingroup. com. **Contact:** Francesco Sedita, president/publisher. "Price Stern Sloan publishes quirky mass market novelty series for childrens as well as licensed movie tie-in books." Price Stern Sloan only responds to submissions it's interested in publishing.

○ Price Stern Sloan does not accept e-mail submissions.

FICTION Publishes picture books and novelty/board books including Mad Libs Movie and Television Tie-ins, and unauthorized biographies. All book formats except for picture books. "We publish unique novelty formats and fun, colorful paperbacks and activity books. We also publish the Book with Audio Series *Wee Sing* and *Baby Loves Jazz*."

HOW TO CONTACT Submit a summary and first chapter or two for longer works.

TERMS Book catalog online.

TIPS "Price Stern Sloan publishes unique, fun titles."

○ ○ PUFFIN BOOKS

Imprint of Penguin Group (USA), Inc., 375 Hudson St., New York NY 10014. (212)366-2000. **Website:** www.us.penguin.com. **Contact:** Kristin Gilson, editorial director. "Puffin Books publishes high-end trade paperbacks and paperback reprints for preschool children, beginning and middle readers, and young adults." Publishes trade paperback originals and reprints. Publishes 175-200 titles/year. 1% of books from first-time authors. 5% from unagented writers.

FICTION Picture books, young adult novels, middle grade and easy-to-read grades 1-3: fantasy and science fiction, graphic novels, classics. Recently Published *Three Cups of Tea* young readers edition, by Greg Mortenson and David Oliver Relin, adapted for young readers by Sarah Thomson; *The Big Field*, by Mike Lupica; *Geek Charming*, by Robin Palmer.

NONFICTION Biography, illustrated books, young children's concept books (counting, shapes, colors). Subjects include education (for teaching concepts and colors, not academic), women in history. "Women in history books interest us."

HOW TO CONTACT Submit a maximum of 30 pages for longer works (middle grade and YA manuscripts). All novel submissions must include a SASE. Does not accept picture books. Receives 600 queries and mss/year. Responds in 5 months. Publishes book 1 year after acceptance.

ILLUSTRATION Reviews artwork. Send color copies.

PHOTOGRAPHY Reviews photos. Send color copies.

TERMS Royalty varies. Pays varies advance. Book catalog for 9×12 SAE with 7 first-class stamps.

TIPS "Our audience ranges from little children 'first books' to young adult (ages 14-16). An original idea has the best luck."

○ PUSH

Scholastic, 557 Broadway, New York NY 10012. **E-mail:** DLevithan@Scholastic.com. **Website:** www.thisispush.com. **Contact:** David Levithan, editor. PUSH publishes new voices in teen literature. Publishes 6-9 titles/year. 50% of books from first-time authors.

○ PUSH does not accept unsolicited mss or queries; only agented or referred fiction/memoir.

FICTION Young adults: contemporary, multicultural, poetry. Recently published *Splintering*, by Eireann Corrigan; *Never Mind the Goldbergs*, by Matthue Roth; *Perfect World*, by Brian James.

NONFICTION Young adults: poetry, memoir. Recently published *Talking in the Dark*, by Billy Merrell; *You Remind Me of You*, by Eireann Corrigan.

HOW TO CONTACT *Does not accept unsolicited mss.*

TIPS "We only publish first-time writers (and then their subsequent books), so authors who have published previously should not consider PUSH. Also, for young writers in grades 7-12, we run the PUSH Novel Contest with the Scholastic Art & Writing Awards. Every year it begins in October and ends in March. Rules can be found on our website."

G.P. PUTNAM'S SONS HARDCOVER

Imprint of Penguin Group (USA), Inc., 375 Hudson, New York NY 10014. (212)366-2000. **Fax:** (212)366-2664. **Website:** www.penguingroup.com. Publishes hardcover originals.

HOW TO CONTACT For picture books, submit complete ms. For longer works, submit cover letter and a 10 pages maximum from the opening chapter(s).

TERMS Pays variable royalties on retail price. Pays varies advance. Request book catalog through mail order department.

RAINBOW PUBLISHERS

P.O. Box 261129, San Diego CA 92196. (858)277-1167. **E-mail:** info@rainbowpublishers.com. **Website:** www.rainbowpublishers.com; www.legacypresskids.com. "Our mission is to publish Bible based, teacher resource materials that contribute to and inspire spiritual growth and development in kids ages 2-12."

NONFICTION Young readers, middle readers, young adult/teens: activity books, arts/crafts, how-to, reference, religion.

HOW TO CONTACT Responds to queries in 6 weeks; mss in 3 months.

ILLUSTRATION Works with 25 illustrators/year. Reviews ms/illustration packages from artists. Submit ms with 2-5 pieces of final art. Illustrations only: Query with samples. Responds in 6 weeks. Samples returned with SASE; samples filed.

TERMS Pays illustrators by the project (range: $300 and up). For authors work purchased outright (range: $500 and up).

TIPS "Our Rainbow imprint publishes reproducible books for teachers of children in Christian ministries, including crafts, activities, games and puzzles. Our Legacy imprint publishes titles for children such as

devotionals, fiction and Christian living. Please write for guidelines and study the market before submitting material."

RAINTOWN PRESS

1111 E. Burnside St. #309, Portland OR 97214. (503)962-9612. **E-mail:** submissions@raintownpress.com. **Website:** www.raintownpress.com. **Contact:** Misty V'Marie, acquisitions editor. Publishes 1-4 middle readers; 1-4 young adult titles/year. 100% of books from first-time authors.

"We are Portland, Oregon's first independent press dedicated to publishing literature for middle grade and young adult readers. We hope to give rise to their voice, speaking directly to the spirit they embody through our books and other endeavors. The gray days we endure in the Pacific Northwest are custom made for reading a good book—or in our case, making one. The rain inspires, challenges, and motivates us. To that end, we say: Let it drizzle. We will soon publish picture books."

FICTION Middle readers/YA/teens: Wants adventure, animal, contemporary, fantasy, folktales, graphic novels, health, hi-lo, history, humor, multicultural, nature/environment, problem novels, sci-fi, special needs, sports. Catalog available on website.

NONFICTION Middle Readers/YA/Teens: biography, concept, graphic novels, hi-lo, how-to.

HOW TO CONTACT See online submission guide for detailed instructions. Query with first 50 pages. Responds to queries and mss in 1-6 months. Publishes ms 1 year after acceptance.

ILLUSTRATION Reviews ms/illustration packages from artists (will review packages for future titles); uses both color and b&w. Submit query, link to online portfolio. Originals not returned. Does not show dummies to illustrators.

PHOTOGRAPHY Buys stock images and assigned work. Model/property releases required with submissions. Photo captions required. Use high-res digital materials. Send cover letter, client list, portolio (online preferred).

TERMS Pays 8-15% royalty on net sales. Does not pay advance. Catalog available on website. Imprints included in a single catalog. Guidelines available on website for writers, artists, and photographers.

TIPS "The middle grade and YA markets have sometimes very stringent conventions for subject matter, theme, etc. It's most helpful if an author knows his/her genre inside and out. Read, read, read books that have successfully been published for your genre. This will ultimately make your writing more marketable. Also, follow a publisher's submission guidelines to a tee. We try to set writers up for success. Send us what we're looking for."

RANDOM HOUSE CHILDREN'S BOOKS

1745 Broadway, New York NY 10019. (212)782-9000. **E-mail:** rhkidspublicity@randomhouse.com **Website:** www.randomhouse.com. "Producing books for preschool children through young adult readers, in all formats from board to activity books to picture books and novels, Random House Children's Books brings together world-famous franchise characters, multimillion-copy series and top-flight, award-winning authors, and illustrators."

Submit mss through a literary agent.

FICTION "Random House publishes a select list of first chapter books and novels, with an emphasis on fantasy and historical fiction." Chapter books, middle grade readers, young adult.

HOW TO CONTACT *Does not accept unsolicited mss.*

ILLUSTRATION The Random House publishing divisions hire their freelancers directly. To contact the appropriate person, send a cover letter and résumé to the department head at the publisher as follows: "Department Head" (e.g., Art Director, Production Director), "Publisher/Imprint" (e.g., Knopf, Doubleday, etc.), 1745 Broadway New York, NY 10019. Works with 100-150 freelancers/year. Works on assignment only. Send query letter with résumé, tearsheets and printed samples; no originals. Samples are filed. Negotiates rights purchased. Assigns 5 freelance design jobs/year. Pays by the project.

TIPS "We look for original, unique stories. Do something that hasn't been done before."

RAVEN TREE PRESS

A Division of Delta Publishing Company, 1400 Miller Pkwy., McHenry IL 60050. (877)256-0579. **Fax:** (800)909-9901. **E-mail:** raven@deltapublishing.com. **Website:** www.raventreepress.com. "We publish entertaining and educational picture books in a variety of formats. Bilingual (English/Spanish), English-only, Spanish-only, and wordless editions." Publishes hardcover and trade paperback originals. Publishes 8-10

titles/year. 50% of books from first-time authors. 90% from unagented writers.

As of summer 2013, currently closed to submissions. Check website for updates.

HOW TO CONTACT "Submission guidelines available online. Do not query or send mss without first checking submission guidelines on our website for most current information." 1,500 mss received/year.

TERMS Pays royalty. Pays variable advance. Book catalog online. Guidelines online.

TIPS "Submit only based on guidelines. No e-mail or snail mail queries please. Word count is a definite issue, since we are bilingual."

RAZORBILL

Penguin Group, 375 Hudson St., New York NY 10014. (212)414-3448. **Fax:** (212)414-3343. **E-mail:** laura.schechter@us.penguingroup.com; Ben.Schrank@us.penguingroup.com. **Website:** www.razorbillbooks.com. **Contact:** Ben Schrank, president/publisher; Gillian Levinson, associate edtor. "This division of Penguin Young Readers is looking for the best and the most original of commercial contemporary fiction titles for middle grade and YA readers. A select quantity of nonfiction titles will also be considered." Publishes 30 titles/year.

FICTION Middle readers: adventure, contemporary, graphic novels, fantasy, humor, problem novels. Young adults/teens: adventure, contemporary, fantasy, graphic novels, humor, multicultural, suspense, paranormal, science fiction, dystopian, literary, romance. Average word length: middle readers—40,000; young adult—60,000. Recently published *Thirteen Reasons Why*, by Jay Asher (ages 14 and up, a NY Times Bestseller); Vampire Academy series by Richelle Mead (ages 12 and up; NY Times bestselling series); *The Teen Vogue Handbook* (ages 12 and up; a NY Times Bestseller); and *I Am a Genius of Unspeakable Evil and I Want to Be Your Class President*, by Josh Lieb (ages 12 and up; a NY Times Bestseller).

NONFICTION Middle readers and young adults/teens: concept.

HOW TO CONTACT Submit outline/synopsis and 30 pages maximum along with query and SASE. Responds to queries/mss in 1-3 months. Publishes book 1-2 after acceptance.

TERMS Offers advance against royalties.

TIPS "New writers will have the best chance of acceptance and publication with original, contemporary material that boasts a distinctive voice and well-articulated world. Check out www.razorbillbooks.com to get a better idea of what we're looking for."

RENAISSANCE HOUSE

465 Westview Ave., Englewood NJ 07631. (201)408-4048. **E-mail:** info@renaissancehouse.net. **Website:** www.renaissancehouse.net. Publishes biographies, folktales, coffee table books, instructional, textbooks, adventure, picture books, juvenile and young adult. Specializes in multicultural and bilingual titles, Spanish/English. Submit outline/synopsis. Will consider e-mail submissions. Children's, educational, multicultural, and textbooks. Represents 80 illustrators. 95% of artwork handled is children's book illustration. Currently open to illustrators seeking representation. Open to both new and established illustrators.
FICTION Picture books: animal, folktales, multicultural. Young readers: animal, anthology, folktales, multicultural. Middle readers, young adult/teens: anthology, folktales, multicultural, nature/environment.
HOW TO CONTACT Responds to queries/mss in 2 months. Publishes ms 1 year after acceptance.
ILLUSTRATION Works with 25 illustrators/year. Uses color and b&w artwork. Reviews ms/illustration packages from artists. Send ms with dummy. Contact: Raquel Benatar. Responds in 3 weeks. Samples not returned; samples filed.

ROARING BROOK PRESS

175 Fifth Ave., New York NY 10010. (646)307-5151. **E-mail:** david.langva@roaringbrookpress.com. **E-mail:** press.inquiries@macmillanusa.com. **Website:** http://us.macmillan.com/RoaringBrook.aspx. Roaring Brook Press is an imprint of Macmillan, a group of companies that includes Henry Holt and Farrar, Straus & Giroux. Roaring Brook is not accepting unsolicited manuscripts. Roaring Brook title *First the Egg*, by Laura Vaccaro Seeger, won a Caldecott Honor Medal and a Theodor Seuss Geisel Honor in 2008. Their title *Dog and Bear: Two Friends, Three Stories*, also by Laura Vaccaro Seeger, won the Boston Globe-Horn Book Picture Book Award in 2007.
FICTION Picture books, young readers, middle readers, young adults: adventure, animal, contemporary, fantasy, history, humor, multicultural, nature/environment, poetry, religion, science fiction, sports, suspense/mystery. Recently published *Happy Birthday, Bad Kitty*, by Nick Bruel; *Cookie*, by Jacqueline Wilson.

NONFICTION Picture books, young readers, middle readers, young adults: adventure, animal, contemporary, fantasy, history, humor, multicultural, nature/environment, poetry, religion, science fiction, sports, suspense/mystery.
HOW TO CONTACT *Not accepting unsolicited mss or queries.*
ILLUSTRATION Works with 25 illustrators/year. Illustrations only: Query with samples. Do not send original art; copies only through the mail. Samples returned with SASE.
TERMS Pays authors royalty based on retail price.
TIPS "You should find a reputable agent and have him/her submit your work."

SASQUATCH BOOKS

1904 Third Ave., Suite 710, Seattle WA 98101. (206)467-4300. **Fax:** (206)467-4301. **E-mail:** ttabor@sasquatchbooks.com. **Website:** www.sasquatchbooks.com. **Contact:** Gary Luke, president/publisher; Heidi Lenze, acquisitions editor. "Sasquatch Books publishes books for and from the Pacific Northwest, Alaska, and California and is the nation's premier regional press. Sasquatch Books' publishing program is a veritable celebration of regionally written words. Undeterred by political or geographical borders, Sasquatch defines its region as the magnificent area that stretches from the Brooks Range to the Gulf of California and from the Rocky Mountains to the Pacific Ocean. Our top-selling Best Places® travel guides serve the most popular destinations and locations of the West. We also publish widely in the areas of food and wine, gardening, nature, photography, children's books, and regional history, all facets of the literature of place. With more than 200 books brimming with insider information on the West, we offer an energetic eye on the lifestyle, landscape, and worldview of our region. Considers queries and proposals from authors and agents for new projects that fit into our West Coast regional publishing program. We can evaluate query letters, proposals, and complete mss." Publishes regional hardcover and trade paperback originals. Publishes 30 titles/year. 20% of books from first-time authors. 75% from unagented writers.

"When you submit to Sasquatch Books, please remember that the editors want to know about you *and* your project, along with a sense of who will want to read your book."

FICTION Young readers: adventure, animal, concept, contemporary, humor, nature/environment. Recently published *Amazing Alaska*, by Deb Vanasse, illustrated by Karen Lewis; *Sourdough Man*, by Cherie Stihler, illustrated by Barbara Lavallee.

NONFICTION "We are seeking quality nonfiction works about the Pacific Northwest and West Coast regions (including Alaska to California). The literature of place includes how-to and where-to as well as history and narrative nonfiction." Picture books: activity books, animal, concept, nature/environment. Recently published *Larry Gets Lost in New York*, written and illustrated by John Skewes (picture book); *Searching for City Sasqatch*, by Nathaniel Lachenmeyer, illustrated by Vicki Bradley (picture book).

HOW TO CONTACT Query first, then submit outline and sample chapters with SASE. Send submissions to The Editors. E-mailed submissions and queries are not recommended. Please include return postage if you want your materials back. Responds to queries in 3 months. Publishes book 6-9 months after acceptance.

ILLUSTRATION Accepts material from international illustrators. Works with 5 illustrators/year. Uses both color and b&w. Reviews ms/illustration packages. For ms/illustration packages: Query. Submit ms/illustration packages to The Editors. Reviews work for future assignments. If interested in illustrating future titles, query with samples. Samples returned with SASE. Samples filed.

TERMS Pays royalty on cover price. Pays wide range advance. Book catalog for 9×12 envelope and 2 first-class stamps. Guidelines available online.

TIPS "We sell books through a range of channels in addition to the book trade. Our primary audience consists of active, literate residents of the West Coast."

◉ SCHOLASTIC INC.

557 Broadway, New York NY 10012. (212)343-6100. **Website:** www.scholastic.com.

○ Scholastic Trade Books is an award-winning publisher of original children's books. Scholastic publishes more than 600 new hardcover, paperback and novelty books each year. The list includes the phenomenally successful publishing properties Harry Potter®, Goosebumps®, The 39 Clues™, I Spy™, and *The Hunger Games*; bestselling and award-winning authors and illustrators, including Blue Balliett, Jim Benton, Meg Cabot, Suzanne Collins, Christopher Paul Curtis, Ann M. Martin, Dav Pilkey, J.K. Rowling, Pam Muñoz Ryan, Brian Selznick, David Shannon, Mark Teague, and Walter Wick, among others, as well as licensed properties such as Star Wars® and Rainbow Magic®.

▲ SCHOLASTIC LIBRARY PUBLISHING

90 Old Sherman Turnpike, Danbury CT 06816. (203)797-3500. **Fax:** (203)797-3197. **Website:** www.scholastic.com. **Contact:** Marie O'Neil, director of publishing. "Scholastic Library is a leading publisher of reference, educational, and children's books. We provide parents, teachers, and librarians with the tools they need to enlighten children to the pleasure of learning and prepare them for the road ahead. Publishes informational (nonfiction) for K-12; picture books for young readers, grades 1-3." Publishes hardcover and trade paperback originals.

○ *Accepts unsolicited ideas in the area of professional books only.*

FICTION Publishes 1 picture book series, Rookie Readers, for grades 1-2. Does not accept unsolicited mss.

NONFICTION Photo-illustrated books for all levels: animal, arts/crafts, biography, careers, concept, geography, health, history, hobbies, how-to, multicultural, nature/environment, science, social issues, special needs, sports. Average word length: young readers—2,000; middle readers—8,000; young adult—15,000.

ILLUSTRATION Works with 15-20 illustrators/year. Uses color artwork and line drawings. Illustrations only: Query with samples or arrange personal portfolio review. Responds only if interested. Samples returned with SASE. Samples filed. Do not send originals. No phone or e-mail inquiries; contact only by mail.

TERMS Pays authors royalty based on net or work purchased outright. Pays illustrators at competitive rates.

▲ SCHOLASTIC PRESS

Imprint of Scholastic, Inc., 557 Broadway, New York NY 10012. (212)343-6100. **Fax:** (212)343-4713. **Website:** www.scholastic.com. Scholastic Press publishes fresh, literary picture book fiction and nonfiction; fresh, literary nonseries or nongenre-oriented middle grade and young adult fiction. Currently emphasizing subtly handled treatments of key relationships in children's lives; unusual approaches to commonly dry subjects, such as biography, math, history, or science. De-emphasizing fairy tales (or retellings), board books, genre, or series fiction (mystery, fantasy, etc.). Publishes hardcover originals. Publishes 60 titles/year. 1% of books from first-time authors.

FICTION Looking for strong picture books, young chapter books, appealing middle grade novels (ages 8-11) and interesting and well-written young adult novels. Wants fresh, exciting picture books and novels—inspiring, new talent. Published *Chasing Vermeer*, by Blue Balliett; *Here Today*, by Ann M. Martin; *Detective LaRue*, by Mark Teague.

HOW TO CONTACT *Agented submissions and previously published authors only.* 2,500 queries received/year. Responds in 3 months to queries; 6-8 months to mss. Publishes book 2 years after acceptance.

ILLUSTRATION Works with 30 illustrators/year. Uses both b&w and color artwork. Illustrations only: Query with samples; send tearsheets. Responds only if interested. Samples returned with SASE. Original artwork returned at job's completion.

TERMS Pays royalty on retail price. Pays variable advance.

TIPS "Read *currently* published children's books. Revise, rewrite, rework and find your own voice, style and subject. We are looking for authors with a strong and unique voice who can tell a great story and have the ability to evoke genuine emotion. Children's publishers are becoming more selective, looking for irresistible talent and fairly broad appeal, yet still very willing to take risks, just to keep the game interesting."

SECOND STORY PRESS

20 Maud St., Suite 401, Toronto Ontario M5V 2M5, Canada. (416)537-7850. **Fax:** (416)537-0588. **E-mail:** info@secondstorypress.ca; marketing@secondstorypress.com. **Website:** www.secondstorypress.ca. Fiction Considers non-sexist, non-racist, and non-violent stories, as well as historical fiction, chapter books, picture books. Recently published: *Writing the Revolution*, by Michele Landsberg; *Shannen and the Dream for a School*, by Janet Wilson.

NONFICTION Picture books: biography. Recently published: *We Are Their Voice: Young People Respond to the Holocaust*, by Kathy Kacer (a new addition to our Holocaust remembrance series for young readers).

HOW TO CONTACT *Accepts appropriate material from residents of Canada only.* Submit outline and sample chapters by postal mail only. No electronic submissions or queries. No electronic submissions or queries.

SEEDLING CONTINENTAL PRESS

520 E. Bainbridge St., Elizabethtown PA 17022. (806)223-0759. **Website:** www.continentalpress.com. **Contact:** Megan Bergonzi. Publishes books for classroom use only for the beginning reader in English. "Natural language and predictable text are requisite. Patterned text is acceptable, but must have a unique story line. Poetry, books in rhyme and full-length picture books are not being accepted. Illustrations are not necessary."

FICTION Young readers: adventure, animal, folktales, humor, multicultural, nature/environment. Does not accept texts longer than 12 pages or over 300 words. Average word length: young readers—100.

NONFICTION Young readers: animal, arts/crafts, biography, careers, concept, multicultural, nature/environment, science. Does not accept texts longer than 12 pages or over 300 words. Average word length: young readers—100.

HOW TO CONTACT Submit complete ms. Responds to mss in 6 months. Publishes book 1-2 years after acceptance.

ILLUSTRATION Works with 8-10 illustrators/year. Uses color artwork only. Reviews ms/illustration packages from artists. Submit ms with dummy. Illustrations only: Color copies or line art. Responds only if interested. Samples returned with SASE only; samples filed if interested.

PHOTOGRAPHY Buys photos from freelancers. Works on assignment only. Model/property releases required. Uses color prints and 35mm transparencies. Submit cover letter and color promo piece.

TERMS Work purchased outright from authors.

TIPS "See our website. Follow writers' guidelines carefully and test your story with children and educators."

SHEN'S BOOKS

1547 Palos Verdes Mall #291, Walnut Creek CA 94597. (925)262-8108. **Fax:** (888)269-9092. **E-mail:** info@shens.com. **Website:** www.shens.com. **Contact:** Renee Ting, president.

FICTION Picture books, young readers: folktales, multicultural with Asian Focus. recently published *Selvakumar Knew Better*, by Virginia Kroll, illustrated by Xiaojun Li (ages 4-8).

NONFICTION Picture books, young readers: multicultural. Recently published *Chinese History Stories* edited by Renee Ting.

HOW TO CONTACT Responds to queries in 1-2 weeks; mss in 6-12 months. Publishes book 1-2 years after acceptance.

ILLUSTRATION Accepts material from international illustrators. Works with 2 illustrators/year. Uses color artwork only. Reviews ms/illustration packages. For ms/illustration packages: Send ms with dummy. Submit ms/illustration packages to Renee Ting, president. Reviews work for future assignments. If interested in illustrating future titles, query with samples. Submit samples to Renee Ting, president. Samples not returned. Samples filed.

PHOTOGRAPHY Works on assignment only. Submit photos to Renee Ting, president.

TERMS Authors pay negotiated by project. Catalog available on website.

TIPS "Be familiar with our catalog before submitting."

SIMON & SCHUSTER BOOKS FOR YOUNG READERS

Imprint of Simon & Schuster Children's Publishing, 1230 Avenue of the Americas, New York NY 10020. (212)698-7000. **Fax:** (212)698-2796. **Website:** www.simonsayskids.com. "Simon and Schuster Books for Young Readers is the flagship imprint of the S&S Children's Division. We are committed to publishing a wide range of contemporary, commercial, award-winning fiction and nonfiction that spans every age of children's publishing. BFYR is constantly looking to the future, supporting our foundation authors and franchises, but always with an eye for breaking new ground with every publication. We publish high-quality fiction and nonfiction for a variety of age groups and a variety of markets. Above all, we strive to publish books that we are passionate about." Publishes hardcover originals. Publishes 75 titles/year.

◐ All unsolicited mss returned unopened. Queries are accepted via mail.

NONFICTION Picture books: concept. All levels: narrative, current events, biography, history. "We're looking for picture books or middle grade nonfiction that have a retail potential. No photo essays." Recently published Insiders Series (picture book nonfiction, all ages).

HOW TO CONTACT Query with SASE only. Responds in 2 months to queries and mss. Publishes ms 2-4 years after acceptance.

ILLUSTRATION Works with 70 illustrators/year. Do not submit original artwork. Does not accept unsolicited or unagented illustration submissions.

TERMS Pays variable royalty on retail price. Guidelines for #10 SASE.

TIPS "We're looking for picture books centered on a strong, fully-developed protagonist who grows or changes during the course of the story; YA novels that are challenging and psychologically complex; also imaginative and humorous middle grade fiction. And we want nonfiction that is as engaging as fiction. Our imprint's slogan is 'Reading You'll Remember.' We aim to publish books that are fresh, accessible and family-oriented; we want them to have an impact on the reader."

SKINNER HOUSE BOOKS

The Unitarian Universalist Association, 25 Beacon St., Boston MA 02108. (617)742-2100 ext. 603. **Fax:** (617)367-3237. **E-mail:** info@uua.org. **Website:** www.uua.org/skinner. **Contact:** Mary Benard, senior editor. "We publish titles in Unitarian Universalist faith, liberal religion, history, biography, worship, and issues of social justice. Most of our children's titles are intended for religious education or worship use. They reflect Unitarian Universalist values. We also publish inspirational titles of poetic prose and meditations. Writers should know that Unitarian Universalism is a liberal religious denomination committed to progressive ideals. Currently emphasizing social justice concerns." Publishes trade paperback originals and reprints. Publishes 10-20 titles/year. 50% of books from first-time authors. 100% from unagented writers.

FICTION All levels: anthology, multicultural, nature/environment, religion. Recently published *A Child's Book of Blessings and Prayers*, by Eliza Blanchard (ages 4-8, picture book); *Meet Jesus: The Life and Lessons of a Beloved Teacher*, by Lynn Gunney (ages 5-8, picture book); *Magic Wanda's Travel Emporium*, by Joshua Searle-White (ages 9 and up, stories).

NONFICTION All levels: activity books, multicultural, music/dance, nature/environment, religion. *Unitarian Universalism Is a Really Long Name*, by Jennifer Dant (picture book, resource that answers children's questions about Unitarian Universalism, ages 5-9).

HOW TO CONTACT Query or submit outline/synopsis and 2 sample chapters. Responds to queries in 3 weeks. Publishes book 1 year after acceptance.

ILLUSTRATION Works with 2 illustrators/year. Uses both color and b&w. Reviews ms/illustration packages from artists. Query. Responds only if interested. Samples returned with SASE.

PHOTOGRAPHY Buys stock images and assigns work. Uses inspirational types of photo's. Model/property releases required; captions required. Uses color, b&w. Submit cover letter, resume.

TERMS Book catalog for 6×9 SAE with 3 first-class stamps. Guidelines available online.

TIPS "From outside our denomination, we are interested in manuscripts that will be of help or interest to liberal churches, Sunday school classes, parents, ministers, and volunteers. Inspirational/spiritual and children's titles must reflect liberal Unitarian Universalist values."

SLEEPING BEAR PRESS

315 East Eisenhower Pkwy, Suite 200, Ann Arbor MI 48108. (800)487-2323. **Fax:** (734)794-0004. **E-mail:** customerservice@sleepingbearpress.com. **Website:** www.sleepingbearpress.com. **Contact:** Heather Hughes.

○ *Currently not accepting ms submissions or queries. "Please check back for further updates."*

FICTION Picture books: adventure, animal, concept, folktales, history, multicultural, nature/environment, religion, sports. Young readers: adventure, animal, concept, folktales, history, humor, multicultural, nature/environment, religion, sports. Average word length: picture books—1,800.

TERMS Book catalog available via e-mail.

➕ SOHO TEEN

An imprint of Soho Press, 853 Broadway, New York, NY 10003. **E-mail:** rkowal@sohopress.com. **Website:** www.sohopress.com. **Contact:** Rachel Kowal.

○ "In part, it was conceived as a natural complement to Soho Press—in particular, its legendary Soho Crime imprint. But it was also conceived with a simple question in mind: What recent YA bestseller doesn't involve a mystery in some part? How many times does a YA reader ask: What don't I know? And what will I discover? Soho Teen offers an unapologetic take on that thrill, putting mystery at the front and center of all our titles. In our list, you'll find the paranormal and dystopian. You'll also find hilarity, heartbreak, tragedy, euphoria, reflection, jealousy, love, loss and gain: the entire spectrum of the teen experience. You'll meet characters you trust at first glance and others who make your blood boil."

FICTION Publishes 12 titles/yr. All titles feature a unique protagonist, aged 14-17, who plays a crucial role in resolving a high-stakes mystery.

HOW TO CONTACT Must first submit a query. Will respond to queries in 6-8 weeks. "Start by sending three chapters (or fifty pages) and a cover letter to Soho Press at 853 Broadway, New York, NY 10003, care of acquisitions editor. Please accompany all submissions and queries with postage and packing materials for their return. It's not advised to send a query letter without sample pages. Without seeing the actual writing, it's hard to get enthusiastic about a book." Although you can submit sample pages, do not submit the entire ms.

TIPS This publisher is open to submissions from writers, but tends to buy submissions from agencies. "As of now we are not interested in acquiring series. If your stand-alone title has the potential to become a series, please include future plots at the end of your synopsis."

◯ SOUNDPRINTS/STUDIO MOUSE

Palm Publishing. LLC, 50 Washington St., 12th Floor, Norwalk CT 06854. (800)409-2457. **Fax:** (203)864-1776. **E-mail:** customercare@palmkids.com **Website:** www.soundprints.com.

FICTION Picture books, young readers: adventure, animal, fantasy, history, multicultural, nature/environment, sports. Recently published *Alphabet of Earth: a Smithsonian Alphabet*, by Barbie Heit Schwaeber, and illustrated by Sally Vitsky (ages preschool-2, hardcover and paperback available with audio CD plus bonus audiobook and e-book downloads); *First Look at Insects*, by Laura Gates Galvin, illustrated by Charlotte Oh. Ages 18 months-5 years board book plus e-book and activities download.

HOW TO CONTACT Query or submit complete ms. Responds to queries and mss in 6 months. Publishes book 1-2 years after acceptance.

ILLUSTRATION Illustration: Works with 3-7 illustrators/year. Uses color artwork only. Send tearsheets with contact information, "especially web address if applicable." Samples not returned; samples filed.

PHOTOGRAPHY Buys stock and assign work. Model/property release and captions required. Send color promo sheet.

TERMS Catalog available on website. Guidelines for SASE.

SPINNER BOOKS

University Games, 2030 Harrison St., San Francisco CA 94110. (415)503-1600. **Fax:** (415)503-0085. **E-mail:** info@ugames.com. **Website:** www.ugames.com. "Spinners Books publishes books of puzzles, games and trivia."

NONFICTION Picture books: games & puzzles. Recently published *20 Questions*, by Bob Moog (adult); *20 Questions for Kids*, by Bob Moog (young adult).

HOW TO CONTACT *Only interested in agented material.* Query. Responds to queries in 3 months; mss in 2 months only if interested. Publishes book 6 months after acceptance.

ILLUSTRATION Only interested in agented material. Uses both color and b&w. Illustrations only: Query with samples. Responds in 3 months only if interested. Samples not returned.

STANDARD PUBLISHING

8805 Governor's Hill Dr., Suite 400, Cincinnati OH 45249. (800)543-1353. **E-mail:** customerservice@standardpub.com; adultministry@standardpub.com; ministrytochildren@standardpub.com; ministrytoyouth@standardpub.com. **Website:** www.standardpub.com. Publishes resources that meet church and family needs in the area of children's ministry.

TERMS Guidelines and current publishing objectives available online.

STERLING PUBLISHING CO., INC.

387 Park Ave. S, New York NY 10016. (212)532-7160. **Fax:** (212)981-0508. **E-mail:** custserviceeditorial@sterlingpublishing.com. **Website:** www.sterlingpublishing.com. "Sterling publishes highly illustrated, accessible, hands-on, practical books for adults and children." Publishes hardcover and paperback originals and reprints. 15% of books from first-time authors.

○ "Our mission is to publish high-quality books that educate, entertain, and enrich the lives of our readers."

FICTION Picture books. "At present we do not accept fiction."

NONFICTION Proposals on subjects such as crafting, decorating, outdoor living, and photography should be sent directly to Lark Books at their Asheville, North Carolina offices. Complete guidelines can be found on the Lark site: www.larkbooks.com/submissions. Publishes nonfiction only.

HOW TO CONTACT Submit outline, publishing history, 1 sample chapter (typed and double-spaced), SASE. Explain your idea. Send sample illustrations where applicable. For children's books, please submit full mss. We do not accept electronic (e-mail) submissions. Be sure to include information about yourself with particular regard to your skills and qualifications in the subject area of your submission. It is helpful for us to know your publishing history—whether or not you've written other books and, if so, the name of the publisher and whether those books are currently in print.

ILLUSTRATION Works with 50 illustrators/year. Reviews ms/illustration packages from artists. Illustrations only: Send promo sheet. Contact: Karen Nelson, creative director. Responds in 6 weeks. Samples returned with SASE; samples filed.

PHOTOGRAPHY Buys stock and assigns work. Contact: Karen Nelson.

TERMS Pays royalty or work purchased outright. Offers advances (average amount: $2,000). Catalog available on website. Guidelines available online.

TIPS "We are primarily a nonfiction activities-based publisher. We have a picture book list, but we do not publish chapter books or novels. Our list is not trend-driven. We focus on titles that will backlist well. "

STOREY PUBLISHING

210 MASS MoCA Way, North Adams MA 01247. (800)793-9396. **Fax:** (413)346-2196. **E-mail:** webmaster@storey.com. **Website:** www.storey.com. **Contact:** Deborah Balmuth, editorial director (building, sewing, gift). "The mission of Storey Publishing is to serve our customers by publishing practical information that encourages personal independence in harmony with the environment. We seek to do this in a positive atmosphere that promotes editorial quality, team spirit, and profitability. The books we select to carry out this mission include titles on gardening, small-scale farming, building, cooking, homebrewing, crafts, part-time business, home improvement, woodworking, animals, nature, natural living, personal care, and country living. We are always pleased to review new proposals, which we try to process expeditiously. We offer both work-for-hire and standard royalty contracts." Publishes hardcover and trade paperback originals and reprints. Publishes 40 titles/

year. 25% of books from first-time authors. 60% from unagented writers.

HOW TO CONTACT 600 queries received/year. 150 mss received/year. Responds in 1 month to queries; 3 months to proposals/mss. Publishes book 2 years after acceptance.

TERMS Pays advance. Book catalog available free. Guidelines available online at website.

SYLVAN DELL PUBLISHING

612 Johnnie Dodds Blvd., Suite A2, Mt. Pleasant SC 29464. (843)971-6722. **Fax:** (843)216-3804. **E-mail:** don nagerman@sylvandellpublishing.com; info@sylvandellpublishing.com. **Website:** www.sylvandellpublishing.com. **Contact:** Donna German, editor. "The picture books we publish are usually, but not always, fictional stories that relate to animals, nature, the environment, and science. All books should subtly convey an educational theme through a warm story that is fun to read and that will grab a child's attention. Each book has a 3-5 page 'For Creative Minds' section to reinforce the educational component. This section will have a craft and/or game as well as 'fun facts' to be shared by the parent, teacher, or other adult. Authors do not need to supply this information. Mss should be less than 1,500 words and meet all of the following 4 criteria: fun to read—mostly fiction with nonfiction facts woven into the story; national or regional in scope; must tie into early elementary school curriculum; must be marketable through a niche market such as a zoo, aquarium, or museum gift shop." Publishes hardcover, trade paperback, and electronic originals. Publishes 10 titles/year. 50% of books from first-time authors. 100% from unagented writers.

FICTION Picture books: animal, folktales, nature/ environment, math-related. Word length—picture books: no more than 1500. Recently published *Whistling Wings*, by first-time author Laura Goering, illustrated by Laura Jacques; *Sort it Out!*, by Barbara Mariconda, illustrated by Sherry Rogers; *River Beds: Sleeping in the World's Rivers,* by Gail Langer Karwoski, illustrated by Connie McLennan; *Saturn for My Birthday,* by first-time author John McGranaghan, illustrated by Wendy Edelson.

NONFICTION "We are not looking for mss. about: pets (dogs or cats in particular); new babies; local or state-specific; magic; biographies; history-related; ABC books; poetry; series; young adult books or novels; holiday-related books. We do not consider mss.

that have been previously published in any way, including e-books or self-published."

HOW TO CONTACT Accepts electronic submissions only. Snail mail submissions are discarded without being opened. 2,000 mss received/year. Acknowledges receipt of ms submission within one week. Publishes book 18 months after acceptance. May hold onto mss of interest for 1 year until acceptance.

ILLUSTRATION Works with 10 illustrators/year. Prefers to work with illustrators from the US and Canada. Uses color artwork only. Submit Web link or 2-3 electronic images. Contact: Donna German. "I generally keep submissions on file until I match the manuscripts to illustration needs."

TERMS Pays 6-8% royalty on wholesale price. Pays small advance. Book catalog and guidelines available online.

TIPS "Please make sure that you have looked at our website to read our complete submission guidelines and to see if we are looking for a particular subject. Manuscripts must meet all four of our stated criteria. We look for fairly realistic, bright and colorful art- no cartoons. We want the children excited about the books. We envision the books being used at home and in the classroom."

SYNERGEBOOKS

948 New Highway 7, Columbia TN 38401. (931)223 5990. **Fax:** (863)588-2198. **E-mail:** synergebooks@ aol.com. **Website:** www.synergebooks.com. **Contact:** Debra Staples, publisher/acquisitions editor. "SynergEbooks is first and foremost a digital publisher, so most of our marketing budget goes to those formats. Authors are required to direct-sell a minimum of 100 digital copies of a title before it's accepted for print." Publishes trade paperback and electronic originals. Publishes 40-60 titles/year. 95% of books from first-time authors. 99.9% from unagented writers.

FICTION SynergEbooks publishes at least 40 new titles a year, and only 1-5 of those are put into print in any given year.

HOW TO CONTACT Submit proposal package, including synopsis, 1-3 sample chapters, and marketing plans. 250 queries received/year. 250 mss received/ year.

TERMS Pays 15-40% royalty; makes outright purchase. Book catalog and guidelines available online.

TIPS "At SynergEbooks, we work with the author to promote their work."

TANGLEWOOD BOOKS

P.O. Box 3009, Terre Haute IN 47803. E-mail: khamlinptierney@tanglewood-books.com Website: www.tangle woodbooks.com. Contact: Kairi Hamlin, acquisitions editor; Peggy Tierney, publisher. "Tanglewood Press strives to publish entertaining, kid-centric books." Publishes 10 titles/year. 20% of books from first-time authors.

FICTION Picture books: adventure, animal, concept, contemporary, fantasy, humor. Average word length: picture books—800. Recently published *68 Knots*, by Micheal Robert Evans (young adult); *The Mice of Bistrot des Sept Frères*, written and illustrated by Marie Le Tourneau; *Chester Raccoon and the Acorn Full of Memories*, by Audrey Penn and Barbara Gibson.

NONFICTION Does not generally publish nonfiction.

HOW TO CONTACT Query with 3-5 sample chapters. Responds to mss in up to 18 months. Publishes book 2 years after acceptance.

ILLUSTRATION Accepts material from international illustrators. Works with 3-4 illustrators/year. Uses both color and b&w. Reviews ms/illustration packages. For ms/illustration packages: Send ms with sample illustrations. Submit ms/illustration packages to Peggy Tierney, publisher. If interested in illustrating future titles, query with samples. Submit samples to Peggy Tierney. Samples not returned. Samples filed.

TERMS Illustrators paid by the project for covers and small illustrations; royalty of 3-5% for picture books. Author sees galleys for review. Illustrators see dummies for review. Originals returned to artist at job's completion.

TIPS "Please see lengthy 'Submissions' page on our website."

◑ THISTLEDOWN PRESS LTD.

118 20th Street West, Saskatoon Saskatchewan S7M 0W6, Canada. (306)244-1722. Fax: (306)244-1762. E-mail: editorial@thistledownpress.com. Website: www.thistledownpress.com. Contact: Allan Forrie, publisher.

◑ "Thistledown originates books by Canadian authors only, although we have co-published titles by authors outside Canada. We do not publish children's picture books."

FICTION Middle readers, young adults: adventure, anthology, contemporary, fantasy, humor, poetry, romance, science fiction, suspense/mystery, short sto-ries. Average word length: young adults—40,000. Recently published *Cheeseburger Subversive*, by Richard Scarsbrook and *The Alchemist's Daughter*, by Eileen Kernaghan.

HOW TO CONTACT Submit outline/synopsis and sample chapters. *Does not accept mss.* Do not query by e-mail. Responds to queries in 4 months. Publishes book 1 year after acceptance.

ILLUSTRATION Prefers agented illustrators but "not mandatory." Works with few illustrators. Illustrations only: Query with samples, promo sheet, slides, tearsheets. Responds only if interested. Samples returned with SASE; samples filed.

TERMS Pays authors royalty of 10-12% based on net dollar sales. Pays illustrators and photographers by the project (range: $250-750). Book catalog free on request. Guidelines available for #10 envelope and IRC.

TIPS "Send cover letter including publishing history and SASE."

◑ TIGHTROPE BOOKS

602 Markham St., Toronto ON M6G 2L8, Canada. (647)348-4460. E-mail: info@tightropebooks.com. Website: www.tightropebooks.com. Contact: Halli Villegas, publisher. Publishes hardcover and trade paperback originals. Publishes 12 titles/year. 70% of books from first-time authors. 100% from unagented writers.

◑ Temporarily suspending all submissions.

HOW TO CONTACT Responds if interested. Publishes book 1 year after acceptance.

TERMS Pays 5-15% royalty on retail price. Pays advance of $200-300. Catalog and guidelines free on request and online.

TIPS "Audience is young, urban, literary, educated, unconventional."

TILBURY HOUSE

Harpswell Press, Inc., 103 Brunswick Ave., Gardiner ME 04345. (800)582-1899. Fax: (207)582-8227. E-mail: tilbury@tilburyhouse.com. Website: www.tilburyhouse.com. Contact: Jennifer Bunting, publisher. Publishes 10 titles/year.

FICTION Picture books: multicultural, nature/environment. Special needs include books that teach children about tolerance and honoring diversity. Recently published *One of Us*, by Peggy Moss; *Moon Watchers: Shirin's Ramadan Miracle*, by Reza Jalali; and *The Lunch Thief*, by Anne Bromley, illustrated by Rober Casilla.

NONFICTION Regional adult biography/history/maritime/nature, and children's picture books that deal with issues, such as bullying, multiculturalism, etc.

HOW TO CONTACT Submit complete ms or outline/synopsis. Responds to mss in 2 months. Publishes ms 1 year after acceptance.

ILLUSTRATION Works with 2-3 illustrators/year. Illustrations only: Query with samples. Responds in 1 month. Samples returned with SASE. Original artwork returned at job's completion.

PHOTOGRAPHY Buys photos from freelancers. Works on assignment only.

TERMS Pays royalty based on wholesale price. Book catalog available free. Guidelines available online.

TIPS "We are always interested in stories that will encourage children to understand the natural world and the environment, as well as stories with social justice themes. We really like stories that engage children to become problem solvers as well as those that promote respect, tolerance and compassion." We do not publish books with personified animal characters; historical fiction; chapter books; fantasy."

TOR BOOKS

175 Fifth Ave., New York NY 10010. **Website:** www.tor-forge.com. **Contact:** Juliet Pederson, publishing coordinator. Publishes Publishes 5-10 middle readers/year; 5-10 young adult titles/year. titles/year.

Tor Books is the "world's largest publisher of science fiction and fantasy, with strong category publishing in historical fiction, mystery, western/Americana, thriller, YA."

FICTION Average word length: middle readers—30,000; young adults—60,000-100,000.

NONFICTION Middle readers and young adult: geography, history, how-to, multicultural, nature/environment, science, social issues. Does not want to see religion, cooking. Average word length: middle readers—25,000-35,000; young adults—70,000. Published Strange Unsolved Mysteries by Phyllis Raybin Emert.

HOW TO CONTACT We do not accept queries.

TERMS Pays author royalty. Pays illustrators by the project. Book catalog available for 9x12 SAE and 3 first-class stamps. See website for latest submission guidelines.

TIPS "Know the house you are submitting to, familiarize yourself with the types of books they are publishing. Get an agent. Allow him/her to direct you to publishers who are most appropriate. It saves time and effort."

⊕ TURN THE PAGE PUBLISHING LLC

P.O. Box 3179, Upper Montclair NJ 07043. **E-mail:** rlentin@turnthepagepublishing.com; inquiry@turnthepagepublishing.com. **Website:** www.turnthepagepublishing.com. **Contact:** Roseann Lentin, president. Publishes hardcover, trade paperback, electronic originals and trade paperback, electronic reprints. Publishes 12-15 titles/year. 95% of books from first-time authors. 100% from unagented writers.

FICTION "We like new, fresh voices who are not afraid to 'step outside the box,' with unique ideas and storylines. We prefer 'edgy' rather than 'typical.'"

HOW TO CONTACT Submit proposal package including outline, 3 sample chapters, author bio. Receives 100 queries/year; 50 mss/year. Responds in 3 months to queries; 2 months to proposals/mss. Publishes ms 8 months after acceptance.

TERMS Pays 8-15% royalty on retail price. Book catalog available online at website. Guidelines by e-mail.

TIPS "Our audience is made up of intelligent, sophisticated, forward-thinking, progressive readers, who are not afraid to consider reading something different to Turn the Page of their lives. We're an independent publisher, we're avant-garde, so if you're looking for run of the mill, don't submit here."

⊘ TYNDALE HOUSE PUBLISHERS, INC.

351 Executive Dr., Carol Stream IL 60188. (800)323-9400. **Fax:** (800)684-0247. **Website:** www.tyndale.com. **Contact:** Katara Washington Patton, acquisitions; Talinda Iverson, art acquisitions. "Tyndale House publishes practical, user-friendly Christian books for the home and family." Publishes hardcover and trade paperback originals and mass paperback reprints. Publishes 15 titles/year.

FICTION "Christian truths must be woven into the story organically. No short story collections. Youth books: character building stories with Christian perspective. Especially interested in ages 10-14. We primarily publish Christian historical romances, with occasional contemporary, suspense, or standalones."

HOW TO CONTACT Agented submissions only. *No unsolicited mss.*

ILLUSTRATION Uses full-color for book covers, b&w or color spot illustrations for some nonfiction. Illustrations only: Query with photocopies (color or b&w) of samples, résumé.

PHOTOGRAPHY Buys photos from freelancers. Works on assignment only.

TERMS Pays negotiable royalty. Pays negotiable advance. Guidelines for 9×12 SAE and $2.40 for postage or visit website.

TIPS "All accepted manuscripts will appeal to Evangelical Christian children and parents."

UNTREED READS PUBLISHING

506 Kansas St., San Francisco CA 94107. (415)621-0465. **Fax:** (415)621-0465. **E-mail:** general@untreedreads.com. **E-mail:** submissions@untreedreads.com. **Website:** www.untreedreads.com. **Contact:** Jay A. Hartman, editor-in-chief (fiction, all genres). Publishes electronic originals and reprints. Publishes 35 titles/year. 80% of books from first-time authors. 75% from unagented writers.

FICTION "We look forward to long-term relationships with our authors. We encourage works that are either already a series or could develop into a series. We are one of the few publishers publishing short stories and are happy to be a resource for these good works. We welcome short story collections. Also, we look forward to publishing children's books, cookbooks, and other works that have been known for illustrations in print as the technology in the multiple e-readers improves. We hope to be a large platform for diverse content and authors. We seek mainstream content, but if you're an author or have content that doesn't seem to always 'fit' into traditional market we'd like to hear from you." No erotica, picture books, poetry, poetry in translation, or romance.

NONFICTION "We are very interested in developing our textbook market. E-readers don't currently support graphs, tables, images, etc. as well as print books; however, we plan to be trendsetters in this as the technology in the e-readers improves. Also we are eager to increase our number of business books. We always look for series or works that could develop into a series."

HOW TO CONTACT Submit porposal package with 3 sample chapters. Submit completed ms. Submit proposal package, including 3 sample chapters. Submit completed mss. Receives 50 submissions/year. Responds in 1/2 month on queries, 1 month on proposals, and 1 1/2 months on mss.

TERMS Pays 50-60% royalty on retail price. Catalog and guidelines available online at website.

TIPS "For our fiction titles we lean toward a literary audience. For nonfiction titles, we want to be a platform for business people, entrepreneurs, and speakers to become well known in their fields of expertise. However, for both fiction and nonfiction we want to appeal to many audiences."

URJ BOOKS AND MUSIC

633 Third Ave., 7th Floor, New York NY 10017. (212)650-4120. **Fax:** (212)650-4119. **E-mail:** press@urj.org. **Website:** www.urjbooksandmusic.com. **Contact:** Rabbi Hara Person, editor-in-chief. "URJ publishes textbooks for the religious classroom, children's tradebooks and scholarly work of Jewish education import—no adult fiction and no YA fiction." Publishes hardcover and trade paperback originals. Publishes 22 titles/year. 70% of books from first-time authors. 90% from unagented writers.

○ *URJ Press publishes books related to Judaism.*

FICTION Picture books: religion. Average word length: picture books—1,500. Recently published *The Purim Costume*, by Peninnah Schram, illustrated by Tammy L. Keiser (ages 4-8, picture book); *A Year of Jewish Stories: 52 Tales for Young Children and Their Families*, by Grace Ragues Maisel and Samantha Shubert, illustrated by Tammy L. Keiser (ages 4-12, picture book).

NONFICTION Picture books, young readers, middle readers: religion. Average word length: picture books—1,500.

HOW TO CONTACT Submit complete ms with author bio. Submit proposal package, outline, bio, 1-2 sample chapters. 500 queries received/year. 400 mss received/year. Responds to queries/mss in 4 months. Publishes book 18-24 months after acceptance.

ILLUSTRATION Works with 5 illustrators/year. Reviews ms/illustration packages from artists. Send ms with dummy. Illustrations only: Send portfolio to be kept on file. Responds in 2 months. Samples returned with SASE. Looking specifically for Jewish themes.

PHOTOGRAPHY Buys stock and assigns work. Uses photos with Jewish content. Prefers modern settings. Submit cover letter and promo piece.

TERMS Pays 3-5% royalty on retail price. Makes outright purchase of 500-2,000. Pays $500-2,000 advance. Book catalog and ms guidelines free or on website.

TIPS "Look at some of our books. Have an understanding of the Reform Judaism community. In addition to bookstores, we sell to Jewish congregations and Hebrew day schools."

VIEWPOINT PRESS

PMB 400 785 Tucker Rd. #G, Tehachapi CA 93561. (661)821-5110. **Fax:** (661)821-7515. **E-mail:** joie99@ aol.com. **Website:** http://www.viewpointpress.com/ products.html. We have been in business for 25 years and have three children's books: *Seeds of Violence: the Autobiography of a Subversive; Fiddler of the Opry: The Howdy Forrester Story; and Footprints of the Soul: a Novel.*

○ *Not currently accepting mss.*

Ⓐ Ⓞ VIKING CHILDREN'S BOOKS

375 Hudson St., New York NY 10014. **E-mail:** avery studiopublicity@us.penguingroup.com. **Website:** www.penguingroup.com. **Contact:** Catherine Frank, executive editor. "Viking Children's Books is known for humorous, quirky picture books, in addition to more traditional fiction. We publish the highest quality fiction, nonfiction, and picture books for preschoolers through young adults." Publishes hardcover originals. Publishes 70 titles/year.

○ *Does not accept unsolicited submissions.*

FICTION All levels: adventure, animal, contemporary, fantasy, history, humor, multicultural, nature/environment, poetry, problem novels, romance, science fiction, sports, suspense/mystery. Recently published *Llama Llama Misses Mama*, by Anna Dewdney (ages 2 up, picture book); *Wintergirls*, by Laurie Halse Anderson (ages 12 and up); *Good Luck Bear*, by Greg Foley (ages 2 up); *Along for the Ride*, by Sarah Dessen (ages 12 up).

NONFICTION All levels: biography, concept, history, multicultural, music/dance, nature/environment, science, and sports. Recently published *Harper Lee*, by Kerry Madden (ages 11 up, biography); *Knucklehead*, by Jon Scieszka (ages 7up, autobiography); *Marching for Freedom*, by Elizabeth Partridge (ages 11 up, nonfiction).

HOW TO CONTACT *Accepts agented mss only.* Query with SASE, or submit outline, 3 sample chapters, SASE. Responds to queries/mss in 6 months. Publishes book 1-2 years after acceptance.

ILLUSTRATION Works with 30 illustrators/year. Responds to artist's queries/submissions only if interested. Samples returned with SASE only or samples filed. Originals returned at job's completion.

TERMS Pays 2-10% royalty on retail price or flat fee. Pays negotiable advance.

TIPS No "cartoony" or mass-market submissions for picture books.

WALKER AND CO.

Walker Publishing Co., 175 Fifth Ave., 7th Floor, New York NY 10010. (212)727-8300. **Fax:** (212)727-0984. **Website:** bloomsbury.com. **Contact:** Emily Easton, publisher (picture books, middle grade & young adult novels); Mary Kate Castellani, editor (picture books, middle grade, and young adult novels). "Walker publishes general nonfiction on a variety of subjects, as well as children's books." Publishes hardcover trade originals.

FICTION Accepts unsolicited mss. Query with SASE. Include "a concise description of the story line, including its outcome, word length of story, writing experience, publishing credits, particular expertise on this subject and in this genre. Common mistake: not researching our publishing program and forgetting SASE."

HOW TO CONTACT Query with SASE. Send complete ms for picture books. *Adult fiction: agented submissions only*; juvenile: send synopsis. Publishes ms 1 year after acceptance.

TERMS Pays 5-10% royalty. Book catalog for 9×12 envelope and 3 first-class stamps.

Ⓞ WEIGL PUBLISHERS INC.

350 5th Ave, 59th Floor, New York NY 10118. (866)649-3445. **Fax:** (866)449-3445. **E-mail:** lin da@weigl.com. **Website:** www.weigl.com. **Contact:** Heather Kissock, acquisitions. Publishes 25 young readers/year; 40 middle readers/year; 20 young adult titles/year. "Our mission is to provide innovative high-quality learning resources for schools and libraries worldwide at a competitive price." Publishes 85 titles/year. 15% of books from first-time authors.

NONFICTION Young readers: animal, biography, geography, history, multicultural, nature/environment, science. Middle readers: animal, biography, geography, history, multicultural, nature/environment, science, social issues, sports. Young adults: biography, careers, geography, history, multicultural, nature/environment, social issues. Average word length: young readers—100 words/page; middle readers—200 words/page; young adults—300 words/page. Recently published *Amazing Animals* (ages 9 and up, science series) and *Science Q&A* (ages 9 and up, social studies series).

HOW TO CONTACT Query by e-mail only. Publishes book 6-9 months after acceptance.

ILLUSTRATION Pays illustrators by the project. Book catalog available for 912×11 SASE. Catalog available on website.

PHOTOGRAPHY Pays per photo.

TERMS Book catalog available for 912×11 SASE. Catalog available on website.

WHITE MANE KIDS

73 W. Burd St., P.O. Box 708, Shippensburg PA 17257. (717)532-2237. **Fax:** (717)532-6110. **E-mail:** marketing@whitemane.com. **Website:** www.whitemane.com. **Contact:** Harold Collier, acquisitions editor.

FICTION Middle readers, young adults: history (primarily American Civil War). Average word length: middle readers—30,000. Does not publish picture books. Recently published *The Witness Tree and the Shadow of the Noose: Mystery, Lies, and Spies in Manassas,* by K.E.M. Johnston, and *Drumbeat: The Story of a Civil War Drummer Boy,* by Robert J. Trout (grades 5 and up).

NONFICTION Middle readers, young adults: history. Average word length: middle readers—30,000. Does not publish picture books. Recently published *Hey, History Isn't Boring Anymore! A Creative Approach to Teaching the Civil War,* by Kelly Ann Butterbaugh (young adult).

HOW TO CONTACT Query. Submit outline/synopsis and 2-3 sample chapters. Responds to queries in 1 month, mss in 3 months. Publishes book 18 months after acceptance.

ILLUSTRATION Works with 4 illustrators/year. Illustrations used for cover art only. Responds only if interested. Samples returned with SASE.

PHOTOGRAPHY Buys stock and assigns work. Submit cover letter and portfolio.

TERMS Pays authors royalty of 7-10%. Pays illustrators and photographers by the project. Book catalog and writer's guidelines available for SASE.

TIPS "Make your work historically accurate. We are interested in historically accurate fiction for middle and young adult readers. We do *not* publish picture books. Our primary focus is the American Civil War and some America Revolution topics."

○ ⊕ ALBERT WHITMAN & COMPANY

250 S. Northwest Hwy., Suite 320, Park Ridge IL 60068. (800)255-7675. **Fax:** (847)581-0039. **E-mail:** mail@awhitmanco.com. **Website:** www.albertwhitman.com. "Albert Whitman & Company publishes books for the trade, library, and school library market. We have an open submissions policy: we read unsolicited work, which means that it is not necessary for writers to submit through a literary agent. We are interested in reviewing the following types of projects: picture book manuscripts for ages 2-8; Novels and chapter books for ages 8-12; young adult novels; nonfiction for ages 3-12 and YA; art samples showing pictures of children." Best known for the classic series The Boxcar Children® Mysteries, its highly-praised picture books, novels, and nonfiction titles for ages 2-12, delighting children and reaching out to children of all backgrounds and experiences. "Albert Whitman publishes good books for children on a variety of topics: holidays (i.e., Halloween), special needs (such as diabetes), and problems like divorce. The majority of our titles are picture books with less than 1,500 words. De-emphasizing bedtime stories." Albert Whitman's special interest and issue titles address subjects such as disease, social issues, and disabilities. Many books deal in a caring and respectful manner with the challenging situations and learning experiences encountered by children, helping them to grow intellectually and emotionally. Publishes in original hardcover, paperback, boardbooks. Publishes 40 titles/year. 10% of books from first-time authors. 50% from unagented writers.

○ "We have a new policy for unsolicited submissions. After November 2010, we will respond only to submissions of interest. We read every submission within 4 months of receipt, but we can no longer respond to every one. If you do not receive a response from us after 4 months, we have declined to publish your submission. Please do not enclose an SASE. We will not be returning materials received after that date. Please be sure to include current contact information (mail address, e-mail, and phone number) on cover letter and first page of manuscript."

FICTION Picture books, young readers, middle readers: adventure, concept (to help children deal with problems), fantasy, history, humor, multicultural, suspense. Middle readers: problem novels, suspense/mystery. "We are interested in contemporary multicultural stories—stories with holiday themes, and exciting distinctive novels. We publish a wide variety of topics and are interested in stories that help children deal with their problems and concerns. Does not want to see, "religion-oriented, ABCs, pop-up, romance, counting."

NONFICTION Picture books, young readers, middle readers: animal, arts/crafts, health, history, hobbies, multicultural, music/dance, nature/environment, science, sports, special needs. Does not want to see, "religion, any books that have to be written in, or fictionalized biographies."

HOW TO CONTACT Submit query, outline, and sample chapter. For picture books send entire ms. Include cover letter. Responds within 3 months to queries; 4 months to proposals and mss. Publishes a book 18 months after acceptance.

ILLUSTRATION *"We are not accepting illustration samples at this time. Submissions will not be returned."*

PHOTOGRAPHY Publishes books illustrated with photos, but not stock photos—desires photos all taken for project. "Our books are for children and cover many topics; photos must be taken to match text. Books often show a child in a particular situation (e.g. kids being home-schooled, a sister whose brother is born prematurely)." Photographers should query with samples; send unsolicited photos by mail.

TERMS On retail price: Pays 10% royalty for novels; 5% for picture books. Pays advance. "Send a self-addressed, stamped 9x12 envelope with your request, and address your letter to "Catalog Request" at our main address. Please include three first-class stamps (U.S. postage) with your SASE. Unless you specify otherwise, we will send our most recent catalog." Guidelines available on website.

TIPS "In both picture books and nonfiction, we are seeking stories showing life in other cultures and the variety of multicultural life in the U.S. We also want fiction and nonfiction about mentally or physically challenged children; some recent topics have been autism, stuttering, and diabetes. Look up some of our books first to be sure your submission is appropriate for Albert Whitman & Co. We publish trade books that are especially interesting to schools and libraries. We recommend you study our website before submitting your work."

WILLIAMSON BOOKS

2630 Elm Hill Pike, Suite 100, Nashville TN 37214. **E-mail:** pjay@guideposts.org. **Website:** www.idealspublications.com. Publishes "very successful nonfiction series (Kids Can! Series) on subjects such as history, science, arts/crafts, geography, diversity, multiculturalism. Little Hands series for ages 2-6, Kaleidoscope Kids series (age 7 and up) and Quick Starts for Kids! series (ages 8 and up). Our goal is to help every child fulfill his/her potential and experience personal growth."

NONFICTION Hands-on active learning books, animals, African-American, arts/crafts, Asian, biography, diversity, careers, geography, health, history, hobbies, how-to, math, multicultural, music/dance, nature/environment, Native American, science, writing and journaling. Does not want to see textbooks, picture books, fiction. "Looking for all things African American, Asian American, Hispanic, Latino, and Native American including crafts and traditions, as well as their history, biographies, and personal retrospectives of growing up in U.S. for grades pre K-8th. We are looking for books in which learning and doing are inseparable." Recently published *Keeping Our Earth Green; Leap Into Space; China; Big Fun Craft Book.*

HOW TO CONTACT Query with annotated TOC/synopsis and 1 sample chapter. Responds to queries and mss in 4 months. Publishes book 1 year after acceptance.

ILLUSTRATION Works with at least 2 illustrators and 2 designers/year. "We're interested in expanding our illustrator and design freelancers." Uses primarily 2-color and 4-color artwork. Responds only if interested. Samples returned with SASE; samples filed.

PHOTOGRAPHY Buys photos from freelancers; uses archival art and photos.

TERMS Pays authors advance against future royalties based on wholesale price or purchases outright. Pays illustrators by the project. Pays photographers per photo. Guidelines available for SASE.

TIPS "Please do not send any fiction or picture books of any kind—those should go to Ideals Children's Books. Look at our books to see what we do. We're interested in interactive learning books with a creative approach packed with interesting information, written for young readers ages 3-7 and 8-14. In nonfiction children's publishing, we are looking for authors with a depth of knowledge shared with children through a warm, embracing style. Our publishing philosophy is based on the idea that all children can succeed and have positive learning experiences. Children's lasting learning experiences involve their participation."

WINDRIVER PUBLISHING, INC.

3280 Madison Ave., Ogden UT 84403. (801)689-7440. **E-mail:** info@windriverpublishing.com. **Website:** www.windriverpublishing.com. **Contact:** E. Keith Howick, Jr., president; Gail Howick, vice president/editor-in-chief. "Authors who wish to submit book proposals for review must do so according to our Submissions Guidelines, which can be found on our website, along with an on-line submission form, which is our preferred submission method. *We do not accept submissions of any kind by e-mail.*" Publishes hardcover originals and reprints, trade paperback originals, and mass market originals. Publishes 8 titles/year. 95% of books from first-time authors. 90% from unagented writers.

HOW TO CONTACT *Currently not accpeting unsolicited submissions. Check website for further details.* 1,000 queries received/year. 300 mss received/year. Responds in 1-2 months to queries; 4-6 months to proposals/mss. Publishes book 1 year after acceptance.

TERMS Book catalog available online. Guidelines available online.

TIPS "We do not accept manuscripts containing graphic or gratuitous profanity, sex, or violence. See online instructions for details."

◐ WISDOM TALES

P.O. Box 2682 Bloomington, IN 47402-2682 (812)330-3232 **Website:** www.wisdomtalespress.com/contact_us.shtml.

◑ "We are looking for stories that focus on themes from around the world and illustrations that will compliment the text with their beauty. Wisdom Tales publishes both children's and teen titles and was created for the purpose of sharing the wisdom, beauty, and values of traditional cultures and peoples from around the world with young readers and their families. The content, illustrations, and production quality of these books is intended to assure them a lasting value for children, parents, teachers, and librarians."

FICTION Does not accept fiction manuscripts for teens.

NONFICTION For teen books, only submit one sample chapter of fewer than 4,000 words.

HOW TO CONTACT Does not accept phone call inquiries about submissions. All submissions of manuscripts for children's and teen books must be made

on the following webpage: http://www.worldwisdom.com/public/aboutus/submissions/submission.aspx.

ILLUSTRATION All artwork submissions must be e-mailed to acquisitions@wisdomtalespress.com and must be in a PDF format. Will accept up to 6 different sample illustrations in separate PDFs and total size of e-mail cannot exceed 2MB. For further e-mail specifications for illustration, see guidelines on website. If chosen, author or artist will be contacted within 4 months after submission.

PAULA WISEMAN BOOKS

1230 Sixth Ave., New York NY 10020. (212)698-7272. **Fax:** (212)698-2796. **E-mail:** paula.wiseman@simonandschuster.com. **Website:** http://kids.simonandschuster.com. Publishes 20 titles/year. 10% of books from first-time authors.

FICTION Considers all categories. Average word length: picture books—500; others standard length. Recently published *Outfoxed*, by Mike Twohy.

NONFICTION Picture books: animal, biography, concept, history, nature/environment. Young readers: animal, biography, history, multicultural, nature/environment, sports. Average word length: picture books—500; others standard length.

HOW TO CONTACT *Does not accept unsolicited or unagented mss.*

ILLUSTRATION Works with 15 illustrators/year. Does not accept unsolicited or unagented illustrations or submissions.

WIZARDS OF THE COAST BOOKS FOR YOUNG READERS

P.O. Box 707, Renton WA 98057. (800)324-6496. **E-mail:** nina.hess@wizards.com. **Website:** www.wizards.com. **Contact:** Nina Hess. Wizards of the Coast publishes only science fiction and fantasy shared-world titles. Currently emphasizing solid fantasy writers. De-emphasizing gothic fiction. Dragonlance; Forgotten Realms; Magic: The Gathering; Eberron. Wizards of the Coast publishes games as well, including Dungeons & Dragons® role-playing game. Publishes hardcover and trade paperback originals and trade paperback reprints. Publishes 10 titles/year. 5% of books from first-time authors.

FICTION Young readers, middle readers, young adults: fantasy only. Average word length: middle readers—30,000-40,000; young adults—60,000-75,000. Recently published *A Practical Guide to Dragon Rid-*

ing, by Lisa Trumbauer (ages 6 and up); *The Stowaway*, by R.A. Salvatore and Geno Salvatore (10 and up), *Red Dragon Codex*, by R.D. Henham (ages 8-12).

HOW TO CONTACT Query with samples. Publishes book 9-24 months after acceptance.

ILLUSTRATION Works with 4 illustrators/year. Query. Illustrations only: Query with samples, résumé.

TERMS Pays authors 4-6% based on retail price. Pays illustrators by project. Offers advances (average amount: $4,000). Catalog available on website. Ms guidelines available on website.

TIPS Editorial staff attended or plans to attend ALA conference.

WORDSONG

Boyds Mills Press, 815 Church St., Honesdale PA 18431. **Fax:** (570)253-1164. **E-mail:** submissions@boydsmillspress.com; eagarrow@boydsmillspress.com. **Website:** www.wordsongpoetry.com. "We publish fresh voices in contemporary poetry."

FICTION Submit complete ms or submit through agent. Label package "Manuscript Submission" and include SASE. "Please send a book-length collection of your own poems. Do not send an initial query."

HOW TO CONTACT Responds to mss in 3 months.

ILLUSTRATION Works with 7 illustrators/year. Reviews ms/illustration packages from artists. Submit complete ms with 1 or 2 pieces of art. Illustrations only: Query with samples best suited to the art (postcard, 8½ × 11, etc.) Label package "Art Sample Submission." Responds only if interested. Samples returned with SASE.

PHOTOGRAPHY Assigns work.

TERMS Pays authors royalty or work purchased outright.

TIPS "Collections of original poetry, not anthologies, are our biggest need at this time. Keep in mind that the strongest collections demonstrate a facility with multiple poetic forms and offer fresh images and insights. Check to see what's already on the market and on our website before submitting."

WORLD BOOK, INC.

233 N. Michigan Ave. Suite 2000, Chicago IL 60601. (312)729-5800. **Fax:** (312)729-5600. **Website:** www.worldbook.com. **Contact:** Paul A. Kobasa, editor-in-chief. World Book, Inc. (publisher of The World Book Encyclopedia), publishes reference sources and nonfiction series for children and young adults in the areas of science, mathematics, English-language skills, basic academic and social skills, social studies, history, and health and fitness. We publish print and non-print material appropriate for children ages 3-14. WB does not publish fiction, poetry, or wordless picture books."

NONFICTION Young readers: animal, arts/crafts, careers, concept, geography, health, reference. Middle readers: animal, arts/crafts, careers, geography, health, history, hobbies, how-to, nature/environment, reference, science. Young adult: arts/crafts, careers, geography, health, history, hobbies, how-to, nature/environment, reference, science.

HOW TO CONTACT Submit outline/synopsis only; no mss. Responds to queries in 2 months. Publishes book 18 months after acceptance.

ILLUSTRATION Works with 10-30 illustrators/year. Illustrations only: Query with samples. Responds only if interested. Samples returned with SASE; samples filed "if extra copies and if interested."

PHOTOGRAPHY Buys stock and assigns work. Needs broad spectrum; editorial concept, specific natural, physical and social science spectrum. Model/property releases required; captions required. Uses color 8×10 glossy and matte prints, 35mm, 214×214, 4×5, 8×10 transparencies. Submit cover letter, résumé, promo piece (color and b&w).

TERMS Payment negotiated on project-by-project basis.

YOUNG PALMETTO PRESS

An imprint of South Carolina Press. South Carolina Center for Children's Books and Literacy Davis College, 1501 Greene Street, Columbia, SC 29208. **E-mail:** kimj@sc.edu. **Website:** www.sc.edu/uscpress/microsites/ypbooks/index.html. **Contact:** Kim Shealy Jeffcoat, Young Palmetto Books series editor.

"Young Palmetto Books is a new series of educational South Carolina focused books for young readers. This series, published by the University of South Carolina Press, will highlight South Carolina writers and subjects in smartly crafted books for children and young adults featuring educational themes and supporting materials for teachers and parents."

FICTION This imprint publishers a few novels a year.

NONFICTION This imprint publishers several education nonfiction books a year

HOW TO CONTACT Submit via U.S. mail and include a cover letter, a curriculum vitae or résumé, and a table of contents and representative chapter, if the work is a completed manuscript, or a detailed prospectus. If submitting a picture book, please submit completed manuscript. Include representative samples of illustrations (if there are any) and a description of what will be illustrated. See guidelines on website.

TERMS "Projects must meet the approval of the YPB series editorial board, two anonymous peer reviewers, and the USC Press Committee to gain approval for a publishing contract."

TIPS "To learn more about us, see our blog: http://youngpalmettobooks.wordpress.com/."

ZUMAYA PUBLICATIONS, LLC

3209 S. Interstate 35, Austin TX 78741. **E-mail:** business@zumayapublications.com; productions@zumayapublications.com. **Website:** www.zumayapublications.com. Publishes trade paperback and electronic originals and reprints. Publishes 20-25 titles/year. 75% of books from first-time authors. 98% from unagented writers.

○ "We accept only electronic queries; all others will be discarded unread. A working knowledge of computers and relevant software is a necessity, as our production process is completely digital."

FICTION "We are currently oversupplied with speculative fiction and are reviewing submissions in SF, fantasy and paranormal suspense by invitation only. We are much in need of GLBT and YA/middle grade, historical and western, New Age/inspirational (no overtly Christian materials, please), non-category romance, thrillers. As with nonfiction, we encourage people to review what we've already published so as to avoid sending us more of the same, at least insofar as the plot is concerned. While we're always looking for good specific mysteries, we want original concepts rather than slightly altered versions of what we've already published."

NONFICTION "The easiest way to figure out what we're looking for is to look at what we've already done. Our main nonfiction interests are in collections of true ghost stories, ones that have been investigated or thoroughly documented, memoirs that address specific regions and eras and books on the craft of writing. That doesn't mean we won't consider something else."

HOW TO CONTACT Electronic query only. 1,000 queries received/year. 100 mss received/year. Responds in 6 months to queries and proposals; 9 months to mss. Publishes book 2 years after acceptance.

TERMS Guidelines available online.

TIPS "We're catering to readers who may have loved last year's best seller but not enough to want to read 10 more just like it. Have something different. If it does not fit standard pigeonholes, that's a plus. On the other hand, it has to have an audience. And if you're not prepared to work with us on promotion and marketing, it would be better to look elsewhere."

CANADIAN & INTER-NATIONAL BOOK PUBLISHERS

///

While the United States is considered the largest market in children's publishing, the children's publishing world is by no means strictly dominated by the U.S. After all, the most prestigious children's book extravaganza in the world occurs each year in Bologna, Italy, at the Bologna Children's Book Fair, and some of the world's most beloved characters were born in the United Kingdom (i.e., Winnie-the-Pooh and Mr. Potter).

In this section you'll find book publishers in English-speaking countries around the world: Canada, Australia, New Zealand and the United Kingdom. The listings in this section look just like the U.S. Book Publishers section; and the publishers listed are dedicated to the same goal—publishing great books for children.

Like always, be sure to study each listing and research each publisher carefully before submitting material. Determine whether a publisher is open to U.S. or international submissions, as many publishers accept submissions only from residents of their own country. Some publishers accept illustration samples from foreign artists, but do not accept manuscripts from foreign writers. Illustrators do have a slight edge in this category as many illustrators generate commissions from all around the globe. Visit publishers' websites to be certain they publish the sort of work you do. Visit online bookstores to see if publishers' books are available there. Write or e-mail to request catalogs and submission guidelines.

When mailing requests or submissions out of the United States, remember that U.S. postal stamps are useless on your SASE. Always include International Reply Coupons (IRCs) with your SAE. Each IRC is good for postage for one letter. So if you want the publisher to return your manuscript or send a catalog, be sure to enclose enough IRCs to pay the postage. For more help visit the United State Postal Service website at usps.com/global. Visit www.timeanddate.com/worldclock and American Computer Resources, Inc.'s International Calling Code Directory at www.the-acr.com/codes/cntrycd.htm before calling or faxing internationally to make sure you're calling at a reasonable time and using the correct numbers.

As in the rest of *Children's Writer's & Illustrator's Market*, the maple leaf symbol identifies Canadian markets. Look for International symbols throughout *Children's Writer's & Illustrator's Market* as well. Several of the Society of Children's Book Writers and Illustrator's (SCBWI) international conferences are listed in the Conferences & Workshops section along with other events in locations around the globe. Look for more information about SCBWI's international chapters on the organization's website, scbwi.org. See "Useful Online Resources" in this book for sites that offer additional international information.

ANNICK PRESS, LTD.

15 PATRICIA Ave., Toronto ON M2M 1H9, Canada. (416)221-4802. Fax: (416)221-8400. E-mail: annick press@annickpress.com. Website: www.annickpress. com. **Contact:** Rick Wilks, director; Colleen MacMillan, associate publisher; Sheryl Shapiro, creative director. "Annick Press maintains a commitment to high quality books that entertain and challenge. Our publications share fantasy and stimulate imagination, while encouraging children to trust their judgment and abilities." Publishes 5 picture books/year; 6 young readers/year; 8 middle readers/year; 9 young adult titles/year. Publishes picture books, juvenile and YA fiction and nonfiction; specializes in trade books. Publishes 25 titles/year. 20% of books from first-time authors. 80-85% from unagented writers.

Does not accept unsolicited mss.

FICTION Publisher of children's books. Publishes hardcover and trade paperback originals. Average print order: 9,000. First novel print order: 7,000. Plans 18 first novels this year. Averages 25 total titles/year. Distributes titles through Firefly Books Ltd. Juvenile, young adult. Recently published *The Apprentice's Masterpiece: A Story of Medieval Spain*, by Melanie Little, ages 12 and up; the Chicken, Pig, Cow series, written and illustrated by Ruth Ohi, ages 2-5; the Single Voices series, Melanie Little, Editor, ages 14 and up; *Crusades*, by Laura Scandiffio, illustrated by John Mantha, ages 9-11. Not accepting picture books at this time.

NONFICTION Recently published *Pharaohs and Foot Soldiers: One Hundred Ancient Egyptian Jobs you Might Have Desired or Dreaded*, by Kristin Butcher, illustrations by Martha Newbigging, ages 9-12; *The Bite of the Mango*, by Mariatu Kamara with Susan McClelland, ages 14 and up; *Adventures on the Ancient Silk Road*, by Priscilla Galloway with Dawn Hunter, ages 10 and up; *The Chinese Thought of it: Amazing Inventions and Innovations*, by Ting-xing Ye, ages 9-11.

HOW TO CONTACT 5,000 queries received/year. 3,000 mss received/year. Publishes a book 2 years after acceptance.

TERMS Pays authors royalty of 5-12% based on retail price. Offers advances (average amount: $3,000). Pays illustrators royalty of 5% minimum. Book catalog and guidelines available online.

BOREALIS PRESS, LTD.

8 MOHAWK Crescent, Napean ON K2H 7G6, Canada. (613)829-0150. Fax: (613)829-7783. E-mail: drt@borealispress.com. Website: www.borealispress.com. Our mission is to publish work that will be of lasting interest in the Canadian book market. Currently emphasizing Canadian fiction, nonfiction, drama, poetry. De-emphasizing children's books. Publishes hardcover and paperback originals and reprints. Publishes 20 titles/year. 80% of books from first-time authors. 95% from unagented writers.

FICTION Only material Canadian in content and dealing with significant aspects of the human situation.

NONFICTION Only material Canadian in content. Looks for style in tone and language, reader interest, and maturity of outlook.

HOW TO CONTACT Query with SASE. Submit clips, 1-2 sample chapters. *No unsolicited mss.* Query with SASE. Submit outline, 2 sample chapters. *No unsolicited mss.* Responds in 2 months to queries; 4 months to mss. Publishes book 18 months after acceptance.

TERMS Pays 10% royalty on net receipts; plus 3 free author's copies. Book catalog available online. Guidelines available online.

THE BRUCEDALE PRESS

P.O. BOX 2259, Port Elgin ON N0H 2C0, Canada. (519)832-6025. E-mail: brucedale@bmts.com. Website: brucedalepress.ca. The Brucedale Press publishes books and other materials of regional interest and merit, as well as literary, historical, and/or pictorial works. Publishes hardcover and trade paperback originals. Publishes 3 titles/year. 75% of books from first-time authors. 100% from unagented writers.

Accepts works by Canadian authors only. Submissions accepted in September and March ONLY.

HOW TO CONTACT 50 queries received/year. 30 mss received/year. Publishes book 1 year after acceptance.

TERMS Pays royalty. Book catalog for #10 SASE (Canadian postage or IRC) or online. Guidelines available online.

TIPS Our focus is very regional. In reading submissions, I look for quality writing with a strong connection to the Queen's Bush area of Ontario. All authors should visit our website, get a catalog, and read our books before submitting.

BUSTER BOOKS

9 LION Yard, Tremadoc Rd., London WA SW4 7NQ, United Kingdom. 020 7720 8643. Fax: 022 7720 8953. E-mail: enquiries@michaelomarabooks.com. Website: www.busterbooks.co.uk. "We are dedicated to providing irresistible and fun books for children of all ages. We typically publish black-and-white nonfiction for children aged 8-12 novelty titles-including doodle books."

HOW TO CONTACT Prefers synopsis and sample text over complete ms.

TIPS "We do not accept fiction submissions. Please do not send original artwork as we cannot guarantee its safety." Visit website before submitting.

CHILD'S PLAY (INTERNATIONAL) LTD.

CHILDREN'S PLAY International, Ashworth Rd. Bridgemead, Swindon, Wiltshire SN5 7YD, United Kingdom. E-mail: allday@childs-play.com; neil@childs-play.com; office@childs-play.com. Website: www.childs-play.com. **Contact:** Sue Baker, Neil Burden, manuscript acquisitions. Specializes in nonfiction, fiction, educational material, multicultural material. Produces 30 picture books/year; 10 young readers/year; 2 middle readers/year. "A child's early years are more important than any other. This is when children learn most about the world around them and the language they need to survive and grow. Child's Play aims to create exactly the right material for this all-important time." Publishes 45 titles/year. 20% of books from first-time authors.

FICTION Picture books: adventure, animal, concept, contemporary, folktales, multicultural, nature/environment. Young readers: adventure, animal, anthology, concept, contemporary, folktales, humor, multicultural, nature/environment, poetry. Average word length: picture books—1,500; young readers—2,000. Recently published *Snug*, by Carol Thompson (ages 0-2, picture book); *The Lost Stars*, by Hannah Cumming (ages 4-8 yrs, picture book); *Uuggh!*, by Claudia Boldt (ages 4-8 yrs, picture book); *First Time Doctor/Dentist/Hospital/Vet*, by Jess Stockham (ages 2-5 yrs, picture book); New Baby Series, by Rachel Fuller (ages 1-3, board book).

NONFICTION Picture books: activity books, animal, concept, multicultural, music/dance, nature/environment, science. Young readers: activity books, animal, concept, multicultural, music/dance, nature/environment, science. Average word length: picture books—2,000; young readers—3,000. Recently published *Roly Poly Discovery*, by Kees Moerbeek (ages 3+ years, novelty).

HOW TO CONTACT Responds to queries in 10 weeks; mss in 15 weeks. Publishes book 2 years after acceptance.

ILLUSTRATION Accepts material from international illustrators. Works with 10 illustrators/year. Uses color artwork only. Reviews ms/illustration packages. For ms/illustration packages: Query or submit ms/illustration packages to Sue Baker, editor. Reviews work for future assignments. If interested in illustrating future titles, query with samples, CD, website address. Submit samples to Annie Kubler, art director. Responds in 10 weeks. Samples not returned. Samples filed.

TIPS "Look at our website to see the kind of work we do before sending. Do not send cartoons. We do not publish novels. We do publish lots of books with pictures of babies/toddlers."

CHRISTIAN FOCUS PUBLICATIONS

GEANIES HOUSE, Tain Ross-shire IV20 1TW, United Kingdom. 44 (0) 1862 871 011. Fax: 44 (0) 1862 871 699. E-mail: info@christianfocus.com. Website: www.christianfocus.com. **Contact:** Catherine Mackenzie, publisher. Specializes in Christian material, nonfiction, fiction, educational material. Publishes 22-32 titles/year. 2% of books from first-time authors.

FICTION Picture books, young readers, adventure, history, religion. Middle readers: adventure, problem novels, religion. Young adult/teens: adventure, history, problem novels, religion. Average word length: young readers—5,000; middle readers—max 10,000; young adult/teen—max 20,000. Recently published *Back Leg of a Goat*, by Penny Reeve, illustrated by Fred Apps (middle reader Christian/world issues); *Trees in the Pavement,* by Jennifer Grosser (teen fiction/Christian/Islamic and multicultural issues); *The Duke's Daughter*, by Lachlan Mackenzie; illustrated by Jeff Anderson (young reader folk tale/Christian).

NONFICTION All levels: activity books, biography, history, religion, science. Average word length: picture books—5,000; young readers—5,000; middle readers—5,000-10,000; young adult/teens—10,000-20,000. Recently published *Moses the Child-Kept by God*, by Carine Mackenzie, illustrated by Graham Kennedy (young reader, Bible story); *Hearts and Hands-History Lives vol. 4*, by Mindy Withrow, cover illustration by Jonathan Williams (teen, church history); *Little Hands Life of Jesus*, by Carine Mackenzie, illustrated by Rafaella Cosco (picture book, Bible stories about Jesus).

HOW TO CONTACT Query or submit outline/synopsis and 3 sample chapters. Will consider electronic submissions and previously published work. Query or submit outline/synopsis and 3 sample chapters. Will consider electronic submissions and previously published work. Responds to queries in 2 weeks; mss in 3 months. Publishes book 1 year after acceptance.

ILLUSTRATION Works on 15-20 potential projects. "Some artists are chosen to do more than one. Some projects just require a cover illustration, some require full color spreads, others black and white line art." **Contact:** Catherine Mackenzie, children's editor. Responds in 2 weeks only if interested. Samples are not returned.

PHOTOGRAPHY "We only purchase royalty free photos from particular photographic associations. However portfolios can be presented to our designer." **Contact:** Daniel van Straaten. Photographers should send cover letter, résumé, published samples, client list, portfolio.

TIPS "Be aware of the international market as regards writing style/topics as well as illustration styles. Our company sells rights to European as well as Asian countries. Fiction sales are not as good as they were. Christian fiction for youngsters is not a product that is performing well in comparison to nonfiction such as Christian biography/Bible stories/church history, etc."

☉ COTEAU BOOKS

(306)777-0170. FAX: (306)522-5152. E-mail: coteau@coteaubooks.com. Website: www.coteaubooks.com. **Contact:** Geoffrey Ursell, publisher. "Our mission is to publish the finest in Canadian fiction, nonfiction, poetry, drama, and children's literature, with an emphasis on Saskatchewan and prairie writers. De-emphasizing science fiction, picture books." Publishes trade paperback originals and reprints. Publishes 16 titles/year. 25% of books from first-time authors. 90% from unagented writers.

FICTION *Canadian authors only.* No science fiction. No children's picture books.

NONFICTION *Canadian authors only.*

HOW TO CONTACT Submit bio, complete ms, SASE. Submit bio, 3-4 sample chapters, SASE. 200 queries

received/year. 200 mss received/year. Responds in 3 months to queries and manuscripts.

TERMS Pays 10% royalty on retail price. 12 months. Book catalog available free. Guidelines available online.

TIPS "Look at past publications to get an idea of our editorial program. We do not publish romance, horror, or picture books but are interested in juvenile and teen fiction from Canadian authors. Submissions, even queries, must be made in hard copy only. We do not accept simultaneous/multiple submissions. Check our website for new submission timing guidelines."

☉ DUNDURN PRESS, LTD.

3 CHURCH St., Suite 500, Toronto ON M5E 1M2, Canada. (416)214-5544. E-mail: info@dundurn.com. Website: www.dundurn.com. **Contact:** Allison Hirst; Kirk Howard, president and publisher. Dundurn publishes books by Canadian authors. Publishes hardcover, trade paperback, and ebook originals and reprints. 25% of books from first-time authors. 50% from unagented writers.

☉ "We *do not* publish poetry, short stories, children's books for readers under seven years of age, or picture books."

FICTION No romance, science fiction, or experimental.

HOW TO CONTACT Submit cover letter, 3 sample chapters, synopsis, CV, e-mail contact. Accepts submissions via postal mail only. Submissions will not be returned. Submit cover letter, synopsis, CV, table of contents, writing sample, e-mail contact. Accepts submissions via postal mail only. Do not submit original materials. Submissions will not be returned. 600 queries received/year. Responds in 3 months to queries. Publishes ms 1-2 year after acceptance.

TERMS Guidelines available on website.

☉ DAVID FICKLING BOOKS

31 BEAMONT St., Oxford En OX1 2NP, United Kingdom. (018)65-339000. Fax: (018)65-339009. E-mail: DFickling@randomhouse.co.uk; tburgess@randomhouse.co.uk. Website: www.davidficklingbooks.co.uk. Publishes 12 titles/year.

FICTION Considers all categories. Recently published *Once Upon a Time in the North*, by Phillip Pullman; *The Curious Incident of the Dog in the Night-time*, by Mark Haddon; *The Boy in the Striped Pyjamas*, by John Boyne.

HOW TO CONTACT Submit 3 sample chapters. Responds to mss in 3 months.

ILLUSTRATION Reviews ms/illustration packages from artists. Illustrations only: query with samples.

PHOTOGRAPHY Submit cover letter, résumé, promo pieces.

✪ FITZHENRY & WHITESIDE LTD.

195 ALLSTATE Pkwy., Markham ON L3R 4T8, Canada. (905)477-9700. Fax: (905)477-9179. E-mail: fitz kids@fitzhenry.ca; godwit@fitzhenry.ca; charkin@fitzhenry.ca. Website: www.fitzhenry.ca/. **Contact:** Sharon Fitzhenry, president; Cathy Sandusky, children's publisher; Christie Harkin, submissions editor. Emphasis on Canadian authors and illustrators, subject or perspective. Publishes 15 titles/year. 10% of books from first-time authors.

HOW TO CONTACT Publishes book 1-2 years after acceptance.

ILLUSTRATION Works with approximately 10 illustrators/year. Reviews ms/illustration packages from artists. Submit outline and sample illustration (copy). Illustrations only: Query with samples and promo sheet. Samples not returned unless requested.

PHOTOGRAPHY Buys photos from freelancers. Buys stock and assigns work. Captions required. Uses b&w 8×10 prints; 35mm and 4×5 transparencies, 300+ dpi digital images. Submit stock photo list and promo piece.

TERMS Pays authors 8-10% royalty with escalations. Offers "respectable" advances for picture books, split 50/50 between author and illustrator. Pays illustrators by project and royalty. Pays photographers per photo.

TIPS "We respond to quality."

✪ FRANCES LINCOLN CHILDREN'S BOOKS

FRANCES LINCOLN, 74-77 White Lion St., Islington, London N1 9PF, United Kingdom. 00442072844009. E-mail: flcb@franceslincoln.com. Website: www. franceslincoln.com. "Our company was founded by Frances Lincoln in 1977. We published our first books two years later, and we have been creating illustrated books of the highest quality ever since, with special emphasis on gardening, walking and the outdoors, art, architecture, design and landscape. In 1983, we started to publish illustrated books for children. Since then we have won many awards and prizes with both fiction and nonfiction children's books." Publishes 100 titles/year. 6% of books from first-time authors.

FICTION Picture books, young readers, middle readers, young adults: adventure, animal, anthology, fantasy, folktales, health, history, humor, multicultural, nature/environment, special needs, sports. Average word length: picture books—1,000; young readers—9,788; middle readers— 20,653; young adults— 35,407. Recently published *The Sniper*, by James Riordan (young adult/teen novel); *Amazons! Women Warriors of the World*, by Sally Pomme Clayton, illustrated by Sophie Herxheimer (picture book); *Young Inferno*, by John Agard, illustrated by Satoshi Kitamura (graphic novel/picture book).

NONFICTION Picture books, young readers, middle readers, young adult: activity books, animal, biography, careers, cooking, graphic novels, history, multicultural, nature/environment, religion, social issues, special needs. Average word length: picture books—1,000; middle readers—29,768. Recently published *Tail-End Charlie*, by Mick Manning and Brita Granstroöm (picture book); *Our World of Water*, by Beatrice Hollyer, with photographers by Oxfam (picture book); *Look! Drawing the Line in Art*, by Gillian Wolfe (picture book).

HOW TO CONTACT Query by e-mail. Query by e-mail. Responds to mss in minimum of 6 weeks. Publishes book 18 months after acceptance.

ILLUSTRATION Works with approx 56 illustrators/year. Uses both color and b&w. Reviews ms/illustration packages from artist. Sample illustrations. Illustrations only: Query with samples. Responds only if interested. Samples are returned with SASE. Samples are kept on file only if interested.

PHOTOGRAPHY Buys stock images and assign work. Uses children, multicultural photos. Submit cover letter, published samples, or portfolio.

FRANKLIN WATTS

338 EUSTON Rd., London NW1 3BH, United Kingdom. +44 (0)20 7873 6000. Fax: +44 (0)20 7873 6024. E-mail: ad@hachettechildrens.co.uk. Website: www. franklinwatts.co.uk. Franklin Watts is well known for its high quality and attractive information books, which support the National Curriculum and stimulate children's enquiring minds. Reader Development is one of Franklin Watts' specialisations; the list offers titles on a wide array of subjects for beginner readers. It is also the proud publisher of many award-winning authors/illustrators, including Mick Manning and Brita Granstrom.

Generally does not accept unsolicited mss.

GROUNDWOOD BOOKS

110 SPADINA Ave. Suite 801, Toronto ON M5V 2K4, Canada. (416)363-4343. Fax: (416)363-1017. E-mail: ssutherland@groundwoodbooks.com. Website: www.houseofanansi.com. Publishes 13 picture books/year; 3 young readers/year; 5 middle readers/year; 5 young adult titles/year, approximately 2 nonfiction titles/year.

FICTION Recently published: *One Year in Coal Harbour*, by Polly Horvath; *That Night's Train*, by Ahmad Akbarpour; *Nobody Knows*, by Shelley Tanaka; *My Name is Parvana*, by Deborah Ellis; *My Book of Life by Angel*, by Martine Leavitt.

NONFICTION Recently published: *La Malinche*, by Francisco Serrano, illustrated by Pablo Serrano. Picture books recently published: *Stephen and the Beetle*, by Jorge Luján, illustrated by Chiara Carrer; *Applesauce*, by Klaas Verplancke; *Snow Children*, by Masako Yamashita; *Stella! A Treasury*, by Marie-Louise Gay; *Nocturne*, by Isol; *A Few Bites*, by Cybèle Young.

HOW TO CONTACT Submit synopsis and sample chapters. Responds to mss in 6-8 months.

TERMS Offers advances. Visit website for guidelines: www.houseofanansi.com/Groundwoodsubmissions.aspx.

HINKLER

45-55 FAIRCHILD St., Heatherton VI 3202, Australia. (61)(3)9552-1333. Fax: (61)(3)9558-2566. E-mail: enquiries@hinkler.com.au; Stevie.Brockley@hinkler.com.au. Website: www.hinklerbooks.com. **Contact:** Stephen Ungar, CEO/publisher. "Packaged entertainment affordable to every family."

KIDS CAN PRESS

25 DOCKSIDE Dr., Toronto ON M5A 0B5, Canada. (416)479-7000. Fax: (416)960-5437. E-mail: info@kidscan.com; kkalmar@kidscan.com. Website: www.kidscanpress.com. U.S. address: 2250 Military Rd., Tonawanda, NY 14150. **Contact:** Corus Quay, acquisitions.

Kids Can Press is currently accepting unsolicited mss from Canadian adult authors only.

FICTION Picture books, young readers: concepts. We do not accept young adult fiction or fantasy novels for any age. Adventure, animal, contemporary, folktales, history, humor, multicultural, nature/environment, special needs, sports, suspense/mystery. Average word length: picture books 1,000-2,000; young readers 750-1,500; middle readers 10,000-15,000; young adults over 15,000. Recently published *Rosie & Buttercup* by Chieri Ugaki, illustrated by Shephane Jorisch (picture book); *The Landing* by John Ibbitson (novel); *Scaredy Squirrel* by Melanie Watt, illustrated by Melanie Watt (picture book).

NONFICTION Picture books: activity books, animal, arts/crafts, biography, careers, concept, health, history, hobbies, how-to, multicultural, nature/environment, science, social issues, special needs, sports. Young readers: activity books, animal, arts/crafts, biography, careers, concept, history, hobbies, how-to, multicultural. Middle readers: cooking, music/dance. Average word length: picture books 500-1,250; young readers 750-2,000; middle readers 5,000-15,000. Recently published *The Kids' Book of Canadian Geography*, by Jane Drake and Ann Love, illustrated by Heather Collins (informational activity); *Science, Nature, Environment*; *Moving Day*, by Pamela Hickman, illustrated by Geraldo Valerio (animal/nature); *Everywear*, by Ellen Warwick, illustrated by Bernice Lum (craft book).

HOW TO CONTACT Submit outline/synopsis and 2-3 sample chapters. For picture books submit complete ms. Submit outline/synopsis and 2-3 sample chapters. For picture books submit complete ms. Responds in 6 months only if interesed. Publishes book 18-24 months after acceptance.

ILLUSTRATION Works with 40 illustrators/year. Reviews mss/illustration packages from artists. Send color copies of illustration portfolio, cover letter outlining other experience. Contact: Art Director. Illustrations only: Send tearsheets, color photocopies. Responds only if interested.

LITTLE TIGER PRESS

1 THE Coda Centre, 189 Munster Rd., London En SW6 6AW, United Kingdom. 44)20-7385 6333. E-mail: info@littletiger.co.uk; malperin@littletiger.co.uk. Website: www.littletigerpress.com.

FICTION Picture books: animal, concept, contemporary, humor. Average word length: picture books—750 words or less. Recently published *Gruff the Grump*, by Steve Smallman and Cee Biscoe (ages 3-7, picture book); *One Special Day*, by M. Christina Butler and Tina Macnaughton (ages 3-7, touch-and-feel, picture book).

ILLUSTRATION Digital submissions preferred please send in digital samples as pdf or jpeg attachments to artsubmissions@littletiger.co.uk. Files should be flattened and no bigger than 1 MB per attachment. Include name and contact details on any attachments. Printed submissions please send in printed color samples as A4 printouts. Do not send in original artwork as we cannot be held responsible for unsolicited original artwork being lost or damaged in the post. We aim to acknowledge unsolicited material and to return material if so requested within three months. Please include S.A.E. if return of material is requested.

TIPS "Every reasonable care is taken of the manuscripts and samples we receive, but we cannot accept responsibility for any loss or damage. Try to read or look at as many books on the Little Tiger Press list before sending in your material. Refer to our website www.littletigerpress.com for further details."

☉ MANOR HOUSE PUBLISHING, INC.

452 COTTINGHAM Crescent, Ancaster ON L9G 3V6, Canada. E-mail: mbdavie@manor-house.biz. Website: www.manor-house.biz. **Contact:** Mike Davie, president (novels, poetry, and nonfiction). Publishes hardcover, trade paperback, and mass market paperback originals reprints. Publishes 5-6 titles/year. 90% of books from first-time authors. 90% from unagented writers.

FICTION Stories should have Canadian settings and characters should be Canadian, but content should have universal appeal to wide audience.

NONFICTION "We are a Canadian publisher, so mss should be Canadian in content and aimed as much as possible at a wide, general audience. At this point in time, we are only publishing books by Canadian citizens residing in Canada."

HOW TO CONTACT Query via e-mail. Submit proposal package, clips, bio, 3 sample chapters. Submit complete ms. Query via e-mail. Submit proposal package, outline, bio, 3 sample chapters. Submit complete ms. 30 queries received/year; 20 mss received/year. Queries and mss to be sent by e-mail only. "We will respond in 30 days if interested-if not, there is no response. Do not follow up unless asked to do so." Publishes book 1 year after acceptance.

TERMS Pays 10% royalty on retail price. Book catalog available online. Guidelines available via e-mail.

TIPS "Our audience includes everyone-the general public/mass audience. Self-edit your work first, make sure it is well written with strong Canadian content."

☉ MANTRA LINGUA

GLOBAL HOUSE, 303 Ballards Ln., London N12 8NP, United Kingdom. (44)(208)445-5123. E-mail: jean@mantralingua.com. Website: www.mantralingua.com.

◯ Mantra Lingua publishes dual-language books in English and more that 42 languages. They also publish talking books and resources with their Talking Pen technology, which brings sound and interactivity to their products. They will consider good contemporary stories, myths and folklore for picture books only.

FICTION Picture books, young readers, middle readers: folktales, multicultural stories, myths. Average word length: picture books—1,000-1,500; young readers—1,000-1,500. Recently published *Keeping Up With Cheetah*, by Lindsay Camp, illustrated by Jill Newton (ages 3-7); *Lion Fables*, by Heriette Barkow, illustrated by Jago Ormerod (ages 6-10).

HOW TO CONTACT Submit outline/synopsis (250 words) via postal mail. Incluse SASE for returns.

ILLUSTRATION Uses 2D animations for CD-ROMs. Query with samples. Responds only if interested. Samples not returned; samples filed.

☉ MOOSE ENTERPRISE BOOK & THEATRE PLAY PUBLISHING

684 WALLS Rd., Sault Ste. Marie ON P6A 5K6, Canada. (705) 779-3331. Fax: (705) 779-3331. E-mail: mooseenterprises@on.aibn.com. Website: www.moosehidebooks.com. **Contact:** Edmond Alcid. Editorial philosophy: "To assist the new writers of moral standards."

◯ This publisher does not offer payment for stories published in its anthologies and/or book collections. Be sure to send a SASE for guidelines.

FICTION Middle readers, young adults: adventure, fantasy, humor, suspense/mystery, story poetry. Recently published *Realm of the Golden Feather*, by C.R. Ginter (ages 12 and up, fantasy); *Tell Me a Story*, short story collection by various authors (ages 9-11, humor/adventure); *Spirits of Lost Lake*, by James Walters (ages 12 and up, adventure); *Rusty Butt-Treasure of the Ocean Mist*, by R.E. Forester.

NONFICTION Middle readers, young adults: biography, history, multicultural.

HOW TO CONTACT Query. Query. Responds to queries in 1 month; mss in 3 months. Publishes book 1 year after acceptance.

ILLUSTRATION Uses primarily b&w artwork for interiors, cover artwork in color. Illustrations only: Query with samples. Responds in 1 month, if interested. Samples returned with SASE; samples filed.

TERMS Pays royalties. Ms guidelines available for SASE.

TIPS "Do not copy trends; be yourself—give me something new, something different."

⊙ ORCA BOOK PUBLISHERS

P.O. BOX 5626, Stn. B, Victoria BC V8R 6S4, Canada. Fax: (877)408-1551. E-mail: orca@orcabook. com. Website: www.orcabook.com. **Contact:** Christi Howes, editor (picture books); Sarah Harvey, editor (young readers); Andrew Wooldridge, editor (juvenile and teen fiction); Bob Tyrrell, publisher (YA, teen). Publishes hardcover and trade paperback originals, and mass market paperback originals and reprints. Publishes 30 titles/year. 20% of books from first-time authors. 75% from unagented writers.

◑ Only publishes Canadian authors.

FICTION Picture books: animals, contemporary, history, nature/environment. Middle readers: contemporary, history, fantasy, nature/environment, problem novels, graphic novels. Young adults: adventure, contemporary, hi-lo (Orca Soundings), history, multicultural, nature/environment, problem novels, suspense/mystery, graphic novels. Average word length: picture books—500-1,500; middle readers—20,000-35,000; young adult—25,000-45,000; Orca Soundings—13,000-15,000; Orca Currents—13,000-15,000. Published *Tall in the Saddle,* by Anne Carter, illustrated by David McPhail (ages 4-8, picture book); *Me and Mr. Mah*, by Andrea Spalding, illustrated by Janet Wilson (ages 5 and up, picture book); *Alone at Ninety Foot*, by Katherine Holubitsky (young adult). No romance, science fiction.

NONFICTION Only publishes Canadian authors.

HOW TO CONTACT Query with SASE. Submit proposal package, outline, clips, 2-5 sample chapters, SASE. Query with SASE. 2,500 queries received/year. 1,000 mss received/year. Responds in 1 month to queries; 2 months to proposals and mss. Publishes book 12-18 months after acceptance.

ILLUSTRATION Works with 8-10 illustrators/year. Reviews ms/illustration packages from artists. Submit ms with 3-4 pieces of final art. "Reproductions only, no original art please." Illustrations only: Query with samples; provide résumé, slides. Responds in 2 months. Samples returned with SASE; samples filed.

TERMS Pays 10% royalty. Book catalog for 8½x11 SASE. Guidelines available online.

TIPS "Our audience is students in grades K-12. Know our books, and know the market."

⊙ PEMMICAN PUBLICATIONS, INC.

90 SUTHERLAND Ave., Winnipeg MB R2W 3C7, Canada. (204)589-6346. Fax: (204)589-2063. E-mail: pemmican@pemmican.mb.ca. Website: www.pemmicanpublications.ca. **Contact:** Randal McIlroy, managing editor (Metis culture & heritage). "Pemmican Publications is a Metis publishing house, with a mandate to publish books by Metis authors and illustrators and with an emphasis on culturally relevant stories. We encourage writers to learn a little about Pemmican before sending samples. Pemmican publishes titles in the following genres: Adult Fiction, which includes novels, story collections and anthologies; Nonfiction, with an emphasis on social history and biography reflecting Metis experience; Children's and Young Adult titles; Aboriginal languages, including Michif and Cree." Publishes trade paperback originals and reprints. Publishes 5-6 titles/year. 50% of books from first-time authors. 100% from unagented writers.

FICTION All manuscripts must be Metis culture and heritage related.

NONFICTION All mss must be Metis culture and heritage related.

HOW TO CONTACT Submit proposal package including outline and 3 sample chapters. Submit proposal package including outline and 3 sample chapters. 120 queries received/year. 120 mss received/year. Responds to queries, proposals, and mss in 3 months. Publishes book 1-2 years after acceptance.

TERMS Pays 10% royalty on retail price. Book catalog available free with SASE. Guidelines available online.

TIPS "Our mandate is to promote Metis authors, illustrators and stories. No agent is necessary."

⊙ PICCADILLY PRESS

5 CASTLE Rd., London NW1 8PR, United Kingdom. (44)(207)267-4492. Fax: (44)(207)267-4493. E-mail: books@piccadillypress.co.uk. Website: www.picca

dillypress.co.uk. "Piccadilly Press is the perfect choice for variety of reading for everyone aged 2-16! We're an independent publisher, celebrating 26 years of specialising in teen fiction and nonfiction, childrens fiction, picture books and parenting books by highly acclaimed authors and illustrators and fresh new talents too. We hope you enjoy reading the books as much as we enjoy publishing them."

FICTION Picture books: animal, contemporary, fantasy, nature/environment. Young adults: contemporary, humor, problem novels. Average word length: picture books—500-1,000; young adults—25,000-35,000.

NONFICTION Young adults: self help (humorous). Average word length: young adults—25,000-35,000.

HOW TO CONTACT Submit complete ms for picture books or submit outline/synopsis and 2 sample chapters for YA. Enclose a brief cover letter and SASE for reply. Submit outline/synopsis and 2 sample chapters. Responds to mss in 6 weeks.

ILLUSTRATION Illustrations only: Query with samples (do not send originals).

TIPS "Take a look in bookshops to see if there are many other books of a similar nature to yours—this is what your book will be competing against, so make sure there is something truly unique about your story. Looking at what else is available will give you ideas as to what topics are popular, but reading a little of them will also give you a sense of the right styles, language and length appropriate for the age-group."

RAINCOAST BOOK DISTRIBUTION, LTD.

2440 VIKING Way, Richmond BC V6V 1N2, Canada. (604)448-7100. Fax: (604)270-7161. E-mail: info@raincoast.com. Website: www.raincoast.com. Publishes hardcover and trade paperback originals and reprints. Publishes 60 titles/year. 10% of books from first-time authors. 40% from unagented writers.

FICTION *No unsolicited mss.*

NONFICTION *No unsolicited mss.*

HOW TO CONTACT Query with SASE. 3,000 queries received/year. Publishes book within 2 years of acceptance.

TERMS Pays 8-12% royalty on retail price. Pays $1,000-6,000 advance. Book catalog for #10 SASE.

RANDOM HOUSE CHILDREN'S BOOKS

61-63 UXBRIDGE Rd., London En W5 5SA, United Kingdom. (44)(208)231-6000. Fax: (44)(208)231-6737. E-mail: enquiries@randomhouse.co.uk; lduffy@randomhouse.co.uk. Website: www.kidsatrandomhouse.co.uk. **Contact:** Philippa Dickinson, managing director. Publishes 250 titles/year.

Only interested in agented material.

FICTION Picture books: adventure, animal, anthology, contemporary, fantasy, folktales, humor, multicultural, nature/environment, poetry, suspense/mystery. Young readers: adventure, animal, anthology, contemporary, fantasy, folktales, humor, multicultural, nature/environment, poetry, sports, suspense/mystery. Middle readers: adventure, animal, anthology, contemporary, fantasy, folktales, humor, multicultural, nature/environment, problem novels, romance, sports, suspense/mystery. Young adults: adventure, contemporary, fantasy, humor, multicultural, nature/environment, problem novels, romance, science fiction, suspense/mystery. Average word length: picture books—800; young readers—1,500-6,000; middle readers—10,000-15,000; young adults—20,000-45,000.

ILLUSTRATION Works with 50 illustrators/year. Reviews ms/illustration packages from artists. Query with samples. Contact: Margaret Hope. Samples are returned with SASE (IRC).

PHOTOGRAPHY Buys photos from freelancers. Contact: Margaret Hope. Photo captions required. Uses color or b&w prints. Submit cover letter, published samples.

TERMS Pays authors royalty. Offers advances.

TIPS "Although Random House is a big publisher, each imprint only publishes a small number of books each year. Our lists for the next few years are already full. Any book we take on from a previously unpublished author has to be truly exceptional. Manuscripts should be sent to us via literary agents."

RANSOM PUBLISHING

RADLEY HOUSE, 8 St. Cross Road, Winchester Hampshire SO23 9HX, United Kingdom. +44 (0) 01962 862307. Fax: +44 (0) 05601 148881. E-mail: ransom@ransom.co.uk. Website: www.ransom.co.uk. **Contact:** Jenny Ertle, editor. Independent UK publisher with distribution in English speaking markets throughout the world. Specializes in books for reluctant and struggling readers. Our high quality, visually stimulating, age appropriate material has achieved wide acclaim for its ability to engage and motivate those who either can't or won't read. One of the few

English language publishers to publish books with very high interest age and very low reading age. Has a developing list of children's books for home and school use. Specializes in phonics and general reading programs. Publishes paperback originals.

FICTION Easy reading for young adults. Books for reluctant and struggling readers.

HOW TO CONTACT Accepts unsolicited mss. Query with SASE or submit outline/proposal. Prefers queries by e-mail. Include estimated word count, brief bio, list of publishing credits. Responds to mss in 3-4 weeks.

TERMS Pays 10% royalty on net receipts. Ms guidelines by e-mail.

RONSDALE PRESS

3350 W. 21st Ave., Vancouver BC V6S 1G7, Canada. (604)738-4688. Fax: (604)731-4548. E-mail: ronsdale@shaw.ca. Website: http://ronsdalepress.com. **Contact:** Ronald B. Hatch (fiction, poetry, nonfiction, social commentary); Veronica Hatch (YA novels and short stories). "Ronsdale Press is a Canadian literary publishing house that publishes 12 books each year, four of which are young adult titles. Of particular interest are books involving children exploring and discovering new aspects of Canadian history." Publishes trade paperback originals. Publishes 12 titles/year. 40% of books from first-time authors. 95% from unagented writers.

FICTION Young adults: Canadian novels. Average word length: middle readers and young adults—50,000. Recently published *Torn from Troy*, by Patrick Bowman (ages 10-14); *Hannah & The Salish Sea*, by Carol Anne Shaw (ages 10-14); *Dark Times*, edited by Ann Walsh (anthology of short stories, ages 10 and up); *Outlaw in India*, by Philip Roy; *Freedom Bound*, by Jean Rae Baxter (ages 10-14).

NONFICTION Middle readers, young adults: animal, biography, history, multicultural, social issues. Average word length: young readers—90; middle readers—90. "We publish a number of books for children and young adults in the age 10 to 15 range. We are especially interested in YA historical novels. **We regret that we can no longer publish picture books.**"

HOW TO CONTACT Submit complete ms. Submit complete ms. 40 queries received/year. 800 mss received/year. Responds to queries in 2 weeks; mss in 2 months. Publishes book 1 year after acceptance.

ILLUSTRATION Works with 2 illustrators/year. Reviews ms/illustration packages from artists. Requires only cover art. Responds in 2 weeks. Samples returned with SASE. Originals returned to artist at job's completion.

TERMS Pays 10% royalty on retail price. Book catalog for #10 SASE. Guidelines available online.

TIPS "Ronsdale Press is a literary publishing house, based in Vancouver, and dedicated to publishing books from across Canada, books that give Canadians new insights into themselves and their country. We aim to publish the best Canadian writers."

SECOND STORY PRESS

20 MAUD St., Suite 401, Toronto ON M5V 2M5, Canada. (416)537-7850. Fax: (416)537-0588. E-mail: info@secondstorypress.ca; marketing@secondstorypress.com. Website: www.secondstorypress.ca.

FICTION Considers non-sexist, non-racist, and non-violent stories, as well as historical fiction, chapter books, picture books. **Recently published:** *Writing the Revolution*, by Michele Landsberg; *Shannen and the Dream for a School*, by Janet Wilson.

NONFICTION Picture books: biography. **Recently published:** *We Are Their Voice: Young People Respond to the Holocaust*, by Kathy Kacer (a new addition to our Holocaust remembrance series for young readers).

HOW TO CONTACT *Accepts appropriate material from residents of Canada only.* Submit outline and sample chapters by postal mail only. No electronic submissions or queries.

TAFELBERG PUBLISHERS

IMPRINT OF NB Publishers, P.O. Box 879, Cape Town 8000, South Africa. (27)(21)406-3033. Fax: (27)(21)406-3812. E-mail: nb@nb.co.za. Website: www.tafelberg.com. **Contact:** Danita van Romburgh, editorial secretary; Louise Steyn, publisher. General publisher best known for Afrikaans fiction, authoritative political works, children's/youth literature, and a variety of illustrated and nonillustrated nonfiction. Publishes 10 titles/year.

FICTION Picture books, young readers: animal, anthology, contemporary, fantasy, folktales, hi-lo, humor, multicultural, nature/environment, scient fiction, special needs. Middle readers, young adults: animal (middle reader only), contemporary, fantasy, hi-lo, humor, multicultural, nature/environment, problem novels, science fiction, special needs, sports, suspense/mystery. Average word length: picture books—1,500-7,500; young readers—25,000; middle readers—15,000; young adults—40,000. Recently published *Because Pula Means Rain*, by Jenny Robson (ages 12-15, realism); *BreinBliksem*, by Fanie Viljoen (ages 13-18, realism); *SuperZero*, by Darrel Bristow-Bovey (ages 9-12, realism/humor).

HOW TO CONTACT Query or submit complete ms. Submit complete ms. Responds to queries in 2 weeks; mss in 6 months. Publishes book 1 year after acceptance.

ILLUSTRATION Works with 2-3 illustrators/year. Reviews ms/illustration packages from artists. Send ms with dummy or e-mail and jpegs. Contact: Louise Steyn, publisher. Illustrations only: Query with brochure, photocopies, résumé, URL, JPEGs. Responds only if interested. Samples not returned.

TERMS Pays authors royalty of 15-18% based on wholesale price.

TIPS "Writers: Story needs to have a South African or African style. Illustrators: I'd like to look, but the chances of getting commissioned are slim. The market is small and difficult. Do not expect huge advances. Editorial staff attended or plans to attend the following conferences: IBBY, Frankfurt, SCBWI Bologna."

☯ THISTLEDOWN PRESS LTD.

118 20TH Street West, Saskatoon SK S7M 0W6, Canada. (306)244-1722. Fax: (306)244-1762. E-mail: editorial@thistledownpress.com. Website: www.thistledownpress.com. **Contact:** Allan Forrie, publisher.

"Thistledown originates books by Canadian authors only, although we have co-published titles by authors outside Canada. We do not publish children's picture books."

FICTION Middle readers, young adults: adventure, anthology, contemporary, fantasy, humor, poetry, romance, science fiction, suspense/mystery, short stories. Average word length: young adults—40,000. Recently published *Up All Night*, edited by R.P. MacIntyre (young adult, anthology); *Offside*, by Cathy Beveridge (young adult, novel); *Cheeseburger Subversive*, by Richard Scarsbrook; *The Alchemist's Daughter*, by Eileen Kernaghan.

HOW TO CONTACT Submit outline/synopsis and sample chapters. *Does not accept mss.* Do not query by e-mail. Responds to queries in 4 months. Publishes book 1 year after acceptance.

ILLUSTRATION Prefers agented illustrators but "not mandatory." Works with few illustrators. Illustrations only: Query with samples, promo sheet, slides,

tearsheets. Responds only if interested. Samples returned with SASE; samples filed.

TERMS Pays authors royalty of 10-12% based on net dollar sales. Pays illustrators and photographers by the project (range: $250-750). Book catalog free on request. Guidelines available for #10 envelope and IRC.

TIPS "Send cover letter including publishing history and SASE."

☯ TRADEWIND BOOKS

(604)662-4405. E-MAIL: tradewindbooks@mail.lycos.com. Website: www.tradewindbooks.com. **Contact:** Michael Katz, publisher; Carol Frank, art director; R. David Stephens, senior editor. "Tradewind Books publishes juvenile picture books and young adult novels. Requires that submissions include evidence that author has read at least 3 titles published by Tradewind Books." Publishes hardcover and trade paperback originals. Publishes 5 titles/year. 15% of books from first-time authors. 50% from unagented writers.

FICTION Picture books: adventure, multicultural, folktales. Average word length: 900 words. Recently published *City Kids*, by X.J. Kennedy and illustrated by Phillpe Beha; *Roxy* by PJ Reece; *Viva Zapata!* by Emilie Smith and illustrated by Stefan Czernecki.

HOW TO CONTACT Send complete ms for picture books. *YA novels by Canadian authors only. Chapter books by US authors considered.* Responds to mss in 2 months. Publishes book 3 years after acceptance.

ILLUSTRATION Works with 3-4 illustrators/year. Reviews ms/illustration packages from artists. Send illustrated ms as dummy. Illustrations only: Query with samples. Responds only if interested. Samples returned with SASE; samples filed.

TERMS Pays 7% royalty on retail price. Pays variable advance. Book catalog and ms guidelines online.

● USBORNE PUBLISHING

83-85 SAFFRON Hill, London En EC1N 8RT, United Kingdom. (44)(020)7430-2800. Fax: (44)(020)7430-1562. E-mail: mail@usborne.co.uk; pippas@usborne.co.uk; alicep@usborne.co.uk; Graeme@usborne.co.uk. Website: www.usborne.com. "Usborne Publishing is a multiple-award winning, world-wide children's publishing company specializing in superbly researched and produced information books with a unique appeal to young readers."

FICTION Young readers, middle readers: adventure, contemporary, fantasy, history, humor, multicultural, nature/environment, science fiction, suspense/mystery, strong concept-based or character-led series. Average word length: young readers—5,000-10,000; middle readers—25,000-50,000. Recently published *Secret Mermaid* series by Sue Mongredien (ages 7 and up); *School Friends*, by Ann Bryant (ages 9 and up).

ILLUSTRATION Works with 100 illustrators per year. Illustrations only: Query with samples. Samples not returned; samples filed.

PHOTOGRAPHY Contact: Usborne Art Department. Submit samples.

TERMS Pays authors royalty.

TIPS "Do not send any original work and, sorry, but we cannot guarantee a reply."

○ WEIGL EDUCATIONAL PUBLISHERS, LTD.

6325 10TH St. SE, Calgary AB T2H 2Z9, Canada. (403)233-7747. Fax: (403)233-7769. E-mail: linda@weigl.com. Website: www.weigl.ca. "Textbook publisher catering to juvenile and young adult audience (K-12)." Makes outright purchase. Responds ASAP to queries. Query with SASE. Publishes hardcover originals and reprints, school library softcover. Publishes 104 titles/year. 100% from unagented writers.

TERMS Book catalog available for free.

○ WHITECAP BOOKS, LTD.

(905)477-9700 EXT. 244. Fax: (905)477-9179. E-mail: whitecap@whitecap.ca. Website: www.whitecap.ca. "Whitecap Books is a general trade publisher with a focus on food and wine titles. Although we are interested in reviewing unsolicited ms submissions, please note that we only accept submissions that meet the needs of our current publishing program. Please see some of most recent releases to get an idea of the kinds of titles we are interested in." Publishes hardcover and trade paperback originals. Publishes 40 ti-

tles/year. 20% of books from first-time authors. 90% from unagented writers.

FICTION No children's picture books or adult fiction.

NONFICTION Young children's and middle readers nonfiction focusing mainly on nature, wildlife and animals. "Writers should take the time to research our list and read the submission guidelines on our website. This is especially important for children's writers and cookbook authors. We will only consider submissions that fall into these categories: cookbooks, wine and spirits, regional travel, home and garden, Canadian history, North American natural history, juvenile series-based fiction. At this time, we are not accepting the following categories: self-help or inspirational books, political, social commentary, or issue books, general how-to books, biographies or memoirs, business and finance, art and architecture, religion and spirituality."

HOW TO CONTACT See guidelines. Submit cover letter, synopsis, SASE via ground mail. See guidelines online at website. 500 queries received/year; 1,000 mss received/year. Responds in 2-3 months to proposals. Publishes book 1 year after acceptance.

ILLUSTRATION Works with 1-2 illustrators/year. Uses color artwork only. Reviews ms/illustration packages from artists. Query. Contact: Rights and Acquisitions. Illustrations only: Send postcard sample with tearsheets. Contact: Michelle Furbacher, art director. Responds only if interested.

PHOTOGRAPHY Only accepts digital photography. Submit stock photo list. Buys stock and assigns work. Model/property releases required.

TERMS Pays royalty. Pays negotiated advance. Catalog and guidelines available online at website.

TIPS "We want well-written, well-researched material that presents a fresh approach to a particular topic."

MAGAZINES

Children's magazines are a great place for unpublished writers and illustrators to break into the market. Writers, illustrators and photographers alike may find it easier to get book assignments if they have tearsheets from magazines. Having magazine work under your belt shows you're professional and have experience working with editors and art directors and meeting deadlines.

But magazines aren't merely a breaking-in point. Writing, illustration and photo assignments for magazines let you see your work in print quickly, and the magazine market can offer steady work and regular paychecks (a number of them pay on acceptance). Book authors and illustrators may have to wait a year or two before receiving royalties from a project. The magazine market is also a good place to use research material that didn't make it into a book project you're working on. You may even work on a magazine idea that blossoms into a book project.

TARGETING YOUR SUBMISSIONS

It's important to know the topics typically covered by different children's magazines. To help you match your work with the right publications, we've included several indexes in the back of this book. The **Subject Index** lists both book and magazine publishers by the fiction and nonfiction subjects they're seeking.

If you're a writer, use the Subject Index in conjunction with the **Age-Level Index** to narrow your list of markets. Targeting the correct age group with your submission is an important consideration. Many rejection slips are sent because a writer has not targeted a manuscript to the correct age. Few magazines are aimed at children of all ages, so you must be certain your manuscript is written for the audience level of the particular magazine you're submitting to. Magazines for children (just like magazines for adults) may also target a specific gender.

If you're a poet, refer to the **Poetry Index** to find which magazines publish poems.

Each magazine has a different editorial philosophy. Language usage also varies between periodicals, as does the length of feature articles and the use of artwork and photographs. Reading magazines *before* submitting is the best way to determine if your material is appropriate. Also, because magazines targeted to specific age groups have a natural turnover in readership every few years, old topics (with a new slant) can be recycled.

If you're a photographer, the **Photography Index** lists books and children's magazines that use photos from freelancers. Using it in combination with the Subject Index can narrow your search. For instance, if you photograph sports, compare the Magazine list in the Photography Index with the list under Sports in the Subject Index. Highlight the markets that appear on both lists, then read those listings to decide which magazines might be best for your work.

Since many kids' magazines sell subscriptions through direct mail or schools, you may not be able to find a particular publication at bookstores or newsstands. Check your local library, or send for copies of the magazines you're interested in. Most magazines in this section have sample copies available and will send them for a SASE or small fee.

If you're an illustrator, you can use the **Illustration Index** to take a similar approach. Many magazines use illustrations from freelancers to fill and color their pages. As with photography, you can use the **Subject Index** in conjunction with the Illustration Index to determine where your work's style and subject matter might fit best.

Also, many magazines have submission guidelines and theme lists available for a SASE. Check magazines' websites, too. Many offer excerpts of articles, submission guidelines, and theme lists and will give you a feel for the editorial focus of the publication.

Watch for the Canadian and International symbols. These publications' needs and requirements may differ from their U.S. counterparts.

ADVOCATE, PKA'S PUBLICATION

1881 Little Westkill Rd., Prattsville NY 12468. (518)299-3103. **Website:** Advocatepka.weebly.com; www.facebook.com/GaitedHorseAssociation. **Contact:** Patricia Keller, publisher. *Advocate, PKA's Publication*, published bimonthly, is an advertiser-supported tabloid using "original, previously unpublished works, such as feature stories, essays, 'think' pieces, letters to the editor, profiles, humor, fiction, poetry, puzzles, cartoons, or line drawings. Advocates for good writers and quality writings. We publish art, fiction, photos and poetry. *Advocate*'s submitters are talented people of all ages who do not earn their livings as writers. We wish to promote the arts and to give those we publish the opportunity to be published." Estab. 1987. Circ. 7,000.

○ "This publication has a strong horse orientation." Includes Gaited Horse Association newsletter. Horse-oriented stories, poetry, art and photos are currently needed."

FICTION Middle readers, young adults/teens, adults: adventure, animal, contemporary, fantasy, folktales, health, humorous, nature/environment, problemsolving, romance, science fiction, sports, suspense/mystery. Looks for "well written, entertaining work, whether fiction or nonfiction." Buys approximately 42 mss/year. Prose pieces should not exceed 1,500 words. Wants to see more humorous material, nature/environment and romantic comedy. "Nothing religious, pornographic, violent, erotic, pro-drug or anti-environment." Send complete ms.

NONFICTION Middle readers, young adults/teens: animal, arts/crafts, biography, careers, concept, cooking, fashion, games/puzzles, geography, history, hobbies, how-to, humorous, interview/profile, nature/environment, problem-solving, science, social issues, sports, travel. Buys 10 mss/year. Prose pieces should not exceed 1,500 words. Send complete ms.

POETRY Wants "nearly any kind of poetry, any length." Occasionally comments on rejected poems. No religious or pornographic poetry. Pays 2 contributor copies.

HOW TO CONTACT Responds to queries in 6 weeks; mss in 2 months. Publishes ms 2-18 months after acceptance.

ILLUSTRATION Uses b&w artwork only. Uses cartoons. Reviews ms/illustration packages from artists. Submit a photo print (b&w or color), an excellent copy of work (no larger than 8×10) or original. Prints in black and white but accepts color work that converts well to gray scale. Illustrations only: "Send previous unpublished art with SASE, please." Responds in 2 months. Samples returned with SASE; samples not filed. Credit line given.

PHOTOS Buys photos from freelancers. Model/property releases required. Uses color and b&w prints (no slides). Send unsolicited photos by mail with SASE. Responds in 2 months. Wants nature, artistic and humorous photos.

TERMS Acquires first rights for mss, artwork, and photographs. Pays on publication with contributor's copies. Sample copy: $5 (includes guidelines). Subscription: $18.50 (6 issues). Previous three issues are on website.

TIPS "Please, no simultaneous submissions, work that has appeared on the Internet, pornography, overt religiosity, anti-environmentalism or gratuitous violence. Artists and photographers should keep in mind that we are a b&w paper. Please do not send postcards. Use envelope with SASE."

AMERICAN CAREERS

Career Communications, Inc., 6701 W. 64th St., Suite 210, Overland Park KS 66202. (800)669-7795. **E-mail:** ccinfo@carcom.com. **Website:** www.carcom.com; www.americancareersonline.com. **Contact:** Mary Pitchford, editor-in-chief. "*American Careers* provides career, salary, and education information to middle school and high school students. Self-tests help them relate their interests and abilities to future careers." Estab. 1989. Circ. 500,000.

NONFICTION Query by mail only with published clips. Length: 300-1,000 words. Pays $100-450.

HOW TO CONTACT Accepts queries by mail.

PHOTOS State availability. Captions, identification of subjects, model releases required. Negotiates payment individually.

TERMS Buys all rights. Makes work-for-hire assignments. Byline given. Pays 1 month after acceptance. No kill fee. 10% freelance written. Sample copy for $4. Guidelines for #10 SASE.

TIPS "Letters of introduction or query letters with samples and résumés are ways we get to know writers. Samples should include how-to articles and career-related articles. Articles written for teenagers also would make good samples. Short feature articles on careers, career-related how-to articles, and self-assessment tools (10-20 point quizzes with scoring information) are primarily what we publish."

AMERICAN CHEERLEADER

Macfadden Performing Arts Media LLC, 110 William St., 23rd Floor, New York NY 10038. (646)459-4800. **Fax:** (646)459-4900. **E-mail:** mwalker@american cheerleader.com; acmail@americancheerleader.com. **Website:** www.americancheerleader.com. **Contact:** Marisa Walker, editor-in-chief. Bimonthly magazine covering high school, college, and competitive cheerleading. "We try to keep a young, informative voice for all articles—'for cheerleaders, by cheerleaders.'" Estab. 1995. Circ. 200,000.

NONFICTION Needs young adults: biography, interview/profile (sports personalities), careers, fashion, beauty, health, how-to (cheering techniques, routines, pep songs, etc.), problem-solving, sports, cheerleading-specific material. Query with published clips; provide résumé, business card, and tearsheets to be kept on file. "We're looking for authors who know cheerleading." Length. 750-2,000 words. Pays $100-250 for assigned articles; $100 maximum for unsolicited articles.

HOW TO CONTACT Editorial lead time 3 months. Responds in 4 weeks to queries. Responds in 2 months to mss. Publishes ms an average of 4 months after acceptance. Accepts queries by mail, e-mail, online submission form.

ILLUSTRATION Reviews ms/illustration packages from artists. Illustrations only. Query with samples; arrange portfolio review. Responds only if interested. Samples filed. Originals not returned at job's completion. Credit line given.

PHOTOS State availability. Model releases required. Reviews transparencies, 5x7 prints. Offers $50/photo.

TERMS Buys all rights. Byline given. Pays on publication. Offers 25% kill fee. 30% freelance written. Sample copy for $2.95. Guidelines free.

TIPS "We invite proposals from freelance writers who are involved in or have been involved in cheerleading—i.e., coaches, sponsors, or cheerleaders. Our writing style is upbeat and 'sporty' to catch and hold the attention of our teenaged readers. Articles should be broken down into lots of sidebars, bulleted lists, Q&As, etc."

APPLESEEDS

30 Grove St., Suite C, Peterborough NH 03458. (800)821-0115. **Fax:** (603)924-7380. **E-mail:** susan buckleynyc@gmail.com. **Website:** www.cobblestone pub.com; customerservice@caruspub. **Contact:** Susan Buckley, editor. AppleSeeds is a 36-page, multidisciplinary, nonfiction social studies magazine from Cobblestone Publishing for ages 6-9 (primarily grades 3 and 4). Each issue focuses on 1 theme.

◐   *Does not accept unsolicited mss.*

NONFICTION Query only (via e-mail). See website for submission guidelines and theme list.

HOW TO CONTACT Accepts queries by e-mail only.

ILLUSTRATION Contact Ann Dillon at Cobblestone. See website for illustration guidelines.

TERMS Requests for sample issues should be mailed to Cobblestone directly. See website for current theme list. Guidelines available on website.

TIPS "Submit queries specifically focused on the theme of an upcoming issue. We generally work 6 months ahead on themes. We look for unusual perspectives, original ideas, and excellent scholarship. Writers should check our website at www.cobble stonepub.com/guides_APP.html for current guidelines, topics, and query deadlines. We use very little fiction. Illustrators should not submit unsolicited art."

AQUILA

Studio 2, 67A Willowfield Rd., Eastbourne BN22 8AP, United Kingdom. (44)(132)343-1313. **Fax:** (44)(132)373-1136. **Website:** www.aquila.co.uk. "*Aquila* is an educational magazine for readers ages 8-13 including factual articles (no pop/celebrity material), arts/crafts and puzzles." Entire publication aimed at juvenile market. Estab. 1993. Circ. Monthly.

FICTION Young readers: animal, contemporary, fantasy, folktales, health, history, humorous, multicultural, nature/environment, problem solving, religious, science fiction, sports, suspense/mystery. Middle readers: animal, contemporary, fantasy, folktales, health, history, humorous, multicultural, nature/environment, problem solving, religious, romance, science fiction, sports, suspense/mystery. Buys 6-8 mss/year. Query with published clips.

NONFICTION Considers young readers: animal, arts/crafts, concept, cooking, games/puzzles, health, history, how-to, interview/profile, math, nature/environment, science, sports. Middle readers: animal, arts/crafts, concept, cooking, games/puzzles, health, history, interview/profile, math, nature/environment, science, sports. Buys 48 mss/year. Average word length—350-750.

HOW TO CONTACT Responds to queries in 6-8 weeks. Publishes ms 1 year after acceptance.

ILLUSTRATION Color artwork only. Works on assignment only. For first contact, query with samples. Responds only if interested. Samples not returned. Samples filed.

TERMS Buy exclusive magazine rights. Pays $150-200 for stories; $50-100 for articles. Writer's guidelines online at website.

TIPS "We only accept a high level of educational material for children ages 8-13 with a good standard of literacy and ability."

ASK

Carus Publlishing, 70 E. Lake St., Suite 300, Chicago IL 60601. **E-mail:** ask@caruspub.com. **Website:** www.cricketmag.com. **Contact:** Liz Huyck, editor. Magazine published 9 times/year covering science for children ages 6-9. "*ASK* is a magazine of arts and sciences for curious kids who like to find out how the world works." Estab. 2002.

NONFICTION Needs young readers, middle readers: science, engineering, invention, machines, archaeology, animals, nature/environment, history, history of science. "*ASK* commissions most articles but welcomes queries from authors on all nonfiction subjects. Particularly looking for odd, unusual, and interesting stories likely to interest science-oriented kids. Writers interested in working for *ASK* should send a résumé and writing sample (including at least 1 page unedited) for consideration." Average word length: 150-1,600.

ILLUSTRATION Buys 10 illustrations/issue; 60 illustrations/year. Works on assignment only. For illustrations, send query with samples.

PHOTOS Buys 10 illustrations/issue; 60 illustrations/year. Works on assignment only. For illustrations, send query with samples.

TERMS Byline given. Guidelines and current theme list available online.

AUSTRALASIAN JOURNAL OF EARLY CHILDHOOD

Early Childhood Australia, P.O. Box 86, Deakin West ACT 2600, Australia. (61)(2)6242-1800. **Fax:** (61)(2)6242-1818. **E-mail:** publishing@earlychildhood.org.au. **Website:** www.earlychildhoodaustralia.org.au. **Contact:** Chris Jones, publishing manager. Nonprofit early childhood advocacy organization, acting in the interests of young children aged from birth to 8 years of age, their families and those in the early childhood field. Specialist publisher of early childhood magazines, journals, and booklets.

NONFICTION Needs essays. Send complete ms. Length: Magazine articles, 600-1,000 words; research-based papers, 3,000-6,500 words; submissions for booklets, approximately 5,000 words.

TERMS Guidelines available online.

BABYBUG

Carus Publishing, 70 East Lake St., Chicago IL 60601. **E-mail:** babybug@caruspub.com. **Website:** www.cricketmag.com. **Contact:** Marianne Carus, editor-in-chief; Suzanne Beck, art director. "A listening and looking magazine for infants and toddlers ages 6 to 24 months, *Babybug* is 6×7, 24 pages long, printed in large type on high-quality cardboard stock with rounded corners and no staples." Estab. 1994. Circ. 45,000.

FICTION Looking for very simple and concrete stories. rhythmic, rhyming Length: 4-6 short sentences. $25 min.

NONFICTION Must use very basic words and concepts. Submit complete ms, SASE. Length: 10 words maximum. Pays $25.

POETRY Submit no more than 5 poems at a time. Lines/poem: 8 lines maximum. Considers previously published poems. Pays $25 minimum on publication. Acquires North American publication rights for previously published poems; rights vary for unpublished poems.

HOW TO CONTACT Responds in 6 months to mss.

ILLUSTRATION Uses color artwork only. Works on assignment only. Reviews ms/illustration packages from artists. "The manuscripts will be evaluated for quality of concept and text before the art is considered." Contact: Suzanne Beck. Illustrations only: Send tearsheets or photo prints/photocopies with SASE. "Submissions without SASE will be discarded." Responds in 3 months. Samples filed.

PHOTOS Pays $500/spread; $250/page.

TERMS Byline given. 50% freelance written. Guidelines available online.

TIPS "Imagine having to read your story or poem—out loud—50 times or more! That's what parents will have to do. Babies and toddlers demand, 'Read it again!' Your material must hold up under repetition. And humor is much appreciated by all."

BOYS' LIFE

Boy Scouts of America, P.O. Box 152079, Irving TX 75015. (972)580-2366. **Fax:** (972)580-2079. **Website:** www.boyslife.org. **Contact:** J.D. Owen, editor-in-chief; Michael Goldman, managing editor; Paula Murphey. *Boys' Life* is a monthly 4-color general interest magazine for boys 7-18, most of whom are Cub Scouts, Boy Scouts or Venturers. Estab. 1911. Circ. 1.1 million.

FICTION All fiction is assigned.

NONFICTION Scouting activities and general interests (nature, Earth, health, cars, sports, science, computers, space and aviation, entertainment, history, music, animals, how-to's, etc.) Query with SASE. No phone queries. Averge word length for articles: 500-1,500 words, including sidebars and boxes. Average word length for columns: 300-750. Pay ranges from $300 and up.

HOW TO CONTACT Responds to queries/mss in 2 months. Publishes approximately one year after acceptance. Accepts queries by mail.

ILLUSTRATION Buys 10-12 illustrations/issue; 100-125 illustrations/year. Works on assignment only. Reviews ms/illustration packages from artists. "Query first." Illustrations only: Send tearsheets. Responds to art samples only if interested. Samples returned with SASE. Original artwork returned at job's completion. Works on assignment only.

PHOTOS Photo guidelines free with SASE. Boy Scouts of America Magazine Division also publishes *Scouting* magazine. "Most photographs are from specific assignments that freelance photojournalists shoot for *Boys' Life*. Interested in all photographers, but do not send unsolicited images." Pays $500 base editorial day rate against placement fees, plus expenses. Pays on acceptance. Buys one-time rights.

TERMS Buys one-time rights. Byline given. Pays on acceptance. 75% freelance written. Prefers to work with published/established writers; works with small number of new/unpublished writers each year. Sample copies for $3.95 plus 9x12 SASE. Guidelines available with SASE and online.

TIPS "We strongly recommend reading at least 12 issues of the magazine before submitting queries. We are a good market for any writer willing to do the necessary homework. Write for a boy you know who is 12. Our readers demand punchy writing in relatively short, straightforward sentences. The editors demand well-reported articles that demonstrate high standards of journalism. We follow the Associated Press manual of style and usage. Learn and read our publications before submitting anything."

BOYS' QUEST

P.O. Box 227, Bluffton OH 45817-0227. (419)358-4610, ext. 101. **Fax:** (419)358-8020. **Website:** www.funforkidzmagazines.com. **Contact:** Marilyn Edwards, editor. Bimonthly magazine. "*Boys' Quest* is a magazine created for boys from 5 to 14 years, with youngsters 8, 9 and 10 the specific target age. Our point of view is that every young boy deserves the right to be a young boy for a number of years before he becomes a young adult." Estab. 1995. Circ. 10,000.

FICTION Picture-oriented material, young readers, middle readers: adventure, animal, history, humorous, multicultural, nature/environment, problem-solving, sports. Does not want to see violence, teenage themes. Buys 30 mss/year. Query or send complete ms (preferred). Send SASE with correct postage. No faxed or e-mailed material. Length: 200-500 words.

NONFICTION Needs nonfiction pieces that are accompanied by clear photos. Articles accompanied by photos with high resolution are far more likely to be accepted than those that need illustrations. Query or send complete ms (preferred). Send SASE with correct postage. No faxed or e-mailed material. Length: 500 words.

POETRY Reviews poetry. Limit submissions to 6 poems. Length: 21 lines maximum.

HOW TO CONTACT Responds to queries in 2 weeks; mss in 2 weeks (if rejected); 6 weeks (if scheduled). Accepts queries by mail.

ILLUSTRATION Buys 10 illustrations/issue; 60-70 illustrations/year. Uses b&w artwork only. Works on assignment only. Reviews ms/illustration packages from artists. Illustrations only: Query with samples, tearsheets. Responds in 1 month only if interested and a SASE. Samples returned with SASE; samples filed. Credit line given.

PHOTOS Photos used for support of nonfiction. "Excellent photographs included with a nonfiction story is considered very seriously." Model/property releases required. Uses b&w, 5x7 or 3x5 prints. Query with samples; send unsolicited photos by mail. Responds in 3 weeks. "We use a number of photos, printed in b&w, inside the magazine. These photos support the articles." $5/photo.

TERMS Buys first North American serial rights for mss. Byline given. Pays on publication. Guidelines and open themes available for SASE, or visit www.funforkidz.com and click on 'Writers' at the bottom of the homepage.

TIPS "First be familiar with our magazines. We are looking for lively writing, most of it from a young boy's point of view—with the boy or boys directly involved in an activity that is both wholesome and unusual. We need nonfiction with photos and fiction stories—around 500 words—puzzles, poems, cooking, carpentry projects, jokes and riddles. Nonfiction pieces that are accompanied by b&w photos are far more likely to be accepted than those that need illustrations. We will entertain simultaneous submissions as long as that fact is noted on the ms."

BREAD FOR GOD'S CHILDREN

P.O. Box 1017, Arcadia FL 34265. (863)494-6214. **Fax:** (863)993-0154. **E-mail:** bread@breadministries.org. **Website:** www.breadministries.org. **Contact:** Judith M. Gibbs, editor. An interdenominational Christian teaching publication published 6-8 times/year written to aid children and youth in leading a Christian life. Estab. 1972. Circ. 10,000 (U.S. & Canada).

FICTION "We are looking for writers who have a solid knowledge of Biblical principles and are concerned for the youth of today living by those principles. Our stories must be well written, with the story itself getting the message across—no preaching, moralizing, or tag endings." Young readers, middle readers, young adult/teen: adventure, religious, problem-solving, sports. Looks for "teaching stories that portray Christian lifestyles without preaching." Buys approximately 10-15 mss/year. Send complete ms. Length: young children—600-800 words; older children—900-1,500 words. Pays $40-50.

NONFICTION All levels: how-to. "We do not want anything detrimental to solid family values. Most topics will fit if they are slanted to our basic needs." Buys 3-4 mss/year. Length: 500-800 words.

HOW TO CONTACT Responds to mss in 6 months. Publishes ms an average of 6 months after acceptance. Accepts queries by mail.

ILLUSTRATION "The only illustrations we purchase are those occasional good ones accompanying an accepted story."

TERMS Pays on publication. Pays $30-50 for stories; $30 for articles. Sample copies free for 9×12 SAE and

5 first-class stamps (for 2 copies). Buys first rights. Byline given. No kill fee. 10% freelance written. Three sample copies for 9x12 SAE and 5 first-class stamps. Guidelines for #10 SASE.

TIPS "We want stories or articles that illustrate overcoming obstacles by faith and living solid, Christian lives. Know our publication and what we have used in the past. Know the readership and publisher's guidelines. Stories should teach the value of morality and honesty without preaching. Edit carefully for content and grammar."

◑☺ BRILLIANT STAR

1233 Central St., Evanston IL 60201. (847)853-2354. **Fax:** (847)256-1372. **E-mail:** brilliant@usbnc.org; sengle@usbnc.org. **Website:** www.brilliantstarmagazine.org. **Contact:** Susan Engle, associate editor; Amethel Parel-Sewell, editor/creative director. "*Brilliant Star* presents Bahá'í history and principles through fiction, nonfiction, activities, interviews, puzzles, cartoons, games, music, and art. Universal values of good character, such as kindness, courage, creativity, and helpfulness are incorporated into the magazine." Estab. 1969.

FICTION Middle readers: contemporary, fantasy, folktale, multicultural, nature/environment, problem-solving, religious. Submit complete ms. Length: 700-1,400 words.

NONFICTION Middle readers: arts/crafts, games/puzzles, geography, how-to, humorous, multicultural, nature/environment, religion, social issues. Buys 6 mss/year. Query. Length: 300-700 words.

POETRY "We only publish poetry written by children at the moment."

ILLUSTRATION Reviews ms/illustration packages from artists. Illustrations only; query with samples. Contact: Aaron Kreader, graphic designer. Responds only if interested. Samples kept on file. Credit line given.

PHOTOS Buys photos with accompanying ms only. Model/property release required; captions required. Responds only if interested.

TERMS Buys first rights and reprint rights for mss, artwork, and photos. Byline given. Pays 2 contributor's copies. Guidelines available for SASE or via e-mail.

TIPS "*Brilliant Star*'s content is developed with a focus on children in their 'tween' years, ages 8-12. This is a period of intense emotional, physical, and psychological development. Familiarize yourself with the interests and challenges of children in this age range. Protagonists in our fiction are usually in the upper part of our age range: 10-12 years old. They solve their problems without adult intervention. We appreciate seeing a sense of humor but not related to bodily functions or put-downs. Keep your language and concepts age-appropriate. Use short words, sentences, and paragraphs. Activities and games may be submitted in rough or final form. Send us a description of your activity along with short, simple instructions. We avoid long, complicated activities that require adult supervision. If you think they will be helpful, please try to provide step-by-step rough sketches of the instructions. You may also submit photographs to illustrate the activity."

◑☺ CADET QUEST MAGAZINE

P.O. Box 7259, Grand Rapids MI 49510-7259. (616)241-5616. **Fax:** (616)241-5558. **E-mail:** submissions@calvinistcadets.org. **Website:** www.calvinistcadets.org. **Contact:** G. Richard Broene, editor. Magazine published 7 times/year. "*Cadet Quest Magazine* shows boys 9-14 how God is at work in their lives and in the world around them." Estab. 1958. Circ. 6,000.

○ Accepts submissions by mail, or by e-mail (must include ms in text of e-mail). Will not open attachments.

FICTION Middle readers, boys/early teens: adventure, arts/craft, games/puzzles, hobbies, how-to, humorous, interview/profile, multicultural, problem-solving, religious, science, sports. Fast-moving stories that appeal to a boy's sense of adventure or sense of humor are welcome. Needs adventure, religious, spiritual, sports. Avoid preachiness. Avoid simplistic answers to complicated problems. Avoid long dialogue and little action. No fantasy, science fiction, fashion, horror or erotica. Send complete ms. Length: 900-1,500 words. Pays 4-6¢/word, and 1 contributor's copy.

NONFICTION Needs how-to, humor, inspirational, interview, personal experience. informational Send complete ms. Length: 500-1,500 words. Pays 4-6¢/word.

HOW TO CONTACT Responds in 2 months to mss. Publishes ms an average of 4-11 months after acceptance.

ILLUSTRATION Buys 2 illustrations/issue; buys 12 illustrations/year. Works on assignment only. Reviews ms/illustration packages from artists.

PHOTOS Pays $20-30 for photos purchased with ms.

TERMS Buys first North American serial rights, buys one time rights, buys second serial (reprint) rights, buys simultaneous rights. Rights purchased vary with author and material. Byline given. Pays on acceptance. No kill fee. 40% freelance written. Works with a small number of new/unpublished writers each year. Sample copy for 9x12 SASE. Guidelines for #10 SASE.

TIPS "Best time to submit stories/articles is early in the year (January-April). Also remember readers are boys ages 9-14. Stories must reflect or add to the theme of the issue and be from a Christian perspective."

♋ CALLIOPE

30 Grove St., Suite C, Peterborough NH 03458-1454. (603)924-7209. **Fax:** (603)924-7380. **E-mail:** customerservice@caruspub.com. **Website:** www.cobblestonepub.com. **Contact:** Rosalie Baker and Charles Baker, co-editors; Lou Waryncia, editorial director; Ann Dillon, art director. Magazine published 9 times/year covering world history (East and West) through 1800 AD for 8 to 14-year-old kids. Articles must relate to the issue's theme. Lively, original approaches to the subject are the primary concerns of the editors in choosing material. Estab. 1990. Circ. 13,000.

FICTION Middle readers and young adults: adventure, folktales, plays, history, biographical fiction. Material must relate to forthcoming themes. Needs adventure, historical. biographical, retold legends Length: no more than 1,000 words. Pays 20-25¢/word.

NONFICTION Needs essays, general interest, historical, how-to, crafts/woodworking, humor, interview, personal experience, photo feature, technical, travel. recipes Query with writing sample, 1-page outline, bibliography, SASE. Length: 400-1000 words/feature articles; 300 600 words/supplemental nonfiction. Pays 20-25¢/word.

HOW TO CONTACT If interested, responds 5 months before publication date. Accepts queries by mail.

PHOTOS "Illustrations only: Send tearsheets, photocopies. Original work returned upon job's completion (upon written request). Buys photos from freelancers. Wants photos pertaining to any upcoming themes. Uses b&w/color prints, 35mm transparencies and 300 DPI digital images. Send unsolicited photos by mail (on speculation). Buys all rights for mss and artwork." If you have photographs pertaining to any upcoming theme, please contact the editor by mail or fax, or send them with your query. You may also send images on speculation. Model/property release preferred. Reviews b&w prints, color slides. Reviews photos with or without accompanying manuscript. We buy one-time use. Suggested fee range for professional quality photographs follows: ¼ page to full page b/w $15-100; color $25-100. Please note that fees for non-professional quality photographs are negotiated. Cover fees are set on an individual basis for one-time use, plus promotional use. All cover images are color. Prices set by museums, societies, stock photography houses, etc., are paid or negotiated. Photographs that are promotional in nature (e.g., from tourist agencies, organizations, special events, etc.) are usually submitted at no charge. Pays on publication. Credit line given. Buys one-time rights; negotiable.

TERMS Buys all rights. Byline given. Pays on publication. Kill fee. 50% freelance written. Sample copy for $5.95, $2 shipping and handling, and 10x13 SASE. Guidelines available online.

TIPS "A query must consist of the following to be considered: a brief cover letter stating subject and word length of the proposed article; a detailed one-page outline explaining the information to be presented in the article; a bibliography of materials the author intends to use in preparing the article; a SASE. Writers new to *Calliope* should send a writing sample with query. In all correspondence, please include your complete address as well as a telephone number where you can be reached. A writer may send as many queries for one issue as he or she wishes, but each query must have a separate cover letter, outline and bibliography as well as a SASE. Telephone and e-mail queries are not accepted. Handwritten queries will not be considered. Queries may be submitted at any time, but queries sent well in advance of deadline may not be answered for several months."

CARUS PUBLISHING COMPANY

30 Grove St., Suite C, Peterborough NH 03458. **Website:** www.cricketmag.com. "We do not accept e-mailed submissions. Mss must be typed and accompanied by an SASE so that we may respond to your submission. Mss without an accompanying SASE will not be considered. Unfortunately, we are unable to return mss. Please do not send us your only copy. When submitting poetry, please send us no more than 6 poems at a time. Be sure to include phone and e-mail contact information. Please allow us up to 8

months for careful consideration of your submission. No phone calls, please."

○ See listings for *Babybug*, *Cicada*, *Click*, *Cricket*, *Ladybug*, *Muse*, *Spider* and *ASK*. Carus Publishing owns Cobblestone Publishing, publisher of *AppleSeeds*, *Calliope*, *Cobblestone*, *Dig*, *Faces* and *Odyssey*.

CATHOLIC FORESTER

Catholic Order of Foresters, 355 Shuman Blvd., P.O. Box 3012, Naperville IL 60566-7012. **Fax:** (630)983-3384. **E-mail:** magazine@catholicforester.org. **Website:** www.catholicforester.org. **Contact:** Editor; art director. Quarterly magazine for members of the Catholic Order of Foresters, a fraternal insurance benefit society. "*Catholic Forester* is a quarterly magazine filled with product features, member stories, and articles affirming fraternalism, unity, friendship, and true Christian charity among members. Although a portion of each issue is devoted to the organization and its members, a few freelance pieces are published in most issues. These articles cover varied topics to create a balanced issue for the purpose of informing, educating, and entertaining our readers." Estab. 1883. Circ. 77,000.

FICTION Needs humorous, religious. inspirational Length: 500-1,500 words. Pays 50¢/word.

NONFICTION Needs health and wellness, money management and budgeting, parenting and family life, insurance, nostalgia, humor, inspirational, religious. Will consider previously published work. Send complete ms by mail, fax, or e-mail. Rejected material will not be returned without accompanying SASE. Length: 500-1,000 words. Pays 50¢/word.

POETRY Length: 15 lines maximum. Pays 30¢/word.

HOW TO CONTACT Editorial lead time 6 months. Responds in 3 months to mss.

ILLUSTRATION Buys 2-4 illustrations/issue. Uses color artwork only.

PHOTOS State availability. Negotiates payment individually.

TERMS Buys first North American serial rights. Pays on acceptance. 20% freelance written. Sample copy for 9x12 SAE and 4 first-class stamps. Guidelines available on website.

TIPS "Our audience includes a broad age spectrum, ranging from youth to seniors. A good children's story with a positive lesson or message would rate high on our list."

CHEMMATTERS

1155 16th St., NW, Washington DC 20036. (202)872-6164. **Fax:** (202)833-7732. **E-mail:** chemmatters@acs.org. **Website:** www.acs.org/chemmatters. **Contact:** Pat Pages, editor; Cornithia Harris, art director. Covers content covered in a standard high school chemistry textbook. Estab. 1983.

NONFICTION Query with published clips. Pays $500-1,000 for article. Additional payment for mss/illustration packages and for photos accompanying articles.

HOW TO CONTACT Responds to queries/mss in 2 weeks. Publishes ms 6 months after acceptance. Accepts queries by mail, e-mail.

ILLUSTRATION Buys 3 illustrations/issue; 12 illustrations/year. Uses color artwork only. Works on assignment only. Reviews ms/illustration packages from artists. Query. Illustrations only: Query with promo sheet, résumé. Responds in 2 weeks. Samples returned with self-addressed stamped envelope; samples not filed. Credit line given.

PHOTOS Looking for photos of high school students engaged in science-related activities. Model/property release required; captions required. Uses color prints, but prefers high-resolution PDFs. Query with samples. Responds in 2 weeks.

TERMS Minimally buys first North American serial rights, but prefers to buy all rights, reprint rights, electronic rights for mss. Buys all rights for artwork; non-exclusive first rights for photos. Pays on acceptance. Sample copies free for 10x13 SASE and 3 first-class stamps. Writer's guidelines free for SASE (available as e-mail attachment upon request).

TIPS "Be aware of the content covered in a standard high school chemistry textbook. Choose themes and topics that are timely, interesting, fun, *and* that relate to the content and concepts of the first-year chemistry course. Articles should describe real people involved with real science. Best articles feature young people making a difference or solving a problem."

CICADA MAGAZINE

Cricket Magazine Group, 70 E. Lake St., Suite 300, Chicago IL 60601. (312)701-1720. **Fax:** (312)701-1728. **E-mail:** cicada@cicadamag.com. **Website:** www.cicadamag.com. **Contact:** Marianne Carus, editor-in-chief; Deborah Vetter, executive editor; John Sandford, art director. Bimonthly literary magazine for ages 14 and up. Publishes original short stories, poems, and first-person essays written for teens and young adults. *Cicada* publishes fiction and poetry with a genuine teen sensibility, aimed at the high school and college-age market. The editors are looking for stories and poems that are thought-provoking but entertaining. Estab. 1998. Circ. 10,000.

FICTION Young adults: adventure, contemporary, fantasy, historical, humor/satire, mainstream, multicultural, nature/environment, novel excerpts, novellas (1/issue), realistic, romance, science fiction, sports, suspense/mystery. Buys up to 42 mss/year. The main protagonist should be at least 14 and preferably older. Stories should have a genuine teen sensibility and be aimed at readers in high school or college. Length: 5,000 words maximum (up to 9,000 words/novellas). Pays up to 25¢/word.

NONFICTION Needs essays, personal experience. First-person, coming-of-age experiences that are relevant to teens and young adults (example: life in the Peace Corps). Buys up to 6 mss/year. Submit complete ms, SASE. Length: 5,000 words maximum; Pays up to 25¢/word.

POETRY Reviews serious, humorous, free verse, rhyming (if done well) poetry. Limit submissions to 5 poems. Length: 25 lines maximum. Pays up to $3/line on publication.

HOW TO CONTACT Responds in 4-6 months to mss.

ILLUSTRATION Buys 10 illustrations/issue; 60 illustrations/year. Uses color artwork for cover; b&w for interior. Works on assignment only. Reviews ms/illustration packages from artists. "To submit samples, e-mail a link to your online portfolio to: cicada@cicadamag.com. You may also e-mail a sample up to a maximum attachment size of 50 KB. We will keep your samples on file and contact you if we find an assignment that suits your style."

PHOTOS Wants documentary photos (clear shots that illustrate specific artifacts, persons, locations, phenomena, etc., cited in the text) and "art" shots of teens in photo montage/lighting effects etc. Send photocopies/tearsheets of artwork.

TERMS Byline given. Pays on publication. 80% freelance written. Guidelines available online at www.cricketmag.com (adults) and www.cicadamag.com (young adults 14-23)

TIPS "Quality writing, good literary style, genuine teen sensibility, depth, humor, good character development, avoidance of stereotypes. Read several issues to familiarize yourself with our style."

MAGAZINES

CLICK

Carus Publishing, 30 Grove St., Suite C, Peterborough NH 03458. **E-mail:** click@caruspub.com. **Website:** www.cricketmag.com. **Contact:** Amy Tao, editor; Deb Porter, art director. "*Click* is a science and exploration magazine for children ages 3 to 7. Designed and written with the idea that it's never too early to encourage a child's natural curiosity about the world, *Click*'s 40 full-color pages are filled with amazing photographs, beautiful illustrations, and stories and articles that are both entertaining and thought-provoking."

Does not accept unsolicited mss.

ILLUSTRATION Buys 10 illustrations/issue; 100 illustrations/year. Works on assignment only. Query with samples. Responds only if interested. Credit line given.

COBBLESTONE

Carus Publishing, 30 Grove St., Suite C, Peterborough NH 03458. (800)821-0115. **Fax:** (603)924-7380. **E-mail:** customerservice@caruspub.com. **Website:** www.cobblestonepub.com. Covers American history for ages 9-14. "We are interested in articles of historical accuracy and lively, original approaches to the subject at hand. Writers are encouraged to study recent *Cobblestone* back issues for content and style. All material must relate to the theme of a specific upcoming issue in order to be considered. To be considered, a query must accompany each individual idea (however, you can mail them all together) and must include the following: a brief cover letter stating the subject and word length of the proposed article, a detailed one-page outline explaining the information to be presented in the article, an extensive bibliography of materials the author intends to use in preparing the article, and a SASE. Authors are urged to use primary resources and up-to-date scholarly resources in their bibliography. Writers new to Cobblestone° should send a writing sample with the query. If you would like to know if your query has been received, please also include a stamped postcard that requests acknowledgment of receipt. In all correspondence, please include your complete address as well as a telephone number where you can be reached. A writer may send as many queries for one issue as he or she wishes, but each query must have a separate cover letter, outline, bibliography, and SASE. All queries must be typed. Please do not send unsolicited manuscripts—queries only! Prefers to work with published/established writers. Each issue presents a particular theme, making it exciting as well as informative. Half of all subscriptions are for schools. All material must relate to monthly theme." Circ. 15,000.

"*Cobblestone* stands apart from other children's magazines by offering a solid look at one subject and stressing strong editorial content, color photographs throughout, and original illustrations." *Cobblestone* themes and deadline are available on website or with SASE.

FICTION Needs adventure, historical. biographical, retold legends, folktales, multicultural Query. Length: 800 words maximum. Pays 20-25¢/word.

NONFICTION Needs historical, humor, interview, personal experience, photo feature, travel. crafts, recipes, activities Query with writing sample, 1-page outline, bibliography, SASE. Length: 800 words/feature articles; 300-600 words/supplemental nonfiction; 700 words maximum/activities. Pays 20-25¢/word.

POETRY Serious and light verse considered. Must have clear, objective imagery. Length: 100 lines maximum. Pays on an individual basis. Acquires all rights.

HOW TO CONTACT Accepts queries by mail, fax.

ILLUSTRATION Reviews ms/illustration packages from artists. Query. Illustrations only: Send photocopies, tearsheets, or other nonreturnable samples. "Illustrators should consult issues of *Cobblestone* to familiarize themselves with our needs." Responds to art samples in 1 month. Samples are not returned; samples filed. Original artwork returned at job's completion (upon written request). Credit line given. Illustrators: "Submit color samples, not too juvenile. Study past issues to know what we look for. The illustration we use is generally for stories, recipes and activities."

PHOTOS Captions, identification of subjects required, model release. Reviews contact sheets, transparencies, prints. $15-100/b&w. Pays on publication. Credit line given. Buys one-time rights. Our suggested fee range for professional quality photographs follows: ¼ page to full page b/w $15 to $100; color $25 to $100. Please note that fees for non-professional quality photographs are negotiated.

TERMS Buys all rights. Byline given. Pays on publication. Offers 50% kill fee. 50% freelance written. Guidelines available on website or with SASE; sample copy for $6.95, $2 shipping/handling, 10x13 SASE.

TIPS "Review theme lists and past issues to see what we're looking for."

COLLEGEXPRESS MAGAZINE

Carnegie Communications, LLC, 2 LAN Dr., Suite 100, Westford MA 01886. **E-mail:** info@carne giecomm.com. **Website:** www.collegexpress.com. "*CollegeXpress Magazine*, formerly *Careers and Colleges*, provides juniors and seniors in high school with editorial, tips, trends, and websites to assist them in the transition to college, career, young adulthood, and independence."

○ Distributed to 760,000 homes of 15- to 17-year-olds and college-bound high school graduates, and 10,000 high schools.

NONFICTION Needs Young adults/teens: careers, college, health, how-to, humorous, interview/profile, personal development, problem-solving, social issues, sports, travel. Query. Length: 1,000-1,500 words.

HOW TO CONTACT Responds to queries in 6 weeks. Accepts queries by mail, e-mail.

ILLUSTRATION Buys 2 illustrations/issue; buys 8 illustrations/year. Works on assignment only. Reviews samples online. Query first. Credit line given.

TERMS Buys all rights. Byline given. Pays on acceptance plus 45 days. Contributor's guidelines available electronically.

TIPS "Articles with great quotes, good reporting, good writing. Rich with examples and anecdotes. Must tie in with the objective to help teenaged readers plan for their futures. Current trends, policy changes and information regarding college admissions, financial aid, and career opportunities."

CRICKET

Carus Publishing Co., 70 E. Lake St., Suite 300, Chicago IL 60601. (312)701-1720, ext. 10. **Website:** www. cricketmag.com. **Contact:** Marianne Carus, editor-in-chief; Lonnie Plecha, editor; Alice Letvin, editorial director; Karen Kohn, senior art director. Monthly magazine for children ages 9-14. "*Cricket* is looking for more fiction and nonfiction for the older end of its 9-14 age range, as well as contemporary stories set in other countries. It also seeks humorous stories and mysteries (not detective spoofs), fantasy and original fairy tales, stand-alone excerpts from unpublished novels, and well-written/researched science articles." Estab. 1973. Circ. 73,000.

FICTION Middle readers, young adults/teens: contemporary, fantasy, folk and fairy tales, history, humorous, legends/myths, realistic, science fiction, suspense/mystery. Buys 70 mss/year. Recently published work by Aaron Shepard, Arnold Adoff, and Nancy Springer. No didactic, sex, religious, or horror stories. Submit complete ms. Length: 200-2,000 words. Pays 25¢/word maximum, and 6 contributor's copies; $2.50 charge for extras.

NONFICTION Middle readers, young adults/teens: adventure, architecture, archaeology, biography, foreign culture, games/puzzles, geography, natural history, science and technology, social science, sports, travel. Multicultural needs include articles on customs and cultures. Requests bibliography with submissions. Buys 30 mss/year. Submit complete ms, SASE. Length: 200-1,500 words. Pays 25¢/word maximum.

POETRY Reviews poems. Limit submission to 5 poems or less. Serious, humorous, nonsense rhymes. Length: 50 lines maximum. Pays $3/line maximum.

HOW TO CONTACT Responds in 4-6 months to mss. Accepts queries by mail.

ILLUSTRATION Buys 22 illustrations (7 separate commissions)/issue; 198 illustrations/year. Preferred theme for style: "stylized realism; strong people, especially kids; good action illustration, whimsical and humorous. All media, generally full color." Reviews ms/illustration packages from artists, "but reserves option to re-illustrate." Send complete ms with sample and query. Illustrations only: Provide link to web site or tearsheets and good quality photocopies to be kept on file. SASE required for response/return of samples.

PHOTOS Purchases photos with accompanying ms only. Model/property releases required. Uses 300 DPI digital files, color glossy prints. Commissions all art separately from the text. Tearsheets/photocopies of both color and b&w work are considered. Accepts artwork done in pencil, pen and ink, watercolor, acrylic, oil, pastels, scratchboard, and woodcut. Does not want work that is overly caricatured or cartoony. It is especially helpful to see pieces showing young people, animals, action scenes, and several scenes from a narrative showing a character in different situations and emotional states.

TERMS Byline given. Pays on publication. Guidelines available online.

TIPS Writers: "Read copies of back issues and current issues. Adhere to specified word limits. *Please* do not query." Would currently like to see more fantasy and science fiction. Illustrators: "Send only your best work and be able to reproduce that quality in assignments. Put name and address on *all* samples. Know a publication before you submit."

DAVEY AND GOLIATH'S DEVOTIONS

Evangelical Lutheran Church in America, ELCA Churchwide Ministries, 8765 W. Higgins Rd., Chicago IL 60631. **E-mail:** daveyandgoliath@elca.org. **Website:** www.daveyandgoliath.org. "*Davey and Goliath's Devotions* is a magazine with concrete ideas that families can use to build Biblical literacy and share faith and serve others. It includes Bible stories, family activities, crafts, games, and a section of puzzles, and mazes."

○ This is a booklet of interactive conversations and activities related to weekly devotional material. Used primarily by Lutheran families with elementary school-aged children.

TERMS Buys all rights. Pays on acceptance of final ms.

TIPS "Pay attention to details in the sample devotional. Follow the process laid out in the information for prospective writers. Ability to interpret Bible texts appropriately for children is required. Content must be doable and fun for families on the go."

DIG

Cobblestone Publishing, 30 Grove St., Suite C, Peterborough NH 03450. (603)924-7209. **Fax:** (603)924-7380. **E-mail:** cfbakeriii@meganet.net. **Website:** www.cobblestonepub.com. **Contact:** Rosalie Baker, editor; Lou Waryncia, editorial director; Ann Dillon, art director. An archaeology magazine for kids ages 8-14. Publishes entertaining and educational stories about discoveries, artifacts, and archaeologists. Estab. 1999.

FICTION Query. "Writers new to *Dig* should send a writing sample with query." Multiple queries accepted, may not be answered for many months.

NONFICTION Query. "A query must consist of all of the following to be considered: a brief cover letter stating the subject and word length of the proposed article, a detailed one-page outline explaining the information to be presented in the article, a bibliography of materials the author intends to use in preparing the article, and a SASE. Writers new to *Dig* should send a writing sample with query." Multiple queries accepted; may not be answered for many months.

ILLUSTRATION Buys 10-15 illustrations/issue; 60-75 illustrations/year. Prefers color artwork. Works on assignment only. Reviews ms/illustration packages from artists. Query. Illustrations only: Query with samples. Arrange portfolio review. Send tearsheets. Responds in 2 months only if interested. Samples not returned; samples filed. Credit line given.

PHOTOS Uses anything related to archaeology, history, artifacts, and current archaeological events that relate to kids. Uses color prints and 35mm transparencies and 300 dpi digital images. Provide résumé, promotional literature or tearsheets to be kept on file. Responds only if interested.

TERMS Buys all rights for mss. Buys first North American rights for photos. Pays on publication.

TIPS "We are looking for writers who can communicate archaeological concepts in a conversational, interesting, informative and *accurate* style for kids. Writers should have some idea where photography can be located to support their articles."

DRAMATICS MAGAZINE

Educational Theatre Association, 2343 Auburn Ave., Cincinnati OH 45219. (513)421-3900. **E-mail:** dcorathers@edta.org. **Website:** www.edta.org. **Contact:** Don Corathers, editor. "*Dramatics* is for students (mainly high school age) and teachers of theater. Mix includes how-to (tech theater, acting, directing, etc.), informational, interview, photo feature, humorous, profile, technical. We want our student readers to grow as theater artists and become a more discerning and appreciative audience. Material is directed to both theater students and their teachers, with strong student slant." Estab. 1929. Circ. 35,000.

FICTION Young adults: drama (one-act and full-length plays). "We prefer unpublished scripts that have been produced at least once." Does not want to see plays that show no understanding of the conventions of the theater. No plays for children, no Christmas or didactic "message" plays. Submit complete ms. Buys 5-9 plays/year. Emerging playwrights have better chances with résumé of credits. Length: 750-3,000 words. Pays $100-500 for plays.

NONFICTION Needs Young adults: arts/crafts, careers, how-to, interview/profile, multicultural (all theater-related). "We try to portray the theater community in all its diversity." Submit complete ms. Length: 750-3,000 words. Pays $50-500 for articles.

HOW TO CONTACT Publishes ms 3 months after acceptance.

ILLUSTRATION Buys 0-2 illustrations/year. Works on assignment only. Arrange portfolio review; send résumé, promo sheets and tearsheets. Responds only if interested. Samples returned with SASE; sample not filed. Credit line given. Pays up to $100 for illustrations.

PHOTOS Buys photos with accompanying ms only. Looking for "good-quality production or candid photography to accompany article. We very occasionally publish photo essays." Model/property release and captions required. Prefers hi-res JPG files. Will consider prints or transparencies. Query with résumé of credits. Responds only if interested.

TERMS Byline given. Pays on acceptance. Sample copy available for 9x12 SAE with 4-ounce first-class postage. Guidelines available for SASE.

TIPS "Obtain our writer's guidelines and look at recent back issues. The best way to break in is to know our audience—drama students, teachers, and others interested in theater—and write for them. Writers who have some practical experience in theater, especially in technical areas, have an advantage, but we'll work with anybody who has a good idea. Some freelancers have become regular contributors."

FACES

Cobblestone Publishing, 30 Grove St., Suite C, Peterborough NII 03458. (603)924-7209; (800)821-0115. **Fax:** (603)924-7380. **E-mail:** customerservice@caruspub.com. **Website:** www.cobblestonepub.com. "Published 9 times/year, *Faces* covers world culture for ages 9-14. It stands apart from other children's magazines by offering a solid look at one subject and stressing strong editorial content, color photographs throughout, and original illustrations. *Faces* offers an equal balance of feature articles and activities, as well as folktales and legends." Estab. 1984. Circ. 15,000.

FICTION Needs ethnic, historical, retold legends/folktales, original plays Length: 800 words maximum. Pays 20-25¢/word.

NONFICTION Needs historical, humor, interview, personal experience, photo feature, travel, recipes, activities, crafts Query with writing sample, 1-page outline, bibliography, SASE. Length: 800 words/feature articles; 300-600/supplemental nonfiction; 700 words maximum/activities. Pays 20-25¢/word.

POETRY Serious and light verse considered. Must have clear, objective imagery. Length: 100 lines maximum. Pays on an individual basis.

HOW TO CONTACT Accepts queries by mail, e-mail.

ILLUSTRATION "Submit b&w samples, not too juvenile. Study past issues to know what we look for. The illustration we use is generally for retold legends, recipes and activities." Buys 3 illustrations/issue; buys 27 illustrations/year. Preferred theme or style: Material that is meticulously researched (most articles are written by professional anthropologists); simple, direct style preferred, but not too juvenile. Works on assignment only. Roughs required. Reviews ms/illustration packages from artists. Illustrations only: Send samples of b&w work. "Illustrators should consult issues of *Faces* to familiarize themselves with our needs." Responds to art samples only if interested. Samples returned with SASE. Original artwork returned at job's completion (upon written request). Credit line given.

PHOTOS Wants photos relating to forthcoming themes. "Contact the editor by mail or fax, or send photos with your query. You may also send images on speculation." Captions, identification of subjects, model releases required. Reviews contact sheets, transparencies, prints. Pays $15-100/b&w; $25-100/color; cover fees are negotiated.

TERMS Buys all rights. Byline given. Pays on publication. Offers 50% kill fee. 90-100% freelance written. Sample copy for $6.95, $2 shipping and handling, 10 x 13 SASE. Guidelines with SASE or online.

TIPS "Writers are encouraged to study past issues of the magazine to become familiar with our style and content. Writers with anthropological and/or travel experience are particularly encouraged; *Faces* is about world cultures. All feature articles, recipes and activities are freelance contributions."

FCA MAGAZINE

Fellowship of Christian Athletes, 8701 Leeds Rd., Kansas City MO 64129. (816)921-0909. **Fax:** (816)921-8755. **E-mail:** mag@fca.org. **Website:** www.fca.org/mag. **Contact:** Clay Meyer, editor; Matheau Casner, creative director. Published 6 times/year. "We seek to serve as a ministry tool of the Fellowship of Christian Athletes by informing, inspiring, and involving coaches, athletes, and all whom they influence, that they may make an impact for Jesus Christ." Estab. 1959. Circ. 80,000.

NONFICTION Needs inspirational, interview (with name athletes and coaches solid in their faith), personal experience, photo feature. "Articles should be accompanied by at least 3 quality photos." Query. Considers electronic sumbissions via e-mail. Length: 1,000-2,000 words. Pays $150-400 for assigned and unsolicited articles.

HOW TO CONTACT Responds to queries/mss in 3 months. Publishes ms an average of 4 months after acceptance.

PHOTOS Purchases photos separately. Looking for photos of sports action. Uses color prints and high resolution electronic files of 300 dpi or higher. State availability. Reviews contact sheets. Payment based on size of photo.

TERMS Buys first rights and second serial (reprint) rights. Byline given. Pays on publication. No kill fee. 50% freelance written. Prefers to work with published/established writers, but works with a growing number of new/unpublished writers each year. Sample copy for $2 and 9x12 SASE with 3 first-class stamps. Guidelines available at www.fca.org/mag/media-kit.

TIPS "Profiles and interviews of particular interest to coed athlete, primarily high school and college age. Our graphics and editorial content appeal to youth. The area most open to freelancers is profiles on or interviews with well-known athletes or coaches (male, female, minorities) who have been or are involved in some capacity with FCA."

THE FRIEND MAGAZINE

The Church of Jesus Christ of Latter-day Saints, 50 E. North Temple St., Salt Lake City UT 84150. (801)240-2210. **E-mail:** friend@ldschurch.org. **Website:** www.lds.org/friend. **Contact:** Paul B. Pieper, editor; Mark W. Robison, art director. Monthly magazine for 3-12 year olds. "*The Friend* is published by The Church of Jesus Christ of Latter-day Saints for boys and girls up to 12 years of age. Estab. 1971. Circ. 275,000.

NONFICTION Needs historical, humor, inspirational, religious, adventure, ethnic, nature, family- and gospel-oriented puzzles, games, cartoons. Submit complete ms. Length: 1,000 words maximum. Pays $100-150 (400 words and up) for stories; $20 minimum for activities and games.

POETRY "We are looking for easy-to-illustrate poems with catchy cadences. Poems should convey a sense of joy and reflect gospel teachings. Also brief poems that will appeal to preschoolers." Length: 20 lines maximum. Pays $30 for poems.

HOW TO CONTACT Responds in 2 months to mss.

ILLUSTRATION Illustrations only: Query with samples; arrange personal interview to show portfolio; provide résumé and tearsheets for files.

TERMS Pays on acceptance. Buys all rights for mss. Pays $100-150 (400 words and up) for stories; $30 for

poems; $20 minimum for activities and games. Contributors are encouraged to send for sample copy for $1.50, 9×12 envelope and four 41-cent stamps. Free writer's guidelines. Buys all rights for mss. Pays on acceptance. Sample copy for $1.50, 9x12 envelope, and 4 first-class stamps.

TIPS "All submissions are carefully read by the *Friend* staff, and those not accepted are returned within 2 months for SASE. Submit seasonal material at least 1 year in advance. Query letters and simultaneous submissions are not encouraged. Authors may request rights to have their work reprinted after their ms is published."

FUN FOR KIDZ

P.O. Box 227, Bluffton OH 45817-0227. (419)358-4610. **Fax:** (419)358-8020. **Website:** http://funforkidz.com. **Contact:** Marilyn Edwards, articles editor. "*Fun for Kidz* is a magazine created for boys and girls ages 5-14, with youngsters 8, 9, and 10 the specific target age. The magazine is designed as an activity publication to be enjoyed by both boys and girls on the alternative months of *Hopscotch* and *Boys' Quest* magazines." Estab. 2002.

○ *Fun for Kidz* is theme-oriented. Send SASE for theme list and writer's guidelines or visit www.funforkidz.com and click on 'Writers' at the bottom of the homepage.

FICTION picture-oriented material, young readers, middle readers: adventure, animal, history, humorous, problem-solving, multicultural, nature/environment, sports. Length: 300-700 words.

NONFICTION picture-oriented material, young readers, middle readers: animal, arts/crafts, cooking, games/puzzles, history, hobbies, how-to, humorous, problem-solving, sports, carpentry projects. Submit complete ms. Length: 300-700 words.

HOW TO CONTACT Responds in 2 weeks to queries; 6 weeks to mss. Accepts queries by mail.

ILLUSTRATION Works on assignment mostly. "We are anxious to find artists capable of illustrating stories and features. Our inside art is pen and ink." Query with samples. Samples kept on file.

PHOTOS "We use a number of b&w photos inside the magazine; most support the articles used."

TERMS Buys first North American serial rights. Byline given. Pays on acceptance.

TIPS "Our point of view is that every child deserves the right to be a child for a number of years before he or she becomes a young adult. As a result, *Fun for Kidz* looks for activities that deal with timeless topics, such as pets, nature, hobbies, science, games, sports, careers, simple cooking, and anything else likely to interest a child."

GIRLS' LIFE

Monarch Publishing, 4529 Harford Rd., Baltimore MD 21214. (410)426-9600. **Fax:** (410)254-0991. **E-mail:** jessica@girlslife.com. **Website:** www.girlslife.com. **Contact:** Jessica D'Argenio Waller, associate fashion editor; Chun Kim, art director. Bimonthly magazine covering girls ages 9-15. Estab. 1994. Circ. 363,000.

FICTION "We accept short fiction. They should be stand-alone stories and are generally 2,500-3,500 words."

NONFICTION Needs book excerpts, essays, general interest, how-to, humor, inspirational, interview, new product, travel. Query by mail with published clips. Submit complete mss on spec only. "Features and articles should speak to young women ages 10-15 looking for new ideas about relationships, family, friends, school, etc. with fresh, savvy advice. Front-of-the-book columns and quizzes are a good place to start." Length: 700-2,000 words. Pays $350/regular column; $500/feature.

HOW TO CONTACT Editorial lead time 4 months. Responds in 1 month to queries. Publishes ms an average of 3 months after acceptance. Accepts queries by mail, e-mail.

PHOTOS State availability with submission if applicable. Reviews contact sheets, negatives, transparencies. Negotiates payment individually. Captions, identification of subjects, model releases required. State availability. Captions, identification of subjects, model releases required. Reviews contact sheets, negatives, transparencies. Negotiates payment individually.

TERMS Buys all rights. Byline given. Pays on publication. Sample copy for $5 or online. Guidelines available online.

TIPS "Send thought-out queries with published writing samples and detailed résumé. Have fresh ideas and a voice that speaks to our audience-not down to them. And check out a copy of the magazine or visit girlslife.com before submitting."

GREEN TEACHER

Green Teacher, 95 Robert St., Toronto ON M2S 2K5, Canada. (416)960-1244. **Fax:** (416)925-3474. **E-mail:** tim@greenteacher.com; info@greenteacher.com. **Website:** www.greenteacher.com. **Contact:** Tim Grant, co-editor; Brandon Quigley, editorial assistant. "*Green Teacher* is a magazine that helps youth educators enhance environmental and global education inside and outside of schools." Estab. 1991. Circ. 15,000.

NONFICTION multicultural, nature, environment Query. Submit one-page summary or outline. Length: 750-2,500 words.

HOW TO CONTACT Responds to queries in 1 week. Publishes ms 8 months after acceptance. Accepts queries by mail, e-mail.

ILLUSTRATION Buys 3 illustrations/issue from freelancers; 10 illustrations/year from freelancers. Black & white artwork only. Works on assignment only. Reviews ms/illustration packages from artists. Query with samples; tearsheets. Responds only if interested. Samples not returned. Samples filed. Credit line given.

PHOTOS Purchases photos both separately and with accompanying mss. "Activity photos, environmental photos." Uses b&w prints. Query with samples. Responds only of interested.

TERMS Pays on acceptance.

GUIDE

55 W. Oak Ridge Dr., Hagerstown MD 21740. (301)393-4037. **Fax:** (301)393-4055. **E-mail:** guide@rhpa.org. **Website:** www.guidemagazine.org. **Contact:** Randy Fishell, editor; Brandon Reese, designer. "*Guide* is a Christian story magazine for young people ages 10-14. The 32-page, 4-color publication is published weekly by the Review and Herald Publishing Association. Our mission is to show readers, through stories that illustrate Bible truth, how to walk with God now and forever." Estab. 1953.

NONFICTION Send complete ms. "Each issue includes 3-4 true stories. *Guide* does not publish fiction, poetry, or articles (devotionals, how-to, profiles, etc.). However, we sometimes accept quizzes and other unique nonstory formats. Each piece should include a clear spiritual element." Length: 1,000-1,200 words. Pays 6-12¢/word.

HOW TO CONTACT Responds in 6 weeks to mss. Accepts queries by mail, e-mail.

TERMS Byline given. Pays on acceptance. Sample copy free with 6x9 SAE and 2 first-class stamps. Guidelines available on website.

TIPS "Children's magazines want mystery, action, discovery, suspense, and humor—no matter what the topic. For us, truth is stronger than fiction."

HIGHLIGHTS FOR CHILDREN

803 Church St., Honesdale PA 18431. (570)253-1080. **Fax:** (570)251-7847. **Website:** www.highlights.com. **Contact:** Christine French Cully, editor-in-chief; Drew Hires, art director. Monthly magazine for children up to age 12. "This book of wholesome fun is dedicated to helping children grow in basic skills and knowledge, in creativeness, in ability to think and reason, in sensitivity to others, in high ideals, and worthy ways of living—for children are the world's most important people. We publish stories for beginning and advanced readers. Up to 500 words for beginners (ages 3-7), up to 800 words for advanced (ages 8-12)." Estab. 1946. Circ. approximately 2 million.

FICTION Meaningful stories appealing to both girls and boys, up to age 12. Vivid, full of action. Engaging plot, strong characterization, lively language. Prefers stories in which a child protagonist solves a dilemma through his or her own resources. Seeks stories that the child ages 8-12 will eagerly read, and the child ages 2-7 will like to hear when read aloud (500-800 words). Stories require interesting plots and a number of illustration possiblities. Also need rebuses (picture stories 120 words or under), stories with urban settings, stories for beginning readers (100-500 words), sports and humorous stories, adventures, holiday stories, and mysteries. We also would like to see more material of 1-page length (300 words), both fiction and factual. Needs adventure, fantasy, historical, humorous. animal, contemporary, folktales, multi-cultural, problem-solving, sports No war, crime or violence. Send complete ms. Pays $100 minimum plus 2 contributor's copies.

NONFICTION "Generally we prefer to see a manuscript rather than a query. However, we will review queries regarding nonfiction." Length: 800 words maximum. Pays $25 for craft ideas and puzzles; $25 for fingerplays; $150 and up for articles.

POETRY Lines/poem: 16 maximum ("most poems are shorter"). Considers simultaneous submissions ("please indicate"); no previously published poetry. No e-mail submissions. "Submit typed manuscript with very brief cover letter." Occasionally comments on submissions "if manuscript has merit or author seems to have potential for our market." Guidelines available for SASE. Responds "generally within one month." Always sends prepublication galleys. Pays 2 contributor's copies; "money varies." Acquires all rights.

HOW TO CONTACT Responds in 2 months to queries. Accepts queries by mail.

ILLUSTRATION Buys 25-30 illustrations/issue. Preferred theme or style: Realistic, some stylization. Works on assignment only. Reviews ms/illustration packages from artists. Illustrations only: photocopies, promo sheet, tearsheets, or slides. Résumé optional. Portfolio only if requested. Contact: Art Director. Responds to art samples in 2 months. Samples returned with SASE; samples filed. Credit line given.

PHOTOS Reviews color 35mm slides, photos, or electronic files.

TERMS Buys all rights. Pays on acceptance. 80% freelance written. Sample copy free. Guidelines on website in "About Us" area.

TIPS "Know the magazine's style before submitting. Send for guidelines and sample issue if necessary." Writers: "At *Highlights* we're paying closer attention to acquiring more nonfiction for young readers than we have in the past." Illustrators: "Fresh, imaginative work encouraged. Flexibility in working relationships a plus. Illustrators presenting their work need not confine themselves to just children's illustrations as long as work can translate to our needs. We also use animal illustrations, real and imaginary. We need crafts, puzzles and any activity that will stimulate children mentally and creatively. We are always looking for imaginative cover subjects. Know our publication's standards and content by reading sample issues, not just the guidelines. Avoid tired themes, or put a fresh twist on an old theme so that its style is fun and lively. We'd like to see stories with subtle messages, but the fun of the story should come first. Write what inspires you, not what you think the market needs. We are pleased that many authors of children's literature report that their first published work was in the pages of *Highlights*. It is not our policy to consider fiction on the strength of the reputation of the author. We judge each submission on its own merits. With factual material, however, we do prefer that writers be authorities in their field or people with first-hand experience. In this manner we can avoid the encyclopedic article that merely restates information readily available elsewhere. We don't make assignments. Query with simple letter to establish whether the nonfiction subject is likely to be of interest. A beginning writer should first become familiar with the type of material that *Highlights* publishes. Include special qualifications, if any, of author. Write for the child, not the editor. Write in a voice that children understand and relate to. Speak to today's kids, avoiding didactic, overt messages. Even though our general principles haven't changed over the years, we are contemporary in our approach to issues. Avoid worn themes."

HIGHLIGHTS HIGH FIVE

807 Church St., Honesdale PA 18431. **Fax:** (570)251-7847. **Website:** www.highlights.com/high-five. **Contact:** Kathleen Hayes, editor. "*Highlights High Five* was created to help you encourage your young child's development—and have fun together at the same time. Based on sound educational principles and widely accepted child-development theories, each monthly issue brings a 40-page, high-quality mix of read-aloud stories and age appropriate activities that will help you set your child firmly on the path to becoming a lifelong learner. Stories for younger readers should have 170 words or less and should appeal to children ages 2-6." Estab. 2009.

HOW TO CONTACT At this time, accepts very few mss. Most articles are commissioned or written in-house. Accepts queries by mail.

HOPSCOTCH

P.O. Box 164, Bluffton OH 45817. (419)358-4610. **Fax:** (419)358-8020. **E-mail:** customerservice@funforkidz.com ("we do not accept submissions via e-mail"). **Website:** www.hopscotchmagazine.com. **Contact:** Marilyn Edwards, editor. "For girls from ages 5-14, featuring traditional subjects—pets, games, hobbies, nature, science, sports, etc.—with an emphasis on articles that show girls actively involved in unusual and/or worthwhile activities." Estab. 1989. Circ. 14,000.

FICTION Needs picture-oriented material, young readers, middle readers: adventure, animal, history, humorous, nature/environment, sports, suspense/mystery. Does not want to see stories dealing with dating, sex, fashion, hard rock music. Submit complete ms. Length: 300-700 words.

NONFICTION Picture-oriented material, young readers, middle readers: animal, arts/crafts, biography, cooking, games/puzzles, geography, hobbies,

how-to, humorous, math, nature/environment, science. "Need more nonfiction with quality photos about a *Hopscotch*-age girl involved in a worthwhile activity." Query or submit complete ms. Length: 400-700 words.

HOW TO CONTACT Responds in 2 weeks to queries; 5 weeks to mss.

ILLUSTRATION Buys approximately 10 illustrations/issue; buys 60-70 articles/year. "Generally, the illustrations are assigned after we have purchased a piece (usually fiction). Occasionally, we will use a painting—in any given medium—for the cover, and these are usually seasonal." Uses b&w artwork only for inside; color for cover. Reviews ms/illustration packages from artists. Query first or send complete ms with final art. Illustrations only: Send résumé, portfolio, client list and tearsheets. Responds to art samples only if interested and SASE in 1 month. Samples returned with SASE. Credit line given.

PHOTOS Purchases photos separately (cover only) and with accompanying ms only. Looking for photos to accompany article. Model/property releases required. Uses 5x7, b&w prints; 35mm transparencies. Black & white photos should go with ms. Should show girl or girls ages 6-12.

TERMS Byline given. Pays on publication.

TIPS "Remember we publish only 6 issues a year, which means our editorial needs are extremely limited. Please look at our guidelines and our magazine. Remember, we use far more nonfiction than fiction. Guidelines and current theme list can be downloaded from our website. If decent photos accompany the piece, it stands an even better chance of being accepted. We believe it is the responsibility of the contributor to come up with photos. Please remember, our readers are 6-12 years—most are 8-10—and your text should reflect that. Many magazines try to entertain first and educate second. We try to do the reverse. Our magazine is more simplistic, like a book to be read from cover to cover. We are looking for wholesome, non-dated material."

☺ HORSEPOWER

Box 670, Aurora ON L4G 4J9, Canada. (800)505-7428. **Fax:** (905)841-1530. **E-mail:** ftdesk@horse-canada.com. **Website:** www.horsepowermagazine.ca. **Contact:** Susan Stafford, managing editor. Bimonthly 16-page magazine, bound into *Horse Canada*, a bimonthly family horse magazine. "*Horsepower* offers how-to articles and stories relating to horse care for kids ages 6-16, with a focus on safety." Estab. 1988. Circ. 17,000.

🌢 *Horsepower no longer accepts fiction.*

NONFICTION Needs Middle readers, young adults: arts/crafts, biography, careers, fashion, games/puzzles, health, history, hobbies, how-to, humorous, interview/profile, problem-solving, travel. Submit complete ms. Length: 500-1,200 words.

HOW TO CONTACT Responds to mss in 3 months.

ILLUSTRATION Buys 3 illustrations/year. Reviews ms/illustration packages from artists. Contact: Editor. Query with samples. Responds only if interested. Samples returned with SASE; samples kept on file. Credit line given.

PHOTOS Looks for photos of kids and horses, instructional/educational, relating to riding or horse care. Uses color matte or glossy prints. Query with samples. Responds only if interested. Accepts TIFF or JPEG 300 dpi, disk or e-mail. Children on horseback must be wearing riding helmets or photos cannot be published.

TERMS Buys one-time rights for mss. Pays on publication. Guidelines available for SASE.

TIPS "Articles must be easy to understand, yet detailed and accurate. How-to or other educational features must be written by, or in conjunction with, a riding/teaching professional. Fiction is not encouraged, unless it is outstanding and teaches a moral or practical lesson. Note: Preference will be given to Canadian writers and photographers due to Canadian content laws. Non-Canadian contributors accepted on a very limited basis."

🌐 HUNGER MOUNTAIN

Vermont College of Fine Arts, 36 College St., Montpelier VT 05602. (802)828-8517. **E-mail:** hungermtn@vcfa.edu. **Website:** www.hungermtn.org. "We accept picture book, middle grade, YA and YA crossover work (text only—for now). We're looking for polished pieces that entertain, that show the range of adolescent experience, and that are compelling, creative and will appeal to the devoted followers of the kid-lit craft, as well as the child inside us all." Monthly online publication and annual perfect-bound journal covering high quality fiction, poetry, creative nonfiction, craft essaus, writing for children, and artwork. Accepts high quality work from unknown, emerging, or successful writers. No genre fiction, drama, or academic articles, please. *Hunger Mountain* is about 200 pages, 7x10, professionally printed, perfect-bound, with full-bleed color artwork on cover. Press run is 1,000; 10,000 visits online monthly. Single copy: $10; subscription: $12/year, $22 for 2 years. Make checks payable to Vermont College of Fine Arts. Member: CLMP. Estab. 2002.

🌢 Uses online submissions manager.

FICTION "We look for work that is beautifully crafted and tells a good story, with characters that are alive and kicking, storylines that stay with us long after we've finished reading, and sentences that slay us with their precision." Needs adventure. high quality short stories and short shorts No genre fiction, meaning science fiction, fantasy, horror, erotic, etc. Submit ms using online submissions manager. Length: no more than 10,000 words. Pays $25-100.

NONFICTION "We welcome an array of traditional and experimental work, including, but not limited to, personal, lyrical, and meditative essays, memoirs, collages, rants, and humor. The only requirements are recognition of truth, a unique voice with a firm command of language, and an engaging story with multiple pressure points." Submit complete ms using online submissions manager. Length: no more than 10,000 words.

POETRY Submit 3-10 poems at a time. All poems should be in ONE file. "We look for poetry that is as much about the world as about the self, that's an invitation, an opening out, a hand beckoning. We like poems that name or identify something essential that we may have overlooked. We like poetry with acute, precise attention to both content and diction." Submit using online submissions manager. No light verse, humor/quirky/catchy verse, greeting card verse.

HOW TO CONTACT Responds in 4 months to mss. Publishes ms an average of 1 year after acceptance. Accepts queries by online submission form.

PHOTOS Send photos. Reviews contact sheets, transparencies, prints, GIF/JPEG files. Slides preferred. Negotiates payment individually.

TERMS Buys first worldwide serial rights. Byline given. Pays on publication. No kill fee. Sample copy for $10. Writer's guidelines online.

TIPS "Mss must be typed, prose double-spaced. Poets submit at least 3 poems. No multiple genre submissions. Fresh viewpoints and human interest are very important, as is originality. We are committed to publishing an outstanding journal of the arts. Do not send entire novels, mss, or short story collections. Do not send previously published work."

IMAGINATION CAFÉ

Imagination Café, P.O. Box 1536, Valparaiso IN 46384. (219)510-4467. **E-mail:** editor@imagination -cafe.com; submissions@imagination-cafe.com. **Website:** www.imagination-cafe.com. **Contact:** Rosanne Tolin, articles editor. "*Imagination Café* is dedicated to empowering kids and tweens by encouraging curiosity in the world around them, as well as exploration of their talents and aspirations. *Imagination Café*'s mission is to offer children tools to discover their passions by providing them with reliable information, resources and safe opportunities for self-expression. *Imagination Café* publishes general interest articles with an emphasis on career exploration for kids. There is also material on school, science, history, and sports. Plus, celebrity briefs, recipes, animals, and other general interest pieces." Estab. 2006.

NONFICTION Query with published clips.

HOW TO CONTACT Responds to queries in 1 day to 2 weeks.

TERMS Buys electronic and non-exclusive print rights.

TIPS "*Imagination Café* is not a beginner's market. Most of our contributors are published writers. Please study the website before submitting, and make sure your writing is clearly directed to a kid audience, no adults. That means informative, interesting text written in a clear, concise, even clever manner that suitable for the online reader. Have fun with it and be sure include web-friendly, relevant links and sidebars."

INSIGHT

The Review and Herald Publishing Association, 55 W. Oak Ridge Dr., Hagerstown MD 21740. (301)393-4038. **E-mail:** insight@rhpa.org. **Website:** www.insight magazine.org. Weekly magazine covering spiritual life of teenagers. *Insight* publishes true dramatic stories, interviews, and community and mission service features that relate directly to the lives of Christian teenagers, particularly those with a Seventh-day Adventist background. Estab. 1970. Circ. 8,000.

○ "Big Deal" appears in *Insight* often, covering a topic of importance to teens. Each feature contains: An opening story involving real teens (can be written in first-person), Scripture Picture (a sidebar that discusses what the Bible says about the topic) and another sidebar (optional) that adds more perspective and help.

NONFICTION Needs how-to, teen relationships and experiences, humor, interview, personal experience, photo feature, religious. Send complete ms. Length: 500-1,000 words. Pays $25-150 for assigned articles. Pays $25-125 for unsolicited articles.

HOW TO CONTACT Editorial lead time 6 months. Responds in 1 month to mss. Publishes ms an average of 4 months after acceptance. Accepts queries by mail, e-mail, fax.

PHOTOS State availability. Model releases required. Reviews contact sheets, negatives, transparencies, prints. Negotiates payment individually.

TERMS Buys first rights, buys second serial (reprint) rights. Byline given. Pays on publication. No kill fee. 80% freelance written. Sample copy for $2 and #10 SASE. Guidelines available online.

TIPS "Skim 2 months of *Insight*. Write about your teen experiences. Use informed, contemporary style and vocabulary. Follow Jesus' life and example."

JACK AND JILL

U.S. Kids, 1100 Waterway Blvd., Indianapolis IN 46206-0567. (317)634-1100. **E-mail:** editor@satur dayeveningpost.com. **Website:** www.jackandjillmag. org. Bimonthly magazine published for children ages 8-12. Estab. 1938. Circ. 200,000.

○ "Please do not send artwork. We prefer to work with professional illustrators of our own choosing."

FICTION Needs Young readers and middle readers: adventure, contemporary, folktales, health, history, humorous, nature, sports. Submit complete ms. Queries not accepted. Length: 600-800 words. Pays 30¢/ word.

NONFICTION Needs Young readers, middle readers: animal, arts, crafts, cooking, games, puzzles, history, hobbies, how-to, humorous, interviews, profile, nature, science, sports. Submit complete ms. Queries not accepted. Length: 700 words. Pays 30¢/word.

POETRY Wants light-hearted poetry appropriate for the age group. Mss must be typewritten with poet's contact information in upper right-hand corner of each poem's page. SASE required. Pays $25-50.

HOW TO CONTACT Responds to mss in 3 months. Publishes ms an average of 8 months after acceptance.

ILLUSTRATION Buys 15 illustrations/issue; 90 illustrations/year. Credit line given.

TERMS Buys all rights. Byline given. Pays on publication. 50% freelance written. Guidelines available online.

TIPS "We are constantly looking for new writers who can tell good stories with interesting slants—stories that are not full of outdated and time-worn expressions. We like to see stories about kids who are smart and capable, but not sarcastic or smug. Problem-solving skills, personal responsibility, and integrity are good topics for us. Obtain current issues of the magazine and study them to determine our present needs and editorial style."

JUNIOR BASEBALL

(203)210-5726. **E-mail:** publisher@juniorbaseball.com. **Website:** www.juniorbaseball.com. **Contact:** Jim Beecher, publisher. Bimonthly magazine focused on youth baseball players ages 7-17 (including high school) and their parents/coaches. Edited to various reading levels, depending upon age/skill level of feature. Estab. 1996. Circ. 20,000.

NONFICTION Needs how-to, skills, tips, features, how-to play better baseball, etc., interview, with major league players; only on assignment, personal experience, from coaches' or parents' perspective. Query. Length: 500-1,000 words. Pays $50-100.

HOW TO CONTACT Editorial lead time 3 months. Responds in 2 weeks to queries; 1 month to mss. Publishes ms an average of 4 months after acceptance.

PHOTOS Photos can be e-mailed in 300 dpi JPEGs. State availability. Captions, identification of subjects required. Reviews 35mm transparencies, 3x5 prints. Offers $10-100/photo; negotiates payment individually.

TERMS Buys all rights. Byline given. Pays on publication. No kill fee. 25% freelance written. Sample copy for $5 and online.

TIPS "Must be well-versed in baseball! Have a child who is very involved in the sport, or have extensive hands-on experience in coaching baseball, at the youth, high school or higher level. We can always use accurate, authoritative skills information, and good photos to accompany is a big advantage! This magazine is read by experts. No fiction, poems, games, puzzles, etc." Does not want first-person articles about your child.

◑ THE KERF

College of the Redwoods, 883 W. Washington Blvd., Crescent City CA 95531. **E-mail:** david-holper@red woods.edu. **Website:** www.redwoods.edu/Depart ments/english/poets&writers/clm.htm. **Contact:** David Holper. *The Kerf*, published annually in fall, features "poetry that speaks to the environment and humanity." Wants "poetry that exhibits an environmental consciousness." Considers poetry by children and teens. Estab. 1995.

◑ *The Kerf* is 54 pages, digest-sized, printed via Docutech, saddle-stapled, with CS2 coverstock. Receives about 1,000 poems/year, accepts up to 3%. Press run is 400 (150 shelf sales); 100 distributed free to contributors and writing centers. Sample: $5. Make checks payable to College of the Redwoods. Has published poetry by Ruth Daigon, Alice D'Alessio, James Grabill, George Keithley, and Paul Willis.

POETRY Submit up to 5 poems (7 pages maximum) at a time. No previously published poems or simultaneous submissions. Reads submissions January 15-March 31 only.

KEYS FOR KIDS

Box 1001, Grand Rapids MI 49501-1001. (616)647-4950. **Fax:** (616)647-4950. **E-mail:** hazel@cbhminis tries.org. **Website:** www.cbhministries.org. **Contact:** Hazel Marett, fiction editor. "CBH Ministries is an international Christian ministry based on the gospel of Jesus Christ, which produces and distributes excellent media resources to evangelize and disciple kids and their families." Estab. 1982.

FICTION Buys 40 mss/year. Needs religious. "Tell a story (not a Bible story) with a spiritual application." Submit complete ms. Length: 400 words. Pays $25 for stories.

TERMS Buys reprint rights or first rights for mss. Pays on acceptance. Sample copy for 6x9 SAE and 3 first-class stamps. Guidelines for SASE.

TIPS "Be sure to follow guidelines after studying sample copy of the publication."

KIDS LIFE MAGAZINE

1426 22nd Ave., Tuscaloosa AL 35401. (205)345-1193. **E-mail:** kidslife@comcast.net. **Contact:** Mary Jane Turner, publisher. "Kids Life Magazine, established in 2000, prides itself in bringing you a publication that showcases all the Tuscaloosa area has to offer its families. Not only does our community offer many activities and family-oriented events, we also have wonderful shopping and dining!" Estab. 2000. Circ. 30,000.

KIDZ CHAT

8805 Governor's Hill Dr., Suite 400, Cincinnati OH 45249. (513)931-4050. **Fax:** (877)867-5751. **E-mail:** mredford@standardpub.com. **Website:** www.standardpub.com. **Contact:** Marjorie Redford, editor. Circ. 55,000.

○ *Kidz Chat* has decided to reuse much of the material that was a part of the first publication cycle. They will not be sending out theme lists, sample copies or writers guidelines or accepting any unsolicited material because of this policy.

◐ ☺ LADYBUG

Carus Publishing Co., 700 E. Lake St., Suite 300, Chicago IL 60601. (312)701-1720. **Website:** www.cricketmag.com. **Contact:** Marianne Carus, editor-in-chief; Suzanne Beck, managing art director. Monthly magazine for children ages 2-6. *LADYBUG Magazine*, published monthly, is a reading and listening magazine for young children (ages 2-6). "We look for quality literature and nonfiction." Subscription: $35.97/year (12 issues). sample: $5; sample pages available on website. Estab. 1990. Circ. 125,000.

FICTION Picture-oriented material: adventure, animal, fantasy, folktales, humorous, multicultural, nature/environment, problem-solving, science fiction, sports, suspense/mystery. "Open to any easy fiction stories." Buys 50 mss/year. Submit complete ms, include SASE. Length: 800 words maximum. Pays 25¢/word minimum.

NONFICTION Picture-oriented material: activities, animal, arts/crafts, concept, cooking, humorous, math, nature/environment, problem-solving, science. Send complete ms, SASE. Length: 400-700 words. Pays 25¢/word minimum.

POETRY Wants poetry that is "rhythmic, rhyming; serious, humorous, active." Length: 20 lines maximum. Pays $3/line ($25 minimum).

HOW TO CONTACT Responds in 6 months to mss.

ILLUSTRATION Prefers "bright colors; all media, but uses watercolor and acrylics most often; same size as magazine is preferred but not required." To be considered for future assignments: Submit promo sheet, slides, tearsheets, color and b&w photocopies. Responds to art samples in 3 months. Submissions without SASE will be discarded.

PHOTOS Artists should submit tearsheets/photocopies of artwork to be kept in our illustrator files. Pays $500/spread; $250/page.

TERMS Byline given. Pays on publication. Guidelines available online.

TIPS "Reread manuscript before sending. Keep within specified word limits. Study back issues before submitting to learn about the types of material we're looking for. Writing style is paramount. We look for rich, evocative language and a sense of joy or wonder. Remember that you're writing for preschoolers—be age-appropriate, but not condescending or preachy. A story must hold enjoyment for both parent and child through repeated read-aloud sessions. Remember that people come in all colors, sizes, physical conditions, and have special needs. Be inclusive!"

LEADING EDGE

4087 JKB, Provo UT 84602. **E-mail:** editor@leadingedgemagazine.com; fiction@leadingedgemagazine.com; art@leadingedgemagazine.com. **Website:** www.leadingedgemagazine.com. **Contact:** Nyssa Silvester, senior editor. Semiannual magazine covering science fiction and fantasy. "We strive to encourage developing and established talent and provide high quality speculative fiction to our readers." Does not accept mss with sex, excessive violence, or profanity. "*Leading Edge* is a magazine dedicated to new and upcoming talent in the field of science fiction and fantasy." Estab. 1980. Circ. 200.

○ Accepts unsolicited submissions.

FICTION Needs fantasy, science fiction. Send complete ms with cover letter and SASE. Include estimated word count. Length: 15,000 words maximum. Pays 1¢/word; $10 minimum.

POETRY "Publishes 2-4 poems per issue. Poetry should reflect both literary value and popular appeal and should deal with science fiction- or fantasy-related themes." Submit 1 or more poems at a time. No e-mail submissions. Cover letter is preferred. Include name, address, phone number, length of poem, title, and type of poem at the top of each page. Please include SASE with every submission." Pays $10 for first 4 pages; $1.50/each subsequent page.

HOW TO CONTACT Responds in 2-4 months to mss. Publishes ms an average of 2-4 months after acceptance.

ILLUSTRATION Buys 24 illustrations/issue; 48 illustrations/year. Uses b&w artwork only. Works on assignment only. Contact: Art Director. Illustrations only: Send postcard sample with portfolio, samples, URL. Responds only if interested. Samples filed. Credit line given.

TERMS Buys first North American serial rights. Byline given. Pays on publication. No kill fee. 90% freelance written. Single copy: $5.95; subscription: $10 (2 issues), $20 (4 issues), $27.50 (6 issues). Guidelines available online at website.

TIPS "Buy a sample issue to know what is currently selling in our magazine. Also, make sure to follow the writer's guidelines when submitting."

LISTEN

55 West Oak Ridge Dr., Hagerstown MD 21740. (301)393-4019; (301)393-4082. **Fax:** (301) 393-3294. **E-mail:** editor@listenmagazine.org. **Website:** www. listenmagazine.org. **Contact:** Celest Perrino-Walker, editor. Monthly magazine, 9 issues. "*Listen* offers positive alternatives to drug use for its teenage readers. Helps them have a happy and productive life by making the right choices." Estab. 1948. Circ. 12,000.

○ *Considers mss only once a year, in October.*

NONFICTION How-to, health, humorous, life skills, problem-solving, social issues, drug facts, drug-free living. Wants to see more factual articles on drug abuse. Buys 50 mss/year. Query. Length: 700 words.

ILLUSTRATION Buys 3-6 illustrations/issue; 50 illustrators/year. Reviews ms/illustration packages from artists. Manuscript/illustration packages and illustration only: Query. Responds only if interested. Originals returned at job's completion. Samples returned with SASE. Credit line given.

PHOTOS Purchases photos from freelancers. Photos purchased with accompanying ms only. Uses color and b&w photos; digital, 35mm, transparencies or prints. Query with samples. Looks for "youth oriented—action (sports, outdoors), personality photos."

TERMS Buys exclusive magazine rights for mss. Byline given. Pays on acceptance.

TIPS "*Listen* is a magazine for teenagers. It encourages development of good habits and high ideals of physical, social and mental health. It bases its editorial philosophy of primary drug prevention on total abstinence from tobacco, alcohol, and other drugs. Because it is used extensively in public high school classes, it does not accept articles and stories with overt religious emphasis. Four specific purposes guide the editors in selecting materials for *Listen*: (1) To portray a positive lifestyle and to foster skills and values that will help teenagers deal with contemporary problems, including smoking, drinking, and using drugs. This is *Listen*'s primary purpose. (2) To offer positive alternatives to a lifestyle of drug use of any kind. (3) To present scientifically accurate information about the nature and effects of tobacco, alcohol, and other drugs. (4) To report medical research, community programs, and educational efforts that are solving problems connected with smoking, alcohol, and other drugs. Articles should offer their readers activities that increase one's sense of self-worth through achievement and/or involvement in helping others. They are often categorized by three kinds of focus: (1) Hobbies. (2) Recreation. (3) Community Service."

LIVE WIRE

8805 Governor's Hill Dr., Suite 400, Cincinnati OH 45249. (513)931-4050. **Fax:** (877)867-5751. **E-mail:** mredford@standardpub.com. **Website:** www.stan dardpub.com. Estab. 1949.

○ *Live Wire* has decided to reuse much of the material that was a part of the first publication cycle. They will not be sending out theme lists, sample copies, or writers guidelines or accepting any unsolicited material because of this policy.

◐ THE LOUISVILLE REVIEW

Spalding University, 851 S. Fourth St., Louisville KY 40203. (502)585-9911, ext. 2777. **Fax:** (502)992-2409. **E-mail:** louisvillereview@spalding.edu. **Website:** www.louisvillereview.org. **Contact:** Kathleen Driskell, associate editor. *The Louisville Review*, published twice/year, prints all kinds of poetry. Has a section devoted to poetry by children and teens (grades K-12) called The Children's Corner. Has published poetry by Wendy Bishop, Gary Fincke, Michael Burkard, and Sandra Kohler. *The Louisville Review* is 150 pages, digest-sized, flat-spined. Receives about 700 submissions/year, accepts about 10%. Single copy: $8; subscription: $14/year, $27/2 years, $40/3 years (foreign subscribers add $6/year for s&h). Sample: $5. Estab. 1976.

POETRY Considers simultaneous submissions; no previously published poems. Accepts submissions via online manager; please see website for more information. "Poetry by children must include permission of parent to publish if accepted. Address those submissions to The Children's Corner." Reads submissions year round. Pays in contributor's copies.

⊕ ● LYRICAL PASSION POETRY E-ZINE

P.O. Box 17331, Arlington VA 22216. **Website:** http://lyricalpassionpoetry.yolasite.com. **Contact:** Raquel D. Bailey, founding editor. Founded by award-winning poet Raquel D. Bailey, Lyrical Passion Poetry E-Zine is an attractive monthly online literary magazine specializing in Japanese short form poetry. Publishes quality artwork, well-crafted short fiction and poetry in English by emerging and established writers. Literature of lasting literary value will be considered. Welcomes the traditional to the experimental. Poetry works written in German will be considered if accompanied by translations. Offers annual short fiction and poetry contests. Estab. 2007. Circ. 500 online visitors/month.

FICTION Send complete mss, typed, double-spaced. Cover letter preferred.

POETRY Multiple submissions are permitted, but no more than 3 submissions in a 6-month period. Submissions from minors should be accompanied by a cover letter from parent with written consent for their child's submission to be published on the website with their child's first initial and last name accompanied by their age at the time of submission. Does not want: dark, cliché, limerick, erotica, extremely explicit, violent, or depressing literature. Free verse poetry length: between 1 and 40/lines.

HOW TO CONTACT Responds in 2 months. Publishes ms 1 month after acceptance. Accepts queries by e-mail.

TERMS Acquires first-time rights, electronic rights (must be the first literary venue to publish online or in any electronic format). Rights revert to poets upon publication. Guidelines and upcoming themes available on website.

MUSE

E-mail: muse@caruspub.com. **Website:** www.cricketmag.com. "The goal of *Muse* is to give as many children as possible access to the most important ideas and concepts underlying the principal areas of human knowledge. Articles should meet the highest possible standards of clarity and transparency aided, wherever possible, by a tone of skepticism, humor, and irreverence." All articles are commissioned. To be considered for assignments, experienced science writers

may send a résumé and 3 published clips. Estab. 1996. Circ. 40,000.

💬 *Muse is not accepting unsolicited mss or queries.*

NONFICTION Middle readers, young adult: animal, arts, history, math, nature/environment, problem-solving, science, social issues.

ILLUSTRATION Works on assignment only. Credit line given. Send prints or tearsheets, but please, no portfolios or original art, and above all, *do not send samples that need to be returned.*

PHOTOS Needs vary. Query with samples to photo editor.

NATIONAL GEOGRAPHIC KIDS

National Geographic Society, 1145 17th St. NW, Washington DC 20036. **Website:** www.kidsnationalgeographic.com. **Contact:** Catherine Hughes, science editor; Andrea Silen, associate editor; Jay Sumner, photo director. Magazine published 10 times/year. "It's our mission to excite kids about their world. We are the children's magazine that makes learning fun." Estab. 1975. Circ. 1.3 million.

💬 "We do not want poetry, sports, fiction, or story ideas that are too young—our audience is between ages 8-14."

NONFICTION Needs general interest, humor, interview, technical, travel, animals, human interest, science, technology, entertainment, archaeology, pets. Query with published clips and résumé. Length: 100-1,000 words. Pays $1/word for assigned articles.

HOW TO CONTACT Editorial lead time 6+ months. Publishes ms an average of 6 months after acceptance. Accepts queries by mail.

PHOTOS State availability. Captions, identification of subjects, model releases required. Reviews contact sheets, negatives, transparencies, prints. Negotiates payment individually.

TERMS Buys all rights. Makes work-for-hire assignments. Byline given. Pays on acceptance. Offers 10% kill fee. 70% freelance written. Sample copy for #10 SASE. Guidelines free.

TIPS "Submit relevant clips. Writers must have demonstrated experience writing for kids. Read the magazine before submitting. Send query and clips via snail mail—materials will not be returned. No SASE required unless sample copy is requested."

◐ NATURE FRIEND MAGAZINE

4253 Woodcock Lane, Dayton VA 22821. (540)867-0764. **E-mail:** info@naturefriendmagazine.com; ed

MAGAZINES

itor@naturefriendmagazine.com; photos@nature friendmagazine.com. **Website:** www.naturefriend magazine.com. **Contact:** Kevin Shank, editor. Monthly children's magazine covering creation-based nature. "*Nature Friend* includes stories, puzzles, science experiments, nature experiments—all submissions need to honor God as creator." Estab. 1982. Circ. 13,000.

○ Picture-oriented material and conversational material needed.

NONFICTION Needs how-to, nature, photo feature, science experiments (for ages 8-12), articles about interesting/unusual animals. Send complete ms. Length: 250-900 words. Pays 5¢/word.

HOW TO CONTACT Editorial lead time 4 months. Responds in 6 months to mss.

PHOTOS Send photos. Captions, identification of subjects required. Reviews prints. Offers $20-75/photo.

TERMS Buys first rights, buys one-time rights. Byline given. Pays on publication. No kill fee. 80% freelance written. Sample copy for $5 postage paid. Guidelines available on website.

TIPS "We want to bring joy and knowledge to children by opening the world of God's creation to them. We endeavor to create a sense of awe about nature's creator and a respect for His creation. We'd like to see more submissions on hands-on things to do with a nature theme (not collecting rocks or leaves—real stuff). Also looking for good stories that are accompanied by good photography."

NEW MOON GIRLS

New Moon Girl Media, P.O. Box 161287, Duluth MN 55816. (218)728-5507. **Fax:** (218)728-0314. **E-mail:** newmoon@newmoon.com. **Website:** www.new moon.org. Bimonthly magazine covering girls ages 8-14, edited by girls aged 8-14. "*New Moon Girls* is for every girl who wants her voice heard and her dreams taken seriously. *New Moon* celebrates girls, explores the passage from girl to woman, and builds healthy resistance to gender inequities. The *New Moon* girl is true to herself and *New Moon Girls* helps her as she pursues her unique path in life, moving confidently into the world." Estab. 1992. Circ. 30,000.

○ In general, all material should be pro-girl and feature girls and women as the primary focus.

FICTION Prefers girl-written material. All girl-centered. Needs adventure, fantasy, historical, humorous, slice-of-life vignettes. Send complete ms. Length: 900-1,600 words. Pays 6-12¢/word.

NONFICTION Needs essays, general interest, humor, inspirational, interview, opinion, personal experience, written by girls, photo feature, religious, travel, multicultural/girls from other countries. Send complete ms. Publishes nonfiction by adults in Herstory and Women's Work departments only. Length: 600 words. Pays 6-12¢/word.

POETRY No poetry by adults.

HOW TO CONTACT Editorial lead time 6 months. Responds in 2 months to mss. Publishes ms an average of 6 months after acceptance. Accepts queries by mail, e-mail, fax.

ILLUSTRATION Buys 6-12 illustrations/year from freelancers. *New Moon* seeks 4-color cover illustrations. Reviews ms/illustrations packages from artists. Query. Submit ms with rough sketches. Illustration only: Query; send portfolio and tearsheets. Samples not returned; samples filed. Responds in 6 months only if interested. Credit line given.

PHOTOS State availability. Captions, identification of subjects required. Negotiates payment individually.

TERMS Buys all rights. Byline given. Pays on publication. 25% freelance written. Sample copy for $7 or online. Guidelines available at website.

TIPS "We'd like to see more girl-written feature articles that relate to a theme. These can be about anything the girl has done personally, or she can write about something she's studied. Please read *New Moon Girls* before submitting to get a sense of our style. Writers and artists who comprehend our goals have the best chance of publication. We love creative articles—both nonfiction and fiction—that are not condescending to our readers. Keep articles to suggested word lengths; avoid stereotypes. Refer to our guidelines and upcoming themes."

ON COURSE

The General Council of the Assemblies of God, 1445 Boonville Ave., Springfield MO 65802-1894. (417)862-2781. **Fax:** (417)862-1693. **E-mail:** oncourse@ag.org. **Website:** www.oncourse.ag.org. **Contact:** Amber Weigand-Buckley, editor; Josh Carter, art director. *On Course* is a magazine to empower students to grow in a real-life relationship with Christ. Estab. 1991.

○ *On Course* no longer uses illustrations, only photos. Works on assignment basis only. Résumés and writing samples will be considered for inclusion in Writer's File to receive story assignments.

FICTION Needs young adults: Christian discipleship, contemporary, humorous, multicultural, problem-solving, sports. Length: 800 words.

NONFICTION Needs young adults: careers, interview/profile, multicultural, religion, social issues, college life, Christian discipleship.

PHOTOS Buys photos from freelancers. "Teen life, church life, college life; unposed; often used for illustrative purposes." Model/property releases required. Uses color glossy prints and 35mm or 2½×2¼ transparencies. Query with samples; send business card, promotional literature, tearsheets or catalog. Responds only if interested.

TERMS Buys first or reprint rights for mss. Byline given. Pays on acceptance. Sample copy free for 9x11 SASE. Guidelines on website.

POCKETS

The Upper Room, P.O. Box 340004, Nashville TN 37203, (615)340-7333. **Fax:** (615)340-7267. **E-mail:** pockets@upperroom.org. **Website:** pockets.upperroom.org. **Contact:** Lynn W. Gilliam, editor. Magazine published 11 times/year. "*Pockets* is a Christian devotional magazine for children ages 8-12. All submissions should address the broad theme of the magazine. Each issue is built around one theme with material which can be used by children in a variety of ways. Scripture stories, fiction, poetry, prayers, art, graphics, puzzles and activities are included. Submissions do not need to be overtly religious. They should help children experience a Christian lifestyle that is not always a neatly-wrapped moral package, but is open to the continuing revelation of God's will. Seasonal material, both secular and liturgical, is desired." Estab. 1981.

🔘 Does not accept e-mail or fax submissions.

FICTION Adventure, ethnic/multicultural, historical (general), religious/inspirational, slice-of-life vignettes. Needs adventure, ethnic, historical, general, religious. No violence, science fiction, romance, fantasy, or talking animal stories. Send complete ms with SASE. Length: 600-1,000 words. Pays 14¢/word.

NONFICTION Picture-oriented, young readers, middle readers: cooking, games/puzzles. "*Pockets* seeks biographical sketches of persons, famous or unknown, whose lives reflect their Christian commitment, written in a way that appeals to children." Does not accept how-to articles. "Nonfiction reads like a story." Mul-

ticultural needs include: stories that feature children of various racial/ethnic groups and do so in a way that is true to those depicted. Length: 400-1,000 words. Pays 14¢/word.

POETRY Considers poetry by children. Length: 4-20 lines. Pays $25 minimum.

HOW TO CONTACT Responds in 8 weeks to mss. Publishes ms an average of 1 year after acceptance.

ILLUSTRATION Buys 25-35 illustrations/issue. Preferred theme or style: varied; both 4-color. Works on assignment only. Illustrations only: Send promo sheet, tearsheets.

PHOTOS Send 4-6 close-up photos of children actively involved in peacemakers at work activities. Send photos, contact sheets, prints, or digital images. Must be 300 dpi. Pays $25/photo.

TERMS Buys first North American serial rights. Byline given. Pays on acceptance. No kill fee. 60% freelance written. Each issue reflects a specific theme. Guidelines on website.

TIPS "Theme stories, role models, and retold scripture stories are most open to freelancers. Poetry is also open. It is very helpful if writers read our writers' guidelines and themes on our website."

RAINBOW RUMPUS

P.O. Box 6881, Minneapolis MN 55406. (612)721-6442. **E-mail:** fictionandpoetry@rainbowrumpus.org; admin@rainbowrumpus.org. **Website:** www.rainbowrumpus.org. **Contact:** Beth Wallace, fiction editor. "*Rainbow Rumpus* is the world's only online literary magazine for children and youth with lesbian, gay, bisexual, and transgender (LGBT) parents. We are creating a new genre of children's and young adult fiction. Please carefully read and observe the guidelines on our website. We purchase first North American online rights. All fiction and poetry submissions should be sent via our contact page. Be sure to select the 'Submissions' category. A staff member will be in touch with you shortly to obtain a copy of your manuscript." Estab. 2005. Circ. 300 visits/day.

FICTION Needs All levels: adventure, animal, contemporary, fantasy, folktales, history, humorous, multicultural, nature/environment, problem solving, science fiction, sports, suspense/mystery. "Stories should be written from the point of view of children or teens with lesbian, gay, bisexual, or transgender parents or other family members, or who are connected to the LGBT community. Stories for 4- to 12-year-old children should be approximately 800 to 2,500 words in length. Stories for 13- to 18-year-olds may be as long as 5,000 words. Stories featuring families of color, bisexual parents, transgender parents, family members with disabilities, and mixed-race families are particularly welcome." Pays $75/story.

NONFICTION Needs interview, profile. social issues Query. Length: 800-5,000 words. Pays $75/story.

ILLUSTRATION Buys 1 illustration/issue. Uses both b&w and color artwork. Reviews ms/illustration packages from artists: Query. Illustrations only: Query with samples. Contact: Beth Wallace, fiction editor. Samples not returned; samples filed depending on the level of interest. Credit line given.

TERMS Buys first rights for mss; may request print anthology and audio or recording rights. Byline given. Pays on publication. Writer's guidelines available on website.

TIPS "Emerging writers encouraged to submit. You do not need to be a member of the LGBT community to participate."

RED LIGHTS

2740 Andrea Drive, Allentown PA 18103-4602. (212)875-9342. **E-mail:** mhazelton@rcn.com; marilynhazelton@rcn.com. **Contact:** Marilyn Hazelton, editor. *red lights tanka journal*, published biannually in January and June, is devoted to English-language tanka and tanka sequences. Wants "print-only tanka, mainly 'free-form' but also strictly syllabic 5-7-5-7-7; will consider tanka sequences and tan-renga." Considers poetry by children and teens. Has published poetry by Sanford Goldstein, Michael McClintock, Laura Maffei, Linda Jeannette Ward, Jane Reichhold, and Michael Dylan Welch. *red lights* is 36-40 pages, offset-printed, saddle-stapled, with Japanese textured paper cover; copies are numbered. Single copy: $8; subscription: $16 U.S., $18 USD Canada, $20 USD foreign. Make checks payable to "red lights" in the U.S. Estab. 2004.

TIPS "Each issue features a 'red lights featured tanka' on the theme of 'red lights.' Poet whose poem is selected receives 1 contributor's copy."

SCIENCE WEEKLY

P.O. Box 70638, Chevy Chase MD 20813. (301)680-8804. **Fax:** (301)680-9240. **E-mail:** scienceweekly@erols.com. **Website:** www.scienceweekly.com. **Contact:** Dr. Claude Mayberry, publisher. *Science Weekly* uses freelance writers to develop and write an entire issue on a single science topic. Send résumé only, not submissions. Authors preferred within the greater D.C./Virginia/Maryland area. *Science Weekly* works on assignment only. Estab. 1984. Circ. 200,000.

○ Submit resume only.

NONFICTION Young readers, middle readers (K-6th grade): science/math education, education, problem-solving.

TERMS Pays on publication. Sample copy free with SAE and 3 first-class stamps.

ⓐ SEVENTEEN MAGAZINE

300 W. 57th St., 17th Floor, New York NY 10019. (917)934-6500. **Fax:** (917)934-6574. **E-mail:** mail@seventeen.com. **Website:** www.seventeen.com. Monthly magazine covering topics geared toward young adult American women. "We reach 14.5 million girls each month. Over the past six decades, *Seventeen* has helped shape teenage life in America. We represent an important rite of passage, helping to define, socialize and empower young women. We create notions of beauty and style, proclaim what's hot in popular culture and identify social issues." Estab. 1944. Circ. 2,000,000.

○ *Seventeen* no longer accepts fiction submissions.

NONFICTION Needs young adults: careers, cooking, hobbies, how-to, humorous, interview/profile, multicultural, social issues. Query. Length: 200-2,000 words.

ILLUSTRATION *Only interested in agented material.* Buys 10 illustrations/issue; 120 illustrations/year. Works on assignment only. Reviews ms/illustration packages. Illustrations only: Query with samples. Responds only if interested. Samples not returned; samples filed. Credit line given.

PHOTOS Looking for photos to match current stories. Model/property releases required; captions required. Uses color, 8×10 prints; 35mm, 2¼×2¼, 4×5 or 8×10 transparencies. Query with samples or résumé of credits, or submit portfolio for review. Responds only if interested.

TERMS Buys first North American serial rights, first rights, or all rights for mss. Buys exclusive rights for 3 months. Byline sometimes given. Pays on publication. Writer's guidelines for SASE.

TIPS "Send for guidelines before submitting."

SHINE BRIGHTLY

GEMS Girls' Clubs, P.O. Box 7259, Grand Rapids MI 49510. (616)241-5616. **Fax:** (616)241-5558. **E-mail:** shinebrightly@gemsgc.org. **Website:** www.gemsgc.org. **Contact:** Jan Boone, executive director; Kelli Gilmore, managing editor. Monthly magazine (with combined June/July, August summer issue). "Our purpose is to lead girls into a living relationship with Jesus Christ and to help them see how God is at work in their lives and the world around them. Puzzles, crafts, stories, and articles for girls ages 9-14." Estab. 1970. Circ. 17,000.

FICTION Does not want "unrealistic stories and those with trite, easy endings. We are interested in manuscripts that show how girls can change the world." Needs adventure experiences girls could have in their hometowns or places they might realistically visit, ethnic, historical, humorous, mystery, religious, omance, slice-of-life vignettes, suspense,. Believable only. Nothing too preachy. Submit complete ms in body of e-mail. No attachments. Length: 700-900 words. Pays up to $35, plus 2 copies.

NONFICTION Needs humor, inspirational, seasonal and holiday, interview, personal experience, photo feature, religious, travel. adventure, mystery Submit complete ms in body of e-mail. No attachments. Length: 100-800 words. Pays up to $35, plus 2 copies.

POETRY Limited need for poetry. Pays $5-15.

HOW TO CONTACT Responds in 2 months to mss. Publishes ms an average of 1 year after acceptance.

ILLUSTRATION Samples returned with SASE. Credit line given.

PHOTOS Purchased with or without ms. Appreciate multicultural subjects. Reviews 5x7 or 8x10 clear color glossy prints. Pays $25-50 on publication.

TERMS Buys first North American serial rights, buys second serial (reprint) rights, buys simultaneous rights. Byline given. Pays on publication. No kill fee. 80% freelance written. Works with new and published/established writers. Sample copy with 9x12 SASE with 3 first class stamps and $1. Guidelines available online.

TIPS Writers: "Please check our website before submitting. We have a specific style and theme that deals with how girls can impact the world. The stories should be current, deal with pre-adolescent problems and joys, and help girls see God at work in their lives through humor as well as problem-solving." Prefers not to see anything on the adult level, secular material, or violence. Writers frequently oversimplify the articles and often write with a Pollyanna attitude. An author should be able to see his/her writing style as exciting and appealing to girls ages 9-14. The style can be fun, but also teach a truth. Subjects should be current and important to *SHINE brightly* readers. Use our theme update as a guide. We would like to receive material with a multicultural slant."

SKIPPING STONES: A MULTICULTURAL LITERARY MAGAZINE

P.O. Box 3939, Eugene OR 97403-0939. (541)342-4956. **E-mail:** editor@skippingstones.org. **Website:** www.skippingstones.org. **Contact:** Arun Toké, editor. "*Skipping Stones* is an award-winning multicultural, nonprofit magazine designed to promote cooperation, creativity and celebration of cultural and ecological richness. We encourage submissions by children of color, minorities and under-represented populations. We want material meant for children and young adults/teenagers with multicultural or ecological awareness themes. Think, live and write as if you were a child, tween or teen. We want material that gives insight to cultural celebrations, lifestyle, customs and traditions, glimpse of daily life in other countries and cultures. Photos, songs, artwork are most welcome if they illustrate/highlight the points. Translations are invited if your submission is in a language other than English." Themes may include cultural celebrations, living abroad, challenging, hospitality customs of various cultures, cross-cultural understanding, African, Asian and Latin American cultures, humor, international understanding, turning points and magical moments in life, caring for the earth, spirituality, and multicultural awareness. *Skipping Stones* is magazine-sized, saddle-stapled, printed on recycled paper. Published bimonthly during the school year (5 issues). Estab. 1988. Circ. 2,000 print, plus Web.

FICTION Middle readers, young adult/teens: contemporary, meaningful, humorous. All levels: folktales, multicultural, nature/environment. Multicultural needs include: bilingual or multilingual pieces; use of words from other languages; settings in other countries, cultures or multi-ethnic communities. Needs adventure, ethnic, historical, humorous. multicultural, international, social issues No suspense or romance stories. Send complete ms. Length: 1,000 words maximum. Pays 2 contributor's copies.

NONFICTION Needs essays, general interest, humor, inspirational, interview, opinion, personal experience, photo feature, travel. All levels: animal, biography, cooking, games/puzzles, history, humorous, interview/profile, multicultural, nature/environment, creative problem-solving, religion and cultural celebrations, sports, travel, social and international awareness. Does not want to see preaching, violence or abusive language. Send complete ms. Length: 1,000 words maximum. Pays 2 contributor's copies.

POETRY Submit up to 5 poems at a time. Considers simultaneous submissions; no previously published poems. Accepts e-mail submissions. Cover letter is preferred. "Include your cultural background, experiences, and the inspiration behind your creation." Time between acceptance and publication is 6-9 months. "A piece is chosen for publication when most of the editorial staff feel good about it." Seldom comments on rejected poems. Publishes multi-theme issues. Responds in up to 4 months. Length: 30 lines maximum. Pays 2 contributor's copies, offers 40% discount for more copies and subscription, if desired.

HOW TO CONTACT Editorial lead time 3-4 months. Responds only if interested. Send nonreturnable samples. Publishes ms an average of 4-8 months after acceptance. Accepts queries by mail, e-mail.

ILLUSTRATION Prefers illustrations by teenagers and young adults. Will consider all illustration packages. Manuscript/illustration packages: Query; submit complete ms with final art; submit tearsheets. Responds in 4 months. Credit line given.

PHOTOS Black & white photos preferred, but color photos with good contrast are welcome. Needs: youth 7-17, international, nature, celebrations. Send photos. Captions required. Reviews 4X6 prints, low-res JPEG files. Offers no additional payment for photos.

TERMS Buys first North American serial rights, non-exclusive reprint, and electronic rights. Byline given. No kill fee. 80% freelance written. Sample: $7. Subscription: $25. Guidelines available online or for SASE.

TIPS "Be original and innovative. Use multicultural, nature, or cross-cultural themes. Multilingual submissions are welcome."

SPARKLE

GEMS Girls' Clubs, P.O. Box 7259, Grand Rapids MI 49510. (616)241-5616. **Fax:** (616)241-5558. **E-mail:** kelli@gemsgc.org. **Website:** www.gemsgc.org. **Contact:** Kelli Gilmore, managing editor; Nicole Zaagman, art director/photo editor. Bimonthly magazine for girls ages 6-9. "Our mission is to prepare young girls to live out their faith and become world-changers. We strive to help girls make a difference in the world. We look at the application of scripture to everyday life. We strive to delight the reader and cause the reader to evalute her own life in light of the truth presented. Finally, we strive to teach practical life skills." Estab. 2002. Circ. 5,000.

FICTION Young readers: adventure, animal, contemporary, ethnic/multcultural, fantasy, folktale, health, history, humorous, music and musicians, mystery, nature/environment, problem-solving, religious, recipes, service projects, slice-of-life, sports, suspense/mystery, vignettes, interacting with family and friends. Send complete ms. Length: 100-400 words. Pays $35 maximum.

NONFICTION Young readers: animal, arts/crafts, biography, careers, cooking, concept, games/puzzles, geography, health, history, hobbies, how-to, humor, inspirational, interview/profile, math, multicultural, music/drama/art, nature/environment, personal experience, photo feature, problem-solving, quizzes, recipes, religious, science, social issues, sports, travel. Looking for inspirational biographies, stories from Zambia, and ideas on how to live a green lifestyle Send complete ms. Length: 100-400 words. Pays $35 maximum.

POETRY Prefers rhyming. "We do not wish to see anything that is too difficult for a first grader to read. We wish it to remain light. The style can be fun, but also teach a truth." No violence or secular material.

HOW TO CONTACT Editorial lead time 3 months. Responds in 3 weeks to queries; 3 months to mss. Accepts queries by mail, e-mail.

ILLUSTRATION Buys 1-2 illustrations/issue; 8-10 illustrations/year. Uses color artwork only. Works on assignment only. Reviews ms/illustration packages from artists. Send ms with dummy. Illustrations only: send promo sheet. Contact: Sara DeRidder. Responds in 3 weeks only if interested. Samples returned with SASE; samples filed. Credit line given.

PHOTOS Send photos. Identification of subjects required. Reviews at least 5X7 clear color glossy prints, GIF/JPEG files on CD. Offers $25-50/photo.

TERMS Buys first North American serial rights, buys first rights, buys one-time rights, buys second serial (reprint) rights, buys simultaneous rights. Byline given. Pays on publication. Offers $20 kill fee. 80% freelance written. Sample copy for 9x13 SAE, 3 first-class stamps, and $1 for coverage/publication cost. Writer's guidelines for #10 SASE or online.

TIPS "Keep it simple. We are writing to 1st-3rd graders. It must be simple yet interesting. Manuscripts should build girls up in Christian character but not be preachy. They are just learning about God and how He wants them to live. Manuscripts should be delightful as well as educational and inspirational.Writers should keep stories simple but not write with a 'Pollyanna' attitude. Authors should see their writing style as exciting and appealing to girls ages 6-9. Subjects should be current and important to *Sparkle* readers. Use our theme as a guide. We would like to receive material with a multicultural slant."

SPIDER

Cricket Magazine Group, 70 East Lake St., Suite 300, Chicago IL 60601. (312)701-1720. **Fax:** (312)701-1728. **Website:** www.cricketmag.com. **Contact:** Marianne Carus, editor-in-chief; Suzanne Beck, managing art director. Monthly reading and activity magazine for children ages 6 to 9. "*Spider* introduces children to the highest quality stories, poems, illustrations, articles, and activities. It was created to foster in beginning readers a love of reading and discovery that will last a lifetime. We're looking for writers who respect children's intelligence." Estab. 1994. Circ. 70,000.

FICTION Stories should be easy to read. Recently published work by Polly Horvath, Andrea Cheng, and Beth Wagner Brust. Needs fantasy, humorous, science fiction. folk tales, fairy tales, fables, myths No romance, horror, religious. Submit complete ms and SASE. Length: 300-1,000 words. Pays 25¢/word maximum.

NONFICTION Submit complete ms, bibliography, SASE. Length: 300-800 words. Pays 25¢/word maximum.

POETRY Length: 20 lines maximum. Pays $3/line maximum.

HOW TO CONTACT Responds in 6 months to mss.

ILLUSTRATION Buys 5-10 illustrations/issue; 45-90 illustrations/year. Uses color artwork only. "We prefer that you work on flexible or strippable stock, no larger than 20 × 22 (image area 19 × 21). This will allow us to put the art directly on the drum of our separator's laser scanner. Art on disk CMYK, 300 dpi. We use more realism than cartoon-style art." Works on assignment only. Reviews ms/illustration packages from artists.

Illustrations only: Send promo sheet and tearsheets. Responds in 3 months. Samples returned with SASE; samples filed. Credit line given.

PHOTOS Buys photos from freelancers. Buys photos with accompanying ms only. Model/property releases and captions required. Uses 35mm, 2¼×2¼ transparencies or digital files. Send unsolicited photos by mail; provide résumé and tearsheets. Responds in 3 months. For art samples, it is especially helpful to see pieces showing children, animals, action scenes, and several scenes from a narrative showing a character in different situations. Send photocopies/tearsheets. Also considers photo essays (prefers color, but b&w is also accepted). Captions, identification of subjects, model releases required. Reviews contact sheets, transparencies, 8×10 prints.

TERMS Byline given. Pays on publication. 85% freelance written. Guidelines available online.

TIPS "We'd like to see more of the following: engaging nonfiction, fillers, and 'takeout page' activities; folktales, fairy tales, science fiction, and humorous stories. Most importantly, do not write down to children."

⊕ STONE SOUP

Children's Art Foundation, P.O. Box 83, Santa Cruz CA 95063-0083. (831)426-5557. **E-mail:** editor@ stonesoup.com. **Website:** http://stonesoup.com. **Contact:** Ms. Gerry Mandel, editor. Bimonthly magazine of writing and art by children age 13 under, including fiction, poetry, book reviews, and art. *Stone Soup* is 48 pages, 7x10, professionally printed in color on heavy stock, saddle-stapled, with coated cover with full-color illustration. Receives 5,000 poetry submissions/year, accepts about 12. Press run is 15,000. Subscription: $37/year (U.S.). "We have a preference for writing and art based on real-life experiences; no formula stories or poems. We only publish writing by children ages 8 to 13. We do not publish writing by adults." Estab. 1973.

○ "Stories and poems from past issues are available online."

FICTION Needs adventure, ethnic, experimental, fantasy, historical, humorous, mystery, science fiction, slice-of-life vignettes, suspense. "We do not like assignments or formula stories of any kind." Send complete ms; no SASE. Length: 150-2,500 words. Pays $40 for stories, a certificate and 2 contributor's copies, plus discounts.

NONFICTION Needs historical, personal experience. book reviews Submit complete ms; no SASE. Pays $40, a certificate and 2 contributor's copies, plus discounts.

POETRY Wants free verse poetry. Does not want rhyming poetry, haiku, or cinquain. Pays $40/poem, a certificate, and 2 contributor's copies, plus discounts.

HOW TO CONTACT Publishes ms an average of 4 months after acceptance.

TERMS Buys all rights. Pays on publication. 100% freelance written. Sample copy by phone only. Guidelines available online.

TIPS "All writing we publish is by young people ages 13 and under. We do not publish any writing by adults. We can't emphasize enough how important it is to read a couple of issues of the magazine. You can read stories and poems from past issues online. We have a strong preference for writing on subjects that mean a lot to the author. If you feel strongly about something that happened to you or something you observed, use that feeling as the basis for your story or poem. Stories should have good descriptions, realistic dialogue, and a point to make. In a poem, each word must be chosen carefully. Your poem should present a view of your subject, and a way of using words that are special and all your own."

TC MAGAZINE (TEENAGE CHRISTIAN)

HU Box 10750, Searcy AR 72149. (501)279-4530. **E-mail:** editor@tcmagazine.org; write@tcmagazine.org. **Website:** www.tcmagazine.org. "*TC Magazine* is published by the Mitchell Center for Leadership & Ministry. We are dedicated to the idea that it is not only possible, but entirely excellent to live in this world with a vibrant and thriving faith. That, and an awesome magazine." Estab. 1961.

FICTION Does not want fiction.

HOW TO CONTACT Accepts queries by e-mail.

ILLUSTRATION Works on assignment only. Send ms with dummy. Illustrations only: URL. Responds only if interested.

PHOTOS Buys photos separately. Model/property release required. Uses hi-res color digital photos. E-mail or URL. Responds only if interested.

TERMS Pays on publication. Guidelines online.

TIPS "Here's what we are looking for: Teenage writers, interviews and first person stories, departments/columns (We regularly run articles about college, style, entertainment, humor and things to do on the weekend. Although these departments are almost all staff-written, we will consider unique queries or submissions.)"

TURTLE MAGAZINE FOR PRESCHOOL KIDS

U.S. Kids, 1100 Waterway Blvd., Indianapolis IN 46202. **Website:** www.turtlemag.org. Bimonthly magazine for children ages 3-5. "Colorful and entertaining..perfect for reading aloud." *Turtle Magazine for Preschool Kids* uses read-aloud stories, especially suitable for bedtime or naptime reading, for children ages 2-5. Also uses poems, simple science experiments, easy recipes and health-related articles. Wants lighthearted poetry appropriate for the age group. Estab. 1978. Circ. 300,000.

FICTION Picture-oriented material: health-related, medical, history, humorous, multicultural, nature/environment, problem-solving. Avoid stories in which the characters indulge in unhealthy activities. *Queries are not accepted.* Send complete ms. Length: 250 words maximum. Pays $70 minimum and 10 contributor's copies.

NONFICTION Picture-oriented material: cooking, health, sports, simple science. "We use very simple experiments illustrating basic science concepts. These should be pretested. We also publish simple, healthful recipes." Submit complete ms. *Queries are not accepted.* Length: 250 words maximum. Pays $70 minimum and 2 contributor's copies.

POETRY "We're especially looking for short poems (4-8 lines) and slightly longer action rhymes to foster creative movement in preschoolers. We also use short verse on our inside front cover and back cover." Pays $25 minimum.

HOW TO CONTACT Responds in 3 months to queries.

TERMS Buys all rights. Byline given. Pays on publication. No kill fee. Sample copy for $3.99. Guidelines free with SASE and on website.

TIPS "Writers should present their material in a way that is appropriate for kids, but which does not talk down to them. Reading our editorial guidelines is not enough. Careful study of current issues will acquaint writers with each title's personality, various departments, and regular features. We are looking for more short rebus stories, easy science experiments, and simple, nonfiction health articles. We are trying to include more material for our youngest readers. Material must be entertaining and written from a healthy lifestyle perspective. Our need for health-related material, especially features that encourage fitness, is ongoing. Health subjects must be age-appropriate. When writing about them, think creatively and lighten up! Always keep in mind that in order for a story or article to educate preschoolers, it first must be entertaining—warm and engaging, exciting, or genuinely funny. Here the trend is toward leaner, lighter writing. There will be a growing need for interactive activities. Writers might want to consider developing an activity to accompany their concise manuscripts."

WEEKLY READER

Website: www.weeklyreader.com.

○ *READ* no longer accepts unsolicited manuscripts. Those that are sent will not be read, responded to, or returned.

YOUNG RIDER

P.O. Box 8237, Lexington KY 40533. (859)260-9800. **Fax:** (859)260-9814. **E-mail:** yreditor@bowtieinc.com. **Website:** www.youngrider.com. **Contact:** Lesley Ward, editor. The Magazine for Horse and Pony Lovers. "*Young Rider* magazine teaches young people, in an easy-to-read and entertaining way, how to look after their horses properly, and how to improve their riding skills safely." Estab. 1994.

FICTION Young adults: adventure, animal, horses. "We would prefer funny stories, with a bit of conflict, which will appeal to the 13-year-old age group. They should be written in the third person, and about kids." Buys 4-5 short stories/year. Length: 800-1,000 words. Pays $150.

NONFICTION Young adults: animal, careers, famous equestrians, health (horse), horse celebrities, riding. Query with published clips. Length: 1,000 words maximum.

HOW TO CONTACT Rsponds to queries in 2 weeks. Publishes ms 6-12 months after acceptance.

ILLUSTRATION Buys 2 illustrations/issue; 10 illustrations/year. Works on assignment only. Reviews ms/illustration packages from artists. Query. Contact: Lesley Ward, editor. Illustrations only: Query with samples. Contact: Lesley Ward, editor. Responds in 2 weeks. Samples returned with SASE. Credit line given.

PHOTOS Buys photos with accompanying ms only. Uses high-res digital images only—in focus, good light. Model/property release required; captions required. Query with samples. Responds in 2 weeks.

TERMS Buys first North American serial rights for mss, artwork, photos. Byline given. Pays on publication. Sample copy for $3.50. Guidelines for SASE.

TIPS "Fiction must be in third person. Read magazine before sending in a query. No 'true story from when I was a youngster.' No moralistic stories. Fiction must be up-to-date and humorous, teen-oriented. Need horsy interest or celebrity rider features. No practical or how-to articles—all done in-house."

AGENTS &
ART REPS

This section features listings of literary agents and art reps who either specialize in, or represent a good percentage of, children's writers and/or illustrators. While there are a number of children's publishers who are open to non-agented material, using the services of an agent or rep can be beneficial to a writer or artist. Agents and reps can get your work seen by editors and art directors more quickly. They are familiar with the market and have insights into which editors and art directors would be most interested in your work. Also, they negotiate contracts and will likely be able to get you a better deal than you could get on your own.

Agents and reps make their income by taking a percentage of what writers and illustrators receive from publishers. The standard percentage for agents is 10 to 15 percent; art reps generally take 25 to 30 percent. We have not included any agencies in this section that charge reading fees.

WHAT TO SEND

When putting together a package for an agent or rep, follow the guidelines given in their listings. Most agents open to submissions prefer initially to receive a query letter describing your work. For novels and longer works, some agents ask for an outline and a number of sample chapters, but you should send these only if you're asked to do so. Never fax or e-mail query letters or sample chapters to agents without their permission. Just as with publishers, agents receive a large volume of submissions. It may take them a long time to reply, so you may want to query several agents at one time. It's best, however, to have a complete manuscript considered by only one agent at a time. Always include a self-addressed, stamped envelope (SASE).

For initial contact with art reps, send a brief query letter and self-promo pieces, following the guidelines given in the listings. If you don't have a flier or brochure, send photocopies. Always include a SASE.

For those who both write and illustrate, some agents listed will consider the work of author/illustrators. Read through the listings for details.

As you consider approaching agents and reps with your work, keep in mind that they are very choosy about who they take on to represent. Your work must be high quality and presented professionally to make an impression on them. For more information on approaching agents and additional listings, see *Guide to Literary Agents* (Writer's Digest Books). For additional listings of art reps see *Artist's & Graphic Designer's Market* (Writer's Digest Books).

AN ORGANIZATION FOR AGENTS

In some listings of agents you'll see references to AAR (The Association of Authors' Representatives). This organization requires its members to meet an established list of professional standards and code of ethics.

The objectives of AAR include keeping agents informed about conditions in publishing and related fields; encouraging cooperation among literary organizations; and assisting agents in representing their author-clients' interests. Officially, members are prohibited from directly or indirectly charging reading fees. They offer writers a list of member agents on their website. They also offer a list of recommended questions an author should ask an agent and other FAQs, all found on their website. They can be contacted at AAR, 676A 9th Ave. #312, New York NY 10036. (212)840-5777. Website: www.aar-online.org.

AGENTS

◑ ADAMS LITERARY

7845 Colony Rd., C4 #215, Charlotte NC 28226. (704)542-1440. **Fax:** (704)542-1450. **E-mail:** info@adamsliterary.com. **E-mail:** submissions@adamsliterary.com. **Website:** www.adamsliterary.com. **Contact:** Tracey Adams, Josh Adams, Quinlan Lee. Adams Literary is a full-service literary agency exclusively representing children's book authors and artists.

REPRESENTS Represents "the finest children's book authors and artists."

TERMS Agent receives 15% commission on domestic sales; 20% on foreign sales. Offers written contract.

HOW TO CONTACT Contact through online form on website only. Send e-mail if that is not operating correctly. "All submissions and queries must be made through the online form on our website. We will not review—and will promptly recycle—any unsolicited submissions or queries we receive by post. Before submitting your work for consideration, please carefully review our complete guidelines. While we have an established client list, we do seek new talent—and we accept submissions from both published and aspiring authors and artists."

TIPS "Guidelines are posted (and frequently updated) on our website."

BOOKSTOP LITERARY AGENCY

67 Meadow View Rd., Orinda CA 94563. (925)254-2664. **Fax:** (925)254-2668. **E-mail:** kendra@bookstopliterary.com; info@bookstopliterary.com. **Website:** www.bookstopliterary.com.

REPRESENTS "Special interest in Hispanic, Asian American, and African American writers; quirky picture books; clever adventure/mystery novels; and authentic and emotional young adult voices."

TERMS Agent receives 15% commission on domestic sales. Offers written contract, binding for 1 year.

HOW TO CONTACT Send: cover letter, entire ms for picture books; first 30 pages of novels; proposal and sample chapters OK for nonfiction. E-mail submissions: Paste cover letter and first 10 pages of ms into body of e-mail, send to info@bookstopliterary.com. Send sample illustrations only if you are an illustrator.

BROWNE & MILLER LITERARY ASSOCIATES, LLC

410 S. Michigan Ave., Suite 460, Chicago IL 60605. (312)922-3063. **Fax:** (312)922-1905. **E-mail:** mail@browneandmiller.com. **Website:** www.browneandmiller.com.

REPRESENTS Considers primarily YA fiction, fiction, young adult. "We love great writing and have a wonderful list of authors writing YA in particular." Not looking for picture books, middle grade.

RECENT SALES Sold 10 books for young readers in the last year.

TERMS Agent receives 15% commission on domestic sales; 20% on foreign sales. Offers written contract. Offers written contract, binding for 2 years. 30 days notice must be given to terminate contract.

HOW TO CONTACT Query with SASE. Accepts queries by e-mail. Obtains clients through recommendations from others.

TIPS "We are very hands-on and do much editorial work with our clients. We are passionate about the books we represent and work hard to help clients reach their publishing goals."

◑ ANDREA BROWN LITERARY AGENCY, INC.

1076 Eagle Dr., Salinas CA 93905. (831)422-5925. **Fax:** (831)422-5915. **E-mail:** andrea@andreabrownlit.com; caryn@andreabrownlit.com; lauraqueries@gmail.com; jennifer@andreabrownlit.com; kelly@andreabrownlit.com; jennL@andreabrownlit.com; jamie@andreabrownlit.com; jmatt@andreabrownlit.com; lara@andreabrownlit.com. **Website:** www.andreabrownlit.com. **Contact:** Andrea Brown, president.

REPRESENTS Specializes in "all kinds of children's books—illustrators and authors." 98% juvenile books. Considers: nonfiction, fiction, picture books, young adult.

RECENT SALES *The Scorpio Races*, by Maggie Stiefvater (Scholastic); *The Raven Boys*, by Maggie Stiefvater (Scholastic); *Wolves of Mercy Falls* series, by Maggie Stiefvater (Scholastic); *The Future of Us*, by Jay Asher; *Triangles*, by Ellen Hopkins (Atria); *Crank*, by Ellen Hopkins (McElderry/S&S); *Burned*, by Ellen Hopkins (McElderry/S&S); *Impulse*, by Ellen Hopkins (McElderry/S&S); *Glass*, by Ellen Hopkins (McElderry/S&S); *Tricks*, by Ellen Hopkins (McElderry/S&S); *Fallout*, by Ellen Hopkins (McElderry/S&S); *Perfect*, by Ellen Hopkins (McElderry/S&S); *The Strange Case of Origami Yoda*, by Tom Angleberger (Amulet/Abrams); *Darth Paper Strikes Back*, by Tom Angleberger (Amulet/Abrams);

Becoming Chloe, by Catherine Ryan Hyde (Knopf); Sasha Cohen autobiography (HarperCollins); *The Five Ancestors*, by Jeff Stone (Random House); *Thirteen Reasons Why*, by Jay Asher (Penguin); *Identical*, by Ellen Hopkins (S&S).

TERMS Agent receives 15% commission on domestic sales. Agent receives 25% commission on foreign sales. Offers written contract.

HOW TO CONTACT For picture books, submit complete ms. For fiction, submit query letter, first 10 pages. For nonfiction, submit proposal, first 10 pages. Illustrators: submit a query letter and 2-3 illustration samples (in jpeg format), link to online portfolio, and text of picture book, if applicable. "We only accept queries via e-mail. No attachments, with the exception of jpeg illustrations from illustrators." Visit the agents' bios on our website and choose only one agent to whom you will submit your e-query. Send a short e-mail query letter to that agent with QUERY in the subject field. Yes Obtains most new clients through referrals from editors, clients and agents. Check website for guidelines and information.

TIPS "ABLA is consistently ranked #1 in juvenile sales in Publishers Marketplace. Several clients have placed in the top 10 of the NY Times Bestseller List in the last year, including Tom Angleberger, Jay Asher, Ellen Hopkins, and Maggie Stiefvater. Awards recently won by ABLA clients include the Michael L. Printz Honor, the APALA Asian/Pacific Award and Honor, Charlotte Zolotow Honor, Cybils Award, EB White Read Aloud Award and Honor, Edgar Award Nominee, Indies Choice Honor Award, Jack Ezra Keats New Writer Award, Odyssey Honor Audiobook, Orbis PIctus Honor, Pura Belpré Illustrator Honor Book; SCBWI Golden Kite Award; Stonewall Honor; Texas Bluebonnet Award; Theodore Seuss Geisel Honor; William C. Morris YA Debut Award."

CURTIS BROWN, LTD.

10 Astor Place, New York NY 10003-6935. (212)473-5400. **E-mail:** gknowlton@cbltd.com. **Website:** www.curtisbrown.com. **Contact:** Ginger Knowlton. Alternate address: Peter Ginsberg, president at CBSF, 1750 Montgomery St., San Francisco CA 94111; (415)954-8566. Represents authors and illustrators of fiction, nonfiction, picture books, middle grade, young adult.

RECENT SALES This agency prefers not to share information on specific sales.

TERMS Agent receives 15% commission on domestic sales; 20% on foreign sales. Offers written contract. 75-day notice must be given to terminate contract. Offers written contract. Charges for some postage (overseas, etc.).

HOW TO CONTACT Prefers to read materials exclusively. *No unsolicited mss.* Query with SASE. If a picture book, send only 1 picture book ms. Considers simultaneous queries, "but please tell us." Returns material only with SASE. Obtains most new clients through recommendations from others, solicitations, conferences.

CORVISIERO LITERARY AGENCY

275 Madison Ave., 14th Floor, New York NY 10016. (646)942-8396. **Fax:** (646)217-3758. **E-mail:** contact@corvisieroagency.com. **E-mail:** query@corvisieroagency.com. **Website:** www.corvisieroagency.com. **Contact:** Marisa A. Corvisiero, senior agent and literary attorney.

MEMBER AGENTS Marisa A. Corvisiero, senior agent and literary attorney (romance, thrillers, adventure, paranormal, fantasy, science fiction, young adult, middle grade, nonfiction); Saritza Hernandez (all genres of romance and erotica; GLBT young adult); Stacey Donaghy; Brittany Howard; Doreen MacDonald; Sarah Negovetich (young adult and middle grade).

HOW TO CONTACT Accepts submissions via e-mail only. Include 5 pages of complete and polished ms pasted into the body of an e-mail, and a 1-2 page synopsis. For nonfiction, include a proposal instead of the synopsis. All sample pages must be properly formatted into 1 inch margins, double-spaced lines, Times New Roman black font size 12.

TIPS "For tips and discussions on what we look for in query letters and submissions, please take a look at Marisa A. Corvisiero's blog: Thoughts From A Literary Agent."

CRAWFORD LITERARY AGENCY

92 Evans Rd., Barnstead NH 03218. (603)269-5851. **E-mail:** crawfordlit@att.net. **Contact:** Susan Crawford. Winter Office: 3920 Bayside Rd., Fort Myers Beach FL 33931. (239)463-4651. **Fax:** (239)463-0125.

REPRESENTS Nonfiction books, commercial fiction. 8—☛ Actively seeking action/adventure stories; medical, legal, and psychological thrillers; true crime; romance and romantic suspense;

self-help; inspirational; how-to; women's issues. No short stories, or poetry.

HOW TO CONTACT Query with cover letter, SASE. Accepts simultaneous submissions. Responds in 3-6 weeks. Obtains most new clients through recommendations from others and conferences.

TERMS Agent receives 15% commission on domestic sales. Agent receives 20% commission on foreign sales. Offers written contract.

RECENT SALES *Sexy Star Cooking: An Astrology Cookbook for Lovers*, by Sabra Ricci; *Date with the Devil*, by Don Lasseter; *Petals from the Sky*, by Mingmei Yip.

WRITERS CONFERENCES Hawaii Spellbinders Conference; Love is Murder Mystery Conference; Puerto Villarta Writers Conference; International Film & Television Workshops; Maui Writers Conference; Emerson College Conference; Suncoast Writers Conference; San Diego Writers Conference; Simmons College Writers Conference; Cape Cod Writers Conference; Maui-Writers Alaskan Cruise; Western Caribbean Cruise and Fiji Island Writers Retreat.

TIPS "Keep learning to improve your craft. Attend conferences and network."

◗ DEFIORE & CO.

47 E. 19th St., 3rd Floor, New York NY 10003. (212)925-7744. **Fax:** (212)925-9803. **E-mail:** info@defioreandco.com; submissions@defioreandco.com. **Website:** www.defioreandco.com. **Contact:** Lauren Gilchrist. Member of AAR. Represents 75 clients. 50% of clients are new/unpublished writers. Currently handles: nonfiction books 70%, novels 30%.

○ Prior to becoming an agent, Mr. DeFiore was publisher of Villard Books (1997-1998), editor-in-chief of Hyperion (1992-1997), and editorial director of Delacorte Press (1988-1992).

MEMBER AGENTS Brian DeFiore (popular nonfiction, business, pop culture, parenting, commercial fiction); Laurie Abkemeier (memoir, parenting, business, how-to/self-help, popular science); Kate Garrick (literary fiction, memoir, popular nonfiction); Matthew Elblonk (young adult, popular culture, narrative nonfiction); Caryn Karmatz-Rudy (popular fiction, self-help, narrative nonfiction); Adam Schear (commercial fiction, humor, YA, smart thrillers, historical fiction, and quirky debut literary novels. For nonfiction: popular science, politics, popular culture, and current events); Meredith Kaffel (smart upmarket

women's fiction, literary fiction [especially debut] and literary thrillers, narrative nonfiction, nonfiction about science and tech, sophisticated pop culture/humor books); Rebecca Strauss (literary and commercial fiction, women's fiction, urban fantasy, romance, mystery, YA, memoir, pop culture, and select nonfiction).

REPRESENTS Nonfiction books, novels. **Considers these nonfiction areas:** autobiography, biography, business, child guidance, cooking, economics, foods, how-to, inspirational, money, multicultural, parenting, popular culture, psychology, religious, self-help, sports, young adult, middle-grade. **Considers these fiction areas:** ethnic, literary, mainstream, mystery, suspense, thriller.

⌇ "Please be advised that we are not considering children's picture books, poetry, adult science fiction and fantasy, romance, or dramatic projects at this time."

HOW TO CONTACT Query with SASE or e-mail to submissions@defioreandco.com. "Please include the word "Query" in the subject line. All attachments will be deleted; please insert all text in the body of the e-mail. For more information about our agents, their individual interests, and their query guidelines, please visit our 'About Us' page." Accepts simultaneous submissions. Responds in 3 weeks to queries. Responds in 2 months to mss. Obtains most new clients through recommendations from others.

TERMS Agent receives 15% commission on domestic sales. Agent receives 20% commission on foreign sales. Offers written contract; 10-day notice must be given to terminate contract. Charges clients for photocopying and overnight delivery (deducted only after a sale is made).

WRITERS CONFERENCES Maui Writers Conference; Pacific Northwest Writers Conference; North Carolina Writers' Network Fall Conference.

◗ SANDRA DIJKSTRA LITERARY AGENCY

1155 Camino del Mar, PMB 515, Del Mar CA 92014. (858)755-3115. **Fax:** (858)794-2822. **E-mail:** elise@dijkstraagency.com. **Website:** www.dijkstraagency.com. Member of AAR. Other memberships include Authors Guild, PEN West, Poets and Editors, MWA. Represents 100+ clients. 30% of clients are new/unpublished writers. Currently handles: nonfiction books 50%, novels 45%, juvenile books 5%.

MARISA CLEVELAND (SEYMOUR AGENCY)

theseymouragency.com
@marisacleveland

ABOUT MARISA: Marisa Cleveland interned with The Seymour Agency for a year before transitioning into associate agent. Her goals have always included writing her romance novels and representing career-driven authors. She loves to laugh, hates to cry, and does both often (when reading an amazing book). As a writer and an agent, she reads and writes every day. She is a member of SCBWI, YA-RWA and RWA.

SHE IS SEEKING: Marisa is accepting queries for middle grade fiction. She is searching for a middle school novel she cannot put down until the last page and cannot stop discussing. She is specifically targeting books that have strong voice. If she's going to sign (and sell) someone or recommend someone, then the writer's voice has to speak to her. She has to be able to listen (vocally and on the page) to that writer through revisions and edits and book after book. She wants to find characters she'd want as her best friends and partners in crime long after the story ends, whether it's in this world or an alternate universe.

HOW TO SUBMIT: If you'd like to query her, please e-mail your query and the first five pages of your manuscript in the body of the e-mail. No attachment. E-mail Marisa@theseymouragency.com.

AGENTS AND ART REPS

MEMBER AGENTS Sandra Dijkstra, president (adult only). Acquiring Sub-agents: Elise Capron (adult only), Jill Marr (adult only), Thao Le (adult and YA), Jennifer Azantian (YA only). Sub-rights agent: Andrea Cavallaro; Roz Foster (associate agent).
REPRESENTS Nonfiction books, novels. **Considers these nonfiction areas:** biography, business, history, memoirs, psychology, science, self-help, narrative. **Considers these fiction areas:** contemporary issues, fantasy, literary, science fiction, suspense, thriller, women's, young adult.
HOW TO CONTACT "Please see guidelines on our website, and please note that we now only accept e-mail submissions. Due to the large number of unso-licited submissions we receive, we are only able to respond those submissions in which we are interested." Accepts simultaneous submissions. Responds to queries of interest within 6 weeks.
TERMS Works in conjunction with foreign and film agents. Agent receives 15% commission on domestic sales and 20% commission on foreign sales. Offers written contract. No reading fee.
TIPS "Be professional and learn the standard procedures for submitting your work. Be a regular patron of bookstores, and study what kind of books are being published and will appear on the shelves next to yours. You'll also find lots of books on writing and the publishing industry that will help you. At conferences,

NEW AGENT SPOTLIGHT

LIAT JUSTIN (SERENDIPITY LITERARY AGENCY)

serendipitylit.com

ABOUT LIAT: Liat Justin is an associate agent with the Serendipity Literary Agency. Liat graduated from Boston University with a Bachelor of Science degree in Communication Studies. As an undergrad, Liat simultaneously enrolled in Boston University's Certificate Program in Book Publishing and Digital Media. Liat then moved back to New York where she began her publishing career as an intern at PMA Literary and Film Management. Soon after, Liat joined the team at Serendipity. In addition to her passion for reading, Liat has a love for film, traveling, going to concerts and doing puzzles.

SHE IS SEEKING: "Liat is actively seeking to represent a broad range of projects and is open to emerging authors. Her sweet spot genres includes YA fiction."

HOW TO SUBMIT: Serendipity requires all submissions through a submission form on their agency website, even if you are querying for your children's books.

ask published writers about their agents. Don't believe the myth that an agent has to be in New York to be successful. We've already disproved it!"

DUNHAM LITERARY, INC.

110 William St., Suite 2202, New York NY 10038. (212)929-0994. **E-mail:** dunhamlit@yahoo.com. **E-mail:** query@dunhamlit.com. **Website:** www.dunhamlit.com. **Contact:** Jennie Dunham.
RECENT SALES Sold 30 books for young readers in the last year. *Peter Pan*, by Robert Sabuda (Little Simon); *Flamingos on the Roof*, by Calef Brown (Houghton); *Adele and Simon in America*, by Barbara McClintock (Farrar, Straus & Giroux); *Caught Between the Pages*, by Marlene Carvell (Dutton); *Waiting For Normal*, by Leslie Connor (HarperCollins), *The Gollywhopper Games*, by Jody Feldman (Greenwillow); *America the Beautiful*, by Robert Sabuda; *Dahlia*, by Barbara McClintock; *Living Dead Girl*, by Tod Goldberg; *In My Mother's House*, by Margaret McMulla; *Black Hawk Down,* by Mark Bowden; *Look Back All*

the Green Valley, by Fred Chappell; *Under a Wing*, by Reeve Lindbergh; *I Am Madame X*, by Gioia Diliberto.
TERMS Agent receives 15% commission on domestic sales. Agent receives 20% commission on foreign sales.
HOW TO CONTACT Query with SASE. Obtains most new clients through recommendations from others, solicitations.

DYSTEL & GODERICH LITERARY MANAGEMENT

1 Union Square W., Suite 904, New York NY 10003. (212)627-9100. **Fax:** (212)627-9313. **E-mail:** mbourret@dystel.com. **Website:** www.dystel.com. **Contact:** Michael Bourret; Jim McCarthy.
REPRESENTS "This agency specializes in cookbooks and commercial and literary fiction and nonfiction." "We are actively seeking fiction for all ages, in all genres. We're especially interested in quality young adult fiction, from realistic to paranormal, and all kinds of middle-grade, from funny boy books to more sentimental fare. Though we are open to author/illustrators, we are not looking for picture book mss.

And, while we would like to see more YA memoir, nonfiction is not something we usually handle." No plays, screenplays, or poetry.

TERMS Agent receives 15% commission on domestic sales. Agent receives 19% commission on foreign sales. Offers written contract.

HOW TO CONTACT Query with SASE. "Please include the first 3 chapters in the body of the e-mail. E-mail queries preferred (Michael Bourret only accepts e-mail queries); will accept mail. See website for full guidelines." Obtains most new clients through recommendations from others, solicitations, conferences.

TIPS "DGLM prides itself on being a full-service agency. We're involved in every stage of the publishing process, from offering substantial editing on mss and proposals, to coming up with book ideas for authors looking for their next project, negotiating contracts and collecting monies for our clients. We follow a book from its inception through its sale to a publisher, its publication, and beyond. Our commitment to our writers does not, by any means, end when we have collected our commission. This is one of the many things that makes us unique in a very competitive business."

○ EDUCATIONAL DESIGN SERVICES LLC

5750 Bou Ave, Suite 1508, N. Bethesda MD 20852. **E-mail:** blinder@educationaldesignservices.com. **Website:** www.educationaldesignservices.com. **Contact:** B. Linder.

REPRESENTS "We specialize in educational materials to be used in classrooms (in class sets), for staff development or in teacher education classes." Actively seeking educational, text materials. Not looking for picture books, story books, fiction; no illustrators.

RECENT SALES *How to Solve Word Problems in Mathematics*, by Wayne (McGraw-Hill*); Preparing for the 8th Grade Test in Social Studies*, by Farran-Paci (Amsco); *Minority Report*, by Gunn-Singh (Scarecrow Education); *No Parent Left Behind,* by Petrosino & Spiegel (Rowman & Littlefield*); Teaching Test-taking Skills* (R&L Education); *10 Languages You'll Need Most in the Classroom,* by Sundem, Krieger, Pickiewicz (Corwin Press*); Kids, Classrooms & Capital Hill,* by Flynn (R&L Education); *Bully Nation*, by Susan Eva Porter (Paragon House).

TERMS Agent receives 15% commission on domestic sales; 25% on foreign sales. Offers written contract,

binding until any party opts out. Terminate contract through certified letter.

HOW TO CONTACT Query by e-mail or with SASE or send outline and 1 sample chapter. Considers simultaneous queries and submissions if so indicated. Returns material only with SASE. Obtains clients through recommendations from others, queries/solicitations, or through conferences.

◑ ETHAN ELLENBERG LITERARY AGENCY

548 Broadway, #5-E, New York NY 10012. (212)431-4554. **Fax:** (212)941-4652. **E-mail:** agent@ethanellenberg.com. **Website:** http://ethanellenberg.com. **Contact:** Ethan Ellenberg.

REPRESENTS "This agency specializes in commercial fiction—especially thrillers, romance/women's, and specialized nonfiction. We also do a lot of children's books." "Actively seeking commercial fiction as noted above—romance/fiction for women, science fiction and fantasy, thrillers, suspense and mysteries. Our other two main areas of interest are children's books and narrative nonfiction. We are actively seeking clients, follow the directions on our website." Does not want to receive poetry, short stories, or screenplays.

TERMS Agent receives 15% commission on domestic sales. Agent receives 10% commission on foreign sales. Offers written contract. Charges clients (with their consent) for direct expenses limited to photocopying and postage.

HOW TO CONTACT For fiction, send introductory letter, outline, first 3 chapters, SASE. For nonfiction, send query letter, proposal, 1 sample chapter, SASE. For children's books, send introductory letter, up to 3 picture book mss, outline, first 3 chapters, SASE. Yes

TIPS We do consider new material from unsolicited authors. Write a good, clear letter with a succinct description of your book. We prefer the first 3 chapters when we consider fiction. For all submissions, you must include a SASE or the material will be discarded. It's always hard to break in, but talent will find a home. Check our website for complete submission guidelines. We continue to see natural storytellers and nonfiction writers with important books.

◑ THE ELAINE P. ENGLISH LITERARY AGENCY

4710 41st St. NW, Suite D, Washington DC 20016. (202)362-5190. **Fax:** (202)362-5192. **E-mail:** que ries@elaineenglish.com. **E-mail:** elaine@elaineeng lish.com. **Website:** www.elaineenglish.com/literary. php. **Contact:** Elaine English, Lindsey Skouras.

REPRESENTS Actively seeking women's fiction, including single-title romances. Does not want to receive any science fiction, time travel, or picture books.

RECENT SALES Have been to Sourcebooks, Tor, Harlequin.

TERMS Agent receives 15% commission on domestic sales. Agent receives 20% commission on foreign sales. Offers written contract; 30-day notice must be given to terminate contract. Charges only for shipping expenses; generally taken from proceeds.

HOW TO CONTACT Generally prefers e-queries sent to queries@elaineenglish.com. If requested, submit synopsis, first 3 chapters, SASE. "Please check our website for further details." Obtains most new clients through recommendations from others, conferences, submissions.

◑ FLANNERY LITERARY

1140 Wickfield Ct., Naperville IL 60563. (630)428-2682. **Fax:** (630)428-2683. **E-mail:** FlanLit@aol.com. **Contact:** Jennifer Flannery.

REPRESENTS This agency specializes in children's and young adult fiction and nonfiction. It also accepts picture books. 100% juvenile books.

TERMS Agent receives 15% commission on domestic sales. Agent receives 20% commission on foreign sales. Offers written contract, binding for life of book in print; 1-month notice must be given to terminate contract.

HOW TO CONTACT Query by mail with SASE or e-mail query. Obtains new clients through referrals and queries.

TIPS "Write an engrossing, succinct query describing your work. We are always looking for a fresh new voice."

⊕ FOREWORD LITERARY

Silicon Valley, CA. **Website:** www.forewordliterary. com.

MEMBER AGENTS Laurie McLean (adult genre fiction (romance, fantasy, science fiction, mystery, thrillers, suspense, horror, etc.) plus middle-grade and young adult children's books; querylaurie@fore-wordliterary.com. Gordon Warnock (nonfiction and fiction, querygordon@forewordliterary.com). Pam van Hylckama Vlieg (young adult, middle grade,

new adult, romance, urban fantasy, paranormal, and epic/high fantasy; querypam@forewordliter-ary.com). Jen Karsbaek (women's fiction, upmarket commercial fiction, historical fiction, and literary fiction, mystery, fantasy, and occasionally romance approaches to any of the genres listed; queryjen@ forewordliterary.com). Danielle Smith (middle grade, picture books, chapter books; querydanielle@ forewordliterary.com). x.

HOW TO CONTACT Query only one agent at this agency. Send a query letter only to start.

● SARAH JANE FREYMANN LITERARY AGENCY

59 W. 71st St., Suite 9B, New York NY 10023. (212)362-9277. **E-mail:** sarah@sarahjanefreymann.com; Sub missions@SarahJaneFreymann.com. **Website:** www. sarahjanefreymann.com. **Contact:** For young adult submissions, the contact is Jessica Sinsheimer. Represents 100 clients. 20% of clients are new/unpub-lished writers. Currently handles: nonfiction books 75%, novels 23%, juvenile books 2%.

MEMBER AGENTS Sarah Jane Freymann; (non-fiction books, novels, illustrated books); Jessica Sin-sheimer, Jessica@sarahjanefreymann.com (young adult fiction); Steven Schwartz, steve@sarahjane freymann.com; Katharine Sands (general fiction and nonfiction).

HOW TO CONTACT Query with SASE. Responds in 2 weeks to queries. Responds in 6 weeks to mss. Obtains most new clients through recommendations from others.

TERMS Agent receives 15% commission on domes-tic sales. Agent receives 20% commission on foreign sales. Offers written contract. Charges clients for long distance, overseas postage, photocopying. 100% of business is derived from commissions on ms sales.

TIPS "[We] love fresh, new, passionate works by au-thors who love what they are doing and have both natural talent and carefully honed skill."

BARRY GOLDBLATT LITERARY LLC

320 Seventh Ave. #266, Brooklyn NY 11215. (718)832-8787. **E-mail:** query@bgliterary.com. **Con-tact:** Barry Goldblatt.

REPRESENTS "Please see our website for specific submission guidelines and information on agents' particular tastes."

RACHEL HECHT (FOUNDRY LITERARY + MEDIA)

foundrymedia.com

ABOUT RACHEL: Rachel Hecht serves as Foundry's Foreign Rights Director for Children's Books, and also develops her own list of authors. Before joining Foundry in 2011, Rachel served as the children's book scout for Mary Anne Thompson Associates, where she provided exclusive insight into the U.S. publishing world for a diverse roster of foreign publishers. A graduate of Kenyon College with a degree in English, she began her career in New York at Condé Nast before moving into book publishing.

SHE IS SEEKING: As a domestic agent, Rachel seeks children's projects of all stripes, from picture books through to young adult fiction.

HOW TO CONTACT: Rachel accepts paper and e-mail submissions. Please send all digital queries for Rachel rhsubmissions@foundrymedia.com. For more information on submitting your project, see the Foundry website.

AGENTS AND ART REPS

RECENT SALES *Ambassador,* by Will Alexander; *Dangerous,* by Shannon Hale; *Glad Rags,* by Genevieve Valentine; *The Retribution of Mara Dyer,* by Michelle Hodkin.

TERMS Agent receives 15% commission on domestic sales; 20% on foreign and dramatic sales. Offers written contract. 60 days notice must be given to terminate contract.

HOW TO CONTACT Obtains clients through referrals, queries, and conferences.

TIPS "We're a hands-on agency, focused on building an author's career, not just making an initial sale. We don't care about trends or what's hot; we just want to sign great writers."

DOUG GRAD LITERARY AGENCY, INC.

156 Prospect Park West, Brooklyn NY 11215. (718)788-6067. **E-mail:** doug.grad@dgliterary.com. **E-mail:** query@dgliterary.com. **Website:** www.dgliterary.com. **Contact:** Doug Grad.

RECENT SALES *Drink the Tea,* by Thomas Kaufman (St. Martin's); *15 Minutes: The Impossible Math of Nuclear War,* by L. Douglas Keeney (St. Martin's).

HOW TO CONTACT Query by e-mail first at query@dgliterary.com. No sample material unless requested.

● ASHLEY GRAYSON LITERARY AGENCY

1342 W. 18th St., San Pedro CA 90732. **Fax:** (310)514-1148. **E-mail:** graysonagent@earthlink.net. **Website:** www.graysonagency.com/blog.

REPRESENTS "We prefer to work with published (traditional print), established authors. We will give first consideration to authors who come recommended to us by our clients or other publishing professionals. We accept a very small number of new, previously unpublished authors. The agency is temporarily closed to queries from writers who are not published at book length (self published or print-on-demand do not count). There are only three exceptions to this policy: (1) Unpublished authors who have received an offer from a reputable publisher, who need an agent before beginning contract negotiations; (2) Authors who are recommended by a published author, editor or agent who has read the work in question; (3) Authors whom we have met at conferences and from whom we have requested submissions. Authors who are recognized within their field or area may still query with proposals. We are seeking more mysteries and thrillers."

RECENT SALES Sold 25+ books last year. *Juliet Dove, Queen of Love*, by Bruce Coville (Harcourt); *Alosha*, by Christopher Pike (TOR); *Sleeping Freshmen Never Lie*, by David Lubar (Dutton); *Ball Don't Lie*, by Matt de la Peña (Delacorte); *Wiley & Grampa's Creature Features*, by Kirk Scroggs (10-book series, Little Brown); *Snitch*, by Allison van Diepen (Simon Pulse). Also represents: J.B. Cheaney (Knopf), Bruce Wetter (Atheneum).

TERMS Agent receives 15% commission on domestic sales. Agent receives 20% commission on foreign sales.

HOW TO CONTACT As of early 2008, the agency was only open to fiction authors with publishing credits (no self-published). For nonfiction, only writers with great platforms will be considered.

TIPS "We do request revisions as they are required. We are long-time agents, professional and known in the business. We perform professionally for our clients and we ask the same of them."

◑ THE GREENHOUSE LITERARY AGENCY

11308 Lapham Dr., Oakton VA 22124. **E-mail:** submissions@greenhouseliterary.com. **Website:** www.greenhouseliterary.com. **Contact:** Sarah Davies, vice president; John M. Cusick, agent (US); Julia Churchill, agent (UK).

◔ "At Greenhouse we aim to establish strong, long-term relationships with clients and work hard to find our authors the very best publisher and deal for their writing. We often get very involved editorially, working creatively with authors where necessary. Our goal is to submit high-quality manuscripts to publishers while respecting the role of the editor who will have their own publishing vision."

REPRESENTS "We exclusively represent authors writing fiction for children and teens. The agency has offices in both the USA and UK, and Sarah Davies (who is British) personally represents authors to both markets. The agency's commission structure reflects this—taking 15% for sales to both US and UK, thus treating both as 'domestic' market.'" All genres of children's and YA fiction—ages 5+. Does not want to receive nonfiction, poetry, picture books (text or illustration) or work aimed at adults; short stories, educational or religious/inspirational work, pre-school/novelty material, or screenplays.

RECENT SALES *Fracture*, by Megan Miranda (Walker); *Paper Valentine*, by Brenna Yovanff (Razorbill); *Uses for Boys*, by Erica L. Scheidt (St Martin's); *Dark Inside*, by Jeyn Roberts (Simon & Schuster); *Breathe*, by Sarah Crossan (HarperCollins); *After the Snow*, by SD Crockett (Feiwel/Macmillan); *Sean Griswold's Head*, by Lindsey Leavitt (Hyperion).

TERMS Agent receives 15% commission on domestic sales. Agent receives 25% commission on foreign sales. Offers written contract. This agency occasionally charges for submission copies to film agents or foreign publishers.

HOW TO CONTACT E-mail queries only; short letter containing a brief outline, biography and any writing 'credentials'. The first five pages of text should be pasted into the e-mail. All submissions are answered Obtains most new clients through recommendations from others, solicitations, conferences.

TIPS "Before submitting material, authors should read the Greenhouse's 'Top 10 Tips for Authors of Children's Fiction' and carefully follow our submission guidelines which can be found on the website."

◑ HERMAN AGENCY

350 Central Park West, New York NY 10025. (212)749-4907. **E-mail:** Ronnie@HermanAgencyInc.com. **Website:** www.hermanagencyinc.com. Literary and artistic agency. Member of SCBWI, Graphic Artists' Guild and Authors' Guild. Some of the illustrators represented: Joy Allen, Seymour Chwast, Troy Cummings, Barry Gott, Jago, Gideon Kendall, Ana Martin Larranaga, Mike Lester, John Nez, Michael Rex, Richard Torrey, Deborah Zemke. Some of the authors represented: Martha Alderson, Larry Brimner. Martha Brockenbrough, Shelley Corielli, Ralph Fletcher, Janet Gurtler, Deloris Jordan, Robin Mellon, Anastasia Suen. Currently not accepting new clients unless they have been successfully published by major trade publishing houses.

TERMS Receives 25% commission for illustration assignments; 15% for ms assignments. Artists pay 75%

JENNIE GOLOBOY (RED SOFA LITERARY)

redsofaliterary.com
@JennieGoloboy

ABOUT JENNIE: Jennie Goloboy is an associate agent with Red Sofa Literary. Jennie has a Ph.D. in the History of American Civilization from Harvard. She is also a published author of both history and fiction, and a member of SFWA, RWA, SHEAR, OAH, the AHA, and Codex Writer's Group. Her funny, specific short stories appear under her pen name, Nora Fleischer.

SHE IS SEEKING: Young adult and middle grade fiction, especially science fiction/fantasy.

HOW TO SUBMIT: jennie@redsofaliterary.com. "We highly encourage everyone to send an e-mail and/or query letter initially, before attempting to send a full book proposal or sample chapters. Ultimately, it will save postage and time. If there is an interest, we will directly contact the author. Once these materials are received, there is usually a response time of 4-6 weeks, sometimes sooner. If querying via e-mail, please only put the contents of your query in the e-mail. We will not open attachments unless they have been requested in advance."

of costs for promotional material, about $200 a year. Offers written contract. Advertising costs are split: 75% paid by illustrator; 25% paid by rep.

HOW TO CONTACT Exclusive representation required. For first contact, e-mail only. Responds in 4-6 weeks. For first contact, artists or author/artists should e-mail a link to their website with bio and list of published books as well as new picture book manuscript or dummy to Ronnie or Katia. We will contact you in a month only if your samples are right for us. For first contact, authors of middle-grade or YA should e-mail bio, list of published books and first ten pages to Jill Corcoran. Jill will contact you within a month if she is interested in seeing more of your manuscript. Finds illustrators and authors through recommendations from others, conferences, queries/

solicitations. Submit via e-mail to one of the agents listed above. See website for specific agents' specialties. **TIPS** "Check our website to see if you belong with our agency."

⊕ INKLINGS LITERARY

3419 Virginia Beach Blvd. #C-12, Virginia Beach, VA 23452. (757)340.1860. **E-mail:** michelle@inklingsliterary.com; jamie@inklingsliterary.com. **Website:** www.inklingsrliterary.com. Estab. 2012.

▢ Ms. Johnson was formerly an agent at the Corvisiero Literary Agency. Ms. Bail was formerly an agent at Andrea Hurst & Associates.

MEMBER AGENTS Michelle Johnson (in adult, new adult and YA fiction, Michelle looks for contemporary, suspense, thriller, mystery, horror, fantasy, and also

AGENTS AND ART REPS

loves paranormal and supernatural elements within those genres); Dr. Jamie Brodnar Drowley (in adult, new adult and young adult fiction, Jamie is seeking fantasy, mystery, romance, paranormal, historical, contemporary, horror, light sci-fi and thrillers; she also reps middle grade); Margaret Bail (adult fiction only. Specifically, she seeks romance, science fiction, thrillers, action/adventure, historical fiction, Western, fantasy—think Song of Fire and Ice or Dark Tower, NOT Lord of the Rings or Chronicles of Narnia). .

REPRESENTS Novels, juvenile books.

HOW TO CONTACT Each agent's openness to queries varies from season to season. Check the website. When open to submissions, they ask for a query, first five pages, and a one page synopsis to query@inklings literary.com

JANKLOW & NESBIT ASSOCIATES

445 Park Ave., New York NY 10022. (212)421-1700. **Fax:** (212)980-3671. **E-mail:** info@janklow.com. **Website:** janklowandnesbit.com. **Contact:** Julie Just, literary agent.

REPRESENTS Does not want to receive unsolicited submissions or queries.

HOW TO CONTACT Query with samples. Considers electronic submissions. Yes Obtains most new clients through recommendations from others.

TIPS "Please send a short query with first 10 pages or artwork."

BARBARA S. KOUTS, LITERARY AGENT

P.O. Box 560, Bellport NY 11713. (631)286-1278. **Fax:** (631) 286-1538. **Contact:** Barbara S. Kouts.

Currently not accepting submissions.

REPRESENTS This agency specializes in children's books.

RECENT SALES *Code Talker*, by Joseph Bruchac (Dial); *The Penderwicks*, by Jeanne Birdsall (Knopf); *Froggy's Baby Sister*, by Jonathan London (Viking).

TERMS Agent receives 10% commission on domestic sales. Agent receives 20% commission on foreign sales. This agency charges clients for photocopying.

HOW TO CONTACT Query with SASE. Accepts queries by mail only. Yes Obtains most new clients through recommendations from others, solicitations, conferences.

TIPS "Write, do not call. Be professional in your writing."

LIZA DAWSON ASSOCIATES

350 Seventh Ave., Suite 2003, New York NY 10001. (212)465-9071. **Fax:** (212)947-0460. **E-mail:** queryl iza@lizadawsonassociates.com. **Website:** www.liza dawsonassociates.com. **Contact:** Anna Olswanger.

REPRESENTS This agency specializes in readable literary fiction, thrillers, mainstream historicals, women's fiction, academics, historians, business, journalists, and psychology.

TERMS Agent receives 15% commission on domestic sales. Agent receives 20% commission on foreign sales. Offers written contract. Charges clients for photocopying and overseas postage.

HOW TO CONTACT Query by e-mail only. No phone calls. Obtains most new clients through recommendations from others, conferences.

GINA MACCOBY LITERARY AGENCY

P.O. Box 60, Chappaqua NY 10514. (914)238-5630. **E-mail:** query@maccobylit.com; gmaccoby@aol.com. **Contact:** Gina Maccoby.

RECENT SALES This agency sold 21 titles last year.

TERMS Agent receives 15% commission on domestic sales. Agent receives 25% commission on foreign sales. Charges clients for photocopying. May recover certain costs, such as legal fees or the cost of shipping books by air to Europe or Japan.

HOW TO CONTACT Query with SASE. If querying by e-mail, put "query" in subject line. Obtains most new clients through recommendations from clients and publishers.

MCINTOSH & OTIS, INC.

353 Lexington Ave., New York NY 10016. (212)687-7400. **Fax:** (212)687-6894. **E-mail:** info@mcintoshan dotis.com. **Website:** www.mcintoshandotis.com. **Contact:** Eugene H. Winick, Esq.. McIntosh & Otis has a long history of representing authors of adult and children's books. The children's department is a separate division.

Prefers e-mail submissions.

REPRESENTS Actively seeking "books with memorable characters, distinctive voices, and great plots." Not looking for educational, activity books, coloring books.

TERMS Agent receives 15% commission on domestic sales; 20% on foreign sales.

HOW TO CONTACT Query with SASE. Obtains clients through recommendations from others, editors, conferences and queries.

BRITTANY HOWARD (CORVISIERO LITERARY)

corvisieroagency.com
@brittanydhoward

ABOUT BRITTANY: Brittany Howard of Corvisiero Literary is all about experiences. She's lived in small towns, big cities and traveled the world. She has a degree in theatre and is currently pursuing an MFA in Creative Writing. When reading, she loves to be introduced to new and interesting people and places. She looks for strong voice, good storytelling and fascinating relationships between characters. More than anything, she loves when a book surprises her.

SHE IS SEEKING: Her first love is YA fiction—from high fantasy to paranormal to soft sci-fi to contemporary—she loves all young adult. She also likes high concept, adventure themed and funny middle grade fiction, but a strong voice is must for her in MG. She's willing to look at picture books, but is very selective.

HOW TO SUBMIT: Brittany prefers that you paste a 1-2 page synopsis and the first 5 pages directly into the query e-mail. Do not send Brittany attachments. E-mail your query with pasted material to query@corvisieroagency.com with "Query For Brittany" in the subject line.

⊘ ERIN MURPHY LITERARY AGENCY

2700 Woodlands Village, #300-458, Flagstaff AZ 86001. **Fax:** (928)525-2480. **Website:** http://emliterary.com. **Contact:** Erin Murphy, president; Ammi-Joan Paquette, agent; Tricia Lawrence, associate agent. "This agency only represents children's books. We do not accept unsolicited manuscripts or queries. We consider new clients by referral or personal contact only."

REPRESENTS Specializes in children's books only.

TERMS Agent receives 15% commission on domestic sales; 20-30% on foreign sales. Offers written contract. 30 days notice must be given to terminate contract.

◑ MUSE LITERARY MANAGEMENT

189 Waverly Place., #4, New York NY 10014. (212)925-3721. **E-mail:** museliterarymgmt@museliterary.com.

Website: www.museliterary.com. **Contact:** Deborah Carter.

REPRESENTS Specializes in development of book manuscripts and associated journalism, the sale and administration of print, performance, and foreign rights. Actively seeking "writers with formal training who bring a unique outlook to their manuscripts. Those who submit should be receptive to editorial feedback and willing to revise during the submission process to remain competitive." Does not want romance, chick lit, sci-fi, fantasy, horror, stories about pets, vampires or serial killers, fiction or nonfiction with religious or spiritual subject matter."

TERMS Agent receives 15% commission on gross domestic sales, 20% on gross foreign sales. One-year contract offered when writer and agent agree that the

NEW AGENT SPOTLIGHT

STEVE KASDIN (CURTIS BROWN LTD.)

curtisbrown.com

ABOUT STEVE: Steve Kasdin joined Curtis Brown in 2012. He has more than 20 years' experience in books and publishing, beginning his career as the mystery buyer at Barnes & Noble. He has been a Marketing executive at St. Martin's Press, Scholastic and Harcourt, an agent at the Sandra Dijkstra Agency and worked on Content Acquisition in the Kindle group at Amazon.com. In addition to representing clients at Curtis Brown, he is also the agency's Director of Digital Strategy, advising clients on all aspects of electronic publishing.

HE IS SEEKING: "The most important thing I've learned in over 20 years in publishing is also the simplest: Plot sells. And the definition of what makes a great plot is also very simple: interesting, well-drawn characters thrown into unpredictable situations. I'm looking for young adult fiction, particularly if it has adult crossover appeal."

HOW TO SUBMIT: skasdin@cbltd.com. Responds in 4-6 weeks. Please send a query letter about what makes your book unique, a 1-3 page plot synopsis, a brief bio (including a description of your publishing history, if you have one), and the first 40-50 pages of your manuscript as a Word attachment to the e-mail. "Let me know in your query letter if I am reading your work exclusively, in which case, I shall give it priority. If the book has been self-published or previously published, please let me know all the details—publisher, date, etc."

manuscript is ready for submission. All expenses are preapproved by the client.

HOW TO CONTACT Query with SASE. Query via e-mail (no attachments). Discards unwanted queries. Obtains most new clients through referrals and conferences.

TIPS "Since we all look for books by familiar names, new writers need a plan for building an audience through their professional affiliations and in freelance journalism. All agreements are signed by the writers. Reimbursement for expenses is subject to client's approval, limited to photocopying and postage."

● **JEAN V. NAGGAR LITERARY AGENCY, INC.**

216 E. 75th St., Suite 1E, New York NY 10021. (212)794-1082. **E-mail:** jweltz@jvnla.com; jvnla@jvnla.com. **E-mail:** jweltz@jvnla.com; jregel@jvnla.com; atasman@jvnla.com; atasman@jvnla.com. **Website:** www.jvnla.com. **Contact:** Jean Naggar.

REPRESENTS This agency specializes in mainstream fiction and nonfiction and literary fiction with commercial potential.

RECENT SALES *Night Navigation*, by Ginnah Howard; *After Hours at the Almost Home*, by Tara Yelen;

An Entirely Synthetic Fish: A Biography of Rainbow Trout, by Anders Halverson; *The Patron Saint of Butterflies*, by Cecilia Galante; *Wondrous Strange*, by Lesley Livingston; *6 Sick Hipsters*, by Rayo Casablanca; *The Last Bridge*, by Teri Coyne; *Gypsy Goodbye*, by Nancy Springer; *Commuters*, by Emily Tedrowe; *The Language of Secrets*, by Dianne Dixon; *Smiling to Freedom*, by Martin Benoit Stiles; *The Tale of Halcyon Crane*, by Wendy Webb; *Fugitive*, by Phillip Margolin; *BlackBerry Girl*, by Aidan Donnelley Rowley; *Wild Girls*, by Pat Murphy.

TERMS Agent receives 15% commission on domestic sales. Agent receives 20% commission on foreign sales. Offers written contract. Charges for overseas mailing, messenger services, book purchases, long-distance telephone, photocopying—all deductible from royalties received.

HOW TO CONTACT Query via e-mail. Prefers to read materials exclusively. No fax queries. Consult website for specific guidelines for each agent. No Obtains most new clients through recommendations from others.

TIPS "Use a professional presentation. Because of the avalanche of unsolicited queries that flood the agency every week, we have had to modify our policy. We will now only guarantee to read and respond to queries from writers who come recommended by someone we know. Our areas are general fiction and nonfiction—no children's books by unpublished writers, no multimedia, no screenplays, no formula fiction, and no mysteries by unpublished writers. We recommend patience and fortitude: the courage to be true to your own vision, the fortitude to finish a novel and polish it again and again before sending it out, and the patience to accept rejection gracefully and wait for the stars to align themselves appropriately for success."

HOW TO CONTACT Query via e-mail. Prefers to read materials exclusively. No fax queries. Consult website for specific guidelines for each agent. Responds in 1 day to queries. Responds in 2 months to mss. Obtains most new clients through recommendations from others.

TERMS Agent receives 15% commission on domestic sales. Agent receives 20% commission on foreign sales. Offers written contract. Charges for overseas mailing, messenger services, book purchases, long-distance telephone, photocopying—all deductible from royalties received.

RECENT SALES *Night Navigation*, by Ginnah Howard; *After Hours at the Almost Home*, by Tara Yelen; *An Entirely Synthetic Fish: A Biography of Rainbow Trout*, by Anders Halverson; *The Patron Saint of Butterflies*, by Cecilia Galante; *Wondrous Strange*, by Lesley Livingston; *6 Sick Hipsters*, by Rayo Casablanca; *The Last Bridge*, by Teri Coyne; *Gypsy Goodbye*, by Nancy Springer; *Commuters*, by Emily Tedrowe; *The Language of Secrets*, by Dianne Dixon; *Smiling to Freedom*, by Martin Benoit Stiles; *The Tale of Halcyon Crane*, by Wendy Webb; *Fugitive*, by Phillip Margolin; *BlackBerry Girl*, by Aidan Donnelley Rowley; *Wild Girls*, by Pat Murphy.

WRITERS CONFERENCES Willamette Writers Conference; Pacific Northwest Writers Conference; Bread Loaf Writers Conference; Marymount Manhattan Writers Conference; SEAK Medical & Legal Fiction Writing Conference.

TIPS "Use a professional presentation. Because of the avalanche of unsolicited queries that flood the agency every week, we have had to modify our policy. We will now only guarantee to read and respond to queries from writers who come recommended by someone we know. Our areas are general fiction and nonfiction—no children's books by unpublished writers, no multimedia, no screenplays, no formula fiction, and no mysteries by unpublished writers. We recommend patience and fortitude: the courage to be true to your own vision, the fortitude to finish a novel and polish it again and again before sending it out, and the patience to accept rejection gracefully and wait for the stars to align themselves appropriately for success."

NELSON LITERARY AGENCY

1732 Wazee St., Suite 207, Denver CO 80202. (303)292-2805. **E-mail:** query@nelsonagency.com. **Website:** www.nelsonagency.com. **Contact:** Kristin Nelson, president and senior literary agent; Sara Megibow, associate literary agent. Member of AAR. RWA, SCBWI, SFWA.

Prior to opening her own agency, Ms. Nelson worked as a literary scout and subrights agent for agent Jody Rein.

REPRESENTS Novels, select nonfiction. **Considers these nonfiction areas:** memoirs. **Considers these fiction areas:** commercial, literary, mainstream, romance (includes fantasy with romantic elements, science fiction, fantasy, young adult).

NLA specializes in representing commercial fiction and high-caliber literary fiction. Actively seeking stories with multicultural elements. Does not want short story collections, mysteries, thrillers, Christian, horror, children's picture books, or screenplays.

HOW TO CONTACT Query by e-mail only.

RECENT SALES *Prodigy*, by Marie Lu (young adult); *Wool*, by Hugh Howey (science fiction); *The Peculiar*, by Stefan Bachmann (middle grade); *Catching Jordan*, by Miranda Kenneally (young adult); *Broken Like This*, by Monica Trasandes (debut literary fiction); *The Darwin Elevator*, by Jason Hough (debut science fiction)

NEW LEAF LITERARY & MEDIA, INC.

110 W. 40th St., Suite 410, New York NY 10018. (646)248-7989. **Fax:** (646)861-4654. **E-mail:** assist@newleafliterary.com. **Contact:** Joanna Volpe; Kathleen Ortiz; Suzie Townsend; Pouya Shahbazian. "At New Leaf Literary & Media we believe in total client representation, before and beyond the sale. While it all begins with a good story, there is so much more that goes into a career as an author. It is our goal to not only advise and assist in this journey, but to stand with our clients at each stage. We provide editorial direction for each and every project in the development stages, and before a book is published, we work with our clients to develop promotion plans that enhance and support the publisher's outreach. With a comprehensive subrights department and film representation in-house, we are always considering the global and multimedia possibilities for each project we take on."

MEMBER AGENTS Joanna Volpe (women's fiction, thriller, horror, speculative fiction, literary fiction and historical fiction.); Kathleen Ortiz; Suzie Townsend (In adult, she's specifically looking for romance (historical and paranormal), and fantasy (urban fantasy, science fiction, steampunk, epic fantasy). In children's, she loves YA (all subgenres) and is dying to find great middle grade projects); Pouya Shahbazian, film and television agent.

HOW TO CONTACT E-mail queries only. "The word QUERY must be in subject line, plus the agent's name." No attachments. Responds only if interested.

RECENT SALES *Hunted*, by Holly McDowell; Divergent series, by Veronica Roth

WRITERS Conferences Pennwriters Conference, Writer's Digest Conference (NYC).

PEMA BROWNE LTD.

71 Pine Rd., Woodbourne NY 12788. (845)268-0029. **E-mail:** ppbltd@optonline.net. **Website:** www.pemabrowneltd.com. **Contact:** Pema Browne.

Looking for "professional and unique" talent.

REPRESENTS Specializes in general commercial.

RECENT SALES *The Daring Miss Quimby*, by Suzanne Whitaker, illustrated by Catherine Stock (Holiday House).

TERMS Rep receives 30% illustration commission; 20% author commission. Exclusive area representation is required. For promotional purposes, talent must provide color mailers to distribute. Representative pays mailing costs on promotion mailings.

HOW TO CONTACT For first contact, send query letter, direct mail flier/brochure, and SASE. If interested will ask to mail appropriate materials for review. Portfolios should include tearsheets and transparencies or good color photocopies, plus SASE. Accepts queries by mail only. Obtains new talent through recommendations and interviews (portfolio review). Current clients include HarperCollins, Holiday House, Bantam Doubleday Dell, Nelson/Word, Hyperion, Putnam. Client list available upon request.

TIPS "We are doing more publishing—all types—less advertising." Looks for "continuity of illustration and dedication to work."

ALISON J. PICARD, LITERARY AGENT

P.O. Box 2000, Cotuit MA 02635. Phone/**Fax:** (508)477-7192. **E-mail:** ajpicard@aol.com. **Contact:** Alison Picard.

REPRESENTS "Many of my clients have come to me from big agencies, where they felt overlooked or ignored. I communicate freely with my clients and offer a lot of career advice, suggestions for revising manuscripts, etc. If I believe in a project, I will submit it to a dozen or more publishers, unlike some agents who give up after four or five rejections." No science fiction/fantasy, westerns, poetry, plays or articles.

RECENT SALES *Zitface*, by Emily Ormand (Marshall Cavendish); *Totally Together*, by Stephanie O'Dea (Running Press); *The Ultimate Slow Cooker Cookbook*, by Stephanie O'Dea (Hyperion); Two Untitled Cookingbooks, by Erin Chase (St. Martin's Press);

LAURA BIAGI (JEAN V. NAGGAR LITERARY AGENCY)

jvnla.com
@LauraJBiagi

ABOUT LAURA: Laura Biagi joined the Jean V. Naggar Literary Agency Inc. (JVNLA) in 2009. She is actively building her own client list, seeking young readers books. She also handles the sale of Australian and New Zealand rights for the agency. She has worked closely with Jean Naggar and Jennifer Weltz on their titles, as well as Jennifer Weltz on the submission of JVNLA's titles internationally. Laura's writing background has honed her editorial eye and has driven her enthusiasm for discovering and developing literary talent. She studied creative writing and anthropology at Northwestern University. As a writer, she has participated in workshops at the Squaw Valley Community of Writers, the Juniper Summer Writing Institute, and the New York State Summer Writers Institute. She is the recipient of a Kentucky Emerging Artist Award for fiction writing. Laura grew up in a small town in Kentucky and maintains a fondness for Southern biscuits and unobstructed views of the stars.

SHE IS SEEKING: In the young readers realm, she is seeking young adult novels, middle grade novels, and picture books. She loves young readers books that have a magical tinge to them and vivid writing. She also looks for titles that incorporate high concept, dark/edgy and quirky elements, as well as titles that challenge the way we typically view the world.

HOW TO SUBMIT TO LAURA: Please e-mail your query to lbiagi@jvnla.com or submit your query to her via the website. Please include the first page of your manuscript when submitting your query.

A Journal of the Flood Year, by David Ely (Portobello Books-United Kingdom, L'Ancora, — Italy); *A Mighty Wall*, by John Foley (Llewellyn/Flux); *Jelly's Gold*, by David Housewright (St. Martin's Press). **TERMS** Agent receives 15% commission on domestic sales. Agent receives 20% commission on foreign sales. Offers written contract, binding for 1 year; 1-week notice must be given to terminate contract.

HOW TO CONTACT Query with SASE. Obtains most new clients through recommendations from others, solicitations.
TIPS "Please don't send material without sending a query first via mail or e-mail. I don't accept phone or fax queries. Always enclose an SASE with a query."

⊙ PIPPIN PROPERTIES, INC.
110 West 40th St., Suite 1704, New York, NY 10018. (212)338-9310. **Fax:** (212)338-9579. **E-mail:** info@pip

pinproperties.com. **Website:** www.pippinproperties.com. **Contact:** Holly McGhee. Represents 52 clients. Currently handles: juvenile books 100%.

Prior to becoming an agent, Ms. McGhee was an editor for 7 years and in book marketing for 4 years. Prior to becoming an agent, Ms. van Beek worked in children's book editorial for 4 years.

MEMBER AGENTS Holly McGhee, Emily van Beek, Elena Mechlin.

REPRESENTS Juvenile.

"We are strictly a children's literary agency devoted to the management of authors and artists in all media. We are small and discerning in choosing our clientele." Actively seeking middle-grade and young-adult novels.

HOW TO CONTACT Query via e-mail. Include a synopsis of the work(s), your background and/or publishing history, and anything else you think is relevant. Accepts simultaneous submissions. Responds in 3 weeks to queries if interested. Responds in 10 weeks to mss. Obtains most new clients through recommendations from others.

TERMS Agent receives 15% commission on domestic sales. Agent receives 25% commission on foreign sales. Offers written contract; 30-day notice must be given to terminate contract. Charges for color copying and UPS/FedEx.

TIPS "Please do not start calling after sending a submission."

PROSPECT AGENCY

551 Valley Road, PMB 377, Upper Montclair NJ 07043. (718)788-3217. **Fax:** (718)360-9582. **E-mail:** esk@prospectagency.com. **Website:** www.prospectagency.com. **Contact:** Emily Sylvan Kim, Becca Stumpf, Rachel Orr, Teresa Keitlinski. "Prospect Agency focuses on adult and children's literature, and is currently looking for the next generation of writers and illustrators to shape the literary landscape. We are a small, personal agency that focuses on helping each client reach success through hands-on editorial assistance and professional contract negotiations. We also strive to be on the cutting edge technologically. The agents here spend a lot of time forming personal relationships with authors and their work. Every agent here has incredibly strong editorial skills, and works directly with clients to balance the goals of selling individual books and managing a career."

All submissions are elcetronic.

REPRESENTS Handles nonfiction, fiction, picture books, middle grade, young adult. "We're looking for strong, unique voices and unforgettable stories and characters."

RECENT SALES Sold 15 books for young readers in the last year. (Also represents adult fiction.) Recent sales include: *Ollie and Claire* (Philomel), *Vicious* (Bloomsbury), *Temptest Rising* (Walker Books), *Where do Diggers Sleep at Night* (Random House Children's), *A DJ Called Tomorrow* (Little, Brown), *The Princesses of Iowa* (Candlewick).

TERMS Agent receives 15% on domestic sales, 20% on foreign sales sold directly and 25% on sales using a subagent. Offers written contract.

HOW TO CONTACT Send outline and 3 sample chapters. Accepts queries through website only. "We do not accept submissions to multiple Prospect agents (please submit to only 1 agent at Prospect Agency). Manuscripts and queries that are not a good fit for our agency are rejected via e-mail." Consult website for complete submission guidelines. Obtains new clients through conferences, recommendations, queries, and some scouting.

⊕ SADLER-CARAVETTE CHILDREN'S LITERARY.

1915 Whitestone Drive, Rockton, IL 61072. **E-mail:** sadlercaravettesubmissions@gmail.com. **Website:** www.sadler-caravetteliterary.com. **Contact:** Jodell Sadler. Currently handles: juvenile books 100%.

Prior to becoming an agent, Ms. Sadler was an instructional author on kidlit writing.

MEMBER AGENTS Jodell Sadler (YA, MG (especially funny), fiction and nonfiction, book proposals, and picture books); Laura Caravette (MG fiction and early readers, agency film rights management).

REPRESENTS Juvenile.

"We are both an active members of Society of Children's Book Writers and Illustrators (SCBWI) and open to speaking at conferences around the country."

HOW TO CONTACT "We only accept queries and submissions via e-mail. Please be sure your subject line reads: "QUERY: (Name or Title, Genre). You are free to submit to other agencies simultaneously, but exclusive is nice; however, if you do send out to others, please mark your query as a multiple submission. You need only send one manuscript at a time. We will

GEMMA COOPER (BENT AGENCY)

jennybent.blogspot.com
@gemma_cooper

ABOUT GEMMA: She is a new agent at The Bent Agency, run by Jenny Bent. In her own words: "Although I'm in London now, I lived in NYC for three years and regularly visit, so I'm going to be representing authors from the UK and the U.S. I look forward to reading your work and really appreciate you sharing it with me. I'm lucky to represent Mo O'Hara, author of *My Big Fat Zombie Goldfish* (Macmillan UK/Feiwel and Friends 2013) and I'd love to find other fantastic chapter books (7+ fiction) with an obvious hook and a laugh on every page. One of my all time favorite books is *When You Reach Me* by Rebecca Stead. I love that it blends genres, and has an amazing literary feel to the writing. Anything similar would make me sit up and take notice."

SHE IS SEEKING: "I love boy-voice YA fiction—it's my favorite thing in YA and so hard to strike the right balance. Think John Green or Erin Jade Lange's *Butter*. In YA, I'm seeing a lot of urban fantasy and am not really looking for this or paranormal romance. However, I'd love a nice juicy contemporary or issues driven YA. Think Jenny Valentine or Sara Zarr. A YA or middle grade fiction crime novel or some sort of heist would be great. My favorite detectives are Poriot and Sherlock Holmes, and I've love to read something with the same feel written for younger audiences—red herrings, opulent settings and gathering everyone in a room for the reveal! Please send me historical fiction with a realistic narrator that almost has a diary feel to it. Think the Once, Then, After series by Morris Gleitzman I would like to see some of the paranormal elements that work so well in YA filtered down into MG or chapter books ideally with humor. I'm obsessed with *Hitchhiker's Guide to the Galaxy* and the TV series "Red Dwarf," so I'd love to see funny sci-fi stories for a younger audience. The more off the wall the better.

HOW TO SUBMIT: Query cooperqueries@thebentagency.com.

contact you to request additional material. Please include a contact phone or cell as well as an e-mail address. Manuscripts should be attached in a Word.doc. If you include illustrations, as an author/illustrator, please attach a PDF file or JPGs. See online submission guidelines for more details. For picture books, please send query and entire manuscript. For CB, MG, YA, please send a query and first 10 pages."

TIPS "As a general rule, if you have not received a response from your queried within 6 months, please assume that Sadler-Caravette Children's Literary is not interested in your work."

WENDY SCHMALZ AGENCY

402 Union St., #831, Hudson NY 12534. (518)672-7697. **E-mail:** wendy@schmalzagency.com. **Website:** www.schmalzagency.com. **Contact:** Wendy Schmalz.

○ Prior to opening her agency, Wendy Schmalz was an agent for 23 years at Harold Ober Associates.

REPRESENTS Actively seeking young adult novels, middle grade novels. Obtains clients through recommendations from others. Not looking for picture books, science fiction or fantasy.

TERMS Agent receives 15% commission on domestic sales; 20% on foreign sales; 25% for Asian sales.

HOW TO CONTACT Accepts only e-mail queries. Do not attach the ms or sample chapters. Replies to queries only if they want to read the ms. Obtains clients through recommendations from others.

◑ SUSAN SCHULMAN LITERARY AGENCY

454 W. 44th St., New York NY 10036. (212)713-1633. **Fax:** (212)581-8830. **E-mail:** schulmanqueries@yahoo.com. **Contact:** Susan Schulman.

REPRESENTS "We specialize in books for, by and about women and women's issues including nonfiction self-help books, fiction and theater projects. We also handle the film, television and allied rights for several agencies as well as foreign rights for several publishing houses." Actively seeking new nonfiction. Considers plays. Does not want to receive poetry, television scripts or concepts for television.

RECENT SALES Sold 50 titles in the last year; hundred of subsidiary rights deals.

TERMS Agent receives 15% commission on domestic sales. Agent receives 20% commission on foreign sales. Offers written contract; 30-day notice must be given to terminate contract.

HOW TO CONTACT Query with SASE. Submit outline, synopsis, author bio, 3 sample chapters. Obtains most new clients through recommendations from others, solicitations, conferences.

TIPS "Keep writing!" Schulman describes her agency as "professional boutique, long-standing, eclectic."

◑ SERENDIPITY LITERARY AGENCY, LLC

305 Gates Ave., Brooklyn NY 11216. (718)230-7689. **Fax:** (718)230-7829. **E-mail:** rbrooks@serendipitylit.com; info@serendipitylit.com. **Website:** www.serendipitylit.com; facebook.com/serendipitylit. **Contact:** Regina Brooks.

○ "Authors who have a hook, platform, and incredible writing are ideal. Must be willing to put efforts into promotion."

REPRESENTS African-American nonfiction, commercial fiction, young adult novels with an urban flair and juvenile books. No stage plays, screenplays or poetry.

RECENT SALES *Putting Makeup on the Fat Boy*, by Bil Wright; *You Should Really Write a Book: How to Write Sell, and Market Your Memoir*, by Regina Brooks; *Living Color*, by Nina Jablonski; *Swirling*, by Christelyn D. Kazarin and Janice R. Littlejohn; *Red Thread Sisters*, by Carol Peacock; *Nicki Minaj: Hop Pop Moments 4 Life*, by Isoul Harris; *Forgotten Burial*, by Jodi Foster.

TERMS Agent receives 15% commission on domestic sales. Agent receives 20% commission on foreign sales. Offers written contract; 2-month notice must be given to terminate contract. Charges clients for office fees, which are taken from any advance.

HOW TO CONTACT Only accepts electronic submissions. "For nonfiction, submit proposal, query, 1 sample chapter (electronically). For adult fiction, please send a query letter that includes basic information that describes your project. Your query letter should include the title, premise, and length of the manuscript. See our guidelines and submission form online. Based on your initial query letter and synopsis, our office may request sample chapters, or your ms in its entirety. Obtains most new clients through conferences, referrals.

TIPS "See the book *Writing Great Books for Young Adults*. Looking for high concept ideas with big hooks. If you get writer's block try possibiliteas.co, it's a muse in a cup."

● THE SPIELER AGENCY

27 W. 20 St., Suite 305, New York NY 10011. **E-mail:** thespieleragency@gmail.com. **Contact:** Joe Spieler.

TERMS Agent receives 15% commission on domestic sales. Charges clients for messenger bills, photocopying, postage.

MICHELLE WITTE
(MANSION STREET LITERARY MANAGEMENT)

mansionstreet.com

ABOUT MICHELLE: As a new literary agent at Mansion Street Literary Management, Michelle Witte brings with her a wealth of experience, not only with juvenile fiction, but with the publishing industry as a whole. Michelle began her career as a journalist, first reporting and then later copyediting for the *Deseret News* in Salt Lake City, Utah, the second largest paper in the state. From there, she transitioned with her editing skills to nonfiction publisher Gibbs Smith, where she oversaw creation, editing and production of more than 30 titles, including children's activity, humor, gift, cookbooks, and a smattering of other topics from blacksmithing to green living. In her spare time she writes on a variety of topics and genres, though her great love is young adult fiction. Her first book, *The Craptastic Guide to Pseudo-Swearing*, hit stores on June 26, 2012.

SHE IS SEEKING: Michelle primarily represents young adult and middle grade works. She also reps children's nonfiction.

HOW TO CONTACT: querymichelle@mansionstreet.com. "Send a query letter and no more than the first 10 pages of your manuscript in the body of an e-mail. No attachments. Include 'QUERY' as well as your name and title in the subject line of the e-mail. Response time for queries is anything from a few days to six weeks."

HOW TO CONTACT Accepts electronic submissions, or send query letter and sample chapters. Returns materials only with SASE; otherwise materials are discarded when rejected. Obtains most new clients through recommendations, listing in *Guide to Literary Agents*.

TIPS "Check http://www.publishersmarketplace.com/members/spielerlit/."

STIMOLA LITERARY STUDIO

308 Livingston Ct., Edgewater NJ 07020. **Fax:** / Phone: (201)945-9353. **E-mail:** info@stimolaliterarystudio.com. **Website:** www.stimolaliterarystudio.com. **Contact:** Rosemary B. Stimola. "A full service literary agency devoted to representing authors and author/illustrators of fiction and nonfiction, preschool through young adult, who bring unique and substantive contributions to the industry."

○ Prior to opening her agency, Rosemary Stimola was an independent children's bookseller.

REPRESENTS Actively seeking remarkable young adult fiction and debut picture book author/illustrators. No institutional books.

AGENTS AND ART REPS

RECENT SALES Sold 40 books for young readers in the past 2 years. Among these, *A Touch Mortal*, by Leah Clifford (Greenwillow/Harper Collins); *Black Hole Sun*, by David Gill (Greenwillow/Harper Collins); *Dot*, by Patricia Intriago (FSG/Macmillan); *Inside Out and Back Again*, by Thanhha Lai (Harper Collins); *The Fox Inheritance*, by Mary Pearson (Henry Holt/Macmillan); *Henry Aaron's Dream*, by Matt Tavares (Candlewick Press); *Throat*, by R.A. Nelson (Knopf/RH).

TERMS Agent receives 15% commission on domestic sales. Agent receives 20% (if subagents are employed) commission on foreign sales. Offers written contract, binding for all children's projects. 60 days notice must be given to terminate contract. Charges $85 one-time fee per project to cover expenses.

HOW TO CONTACT Query via e-mail. "No attachments, please!" While unsolicited queries are welcome, most clients come through editor, agent, client referrals.

TIPS Agent is hands-on, no-nonsense. May request revisions. Does not edit but may offer suggestions for improvement. Well-respected by clients and editors. "A firm but reasonable deal negotiator."

THE STRINGER LITERARY AGENCY, LLC

E-mail: stringerlit@comcast.net. **Website:** www.stringerlit.com. **Contact:** Marlene Stringer.

REPRESENTS This agency specializes in fiction. Does not want to receive picture books, plays, short stories, or poetry.

RECENT SALES *Out for Blood* and *Stolen*, by Alyxandra Harvey (Walker Books); *Change of Heart*, by Shari Maurer (WestSide Books); *I Stole Johnny Depp's Alien Girlfriend*, by Gary Ghislain (Chronicle Books); *The Land of Hope & Glory Trilogy*, by Geoffrey Wilson (Hodder); *...And On The Piano, Nicky Hopkins!*, by Julian Dawson (Plus One Press); *Poison Kissed*, by Erica Hayes (St. Martin's); *Possum Summer*, by Jen K. Blom (Holiday House).

HOW TO CONTACT Electronic submissions only. Yes

TIPS "If your ms falls between categories, or you are not sure of the category, query and we'll let you know if we'd like to take a look. We strive to respond as quickly as possible. If you have not received a response in the time period indicated, please re-query."

UPSTART CROW LITERARY

P.O. Box 25404, Brooklyn NY 11202. **E-mail:** info@upstartcrowliterary.com. **E-mail:** danielle.submission@gmail.com; alexandra.submission@gmail.com. **Website:** www.upstartcrowliterary.com. **Contact:** Danielle Chiotti, Alexandra Penfold.

HOW TO CONTACT Upstart Crow agents that are currently accepting submissions are Danielle Chiotti and Alexandra Penfold. See website for what they are seeking.

CK WEBBER ASSOCIATES LITERARY MANAGEMENT

Website: www.ckwebber.com. **Contact:** Carlie Webber. Estab. 2012.

Prior to forming her own agency, Ms. Webber was an agent with the Jane Rotrosen Agency.

REPRESENTS Fiction, novels, memoir. **Considers these fiction areas:** young adult, middle grade, women's fiction, literary and general fiction, mystery, thriller, suspense, romance, science fiction, fantasy, memoir.

HOW TO CONTACT Send a query letter, synopsis, and the first 30 pages or three chapters of your work, whichever is more, to carlie@ckwebber.com and put the word "query" in the subject line of your e-mail. You may include your materials either in the body of your e-mail or as a Word or PDF attachment. Blank e-mails that include an attachment will be deleted unread.

WERNICK & PRATT AGENCY

E-mail: info@wernickpratt.com. **Website:** www.wernickpratt.com. **Contact:** Marcia Wernick; Linda Pratt. "Wernick & Pratt Agency provides each client with personal attention and the highest quality of advice and service that has been the hallmark of our reputations in the industry. We have the resources and accumulated knowledge to assist clients in all aspects of their creative lives including editorial input, contract negotiations, and subsidiary rights management. Our goal is to represent and manage the careers of our clients so they may achieve industry wide and international recognition, as well as the highest level of financial potential."

Dedicated to children's books.

REPRESENTS "Wernick & Pratt Agency specializes in children's books of all genres, from picture books through young adult literature and everything in between. We represent both authors and illustrators. We do not represent authors of adult books." Wants people who both write and illustrate in the picture book

POOJA MENON (KIMBERLEY CAMERON & ASSOCIATES)

kimberleycameron.com
@FriscoDreamer

ABOUT POOJA: Pooja Menon earned her BA from Nottingham Trent University in England, and an MFA from The Otis School of Art & Design in Los Angeles. In the fall of 2011, she joined Kimberley Cameron & Associates as an intern, wanting to immerse herself more fully into the elusive world of books and publishing.

SHE REPRESENTS: Pooja is actively seeking to build her client list. In YA fiction, she's eagerly looking for submissions across all genres (contemporary, adventure, realist, paranormal romance, gothic, horror, historical, steampunk, dystopian, magical realism, urban fantasy and new age).

HOW TO SUBMIT: "Send e-mail queries to pooja@kimberleycameron.com. Include a one-page synopsis and the first 50 pages in word attachments. I will get in touch with you for extra pages or a hardcopy. In the case of nonfiction, please submit a well-crafted proposal and the first three chapters of your work in similar format."

genre; humorous young chapter books with strong voice, and which are unique and compelling; middle grade/YA novels, both literary and commercial. No picture book mss of more than 750 words, or mood pieces; work specifically targeted to the educational market; fiction about the American Revolution, Civil War, or World War II unless it is told from a very unique perspective.
HOW TO CONTACT Submit via e-mail only. "Please indicate to which agent you are submitting." Detailed submission guidelines available on website.

⚫ WRITERS HOUSE

21 W. 26th St., New York NY 10010. (212)685-2400. **Fax:** (212)685-1781. **Website:** www.writershouse.com. **Contact:** Michael Mejias.

REPRESENTS This agency specializes in all types of popular fiction and nonfiction. Does not want to receive scholarly, professional, poetry, plays, or screenplays.
TERMS Agent receives 15% commission on domestic sales. Agent receives 20% commission on foreign sales. Offers written contract, binding for 1 year. Agency charges fees for copying mss/proposals and overseas airmail of books.
HOW TO CONTACT Query with SASE. "Please send us a query letter of no more than 2 pages, which includes your credentials, an explanation of what makes your book unique and special, and a synopsis. (If submitting to Steven Malk: Writers House, 7660 Fay Ave., #338H, La Jolla, CA 92037). Please do not query 2 agents within our agency simultaneously." No

Obtains most new clients through recommendations from authors and editors.

TIPS "Do not send mss. Write a compelling letter. If you do, we'll ask to see your work. Follow submission guidelines and please do not simultaneously submit your work to more than 1 Writers House agent."

WRITERS HOUSE

7660 Fay Ave., #338H, La Jolla CA 92037. **E-mail:** smalk@writershouse.com. **Website:** http://writershouse.com. (West Coast Office), 7660 Fay Ave., #338H, La Jolla, CA 92037. **Contact:** Steven Malk. e-mail: smalk@WritersHouse.com New York office: 21 W. 26th St., New York, NY 10010; (212)685-2400 (phone); (212)685-1781 (fax).

See Writers House listing above for more information. This is a large agency that has several agents who rep picture books. Only submit to one agent at this agency. Target agents Brianne Johnson, Stephen Barr and Steven Malk.

REPRESENTS Children's nonfiction, fiction, picture books, middle-grade novels, young adult, illustrators.

ART REPS

CAROL BANCROFT & FRIENDS

P.O. Box 2030, Danbury CT 06813. (203)730-8270 or (800)720-7020. **Fax:** (203)730-8275. **E-mail:** cb_friends8270@sbcglobal.net; cbfriends@sbcglobal.net. **Website:** www.carolbancroft.com. **Contact:** Joy Elton Tricarico, owner; Carol Bancroft, founder. "Internationally known for representing artists who specialize in illustrating art for all aspects of the children's market. We also represent many artists who are well known in other aspects of the field of illustration." Clients include, but not limited to, Scholastic, Houghton Mifflin, HarperCollins, Dutton, Harcourt, Marshall Cavendish, McGraw Hill, Hay House.

REPRESENTS Specializes in illustration for children's publishing-text and trade; any children's-related material.

TERMS Rep receives 25% commission. Advertising costs are split: 75% paid by talent; 25% paid by representative.

HOW TO CONTACT Either e-mail 2-3 samples with your address or mail 6-10 samples, along with a SASE to the P.O. box address. For promotional purposes, artists must provide "laser copies (not slides), tearsheets, promo pieces, good color photocopies,

etc.; 6 pieces or more is best; narrative scenes and children interacting."

TIPS "We look for artists who can draw animals and people with imagination and energy, depicting engaging characters with action in situational settings."

BOOKMAKERS LTD.

32 Parkview Avenue, Wolfville NS., Canada B4P 2K8. (902)697-2569. **E-mail:** reg@bookmakersltd.com. **Website:** www.bookmakersltd.com

REPRESENTS Over 20 illustrators of children's books.

RECENT SALES Works with "most major book publishers."

HOW TO CONTACT E-mail with inquiries at reg@bookmakersltd.com.

CORNELL & MCCARTHY LLC

2-D Cross Highway, Westport CT 06880. (203)454-4210. **Fax:** (203)454-4258. **E-mail:** contact@cmartreps.com. **Website:** www.cmartreps.com. **Contact:** Merial Cornell.

REPRESENTS Specializes in children's books: trade, mass market, educational. Obtains new talent through recommendations, solicitation, conferences.

TERMS Agent receives 25% commission. Advertising costs are split: 75% paid by talent; 25% paid by representative.

HOW TO CONTACT For first contact, send query letter, direct mail flier/brochure, tearsheets, photocopies and SASE or preferably e-mail. For promotional purposes, talent must provide 10-12 strong portfolio pieces relating to children's publishing.

CRAVEN DESIGN, INC.

1202 Lexington Ave., Box 242, New York, NY 10028. (212)288-1022. **Fax:** (212)249-9910 **E-mail:** cravendesign@mac.com. **Website:** www.cravendesignstudios.com. **Contact:** Meryl Jones.

REPRESENTS "We represent more than 20 professional illustrators with experience in a full range of genres, from humorous to realistic, decorative and technical, electronic and traditional, including maps, charts and graphs."

RECENT SALES Specializes in textbook illustration for all ages, juvenile through adult, elementary through secondary school.

HOW TO CONTACT E-mail with any inquiries.

THAO LE (SANDRA DIJKSTRA LITERARY AGENCY)

dijkstraagency.com
@ThaoLe8

ABOUT THAO: She is a graduate of the University of California, San Diego with a double major in Econ-Management Science and Chinese Studies. While interning at the agency during college, she realized where her true love lies—books—and joined the Sandra Dijkstra Literary Agency fulltime in 2011.

SHE IS SEEKING: Thao is currently building her list and is specifically interested in middle grade and YA fiction. She's particularly drawn to smart, strong and sassy characters and twisty plots with a compelling narrative. She's always on the lookout for the type of stories that make you stay curled up in bed, turning page after page even after the sun has come up.

HOW TO CONTACT: thao@dijkstraagency.com. "We only accept electronic submissions. Any hardcopy submissions received by mail will be recycled unopened. Please send a query letter, a one-page synopsis, a brief bio (including a description of your publishing history), and the first 10-15 pages of your manuscript. Send all items in the body of the e-mail, not as an attachment.

⊕ FAMOUS FRAMES

5839 Green Valley Circle, Suite 104, Culver City, CA 90230. (855)530-3375. **Fax:** 310.642.2728 **E-mail:** artincgw@gmail.com. www.famousframes.com.
REPRESENTS A "roster of 100+ of the world's top illustrators."
RECENT SALES Sells to a wide client base made up of many commercial organizations and some publishers.
HOW TO CONTACT E-mail portfolio@famousframes.com and include samples/links along with contact information within the body of the e-mail.

⊕ FRIEND + JOHNSON

Contact information varies based upon location. *East*: 37 W 26th St. Suite 313, New York, NY 10010. (212)337-0055. **E-mail:** rsaxon@friendandjohnson.com. **Contact:** Gwen Walters. *West/Southwest*:

870 Market St. Suite 1017, San Francisco, CA 94102. (415)927-4500. **E-mail:** bjohnson@friendandjohnson.com. **Contact:** Beth Johnson. *Midwest*: 901 W Madison St Suite 918., Chicago, IL 60607. (312)435-0055. **E-mail:** sfriend@friendandjohnson.com. **Contact:** Simone Friend .**Website:** www.friendandjohnson.com
REPRESENTS A diverse and original group of artists, photographers, designers, illustrators and typographists.
HOW TO CONTACT Please send your inquiry and a link to your website in an e-mail to agent@friendandjohnson.com. Don't contact the agents directly. Will reply only if interested.

HANNAH REPRESENTS

1472 Dudley Ave., Ventura CA 93004. **E-mail:** hannahrepresents@yahoo.com.

⊕ HEART ARTIST'S AGENCY

Heart USA Inc., 611 Broadway Suite 734, New York, NY 10012 . (212)995-9386 **Fax:** (212)995-9386. **E-mail:** mail@heartagency.com. **Website:** www.heartagency.com

REPRESENTS Currently open to illustrators seeking representation. Is highly selective.

HOW TO CONTACT Accepts submissions in the form of website links via e-mail to mail@heartagency.com. If no website exists please provide printed samples by post. If you would like your samples returned, please supply a stamped self-addressed-envelope in your package.

⊕ SCOTT HULL ASSOCIATES

3875 Ferry Road, Bellbrook, Ohio 45305. (937)433-8383. **Fax:** (937)433-0434 **E-mail:** scott@scotthull.com. **Website:** www.scotthull.com.

REPRESENTS A very large group of illustrators who specialize in a vairety of fields, including publishing.

RECENT SALES Has done business with Scholastic, Harper Collins, Chronicle Books, Crown Publishing, Bantam Books, and many other publishers

HOW TO CONTACT E-mail with inquiries or fill out the form on the website.

⊕ ILLUSTRATORSREP.COM

5 W. Fifth Street, Suite 300, Covington, KY 41011. (513)861-1400. **Fax:** (859)980-0820. **E-mail:** bob@illustratorsrep.com. **Website:** www.illustratorsrep.com.

REPRESENTS Small group of illustrators and photographers.

RECENT SALES "We have serviced such accounts as Disney, Rolling Stone Magazine and Procter & Gamble, just to name a few."

HOW TO CONTACT For information about representation, e-mail samples to info@illustratorsrep.com.

⊕ THE JULY GROUP

(212) 932-8583. **Website:** www.thejulygroup.com.

REPRESENTS Currently open to illustrators seeking representation. Their current group of illustrators' and animators' professional skills include: licensed images, children's book illustration, science fiction and fantasy art, graphic novels, CD art, educational illustration, and multimedia animation."

RECENT SALES Works with a variety of clients, including publishers and commercial.

HOW TO CONTACT Work can be submitted via a form on the website.

⊕ KID SHANNON

Shannon Associates, 333 West 57th Street, Suite 809, New York, New York 10019. (212)333-2551. **E-mail:** information@kidshannon.com. **Website:** www.shannonassociates.com/kidshannon.

REPRESENTS Very large group of illustrators, some photographers and some authors.

RECENT SALES Sells to many major publishing companies, including Penguin and Random House,

HOW TO CONTACT Fill out the form on the website.

TIPS The website has a "Resources" tab that contains great advice, articles and tips for beginning and/or freelance illustrators

⊕ LEMONADE ILLUSTRATION AGENCY

347 Fifth Ave. Suite 1402, New York, NY 10016. **E-mail:** studio@lemonadeillustration.com. **Website:** www.lemonadeillustration.com.

REPRESENTS A wide variety of illustrators, including those for children's books.

RECENT SALES Sells to many major book publishers, including Penguin Books, Pearson, McGraw-Hill, Scholastic, and Random House.

HOW TO CONTACT Does not accept unsolicited attachments via e-mail or CD/DVD's in the post. Please address Lemonade in your e-mail inquiry. Only accepts links to website or sample copies via the post (addressed to the submissions dept). Will reply only if interested.

TIPS "Please try and write a little about yourself and your work in your e-mail. A professional presentation of your illustrations is key."

⊕ MARTHA PRODUCTIONS, INC.

7550 West 82nd Street, Playa Del Rey, CA 90293. (310)670-5300. **Fax:** (310) 670-3644. **E-mail:** contact@marthaproductions.com. **Website:** www.marthaproductions.com.

REPRESENTS Wide range of illustration styles, all categorized on website.

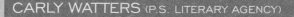
CARLY WATTERS (P.S. LITERARY AGENCY)

psliterary.com
@carlywatters

ABOUT CARLY: Carly began her publishing career in London, England at the Darley Anderson Literary, TV and Film Agency and Bloomsbury PLC. She completed her BA in English Language and Literature at Queen's University and her MA in Publishing Studies at City University London with a thesis on the social, political and economic impact of literary prizes on trade publishing. Now an associate agent at the P.S. Literary Agency she is actively building her list and looking for new writers. Never without a book on hand she reads across categories which is reflected in the genres she acquires.

SHE IS SEEKING: Carly is looking for material contemporary YA fiction and high-concept picture books.

HOW TO SUBMIT: Keep your query to one page. "Please do not submit a full-length manuscript/proposal unless requested. Always let us know if your manuscript/proposal is currently under consideration by other agents/publishers. Do not send attachments. Please use text within the body of your e-mail. We only accept submissions via e-mail. We do not accept or respond to phone/paper queries. Please Note: We normally respond within 4-6 weeks. However, the process may take longer depending on the volume of submissions we may be reviewing at a particular time. Please do not call to check on the status of your submission—if you have a question or concern with regard to your submission, e-mail is the best way to inquire."

HOW TO CONTACT "We always welcome submissions from illustrators considering representation. Please e-mail us a few small digital files of your work or mail us non-returnable samples. We will contact you if we think we would be able to sell your work or if we'd like to see more."

⊕ MGI KIDS (MORGAN GAYNIN INC.)

194 Third Avenue #3, New York, NY 10003. (212)475-0440. **E-mail:** info@morgangaynin.com. **Website:** www.morgangaynin.com.

REPRESENTS "Select international illustrators." Features many of Morgan Gaynin's illustrators who also specialize in children's illustration.
RECENT SALES Has a wide client base. Artists have won several awards from organizations like American Illustration and Society of Illustrators New York and Los Angles.
HOW TO CONTACT Not accepting submissions at this time.

PEMA BROWNE LTD.

71 Pine Rd., Woodbourne NY 12788. (845)268-0029.
E-mail: ppbltd@optonline.net. **Website:** www.pem-abrowneltd.com. **Contact:** Pema Browne.

Looking for "professional and unique" talent.
REPRESENTS Specializes in general commercial.
RECENT SALES *The Daring Miss Quimby*, by Suzanne Whitaker, illustrated by Catherine Stock (Holiday House).
TERMS Rep receives 30% illustration commission; 20% author commission. Exclusive area representation is required. For promotional purposes, talent must provide color mailers to distribute. Representative pays mailing costs on promotion mailings.
HOW TO CONTACT For first contact, send query letter, direct mail flier/brochure, and SASE. If interested will ask to mail appropriate materials for review. Portfolios should include tearsheets and transparencies or good color photocopies, plus SASE. Accepts queries by mail only. Obtains new talent through recommendations and interviews (portfolio review). Current clients include HarperCollins, Holiday House, Bantam Doubleday Dell, Nelson/Word, Hyperion, Putnam. Client list available upon request.
TIPS "We are doing more publishing—all types—less advertising." Looks for "continuity of illustration and dedication to work."

⊕ VICKI PRENTICE ASSOCIATES, INC.

International Building, 630 Fifth Avenue, 20th floor, Rockefeller Center, New York, NY, 10111. (212)332-3460. **Fax:** (212)332-3401 **E-mail:** SayItWithArt@VickiPrenticeAssociatesInc.com. **Website:** www.vickiprenticeassociatesinc.com.
REPRESENTS Almost 20 illustrators with a variety of styles.
RECENT SALES Works with a variety of publishers, including Rising Moon Publishing, William H. Sadlier, and McGraw-Hill.
HOW TO CONTACT E-mail with inquiries.

⊕ RED PAINTBOX

1676A Ninth Avenue, New York, New York 10036. (212)397-7330. **E-mail:** representation@redpaintbox.com. **Website:** www.redpaintbox.com.
REPRESENTS Represents many illustrators and artists, over 30 of them being children's books illustrators.
RECENT SALES Has "world-wide access to clients."

HOW TO CONTACT For representation inquiries, please e-mail one or two jpgs to representation@redpaintbox.com. Will reply only if interested

⊕ RILEY ILLUSTRATION

PO Box 92, New Paltz, NY 12561. (845)255-3309. **E-mail:** info@rileyillustration.com. **Website:** www.rileyillustration.com.
REPRESENTS Several award winning illustrators.
RECENT SALES Works with "art directors and designers, publishers, corporations, organizations, architects, and product developers."
HOW TO CONTACT E-mail any inquiries to info@rileyillustration.com.

LIZ SANDERS AGENCY

2415 E. Hangman Creek Ln., Spokane WA 99224-8514. (509)993-6400. **E-mail:** liz@lizsanders.com; artsubmissions@lizsanders.com. **Website:** www.lizsanders.com. **Contact:** Liz Sanders, owner. Commercial illustration representative. Represents Kyle Poling, Jared Beckstand, Craig Orback, Amy Ning, Tom Pansini, Chris Lensch, Lynn Gesue, Poozie, Susan Synarski, Sudi McCollum, Suzanne Beaky and more.
REPRESENTS Markets include publishing, licensed properties, entertainment and advertising. Currently open to illustrators seeking representation. Open to both new and established illustrators.
TERMS Receives 30% commission against pro bono mailing program. Offers written contract.
HOW TO CONTACT For first contact, send tearsheets, direct mail flier/brochure, color copies, non-returnable or e-mail to artsubmissions@lizsanders.com. Obtains new talent through recommendations from industry contacts, conferences and queries/solicitations, Literary Market Place.

⊕ RICHARD SOLOMON ARTISTS REPRESENTATIVE, LLC

110E 30th St., Suite 501, New York, NY, 10016. (212)223-9545. **Fax:** (212)223-9633 **E-mail:** richard@richardsolomon.com. **Website:** www.richardsolomon.com.
REPRESENTS "We represent an ever-expanding 'big tent' of award-winning illustrators and fine artists, who work collaboratively with the best art directors and designers throughout the world."
RECENT SALES Has done work with Harper Collins, Random House, Scholastic, and many others

HOW TO CONTACT Send inquiries via e-mail or fill out the submission form on the website.

⊕ STORE 44 REPS

PO Box 251, Flagstaff, AZ 86002 . (323)230-0044. **E-mail:** art@store44.com. **Website:** www.store44.com.

REPRESENTS Photopgraphers, fine artists, and illustrators on an international level.

RECENT SALES Works with a wide client base, including Macmillan Publishing Group

HOW TO CONTACT *By e-mail:* art@store44.com. Be sure to reference "Artist Submission" in the subject line. You should also include keywords in your e-mail like "fashion" and "photographer." *By post:* Please include a self-addressed stamped envelope for any items you would like returned, and mark any packages "Artist Submission." All submissions are categorized and reviewed on a monthly basis. We consider new artists for representation during our four annual portfolio reviews. If selected, we will contact you to request additional materials.

⊕ T2 CHILDREN'S ILLUSTRATORS

2231 Grandview Avenue, Cleveland Heights, OH 44106. (216)707-0854. **E-mail:** nicole@tugeau2.com. **Website:** www.tugeau2.com **Contact:** Nicole Tugeau.

REPRESENTS Currently open to children's illustrators seeking representation.

RECENT SALES Works with a variety of publishers, such as Tricycle (division of Random House), Raven Tree Press, and Piggy Toes Press.

HOW TO CONTACT "To submit your work for consideration, please send Nicole a short e-mail with a link to your personal website and/or five pictures of your best and most recent artwork."

GWEN WALTERS ARTIST REPRESENTATIVE

1801 S. Flagler Dr., #1202, W. Palm Beach FL 33401. (561)805-7739. **E-mail:** artincgw@gmail.com. **Website:** www.gwenwaltersartrep.com. **Contact:** Gwen Walters.

REPRESENTS Currently open to illustrators seeking representation. Looking for established illustrators only.

RECENT SALES Sells to "All major book publishers."

TERMS Receives 30% commission. Artist needs to supply all promo material. Offers written contract.

HOW TO CONTACT For first contact, send tearsheets. Finds illustrators through recommendations from others.

TIPS "You need to pound the pavement for a couple of years to get some experience under your belt. Don't forget to sign all artwork. So many artists forget to stamp their samples."

⊕ WILKINSON STUDIOS, INC.

1121 E. Main St., Suite 310, St. Charles, IL 06174. (630)549-0504. **Website:** www.wilkinsonstudios.com.

REPRESENTS Represents several professional illustrators, including those specializing in children's illustration. "What sets us apart from the other rep firms is that we also offer art management services for large volume blackline and color illustration programs."

RECENT SALES Works with a wide variety of clients, nationally and internationally.

HOW TO CONTACT Accepts appropriate hard copy samples, tear sheets, color copies, or digital print-outs only via mail. Accepts digital submissions from non-US artists only.

CLUBS & ORGANIZATIONS

Contacts made through organizations such as the ones listed in this section can be quite beneficial for children's writers and illustrators. Professional organizations provide numerous educational, business, and legal services in the form of newsletters, workshops, or seminars. Organizations can provide tips about how to be a more successful writer or artist, as well as what types of business cards to keep, health and life insurance coverage to carry, and competitions to consider.

An added benefit of belonging to an organization is the opportunity to network with those who have similar interests, creating a support system. As in any business, knowing the right people can often help your career, and important contacts can be made through your peers. Membership in a writer's or artist's organization also shows publishers you're serious about your craft. This provides no guarantee your work will be published, but it gives you an added dimension of credibility and professionalism.

Some of the organizations listed here welcome anyone with an interest, while others are only open to published writers and professional artists. Organizations such as the Society of Children's Book Writers and Illustrators (SCBWI, scbwi.org) have varying levels of membership. SCBWI offers associate membership to those with no publishing credits, and full membership to those who have had work for children published. International organizations such as SCBWI also have regional chapters throughout the U.S. and the world. Write or call for more information regarding any group that interests you, or check the websites of the many organizations that list them. Be sure to get information about local chapters, membership qualifications, and services offered.

AMERICAN ALLIANCE FOR THEATRE & EDUCATION

4908 Auburn Ave., Bethesda MD MD 20814. (301)200-1944. **Fax:** (301). **E-mail:** info@aate.com. **Website:** www.aate.com. Purpose of organization: to promote standards of excellence in theatre and drama education. "We achieve this by assimilating quality practices in theatre and theatre education, connecting artists, educators, researchers and scholars with each other, and by providing opportunities for our members to learn, exchange and diversify their work, their audiences and their perspectives." Membership cost: $115 annually for individual in U.S. and Canada, $220 annually for organization, $60 annually for students, and $70 annually for retired people, $310 annually for University Departmental memberships; add $30 outside Canada and U.S. Holds annual conference (July or August). Contests held for unpublished play reading project and annual awards in various categories. Awards plaque and stickers for published playbooks. Publishes list of unpublished plays deemed worthy of performance and stages readings at conference. Contact national office at number above or see website for contact information for Playwriting Network Chairpersons. **Contact:** Alexis Truitt, operations manager.

AMERICAN SOCIETY OF JOURNALISTS AND AUTHORS

1501 Broadway, Suite 403, New York NY 10036. (212)-997-0947. **Website:** www.asja.org. Qualifications for membership: "Need to be a professional freelance nonfiction writer. Refer to website for further qualifications." Membership cost: Application fee—$50, annual dues—$210. Group sponsors national conferences. Professional seminars online and in person around the country. Workshops/conferences open to nonmembers. Publishes a newsletter for members that provides confidential information for nonfiction writers. **Contact:** Alexandra Owens, executive director.

◉ ARIZONA AUTHORS ASSOCIATION

6145 West Echo Lane, Glendale AZ 85302. (623)847-9343. **E-mail:** info@azauthors.com. **Website:** www.azauthors.com. Purpose of organization: to offer professional, educational and social opportunities to writers and authors, and serve as a network. Members must be authors, writing toward publication, agents, publishers, publicists, printers, illustrators, etc. Membership cost: $45/year writers; $30/year students; $60/year other professionals in publishing industry. Holds regular workshops and meetings. Publishes bimonthly newsletter and *Arizona Literary Magazine.* Sponsors Annual Literary Contest in poetry, essays, short stories, novels, and published books with cash prizes and awards bestowed at a public banquet. Winning entries are also published or advertised in the *Arizona Literary Magazine.* First and second place winners in poetry, essay and short story categories are entered in the Pushcart Prize. Winners in published categories receive free listings by www.fivestarpublications.com. Send SASE or view website for guidelines. **Contact:** Toby Heathcote, president.

THE AUTHORS GUILD, INC.

31 E. 32nd St., 7th Floor, New York NY 10016. (212)564-5904. **Fax:** (212)564-5363. **E-mail:** staff@authorsguild.org. **Website:** www.authorsguild.org. Purpose of organization: to offer services and materials intended to help authors with the business and legal aspects of their work, including contract problems, copyright matters, freedom of expression and taxation. Guild has 8,000 members. Qualifications for membership: Must be book author published by an established American publisher within 7 years or any author who has had 3 works (fiction or nonfiction) published by a magazine or magazines of general circulation in the last 18 months. Associate membership also available. Annual dues: $90. Different levels of membership include: associate membership with all rights except voting available to an author who has a firm contract offer or is currently negotiating a royalty contract from an established American publisher. "The Guild offers free contract reviews to its members. The Guild conducts several symposia each year at which experts provide information, offer advice and answer questions on subjects of interest and concern to authors. Typical subjects have been the rights of privacy and publicity, libel, wills and estates, taxation, copyright, editors and editing, the art of interviewing, standards of criticism and book reviewing. Transcripts of these symposia are published and circulated to members. The *Authors Guild Bulletin,* a quarterly journal, contains articles on matters of interest to writers, reports of Guild activities, contract surveys, advice on problem clauses in contracts, transcripts of Guild and League symposia and information on a variety of professional topics. Subscrip-

tion included in the cost of the annual dues." **Contact:** Paul Aiken, executive director.

☯ CANADIAN SOCIETY OF CHILDREN'S AUTHORS, ILLUSTRATORS AND PERFORMERS

104-40 Orchard View Blvd., Lower Level, Toronto ON M4R 1B9Canada . (416)515-1559. **E-mail:** office@ canscaip.org. **Website:** www.canscaip.org. Purpose of organization: development of Canadian children's culture and support for authors, illustrators and performers working in this field. Qualifications for membership: Members—professionals who have been published (not self-published) or have paid public performances/records/tapes to their credit. Friends—share interest in field of children's culture. Membership cost: $85 (Members dues), $45 (Friends dues). Sponsors workshops/conferences. Manuscript evaluation services; publishes newsletter: includes profiles of members; news round-up of members' activities countrywide; market news; news on awards, grants, etc; columns related to professional concerns. **Contact:** Lena Coakley, administrative director.

LEWIS CARROLL SOCIETY OF NORTH AMERICA

11935 Beltsville Dr., Beltsville MD 20705. **E-mail:** secretary@lewiscarroll.org. **Website:** www.lewiscarroll.org. "We are an organization of Carroll admirers of all ages and interests and a center for Carroll studies." Qualifications for membership: "An interest in Lewis Carroll and a simple love for Alice (or the Snark for that matter)." Membership cost: $35 (regular membership), $50 (foreign membership), $100 (sustaining membership). The Society meets twice a year—in spring and in fall; locations vary. Publishes a semi-annual journal, *Knight Letter*, and maintains an active publishing program. **Contact:** Clare Imholtz, secretary.

THE CHILDREN'S BOOK COUNCIL, INC.

54 W. 39th St., 14th Floor, New York NY 10018. (212)966-1990. **Fax:** (212)966-2073. **E-mail:** cbc.info@ cbcbooks.org. **Website:** www.cbcbooks.org. Purpose of organization: A nonprofit trade association of children's and young adult publishers and packagers, CBC promotes the enjoyment of books for children and young adults and works with national and international organizations to that end. The CBC has sponsored Children's Book Week since 1945 and Young People's Poetry Week since 1999. Qualifications for

membership: trade publishers and packagers of children's and young adult books and related literary materials are eligible for membership. Publishers wishing to join should contact the CBC for dues information. Sponsors workshops and seminars for publishing company personnel. Children's Book Week poster and downloadable bookmark available, information at www.bookweekonline.com. **Contact:** Robin Adelson, executive director.

FLORIDA FREELANCE WRITERS ASSOCIATION

P.O. Box A, North Stratford NH 03590. (603)922-8338. **E-mail:** FFWA@writers-editors.com. **Website:** www. ffwamembers.com; www.writers-editors.com. Purpose of organization: To provide a link between Florida writers and buyers of the written word; to help writers run more effective editorial businesses. Qualifications for membership: "None. We provide a variety of services and information, some for beginners and some for established pros." Membership cost: $90/ year. Publishes a newsletter focusing on market news, business news, how-to tips for the serious writer. Annual Directory of Florida Markets included in FFWA newsletter section and electronic download. Publishes annual *Guide to CNW/Florida Writers*, which is distributed to editors around the country. Sponsors contest: annual deadline March 15. Guidelines on website. Categories: juvenile, adult nonfiction, adult fiction and poetry. Awards include cash for top prizes, certificate for others. Contest open to nonmembers. **Contact:** Dana K. Cassell, executive director.

GRAPHIC ARTISTS GUILD

32 Broadway, Suite 1114, New York NY 10004. (212)791-3400. **Fax:** 212-791-0333. **E-mail:** admin@ gag.org; Patricia@gag.org. **Website:** www.graphicartistsguild.org. Purpose of organization: "To promote and protect the economic interests of member artists. It is committed to improving conditions for all creators of graphic arts and raising standards for the entire industry." Qualification for full membership: 50% of income derived from the creation of graphic artwork. Associate members include those in allied fields and students. Initiation fee: $30. Full memberships: $200; student membership: $75/year. Associate membership: $170/year. Publishes *Graphic Artists Guild Handbook*, *Pricing and Ethical Guidelines* (members receive a copy as part of their membership). **Contact:** Patricia McKiernan, executive director.

HORROR WRITERS ASSOCIATION

244 5th Avenue, Suite 2767, New York NY 10001. E-mail: hwa@horror.org; membership@horror.org. Website: www.horror.org. Purpose of organization: To encourage public interest in horror and dark fantasy and to provide networking and career tools for members. Qualifications for membership: Complete membership rules online at www.horror.org/memrule.htm. At least one low-level sale is required to join as an affiliate. Non-writing professionals who can show income from a horror-related field may join as an associate (booksellers, editors, agents, librarians, etc.). To qualify for full active membership, you must be a published, professional writer of horror. Membership cost: $65 annually. Holds annual Stoker Awards Weekend and HWA Business Meeting. Publishes monthly newsletter focusing on market news, industry news, HWA business for members. Sponsors awards. We give the Bram Stoker Awards for superior achievement in horror annually. Awards include a handmade Stoker trophy designed by sculptor Stephen Kirk. Awards open to nonmembers. **Contact:** James Chambers, membership chair.

INTERNATIONAL READING ASSOCIATION

800 Barksdale Rd., P.O. Box 8139, Newark DE 19714. (302)731-1600 ext. 293. **Fax:** (302)731-1057. **E-mail:** councils@reading.org. **Website:** www.reading.org. Purpose of organization: "Formed in 1956, the International Reading Association seeks to promote high levels of literacy for all by improving the quality of reading instruction through studying the reading process and teaching techniques; serving as a clearinghouse for the dissemination of reading research through conferences, journals, and other publications; and actively encouraging the lifetime reading habit. Its goals include professional development, advocacy, partnerships, research, and global literacy development." **Open to students.** Sponsors annual convention. Publishes a newsletter called "Reading Today." Sponsors a number of awards and fellowships. Visit the IRA website for more information on membership, conventions and awards.

INTERNATIONAL WOMEN'S WRITING GUILD

P.O. Box 810, Gracie Station, New York NY 10028. (212)737-7536. **Fax:** (212)737-9469. **E-mail:** iwwg@iwwg.org; dirhahn@iwwg.org. **Website:** www.iwwg.org. IWWG is "a network for the personal and professional empowerment of women through writing." Qualifications: Open to any woman connected to the written word regardless of professional portfolio. Membership cost: $55/65 annually. "IWWG sponsors several annual conferences a year in all areas of the U.S. The major conference is held in June of each year at Yale University in New Haven, Connecticut. It is a week-long conference attracting 350 women internationally." Also publishes a 32-page newsletter, *Network*, 4 times/year; offers dental and vision insurance at group rates, referrals to literary agents. **Contact:** Hannelore Hahn, founder/executive editor.

☯ LEAGUE OF CANADIAN POETS

312-192 Spadina Ave., Toronto ON M5T 2C2Canada . (416)504-1657. **Fax:** (416)504-0096. **E-mail:** joanna@poets.ca. **Website:** www.poets.ca. The L.C.P. is a national organization of published Canadian poets. Our constitutional objectives are to advance poetry in Canada and to promote the professional interests of the members. Qualifications for membership: full—publication of at least 1 book of poetry by a professional publisher; associate membership—an active interest in poetry, demonstrated by several magazine/periodical publication credits; student—an active interest in poetry, 12 sample poems required; supporting—any friend of poetry. Membership fees: full—$175/year, associate—$60, student—$20, supporting—$100. Holds an Annual General Meeting every spring; some events open to nonmembers. "We also organize reading programs in schools and public venues. We publish a newsletter that includes information on poetry/poetics in Canada and beyond. Also publish the books *Poetry Markets for Canadians*; *Who's Who in the League of Canadian Poets*; *Poets in the Classroom* (teaching guide), and online publications. The Gerald Lampert Memorial Award for the best first book of poetry published in Canada in the preceding year and The Pat Lowther Memorial Award for the best book of poetry by a Canadian woman published in the preceding year. Deadline for awards: November 1. Visit www.poets.ca for more details. Sponsors youth poetry competition. Visit www.youngpoets.ca for details. **Contact:** Joanna Poblocka, executive director.

LITERARY MANAGERS AND DRAMATURGS OF THE AMERICAS

P.O. Box 36. 20985 P.A.C.C., New York NY 10129. (800)680-2148. **E-mail:** info@lmda.org. **Website:**

www.lmda.org. LMDA is a not-for-profit service organization for the professions of literary management and dramaturgy. Student Membership: $25/year. Open to students in dramaturgy, performing arts and literature programs, or related disciplines. Proof of student status required. Includes national conference, New Dramaturg activities, local symposia, job phone and select membership meetings. Active Membership: $60/year. Open to full-time and part-time professionals working in the fields of literary management and dramaturgy. All privileges and services including voting rights and eligibility for office. Institutional Membership: $200/year. Open to theaters, universities, and other organizations. Includes all privileges and services except voting rights and eligibility for office. Publishes a newsletter featuring articles on literary management, dramaturgy, LMDA program updates and other articles of interest. Spotlight sponsor membership $500/year; Open to theatres,universities, and other organizations; includes all priviledges for up to six individual members, plus additional promotional benefits.

THE NATIONAL LEAGUE OF AMERICAN PEN WOMEN

Pen Arts Building, 1300 17th St. N.W., Washington D.C. 20036-1973. (202)785-1997. **Fax:** (202)452-8868. **E-mail:** contact@nlapw.org. **Website:** www.americanpenwomen.org. Purpose of organization: to promote professional work in art, letters, and music since 1897. Qualifications for membership: An applicant must show "proof of sale" in each chosen category—art, letters, and music. Levels of membership include: Active, Associate, International Affiliate, Members-at-Large, Honorary Members (in one or more of the following classifications: Art, Letters, and Music). Holds workshops/conferences. Publishes magazine 4 times/year titled *The Pen Woman*. Sponsors various contests in areas of Art, Letters, and Music. Awards made at Biennial Convention. Biannual scholarships awarded to non-Pen Women for mature women. Awards include cash prizes—up to $1,000. Specialized contests open to nonmembers. **Contact:** Nina Brooks, corresponding secretary.

NATIONAL WRITERS ASSOCIATION

10904 S. Parker Rd., #508, Parker CO 80138. (303)841-0246. **Fax:** (303)841-2607. **E-mail:** natlwritersassn@hotmail.com. **Website:** www.nationalwriters.com. Purpose of organization: association for freelance writers. Qualifications for membership: associate membership—must be serious about writing; professional membership—must be published and paid writer (cite credentials). Membership cost: $65 associate; $85 professional; $35 student. Sponsors workshops/conferences: TV/screenwriting workshops, NWAF Annual Conferences, Literary Clearinghouse, editing and critiquing services, local chapters, National Writer's School. Open to non-members. Publishes industry news of interest to freelance writers; how-to articles; market information; member news and networking opportunities. Nonmember subscription: $20. Sponsors poetry contest; short story contest; article contest; novel contest. Awards cash for top 3 winners; books and/or certificates for other winners; honorable mention certificate places 5-10. Contests open to nonmembers.

NATIONAL WRITERS UNION

256 W. 38th St., Suite 703, New York NY 10018. (212)254-0279. **Fax:** (212)-254-0673. **E-mail:** nwu@nwu.org. **Website:** www.nwu.org. Purpose of organization: Advocacy for freelance writers. Qualifications for membership: "Membership in the NWU is open to all qualified writers, and no one shall be barred or in any manner prejudiced within the Union on account of race, age, sex, sexual orientation, disability, national origin, religion or ideology. You are eligible for membership if you have published a book, a play, three articles, five poems, one short story or an equivalent amount of newsletter, publicity, technical, commercial, government or institutional copy. You are also eligible for membership if you have written an equal amount of unpublished material and you are actively writing and attempting to publish your work." Membership cost: annual writing income less than $5,000-$120/year; $5,001-15,000-$195; $15,001-30,000-$265/year; $30,001-$45,000-$315 a year; $45,001- and up -$340/year. Holds workshops throughout the country. Members only section on website offers rich resources for freelance writers. Skilled contract advice and grievance help for members.

PEN AMERICAN CENTER

588 Broadway, Suite 303, New York NY 10012. (212)334-1660. **Fax:** (212)334-2181. **E-mail:** pen@pen.org. **Website:** www.pen.org. Purpose of organization: "An association of writers working to advance literature, to defend free expression, and to foster international literary fellowship." Qualifications for member-

ship: "The standard qualification for a writer to become a member of PEN is publication of two or more books of a literary character, or one book generally acclaimed to be of exceptional distinction. Also eligible for membership: editors who have demonstrated commitment to excellence in their profession (usually construed as five years' service in book editing); translators who have published at least two book-length literary translations; playwrights whose works have been produced professionally; and literary essayists whose publications are extensive even if they have not yet been issued as a book. Candidates for membership may be nominated by a PEN member or they may nominate themselves with the support of two references from the literary community or from a current PEN member. Membership dues are $100 per year and many PEN members contribute their time by serving on committees, conducting campaigns and writing letters in connection with freedom-of-expression cases, contributing to the PEN journal, participating in PEN public events, helping to bring literature into underserved communities, and judging PEN literary awards. PEN members receive a subscription to the PEN journal, the PEN Annual Report, and have access to medical insurance at group rates. Members living in the New York metropolitan and tri-state area, or near the Branches, are invited to PEN events throughout the year. Membership in PEN American Center includes reciprocal privileges in PEN American Center branches and in foreign PEN Centers for those traveling abroad. Application forms are available on the Web at www.pen.org. Associate Membership is open to everyone who supports PEN's mission, and your annual dues ($40; $20 for students) provides crucial support to PEN's programs. When you join as an Associate Member, not only will you receive a subscription to the *PEN Journal* http://pen.org/page.php/prmID/150 and notices of all PEN events but you are also invited to participate in the work of PEN. PEN American Center is the largest of the 141 centers of PEN International, the world's oldest human rights organization and the oldest international literary organization. PEN International was founded in 1921 to dispel national, ethnic, and racial hatreds and to promote understanding among all countries. PEN American Center, founded a year later, works to advance literature, to defend free expression, and to foster international literary fellowship. The Center has a membership of 3,400 distinguished writers, editors,

and translators. In addition to defending writers in prison or in danger of imprisonment for their work, PEN American Center sponsors public literary programs and forums on current issues, sends prominent authors to inner-city schools to encourage reading and writing, administers literary prizes, promotes international literature that might otherwise go unread in the United States, and offers grants and loans to writers facing financial or medical emergencies. In carrying out this work, PEN American Center builds upon the achievements of such dedicated past members as W.H. Auden, James Baldwin, Willa Cather, Robert Frost, Langston Hughes, Thomas Mann, Arthur Miller, Marianne Moore, Susan Sontag, and John Steinbeck. The Children's Book Authors' Committee sponsors annual public events focusing on the art of writing for children and young adults and on the diversity of literature for juvenile readers. The PEN/Phyllis Naylor Working Writer Fellowship was established in 2001 to assist a North American author of fiction for children or young adults (**E-mail:** awards@pen.org). Visit www.pen.org for complete information. Sponsors several competitions per year. Monetary awards range from $2,000-35,000.

PUPPETEERS OF AMERICA, INC.

26 Howard Ave., New Haven CT 06519. (888)568 6235. **E-mail:** membership@puppeteers.org. **Website:** www.puppeteers.org. Purpose of organization: to promote the art and appreciation of puppetry as a means of communications and as a performing art. The Puppeteers of America boasts an international membership. Qualifications for membership: interest in the art form. Membership cost: single adult, $55; seniors (65+) and youth members, (6-17 years of age), $35; full-time college student, $35; family, $75; couple, $65; senior couple, $55, Company, $90. Membership discounts to festivals and puppetry store purchases, access to the Audio Visual Library & Consultants in many areas of puppetry. The *Puppetry Journal*, a quarterly periodical, provides a color photo gallery, news about puppeteers, puppet theaters, exhibitions, touring companies, technical tips, new products, new books, films, television, and events sponsored by the Chartered Guilds in each of the 8 P of A regions. Includes *Playboard, The P of A Newsletter*; subsciption to the *Puppetry Journal* only, $40 (libraries/ institutions only). **Contact:** Fred Thompson, membership officer.

SCIENCE-FICTION AND FANTASY WRITERS OF AMERICA, INC.

P.O. Box 3238, Enfield CT 06083. **Website:** www.sfwa.org. Purpose of organization: to encourage public interest in science fiction literature and provide organization format for writers/editors/artists within the genre. Qualifications for membership: at least 1 professional sale or other professional involvement within the field. Membership cost: annual active dues—$70; affiliate—$55; one-time installation fee of $10; dues year begins July 1. Different levels of membership include: active—requires 3 professional short stories or 1 novel published; associate—requires 1 professional sale; or affiliate—which requires some other professional involvement such as artist, editor, librarian, bookseller, teacher, etc. Workshops/conferences: annual awards banquet, usually in April or May. Open to nonmembers. Publishes quarterly journal, the *SFWA Bulletin*. Nonmember subscription: $18/year in U.S. Sponsors Nebula Awards for best published science fiction or fantasy in the categories of novel, novella, novelette and short story. Awards trophy. Also presents the Damon Knight Memorial Grand Master Award for Lifetime Achievement, and, beginning in 2006, the Andre Norton Award for Outstanding Young Adult Science Fiction or Fantasy Book of the Year.

SOCIETY OFV CHILDREN'S BOOK WRITERS AND ILLUSTRATORS

8271 Beverly Blvd., Los Angeles CA 90048. (323)782-1010. **Fax:** (323)782-1892. **E-mail:** scbwi@scbwi.org. **Website:** www.scbwi.org. Purpose of organization: to assist writers and illustrators working or interested in the field. Qualifications for membership: an interest in children's literature and illustration. Membership cost: $70/year. Plus one time $85 initiation fee. Different levels of membership include: P.A.L. membership—published by publisher listed in SCBWI Market Surveys; full membership—published authors/illustrators (includes self-published); associate membership—unpublished writers/illustrators. Holds 100 events (workshops/conferences) worldwide each year. National Conference open to nonmembers. Publishes bi-monthly magazine on writing and illustrating children's books. Sponsors annual awards and grants for writers and illustrators who are members. **Contact:** Stephen Mooser, president; Lin Oliver, executive director.

SOCIETY OF ILLUSTRATORS

128 E. 63rd St., New York NY 10065. (212)838-2560. **Fax:** (212)838-2561. **E-mail:** info@societyillustrators.org. **Website:** www.societyillustrators.org. "Our mission is to promote the art and appreciation of illustration, its history and evolving nature through exhibitions, lectures and education." Annual dues for nonresident illustrator members (those living more than 125 air miles from SI's headquarters): $300. Dues for resident illustrator members: $500 per year; resident associate members: $500. "Artist members shall include those who make illustration their profession and earn at least 60% of their income from their illustration. Associate members are those who earn their living in the arts or who have made a substantial contribution to the art of illustration. This includes art directors, art buyers, creative supervisors, instructors, publishers and like categories. The candidate must complete and sign the application form, which requires a brief biography, a listing of schools attended, other training and a résumé of his or her professional career. Candidates for illustrators membership, in addition to the above requirements, must submit examples of their work." **Contact:** Anelle Miller, executive director.

SOCIETY OF MIDLAND AUTHORS

P.O. 10419, Chicago IL 60610. **Website:** www.midlandauthors.com. Purpose of organization: create closer association among writers of the Middle West; stimulate creative literary effort; maintain collection of members' works; encourage interest in reading and literature by cooperating with other educational and cultural agencies. Qualifications for membership: membership by invitation only. Must be author or co-author of a book demonstrating literary style and published by a recognized publisher and be identified through residence with Illinois, Indiana, Iowa, Kansas, Michigan, Minnesota, Missouri, Nebraska, North Dakota, Ohio, South Dakota or Wisconsin. **Open to students** (if authors). Membership cost: $35/year dues. Different levels of membership include: regular—published book authors; associate, nonvoting—not published as above but having some connection with literature, such as librarians, teachers, publishers and editors. Program meetings held 5 times a year, featuring authors, publishers, editors or the like individually or on panels. Usually second Tuesday of October, November, February, March and April. Also holds annual awards dinner in May. Publishes a newsletter focusing on news of members and general items of interest to writers. Sponsors contests. "Annual awards in six categories, given at annual dinner in May. Monetary awards for books published that premiered professionally in previous calendar year. Send SASE to contact person for details." Categories include adult fiction, adult nonfiction, juvenile fiction, juvenile nonfiction, poetry, biography. No picture books. Contest open to nonmembers. Deadline for contest: February 1. **Contact:** Robert Loerzel, president.

SOCIETY OF SOUTHWESTERN AUTHORS
Fax: (520)751-7877. **E-mail:** wporter202@aol.com. **Website:** www.ssa-az.org. Purpose of organization: to promote fellowship among professional and associate members of the writing profession, to recognize members' achievements, to stimulate further achievement, and to assist persons seeking to become professional writers. Qualifications for membership: Professional Membership: proof of publication of a book, articles, TV screenplay, etc. Associate Membership: proof of desire to write, and/or become a professional. Self-published authors may receive status of Professional Membership at the discretion of the board of directors. Membership cost: $30 initiation plus $30/year dues. The Society of Southwestern Authors sponsors an annual 2-day writers conference (all genres) held September 26-27; watch website ssa-az.org. SSA publishes a bimonthly newsletter, *The Write Word*, promoting members' published works, advice to fellow writers, and up-to-the-minute trends in publishing and marketing. Yearly writing contest open to all writers; short story, memoir, poetry, children's stories. Applications available in February—e-mail Mike Rom at Mike_Rom@hotmail.com; Subject Line: SSA Writer's Contest. **Contact:** Penny Porter.

○ TEXT & ACADEMIC AUTHORS ASSOCIATION (TAA)
P.O. Box 56359, St. Petersburg FL 33732. (727)563-0020. **E-mail:** richard.hull@taaonline.net; kim.pawlak@taaonline.net. **Website:** www.taaonline.net. TAA's overall mission is to enhance the quality of textbooks and other academic materials, such as journal articles, monographs and scholarly books, in all fields and disciplines. Qualifications for membership: all authors and prospective authors are welcome. Membership cost: $30 first year; graduated levels for following years. Workshops/conferences: June each year. Newsletter focuses on all areas of interest to textbook and academic authors. **Contact:** Richard T. Hall, executive director; Kim Pawlick, associate executive director.

THEATRE FOR YOUNG AUDIENCES/USA
c/o The Theatre School, 2135 N. Kenmore Ave., Chicago IL 60657. (773)325-7981. **Fax:** (773)325-7920. **E-mail:** info@tyausa.org. **Website:** www.assitej-usa.org. Purpose of organization: to promote theater for children and young people by linking professional theaters and artists together; sponsoring national, international and regional conferences and providing publications and information. Also serves as U.S. Center for International Association of the Theatre for Children and Young People. Different levels of memberships include: organizations, individuals, students, retirees, libraries. TYA Today includes original articles, reviews and works of criticism and theory, all of interest to theater practitioners (included with membership). Publishes *Marquee*, a directory that focuses on information on members in U.S.

VOLUNTEER LAWYERS FOR THE ARTS
1 E. 53rd St., 6th Floor, New York NY 10022. (212)319-2787, ext. 1. **Fax:** (212)752-6575. **E-mail:** vlany@vlany.org. **Website:** www.vlany.org. Purpose of organization: Volunteer Lawyers for the Arts is dedicated to providing free arts-related legal assistance to low-income artists and not-for-profit arts organizations in all creative fields. Over 1,000 attorneys in the New York area donate their time through VLA to artists and arts organizations unable to afford legal counsel. Everyone is welcome to use VLA's Art Law Line, a legal hotline for any artist or arts organization needing quick answers to arts-related questions. VLA also provides clinics, seminars and publications designed to educate artists on legal issues which affect their careers. Members receive discounts on publications and seminars as well as other benefits. Some of the many publications we carry are *All You Need to Know About the Music Business*; *Business and Legal Forms for Fine Artists, Photographers & Authors & Self-Publishers*; *Contracts for the Film & TV Industry*, plus many more.

WESTERN WRITERS OF AMERICA, INC.
1012 Mesa Vista Hall, MSCO6 3770, 1 University of NM, Albuquerque NM 87131. (505)277-5234. **E-mail:** wwa@unm.edu. **Website:** www.westernwriters.org. Open to students. Purpose of organization: to further all types of literature that pertains to the

American West. Membership requirements: must be a published author of Western material. Membership cost: $75/year ($90 foreign). Different levels of membership include: Active and Associate—the two vary upon number of books or articles published. Holds annual conference. The 2008 conference held in Scottsdale, AZ; 2009 held in Midwest City, Oklahoma. Publishes bimonthly magazine focusing on Western literature, market trends, bookreviews, news of members, etc. Nonmembers may subscribe for $30 ($50 foreign). Sponsors youth writing contests. Spur Awards given annually for a variety of types of writing. Awards include plaque, certificate, publicity. Contest and Spur Awards open to nonmembers. **Contact:** Candy Moulton, executive director; Rod Miller, membership.

☼ WRITERS' FEDERATION OF NEW BRUNSWICK

P.O. Box 306, Moncton NB E1C 8L4 Canada. (506)459-7228. **E-mail:** info@wfnb.ca. **Website:** www.wfnb.ca. Purpose of organization: "to promote New Brunswick writing and to help writers at all stages of their development." Qualifications for membership: interest in writing. Membership cost: $40, basic annual membership; $20, high school students; $45, family membership; $50, institutional membership; $100, sustaining member; $250, patron; and $1,000, lifetime member. Holds workshops/conferences. Publishes a newsletter with articles concerning the craft of writing, member news, contests, markets, workshops and conference listings. Sponsors annual literary competition, $15 entry fee for members, $20 for nonmembers. Categories: fiction, nonfiction, poetry, children's literature—3 prizes per category of $150, $75, $50; Alfred Bailey Prize of $400 for poetry ms; The Richards Prize of $400 for short novel, collection of short stories or section of long novel; The Sheree Fitch Prize for writing by young people (14-18 years of age). Contest open to nonmembers (residents of Canada only). **Contact:** Lee Thompson, executive director.

☼ WRITERS' FEDERATION OF NOVA SCOTIA

1113 Marginal Rd., Halifax NS B3H 4P7 Canada. (902)423-8116. **Fax:** (902)422-0881. **E-mail:** talk@ writers.ns.ca. **Website:** www.writers.ns.ca. Purpose of organization: "to foster creative writing and the profession of writing in Nova Scotia; to provide advice and assistance to writers at all stages of their careers; and to encourage greater public recognition of Nova Scotian writers and their achievements." Regional organization open to anybody who writes. Currently has 800+ members. Levels of membership/dues: $45 CAD annually ($20 CAD students). Offerings include resource library with over 2,500 titles, promotional services, workshop series, annual festivals, mentorship program. Publishes *Eastword*, a bimonthly newsletter containing "a plethora of information on who's doing what; markets and contests; and current writing events and issues." Members and nationally known writers give readings that are open to the public. Additional information available on website.

☼ WRITERS GUILD OF ALBERTA

11759 Groat Rd., Edmonton AB T5M 3K6 Canada. (780)422-8174. **Fax:** (780)422-2663. **E-mail:** mail@ writersguild.ab.ca. **Website:** www.writersguild. ab.ca. Purpose of organization: to support, encourage and promote writers and writing, to safeguard the freedom to write and to read, and to advocate for the well-being of writers in Alberta. Currently has over 1,000 members. Offerings include retreats/conferences; monthly events; bimonthly magazine that includes articles on writing and a market section; weekly electronic bulletin with markets and event listings; and the Stephan G. Stephansson Award for Poetry (Alberta residents only). Membership cost: $60/year; $30 for seniors/students. Holds workshops/conferences. Publishes a newsletter focusing on markets, competitions, contemporary issues related to the literary arts (writing, publishing, censorship, royalties etc.). Sponsors annual Literary Awards in five categories (novel, nonfiction, children's literature, poetry, drama). Awards include $1,500, leather-bound book, promotion and publicity. Open to nonmembers.

CONFERENCES & WORKSHOPS

Writers and illustrators eager to expand their knowledge of the children's publishing industry should consider attending one of the many conferences and workshops held each year. Whether you're a novice or seasoned professional, conferences and workshops are great places to pick up information on a variety of topics and network with experts in the publishing industry, as well as with your peers.

Listings in this section provide details about what conference and workshop courses are offered, where and when they are held, and the costs. Some of the national writing and art organizations also offer regional workshops throughout the year. Write, call or visit websites for information.

Writers can find listings of more than 1,000 conferences (searchable by type, location, and date) at The Writer's Digest/Shaw Guides Directory to Writers' Conferences, Seminars, and Workshop—writersdigest.com/conferences.

Members of the Society of Children's Book Writers and Illustrators can find information on conferences in national and local SCBWI newsletters. Nonmembers may attend SCBWI events as well. SCBWI conferences are listed in the beginning of this section under a separate subheading. For information on SCBWI's annual national conferences, contact them at (323)782-1010 or check their website for a complete calendar of national and regional events (scbwi.org).

CONFERENCES & WORKSHOPS CALENDAR

To help you plan your conference travel, here is a month-by-month calendar of all the conferences, workshops and retreats included in this section. The calendar lists conferences alphabetically by the month in which they occur.

January

Butler University Children's Literature Conference (Indianapolis IN)

Kindling Words East (Burlington VT)

San Diego State University Writers' Conference (San Diego CA)

SCBWI—Florida Regional Conference (Miami FL)

South Coast Writers Conference (Gold Beach OR)

Winter Poetry & Prose Getaway in Cape May (Cape May NJ)

February

San Francisco Writers Conference (San Francisco CA)

SCBWI; Annual Conference on Writing and Illustrating for Children (New York NY)

SCBWI—Norca (San Francisco/South); Retreat at Asilomar (Pacific Grove CA)

SCBWI—Southern Breeze; Spring Mingle (Atlanta GA)

South Coast Writers Conference (Gold Beach OR)

March

Florida Christian Writers Conference (Bradenton FL)

Kentucky Writer's Workshop (Pineville KY)

Perspectives in Children's Literature Conference (Amherst MA)

SCBWI Bologna Biennial Conference & SCBWI Showcase Booth at the Bologna Children's Book Fair (Bologna, Italy)

SCBWI—Utah; Forum on Children's Literature (Orem UT)

Virginia Festival of the Book (Charlottesville VA)

Whidbey Island Writers' Conference (Langley WA)

Tennessee Williams/New Orleans Literary Festival (New Orleans LA)

April

AEC Conference on Southern Literature (Chattanooga TN)

Central Ohio Writers of Literature for Children (Columbus OH)

Children's Literature Conference (Hempstead NY)

Festival of Children's Literature (Minneapolis MN)

Festival of Faith and Writing (Grand Rapids MI)

Missouri Writers' Guild Annual State Conference (St. Charles MO)

Mount Hermon Christian Writers Conference (Mount Hermon CA)

SCBWI New Mexico Handsprings: A Conference for Children's Writers and Illustrators (Albuquerque NM)

Writer's Digest Conference East (New York, NY; writersdigestconference.com)

May

Annual Spring Poetry Festival (New York NY)

BookExpo America/Writer's Digest Books Writers Conference (New York NY)

Kindling Words West (Abiquiu NM)

Oklahoma Writers' Federation, Inc. Annual Conference (Oklahoma City OK)

Pima Writers' Workshop (Tucson AZ)

June

Aspen Summer Words Writing Retreat (Aspen CO)

"Books in Progress" Conference: The Carnegie Literacy Center (Lexington, KY)

East Texas Christian Writers Conference (Marshall TX)

The Environmental Writers' Conference and Workshop in Honor of Rachel Carson (Boothbay Harbor ME)

Great Lakes Writers Conference (Milwaukee WI)

Highland Summer Conference (Radford VA)

International Creative Writing Camp (Minot ND)

Iowa Summer Writing Festival (Iowa City IA)

Jackson Hole Writers Conference (Jackson Hole, WY)

Manhattanville Summer Writers' Week (Purchase NY)

Outdoor Writers Association of America Annual Conference (Lake Charles LA)

SCBWI—Florida Mid-Year Writing Workshop (Orlando FL)

SCBWI—New Jersey; Annual Spring Conference (Princeton NJ)

Southeastern Writer's Association—Annual Writer's Workshop (Athens GA)

UMKC/Writers Place Writers Workshops (Kansas City MO)

Wesleyan Writers Conference (Middleton CT)

Write! Canada (Guelph ON Canada)

Write-by-the-Lake Writer's Workshop & Retreat (Madison WI)

Write to Publish Conference (Wheaton IL)

Writers League of Texas: Agents & Editors Conference (Austin, TX)

Writers Retreat Workshop (Erlanger KY)

July

Children's Book Workshop at Castle Hill (Truro MA)

Conference for Writers & Illustrators of Children's Books (Corte Madera CA)

Highlights Foundation Writers Workshop at Chautauqua (Chautauqua NY)

Hofstra University Summer Workshop (Hempstead NY)

Maritime Writers' Workshop (Fredericton NB Canada)

Midwest Writers Workshop (Muncie IN)

Montrose Christian Writer's Conference (Montrose PA)

Pacific Northwest Children's Book Conference (Portland OR)

Pacific Northwest Writer Assn. Summer Writer's Conference (Seattle WA)

Robert Quackenbush's Children's Book Writing and Illustrating Workshop (New York NY)

Sage Hill Writing Experience (Saskatoon SK Canada)

Saskatchewan Festival of Words and Workshops (Moose Jaw SK Canada)

Steamboat Springs Writers Conference (Steamboat Springs CO)

The Victoria School of Writing (Victoria BC Canada)

August

Cape Cod Writer's Conference (Cape Cod MA)

The Columbus Writers Conference (Columbus OH)

Green Lake Writers Conference (Green Lake WI)

The Manuscript Workshop in Vermont (Londonderry VT)

Moondance International Film Festival (Hollywood CA)

The Pacific Coast Children's Writer's Workshop (Aptos CA)

SCBWI; Annual Conference on Writing and Illustrating for Children (Los Angeles CA)

Willamette Writers Annual Writers Conference (Portland OR)

September

League of Utah Writers' Roundup (Ogden UT)

Maui Writers Conference (Kihei HI)

SCBWI—Carolinas; Annual Fall Conference (Durham NC)

SCBWI—Eastern Pennsylvania; Fall Philly Conference (Exton PA)

SCBWI—Idaho; Editor Day (Boise ID)

SCBWI—Midsouth Fall Conference (Nashville TN)

SCBWI—Northern Ohio; Annual Conference (Cleveland OH)

SCBWI—Rocky Mountain Events (Lakewood CO)

Society of Southwestern Authors' Wrangling with Writing (Tucson AZ)

South Coast Writers Conference (Gold Beach CO)

Writer's Digest Conference West (Los Angeles, CA; writersdigestconference.com)

October

Flathead River Writers Conference (Whitefish MT)

Ozark Creative Writers, Inc. Conference (Eureka Springs AR)

SCBWI—Iowa Conference (Iowa City IA)

SCBWI—Midatlantic; Annual Fall Conference (Arlington VA)

SCBWI—Oregon Conferences (Portland OR)

SCBWI—Southern Breeze; Writing and Illustrating for Kids (Birmingham AL)
SCBWI—Ventura/Santa Barbara; Fall Conference (Thousand Oaks CA)
SCBWI—Wisconsin; Fall Retreat for Working Writers (Milton WI)
Surrey International Writer's Conference (Surrey BC Canada)
Vancouver Internatinoal Writers Festival (Vancouver BC Canada)
Write on the Sound Writers Conference (Edmonds WA)

November
Jewish Children's Book Writers' Conference (New York NY)
LaJolla Writers Conference (LaJolla CA)
North Carolina Writers' Network Fall Conference (Durham NC)
SCBWI—Illinois; Prairie Writers Day SCBWI—Missouri; Children's Writer's Conference (St. Peters MO)

December
Big Sur Writing Workshop (Big Sur CA)

Multiple or Seasonal Events
The conference listings below include information on multiple or year-round events or events that are seasonal (held in fall or spring, for example). Please read the listings for more information on the dates and locations of these events and check the conferences' websites.

American Christian Writers Conference
Booming Ground Online Writers Studio
Cat Writers' Association Annual Writers Conference
Children's Authors' Bootcamp
Peter Davidson's How to Write a Children's Picture Book Seminar
The DIY Book Festival
Duke University Youth Programs: Creative Writers' Workshop
Duke University Youth Programs: Young Writers' Camp
Gotham Writers' Workshop (New York NY)
Highlights Foundation Founders Workshops (Honesdale PA)
Iowa Summer Writing Festival (Iowa City IA)
The Manuscript Workshop in Vermont (Londonderry VT)
Publishinggame.com Workshop
SCBWI—Arizona; Events
SCBWI—Eastern Canada; Annual Events
SCBWI—Dakotas
SCBWI—Idaho; Editor Day

SCBWI—Iowa Conferences

SCBWI—Los Angeles; Events

SCBWI—Metro New York; Professional Series (New York NY)

SCBWI—New Jersey; First Page Sessions (Princeton NJ)

SCBWI—Oregon Conferences

SCBWI—Pocono Mountains Retreat (Sterling PA)

SCBWI—Taiwan; Events

SCBWI—Ventura/Santa Barbara; Retreat for Children's Authors and Illustrators (Santa Barbara CA)

SCBWI—Western Washington State; Retreats & Conference

Southwest Writers Conferences

Split Rock Arts Program (St. Paul MN)

Sydney Children's Writers and Illustrators Network (Woollahra NSW Australia)

UMKC/Writers Place Writers Workshops (Kansas City MO)

Writers' League of Texas Workshop Series (Austin TX)

The Writers' Retreat Writing Workshop at Castle Hill

SCBWI; ANNUAL CONFERENCES ON WRITING AND ILLUSTRATING FOR CHILDREN

Website: www.scbwi.org. **Contact:** Lin Oliver, conference director. Writer and illustrator workshops geared toward all levels. **Open to students.** Covers all aspects of children's book and magazine publishing—the novel, illustration techniques, marketing, etc. Annual conferences held in August in Los Angeles and in New York in February. Cost of conference (LA): approximately $390; includes all 4 days and one banquet meal. Write for more information or visit website.

SCBWI—ARIZONA; EVENTS

P.O. Box 26384, Scottsdale AZ 85255-0123. **E-mail:** RegionalAdvisor@scbwi-az.org. **Website:** www.scbwi-az.org. **Contact:** Michelle Parker-Rock, regional advisor. SCBWI Arizona will offer a variety of workshops, retreats, intensives, conferences, meetings and other craft and industry related events throughout 2011-2012. Open to members and nonmembers, published and nonpublished. Registration to major events is usually limited. Pre-registration always required. Visit website, write, or e-mail for more information.

SCBWI BOLOGNA BIENNIAL CONFERENCE

E-mail: Angela@SCBWIBologna.org; Kathleen@SCBWIBologna.org. **Website:** www.scbwi.org. The SCBWI Showcase Booth at the Bologna Book Fair: The next SCBWI Showcase Booth will take place during the 2012 Bologna Book Fair. It will feature authors and illustrators from SCBWI regions, SCBWI PAL members, and special author and illustrator events.

SCBWI—CANADA EAST

E-mail: araeast@scbwicanada.org; raeast@scbwicanada.org. **Website:** www.scbwicanada.org/east. **Contact:** Lizann Flatt, regional advisor. Writer and illustrator events geared toward all levels. Usually offers one event in spring and another in the fall. Check website Events pages for updated information.

SCBWI COLORADO/WYOMING (ROCKY MOUNTAIN); EVENTS

E-mail: denise@rmcscbwi.org; todd.tuell@rmcscbwi.org. **Website:** www.rmcscbwi.org. **Contact:** Todd Tuell and Denise Vega, co-regional advisors. SCBWI Rocky Mountain chapter (CO/WY) offers special events, schmoozes, meetings, and conferences throughout the year. Major events: Fall Conference (annually, September); Summer Retreat, "Big Sur in the Rockies" (bi- and triannually). More info on website.

SCBWI—DAKOTAS; SPRING CONFERENCE

2521 S 40th St., Grand Forks ND 58201. **E-mail:** cdrylander@yahoo.com. **Website:** www.dakotas-scbwi.org. **Contact:** Chris Rylander, regional advisor. This is a conference for writers and illustrators of all levels. Previous conferences have included speakers Tim Gilner, S.T. Underdahl, Roxane Salonen, and Marilyn Kratz. Annual event held every spring. Check website for details.

SCBWI—DAKOTAS; WRITERS CONFERENCE IN CHILDREN'S LITERATURE

Grand Forks ND 58201. (701)720-0464. **E-mail:** cdrylaner@yahoo.com. **Website:** www.dakotas-scbwi.org. **Contact:** Chris Rylander, regional advisor. Conference sessions geared toward all levels. "Although the conference attendees are mostly writers, we encourage and welcome illustrators of every level." Open to students. "Our conference offers 3-4 children's authors, editors, publishers, illustrators, or agents. Past conferences have included Kent Brown (publisher, Boyds Mills Press); Alexandra Penfold (editor, Simon & Schuster); Jane Kurtz (author); Anastasia Suen (author); and Karen Ritz (illustrator). Conference held each fall. "Please call or e-mail to confirm dates. Writers and illustrators come from throughout the northern plains, including North Dakota, South Dakota, Montana, Minnesota, Iowa, and Canada." Writing facilities available: campus of University of North Dakota. Local art exhibits and/or concerts may coincide with conference. Cost of conference includes Friday evening reception and sessions, Saturday's sessions, and lunch. A manuscript may be submitted 1 month in advance for critique (extra charge). E-mail for more information.

SCBWI—DAKOTAS/UND WRITERS CONFERENCE IN CHILDREN'S LITERATURE

Dept. of English, Merrifield Hall, Room 110, 276 Centennial Drive Stop 7209, UND, Grand Forks ND 58202. (701)777-3321; (710)777-3984. **E-mail:** cdrylander@yahoo.com. **Website:** www.dakotas-scbwi.org. **Contact:** Chris Rylander, regional advisor. Con-

CONFERENCES

ference for all levels. "Our conference offers 3-4 children's authors, editors, publishers, illustrators or agents. Past conferences have included Elaine Marie Alphin (author), Jane Kurtz (author), Alexandra Penfold (editor), Kent Brown (publisher), and Karen Ritz (illustrator)." Annual conference held every fall. "Please call or e-mail to confirm dates." Cost of conference to be determined. Cost included Friday evening sessions, Saturday sessions, and Saturday lunch. "We welcome writers, illustrators, and others who are interested in children's literature."

SCBWI—EASTERN PENNSYLVANIA

Website: www.scbwiepa.org. This event is hosted by three regions, Eastern PA, Western PA and MD/DE/VA region. This is a first time event that has the large conference opportunities with small retreat appeal. Watch website for more details, www.scbwiepa.org.

SCBWI—FLORIDA; MID-YEAR WRITING WORKSHOP

12973 SW 112 Ct., Miami FL 33186. (305)382-2677. **E-mail:** lindabernfeld@gmail.com. **Website:** www.scbwiflorida.com. **Contact:** Linda Bernfeld, regional advisor. Annual workshop held in June in Orlando. Workshop is geared toward helping everyone hone their writing skills. Attendees choose one track and spend the day with industry leaders who share valuable information about that area of children's book writing. There are a minimum of 3 tracks, picture book, middle grade and young adult. The 4th and 5th tracks are variable, covering subjects such as poetry, nonfiction, humor or writing for magazines. E-mail for more information.

SCBWI—FLORIDA; REGIONAL CONFERENCE

12973 SW 112 Ct., Miami FL 33186. (305)382-2677. **E-mail:** lindabernfeld@gmail.com. **Contact:** Linda Bernfeld, regional advisor. Annual conference held in January in Miami. Past keynote speakers have included Linda Sue Park, Richard Peck, Bruce Coville, Bruce Hale, Arthur A. Levine, Judy Blume, Kate Dicamillo. Cost of conference: approximately $225. The 3-day conference will have workshops Friday afternoon and a field trip to Books and Books Friday evening.

BOISE REGIONAL CONFERENCE FOR UTAH/SOUTHERN IDAHO SCBWI

E-mail: neysajensen@msn.com. Email: neysajensen@msn.com. One day workshop focuses on the craft of writing, as well as getting to know an editor. One-on-one critiques available for an additional fee. Event held in Boise, Idaho every spring. **Contact:** Sydney Husseman, Regional Advisor; Neysa Jensen, Assis. Regional Advisor. "One day workshop focuses on the craft of writing, as well as getting to know an editor. One-on-one critiques available for an additional fee. Event held in Boise, Idaho every spring."

SCBWI—ILLINOIS; PRAIRIE WRITERS DAY

E-mail: biermanlisa@hotmail.com. **Website:** www.scbwi-illinois.org. **Contact:** Lisa Bierman, regional advisor. Full day of guest speakers, editors/agents TBD. Ms critiques available as well as break-out sessions on career and craft. See website for complete description.

SCBWI—IOWA CONFERENCES

P.O. Box 1436, Bettendorf IA 52722-0024. **E-mail:** hecklit@aol.com. **Website:** www.scbwi-iowa.org/. **Contact:** Connie Heckert, regional advisor. Writer and illustrator workshops in all genres of children writing. The Iowa Region offers conferences of high quality events usually over a three-day period with registration options. Recent speakers included Allyn Johnston, Marla Frazee, Julie Romeis, Samantha McFerrin, Scott Treimel. Holds spring and fall events on a regional level, and network events across that state. Individual critiques and portfolio review offerings vary with the program and presenters. For more information e-mail or visit website.

SCBWI—LOS ANGELES; EVENTS

P.O. Box 1728, Pacific Palisades CA 90272. (310)573-7318. **Website:** www.scbwisocal.org. **Contact:** Sarah Laurenson, co-regional advisor; Edie Pagliasotti, co-regional advisor. SCBWI—Los Angeles hosts 6 major events each year: **Writer's Workshop** (winter)—half-day workshop featuring speaker demonstrating nuts and bolts techniques on the craft of writing for childrens; **Writer's Day** (spring)—a one-day conference featuring speakers, a professional forum, writing contests and awards; **Critiquenic** (summer)—a free informal critiquing session for writers and illustrators facilitated by published authors/illustrators, held after a picnic lunch; **Writers & Illustrator's Sunday Field Trip** (fall)—hands-on creative field trip for writers and illustrators; **Working Writer's Retreat** (fall)—a 3-day, 2-night retreat featuring an editor/agent, speakers, and intensive critiquing. **Illustrator's Day** (winter)— A one-day conference featuring speakers, juried art competition, contests, portfolio review/display. See calendar of events on website for more details and dates.

SCBWI—METRO NEW YORK; PROFESSIONAL SERIES

P.O. Box 1475, Cooper Station, New York NY 10276. (212)545-3719. **E-mail:** scbwi_metrony@yahoo.com. **Website:** http://metro.nyscbwi.org. **Contact:** Seta Toroyan, regional advisor. Writer and illustrator workshops geared toward all levels. The Metro New York Professional Series generally meets the second Tuesday of each month, from September to June, 7:30-9:30 p.m. Check website to confirm location, dates, times, and speakers. Cost of workshop: $15 for SCBWI members; $20 for nonmembers. "We feature an informal evening with coffee, cookies, and top editors, art directors, agents, publicity and marketing people, librarians, reviewers and more."

SCBWI—MICHIGAN; CONFERENCES

Website: www.Kidsbooklink.org. **Contact:** Monica Harris, co regional advisor; Leslia Helakoski, co-regional advisor. One-day conference held in April/May and 3-day fall conference held in September. Workshops periodically. Speakers TBA. See website for details on all upcoming events.

SCBWI—MIDATLANTIC; ANNUAL FALL CONFERENCE

P.O. Box 3215, Reston VA 20195. **E-mail:** scbwimidatlantic@gmail.com. **Website:** www.SCBWI-MidAtlantic.org. **Contact:** Sydney Dunlap and Erin Teagan, conference co-chairs; Ellen Braaf, regional advisor. For updates and details visit website. Registration limited to 200. Conference fills quickly. Cost: $115 for SCBWI members; $145 for nonmembers. Includes continental breakfast. Lunch is on your own. (The food court at the Ballston Common Mall is two blocks away.)

SCBWI—MIDSOUTH FALL CONFERENCE

P.O. Box 396, Cordova TN 38088. **E-mail:** expressdog@bellsouth.net; cameron_s_e@yahoo.com. **Website:** www.scbwi-midsouth.org. **Contact:** Genetta Adair and Sharon Cameron, conference coordinators. Conference for writers and illustrators of all experience. 2011 conference will be held September 17-18 in Nashville. In the past, workshops were offered on Plotting Your Novel, Understanding the Language of Editors, Landing an Agent, How to Prepare a Portfolio, Negotiating a Contract, The Basics for Beginners, and many others. Attendees are invited to bring a manuscript and/or art portfolio to share in the optional, no-charge critique group session. Illustrators are invited to bring color copies of their art (not originals) to be displayed in the illustrators' showcase. For an additional fee, attendees may schedule a 15-minute manuscript critique or portfolio critique by the editor, art director or other expert consultant. Annual conference held in September. Registration limited to 130 attendees. Cost to be determined. The 2010 Midsouth Fall Conference included Balzer & Bray editor Ruta Rimas; nonfiction book pakager and editor Lionel Bender from London, England; Andrea Brown agent Kelly Sonnack; ICM agent Tina Wexler; award-winning author Linda Sue Park and more.

SCBWI—MISSOURI; CHILDREN'S WRITER'S CONFERENCE

P.O. Box 76975, 103 CEAC, St. Peters MO 63376-0975. (636)922-8233. **Website:** www.moscbwi.org. **Contact:** Stephanie Bearce, regional advisor. **Open to students.** Speakers include editors, writers, agents, and other professionals. Topics vary from year to year, but each conference offers sessions for both writers and illustrators as well as for newcomers and published writers. Previous topics included: "What Happens When Your Manuscript is Accepted" by Dawn Weinstock, editor; "Writing—Hobby or Vocation?" by Chris Kelleher; "Mother Time Gives Advice: Perspectives from a 25 Year Veteran" by Judith Mathews, editor; "Don't Be a Starving Writer" by Vicki Berger Erwin, author; and "Words & Pictures: History in the Making," by author-illustrator Cheryl Harness. Annual conference held in early November. For exact date, see SCBWI **Website:** www.scbwi.org or the events page of the Missouri SCBWI website. Registration limited to 75-90. Cost of conference includes one day workshop (8 a.m. to 5 p.m.) plus lunch. Write for more information.

SCBWI—NEW ENGLAND; ANNUAL CONFERENCE

Nashua NH 03063. **E-mail:** northernnera@scbwi.org. **Website:** www.nescbwi.org. **Contact:** Anna Boll, regional advisor. Conference is for all levels of writers and illustrators. **Open to students.** "We offer many workshops at each conference, and often there is a multi-day format. Examples of subjects addressed: manuscript development, revision, marketing your work, productive school visits, picture book dummy formatting, adding texture to your illustrations, etc." Annual conference held in mid-May. Registration

CONFERENCES

limited to 450. Cost: TBD; includes pre-conference social, great keynote speaker, many workshop options, lunch, snacks, etc. Keynote speaker for 2008 conference was Laurie Halse Anderson. "Details (additional speakers, theme, number of workshop choices, etc.) will be posted to our website as they become available. Registration will not start until March. Opportunities for one-on-one manuscript critiques and portfolio reviews will be available at the conference."

SCBWI–NEW JERSEY; ANNUAL SPRING CONFERENCE

E-mail: njscbwi@newjerseyscbwi.com. **Website:** www.newjerseyscbwi.com. **Contact:** Kathy Temean, regional advisor. This two-day conference is always held the first weekend in June in Princeton, NJ. "How to" workshops, first page sessions, agent pitches, one-on-one critiques, consultations, portolio reviews, mix and mingle, group critiques, contests, interaction with the faculty of editors, agents, art director and authors are some of the highlights of the weekend. Published authors and illustrators attending the conference are invited to do a book signing and sell their books on Saturday afternoon. Illustrators have the opportunity to exhibit their artwork and display their portolio throughout the conference. Meals are included with the cost of admission. Illustrator and writing craft workshops held before conference for additional cost. Conference is known for its high ratio of faculty to attendees.

SCBWI–NEW JERSEY; ANNUAL SUMMER CONFERENCE

SCBWI-New Jersey: Society of Children's Book Writers & Illustrators, **Website:** www.newjerseyscbwi.com. **Contact:** Kathy Temean, regional advisor. This weekend conference is held in the beginning of June in Princeton, NJ. Multiple one-on-one critiques; "how to" workshops for every level, first page sessions, agent pitches and interaction with the faculty of editors, agents, art director and authors are some of the highlights of the weekend. On Friday attendees can sign up for writing intensives or register for illustrators' day with the art directors. Published authors attending the conference can sign up to participate in the bookfair to sell and autograph their books; illustrators have the opportunity to display their artwork. Attendees have the option to participate in group critiques after dinner on Saturday evening and attend a mix and mingle with the faculty on Friday night. Meals are

included with the cost of admission. Conference is known for its high ratio of faculty to attendees and interaction opportunities.

SCBWI–NEW JERSEY; FIRST PAGE SESSIONS

E-mail: njscbwi@newjerseyscbwi.com; kathy@newjerseyscbwi.com; laurie@newjerseyscbwi.com. **Website:** www.newjerseyscbwi.com. Held 4 times a year in Princeton, NJ. Two editors/agents give their first impression of a first page and let participants know if they would read more. These sessions are held late afternoon during the week and are limited to 30 people. Attendees can choose to have dinner with the editors after the session. Please visit www.newjerseyscbwi.com for more information.

SCBWI–NEW JERSEY; MENTORING WORKSHOPS

Website: www.newjerseyscbwi.com. **Contact:** Kathy Temean, regional advisor. These workshops have become very popular and fill quickly. Workshops provide an inspiring environment for writers to work on their manuscript and have personal contact with their mentor/editor. Each workshop consists of 14 writers and two editors or 28 people and 4 editors. Weekend workshops allow writers to spend 45 minutes, one-on-one, with their mentor to discuss their manuscript and career direction, first-page critiques, pitch sessions and other fun writing activities. One-day workshops consist of 20-minute, one-on-one critiques and Q&A session, plus first-page critiques. These workshops are held in the winter, spring, and fall each year Princeton, New Jersey. Please visit www.newjerseyscbwi.com for more information.

SCBWI–NEW MEXICO; HANDSPRINGS: A CONFERENCE FOR CHILDREN'S WRITERS AND ILLUSTRATORS

PO Box 1084, Socorro NM **E-mail:** handsprings@scbwi-nm.org. **Website:** www.scbwi-nm.org. **Contact:** Lois Bradley, registrar; Chris Eboch, regional advisor. Conference for beginner and intermediate writers and illustrators. "The 2011 conference features four keynote speakers—editors, agents, art directors and/or illustrators and authors. 2011 speakers will lead 2½ hour intensive, craft-based workshops. Annual conference held in October 8, 2011. Registration limited to 100. "Offers intensive craft-based workshops and large-group presentations." Cost: $110-150 for basic Saturday registration dependent on registration; $40-

50 for private critiques (lowest prices are for SCBWI members). "The Friday evening party included social time and mini book launches. Saturday features a full day of keynote speeches by visiting editors, agents and/or art directors; breakout workshops on the craft and business of writing; and optional written critiques with the editors or written portfolio review by the art director."

SCBWI–NORCA (SAN FRANCISCO/ SOUTH); GOLDEN GATE CONFERENCE AT ASILOMAR

Website: www.scbwisf.org. **Contact:** Amy Laughlin and Kristin Howell, co-regional advisors. "We welcome published and 'not-yet-published' writers and illustrators. Lectures and workshops are geared toward professionals and those striving to become professional. Program topics cover aspects of writing or illustrating, and marketing, from picture books to young adult novels. Past speakers include editors, agents, art directors, Newbery Award-winning authors, and Caldecott Award-winning illustrators. Annual conference, generally held third or fourth weekend in February; Friday evening through Sunday lunch. Registration limited to approximately 140. Manuscript or portfolio review available. Most rooms shared with one other person. Additional charge for single when available. Desks available in most rooms. All rooms have private baths. Conference center is set in wooded campus on Asilomar Beach in Pacific Grove, California. Approximate cost: $465 for SCBWI members, $610 for nonmembers; includes shared room, 6 meals and all conference activities. Vegetarian meals available. Coming together for shared meals and activities builds a strong feeling of community among the speakers and conferees. Scholarships available to SCBWI members. Registration opens end of October/November. For more information, including exact costs and dates, visit our website."

SCBWI–NORTHERN OHIO; ANNUAL CONFERENCE

Website: www.nohscbwi.org. **Contact:** Victoria A. Selvaggio, regional advisor. Northern Ohio's conference is crafted for all levels of writers and illustrators of children's literature. The dates for the 2011 conference are September 23 and 24. "Our annual event will be held at the Sheraton Cleveland Airport Hotel. Conference costs will be posted on our website with registration information. SCBWI members receive a dis-

count. Additional fees apply for late registration, critiques, or portfolio reviews. Cost includes an optional Friday evening Opening Banquet from 6-10 p.m. with a keynote speaker; Saturday event from 8:30 a.m. to 5 p.m. which includes breakfast snack, full-day conference with headliner presentations, general sessions, breakout workshops, lunch, panel discussion, bookstore, and autograph session. The Illustrator Showcase is open to all attendees at no additional cost. Grand door prize drawn at the end of the day Saturday, is free admission to the following year's conference. Further information, including Headliner Speakers will be posted on our website. All questions can be directed to vselvaggio@windstream.net."

SCBWI–OREGON CONFERENCES

E-mail: robink@scbwior.com. **Website:** www.scbwior.com. **Contact:** Robin Koontz, regional advisor. Writer and illustrator workshops and presentations geared toward all levels. "We invite editors, art directors, agents, attorneys, authors, illustrators and others in the business of writing and illustrating for children. Faculty members offer craft presentations, workshops, first-page sessions and individual critiques as well as informal networking opportunities. Critique group network opportunities for local group meetings and regional retreats; see website for details. Two main events per year: Writers and Illustrators Retreat: held near Portland Thurs-Sun the 2nd weekend in October. Cost of retreat: $355 plus $35.00 critique fee includes double occupancy and all meals; Spring Conference: Held in the Portland area (2 day event the third Fri-Sat in May (one-day attendance is permitted); cost for presentations and workshops: about $150 includes continental breakfast and lunch on Saturday, critique fee $35-attendees only; Friday: intensive sessions cost about $100 for the day with professional tracks in writing and illustrating. Registration limited to 300 for the conference and 55 for the retreat. SCBWI Oregon is a regional chapter of the Society of Children's Book Writers and Illustrators. SCBWI Members receive a discount for all events. Oregon and South Washington members get preference.

SCBWI–POCONO MOUNTAINS RETREAT

Website: www.scbwiepa.org. Held in the spring at Shawnee Inn, Shawnee on the Delaware, PA. Faculty addresses craft, web design, school visits, writing, illustration and publishing. Registration limited to 150. Cost of retreat: tuition $140, meals, room and board averages $250 for the weekend. For information, online registration and brochure, visit website.

SCBWI—SAN DIEGO; CHAPTER MEETINGS & WORKSHOPS

San Diego CA 92127. **E-mail:** ra-sd@sandiego-scbwi. org. **Website:** www.sandiego-scbwi.org. **Contact:** Janice M. Yuwiler, regional advisor. Writer and illustrator meetings and workshops geared toward all levels. Topics vary but emphasize writing and illustrating for children. Check website, e-mail or call (619)713-5462 for more information. "The San Diego chapter holds meetings the second Saturday of each month from September-May at the University of San Diego from 2-4 p.m.; cost $7 (members), $9 (nonmembers). Check website for room, speaker and directions." Check website for 2012 meeting schedule. Published members share lessons learned and holiday book sale. 2012 conference to be held in February, Writer's Retreat in May. Check website for details. Season tickets include all regular chapter meetings during the season and newsletter issues for one calendar year as well as discounts on conferences/retreats. See the website for conference/workshop dates, times and prices. Chapter also helps members find critique groups for on-going enhancement of skills.

SCBWI—SOUTHERN BREEZE; SPRINGMINGLE

P.O. Box 26282, Birmingham AL 35260. **Website:** www. southern-breeze.net. **Contact:** Jo Kittinger and Claudia Pearson, regional advisors. Writer and illustrator conference geared toward intermediate, advanced and professional levels. Speakers typically include agents, editors, authors, art directors, illustrators. **Open to SCBWI members, non-members and college students.** Annual conference held in Atlanta, Georgia. Usually held in late February. Registration limited. Cost of conference: approximately $225; Typically includes Friday dinner, Saturday lunch and Saturday banquet. Manuscript critiques and portfolio reviews available for additional fee. Pre-registration is necessary. Mail SASE to Southern Breeze or visit **Website:** www.southern-breeze.net.

SCBWI—SOUTHERN BREEZE; WRITING AND ILLUSTRATING FOR KIDS

P.O. Box 26282, Birmingham AL 35260. **E-mail:** sjkit tinger@gmail.com. **Website:** www.southern-breeze. org. **Contact:** Jo Kittinger, regional advisor. Writer and illustrator workshops geared toward all levels. Open to

SCBWI members, non-members and college students. All sessions pertain specifically to the production and support of quality children's literature. This one-day conference offers about 30 workshops on craft and the business of writing. Picture books, chapter books, novels covered. Entry and professional level topics addressed by published writers and illustrators, editors and agents. Annual conference. Fall conference is held the third weekend in October in the Birmingham, AL, metropolitan area. (Museums, shopping, zoo, gardens, universities and colleges are within a short driving distance.) All workshops are limited to 30 or fewer people. Pre-registration is necessary. Some workshops fill quickly. Cost of conference: approximately $110 for members, $135 for nonmembers, $120 for students; program includes keynote speaker, 4 workshops (selected from 30), lunch, and Friday night dessert party. Mss critiques and portfolio reviews are available for an additional fee; mss must be sent early. Registration is by mail ahead of time. Manuscript and portfolio reviews must be pre-paid and scheduled. Send a SASE to: Southern Breeze, P.O. Box 26282, Birmingham AL 35260 or visit website. Fall conference is always held in Birmingham, Alabama. Room block at a hotel near conference site (usually a school) is by individual reservation and offers a conference rate. Keynote for WIK10 was Darcy Pattison. Additional speakers include editors, agents, art directors, authors, and/or illustrators. WIK12 speakers to be announced.

SCBWI—VENTURA/SANTA BARBARA; FALL CONFERENCE

Simi Valley CA 93094-1389. **E-mail:** alexisinca@aol. com. **Website:** www.scbwicencal.org. **Contact:** Alexis O'Neill, regional advisor. Writers' conference geared toward all levels. Speakers include editors, authors, illustrators and agents. Fiction and nonfiction picture books, middle grade and YA novels, and magazine submissions addressed. Annual writing contest in all genres plus illustration display. Conference held October 26, 2013 at California Lutheran University in Thousand Oaks, California in cooperation with the CLU Graduate School of Education. For fees and other information, e-mail or visit website.

SCBWI—VENTURA/SANTA BARBARA; RETREAT FOR CHILDREN'S AUTHORS AND ILLUSTRATORS

E-mail: AlexisInCA@aol.com. **Website:** www.scb wisocal.org. The Winter Retreat, held in Santa Barbara in January, focuses on craft or business issues. Go to website or e-mail for upcoming date, theme and fee.

SCBWI—WESTERN WASHINGTON STATE; CONFERENCE & RETREAT

Western Region of SCBWI, P.O. Box 156, Enumclaw WA 98022. **E-mail:** info@scbwi-washington.org. **Website:** www.scbwi-washington.org. **Contact:** Joni Sensel and Laurie Thompson, co-regional advisors. "The Western Washington region of SCBWI hosts an annual conference in April, a retreat in November, and monthly meetings and events throughout the year. Please visit the website for complete details."

SCBWI—WISCONSIN; FALL RETREAT FOR WORKING WRITERS

Contact: Pam Beres. Writer and illustrator conference geared toward all levels. All our sessions pertain to children's writing/illustration. Faculty addresses writing/illustrating/publishing. Annual conference held October. Go to our website for more information:www.scbwi-wi.com.

OTHER CONFERENCES

ABROAD WRITERS CONFERENCES

17363 Sutter Creek Rd., Sutter Creek CA 95685. (209)296-4050. **E-mail:** abroadwriters@yahoo.com. **Website:** www.abroad-crwf.com/index.html. "Abroad Writers Conferences are devoted to introducing our participants to world views here in the United States and Abroad. Throughout the world we invite several authors to come join us to give readings and to participate on a panel. Our discussion groups touch upon a wide range of topics from important issues of our times to publishing abroad and in the United States. Our objective is to broaden our cultural and scientific perspectives of the world through discourse and writing." Conferences are held throughout the year in various places worldwide. See website for scheduling details. Conference duration: 7-10 days. "Instead of being lost in a crowd at a large conference, Abroad Writers' Conference prides itself on holding small group meetings where participants have personal contact with everyone. Stimulating talks, interviews, readings, Q&A's, writing workshops, film screenings, private consultations and social gatherings all take place within a week to ten days. Abroad Writers' Conference promises you true networking opportunities and full detailed feedback on your writing."

COSTS Prices start at $2,750. Discounts and upgrades may apply. Particpants must apply to program no later than 3 months before departure. To secure a place you must send in a deposit of $1000. Balance must be paid in full twelve weeks before departure. See website for pricing details.

ADDITIONAL INFORMATION Agents participate in conference. Application is online at website.

ASPEN SUMMER WORDS LITERARY FESTIVAL & WRITING RETREAT

Aspen Writers' Foundation, 110 E. Hallam St., #116, Aspen CO 81611. (970)925-3122. **Fax:** (970)925-5700. **E-mail:** info@aspenwriters.org. **Website:** www.aspenwriters.org. **Contact:** Natalie Lacy, programs coordinator. Estab. 1976. ASW is one part laboratory and one part theater. It is comprised of two tracks— the Writing Retreat and the Literary Festival—which approach the written word from different, yet complementary angles. The Retreat features introductory and intensive workshops with some of the nation's most notable writing instructors and includes literature appreciation symposia and professional consultations with literary agents and editors. The Writing Retreat supports writers in developing their craft by providing a winning combination of inspiration, skills, community, and opportunity. The Literary Festival is a booklover's bliss, where the written word takes center stage. Since 2005, each edition of the Festival has celebrated a particular literary heritage and culture by honoring the stories and storytellers of a specific region. Annual conference held the fourth week of June. Conference duration: 5 days. Average attendance: 150 at writing retreat; 300+ at literary festival.

COSTS Check website each year for updates.

ACCOMMODATIONS Discount lodging at the conference site will be available. 2014 rates to be announced. Free shuttle around town.

ADDITIONAL INFORMATION Check website for details on when to buy tickets and passes. Aspen Summer Words runs in June.

ATLANTIC CENTER FOR THE ARTS

1414 Art Center Ave., New Smyrna Beach FL 32168. (386)427-6975. **Fax:** (386)427-5669. **E-mail:** program@atlanticcenterforthearts.org. **Website:** www.atlanticcenterforthearts.org. Internship and residency programs. A Florida artist-in-residence program in which artists of all disciplines work with current prominent artists in a supportive and creative environment.

ACCOMMODATIONS $850; $25 non-refundable application fee. Financial aid is available. Participants responsible for all meals.Accommodations available on site. See website for application schedule and materials.

BACKSPACE AGENT-AUTHOR SEMINAR

P.O. Box 454, Washington MI 48094-0454. (732)267-6449. **Fax:** (586)532-9652. **E-mail:** chrisg@bksp.org. **E-mail:** karendionne@bksp.org. **Website:** www.bksp.org. **Contact:** Karen Dionne. Estab. 2006. Main conference duration: May 23-25. Average attendance: 100. Panels and workshops designed to educate and assist authors in search of a literary agent to represent their work. Only agents will be in program. Past speakers have included Scott Hoffman, Dan Lazar, Scott Miller, Michael Bourret, Katherine Fausset, Jennifer DeChiara, Sharlene Martin and Paul Cirone.

COSTS All 3 days: May 23-25; includes Agent-Author Seminar, Conference Program, Book Signing & Cocktail Reception, Donald Maass workshop—$720. **Backspace Members Receive a $100 discount on a 3-day registration! First 2 days**: May 23-24; includes Agent-Author Seminar, Conference Program, Book Signing & Cocktail Reception—$580. **Friday only**: May 24; Two-track conference program with literary agents, editors and authors. Includes keynote address, book-signing and cocktail reception—$275. **Saturday only**: May 25; Back-to-back craft workshops with bestselling author Jonathan Maberry in the morning and literary agent Donald Maass in the afternoon—$200.

ACCOMMODATIONS Held in the Radisson Martinique, at 49 West 32nd Street, New York, NY 10001. Telephone: (212) 736-3800. Fax: (212) 277-2702. You can call to book a reservation, based on a two-person occupancy.

ADDITIONAL INFORMATION The Backspace Agent-Author Seminar offers plenty of face time with attending agents. This casual, no-pressure seminar is a terrific opportunity to network, ask questions, talk about your work informally and listen from the people who make their lives selling books.

BLUE RIDGE MOUNTAIN CHRISTIAN WRITERS CONFERENCE

No public address available, 1-800-588-7222. **E-mail:** ylehman@bellsouth.net. **Website:** ridgecrestconfer

encecenter.org/event/blueridgemountainchristian writersconference. Annual conference held in May (May 19-May 23). Conference duration: Sunday through lunch on Thursday. Average attendance: 400. A training and networking event for both seasoned and aspiring writers that allows attendees to interact with editors, agents, professional writers, and readers. Workshops and continuing classes in a variety of creative categories are also offered.

COSTS $320, meal package is $141.50 per person (12 meals beginning with dinner Sunday and ending with lunch on Thursday).

ACCOMMODATIONS $59 per night (Standard Accomodations), and $64-69 per night (Deluxe Accomadations), depending on rooms. Located at LifeWay Ridgecrest Conference Center, 1 Ridgecrest Drive, Ridgecrest, NC 28770.

ADDITIONAL INFORMATION The event also features a contest for unpublished writers and ms critiques prior to the conference.

BREAD LOAF WRITERS' CONFERENCE

Middlebury College, Middlebury College, Middlebury VT 05753. (802)443-5286. **Fax:** (802)443-2087. **E-mail:** ncargill@middlebury.edu. **E-mail:** blwc@middlebury.edu. **Website:** www.middlebury.edu/blwc. **Contact:** Michael Collier, Director. Estab. 1926. Annual conference held in late August. Conference duration: 11 days. Offers workshops for fiction, nonfiction, and poetry. Agents, editors, publicists, and grant specialists will be in attendance.

COSTS $2,714 (includes tuition, housing).

ACCOMMODATIONS Bread Loaf Campus in Ripton, Vermont.

ADDITIONAL INFORMATION Conference Date: August 14-24. Location: mountain campus of Middlebury College. Average attendance: 230.

CAPE COD WRITERS CENTER ANNUAL CONFERENCE

P.O. Box 408, Osterville MA 02655. **E-mail:** writers@capecodwriterscenter.org. **Website:** www.capecod writerscenter.org. **Contact:** Nancy Rubin Stuart, executive director. Duration: 5 days; first week in August. Offers workshops in fiction, commercial fiction, nonfiction, poetry, writing for children, humor, memoir, pitching your book, screenwriting, digital communications, getting published, ms evaluation, mentoring sessions with faculty. Held at Resort and Conference Center of Hyannis, Hyannis, MA.

COSTS Vary, depending on the number of courses selected.

CELEBRATION OF SOUTHERN LITERATURE

Southern Lit Alliance, 3069 S. Broad St., Suite 2, Chattanooga TN 37408-3056. (423)267-1218 or (800)267-4232. **Fax:** (423)267-1018. **E-mail:** srobinson@southernlitalliance.org. **Website:** www.southernlitalliance.org. **Contact:** Susan Robinson. "The Celebration of Southern Literature stands out because of its unique collaboration with the Fellowship of Southern Writers, an organization founded by towering literary figures like Eudora Welty, Cleanth Brooks, Walker Percy, and Robert Penn Warren to recognize and encourage literature in the South. The 2013 celebration marked 24 years since the Fellowship selected Chattanooga for its headquarters and chose to collaborate with the Celebration of Southern Literature. Up to 50 members of the Fellowship will participate in this year's event, discussing hot topics and reading from their latest works. The Fellowship will also award 11 literary prizes and induct 2 new members, making this event the place to discover up-and-coming voices in Southern literature. The Southern Lit Alliance's Celebration of Southern Literature attracts more than 1,000 readers and writers from all over the U.S. It strives to maintain an informal atmosphere where conversations will thrive, inspired by a common passion for the written word. The Southern Lit Alliance (formerly The Arts & Education Council) started as 1 of 12 pilot agencies founded by a Ford Foundation grant in 1952. The Alliance is the only organization of the 12 still in existence. The Southern Lit Alliance celebrates southern writers and readers through community education and innovative literary arts experiences."

CRESTED BUTTE WRITERS CONFERENCE

P.O. Box 1361, Crested Butte CO 81224. **E-mail:** coordinator@conf.crestedbuttewriters.org. **Website:** www.crestedbuttewriters.org/conf.php. **Contact:** Barbara Crawford or Theresa Rizzo, co-coordinators. Estab. 2006.

COSTS $330 nonmembers; $300 members; $297 Early Bird; The Sandy Writing Contest Finalist $280; and groups of 5 or more $280.

ACCOMMODATIONS The conference is held at The Elevation Hotel, located at the Crested Butte Mountain Resort at the base of the ski mountain (Mt. Crested Butte, CO). The quaint historic town lies nestled in a stunning mountain valley 3 short miles from the resort area of Mt. Crested Butte. A free bus runs frequently between the 2 towns. The closest airport is 30 miles away, in Gunnison CO. Our website lists 3 lodging options besides rooms at the Event Facility. All condos, motels and hotel options offer special conference rates. No special travel arrangements are made through the conference; however, information for car rental from Gunnison airport or the Alpine Express shuttle is listed on the conference FAQ page.

ADDITIONAL INFORMATION "Our conference workshops address a wide variety of writing craft and business. Our most popular workshop is Our First Pages Readings—with a twist. Agents and editors read opening pages volunteered by attendees-with a few best selling authors' openings mixed in. Think the A/E can identify the bestsellers? Not so much. Each year one of our attendees has been mistaken for a bestseller and obviously garnered requests from some on the panel. Agents attending: Carlie Webber—CK Webber Associates and TBDs. The agents will be speaking and available for meetings with attendees through our Pitch and Pages system. Editors attending: Christian Trimmer, senior editor at Disney Hyperion Books, and Jessica Williams of Harper Collins. Award-winning authors: Mark Coker, CEO of Smashwords; Kristen Lamb, social media guru, Kim Killion, book cover designer; Jennifer Jakes; Sandra Kerns; and Annette Elton. Writers may request additional information by e-mail."

FLATHEAD RIVER WRITERS CONFERENCE

P.O. Box 7711, Kalispell MT 59904-7711, (406)881-4066. **E-mail:** answers@authorsoftheflathead.org. **Website:** www.authorsoftheflathead.org/conference.asp. Estab. 1990. Two day conference packed with energizing speakers. After a focus on publishing the past two years, this year's focus is on writing, getting your manuscripts honed and ready for your readers. Highlights include two agents will review 12 manuscripts one-on-one with the first 24 paid attendees requesting this opportunity, a synopsis writing workshop, a screenwriting workshop, and more.

COSTS Contact for cost information, not currently listed on website.

ACCOMMODATIONS Rooms are available at a discounted rate.

ADDITIONAL INFORMATION Watch website for additional speakers and other details. Register early as seating is limited.

FLORIDA CHRISTIAN WRITERS CONFERENCE

2344 Armour Ct., Titusville FL 32780. (386)295-3902. **E-mail:** FloridaChristianWritersConf@gmail.com. **Website:** floridacwc.net. Estab. 1988. Annual conference held in March (February 26-March 2). Conference duration: 4 days. Average attendance: 275. "The Florida Christian Writers Conference 2014 meets under the stately oaks of Lake Yale Conference Center near Leesburg, Florida. The conference is designed to meet the needs of beginning writers to published authors. This is your opportunity to learn more about the publishing industry, to build your platform, and to follow God's leading to publish the message He has given you."

COSTS $575 (includes tuition, meals).

ACCOMMODATIONS We provide a shuttle from the Orlando airport. $725/double occupancy; $950/ single occupancy.

ADDITIONAL INFORMATION "Each writer may submit 2 works for critique. We have specialists in every area of writing. Brochures/guidelines are available online or for a SASE."

☁ GENEVA WRITERS CONFERENCE

Geneva Writers Group, Switzerland. **E-mail:** info@ GenevaWritersGroup.org. **Website:** www.genevaw ritersgroup.org. Estab. 1993. Biennial conference held at Webster University in Bellevue/Geneva, Switzerland. Conference duration: 2.5 days, welcoming more than 200 writers from around the world. Speakers and presenters have included Peter Ho Davies, Jane Alison, Russell Celyn Jones, Patricia Hampl, Robert Root, Brett Lott, Dinty W. Moore, Naomi Shihab Nye, Jo Shapcott, Wallis Wilde Menozzi, Susan Tiberghien, Jane Dystel, Laura Longrigg, and Colin Harrison.

THE GLEN WORKSHOP

Image, 3307 Third Ave. W., Seattle WA 98119. (206)281-2988. **Fax:** (206)281-2335. **E-mail:** glenwork shop@imagejournal.org. **Website:** glenworkshop.com. Estab. 1995. A pair of annual workshops. Conference duration: 1 week. Workshop focuses on fiction, poetry, spiritual writing, playwriting, screenwriting, songwriting, and mixed media. Writing classes combine general instruction and discussion with the workshop experience, in which each individual's works are read and discussed critically. Glen West held at St. John's College in Santa Fe, NM from July 28-August 4and Glen East held Mt. Holyoke College in South Hadley, MA from June 9-16. The Glen Workshop combines an intensive learning experience with a lively festival of the arts. It takes place in the stark, dramatic beauty of the Sangre de Cristo mountains and within easy reach of the rich cultural, artistic, and spiritual traditions of northern New Mexico. Lodging and meals are included with registration at affordable rates. A low-cost "commuter" rate is also available for those who wish to camp, stay with friends, or otherwise find their own food and lodging.

COSTS See costs online. A limited number of partial scholarships are available.

ACCOMMODATIONS Offers dorm rooms, dorm suites, and apartments.

ADDITIONAL INFORMATION Like *Image*, the Glen is grounded in a Christian perspective, but its tone is informal and hospitable to all spiritual wayfarers. Depending on the teacher, participants may need to submit workshop material prior to arrival (usually 10-25 pages).

GREATER LEHIGH VALLEY WRITERS GROUP 'THE WRITE STUFF' WRITERS CONFERENCE

3650 Nazareth Pike, PMB #136, Bethlehem PA 18020-1115. **E-mail:** writestuffchair@glvwg.org. **Website:** www.glvwg.org. **Contact:** Donna Brennan, chair. Estab. 1993.

COSTS Members: $110 (includes Friday evening session and all Saturday workshops, 2 meals, and a chance to pitch to an editor or agent); non-members: $130. Late registration: $145. Pre-conference workshops require an additional fee.

ADDITIONAL INFORMATION "The Writer's Flash contest is judged by conference participants. Write 100 words or less in fiction, creative nonfiction, or poetry. Brochures available in January by SASE, or by phone, e-mail, or on website. Accepts inquiries by SASE, e-mail or phone. Agents and editors attend conference. For updated info refer to the website. Greater Lehigh Valley Writers Group hosts a friendly conference and gives you the most for your money. Breakout rooms offer craft topics, business of publishing, editor and agent panels. Book fair with book signing by published authors and presenters."

GREEN LAKE CHRISTIAN WRITERS CONFERENCE

W2511 State Road 23, Green Lake Conference Center, Green Lake WI 54941-9599. (920)294-3323. **E-mail:** program@glcc.org. **E-mail:** janet.p.white@gmail.com. **Website:** glcc.org. **Contact:** Janet White, Conference Director. Estab. 1948. Conference duration: 1 week (August 18-23). Attendees may be well-published or beginners, may write for secular and/or Christian markets. Leaders are experienced writing teachers. Attendees can spend 11.5 contact hours in the workshop of their choice: fiction, nonfiction, poetry, inspirational/devotional. Seminars include specific skills: marketing, humor, songwriting, writing for children, self-publishing, writing for churches, interviewing, memoir writing, the magazine market. Evening: panels of experts will answer questions. Social and leisure activities included. GLCC is in south central WI, has 1,000 acres, 2.5 miles of shoreline on Wisconsin's deepest lake, and offers a resort setting. **COSTS** Short Track (Two Days): $65 per person. Full Track: Writers'—$225 per person; Artists'—$40 per person. **ACCOMMODATIONS** Hotels, lodges and all meeting rooms are a/c. Affordable rates, excellent meals. **ADDITIONAL INFORMATION** Brochure and scholarship info from website or contact Jan White (920-294-7327). To register, call 920-294-3323.

GREEN MOUNTAIN WRITERS CONFERENCE

47 Hazel St., Rutland VT 05701. (802)236-6133. **E-mail:** ydaley@sbcglobal.net. **E-mail:** yvonnedaley@me.com. **Website:** vermontwriters.com. **Contact:** Yvonne Daley, director. Estab. 1999. "Annual conference held in the summer. Covers fiction, creative nonfiction, poetry, journalism, nature writing, essay, memoir, personal narrative, and biography. Held at an old dance pavillion on on a remote pond in Tinmouth, Vermont. Speakers have included Stephen Sandy, Grace Paley, Ruth Stone, Howard Frank Mosher, Chris Bohjalian, Joan Connor, Yvonne Daley, David Huddle, David Budbill, Jeffrey Lent, Verandah Porche, Tom Smith, and Chuck Clarino." **COSTS** $600 before June 30; $650 after June 30. Partial scholarships are available. **ACCOMMODATIONS** "We have made arrangements with a major hotel in nearby Rutland and two area bed and breakfast inns for special accommodations and rates for conference participants. You must make your own reservations."

ADDITIONAL INFORMATION Participants' mss can be read and commented on at a cost. Sponsors contests. Conference publishes a literary magazine featuring work of participants. Brochures available in January on website or for SASE, e-mail. Accepts inquiries by SASE, e-mail, phone. "We offer the opportunity to learn from some of the nation's best writers at a small, supportive conference in a lakeside setting that allows one-to-one feedback. Participants often continue to correspond and share work after conferences." Further information available on website, by e-mail or by phone.

HIGHLAND SUMMER CONFERENCE

Box 7014, Radford University, Radford VA 24142-7014. (540)831-5366. **Fax:** (540)831-5951. **E-mail:** tburriss@radford.edu; rbderrick@radford.edu. **Website:** www.radford.edu/content/cehd/home/departments/appalachian-studies.html. **Contact:** Dr. Theresa Burriss, Ruth Derrick. Estab. 1978. The Highland Summer Writers' Conference is a one-week lecture-seminar workshop combination conducted by well-known guest writers. It offers the opportunity to study and practice creative and expository writing within the context of regional culture. The course is graded on Pass/Fail basis for undergraduates and letter grades for graduate students. It may be taken twice for credit. The class runs Monday through Friday 9 a.m.-noon and 1:30-4:30 p.m., with extended hours on Wednesday, and readings and receptions by resident teachers on Tuesday and Thursday evening in McConnell Library 7:30-9:30 p.m. The evening readings are free and open to the public. **ACCOMMODATIONS** "We do not have special rate arrangements with local hotels. We do offer accommodations on the Radford University campus in a recently refurbished residence hall." **ADDITIONAL INFORMATION** Conference leaders typically critique work done during the one-week conference, and because of the one-week format, students will be asked to bring preliminary work when they arrive at the conference, as well as submit a portfolio following the conference. Brochures/guidelines are available in March by request.

HIGHLIGHTS FOUNDATION FOUNDERS WORKSHOPS

814 Court St., Honesdale PA 18431. (570)253-1122. **Fax:** (570)253-0179. **E-mail:** klbrown@highlights foundation.org. **E-mail:** jo.lloy@highlightsfounda tion.org. **Website:** highlightsfoundation.org. **Contact:** Kent L. Brown, Jr. Estab. 2000. Offers more than three dozen workshops per year. Conference duration: 3-7 days. Average attendance: limited to 10-14. Genre specific workshops and retreats on children's writing: fiction, nonfiction, poetry, promotions. "Our goal is to improve, over time, the quality of literature for children by educating future generations of children's authors." Highlights Founders' home in Boyds Mills, PA.

COSTS Prices vary based on workshop. Check website for details.

ACCOMMODATIONS Coordinates pickup at local airport. Offers overnight accommodations. Participants stay in guest cabins on the wooded grounds surrounding Highlights Founders' home adjacent to the house/conference center.

ADDITIONAL INFORMATION Some workshops require pre-workshop assignment. Brochure available for SASE, by e-mail, on website, by phone, by fax. Accepts inquiries by phone, fax, e-mail, SASE. Editors attend conference. "Applications will be reviewed and accepted on a first-come, first-served basis, applicants must demonstrate specific experience in writing area of workshop they are applying for—writing samples are required for many of the workshops."

HIGHLIGHTS FOUNDATION WRITERS WORKSHOP AT CHAUTAUQUA

814 Court St., Honesdale PA 18431. (570)253-1192. **Fax:** (570)253-0179. **E-mail:** klbrown@highlights foundation.org. **E-mail:** jo.lloyd@highlightsfounda tion.org. **Website:** highlightsfoundation.org. Estab. 1985. Average attendance: 100. Workshops are geared toward those who write for children at the beginner, intermediate, and advanced levels. Offers seminars, small group workshops, and one-on-one sessions with authors, editors, illustrators, critics, and publishers. Workshop site is the picturesque community of Chautauqua, New York. Speakers have included Bruce Coville, Candace Fleming, Linda Sue Park, Jane Yolen, Patricia Gauch, Jerry Spinelli, Eileen Spinelli, Joy Cowley and Pam Munoz Ryan.

ACCOMMODATIONS We coordinate ground transportation to and from airports, trains, and bus sta-

tions in the Erie, Pennsylvania and Jamestown/Buffalo, NY area. We also coordinate accommodations for conference attendees.

ADDITIONAL INFORMATION "We offer the opportunity for attendees to submit a ms for review at the conference. Workshop brochures/guidelines are available upon request."

HOFSTRA UNIVERSITY SUMMER WRITING WORKSHOPS

University College for Continuing Education, 250 Hofstra University, Hempstead NY 11549-2500. (516)463-7200. **Fax:** (516)463-4833. **E-mail:** ce@hof stra.edu. **Website:** hofstra.edu/academics/ce. **Contact:** Colleen Slattery, Senior Associate Dean. Estab. 1972. Hofstra University's 2-week Summer Writers Program, a cooperative endeavor of the Creative Writing Program, the English Department, and Hofstra University Continuing Education (Hofstra CE), offers 8 classes which may be taken on a noncredit or credit basis, for both graduate and undergraduate students. Led by master writers, the Summer Writing Program operates on the principle that true writing talent can be developed, nurtured and encouraged by writer-in-residence mentors. Through instruction, discussion, criticism and free exchange among the program members, writers begin to find their voice and their style. The program provides group and individual sessions for each writer. The Summer Writing Program includes a banquet, guest speakers, and exposure to authors such as Oscar Hijuelos, Robert Olen Butler (both Pulitzer Prize winners), Maurice Sendak, Cynthia Ozick, Nora Sayre, and Denise Levertov. Often agents, editors, and publishers make presentations during the conference, and authors and students read from published work and works in progress. These presentations and the conference banquet offer additional opportunities to meet informally with participants, master writers and guest speakers. Average attendance: 65. Conference offers workshops in short fiction, nonfiction, poetry, and occasionally other genres such as screenplay writing or writing for children. Site is the university campus on Long Island, 25 miles from New York City.

COSTS Check website for current fees. Credit is available for undergraduate and graduate students. Choose one of 9 writing genres and spend two intensive weeks studying and writing in that genre.

ACCOMMODATIONS Free bus operates between Hempstead Train Station and campus for those commuting from New York City on the Long Island Rail Road. Dormitory rooms are available.

ADDITIONAL INFORMATION Students entering grades 9-12 can now be part of the Summer Writers Program with a special section for high school students. Through exercises and readings, students will learn how to use their creative impulses to improve their fiction, poetry and plays and learn how to create cleaner and clearer essays. During this intensive 2-week course, students will experiment with memoir, poetry, oral history, dramatic form and the short story, and study how to use character, plot, point of view and language.

HOW TO BE PUBLISHED WORKSHOPS

P.O. Box 100031, Irondale AL 35210-3006. **E-mail:** mike@writing2sell.com. **Website:** www.writing2sell.com. **Contact:** Michael Garrett. Estab. 1986. Workshops are offered continuously year-round at various locations. Conference duration: 1 session. Average attendance: 10-15. Workshops to "move writers of category fiction closer to publication." Focus is not on how to write, but how to get published. Site: Workshops held at college campuses and universities. Themes include marketing, idea development, characterization, and ms critique. Special critique is offered, but advance submission is not required. Workshop information available on website. Accepts inquiries by e-mail.

COSTS $79-99.

INDIANA UNIVERSITY WRITERS' CONFERENCE

464 Ballantine Hall, 1020 E. Kirkwood Ave., Bloomington IN 47405-7103. (812)855-1877. **Fax:** (812)855-9535. **E-mail:** writecon@indiana.edu. **Website:** www.indiana.edu/~writecon. **Contact:** Bob Bledsoe, director. Estab. 1940. Annual. Conference/workshops held in May. Average attendance: 115. "The Indiana University Writers' Conference believes in a craft-based teaching of fiction writing. We emphasize an exploration of creativity through a variety of approaches, offering workshop-based craft discussions, classes focusing on technique, and talks about the careers and concerns of a writing life." 2013 faculty: Alix Lambert, Scott Hutchins, Nathaniel Perry, Lloyd Suh.

COSTS 2013: Workshop, $550/week; classes only, $300/week.

ACCOMMODATIONS Information on accommodations available on website.

ADDITIONAL INFORMATION Fiction workshop applicants must submit up to 25 pages of prose. Registration information available for SASE, by e-mail, or on website. Spaces still available in all workshops and classes for 2013.

IOWA SUMMER WRITING FESTIVAL

The University of Iowa, C215 Seashore Hall, University of Iowa, Iowa City IA 52242. (319)335-4160. **Fax:** (319)335-4743. **E-mail:** iswfestival@uiowa.edu. **Website:** uiowa.edu/~iswfest. Estab. 1987. Annual festival held in June and July. Conference duration: Workshops are 1 week or a weekend. Average attendance: Limited to 12 people/class, with over 1,500 participants throughout the summer. "We offer courses across the genres: novel, short story, poetry, essay, memoir, humor, travel, playwriting, screenwriting, writing for children, and women's writing. Held at the University of Iowa campus." Speakers have included Marvin Bell, Lan Samantha Chang, John Dalton, Hope Edelman, Katie Ford, Patricia Foster, Bret Anthony Johnston, Barbara Robinette Moss, among others.

COSTS $590 for full week; $305 for weekend workshop. Housing and meals are separate.

ACCOMMODATIONS Accommodations available at area hotels. Information on overnight accommodations available by phone or on website.

ADDITIONAL INFORMATION Brochures are available in February. Inquire via e-mail or on website.

JACKSON HOLE WRITERS CONFERENCE

PO Box 1974, Jackson WY 83001. (307)413-3332. **E-mail:** nicole@jacksonholewritersconference.com. **Website:** jacksonholewritersconference.com. Estab. 1991. Annual conference held June 27-29. Conference duration: 4 days. Average attendance: 110. Covers fiction, creative nonfiction, and young adult and offers ms critiques from authors, agents, and editors. Agents in attendance will take pitches from writers. Paid manuscript critique programs are available.

COSTS $365 if registered by May 12. Accompanying teen writer: $175. Pre-Conference Writing Workshop: $150.

ADDITIONAL INFORMATION Held at the Center for the Arts in Jackson, Wyoming and online.

KENYON REVIEW WRITERS WORKSHOP

Kenyon College, Gambier OH 43022. (740)427-5207. **Fax:** (740)427-5417. **E-mail:** kenyonreview@kenyon. edu; writers@kenyonreview.org. **Website:** www.ke nyonreview.org. **Contact:** Anna Duke Reach, director. Estab. 1990. Annual 8-day workshop held in June. Participants apply in poetry, fiction, or creative nonfiction, and then participate in intensive daily workshops which focus on the generation and revision of significant new work. Held on the campus of Kenyon College in the rural village of Gambier, Ohio. Workshop leaders have included David Baker, Ron Carlson, Rebecca McClanahan, Meghan O'Rourke, Linda Gregorson, Dinty Moore, Tara Ison, Jane Hamilton, Lee K. Abbott, and Nancy Zafris.

COSTS $1,995; includes tuition, room and board.

ACCOMMODATIONS The workshop operates a shuttle to and from Gambier and the airport in Columbus, Ohio. Offers overnight accommodations. Participants are housed in Kenyon College student housing. The cost is covered in the tuition.

ADDITIONAL INFORMATION Application includes a writing sample. Admission decisions are made on a rolling basis. Workshop information is available online at www.kenyonreview.org/work shops in November. For brochure send e-mail, visit website, call, fax. Accepts inquiries by SASE, e-mail, phone, fax.

LA JOLLA WRITERS CONFERENCE

P.O. Box 178122, San Diego CA 92177. (858)467-1978. **E-mail:** akuritz@san.rr.com. **Website:** www.lajollaw ritersconference.com. **Contact:** Jared Kuritz, director. Estab. 2001. Annual conference held in October/November. Conference duration: 3 days. Average attendance: 200. "In addition to covering nearly every genre, we also take particular pride in educating our attendees on the business aspect of the book industry by having agents, editors, publishers, publicists, and distributors teach classes. Our conference offers 2 types of classes: lecture sessions that run for 50 minutes, and workshops that run for 110 minutes. Each block period is dedicated to either workshop or lecture-style classes. During each block period, there will be 6-8 classes on various topics from which you can choose to attend. For most workshop classes, you are encouraged to bring written work for review. Literary agents from prestigious agencies such as The Andrea Brown Literary Agency, The Dijkstra Agency,

The McBride Agency and Full Circle Literary Group have participated in the past. The conference creates a strong sense of community, and it has seen many of its attendees successfully published."

COSTS Information available online.

LAS VEGAS WRITERS CONFERENCE

Henderson Writers' Group, 614 Mosswood Dr., Henderson NV 89015. (702)564-2488; or, toll-free, (866)869-7842. **E-mail:** marga614@mysticpublish ers.com. **Website:** www.lasvegaswritersconference. com. Annual. Held in April. Conference duration: 3 days. Average attendance: 150 maximum. "Join writing professionals, agents, industry experts, and your colleagues for 3 days in Las Vegas as they share their knowledge on all aspects of the writer's craft. While there are formal pitch sessions, panels, workshops, and seminars, the faculty is also available throughout the conference for informal discussions and advice. Plus, you're bound to meet a few new friends, too. Workshops, seminars, and expert panels will take you through writing in many genres including fiction, creative nonfiction, screenwriting, journalism, and business and technical writing. There will be many Q&A panels for you to ask the experts all your questions." Site: Sam's Town Hotel and Gambling Hall in Las Vegas.

COSTS $400 before December 31, $450 until conference, and $500 at the door. One day registration is $275.

ADDITIONAL INFORMATION Sponsors contest. Agents and editors participate in conference.

LEAGUE OF UTAH WRITERS' ANNUAL WRITER'S CONFERENCE

Dianne Hardy, League of Utah Writers, 420 W. 750 N., Logan UT 84321. **E-mail:** writerscache435@gmail. com. **Website:** www.luwriters.org/index.html. **Contact:** Tim Keller, president; Irene Hastings, president-elect; Caroll Shreeve, secretary. The League of Utah Writers is a non-profit organization dedicated to offering friendship, education, and encouragement to the writers of Utah. New members are always welcome. Writer workshops geared toward beginner, intermediate or advanced. Annual conference.

THE MACDOWELL COLONY

100 High St., Peterborough NH 03458. (603)924-3886. **Fax:** (603)924-9142. **E-mail:** admissions@macdow ellcolony.org. **Website:** www.macdowellcolony.org. Estab. 1907. Open to writers, playwrights, compos-

ers, visual artists, film/video artists, interdisciplinary artists and architects. Applicants submit information and work samples for review by a panel of experts in each discipline. Application form submitted online at www.macdowellcolony.org/apply.html.

COSTS Travel reimbursement and stipends are available for participants of the residency, based on need. There are no residency fees.

MENDOCINO COAST WRITERS CONFERENCE

1211 Del Mar Dr., Fort Bragg CA 95437. (707)937-9983. **E-mail:** info@mcwc.org. **Website:** www.mcwc.org. Estab. 1988. Annual conference held in July. Average attendance: 80. Provides workshops for fiction, nonfiction, and poetry. Held at a small community college campus on the northern Pacific Coast. Workshop leaders have included Kim Addonizio, Lynne Barrett, John Dufresne, John Lescroart, Ben Percy, Luis Rodriguez, and Ellen Sussman. Agents and publishers will be speaking and available for meetings with attendees.

COSTS $525+ (includes panels, meals, 2 socials with guest readers, 4 public events, 3 morning intensive workshops in 1 of 6 subjects, and a variety of afternoon panels and lectures).

ACCOMMODATIONS Information on overnight accommodations is made available.

ADDITIONAL INFORMATION Emphasis is on writers who are also good teachers. Registration opens March 15. Send inquiries via e-mail.

MIDWEST WRITERS WORKSHOP

Ball State University, Department of Journalism, Muncie IN 47306. (765)282-1055. **E-mail:** midwestwriters@yahoo.com. **Website:** www.midwestwriters.org. **Contact:** Jama Kehoe Bigger, director. Annual workshop held in late July. Writer workshops geared toward intermediate level. Topics include most genres. Faculty/speakers have included Joyce Carol Oates, George Plimpton, Clive Cussler, Haven Kimmel, James Alexander Thom, Wiliam Zinsser, Phillip Gulley, and children's writers Rebecca Kai Dotlich, April Pulley Sayre, Peter Welling, Claire Ewert, and Michelle Medlock Adams. Workshop also includes agent pitch sessions ms evaluation and a writing contest. Registration tentatively limited to 125.

COSTS $135-360. Most meals included.

ADDITIONAL INFORMATION Offers scholarships. See website for more information.

MONTEVALLO LITERARY FESTIVAL

Sta. 6420, University of Montevallo, Montevallo AL 35115. (205)665-6420. **Fax:** (205)665-6422. **E-mail:** murphyj@montevallo.edu. **Website:** www.montevallo.edu/english. **Contact:** Dr. Jim Murphy, director. Estab. 2003. Takes place annually, April 12.

COSTS Readings are free. Readings, plus lunch, reception, and dinner is $20. Master Class only is $30. Master Class with everything else is $50.

ACCOMMODATIONS Offers overnight accommodations at Ramsay Conference Center on campus. Call (205)665-6280 for reservations. Free on-campus parking. Additional information available at www.montevallo.edu/cont_ed/ramsay.shtm.

ADDITIONAL INFORMATION To enroll in a fiction workshop, contact Bryn Chancellor (bchancellor@montevallo.edu). Information for upcoming festival available in February For brochure, visit website. Accepts inquiries by mail (with SASE), e-mail, phone, and fax. Editors participate in conference. "This is a friendly, relaxed festival dedicated to bringing literary writers and readers together on a personal scale." Poetry workshop participants submit up to 5 pages of poetry; e-mail as Word doc to Jim Murphy (murphyj@montevallo.edu) at least 2 weeks prior to festival.

MONTROSE CHRISTIAN WRITERS' CONFERENCE

218 Locust St., Montrose PA 18801. (570)278-1001 or (800)598-5030. **Fax:** (570)278-3061. **E-mail:** info@montrosebible.org. **Website:** montrosebible.org. Estab. 1990. "Annual conference held in July. Offers workshops, editorial appointments, and professional critiques. We try to meet a cross-section of writing needs, for beginners and advanced, covering fiction, poetry, and writing for children. It is small enough to allow personal interaction between attendees and faculty. Speakers have included William Petersen, Mona Hodgson, Jim Fletcher, and Terri Gibbs." Held in Montrose, from July 21-24.

COSTS Tuition is $175.

ACCOMMODATIONS Will meet planes in Binghamton, NY and Scranton, PA. On-site accomodations: room and board $305-350/conference; $60-70/day including food (2009 rates). RV court available.

ADDITIONAL INFORMATION "Writers can send work ahead of time and have it critiqued for a small fee." The attendees are usually church related. The writing has a Christian emphasis. Conference information available in April. For brochure send SASE, visit website, e-mail, call or fax. Accepts inquiries by SASE, e-mail, fax, phone.

MOUNT HERMON CHRISTIAN WRITERS CONFERENCE

PO Box 413, Mount Hermon CA 95041. **E-mail:** info@mounthermon.org. **Website:** mounthermon. org. Estab. 1970. Annual professional conference (always held over the Palm Sunday weekend, Friday noon through Tuesday noon). Average attendance: 450. Sponsored by and held at the 440-acre Mount Hermon Christian Conference Center near San Jose, California in the heart of the coastal redwoods, we are a broad-ranging conference for all areas of Christian writing, including fiction, nonfiction, fantasy, children's, teen, young adult, poetry, magazines, inspirational and devotional writing. This is a working, how-to conference, with Major Morning tracks in all genres (including a track especially for teen writers), and as many as 20 optional workshops each afternoon. Faculty-to-student ratio is about 1 to 6. The bulk of our more than 70 faculty members are editors and publisher representatives from major Christian publishing houses nationwide. Speakers have included T. Davis Bunn, Debbie Macomber, Jerry Jenkins, Bill Butterworth, Dick Foth and others.

COSTS Registration fees include tuition, all major morning sessions, keynote sessions, and refreshment breaks. Room and board varies depending on choice of housing options. Costs vary from $617 to $1565 based on housing rates.

ACCOMMODATIONS Registrants stay in hotel-style accommodations. Meals are buffet style, with faculty joining registrants. See website for cost updates.

ADDITIONAL INFORMATION "The residential nature of our conference makes this a unique setting for one-on-one interaction with faculty/staff. There is also a decided inspirational flavor to the conference, and general sessions with well-known speakers are a highlight. Registrants may submit 2 works for critique in advance of the conference, then have personal interviews with critiquers during the conference. All conference information is online by December 1 of each year. Send inquiries via e-mail. Tapes of past conferences are also available online."

NAPA VALLEY WRITERS' CONFERENCE

Napa Valley College, 1088 College Ave., St. Helena CA 94574. (707)967-2900. **Website:** www.napawriter

sconference.org. **Contact:** John Leggett and Anne Evans, program directors. Estab. 1981. Established 1981. Annual weeklong event, July 28-August 2. Location: Upper Valley Campus in the historic town of St. Helena, 25 miles north of Napa in the heart of the valley's wine growing community. Excellent cuisine provided by Napa Valley Cooking School. Average attendance: 48 in poetry and 48 in fiction. "Serious writers of all backgrounds and experience are welcome to apply." Offers poets workshops, lectures, faculty readings, ms critiques, and meetings with editors. "Poetry session provides the opportunity to work both on generating new poems and on revising previously written ones."

COSTS Total participation fee is $900.

ADDITIONAL INFORMATION The conference is held at the Upper Valley Campus of Napa Valley College, located in the heart of California's Wine Country. During the conference week, attendees' meals are provided by the Napa Valley Cooking School, which offers high quality, intensive training for aspiring chefs. The goal of the program is to provide each student with hands-on, quality, culinary and pastry skills required for a career in a fine-dining establishment. The disciplined and professional learning environment, availability of global externships, low student-teacher ratio and focus on sustainability make the Napa Valley Cooking School unique.

NIMROD ANNUAL WRITERS' WORKSHOP

800 S. Tucker Dr., Tulsa OK 74104. (918)631-3080. **E-mail:** nimrod@utulsa.edu. **Website:** www.utulsa. edu/nimrod. **Contact:** Eilis O'Neal, managing editor. Estab. 1978. Annual conference held in October. Conference duration: 1 day. Offers one-on-one editing sessions, readings, panel discussions, and master classes in fiction, poetry, nonfiction, memoir, and fantasy writing. Speakers have included Myla Goldberg, B.H. Fairchild, Colum McCann, Molly Peacock, Peter S. Beagle, Robert Olen Butler, and Marvin Bell. Full conference details are online in August.

COSTS Approximately $50. Lunch provided. Scholarships available for students.

ADDITIONAL INFORMATION *Nimrod International Journal* sponsors *Nimrod* Literary Awards: The Katherine Anne Porter Prize for fiction and The Pablo Neruda Prize for poetry. Poetry and fiction prizes: $2,000 each and publication (1st prize); $1,000 each and publication (2nd prize). Deadline: must be postmarked no later than April 30.

NORTH CAROLINA WRITERS' NETWORK FALL CONFERENCE

P.O. Box 21591, Winston-Salem NC 27120. (336)293-8844. **E-mail:** mail@ncwriters.org. **Website:** www.ncwriters.org. Estab. 1985. Annual conference held in November in different NC venues. Average attendance: 250. This organization hosts 2 conferences: 1 in the spring and 1 in the fall. Each conference is a weekend full of workshops, panels, book signings, and readings (including open mic). There will be a keynote speaker, a variety of sessions on the craft and business of writing, and opportunities to meet with agents and editors.

COSTS Approximately $250 (includes 4 meals).

ACCOMMODATIONS Special rates are usually available at the Conference Hotel, but conferees must make their own reservations.

ADDITIONAL INFORMATION Available at www.ncwriters.org.

NORWESCON

100 Andover Park W. PMB 150-165, Tukwila WA 98188-2828. (425)243-4692. **Fax:** (520)244-0142. **E-mail:** info@norwescon.org. **Website:** www.norwescon.org. Estab. 1978. Annual conference held on Easter weekend. Average attendance: 2,800. General multi-track convention focusing on science fiction and fantasy literature with wide coverage of other media. Tracks cover science, socio-cultural, literary, publishing, editing, writing, art, and other media of a science fiction/fantasy orientation. Agents will be speaking and available for meetings with attendees.

ACCOMMODATIONS Conference is held at the Doubletree Hotel Seattle Airport.

ADDITIONAL INFORMATION Brochures are available online or for a SASE. Send inquiries via e-mail.

OKLAHOMA WRITERS' FEDERATION, INC. ANNUAL CONFERENCE

3800 Bonaire Place, Edmond OK 73013. **Website:** www.owfi.org. **Contact:** Linda Apple, president. Annual conference. Held first weekend in May each year. Writer workshops geared toward all levels. **Open to students.** "Forty seminars, with 30 speakers consisting of editors, literary agents and many best-selling authors. Topics range widely to include craft, marketing, and all genres of writing." Writing facilities available: book room, autograph party, 2 lunch workshops. "If writers would like to participate in the annual writing contest, they must become members of

OWFI. You don't have to be a member to attend the conference." See website for more information.

COSTS $150 before March 15; $175 after March 15; $70 for single days; $25 for lunch workshops. Full tuition includes 2-day conference (all events except lunch workshops) and 2 dinners, plus 110-minute appointment with an attending editor or agent of your choice (must be reserved in advance).

OZARK CREATIVE WRITERS, INC. CONFERENCE

P.O. Box 424, Eureka Springs AR 72632. **E-mail:** ozarkcreativewriters@gmail.com. **Website:** www.ozarkcreativewriters.org. Open to professional and amateur writers, workshops are geared to all levels and all forms of the creative process and literary arts. Sessions sometimes include songwriting, with presentations by best-selling authors, editors, and agents. The OCW Conference promotes writing by offering competition in all genres. The annual event is held on the second full weekend in October at the Inn of the Ozarks, in the resort town of Eureka Springs, Arkansas. Approximately 200 attend each year; many also enter the creative writing competitions.

PACIFIC COAST CHILDREN'S WRITERS WHOLE-NOVEL WORKSHOP

P.O. Box 244, Aptos CA 95001. **Website:** www.childrenswritersworkshop.com. Estab. 2003. "Our seminar offers semi-advanced through published adult writers an editor and/or agent critique on their full novel or 15-30 page partial. A concurrent workshop is open to students age 14 and up, who give adults target reader feedback. Focus on craft as a marketing tool. Team-taught master classes (open clinics for manuscript critiques) explore such topics as "Story Architecture and Arcs." Continuous close contact with faculty, who have included Andrea Brown, agent, and Simon Boughton, currently VP/executive editor at 3 Macmillan imprints. Registration limited to 12 adults and 6 teens. For the most critique options, submit sample chapters and synopsis with e-application by mid May; open until filled. **Content:** Character-driven novels with protagonists ages 11 and older. Collegial format; 90 percent hands-on. Our faculty critiques early as well as optional later chapters, plus synopses. Our pre-workshop anthology of peer manuscripts maximizes learning and networking. Several enrollees have landed contracts as a direct result of our seminar. **Details:** visit our website and e-mail us via the contact form."

WILLIAM PATERSON UNIVERSITY SPRING WRITER'S CONFERENCE

English Department, Atrium 232, 300 Pompton Rd., Wayne NJ 07470. (973)720-3067. **Fax:** (973)720-2189. **E-mail:** liut@wpunj.edu. **Website:** wpunj.edu/cohss/departments/english/writers-conference/. Annual conference held each spring (April 13). Conference duration: 1 day. Average attendance: 100-125. Small writing workshops and panels address topics such as writing from life, getting your work in print, poetry, playwriting, fiction, creative nonfiction, and book and magazine editing. Sessions are led by William Paterson faculty members and distinguished guest writers and editors of verse and prose. Speakers have included Francine Prose, David Means, Alison Lurie, Russell Banks, Terese Svoboda, and Anthony Swofford.

COSTS $55 (includes lunch).

PHILADELPHIA WRITERS' CONFERENCE

P.O. Box 7171, Elkins Park PA 19027-0171. (215) 619-7422. **E-mail:** dresente@mc3.edu. **E-mail:** info@pwcwriters.org. **Website:** www.pwcwriters.org. **Contact:** Dana Resente. Estab. 1949. Annual. Conference held June 7-9. Average attendance: 160-200. Conference covers many forms of writing: novel, short story, genre fiction, nonfiction book, magazine writing, blogging, juvenile, poetry.

COSTS Advance registration is $205; walk-in registration is $225. The banquet and buffet are $40 each. Master classes are $50.

ACCOMMODATIONS Holiday Inn, Independence Mall, Fourth and Arch Streets, Philadelphia, PA 19106-2170. "Hotel offers discount for early registration."

ADDITIONAL INFORMATION Sponsors contest. "Length is generally 2,500 words for fiction or nonfiction. 1st Prize, in addition to cash and certificate, gets free tuition for following year." Also offers ms critique. Accepts inquiries by e-mail and SASE. Agents and editors attend conference. Visit us on the web for further agent and speaker details."

PIMA WRITERS' WORKSHOP

Pima College, 2202 W. Anklam Rd., Tucson AZ 85709. (520)206-6084. **Fax:** (520)206-6020. **E-mail:** mfiles@pima.edu. **Contact:** Meg Files, director. Writer conference geared toward beginner, intermediate and advanced levels. **Open to students.** The conference features presentations and writing exercises on writing and publishing stories for children and young adults, among other genres. Annual conference. Workshop held in May. Cost: $100 (can include ms critique). Participants may attend for college credit. Meals and accommodations not included. Features a dozen authors, editors, and agents talking about writing and publishing fiction, nonfiction, poetry, and stories for children. Write for more information.

ROCKY MOUNTAIN FICTION WRITERS COLORADO GOLD

Rocky Mountain Fiction Writers, P.O. Box 735, Confier CO 80433. **E-mail:** conference@rmfw.org. **Website:** www.rmfw.org. Estab. 1982. Annual conference held in September. Conference duration: 3 days. Average attendance: 350. Themes include general novel-length fiction, genre fiction, contemporary romance, mystery, science fiction/fantasy, mainstream, young adult, and historical fiction. Speakers have included Jodi Thomas, Bernard Cornwell, Terry Brooks, Dorothy Cannell, PatriciaGardner Evans, Diane Mott Davidson, Constance O'Day, Connie Willis, Clarissa Pinkola Estes, Michael Palmer, Jennifer Unter, Margaret Marr, Ashley Krass, and Andren Barzvi. Approximately 8 editors and 5 agents attend annually.

COSTS Available online.

ACCOMMODATIONS Special rates will be available at conference hotel.

ADDITIONAL INFORMATION Editor-conducted workshops are limited to 8 participants for critique, with auditing available. Pitch appointments available at no charge. Friday morning master classes available. New as of 2013: Writers' retreat available immediately following conference; space is limited.

RT BOOKLOVERS CONVENTION

55 Bergen St., Brooklyn NY 11201. (718)237-1097 or (800)989-8816, ext. 12. **Fax:** (718)624-2526. **E-mail:** jocarol@rtconvention.com. **E-mail:** nancy@rtbookreviews.com. **Website:** rtconvention.com. Features 125 workshops, agent and editor appointments, a book fair, and more.

COSTS See website for pricing and other information.

ACCOMMODATIONS Rooms available at a nearby Sheaton and Westin. Check online to reserve a room.

☺ SAGE HILL WRITING EXPERIENCE

Box 1731, Saskatoon SK S7K 3S1 Canada. (306)652-7395. **E-mail:** sage.hill@sasktel.net. **Website:** sage hillwriting.ca. **Contact:** Philip Adams, Executive Director. Annual workshops held in late July/August

and May. Conference duration: 10-14 days. Average attendance: 40/summer program; 8/spring program. Sage Hill Writing Experience offers a special working and learning opportunity to writers at different stages of development. Top-quality instruction, low instructor-student ratio, and the beautiful Sage Hill setting offer conditions ideal for the pursuit of excellence in the arts of fiction, poetry and playwriting. The Sage Hill location features individual accommodations, in-room writing areas, lounges, meeting rooms, healthy meals, walking woods, and vistas in several directions. Classes being held (may vary from year to year) include: Introduction to Writing Fiction & Poetry, Fiction Workshop, Writing Young Adult Fiction Workshop, Poetry Workshop, Poetry Colloquium, Fiction Colloquium, Novel Colloquium, Playwriting Lab, Fall Poetry Colloquium, and Spring Poetry Colloquium. Speakers have included Nicole Brossard, Steven Galloway, Robert Currie, Jeanette Lynes, Karen Solie and Colleen Murphy.
COSTS Summer program: $1,295 (includes instruction, accommodation, meals). Fall Poetry Colloquium: $1,495. Scholarships and bursaries are available.
ACCOMMODATIONS Located at Lumsden, 45 kilometers outside Regina.
ADDITIONAL INFORMATION For Introduction to Creative Writing, send a 5-page sample of your writing or a statement of your interest in creative writing and a list of courses taken. For workshop and colloquium programs, send a résumé of your writing career and a 12-page sample of your work, plus 5 pages of published work. Guidelines are available for SASE. Inquire via e-mail or fax.

SAN DIEGO STATE UNIVERSITY WRITERS' CONFERENCE

SDSU College of Extended Studies, 5250 Campanile Dr., San Diego State University, San Diego CA 92182-1920. (619)594-2517. **Fax:** (619)594-8566. **E-mail:** sdsuwritersconference@mail.sdsu.edu. **Website:** ces. sdsu.edu/writers. Estab. 1984. Annual conference held in January/February. Conference duration: 2 days. Average attendance: 375. Covers fiction, nonfiction, scriptwriting and e-books. Held at the Doubletree Hotel in Mission Valley. Each year the conference offers a variety of workshops for the beginner and advanced writers. This conference allows the individual writer to choose which workshop best suits his/her needs. In addition to the workshops, editor reading appointments and agent/editor consultation appointments are provided so attendees may meet with editors and agents one-on-one to discuss specific questions. A reception is offered Saturday immediately following the workshops, offering attendees the opportunity to socialize with the faculty in a relaxed atmosphere. Last year, approximately 60 faculty members attended.
COSTS Approximately $365-485
ACCOMMODATIONS Attendees must make their own travel arrangements.

SAN FRANCISCO WRITERS CONFERENCE

1029 Jones St., San Francisco CA 94109. (415)673-0939. **Fax:** (415)673-0367. **E-mail:** Barabara@sfwriters.org. **Website:** sfwriters.org. **Contact:** Barbara Santos, marketing director. Estab. 2003. "Annual conference held President's Day weekend in February. Average attendance: 400+. Top authors, respected literary agents, and major publishing houses are at the event so attendees can make face-to-face contact with all the right people. Writers of nonfiction, fiction, poetry, and specialty writing (children's books, cookbooks, travel, etc.) will all benefit from the event. There are important sessions on marketing, self-publishing, technology, and trends in the publishing industry. Plus, there's an optional 4-hour session called Speed Dating for Agents where attendees can meet with 20+ agents. Speakers have included Jennifer Crusie, Richard Paul Evans, Jamie Raab, Mary Roach, Jane Smiley, Debbie Macomber, Firoozeh Dumas, Zilpha Keatley Snyder, Steve Berry, Jacquelyn Mitchard. More than 20 agents and editors participate each year, many of whom will be available for meetings with attendees."
COSTS Early price (until September) is $575. Check the website for pricing on later dates.
ACCOMMODATIONS The Intercontinental Mark Hopkins Hotel is a historic landmark at the top of Nob Hill in San Francisco. The hotel is located so that everyone arriving at the Oakland or San Francisco airport can take BART to either the Embarcadero or Powell Street exits, then walk or take a cable car or taxi directly to the hotel.
ADDITIONAL INFORMATION "Present yourself in a professional manner and the contact you will make will be invaluable to your writing career. Brochures and registration are online."

SANTA BARBARA WRITERS CONFERENCE

27 W. Anapamu St., Suite 305, Santa Barbara CA 93101. (805)568-1516. **E-mail:** info@sbwriters.com.

Website: www.sbwriters.com. Estab. 1972. Annual conference held June 8-13. Average attendance: 200. Covers fiction, nonfiction, journalism, memoir, poetry, playwriting, screenwriting, travel writing, young adult, children's literature, humor, and marketing. Speakers have included Ray Bradbury, William Styron, Eudora Welty, James Michener, Sue Grafton, Charles M. Schulz, Clive Cussler, Fannie Flagg, Elmore Leonard, and T.C. Boyle. Agents will appear on a panel; in addition, there will be an agents and editors day that allows writers to pitch their projects in one-on-one meetings.

COSTS Conference registration is $550 on or before March 16 and $625 after March 16.

ACCOMMODATIONS Hyatt Santa Barbara.

ADDITIONAL INFORMATION Register online or contact for brochure and registration forms.

☘ SASKATCHEWAN FESTIVAL OF WORDS AND WORKSHOPS

217 Main St. N., Moose Jaw SK S6H 0W1 Canada. **E-mail:** word.festival@sasktel.net. **Website:** www.festivalofwords.com. **Contact:** Donna Lee Howes. Writer workshops geared toward beginner and intermediate levels. **Open to students.** Readings that include a wide spectrum of genres—fiction, creative nonfiction, poetry, songwriting, screenwriting, playwriting, dramatic reading with actors, graphic novels, Great Big Book Club Discussion with author, children's writing, panels, independent film screening, panels, slam poetry, interviews and performances. Annual festival. Workshop held third weekend in July. Cost of workshop varies from $10 for a single reading to $200 for a full pass. Trivia Night Fun ticket is extra. Visit website for more information.

SCIENCE FICTION WRITERS WORKSHOP

English Department/University of Kansas, Wesoce Hall, 1445 Jayhawk Blvd., Room 3001, Lawrence KS 66045-7590. (785)864-2508. **E-mail:** cmckit@ku.edu. **Website:** www.sfcenter.ku.edu/SFworkshop.htm. Estab. 1985. Annual. Workshop held June 2-14. The workshop is "small, informal, and aimed at writers on the edge of publication or regular publication." For writing and marketing science fiction and fantasy. Site: Workshop sessions operate informally in a university housing lounge on the University of Kansas campus where most participants also reside. Established in 1985 by James Gunn and currently led by Christopher McKitterick, with guest authors joining

for the second week. Writer and editor instructors have included Lou Anders, Bradley Denton, James Gunn, Kij Johnson, John Ordover, Frederik Pohl, Pamela Sargent, and George Zebrowski, and each year the winners of the Campbell and Sturgeon Memorial Awards participate in 1 or more days of the workshop. A novel workshop in science fiction and fantasy is also available at the same time, led by Kij Johnson.

COSTS $500, exclusive of meals and housing.

ACCOMMODATIONS Housing information is available. Several airport shuttle services offer reasonable transportation from the Kansas City International Airport to Lawrence.

ADDITIONAL INFORMATION Admission to the workshop is bysubmission of an acceptable story, usually by May. Two additional stories are submitted by the middle of June. These 3 stories are distributed to other participants for critiquing and are the basis for the first week of the workshop. One story is rewritten for the second week, when students also work with guest authors. See website for guidelines. This workshop is intended for writers who have just started to sell their work or need that extra bit of understanding or skill to become a published writer.

SEWANEE WRITERS' CONFERENCE

735 University Ave., 119 Gailor Hall, Stamler Center, Sewanee TN 37383-1000. (931) 598-1654. **E-mail:** al latham@sewanee.edu. **Website:** www.sewaneewriters.org. **Contact:** Adam Latham. Estab. 1990. Annual conference held in the date range of July 23–August 4. Average attendance: 144. "We offer genre-based workshops in fiction, poetry, and playwriting. The conference uses the facilities of Sewanee: The University of the South. The university is a collection of ivy-covered Gothic-style buildings located on the Cumberland Plateau in mid-Tennessee. Editors, publishers, and agents structure their own presentations, but there is always opportunity for questions from the audience." A score of writing professionals will visit. The Conference will offer its customary Walter E. Dakin Fellowships and Tennessee Williams Scholarships as well as awards in memory of Stanley Elkin, Donald Justice, Howard Nemerov, Father William Ralston, Peter Taylor, Mona Van Duyn, and John N. Wall. Additional scholarships have been made possible by Georges and Anne Borchardt and

Gail Hochman. Each participant—whether contributor, scholar, or fellow—receives financial support.

COSTS $1,000 for tuition and $700 for room, board, and activity costs

ACCOMMODATIONS Participants are housed in single rooms in university dormitories. Bathrooms are shared by small groups. Motel or B&B housing is available, but not abundantly so.

SOCIETY OF CHILDREN'S BOOK WRITERS & ILLUSTRATORS ANNUAL SUMMER CONFERENCE ON WRITING AND ILLUSTRATING FOR CHILDREN

8271 Beverly Blvd., Los Angeles CA 90048-4515. (323)782-1010. **Fax:** (323)782-1892. **E-mail:** scbwi@scbwi.org. **Website:** www.scbwi.org. Estab. 1972. Annual conference held in early August. Conference duration: 4 days. Average attendance: 1,000. Held at the Century Plaza Hotel in Los Angeles. Speakers have included Andrea Brown, Steven Malk, Ashley Bryan, Bruce Coville, Karen Hesse, Harry Mazer, Lucia Monfried, and Russell Freedman. Agents will be speaking and sometimes participate in ms critiques.

COSTS Approximately $450 (does not include hotel room).

ACCOMMODATIONS Information on overnight accommodations is made available.

ADDITIONAL INFORMATION Ms and illustration critiques are available. Brochure/guidelines are available in June online or for SASE.

SOUTH COAST WRITERS CONFERENCE

Southwestern Oregon Community College, P.O. Box 590, 29392 Ellensburg Ave., Gold Beach OR 97444. (541)247-2741. **Fax:** (541)247-6247. **E-mail:** scwc@socc.edu. **Website:** www.socc.edu/scwriters. Estab. 1996. Annual conference held Presidents Day weekend in February. Conference duration: 2 days. Covers fiction, poetry, children's, nature, songwriting, and marketing. William Sullivan is the next scheduled keynote speaker, and presenters include Linda Barnes, Merritt "Biff" Barnes, Judy Cox, Bruce Holbert, Elizabeth Lyon, Carolyn J. Rose, Johnny Shaw, Lauren Sheehan, William Sullivan, and Bob Welch.

ADDITIONAL INFORMATION See website for cost and additional details.

STORY WEAVERS CONFERENCE

Oklahoma Writer's Federation, (405)682-6000. **E-mail:** president@owfi.org. **Website:** www.OWFI.org.

Contact: Linda Apple, president. Oklahoma Writer's Federation, Inc. is open and welcoming to writers of all genres and all skill levels. Our goal is to help writers become better and to help beginning writers understand and master the craft of writing.

COSTS Cost is $150 before April. $175 after April. Cost includes awards banquet and famous author banquet. Three extra sessions are available for an extra fee: How to Self-Publish Your Novel on Kindle, Nook, and iPad (and make more money than being published by New York), with Dan Case; When Polar Bear Wishes Came True: Understanding and Creating Meaningful Stories, with Jack Dalton; How to Create Three-Dimensional Characters, with Steven James.

ACCOMMODATIONS The site is at the Embassy Suite using their meeting halls. There are very few stairs and the rooms are close together for easy access.

ADDITIONAL INFORMATION "We have 20 speakers, five agents, and nine publisher/editors for a full list and bios, please see website."

SURREY INTERNATIONAL WRITERS' CONFERENCE

SIWC, P.O. Box 42023 RPO Guildford, Surrey BC V3R 1S5 Canada. **E-mail:** kathychung@siwc.ca. **Website:** www.siwc.ca. **Contact:** Kathy Chung, conference coordinator. Writing workshops geared toward beginner, intermediate, and advanced levels. More than 70 workshops and panels, on all topics and genres. Blue Pencil and Agent/Editor Pitch sessions included. Annual Conference held every October. Different conference price packages available. Check our website for more information.

TAOS SUMMER WRITERS' CONFERENCE

Department of English Language and Literature, MSC 03 2170, 1 University of New Mexico, Albuquerque NM 87131-0001. (505)277-5572. **Fax:** (505)277-2950. **E-mail:** taosconf@unm.edu. **Website:** www.unm.edu/~taosconf. **Contact:** Sharon Oard Warner. Estab. 1999. Annual conference held July 14-21. Offers workshops in novel writing, short story writing, screenwriting, poetry, creative nonfiction, travel writing, historical fiction, memoir, and revision. Participants may also schedule a consultation with a visiting agent/editor.

COSTS Weeklong workshop registrations are $650

ACCOMMODATIONS Held at the Sagebrush Inn and Conference Center.

☁ THE SCHOOL FOR WRITERS SUMMER WORKSHOP

The Humber School for Writers, Humber Institute of Technology & Advanced Learning, 3199 Lake Shore Blvd. W., Toronto ON M8V 1K8 Canada. (416)675-6622. **E-mail:** antanas.sileika@humber.ca; hilary.higgins@humber.ca. **Website:** www.creativeandperformingarts.humber.ca/content/writers.html. The School for Writers Summer Workshop has moved to the fall with the International Festival of Authors. Workshop the last week in October through first week in November. Conference duration: 1 week. Average attendance: 100. New writers from around the world gather to study with faculty members to work on their novels, short stories, poetry, or creative nonfiction. Agents and editors participate in conference. Include a work-in-progress with your registration. Faculty has included Martin Amis, David Mitchell, Rachel Kuschner, Peter Carey, Roddy Doyle, Tim O'Brien, Andrea Levy, Barry Unsworth, Edward Albee, Ha Jin, Julia Glass, Mavis Gallant, Bruce Jay Friedman, Isabel Huggan, Alistair MacLeod, Lisa Moore, Kim Moritsugu, Francine Prose, Paul Quarrington, Olive Senior, and D.M. Thomas, Annabel Lyon, Mary Gaitskill, M. G. Vassanji.

COSTS around $800 (in 2013). Some limited scholarships are available.

ACCOMMODATIONS Nearby hotels are available.

ADDITIONAL INFORMATION Accepts inquiries by e-mail, phone, and fax.

TMCC (RENO) WRITERS' CONFERENCE

Truckee Meadows Community College, 5270 Neil Rd., Reno NV 89502. (775)829-9010. **Fax:** (775)829-9032. **E-mail:** wdce@tmcc.edu. **Website:** wdce.tmcc.edu. Estab. 1991. Annual conference held April 27. Average attendance: 150. Conference focuses on strengthening mainstream/literary fiction and nonfiction works and how to market them to agents and publishers. Site: Truckee Meadows Community College in Reno, Nevada. "There is always an array of speakers and presenters with impressive literary credentials, including agents and editors." Speakers have included Chuck Sambuchino, Sheree Bykofsky, Andrea Brown, Dorothy Allison, Karen Joy Fowler, James D. Houston, James N. Frey, Gary Short, Jane Hirschfield, Dorrianne Laux, and Kim Addonizio

COSTS $119 for a full-day seminar; $32 for a 10-minute one-on-one appointment with an agent or editor.

ACCOMMODATIONS The Silver Legacy, in downtown Reno, offers a special rate and shuttle service to the Reno/Tahoe International Airport, which is less than 20 minutes away.

ADDITIONAL INFORMATION "The conference is open to all writers, regardless of their level of experience. Brochures are available online and mailed in January. Send inquiries via e-mail."

TONY HILLERMAN WRITER'S CONFERENCE

1063 Willow Way, Santa FE NM 87505. (505)471-1565. **E-mail:** wordharvest@wordharvest.com. **Website:** www.wordharvest.com. **Contact:** Jean Schaumberg, co-director. Estab. 2004. Annual. November 7-9, 2013. Conference duration: 3 days. Average attendance: 100. Site: Hilton Santa Fe Historic Plaza. First day: Author/teacher Margaret Coel, focuses on the art of writing to create great characters. Other programs focus on creating memorable plots and the business of writing. "We'll honor the winner of the $10,000 Tony Hillerman Prize for best first mystery at a lunch with keynote speaker Craig Johnson, a *New York Times* bestselling author. A 'flash critique' session, open to any interested attendee, will add to the fun and information. Author attendees will also have a chance to talk about their new books at teh new Book/New Author Breakfast."

COSTS Previous year's costs: $395 per-registration.

ACCOMMODATIONS Hilton Santa Fe Historic Plaza offers $119 single or double occupancy. November 6-10. Book online with the hotel.

ADDITIONAL INFORMATION Sponsors a $10,000 first mystery novel contest with St. Marttin's Press. Brochures available in July for SASE, by phone, e-mail, and on website. Accepts inquiries by SASE, phone, e-mail. Deadline for the Hillerman Mystery Competition is June 1.

UCLA EXTENSION WRITERS' PROGRAM

10995 Le Conte Ave., #440, Los Angeles CA 90024. (310)825-9415 or (800)388-UCLA. **Fax:** (310)206-7382. **E-mail:** writers@uclaextension.edu. **Website:** www. uclaextension.org/writers. Estab. 1891. "As America's largest and most comprehensive continuing education creative writing and screenwriting program, the UCLA Extension Writers' Program welcomes and trains writers at all levels of development whose aspirations range from personal enrichment to professional publication and production. Taught by an instructor corps of 250 professional writers, the Writers' Program curriculum features 530 annual open-enrollment courses onsite and online in novel writing, short fiction, personal essay, memoir, poetry, playwriting, writing for the youth market, publishing, feature film writing, and television writing, and is designed to accommodate your individual writing needs, ambitions, and lifestyle. Special programs and services include certificate programs in creative writing, feature film writing, and television writing; a four-day Writers Studio which attracts a national and international audience; nine-month master classes in novel writing and feature film writing; an online screenwriting mentorship program; one-on-one script and manuscript consultation services; literary and screenplay competitions; advisors who help you determine how best to achieve your personal writing goals; and free annual public events such as Writers Faire and Publication Party which allow you to extend your writing education and network with the literary and entertainment communities."

COSTS Depends on length of the course.

ACCOMMODATIONS Students make their own arrangements. Out-of-town students are encouraged to take online courses.

ADDITIONAL INFORMATION Some advanced-level classes have ms submittal requirements; see the UCLA Extension catalog or see website.

UMKC WRITERS WORKSHOPS

5300 Rockhill Rd., Kansas City MO 64110. (816)235-2736. **Fax:** (816)235-5279. **E-mail:** wittfeldk@umkc.edu. **Website:** www.newletters.org/writingConferences.asp. **Contact:** Kathi Wittfeld. Mark Twain Workshop will not be held in 2013. New Letters Weekend Writing Conference was held on Friday, Saturday and Sunday, June 28-30,2013 at Diastole. New Letters Writer's Conference and Mark Twain Writer's Workshop are geared toward intermediate, advanced and professional levels. Workshops open to students and community. Annual workshops. Workshops held in Summer. Cost of workshop varies. Write for more information.

UNIVERSITY OF NORTH DAKOTA WRITERS CONFERENCE

Department of English, 110 Merrifield Hall, 276 Centennial Drive, Stop 7209, Grand Forks ND 58202.

(701)777-3321. **E-mail:** writersconference@und.nodak.edu. **Website:** www.undwritersconference.org. Estab. 1970. Annual conference held March 19-23. Offers panels, readings, and films focused around a specific theme. Almost all events take place in the UND Memorial Union, which has a variety of small rooms and a 1,000-seat main hall. Past speakers include Art Spiegelman, Truman Capote, Sir Salman Rushdie, Allen Ginsberg, Alice Walker, and Louise Erdrich.

COSTS All events are free and open to the public. Donations accepted.

ACCOMMODATIONS All events are free and open to the public. Accommodations available at area hotels. Information on overnight accommodations available on website.

ADDITIONAL INFORMATION Schedule and other information available on website.

UNIVERSITY OF NORTH FLORIDA WRITERS CONFERENCE

12000 Alumni Dr., Jacksonville FL 32224-2678. (904)620-4200. **E-mail:** sharon.y.cobb@unf.edu. **Website:** www.unfwritersconference.com. **Contact:** Sharon Y. Cobb, conference director. Estab. 2009.

COSTS See website for current registration fees. Full conference attendees receive: workshops, critiques by faculty and fellow students, lunches, Friday wine/cheese reception, and book signings.

ACCOMMODATIONS Nearby accommodations are listed on website. There is free parking provided at the University Center.

⊙ THE VANCOUVER INTERNATIONAL WRITERS & READERS FESTIVAL

202-1398 Cartwright St., Vancouver BC V6H 3R8 Canada. (604)681-6330. **Fax:** (604)681-8400. **E-mail:** info@writersfest.bc.ca. **E-mail:** hwake@writersfest.bc.ca. **Website:** www.writersfest.bc.ca. Estab. 1988. Annual festival held October 22-27. Average attendance: 11,000. The program of events is diverse and includes readings, panel discussions, and seminars. There are lots of opportunities to interact with the writers who attend. Held on Granville Island in the heart of Vancouver. Speakers have included Margaret Atwood, Maeve Binchy, and J.K. Rowling.

ACCOMMODATIONS Local tourist information can be provided upon request.

ADDITIONAL INFORMATION Remember—this is a festival and a celebration, not a conference or workshop. Brochures are available after August for a SASE. Inquire via e-mail or fax, or go online for updates.

VERMONT COLLEGE OF FINE ARTS POSTGRADUATE WRITERS' CONFERENCE

36 College St., Montpelier VT 05602. (802)828-8835. **Fax:** (802)828-8649. **E-mail:** pgconference@vcfa.edu. **Website:** www.vcfa.edu/writing/pwc. Estab. 1996. Annual conference for writers with MFAs or equivalent preparation on the historic campus of Vermont College of Fine Arts. August 12-18. Features intensive small-group workshops taught by an award-winning faculty, plus readings, craft talks, writing exercise sessions and individual consultations. Conference size: 70 participants. Workshops in creative nonfiction, novel, short story, poetry, poetry manuscript and writing for young people.

COSTS Costs: $875 or $995 (Poetry Ms.)/tuition, $330/private room, $180/shared room, $185/meals. Limited scholarships are available.

ACCOMMODATIONS Single or double rooms are available in the VCFA campus dormitories.

VERMONT STUDIO CENTER

P.O. Box 613, 80 Pearl Street, Johnson VT 05656. (802)635-2727. **Fax:** (802)635-2730. **E-mail:** info@ vermontstudiocenter.org. **Website:** www.vermont studiocenter.org. **Contact:** Gary Clark, Writing Program Director. Estab. 1984. Founded by artists in 1984, the Vermont Studio Center is the largest international artists' and writers' Residency Program in the United States, hosting 50 visual artists and writers each month from across the country and around the world. The Studio Center provides 4-12 week studio residencies on an historic 30-building campus along the Gihon River in Johnson, Vermont, a village in the heart of the northern Green Mountains.

ACCOMMODATIONS "The cost of a 4-week residency is $3,750. Generous fellowship and grant assistance available. "Accommodations available on site. "Residents live in single rooms in ten modest, comfortable houses adjacent to the Red Mill Building. Rooms are simply furnished and have shared baths. Complete linen service is provided. The Studio Center is unable to accommodate guests at meals, overnight guests, spouses, children or pets."

ADDITIONAL INFORMATION Fellowships application deadlines are February 15, June 15 and October 1. Writers encouraged to visit website for more information. May also e-mail, call, fax.

VIRGINIA FESTIVAL OF THE BOOK

Virginia Festival of the Book Foundation for the Humanities, 145 Ednam Dr., Charlottesville VA 22903-4629. (434)924-3296. **Fax:** (434)296-4714. **E-mail:** vabook@virginia.edu; spcoleman@virginia.edu. **Website:** www.vabook.org. **Contact:** Nancy Damon, program director. Estab. 1995. Annual. Held March 20-24. Average attendance: 22,000. Festival held to celebrate books and promote reading and literacy. Open to Students. Readings, panel discussions, presentations and workshops by author, and book-related professionals for children and adults. Most programs are free and open to the public. See website for more information. Applications available online from May through September.

COSTS Most events are free and open to the public. Two luncheons, a breakfast, and a reception require tickets.

ACCOMMODATIONS Overnight accommodations available.

ADDITIONAL INFORMATION "The festival is a 5-day event featuring authors, illustrators, and publishing professionals. Authors must apply to the festival to be included on a panel. Applications accepted only online.

WESLEYAN WRITERS CONFERENCE

Wesleyan University, 294 High St., Room 207, Middletown CT 06459. (860)685-3604. **Fax:** (860)685-2441. **E-mail:** agreene@wesleyan.edu. **Website:** www.wesleyan.edu/writing/conference. Estab. 1956. Annual conference held June 12-16. Average attendance: 100. Focuses on the novel, fiction techniques, short stories, poetry, screenwriting, nonfiction, literary journalism, memoir, mixed media work and publishing. The conference is held on the campus of Wesleyan University, in the hills overlooking the Connecticut River. Features a faculty of award-winning writers, seminars and readings of new fiction, poetry, nonfiction and mixed media forms—as well as guest lectures on a range of topics including publishing. Both new and experienced writers are welcome. Participants may attend seminars in all genres. Speakers have included Esmond Harmsworth (Zachary Schuster Agency), Daniel Mandel (Sanford J. Greenburger Associates), Dorian Karchmar, Amy Williams (ICM and Collins McCormick), Mary Sue Rucci (Simon & Schuster), Denise Roy (Simon & Schuster), John Kulka (Harvard University Press), Julie Barer (Barer Literary) and many others. Agents will be speaking and available for meetings with attendees. Participants are often successful in finding agents and publishers for their mss. Wesleyan participants are also frequently featured in the anthology *Best New American Voices*.

ACCOMMODATIONS Meals are provided on campus. Lodging is available on campus or in town.

ADDITIONAL INFORMATION Ms critiques are available, but not required. Scholarships and teaching fellowships are available, including the Joan Jakobson Awards for fiction writers and poets; and the Jon Davidoff Scholarships for nonfiction writers and journalists. Inquire via e-mail, fax, or phone.

WESTERN RESERVE WRITERS & FREELANCE CONFERENCE

7700 Clocktower Dr., Kirtland OH 44094. (440) 525-7812. **E-mail:** deencr@aol.com. **Website:** www.deannaadams.com. **Contact:** Deanna Adams, director/conference coordinator. Estab. 1983. Biannual. Last conference held September 28, 2013. Conference duration: 1 day or half-day. Average attendance: 120. "The Western Reserve Writers Conferences are designed for all writers, aspiring and professional, and offer presentations in all genres—nonfiction, fiction, poetry, essays, creative nonfiction, and the business of writing, including Web writing and successful freelance writing." Site: "Located in the main building of Lakeland Community College, the conference is easy to find and just off the I-90 freeway. The Fall 2013 conference featured top-notch presenters from newspapers and magazines, along with published authors, freelance writers, and professional editors. Presentations included developing issues in today's publishing and publishing options, turning writing into a lifelong vocation, as well as workshops on plotting, creating credible characters, writing mysteries, romance writing, and tips on submissions, getting books into stores, and storytelling for both fiction and nonfiction writers. Included throughout the day are one-on-one editing consults, Q&A panel, and book sale/author signings."

COSTS Fall all-day conference includes lunch: $95. Spring half-day conference, no lunch: $69.

ADDITIONAL INFORMATION Brochures for the conferences are available by January (for spring conference) and July (for fall). Also accepts inquiries by e-mail and phone. Check Deanna Adams' website for all updates. Editors and agents often attend the conferences.

WILLAMETTE WRITERS CONFERENCE

2108 Buck St., Portland OR 97068. (503)305-6729. **Fax:** (503)344-6174. **E-mail:** wilwrite@willamettewriters.com. **Website:** www.willamettewriters.com. Estab. 1981. Annual conference held in August. Conference duration: 3 days. Average attendance: 600. "Williamette Writers is open to all writers, and we plan our conference accordingly. We offer workshops on all aspects of fiction, nonfiction, marketing, the creative process, screenwriting, etc. Also we invite top-notch inspirational speakers for keynote addresses. Recent theme was 'Fresh Brewed.' We always include at least 1 agent or editor panel and offer a variety of topics of interest to both fiction and nonfiction writers and screenwriters." Agents will be speaking and available for meetings with attendees. Recent editors, agents, and film producers in attendance have included April Eberhardt, Katheryn Flynn, Robert Guinsler, Laura Mclean, Tooschis Morin.

COSTS Pricing schedule available online.

ACCOMMODATIONS If necessary, arrangements can be made on an individual basis through the conference hotel. Special rates may be available.

ADDITIONAL INFORMATION Brochure/guidelines are available for a catalog-sized SASE.

⚫ WINCHESTER WRITERS' CONFERENCE, FESTIVAL AND BOOKFAIR, AND IN-DEPTH WRITING WORKSHOPS

University of Winchester, Winchester Hampshire WA S022 4NR United Kingdom. 44 (0) 1962 827238. **E-mail:** Barbara.Large@winchester.ac.uk. **Website:** www.writersconference.co.uk. **Contact:** Barbara Large. "The 33rd Winchester Writers' Conference, Festival, and Bookfair will be launched by Lord Julian Fellowes, author/scriptwriter, internationally famous for many works, including *Downton Abbey*, in-depth writing workshops June 24-25, 2-13, at the University of Winchester, Winchester, Hampshire S022 4NR. Lord Felloews will give the Keynote Address and will lead an outstanding team of 65 professional writers who will offer during 14 masters' courses, 16 Friday evening-Sunday morning, 55 lectures, and 500 one-to-one appointments to help writers harness their creative ideas into marketable work. Participate by entering some of the 17 writing competitions, even if you can't attend. Over 120 writers have now reported major publishing successes as a direct result of their attendance at past conferences. This leading international literary event offers a magnificent source of information and network of support from tutors who are published writers and industry specialists, a support that continues throughout the year with additional short courses. Enjoy a creative writing holiday in Winchester, the oldest city in England, yet within an hour of London. Tours planned to Jane Austen's home and the Chawton Study Centre for Women's Literature, the haunts of Keats and the 12th century illuminated Winchester Bible. To receive the 66-page conference programme, including all the competition details please contact us:sara.gangai@winchester.ac.uk, 44(0)1962-826367; barbara.large@winchester.ac.uk, 44(0)1962-827238; or write to us at University of Winchester, Winchester, Hampshire SO22 4NR, United Kingdom."

WISCONSIN REGIONAL WRITERS' ASSOCIATION CONFERENCES

PO Box 085270, Racine Wisconsin 53408-5270. **E-mail:** cfreg@wiwrite.org. **Website:** www.wiwrite.org. Estab. 1948. Annual conferences are held in May 10 and 11 and September. Conference duration: 2-3 days. Provides presentations for all genres, including fiction, nonfiction, scriptwriting, and poetry. Presenters include authors, agents, editors, and publishers. Speakers have included Jack Byrne, Michelle Grajkowski, Benjamin Leroy, Richard Lederer, and Philip Martin.
COSTS $40-75.
ACCOMMODATIONS Provides a list of area hotels or lodging options. "We negotiate special rates at each facility. A block of rooms is set aside for a specific time period."
ADDITIONAL INFORMATION Award winners receive a certificate and a cash prize. First place winners of the Jade Ring contest receive a jade ring. Must be a member to enter contests. For brochure, call, e-mail or visit website in March/July.

WOMEN WRITERS WINTER RETREAT

Homestead House B&B, 38111 West Spaulding, Willoughby OH 44094. (440)946-1902. **E-mail:** deencr@aol.com. **Website:** www.deannaadams.com. Estab. 2007. Annual. Conference duration: 3 days. Average attendance: 35-40. Retreat. "The Women Writers' Winter Retreat was designed for aspiring and professional women writers who cannot seem to find enough time to devote to honing their craft. Each retreat offers class time and workshops facilitated by successful women writers, as well as allows time to

do some actual writing, alone or in a group. A Friday night dinner and keynote kick-starts the weekend, followed by Saturday workshops, free time, meals, and an open mic to read your works. Sunday wraps up with 1 more workshop and fellowship. All genres welcome. Choice of overnight stay or commuting." Site: Located in the heart of downtown Willoughby, this warm and attractive bed and breakfast is easy to find, around the corner from the main street, Erie Street, and behind a popular Arabica coffee house. Door prizes and book sale/author signings throughout the weekend.
COSTS Single room: $315; shared room: $235 (includes complete weekend package, with B&B stay and all meals and workshops); weekend commute: $165; Saturday only: $125 (prices include lunch and dinner).
ADDITIONAL INFORMATION Brochures for the writers retreat are available by December. Accepts inquiries and reservations by e-mail or phone. See Deanna's website for additional information and updates.

WORDS & MUSIC

624 Pirate's Alley, New Orleans LA 70116. (504)586-1609. **Fax:** (504)522-9725. **E-mail:** info@wordsandmusic.org. **Website:** www.wordsandmusic.org. Estab. 1997. Annual conference held November 20-24. Conference duration: 5 days. Average attendance: 300. Presenters include authors, agents, editors and publishers. Past speakers included agents Deborah Grosvenor, Judith Weber, Stuart Bernstein, Nat Sobel, Jeff Kleinman, Emma Sweeney, Liza Dawson and Michael Murphy; editors Lauren Marino, Webster Younce, Ann Patty, Will Murphy, Jofie Ferrari-Adler, Elizabeth Stein; critics Marie Arana, Jonathan Yardley, and Michael Dirda; fiction writers Oscar Hijuelos, Robert Olen Butler, Shirley Ann Grau, Mayra Montero, Ana Castillo, H.G. Carrillo. Agents and editors critique manuscripts in advance; meet with them one-on-one during the conference.
COSTS See website for a costs and additional information on accommodations. Website will update closer to date of conference.
ACCOMMODATIONS Hotel Monteleone in New Orleans.

WRITE-BY-THE-LAKE WRITER'S WORKSHOP & RETREAT

21 N. Park St., 7th Floor, Madison WI 53715. (608)262-3447. **E-mail:** cdesmet@dcs.wisc.edu. **Website:** www.

dcs.wisc.edu/lsa/writing. **Contact:** Christine DeSmet, director. Open to all writers and students; 12 workshops for all levels. Includes 2 Master Classes for full-novel critique. Held the third week of June on UW-Madison campus. Registration limited to 15; fewer in Master Classes. Writing facilities available; computer labs, wi-fi in all buildings and on the outdoor lakeside terrace.

COSTS $345 before May 20; $395 after May 20. Additional cost for Master Classes and college credits. Cost includes instruction, welcome luncheon, and pastry/coffee each day.

ADDITIONAL INFORMATION E-mail for more information. "Registration opens every December for following June. See web pages online."

♻ WRITE! CANADA

The Word Guild, P.O. Box 1243, Trenton ON K8V 5R9 Canada. **E-mail:** info@thewordguild.com. **E-mail:** writecanada@rogers.com. **Website:** www.writecanada.org. Conference duration: 3 days. Annual conference June 14-16 in Guelph, Ontario for writers who are Christian of all types and at all stages. Offers solid instruction, stimulating interaction, exciting challenges, and worshipful community.

WRITE ON THE SOUND WRITERS' CONFERENCE

Edmonds Arts Commission, 700 Main St., Edmonds WA 98020. (425)771-0228, **Fax:** (425)771-0253. **E-mail:** sarah.cocker@edmondswa.gov. **Website:** www.writeonthesound.com. Estab. 1985. Annual conference held October 4-6. Conference duration: 2.5 days. Average attendance: 200. Features over 30 presenters, a literary contest, ms critiques, a reception and book signing, onsite bookstore, and a variety of evening activities. Held at the Frances Anderson Center in Edmonds, just north of Seattle on the Puget Sound. Speakers have included Elizabeth George, Dan Hurley, Marcia Woodard, Holly Hughes, Greg Bear, Timothy Egan, Joe McHugh, Frances Wood, Garth Stein and Max Grover.

COSTS See website for more information on applying to view costs.

ADDITIONAL INFORMATION Brochures are available in July. Accepts inquiries via phone, e-mail, and fax.

WRITERS@WORK CONFERENCE

P.O. Box 711191, Salt Lake City UT 84171-1191. (801)996-3313. **E-mail:** jennifer@writersatwork.org.

Website: www.writersatwork.org. Estab. 1985. Annual conference held June 5-9. Conference duration: 5 days. Average attendance: 250. Morning workshops (3-hours/day) focus on novel, advanced fiction, generative fiction, nonfiction, poetry, and young adult fiction. Afternoon sessions will include craft lectures, discussions, and directed interviews with authors, agents, and editors. In addition to the traditional, one-on-one manuscript consultations, there will be many opportunities to mingle informally with agents/editors. Held at the Alta Lodge in Alta Lodge, Utah. Speakers have included Steve Almond, Bret Lott, Shannon Hale, Emily Forland (Wendy Weil Agency), Julie Culver (Folio Literary Management, Chuck Adams (Algonquin Press), and Mark A. Taylor (Juniper Press).

COSTS $675-965, based on housing type and consultations.

ACCOMMODATIONS Onsite housing available. Additional lodging and meal information is on the website.

WRITERS' CONFERENCE AT OCEAN PARK

14 Temple Ave., P.O. Box 7296, Ocean Park ME 04063-7296. (207)934-9068. **Fax:** (207)934-2823. **E-mail:** opa@oceanpark.org. **Website:** www.oceanpark.org. Other addresses: P.O. Box 7146, Ocean Park, ME 04063-7146; P.O. Box 172, Assonet, MA 02702 (mailing address for conference). Estab. 1941. Annual conference held in mid-August. Conference duration: 4 days. Average attendance: 50. "We try to present a balanced and eclectic conference. In addition to time and attention given to poetry, we also have children's literature, mystery writing, travel, fiction, nonfiction, journalism, and other issues of interest to writers. Our speakers are editors, writers, and other professionals. Our concentration is, by intention, a general view of writing to publish with supportive encouragement. We are located in Ocean Park, a small seashore village 14 miles south of Portland. Ours is a summer assembly center with many buildings from the Victorian age. The conference meets in Porter Hall, one of the assembly buildings which is listed in the National Register of Historic Places. Speakers have included Michael C. White (novelist/short story writer), Betsy Shool (poet), Suzanne Strempek Shea (novelist), John Perrault (poet), Josh Williamson (newspaper editor), Dawn Potter (poet), Bruce Pratt (fiction writer), Amy McDonald (children's author), Anne Wescott Dodd

(nonfiction writer), Kate Chadbourne (singer/songwriter), Wesley McNair (poet/Maine faculty member), and others. We usually have about 8 guest presenters each year." Publishes writers/editors will be speaking, leading workshops, and available for meetings with attendees.

COSTS $200. The fee does not include housing or meals, which must be arranged separately by conferees.

ACCOMMODATIONS "An accommodations list is available. We are in a summer resort area where motels, guest houses, and restaurants abound."

ADDITIONAL INFORMATION Official summer hours begin in late June, check then for specific dates for 2013 conference. "We have 6 contests for various genres. An announcement is available in the spring. The prizes (all modest) are awarded at the end of the conference and only to those who are registered. Send SASE in June for the conference program."

WRITER'S DIGEST CONFERENCE (EAST IN NYC, AND WEST IN LA)

F+W Media, Inc., 10151 Carver Road, Suite 200, Blue Ash OH 45242. **E-mail:** jill.ruesch@fwmedia.com. **Website:** www.writersdigestconference.com. The Writer's Digest Conferences happen twice a year -- a spring event in New York City and a fall event (2013 LA dates = Sept. 27-29) in Los Angeles. They feature an amazing line up of speakers to help writers with the craft and business of writing. The most popular feature of this conference is the agent pitch slam, in which potential authors are given the ability to pitch their books directly to agents. For the 2014 conference, there will be more than 60 agents in attendance..

WRITERS' LEAGUE OF TEXAS AGENTS & EDITORS CONFERENCE

Writers' League of Texas, 611 S. Congress Ave., Suite 505, Austin TX 78704. (512)499-8914. **Fax:** (512)499-0441. **E-mail:** wlt@writersleague.org. **E-mail:** jennifer@writersleague.org. **Website:** www.writersleague.org. Estab. 1982. Established in 1981, the Writers' League of Texas is a nonprofit professional organization whose primary purpose is to provide a forum for information, support, and sharing among writers, to help members improve and market their writing skills, and to promote the interests of writers and the writing community. The Writers' League of Texas Agents & Editors Conference is for writers at every stage of their career. Beginners can learn more about this mystifying industry and prepare themselves for the journey ahead. Those with completed manuscripts can pitch to agents and get feedback on their manuscripts from professional editors. Published writers can learn about market trends and network with rising stars in the world of writing. No matter what your market, genre, or level, our conference can benefit you.

COSTS Rates vary based on membership and the date of registration. The starting rate (registration through December 15) is $309 for members and $369 for non-members. Rate increases by through later dates. See website for details.

ACCOMMODATIONS 2013 event is at the Hyatt Regency Austin, 208 Barton Springs Road, Austin, TX 78704. Check back often for new information.

ADDITIONAL INFORMATION Event held from June 21-23, 2013. Contests and awards programs are offered separately. Brochures are available upon request.

WRITERS RETREAT WORKSHOP

P.O. Box 4236, Louisville KY 40204. **E-mail:** wrw04@netscape.net. **Website:** www.writersretreatworkshop.com. Estab. 1987. Annual workshop held June 14-23 at the Villa Maria Retreat and Conference Center in Frontenac, Minnesota. Conference duration: 10 days. Focuses on fiction and narrative nonfiction books in progress (all genres). This is an intensive learning experience for small groups of serious-minded writers. Founded by the late Gary Provost (one of the country's leading writing instructors) and his wife Gail (an award-winning author). The goal is for students to leave with a solid understanding of the marketplace, as well as the craft of writing a novel. Speakers have included Becky Motew, Donald Maass, Jennifer Crusie, Michael Palmer, Nancy Pickard, Elizabeth Lyon, Lauren Mosko (Writer's Digest Books), Adam Marsh (Reece Halsey North), and Peter H. McGuigan (Sanford J. Greenburger Literary Agency).

COSTS $1,750 for returning students and $1,825 for new students. Tuition includes private room, three meals daily, all 1-1 meetings with staff and agents, and classes.

WRITERS WEEKEND AT THE BEACH

P.O. Box 877, Ocean Park WA 98640. (360)262-0160. **E-mail:** bhansen6@juno.com. **E-mail:** bobtracie@hotmail.com. **Contact:** John Pelkey. Estab. 1992. Annual conference held in March. Conference duration:

2 days. Average attendance: 60. A retreat for writers with an emphasis on poetry, fiction, and nonfiction. Held at the Ocean Park Methodist Retreat Center & Camp. Speakers have included Wayne Holmes, Miralee Ferrell, Jim Whiting, Birdie Etchison, Colette Tennant, Gail Dunham, Linda Clare and Marion Duckworth.

COSTS $199 for full registration before February 17 and $209 after February 17.

ACCOMMODATIONS Offers on-site overnight lodging.

WRITE-TO-PUBLISH CONFERENCE

WordPro Communication Services, 9118 W. Elmwood Dr., Suite 1G, Niles IL 60714-5820. (847)296-3964. **Fax:** (847)296-0754. **E-mail:** lin@writetopublish.com. **Website:** www.writetopublish.com. **Contact:** Lin Johnson, director. Estab. 1971. Annual. Conference held June 4-7, 2013. Average attendance: 250. Conference is focused for the Christian market and includes classes on writing for children. Writer workshops geared toward all levels. Open to students. Site: Wheaton College, Wheaton, IL (Chicago).

COSTS approximately $485; includes conference and banquet.

ACCOMMODATIONS In campus residence halls. Cost is approximately $280-360.

ADDITIONAL INFORMATION Optional ms evaluation available. College credit available. Conference information available in January. For details, visit website, or e-mail brochure@writetopublish.com. Accepts inquiries by e-mail, fax, phone.

WRITING FOR THE SOUL

Jerry B. Jenkins Christian Writers Guild, 5525 N. Union Blvd., Suite 101, Colorado Springs CO 80918. (866)495-5177. **Fax:** (719)495-5181. **E-mail:** contactus@christianwritersguild.com. **Website:** www.christianwritersguild.com/conference. Annual conference held in February. Workshops and continuing classes cover fiction, nonfiction and magazine writing, children's books, and teen writing. The keynote speakers are nationally known, leading authors. The conference is hosted by Jerry B. Jenkins.

COSTS See website for pricing.

ACCOMMODATIONS The Broadmoor in Colorado Springs.

CONFERENCES

CONTESTS, AWARDS & GRANTS

///

Publication is not the only way to get your work recognized. Contests and awards can also be great ways to gain recognition in the industry. Grants, offered by organizations like SCBWI, offer monetary recognition to writers, giving them more financial freedom as they work on projects.

When considering contests or applying for grants, be sure to study guidelines and requirements. Regard entry deadlines as gospel and follow the rules to the letter.

Note that some contests require nominations. For published authors and illustrators, competitions provide an excellent way to promote your work. Your publisher may not be aware of local competitions such as state-sponsored awards—if your book is eligible, have the appropriate person at your publishing company nominate or enter your work for consideration.

To select potential contests and grants, read through the listings that interest you, then send for more information about the types of written or illustrated material considered and other important details. A number of contests offer information through Web sites given in their listings.

If you are interested in knowing who has received certain awards in the past, check your local library or bookstores or consult *Children's Books: Awards & Honors*, compiled and edited by the Children's Book Council (cbcbooks.org). Many bookstores have special sections for books that are Caldecott and Newbery Medal winners. Visit the American Library Association website, www.ala.org, for information on the Caldecott, Newbery, Coretta Scott King and Printz Awards. Visit www.hbook.com for information on The Boston Globe-Horn Book Award. Visit scbwi.org/awards.htm for information on The Golden Kite Award.

JANE ADDAMS CHILDREN'S BOOK AWARDS

Website: www.janeaddamspeace.org. Jane Addams Peace Association, Inc./Women's International League for Peace and Freedom, 777 United Nations Plaza 6th floor. New York NY 10017. (212)682-8830. **Fax:** (212)286-8211. **E-mail:** japa@igc.org. **Website:** www.janeaddamspeace.org. **Contact:** Linda Belle. "Two copies of published books the previous year only." Annual award. Estab. 1953. Previously published submissions only. Submissions made by author, author's agent, person, group or publisher, submitted by the publisher. Must be published January 1-December 31 of preceding year. Deadline for entries: December 31. Check website for all submission information. Cash awards and certificate, $1,000 to winners (winning book) and $500 each to Honor Book winners (split between author and illustrator, if necessary). Judging by national committee from various N.S. regions (all are members of WILPF). The award ceremony is held in New York the third Friday October annually. The Jane Addams Children's Book Awards are given annually to the children's books published the preceding year that effectively promote the cause of peace, social justice, world community, and the equality of the sexes and all races as well as meeting conventional standards for excellence. See website for specific details on guidelines that books must fulfill. Deadline: December 31. A national committe of WILPF members concerned with children's books and their social values is responsible for making the changes each year.

☺ ALCUIN CITATION AWARD

P.O. Box 3216, Vancouver BC V6B 3X8 Canada. (604)732-5403. **Fax:** (604)985-1091. **E-mail:** awards@alcuinsociety.com. **Website:** www.alcuinsociety.com. **Contact:** Leah Gordon. Previously published submissions from the year prior to the Award's Call for Entries. Submissions made by the publisher, author or designer. Winning books are exhibited nationally and internationally at the Tokyo, Frankfurt, and Leipzig Book Fairs, and are Canada's entries in the international competition in Leipzig, "Book Design from all over the World" in the following spring. Winners are selected from books designed and published in Canada. Awards are presented annually at appropriate ceremonies held in each year. Alcuin Citations are awarded annually for excellence in Canadian book design. Deadline: March 1. Prize: Prizes: 1st, 2nd, and 3rd in each category (at the discretion of the judges). Judging by professionals and those experienced in the field of book design.

AMERICA & ME ESSAY CONTEST

P.O. Box 30400, 7373 W. Saginaw Hwy., Lansing MI 48917. **E-mail:** lfedewa@fbinsmi.com. **Website:** http://www.farmbureauinsurance-mi.com/pages/events/essay.htm. Focuses on encouraging students to write about their personal Michigan heroes: someone they know personally who has encouraged them and inspired them to want to live better and achieve more. Open to Michigan eighth graders. Encourages Michigan youth to explore their roles in America's future. Prize: Prize: $1,000, plaque, and medallion for top tenn winners.

ⓘ AMERICAN ASSOCIATION OF UNIVERSITY WOMEN AWARD IN JUVENILE LITERATURE

4610 Mail Service Center, Raleigh NC 27699-4610. (919)733-9375. **E-mail:** michael.hill@ncdcr.gov. **Contact:** Michael Hill, awards coordinator. Annual award. Book must be published during the year ending June 30. Submissions made by author, author's agent or publisher. Deadline for entries: July 15. SASE for contest rules. Author must have maintained either legal residence or actual physical residence, or a combination of both, in the state of North Carolina for 3 years immediately preceding the close of the contest period. Only published work (books) eligible. Recognizes the year's best work of juvenile literature by a North Carolina resident. Deadline: July 15. Prize: Prize: Awards a cup to the winner and winner's name inscribed on a plaque displayed within the North Carolina Office of Archives and History. Judged by three-judge panel. ♡ Competition receives 10-15 submissions per category.

AMERICAS AWARD

Website: http://www4.uwm.edu/clacs/aa/index.cfm. **Contact:** Claire Gonzalez. The award winners and commended titles are selected for their (1) distinctive literary quality; (2) cultural contextualization; (3) exceptional integration of text, illustration and design; and (4) potential for classroom use. The Américas Award is given in recognition of U.S. works of fiction, poetry, folklore, or selected non-fiction (from picture books to works for young adults) published in the previous year in English or Spanish that authentically and engagingly portray Latin America, the Caribbean, or Latinos in the United States. By combining both and linking the Americas, the award reaches beyond geographic borders, as well as multicultural-international boundaries, focusing instead upon cultural heritages within the hemisphere. Deadline: January 18. Prize: Prize: $500, plaque and a formal presentation at the Library of Congress, Washington DC.

HANS CHRISTIAN ANDERSEN AWARD

Nonnenweg 12, Postfach Ba CH-4003 Switzerland. **E-mail:** liz.page@ibby.org. **E-mail:** ibby@ibby.org. **Website:** www.ibby.org. **Contact:** Liz Page, director. The Hans Christian Andersen Award, is the highest international recognition given to an author and an illustrator of children's books. The Author's Award has been given since 1956, the Illustrator's Award since 1966. Her Majesty Queen Margrethe II of Denmark is the Patron of the Hans Christian Andersen Awards. The Hans Christian Andersen Jury judges the books submitted for medals according to literary and artistic criteria. The awards are presented at the biennial congresses of IBBY. A Hans Christian Andersen Medal shall be awarded every two years by the International Board on Books for Young People (IBBY) to an author and to an illustrator, living at the time of the nomination, who by the outstanding value of their work are judged to have made a lasting contribution to literature for children and young people. The complete works of the author and of the illustrator will be taken into consideration in awarding the medal, which will be accompanied by a diploma. Candidates are nominated by National Sections of IBBY in good standing.

ATLANTIC WRITING COMPETITION FOR UNPUBLISHED MANUSCRIPTS

1113 Marginal Rd., Halifax NS B3H 4P7. (902)423-8116. **Fax:** (902)422-0881. **E-mail:** programs@writers.ns.ca. **Website:** www.writers.ns.ca. **Contact:** Hillary Titley. "Annual contest for beginners to try their hand in a number of categories: adult novel, writing for children, poetry, short story, juvenile/young adult novel, creative non-fiction, and play. Because our aim is to help Atlantic Canadian writers grow, judges return written comments when the competition is concluded." Page lengths and rules vary based on categories. See website for details. Anyone resident in the Atlantic Provinces since September 1, 2012 is eligible to enter. Only one entry per category is allowed. Each entry requires its own entry form and registration fee.

"We encourage writers in Atlantic Canada to explore and expand their talents by sending in their new, untried work." Deadline: November 9. Prize: Prizes vary based on categories. See website for details.

MARILYN BAILLIE PICTURE BOOK AWARD

40 Orchard View Blvd., Suite 217, Toronto ON M4R 1B9 Canada. (416)975-0010, ext. 222. **Fax:** (416)975-8970. **E-mail:** meghan@bookcentre.ca. **Website:** www.bookcentre.ca. To be eligible, the book must be an original work in English, aimed at children ages 3-8, written and illustrated by Canadians and first published in Canada. Eligible genres include fiction, non-fiction and poetry. Books must be published between Jan. 1 and Dec. 31 of the previous calendar year. Honors excellence in the illustrated picture book format. Deadline: February 8. Prize: Prize: $20,000.

JOHN AND PATRICIA BEATTY AWARD

2471 Flores St., San Mateo CA 94403. (650)376-0886. **Fax:** (650)539-2341. **E-mail:** ncole@cla-net.org. **E-mail:** Clio.Hathaway@hayward-ca.gov. **Website:** www.cla-net.org. **Contact:** Clio Hathaway. The California Library Association's John and Patricia Beatty Award, sponsored by Baker & Taylor, honors the author of a distinguished book for children or young adults that best promotes an awareness of California and its people. A committee of CLA members selects the winning title from books published in the United States during the preceding year. Prize: Prize: $500 and an engraved plaque.

THE GEOFFREY BILSON AWARD FOR HISTORICAL FICTION FOR YOUNG PEOPLE

40 Orchard View Blvd., Suite 217, Toronto ON M4R 1B9 Canada. (416)975-0010, ext. 222. **Fax:** (416)975-8970. **Website:** www.bookcentre.ca. **Contact:** Meghan Howe. Open to Canadian citizens and residents of Canada for at least 2 years. Books must be published between January 1 and December 31 of the previous year. Awarded annually to reward excellence in the writing of an outstanding work of historical fiction for young readers, by a Canadian author, published in the previous calendar year. Deadline: February 8. Prize: Prize: $5,000.

THE IRMA S. AND JAMES H. BLACK AWARD

Bank Street College of Education, 610 W. 112th St., New York NY 10025-1898. (212)875-4458.

Fax: (212)875-4558. E-mail: kfreda@bankstreet.edu;apryce@bankstreet.edu. Website: http://www.bankstreet.edu/childrenslibrary/irmasimonton blackhome.html. Contact: Kristin Freda. Purpose of award: "The award is given each spring for a book for young children, published in the previous year, for excellence of both text and illustrations." Entries must have been published during the previous calendar year (between January '11 and December '11 for 2012 award). Deadline for entries: mid-December. "Publishers submit books to us by sending them here to me at the Bank Street Library. Authors may ask their publishers to submit their books. Out of these, three to five books are chosen by a committee of older children and children's literature professionals. These books are then presented to children in selected first-, second , and third grade classes here and at a number of other cooperating schools. These children are the final judges who pick the actual award winner. A scroll (one each for the author and illustrator, if they're different) with the recipient's name and a gold seal designed by Maurice Sendak are awarded in May."

BOSTON GLOBE-HORN BOOK AWARDS

56 Roland St., Suite 200, Boston MA 02129. (617)628-0225. Fax: (617)628-0882. E-mail: info@hbook.com; khedeen@hbook.com. Website: hbook.com/bghb/. Contact: Katrina Hedeen. Offered annually for excellence in literature for children and young adults (published June 1-May 31). Categories: picture book, fiction and poetry, nonfiction. Judges may also name several honor books in each category. Books must be published in the US, but may be written or illustrated by citizens of any country. The Horn Book Magazine publishes speeches given at awards ceremonies. Guidelines for SASE or online. Deadline: May 15. Prize: Prize: $500 and an engraved silver bowl; honor book recipients receive an engraved silver plate. Judged by a panel of 3 judges selected each year.

☺ ANN CONNOR BRIMER AWARD

Website: www.nsla.ns.ca/index.php/about/awards/ann-connor-brimer-award. Contact: Heather MacKenzie, award director. In 1990, the Nova Scotia Library Association established the Ann Connor Brimer Award for writers residing in Atlantic Canada who have made an outstanding contribution to children's literature. Author must be alive and residing in Atlantic Canada at time of nomination. Book intended for youth up to the age of 15. Book in print and readily available. Fiction or non-fiction (except textbooks). To recognize excellence in writing. Prize: Prize: $2,000.

BUCKEYE CHILDREN'S BOOK AWARD

Website: www.bcbookaward.info. Contact: Christine Watters, president. Open to Ohio students. Award offered every year. Awarded annually. Open to Ohio students. The Buckeye Childeren's Book Award Program was designed to encourage children to read literature critically, to promote teacher and librarian involvement in children's literature programs, and to commend authors of such literature, as well as to promote the use of libraries. Deadline: March 15. Nominees submitted by students starting January 1.

RANDOLPH CALDECOTT MEDAL

50 E. Huron, Chicago IL 60611-2795. (312)944-7680. Fax: (312)440-9374. E-mail: alsc@ala.org; lschulte@ala.org. Website: www.ala.org/alsc/caldecott.cfm. The Caldecott Medal was named in honor of nineteenth-century English illustrator Randolph Caldecott. It is awarded annually by the Association for Library Service to Children, a division of the American Library Association, to the artist of the most distinguished American picture book for children. Illustrator must be U.S. citizen or resident. Must be published year preceding award. SASE for award rules. Entries are not returned. Honors the artist of the most outstanding picture book for children published in the U.S. Deadline: December 31.

CALIFORNIA YOUNG PLAYWRIGHTS CONTEST

2590 Truxton Rd., Suite 202, San Diego CA 92106-6145. (619)239-8222. Fax: (619)239-8225. E-mail: write@playwrightsproject.org. Website: www.playwrightsproject.org. Contact: Cecelia Kouma, executive director. Open to Californians under age 19. Annual contest. Estab. 1985. "Our organization and the contest is designed to nurture promising young writers. We hope to develop playwrights and audiences for live theater. We also teach playwriting." Submissions required to be unpublished and not produced professionally. Submissions made by the author. Deadline for entries: June 1. SASE for contest rules and entry form. No entry fee. Judging by professionals in the theater community, a committee of 5-7; changes somewhat each year. Works performed in San Diego at a professional theatre. Writers submitting scripts of 10 or more pages receive a detailed script evaluation letter upon request. "Offered annually for previously unpublished plays by young writers to stimulate young people to create dramatic works, and to nurture promising writers. Scripts must be a minimum of 10 standard typewritten pages; send 2 copies. Scripts will *not* be returned. If requested, entrants receive detailed evaluation letter. Guidelines available online." See website for current year's deadline. Prize: Scripts will be produced in spring at a professional theatre in San Diego.

CALLIOPE FICTION CONTEST

5975 W. Western Way, PMD 116Y, Tucson AZ 85713. **E-mail:** cynthia@theriver.com. **Website:** www.calliopewriters.org. **Contact:** Cynthia Sabelhaus, General Editor. Open to students. Annual contest. Unpublished submissions only (all genres, no violence, profanity or extreme horror). Submissions made by author. Winners must retain sufficient rights to have their stories published in the January/February issue, or their entries will be disqualified; one-time rights. Open to all writers. No special considerations—other than following the guidelines. Contest theme, due dates and sometimes entry fees change annually. The purpose of fiction in Calliope is to entertain its readers, most of whom are writers, or trying to be. Calliope is open to any genre of short fiction, including science fiction, fantasy, horror, mystery, and all their sub-genres. Mixed genre stories and experimental forms are also welcome. Mainstream/literary stories will be considered if they are in some way out of the ordinary. Humor and satire are greatly appreciated. Deadline: Changes annually. Prize: Prize: Up to $75 for 1st place.

CANADA COUNCIL GOVERNOR GENERAL'S LITERARY AWARDS

350 Albert St., P.O. Box 1047, Ottawa ON K1P 5V8 Canada. (613)566-4410, ext. 5573. **Fax:** (613)566-4390. **Website:** www.canadacouncil.ca/prizes/ggla. As Canada's national literary awards, the Governor General's Literary Awards (the GGs) represent the rich diversity of Canadian literature. Some 1,600 books are submitted each year from English and French-language publishers representing authors, translators and illustrators from across Canada, in seven categories (fiction, poetry, drama, non-fiction, children's literature, children's literature illustration, and translation). For each category, a jury makes the final selection. Each year, the GGs honour the best in Canadian literature. Deadline: Depends on the book's publication date.

Prize: Prize: Each GG winner receives $25,000 and a specially-bound copy of their winning book. Non-winning finalists receive $1,000. Judged by fellow authors, translators, and illustrators.

CANADIAN SHORT STORY COMPETITION

Unit #6, 477 Martin St., Penticton BC V2A 5L2 Canada. (778)476-5750. **Fax:** (778)476-5750. **E-mail:** dave@redtuquebooks.ca. **Website:** www.redtuquebooks.ca. **Contact:** David Korinetz, contest director. Offered annually for unpublished works. Purpose of award is "to promote Canada and Canadian publishing. Stories require a Canadian element. There are three ways to qualify. They can be written by a Canadian, or written about Canadians, or take place somewhere in Canada." Deadline: December 31. Prize: 1st Place: $500; 2nd Place: $150; 3rd Place: $100; and 10 prizes of $25 will be given to honourable mentions. All 13 winners will be published in an anthology. They will each receive a complimentary copy. Judged by Canadian authors in the fantasy/sci-fi/horror field. Acquires first print rights. Contest open to anyone.

CHILDREN'S AFRICANA BOOK AWARD

c/o Rutgers University, 132 George St., New Brunswick NJ 08901. (732)932-8173; (301)585-9136. **Fax:** (732)932-3394. **E-mail:** africaaccess@aol.com. **Website:** www.africaaccessreview.org. **Contact:** Brenda Randolph, chairperson. The Children's Africana Book Awards are presented annually to the authors and illustrators of the best books on Africa for children and young people published or republished in the U.S. The awards were created by the Outreach Council of the African Studies Association (ASA) to dispel stereotypes and encourage the publication and use of accurate, balanced children's materials about Africa. The awards are presented in 2 categories: Young Children and Older Readers. Since 1991, 63 books have been recognized. Entries must have been published in the calendar year previous to the award. Work submitted for awards must be suitable for children ages 4-18; a significant portion of books' content must be about Africa; must by copyrighted in the calendar year prior to award year; must be published or republished in the US. Books should be suitable for children and young adults, ages 4-18. A significant portion of the book's content should be about Africa. Books must be copyrighted the previous year to be eligible for the awards.

CHILDREN'S BOOK GUILD AWARD FOR NONFICTION

E-mail: theguild@childrensbookguild.org. **Website:** www.childrensbookguild.org. Annual award. Purpose of award: "to honor an author or illustrator whose total work has contributed significantly to the quality of nonfiction for children." Award includes a cash prize and an engraved crystal paperweight. Judging by a jury of Children's Book Guild specialists, authors, and illustrators. "One doesn't enter. One is selected. Our jury annually selects one author for the award."

CHILDREN'S WRITER WRITING CONTESTS

95 Long Ridge Rd., West Redding CT 06896-0811. (203)792-8600. **Fax:** (203)792-8406. **Website:** www.childrenswriter.com. Contest offered twice a year by *Children's Writer*, the monthly newsletter of writing and publishing trends. Each contest has its own theme. Any original unpublished piece, not accepted by any publisher at the time of submission, is eligible. Submissions made by the author. To obtain the rules and theme for the current contest go to the website and click on "Writing Contests," or send a SASE to *Children's Writer* at the above address. Put "Contest Request" in the lower left of your envelope. Open to any writer. Entries are judged on age targeting, originality, quality of writing and, for nonfiction, how well the information is conveyed and accuracy. Promotes higher quality children's literature. Deadline: Last weekday in February and October. Prize: Prize: 1st place: $250 or $500, a certificate and publication in *Children's Writer*; 2nd place: $100 or $250, and certificate; 3rd-5th places: $50 or $100 and certificates. Judged by a panel of 4 selected from the staff of the Institute of Children's Literature.

CHRISTIAN BOOK AWARDS

9633 S. 48th St., Suite 140, Phoenix AZ 85044. (480)966-3998. **Fax:** (480)966-1944. **E-mail:** info@ecpa.org; mkuyper@ecpa.org. **Website:** www.ecpa.org. **Contact:** Mark W. Kuyper, president and CEO. Since 1978 the Evangelical Christian Publishers Association has recognized quality and encouraged excellence by presenting the ECPA Christian Book Awards (formerly known as Gold Medallion) each year. Categories include children, fiction, nonfiction, Bibles, Bible reference, inspiration, and new author. "All entries must be evangelical in nature and submitted through an ECPA member publisher." Submission period: September 1-30. See website for all details The Christian Book Awards recognize the highest quality in Christian books and is among the oldest and most prestigious awards program in Christian publishing. Deadline: September 30.

COLORADO BOOK AWARDS

(303)894-7951, ext. 21. **Fax:** (303)864-9361. **E-mail:** goff@coloradohumanities.org. **Website:** www.coloradohumanities.org. **Contact:** Christine Goff. An annual program that celebrates the accomplishments of Colorado's outstanding authors, editors, illustrators, and photographers. Awards are presented in at least ten categories including anthology/collection, biography, children's, creative nonfiction, fiction, history, nonfiction, pictorial, poetry, and young adult. To be eligible for a Colorado Book Award, a primary contributor to the book must be a Colorado writer, editor, illustrator, or photographer. Current Colorado residents are eligible, as are individuals engaged in ongoing literary work in the state and authors whose personal history, identity, or literary work reflect a strong Colorado influence. Authors not currently Colorado residents who feel their work is inspired by or connected to Colorado should submit a letter with his/her entry describing the connection. To celebrate books and their creators and promote them to readers.

CRICKET LEAGUE

P.O. Box 300, Peru IL 61354. **E-mail:** cricket@caruspub.com. **E-mail:** mail@cricketmagkids.com. **Website:** www.cricketmagkids.com. There is a contest in each issue. Possible categories include story, poetry, art, or photography. Each contest relates to a specific theme described on each *Cricket* issue's Cricket League page and on the website. Signature verifying originality, age and address of entrant and permission to publish required. Entries which do not relate to the current month's theme cannot be considered. Unpublished submissions only. Cricket League rules, contest theme, and submission deadline information can be found in the current issue of *Cricket* and via website. The purpose of Cricket League contests is to encourage creativity and give young people an opportunity to express themselves in writing, drawing, painting or photography. Deadline: The 25th of each month. Prize: Prize: Certificates. Judged by *Cricket* editors.

CWW ANNUAL WISCONSIN WRITERS AWARDS COMPETITION

Website: www.wisconsinwriters.org. **Contact:** Geoff Gilpin; Jerriane Hayslett and Karla Huston, awards co-chairs; and Carolyn Washburne, Christopher Latham Sholes Award and Major Achievement Award co-chair. Offered annually for work published by Wisconsin writers the previous calendar year. Nine awards: Major/life achievement alternate years; short fiction; short nonfiction; nonfiction book; poetry book; fiction book; children's literature; Lorine Niedecker Poetry Award; Sholes Award for Outstanding Service to Wisconsin Writers Alternate Years; Essay Award for Young Writers. Open to Wisconsin residents. Guidelines, rules, and entry form on website. Deadline: January 31 (postmark). Prize: Prizes: $500 and a week-long residency at Shake Rag Alley or Maplewood Lodge in Mineral Point. Essay Contest: $150. "This year only the Essay Award for Young Writers prize will be $250.".

MARGARET A. EDWARDS AWARD

50 East Huron St., Chicago IL 60611-2795. (312)280-4390 or (800)545-2433. **Fax:** (312)280-5276. **E-mail:** yalsa@ala.org. **Website:** www.ala.org/yalsa/edwards. Annual award administered by the Young Adult Library Services Association (YALSA) of the American Library Association (ALA) and sponsored by *School Library Journal* magazine. "The award will be given annually to an author whose book or books, over a period of time, have been accepted by young adults as an authentic voice that continues to illuminate their experiences and emotions, giving insight into their lives. The book or books should enable them to understand themselves, the world in which they live, and their relationship with others and with society. The book or books must be in print at the time of the nomination." Submissions must be previously published no less than five years prior to the first meeting of the current Margaret A. Edwards Award Committee at Midwinter Meeting. Nomination form is available on the YALSA website. ALA's Young Adult Library Services Association (YALSA), recognizes an author and a specific work or works for significant and lasting contribution to young adult literature. Deadline: December 1. Prize: Prize: $2,000. Judged by members of the Young Adult Library Services Association.

SHUBERT FENDRICH MEMORIAL PLAYWRITING CONTEST

P.O. Box 4267, Englewood CO 80155. (303)779-4035. **Fax:** (303)779-4315. **E-mail:** editors@pioneerdrama.com. **E-mail:** submissions@pioneerdrama.com. **Website:** www.pioneerdrama.com. **Contact:** Lori Conary, submissions editor. Previously unpublished submissions only. Open to all writers not currently published by Pioneer Drama Service. SASE for contest rules and guidelines or view online. No entry fee. Cover letter, SASE for return of ms, and proof of production or staged reading must accompany all submissions. Encourages the development of quality theatrical material for educational and family theater. Deadline: Ongoing contest; a winner is selected by June 1 each year from all eligble submissions received the previous year. Prize: Prize: $1,000 royalty advance in addition to publication. Judged by editors.

DOROTHY CANFIELD FISHER CHILDREN'S BOOK AWARD

578 Paine Tpke. N., Berlin VT 05602. (802)828-6954. **E-mail:** grace.greene@state.vt.us. **Website:** www.dcfaward.org. **Contact:** Mary Linney, chair. Annual award. Purpose of the award: to encourage Vermont children to become enthusiastic and discriminating readers by providing them with books of good quality by living American or Canadian authors published in the current year. Deadline for entries: December of year book was published. E-mail for entry rules. No entry fee. Awards a scroll presented to the winning author at an award ceremony. Judging is by the children grades 4-8. They vote for their favorite book. Requirements for entrants: "Titles must be original work, published in the U.S., and be appropriate to children in grades 4-8. The book must be copyrighted in the current year. It must be written by an American author living in the U.S. or Canada, or a Canadian author living in Canada or the U.S."

☺ THE NORMA FLECK AWARD FOR CANADIAN CHILDREN'S NONFICTION

40 Orchard View Blvd., Suite 217, Toronto ON M4R 1B9 Canada. (416)975-0010 ext. 222. **Fax:** (416)975-8970. **E-mail:** info@bookcentre.ca. **Website:** www.bookcentre.ca. **Contact:** Meghan Howe, library coordinator. The Norma Fleck Award was established by the Fleck Family Foundation in May 1999 to honour the life of Norma Marie Fleck, and to recognize exceptional Canadian nonfiction books for young people.

Publishers are welcome to nominate books using the online form. Offered annually for books published between January 1 and December 31 of the previous calendar year. Open to Canadian citizens or landed immigrants. The jury will always include at least 3 of the following: a teacher, a librarian, a bookseller, and a reviewer. A juror will have a deep understanding of, and some involvement with, Canadian children's books. The Canadian Children's Book Centre will select the jury members. Prize: $10,000 goes to the author (unless 40% or more of the text area is composed of original illustrations, in which case the award will be divided equally between the author and the artist). Deadline: February 8. Prize: Prize: $10,000.

FLICKER TALE CHILDREN'S BOOK AWARD

Morton Mandan Public Library, 609 W. Main St., Mandan ND 58554. **E-mail:** laustin@cdln.info. **Website:** www.ndla.info/ftaward.htm. **Contact:** Linda Austin. Purpose of award: to give children across the state of North Dakota a chance to vote for their book of choice from a nominated list of 20: 4 in the picture book category; 4 in the intermediate category; 4 in the juvenile category (for more advanced readers); 4 in the upper grade level nonfiction category. Also, to promote awareness of quality literature for children. Previously published submissions only. Submissions nominated by librarians and teachers across the state of North Dakota. Awards a plaque from North Dakota Library Association and banquet dinner. Judging by children in North Dakota. Entry deadline in April.

DON FREEMAN MEMORIAL GRANT-IN-AID

8271 Beverly Blvd., Los Angeles CA 90048. (323)782-1010. **Fax:** (323)782-1892. **E-mail:** scbwi@scbwi.org. **Website:** www.scbwi.org. Purpose of award: to "enable picture book artists to further their understanding, training and work in the picture book genre." Applications and prepared materials are available in October and must be postmarked between February 1 and March 1. Grant awarded and announced in August. SASE for award rules and entry forms. SASE for return of entries. No entry fee. Annually awards one grant of $1,500 and one runner-up grant of $500. "The grant-in-aid is available to both full and associate members of the SCBWI who, as artists, seriously intend to make picture books their chief contribution to the field of children's literature."

THEODOR SEUSS GEISEL AWARD

50 E. Huron, Chicago IL 60611. (800)545-2433. **E-mail:** ala@ala.org. **Website:** www.ala.org. The Theodor Seuss Geisel Award, established in 2004, is given annually beginning in 2006 to the author(s) and illustrator(s) of the most distinguished American book for beginning readers published in English in the United States during the preceding year. The award is to recognize the author(s) and illustrator(s) who demonstrate great creativity and imagination in his/her/their literary and artistic achievements to engage children in reading. Deadline for entries: December 31. Entries not returned. Not entry fee. Medal given at awards ceremony during ALA Annual Conference.

AMELIA FRANCES HOWARD GIBBON AWARD FOR ILLUSTRATION

1150 Morrison Drie, Suite 400, Ottawa ON K 2H859 Canada. (613)232-9625. **Fax:** (613) 563-9895. **E-mail:** carol.mcdougall@iwk.nshealth.ca. **Website:** www.cla. ca. Purpose of the award: "to honor excellence in the illustration of children's book(s) in Canada. To merit consideration the book must have been published in Canada and its illustrator must be a Canadian citizen or a permanent resident of Canada." Previously published submissions only; must be published between January 1 and December 31 of the previous year. Deadline for entries: December 31. See website for award rules. Entries not returned. No entry fee. Judging by selection committee of members of Canadian Association of Children's Librarians. Requirements for entrants: illustrator must be Canadian or Canadian resident.

GOLDEN KITE AWARDS

SCBWI Golden Kite Awards, 8271 Beverly Blvd., Los Angeles CA 90048-4515. (323)782-1010. **E-mail:** awards@scbwi.org. **Website:** www.scbwi.org. Society of Children's Book Writers and Illustrators, 8271 Beverly Blvd.Los Angeles CA 90048. (323)782-1010. **E-mail:** scbwi@scbwi.org. **Website:** www.scbwi.org. **Contact:** SCBWI Golden Kite Coordinator. Annual award. Estab. 1973. "The works chosen will be those that the judges feel exhibit excellence in writing, and in the case of the picture-illustrated books—in illustration, and genuinely appeal to the interests and concerns of children. For the fiction and nonfiction awards, original works and single-author collections of stories or poems of which at least half are new and never before published in book form are eligible—anthologies and translations are not. For the picture-illustration awards, the art or photographs must be original works (the texts—which may be fiction or nonfiction—may be original, public domain or previously published). Deadline for entries: December 15. SASE for award rules. No entry fee. Awards, in addition to statuettes and plaques, the four winners receive $2,500 cash award plus trip to LA SCBWI Conference. The panel of judges will consist of professional authors, illustrators, editors or agents." Requirements for entrants: "must be a member of SCBWI and books must be published in that year." Winning books will be displayed at national conference in August. Books to be entered, as well as further inquiries, should be submitted to: The Society of Children's Book Writers and Illustrators, above address. "The works chosen will be those that the judges feel exhibit excellence in writing and, in the case of the picture-illustrated books, in illustration, and genuinely appeal to the interests and concerns of children. For the fiction and nonfiction awards, original works and single-author collections of stories or poems of which at least half are new and never before published in book form are eligible—anthologies and translations are not. For the picture-illustration awards, the art or photographs must be original works (the texts—which may be fiction or nonfiction—may be original, public domain or previously published)." To be eligible to submit your book(s) for the Golden Kite Award, and/or the Sid Fleischman Award, you must be a current member of the SCBWI with your membership current through April 1, 2014. You may submit your book to one category only, except in the case of Picture Book Text and Picture Book Illustration. See website for more details. Deadline: December 4. Prize: Prize: In addition to statuettes and plaques, the 4 winners receive $2,500 cash award plus trip to LA SCBWI Conference.

☘ GOVERNOR GENERAL'S LITERARY AWARD FOR CHILDREN'S LITERATURE

350 Albert St., P.O. Box 1047, Ottawa ON K1P 5V8 Canada. (613)566-4414, ext. 5573. **Fax:** (613)566-4410. **Website:** www.canadacouncil.ca/prizes/ggla. Offered for the best English-language and the best French-language works of children's literature by a Canadian in 2 categories: text and illustration. Publishers submit titles for consideration. Deadline depends on the book's publication date. Books in English: March 15,

June 1, or August 7. Books in French: March 15 or July 15. Prize: Each laureate receives $25,000; non-winning finalists receive $1,000.

☘ GOVERNOR GENERAL'S LITERARY AWARDS

350 Albert St., P.O. Box 1047, Ottawa ON K1P 5V8 Canada. (613)566-4414, ext. 4075. **Website:** www.canadacouncil.ca/prizes/ggla. (Specialized: Canadian citizens/permanent residents; English- and French-language works) Established by Parliament, the Canada Council for the Arts "provides a wide range of grants and services to professional Canadian artists and art organizations in dance, media arts, music, theater, writing, publishing, and the visual arts." The Governor General's Literary Awards, valued at $25,000 CAD each, are given annually for the best English-language and best French-language work in each of 7 categories, including poetry. Non-winning finalists each receive $1,000 CAD. Books must be first edition trade books written, translated, or illustrated by Canadian citizens or permanent residents of Canada and published in Canada or abroad during the previous year (September 1 through the following September 30). Collections of poetry must be at least 48 pages long, and at least half the book must contain work not published previously in book form. In the case of translation, the original work must also be a Canadian-authored title. Books must be submitted by publishers with a Publisher's Submission Form, which is available on request from the Writing and Publishing Section of the Canada Council for the Arts. Guidelines and current deadlines on the website and available by mail, telephone, fax, or e-mail.

HACKNEY LITERARY AWARDS

1305 2nd Ave. N, #103, Birmingham AL 35203. (205)226-4921. **E-mail:** info@hackneyliteraryawards.org. **Website:** www.hackneyliteraryawards.org. **Contact:** Myra Crawford, PhD, executive director. Offered annually for unpublished novels, short stories (maximum 5,000 words) and poetry (50 line limit). Guidelines on website. Deadline: September 30 (novels), November 30 (short stories and poetry). Prize: Prize: $5,000 in annual prizes for poetry and short fiction ($2,500 national and $2,500 state level). 1st Place: $600; 2nd Place: $400; 3rd Place: $250); plus $5,000 for an unpublished novel. Competition winners will be announced on the website each March.

⊕ THE MARILYN HALL AWARDS FOR YOUTH THEATRE

P.O. Box 148, Beverly Hills CA 90213. **Website:** www.beverlyhillstheatreguild.com. **Contact:** Candace Coster, competition coordinator. Unpublished submissions only. Authors must be U.S. citizens or legal residents and must sign entry form personally. "To encourage the creation and development of new plays for youth theatre." Deadline: Postmarked between January 15 and the last day of February. Prize: Prize: 1st Prize: $700; 2nd Prize: $300.

HIGHLIGHTS FOR CHILDREN FICTION CONTEST

803 Church St., Honesdale PA 18431-1824. (570)253-1080. **Fax:** (570)251-7847. **E-mail:** eds@highlights-corp.com. **Website:** www.Highlights.com. **Contact:** Christine French Cully, fiction contest editor. Unpublished submissions only. Open to any writer 16 years of age or older. Winners announced in May. Length up to 800 words. Stories for beginning readers should not exceed 500 words. Stories should be consistent with Highlights editorial requirements. No violence, crime or derogatory humor. Send SASE or visit website for guidelines and current theme. Stimulates interest in writing for children and reward and recognize excellence. Deadline: January 31. Submission period begins January 1. Prize: Prize: Three prizes of $1,000 or tuition for any Highlights Foundation Founders Workshop.

MARILYN HOLINSHEAD VISITING SCHOLARS FELLOWSHIP

113 Anderson Library, 222 21st Ave. South, Minneapolis MN 55455. **Website:** http://special.lib.umn.edu/clrc/kerlan/awards.php. Marilyn Hollinshead Visiting Scholars Fund for Travel to the Kerlan Collection will be available for research study in 2013. Applicants may request up to **$1,500.** Send a letter with the proposed purpose, plan to use specific research materials (manuscripts and art), dates, and budget (including airfare and per diem) to Marilyn Hollinshead Visiting Scholars Fellowship, 113 Andersen Library, 222 21st Ave. S. Mpls, MN 55455. The application deadline is **January 30.** Travel and a written report on the project must be completed and submitted in 2012.

THE JULIA WARD HOWE/BOSTON AUTHORS AWARD

45 Pine Crest Rd., Newton MA 02459. (617)244-0646. **E-mail:** bostonauthors@aol.com; SarahM45@aol. com. **Website:** www.bostonauthorsclub.org. **Contact:** Sarah Lamstein. This annual award honors Julia Ward Howe and her literary friends who founded the Boston Authors Club in 1900. It also honors the membership over 110 years, consisting of novelists, biographers, historians, governors, senators, philosophers, poets, playwrights, and other luminaries. There are 2 categories: trade books and books for young readers (beginning with chapter books through young adult books). Works of fiction, nonfiction, memoir, poetry, and biography published in 2010 are eligible. Authors must live or have lived (college counts) within a 100-mile radius of Boston within the last 5 years. Subsidized books, cook books and picture books are not eligible. Fee is $25 per title.

HRC SHOWCASE THEATRE PLAYWRITING CONTEST

P.O. Box 940, Hudson NY 12534. (518)851-7244. **Website:** www.hrc-showcasetheatre.com. HRC Showcase Theatre is a not-for-profit professional theater company dedicated to the advancement of performing in the Hudson River Valley area through reading of plays and providing opportunities for new and established playwrights. Unpublished submissions only. Submissions made by author and by the author's agent. Deadlines for entries: May 1. SASE for contest rules and entry forms. Entry fee is $5. Awards $500 cash plus concert reading by professional actors for winning play and $100 for each of the four other plays that will be given a staged reading. Judging by panel selected by Board of Directors. Requirements for entrants: Entrants must live in the northeastern U.S.

CAROL OTIS HURST CHILDREN'S BOOK PRIZE

Westfield Athenaeum, 6 Elm St., Westfield MA 01085. (413)568-7833. **Website:** www.westath.org. **Contact:** Ralph Melnick, assistant director, Westfield Athenaeum. The Carol Otis Hurst Children's Book Prize honors outstanding works of fiction and nonfiction written for children and young adults through the age of 18. For a work to be considered, the writer must either be a native or a current resident of New England. While the prize (together with a monetary award of $500) is presented annually to an author whose work best exemplifies the highest standards of writing for this age group regardless of genre or topic or geographical setting, the prize committee is especially interested in those books that treat life in the region.

Further, entries will be judged on how well they succeed in portraying one or more of the following elements: childhood, adolescence, family life, schooling, social and political developments, fine and performing artistic expression, domestic arts, environmental issues, transportation and communication, changing technology, military experience at home and abroad, business and manufacturing, workers and the labor movement, agriculture and its transformation, racial and ethnic diversity, religious life and institutions, immigration and adjustment, sports at all levels, and the evolution of popular entertainment. To date, award recipients have been Milton Meltzer for his young adult book, *Tough Times* (Clarion), Kay Winters for her children's book, *Colonial Voices: Hear Them Speak* (Dutton), and Jane Yolan for her children's book treatment of Emily Dickinson in *My Uncle Emily* (Philomel). Established to celebrate the life and work of noted children's author Carol Otis Hurst. The book's cover, brief excerpts from the text, and its illustrations may be used to publicize the prize and its recipient.

INSIGHT WRITING CONTEST

Fax: (301)393-4055. **E-mail:** insight@rhpa.org. **Website:** www.insightmagazine.org. **Contact:** Dwain Esmond, editor. Annual contest for writers in the categories of student short story, general short story, and student poetry. Unpublished submissions only. General category is open to all writers; student categories must be age 22 and younger. "Your entry must be a true, unpublished work by you, with a strong spiritual message. We appreciate the use of Bible texts." Deadline: June 3. Prize: Prizes: Student Short and General Short Story: 1st Prize: $250; 2nd Prize: $200; 3rd Prize: $150. Student Poetry: 1st Prize: $100; 2nd Prize: $75; 3rd Prize: $50.

INTERNATIONAL READING ASSOCIATION CHILDREN'S BOOK AWARDS

P.O. Box 8139, 800 Barksdale Rd., Newark DE 19714-8139. (302)731-1600, ext. 221. **E-mail:** exec@reading.org. **E-mail:** committees@reading.org. **Website:** reading.org. **Contact:** Kathy Baughman. Provide believable and intriguing characters, truthful and authentic in its presentation of information and attitudes as they existed at the time and place which the story reflects. Children's and Young Adults' Book Awards is intended for newly published authors who show unusual promise in the children's and young adults'

book field. Awards are given for fiction and nonfiction in each of three categories: primary, intermediate, and young adult. Books from all countries and published in English for the first time during the previous calendar year will be considered. Deadline: November 1. Prize: Prize: $1,000.

IRA CHILDREN'S AND YOUNG ADULT'S BOOK AWARD

(302)731-1600. **Fax:** (302)731-1057. **E-mail:** kbaughman@reading.org; exec@reading.org. **Website:** www.reading.org. **Contact:** Kathy Baughman. Awards are given for an author's first or second published book for fiction and nonfiction in 3 categories: primary (ages preschool-8), intermediate (ages 9-13), and young adult (ages 14-17). This award is intended for newly published authors who show unusual promise in the children's book field. Deadline for entries: See website. Awards $1,000. For guidelines, write or e-mail.

EZRA JACK KEATS/KERLAN MEMORIAL FELLOWSHIP

113 Elmer L. Andersen Library, 222 21st Ave. S., University of Minnesota, Minneapolis MN 55455. **E-mail:** clrc@tc.umn.edu. **Website:** http://special.lib.umn.edu/clrc/. **Contact:** Lisa Von Drasek, curator. This fellowship from the Ezra Jack Keats Foundation will provide $1,500 to a "talented writer and/or illustrator of children's books who wishes to use the Kerlan Collection for the furtherance of his or her artistic development." Special consideration will be given to someone who would find it difficult to finance a visit to the Kerlan Collection. The Ezra Jack Keats Fellowship recipient will receive transportation costs and a per diem allotment. See website for application deadline and for digital application materials. For paper copies of the application send a large (6×9 or 9×12) SAE with 97¢ postage.

THE EZRA JACK KEATS NEW WRITER AND NEW ILLUSTRATOR AWARDS

450 14th St., Brooklyn NY 11215. **E-mail:** jchang@nypl.org. **Website:** www.ezra-jack-keats.org. **Contact:** Julia Chang, program coordinator. Annual awards. Purpose of the awards: "The awards will be given to a promising new writer of picture books for children and a promising new illustrator of picture books for children. Selection criteria include books for children (ages 9 and under) that reflect the tradition of Ezra Jack Keats. These books portray: the universal qualities of childhood, strong and supportive family

and adult relationships, the multicultural nature of our world." Submissions made by the publisher. Must be published in the preceding year. Deadline for entries: mid-December. SASE for contest rules and entry forms or e-mail Julia Chang at jchang@nypl.org. No entry fee. Awards $1,000 coupled with Ezra Jack Keats Bronze Medal. Judging by a panel of experts. "The author or illustrator should have published no more than 3 children's books. Entries are judged on the outstanding features of the text, complemented by illustrations. Candidates need not be both author and illustrator. Entries should carry a 2011 copyright (for the 2012 award)." Winning books and authors to be presented at reception at The New York Public Library.

KENTUCKY BLUEGRASS AWARD

Northern Kentucky University, 405 Steely Library, Nunn Drive, Highland Heights KY 41099. (859)572-6620. **Website:** kba.nku.edu. The Kentucky Bluegrass Award is a student choice program. The KBA promotes and encourages Kentucky students in kindergarten through grade 12 to read a variety of quality literature. All Kentucky public and private schools, as well as public libraries, are welcome to participate in the program. To nominate a book, see the website for form and details. Each year, a KBA committee for each grade category chooses the books for the four Master Lists (K-2, 3-5, 6-8 and 9-12). Students read books from the appropriate Master Lists and choose their favorite which they indicate on a ballot. All the ballots are counted and the results are transferred to an online tally sheet which is submitted to the KBA by the volunteer on-site, teacher or librarian coordinator. A winner is declared for each level.

CORETTA SCOTT KING BOOK AWARDS

50 E. Huron St., Chicago IL 60611. (800)545-2433. **Website:** www.ala.org/csk. The Coretta Scott King Book Awards is an annual award celebrating African American experience. A new talent award may also be selected. An awards jury of Children's Librarians judge the books form the previous year, and select the winners in January at the ALA Midwinter meeting. A copy of an entry must be sent to each juror by December 1 of the juried year. A copy of the jury list and directions for submitting titles can be found on website. Call or e-mail ALA Office for Literacy and Outreach Services for jury list. Awards breakfast held on Tuesday morning during ALA. Annual Conference in June. See schedule at website.

LEAGUE OF UTAH WRITERS CONTEST

The League of Utah Writers, P.O. Box 88, Logan UT 84323. (435)755-7609. **E-mail:** luwcontest@gmail.com. **Website:** www.luwriters.org. **Contact:** Tim Keller, Contest Chair. Open to any writer, the LUW Contest provides authors an opportunity to get their work read and critiqued. Multiple categories are offered; see webpage for details. Entries must be the original and unpublished work of the author. Winners are announced at the Annual Writers Round-Up in September. Those not present will be notified by e-mail. Submission Period: Martch 15 to June 15. Entries are judged by professional authors and editors from outside the League.

MCLAREN MEMORIAL COMEDY PLAY WRITING COMPETITION

2000 W. Wadley, Midland TX 79705. (432)682-2544. **Fax:** (432)682-6136. **Website:** www.mctmidland.org. Open to students. Annual contest. Purpose of conference: "The McLaren Memorial Comedy Play Writing Competition was established in 1989 to honor long time MCT volunteer Mike McLaren who loved a good comedy, whether he was on stage or in the front row." Unpublished submissions only. Submissions made by author. Deadline for entries: February 28th (scripts are accepted January 1 through the end of February each year). SASE for contest rules and entry forms. Entry fee is $10 per script. Awards $400 for full-length winner and $200 for one act winner as well as staged readings for 3 finalists in each category. Judging by the audience present at the McLaren festival when the staged readings are performed. Rights to winning material acquired or purchased. 1st right of production or refusal is acquired by MCT. Requirements for entrants: "Yes, the contest is open to any playwright, but the play submitted must be unpublished and never produced in a for-profit setting. One previous production in a nonprofit theatre is acceptable. 'Readings' do not count as productions."

○ THE VICKY METCALF AWARD FOR CHILDREN'S LITERATURE

90 Richmond St. E., Suite 200, Toronto ON M5C 1P1 Canada. (416)504-8222. **Fax:** (416)504-9090. **E-mail:** info@writerstrust.com. **Website:** www.writerstrust.com. **Contact:** Amanda Hopkins, program coordinator. "The Metcalf Award is presented to a Canadian writer for a body of work in children's literature at The Writers' Trust Awards event held in Toronto

each Fall. Open to Canadian citizens and permanent residents only."

MIDLAND AUTHORS AWARD

Society of Midland Authors, P.O. Box 10419, Chicago IL 60610-0419. E-mail: loerzel@comcast.net. Website: www.midlandauthors.com. Contact: Robert Loerzel, President. Since 1957, the Society has presented annual awards for the best books written by Midwestern authors. The contest is open to any title with a recognized publisher that has been published within the year prior to the contest year. Open to authors or poets who reside in, were born in, or have strong ties to a Midland state, which includes Illinois, Indiana, Iowa, Kansas, Michigan, Minnesota, Missouri, Nebraska, North Dakota, South Dakota, Ohio and Wisconsin. Categories: children's nonfiction and fiction, adult nonfiction and fiction, adult biography, and poetry. "Established in 1915, the Society of Midland Authors Award (SMA) is presented to one title in each of six categories 'to stimulate creative effort,' one of SMA's goals, to be honored at the group's annual awards banquet in May." Deadline: February 1. Prize: Prize: cash prize of at least $300 and a plaque that is awarded at the SMA banquet.

MILKWEED NATIONAL FICTION PRIZE

1011 Washington Ave. S., Suite 300, Minneapolis MN 55415. (612)332-3192. Fax: (612)215-2550. E-mail: editor@milkweed.org. Website: www.milkweed.org. Contact: Daniel Slager, award director. Unpublished submissions only "in book form." Please send SASE or visit website for award guidelines. The prize is awarded to the best work for children ages 8-13 that Milkweed agrees to publish in a calendar year. Recognizes an outstanding literary novel for readers ages 8-13 and encourage writers to turn their attention to readers in this age group. Prize: Prize: $5,000 advance against royalties agreed to at the time of acceptance. Judged by the editors of Milkweed Editions.

MINNESOTA BOOK AWARDS

325 Cedar Street, Suite 555, St. Paul MN 55101. E-mail: ann@thefriends.org; mnbookawards@thefriends.org; friends@thefriends.org. Website: www.thefriends.org. Annual award. Purpose of contest: To recognize and honor achievement by members of Minnesota's book community.

☼ MUNICIPAL CHAPTER OF TORONTO IODE JEAN THROOP BOOK AWARD

40 Orchard View Blvd., Suite 219, Toronto ON M4R 1B9 Canada. (416)925-5078. Fax: (416)925-5127. E-mail: ioedtoronto@bellnet.ca. Website: www.bookcentre.ca/awards/iode_book_award_municipal_chapter_toronto. Contact: Jennifer Werry, contest director. The award-winner must be a Canadian citizen, resident in Toronto or the surrounding area, and the book must be published in Canada. Since 1974 the Municipal Chapter of Toronto IODE has presented an award intended to encourage the publication of books for children between the ages of 6 and 12 years. Deadline: November 1. Prize: Prize: Award and cash prize of $2,000. Judged by a selected committee.

● NATIONAL BOOK AWARDS

The National Book Foundation, 90 Broad St., Suite 604, New York NY 10004. (212)685-0261. E-mail: nationalbook@nationalbook.org. Website: www.nationalbook.org. Presents $10,000 in each of 4 categories (fiction, nonfiction, poetry, and young people's literature), plus 16 short-list prizes of $1,000 each to finalists. Submissions must be previously published and **must be entered by the publisher**. General guidelines available on website; interested publishers should phone or e-mail the Foundation. Deadline: See website for current year's deadline.

NATIONAL CHILDREN'S THEATRE FESTIVAL

(305)444-9293, ext. 615. Fax: (305)444-4181. E-mail: maulding@actorsplayhouse.org. Website: www.actorsplayhouse.org. Contact: Earl Maulding. Purpose is to bring together the excitement of the theater arts and the magic of young audiences through the creation of new musical works and to create a venue for playwrights/composers to showcase their artistic products. While scripts should target the appropriate audience, those musicals appealing to adults as well as children will be at an advantage. Contemporary relevance is to be preferred over mere topicality—we seek plays whose appeal will last beyond this season's headlines. Deadline: April 1. Prize: Prize: $500.

NATIONAL FOUNDATION FOR ADVANCEMENT IN THE ARTS

777 Brickell Ave., Suite 370, Miami FL 33131. (305)377-1140 ext 243. Fax: (305)377-1149. E-mail: info@nfaa.org. Website: www.youngARTS.org. Contact: Carla Hill. Created to recognize and reward outstanding

accomplishment in cinematic arts, dance, jazz, music, photography, theater, voice, visual arts and/or writing. youngARTS is an innovative national program of the National Foundation for Advancement in the Arts (NFAA). Established in 1981, youngARTS touches the lives of gifted young people across the country, providing financial support, scholarships and goal-oriented artistic, educational and career opportunities. Each year, from a pool of more than 8,000 applicants, an average of 800 youngARTS winners are chosen for NFAA support by panels of distinguished artists and educators. Deadline for registration: June 1 (early) and October 1. Deadline for submission of work: Nov. 3. Entry fee is $35 (online)/$40 (paper). Fee waivers available based on need. Awards $100-10,000—unrestricted cash grants. Judging by a panel of artists and educators recognized in the field. Rights to submitted/winning material: NFAA/youngARTS retains the right to duplicate work in an anthology or in Foundation literature unless otherwise specified by the artist. Requirements for entrants: Artists must be high school seniors or, if not enrolled in high school, must be 17 or 18 years old. Applicants must be U.S. citizens or residents, unless applying in jazz. Literary and visual works will be published in an anthology distributed during youngARTS Week in Miami when the final adjudication takes place. NFAA invites up to 150 finalists to participate in youngARTS Week in January in Miami-Dade County, Florida. youngARTS Week is a once-in-a-lifetime experience consisting of performances, master classes, workshops, readings, exhibits, and enrichment activities with renowned artists and arts educators. All expenses are paid by NFAA, including airfare, hotel, meals and ground transportation.

NATIONAL OUTDOOR BOOK AWARDS

(208)282-3912. **E-mail:** wattron@isu.edu. **Website:** www.noba-web.org. **Contact:** Ron Watters. "Nine categories: History/biography, outdoor literature, instructional texts, outdoor adventure guides, nature guides, children's books, design/artistic merit, natural history literature, and nature and the environment. Additionally, a special award, the Outdoor Classic Award, is given annually to books which, over a period of time, have proven to be exceptionally valuable works in the outdoor field. Application forms and eligibilty requirements are available online." Applications for the Awards program become available in ear-

ly June. Deadline: September 1. Prize: Winning books are promoted nationally and are entitled to display the National Outdoor Book Award (NOBA) medallion.

NATIONAL PEACE ESSAY CONTEST

United States Institute of Peace, 2301 Constitution Avenue, NW, Washington DC 20037. (202)457-1700. **Fax:** (202)429-6063. **E-mail:** essaycontest@usip.org. **Website:** www.usip.org. The Academy for International Conflict Management and Peacebuilding is the education and training arm of the United States Institute of Peace and runs the National Peace Essay Contest based on the belief that questions about peace, justice, freedom, and security are vital to civic education. Each year over 1,100 students submit entries to the essay contest while thousands more participate in related writing and other classroom exercises in high schools around the country. "Promotes serious discussion among high school students, teachers, and national leaders about international peace and conflict resolution today and in the future; complements existing curricula and other scholastic activities; strengthens students' research, writing, and reasoning skills; and meets National Contents Standards." Deadline: February 1. Prize: Prize: First-place state winners receive scholarships and are invited to Washington for a five-day awards program. The Institute pays for expenses related to the program, including travel, lodging, meals and entertainment. This unique five-day program promotes an understanding of the nature and process of international peacemaking by focusing on a region and/or theme related to the current essay contest.

NATIONAL WRITERS ASSOCIATION NONFICTION CONTEST

10940 S. Parker Rd., #508, Parker CO 80134. (303)841-0246. **E-mail:** natlwritersassn@hotmail.com. **Website:** www.nationalwriters.com. All entries must be postmarked by December 31. Only unpublished works may be submitted. Judging of entries will not begin until the contest ends. Nonfiction in the following areas will be accepted: articles-submission should include query letter, 1st page of manuscript, separate sheet citing 5 possible markets; essay—the complete essay and 5 possible markets on separate sheet; nonfiction book proposal including query letter, chapter by chapter outline, first chapter, bio and market analysis. Those unsure of proper manuscript format should request Research Report #35. "The purpose of the National Writers Association Nonfiction Contest is to encourage the writing of nonfiction and recognize those who excel in this field." Prize: "First through fifth place awards will be presented at the NWAF Conference. Other winners will be notified by March 31st. 1st Prize—$200 and Clearinghouse representation if winner is book proposal; 2nd Prize—$100; 3rd Prize—$50; 4th through 10th places will receive a book. Honorable Mentions receive a certificate.". "Judging will be based on originality, marketability, research, and reader interest. Copies of the judges evaluation sheets will be sent to entrants furnishing an SASE with their entry."

NATIONAL WRITERS ASSOCIATION SHORT STORY CONTEST

10940 S. Parker Rd., #508, Parker CO 80134. (303)841-0246. **E-mail:** natlwritersassn@hotmail.com. **Website:** www.nationalwriters.com. Opens April 1, annually. "Any genre of short story manuscript may be entered. All entries must be postmarked by July 1. Only unpublished works may be submitted. All manuscripts must be typed, double-spaced, in the English language. Maximum length is 5,000. Those unsure of proper manuscript format should request Research Report #35. The entry must be accompanied by entry form (photocopies are acceptable), entry fee of $15 per submission, and return SASE if you wish the material and rating sheets returned. OTHERWISE SUBMISSIONS WILL BE DESTROYED. The U.S. Postal Service will not allow us to use your metered postage unless it is undated. Receipt of entry will not be acknowledged without a return postcard. Author's name and address must appear on the first page. Entries remain the property of the author and may be submitted during the contest as long as they are not published before the final notification of winners. Final prizes will be awarded at the NWAF Workshop in June." The purpose of the National Writers Assn. Short Story Contest is to encourage the development of creative skills, recognize and reward outstanding ability in the area of short story writing. Prize: "First through fifth place awards will be presented at the NWAF Conference. 1st Prize—$250; 2nd Prize—$100; 3rd Prize—$50; 4th through 10th places will receive a book. First through third place winners may be asked to grant one-time rights for publication in AUTHORSHIP magazine. Honorable Mentions receive a certificate. Judging will be based on originality, marketability, research, and reader interest. Copies of the judges evaluation

sheets will be sent to entrants furnishing an SASE with their entry."

JOHN NEWBERY MEDAL

50 E. Huron, Chicago IL 60611. (800)545-2433, ext. 2153. **Fax:** (312)280-5271. **E-mail:** library@ala.org. **Website:** www.ala.org. Purpose of award: to recognize the most distinguished contribution to American children's literature published in the U.S. Previously published submissions only; must be published prior to year award is given. Deadline for entries: December 31. SASE for award rules. Entries not returned. No entry fee. Medal awarded at Caldecott/Newbery banquet during ALA annual conference. Judging by Newbery Award Selection Committee.

● NEW ENGLAND BOOK AWARDS

297 Broadway, #212, Arlington MA 02474. (781)316-8894. **Fax:** (781)316-2605. **E-mail:** nan@neba.org. **Website:** www.newenglandbooks.org/Default. aspx?pageId=234046. **Contact:** Nan Sorenson, assistant executive director. Annual award. Previously published submissions only. Submissions made by New England booksellers; publishers. "Award is given to a specific title, fiction, non-fiction, children's. The titles must be either about New England, set in New England or by an author residing in the New England. The titles must be hardcover, paperback orginal or reissue that was published between September 1 and August 31. Entries must be still in print and available. No entry fee. Judging by NEIBA membership. Requirements for entrants: Author/illustrator must live in New England. Submit written nominations only; actual books should not be sent. Member bookstores receive materials to display winners' books. Submission deadline: July 2.

NEW VOICES AWARD

Website: www.leeandlow.com. **Open to students.** Annual award. Purpose of contest: To encourage writers of color to enter the world of children's books. Lee & Low Books is one of the few minority-owned publishing companies in the country. We have published more than 90 first-time writers and illustrators. Winning titles include *The Blue Roses*, winner of a Patterson Prize for Books for Young People; *Janna and the Kings*, an IRA Children's Book Award Notable; and *Sixteen Years in Sixteen Seconds*, selected for the Texas Bluebonnet Award Masterlist. Submissions made by author. Deadline for entries: September 30. SASE for contest rules or visit website. No entry fee. Awards

New Voices Award—$1,000 prize and standard publication contract (regardless of whether or not writer has an agent) along with an advance against royalties; New Voices Honor Award—$500 prize. Judging by Lee & Low editors. Restrictions of media for illustrators: The author must be a writer of color who is a resident of the U.S. and who has not previously published a children's picture book. For additional information, send SASE or visit Lee & Low's website.

NORTH AMERICAN INTERNATIONAL AUTO SHOW HIGH SCHOOL POSTER CONTEST

1900 W. Big Beaver Rd., Troy MI 48084-3531. (248)643-0250. **Fax:** (248)283-5148. **E-mail:** sherp@dada.org. **Website:** www.naias.com. **Open to students.** Annual contest. Submissions made by the author and illustrator. **Contact:** Detroit Auto Dealers Association (DADA) for contest rules and entry forms or retrieve rules from website. No entry fee. Awards in the High School Poster Contest are as follows: Chairman's Award—$1,000; State Farm Insurance Award—$1,000; Designer's Best of Show (Digital and Traditional)—$500; Best Theme—$250; Best Use of Color—$250; Most Creative—$250. A winner will be chosen in each category from grades 10, 11 and 12. Prizes: 1st place in 10, 11, 12—$500; 2nd place—$250; 3rd place—$100. The winners of the Designer's Best of Show Digital and Traditional will each receive $500. The winner of the Chairman's Award will receive $1,000. Entries will be judged by an independent panel of recognized representatives of the art community. Entrants must be Michigan high school students enrolled in grades 10-12. Winning posters may be displayed at the NAIAS 2012 and reproduced in the official NAIAS program, which is available to the public, international media, corporate executives and automotive suppliers. Winning posters may also be displayed on the official NAIAS website at the sole discretion of the NAIAS.

NORTHERN CALIFORNIA BOOK AWARDS

c/o Poetry Flash, 1450 Fourth St. #4, Berkeley CA 94710. (510)525-5476. **E-mail:** editor@poetryflash.org. **Website:** www.poetryflash.org. **Contact:** Joyce Jenkins, executive director. Annual Northern California Book Award for outstanding book in literature, open to books published in the current calendar year by Northern California authors. Annual award. NCBR presents annual awards to Bay Area (northern California) authors annually in fiction, nonfiction, poetry and children's literature. Previously published books only. Must be published the calendar year prior to spring awards ceremony. Submissions nominated by publishers; author or agent could also nominate published work. Send 3 copies of the book to attention: NCBR. Encourages writers and stimulates interest in books and reading. Deadline: December 28. Prize: Prize: $100 honorarium and award certificate. Judging by voting members of the Northern California Book Reviewers.

OHIOANA BOOK AWARDS

274 E. First Ave., Suite 300, Columbus OH 43201-3673. (614)466-3831. **Fax:** (614)728-6974. **E-mail:** ohioana@ohioana.org. **Website:** www.ohioana.org. **Contact:** Linda Hengst, executive director. Offered annually to bring national attention to Ohio authors and their books, published in the last 2 years. (Books can only be considered once.) Categories: Fiction, nonfiction, juvenile, poetry, and books about Ohio or an Ohioan. Writers must have been born in Ohio or lived in Ohio for at least 5 years, but books about Ohio or an Ohioan need not be written by an Ohioan. Results announced in August or September. Winners notified by mail in May. Deadline: December 31. Prize: Prize: certificate and glass sculpture. Judged by a jury selected by librarians, book reviewers, writers and other knowledgeable people.

OKLAHOMA BOOK AWARDS

200 NE 18th St., Oklahoma City OK 73105. (405)521-2502. **Fax:** (405)525-7804. **E-mail:** carmstrong@oltn.odl.state.ok.us. **Website:** www.odl.state.ok.us/ocb. **Contact:** Connie Armstrong, executive director. Purpose of award: "to honor Oklahoma writers and books about our state." Previously published submissions only. Submissions made by the author, author's agent, or entered by a person or group of people, including the publisher. Must be published during the calendar year preceding the award. Awards are presented to best books in fiction, nonfiction, children's, design and illustration, and poetry books about Oklahoma or books written by an author who was born, is living or has lived in Oklahoma. Deadline for entries: early January. SASE for award rules and entry forms. Entry fee $25. Awards a medal—no cash prize. Judging by a panel of 5 people for each category—a librarian, a working writer in the genre, booksellers, editors, etc. Requirements for entrants: author must be

CONTESTS, GRANTS & AWARDS

an Oklahoma native, resident, former resident or have written a book with Oklahoma theme. Winner will be announced at banquet in Oklahoma City. The Arrell Gibson Lifetime Achievement Award is also presented each year for a body of work.

ONCE UPON A WORLD CHILDREN'S BOOK AWARD

1399 S. Roxbury Dr., Los Angeles CA 90035-4709. (310)772-7605. **Fax:** (310)772-7628. **E-mail:** bookaward@wiesenthal.net. **Website:** www.wiesenthal.com/library. **Contact:** Adaire J. Klein, award director. Submissions made by publishers, author or author's agent. Suggestions from educators, libraries, and others accepted. Must be published January-December of previous year. Deadline for entries: March 31. SASE for contest rules and entry forms. Awards $1,000 each to two authors honoring a book for children age 6-10 and one for age 11 and up. Recognition of Honor Books if deemed appropriate. Judging is by 6 independent judges familiar with children's literature. Award open to any writer with work in English language on subjects of tolerance, diversity, human understanding, and social justice. Book Seals available from the library.

ORBIS PICTUS AWARD FOR OUTSTANDING NONFICTION FOR CHILDREN

1111 W. Kenyon Rd., Urbana IL 61801-1096. (217)328-3870. **Fax:** (217)328-0977. **E-mail:** dzagorski@ncte.org. **Website:** www.ncte.org/awards/orbispictus. Purpose of award: To promote and recognize excellence in the writing of nonfiction for children. Previously published submissions only. Submissions made by author, author's agent, by a person or group of people. Must be published January 1-December 31 of contest year. Deadline for entries: December 31. Call for award information. No entry fee. Awards a plaque given at the NCTE Elementary Section Luncheon at the NCTE Annual Convention in November. Judging by a committee. "The name Orbis Pictus commemorates the work of Johannes Amos Comenius, *Orbis Pictus—The World in Pictures* (1657), considered to be the first book actually planned for children."

● OREGON BOOK AWARDS

925 SW Washington St., Portland OR 97205. (503)227-2583. **Fax:** (503)241-4256. **E-mail:** la@literary-arts.org. **Website:** www.literary-arts.org. **Contact:** Susan Denning. The annual Oregon Book Awards celebrate Oregon authors in the areas of poetry, fiction, nonfiction, drama and young readers' literature published between August 1 and July 31 of the previous calendar year. Entry fee determined by initial print run; see website for details. Entries must be previously published. Oregon residents only. Accepts inquiries by phone and e-mail. Finalists announced in January. Winners announced at an awards ceremony in November. List of winners available in April. Deadline: Last Friday in August. Prize: Prize: Grant of $2,500. (Grant money could vary.). Judged by writers who are selected from outside Oregon for their expertise in a genre. Past judges include Mark Doty, Colson Whitehead and Kim Barnes.

THE ORIGINAL ART

128 E. 63rd St., New York NY 10065. (212)838-2560. **Fax:** (212)838-2561. **E-mail:** kim@societyillustrators.org; info@societyillustrators.org. **Website:** www.societyillustrators.org. **Contact:** Kate Feirtag, exhibition director. Purpose of contest: to celebrate the fine art of children's book illustration. Previously published submissions only. Deadline for entries: July 18. Request "call for entries" to receive contest rules and entry forms. Entry fee is $30/book. Judging by seven professional artists and editors. Works will be displayed at the Society of Illustrators Museum of American Illustration in New York City October-November annually. Medals awarded; catalog published.

HELEN KEATING OTT AWARD FOR OUTSTANDING CONTRIBUTION TO CHILDREN'S LITERATURE

10157 SW Barbur Blvd. #102C, Portland OR 97219. (503)244-6919. **Fax:** (503)977-3734. **E-mail:** csla@worldaccessnet.com. **Website:** www.cslainfo.org. **Contact:** Jeri Baker, chair of committee; Judy Janzen, administrator of CSLA. Annual award. "This award is given to a person or organization that has made a significant contribution to promoting high moral and ethical values through children's literature." Recipient is honored in July during the conference. Awards certificate of recognition, the awards banquet, and one-night's stay in the hotel. "A nomination for an award may be made by anyone. An application form is available by contacting Judy Janzen. Elements of creativity and innovation will be given high priority by the judges. A detailed description of the reasons for the nomination should be given, accompanied by documentary evidence of accomplishment. The nominator should give his or her name,address, telephone number, e-mail addressand a brief explanation of his or herknowledge of the individual's efforts. Elements of creativity and innovation will begiven high priority. Applications should include at least two examples of the your work (published or unpublished, 30 pages maximum) and a short biographical note including a description of your current and anticipated work. Also please indicate what you will work on while attending the Blue Mountain residency. Please send three copies of these writing samples. Samples will not be returned."

PATERSON PRIZE FOR BOOKS FOR YOUNG PEOPLE

One College Blvd., Paterson NJ 07505. (973)523-6085. **Fax:** (973)523-6085. **E-mail:** mgillan@pccc.edu. **Website:** www.pccc.edu/poetry. **Contact:** Maria Mazziotti Gillan, executive director. Award for a book published in the previous year in each age category (Pre-K-Grade 3, Grades 4-6, Grades 7-12). Postmark deadline March 15. Prize: $500.

⊕ THE KATHERINE PATERSON PRIZE FOR YOUNG ADULT AND CHILDREN'S WRITING

Vermont College of Fine Arts, 36 College St., Montpelier VT 05602. (802)828-8517. **E-mail:** hungermtn@vcfa.edu. **Website:** www.hungermtn.org. **Contact:** Miciah Bay Gault, editor. The annual Katherine Paterson Prize for Young Adult and Children's Writing offers $1,000 and publication in *Hunger Mountain*; 3 runners-up receive $100 and are also published. Submit young adult or middle grade mss, and writing for younger children, short stories, picture books, or novel excerpts, under 10,000 words. Guidelines available on website. "An annual prize for Young Adult and Children's Literature. A chance for your YA and Children's Lit to be read by Hunger Mountain editors and guest judges." Deadline: June 30. Prize: Prize: $1,000 and publication for the first place winner; $100 each and publication for the three category winners.

PENNSYLVANIA YOUNG READERS' CHOICE AWARDS PROGRAM

148 S. Bethelehem Pike, Ambler PA 19002-5822. (215)643-5048. **E-mail:** bellavance@verizon.net. **Website:** http://www.psla.org. **Contact:** Jean B. Bellavance, coordinator. Submissions nominated by a person or group. Must be published within 5 years of the award—for example, books published in 2007

to present are eligible for the 2011-2012 award. Deadline for entries: September 1. SASE for contest rules and entry forms. No entry fee. Framed certificate to winning authors. Judging by children of Pennsylvania (they vote). Requirements for entrants: currently living in North America. Reader's Choice Award is to promote reading of quality books by young people in the Commonwealth of Pennsylvania, to promote teacher and librarian involvement in children's literature, and to honor authors whose work has been recognized by the children of Pennsylvania. Four awards are given, one for each of the following grade level divisions: K-3, 3-6, 6-8, YA. View information at the Pennsylvania School Librarians website.

PEN/PHYLLIS NAYLOR WORKING WRITER FELLOWSHIP

PEN American Center, 588 Broadway, Suite 303, New York NY 10012. **E-mail:** awards@pen.org. **Website:** www.pen.org. **Contact:** Nick Burd, awards program director. Offered annually to an author of children's or young-adult fiction. Candidates have published at least two novels for children or young adults which have been received warmly by literary critics, but have not generated suficient income to support the author. Writers must be nominated by an editor or fellow author. See website for eligibility and nomination guidelines. The Fellowship has been developed to help writers whose work is of high literary caliber but who have not yet attracted a broad readership. The Fellowship is designed to assist a writer at a crucial moment in his or her career to complete a book-length work-in-progress. Deadline: February 15. Prize: Prize: $5,000.

PLEASE TOUCH MUSEUM BOOK AWARD

Memorial Hall in Fairmount Park, 4231 Avenue of the Republic, Philadelphia PA 19131. (215)578-5153. **Fax:** (215)578-5171. **E-mail:** hboyd@pleasetouchmuseum.org. **Website:** www.pleasetouchmuseum.org. **Contact:** Heather Boyd. "To be eligible for consideration, a book must: (1) Be distinguished in text, illustration, and ability to explore and clarify an idea for young children (ages 7 and under); (2) be published within the last year by an American publisher; and (3) be by an American author and/or illustrator." Books must be published between September and August of preceeding year. This prestigious award has recognized and encouraged the publication of high quality books for young children. The award is given to books that are imaginative, exceptionally illustrated and help foster a child's life-long love of reading. Deadline: October 1. Judged by a panel of volunteer educators, artists, booksellers and librarians in conjunction with museum staff.

PNWA LITERARY CONTEST

PMB 2717-1420 NW Gilman Blvd., Suite 2, Issaquah WA 98027. (425)673-2665. **Fax:** (425)961-0768. **E-mail:** pnwa@pnwa.org. **Website:** www.pnwa.org. **Contact:** Kelli Liddane. **Open to students.** Annual contest. Purpose of contest: "Valuable tool for writers as contest submissions are critiqued (2 critiques)." Unpublished submissions only. Submissions made by author. Deadline: February 18. Prize: 1st: $700; 2nd: $300.

POCKETS FICTION-WRITING CONTEST

P.O. Box 340004, Nashville TN 37203-0004. (615)340-7333. **Fax:** (615)340-7267. **E-mail:** pockets@upperroom.org. **Website:** www.pockets.upperroom.org. **Contact:** Lynn W. Gilliam, senior editor. Designed for 6- to 12-year-olds, *Pockets* magazine offers wholesome devotional readings that teach about God's love and presence in life. The content includes fiction, scripture stories, puzzles and games, poems, recipes, colorful pictures, activities, and scripture readings. Freelance submissions of stories, poems, recipes, puzzles and games, and activities are welcome. Stories should be 750-1,000 words. Multiple submissions are permitted. Past winners are ineligible. The primary purpose of Pockets is to help children grow in their relationship with God and to claim the good news of the gospel of Jesus Christ by applying it to their daily lives. Pockets espouses respect for all human beings and for God's creation. It regards a child's faith journey as an integral part of all of life and sees prayer as undergirding that journey. Deadline: November 1. Prize: Prize: $500 and publication in magazine.

◑ EDGAR ALLAN POE AWARD

1140 Broadway, Suite 1507, New York NY 10001. (212)888-8171. **Fax:** (212)888-8107. **E-mail:** mwa@mysterywriters.org. **Website:** www.mysterywriters.org. Mystery Writers of America is the leading association for professional crime writers in the United States. Members of MWA include most major writers of crime fiction and non-fiction, as well as screenwriters, dramatists, editors, publishers, and other professionals in the field. Purpose of the award: to honor authors of distinguished works in the mystery field. Previously published submissions only. Submissions

made by the author, author's agent; "normally by the publisher." Work must be published/produced the year of the contest. Deadline: November 30. Prize: Prize: Awards ceramic bust of "Edgar" for winner; scrolls for all nominees. Judged by professional members of Mystery Writers of America (writers).

MICHAEL L. PRINTZ AWARD

50 E. Huron, Chicago IL 60611. **Fax:** (312)280-5276. **E-mail:** yalsa@ala.org. **Website:** www.ala.org/yalsa/printz. Annual award. The Michael L. Printz Award is an award for a book that exemplifies literary excellence in young adult literature. It is named for a Topeka, Kansas school librarian who was a long-time active member of the Young Adult Library Services Association. It will be selected annually by an award committee that can also name as many as 4 honor books. The award-winning book can be fiction, nonfiction, poetry or an anthology, and can be a work of joint authorship or editorship. The books must be published between January 1 and December 31 of the preceding year and be designated by its publisher as being either a young adult book or one published for the age range that YALSA defines as young adult, e.g. ages 12 through 18. The deadline for both committee and field nominations will be December 1.

PURPLE DRAGONFLY BOOK AWARDS

4696 W. Tyson St., Chandler AZ 85226-2903. (480)940-8182. **Fax:** (480)940-8787. **E-mail:** info@fivestarpublications.com. **Website:** www.purpledragonflybookawards.com; www.fivestarpublications.com; www.fivestarbookawards.com. **Contact:** Lisa Goldman, Lynda Exley, contest coordinators. "Five Star Publications is proud to present the Purple Dragonfly Book Awards, which were conceived and designed with children in mind. Not only do we want to recognize and honor accomplished authors in the field of children's literature, but we also want to highlight and reward up-and-coming, newly published authors and younger published writers. In our efforts to include everyone, the Purple Dragonfly Book Awards are divided into 35 distinct subject categories, ranging from books on the environment and cooking to sports and family issues. (Please click on the 'Categories' tab for a complete list.) The Purple Dragonfly Book Awards are geared toward stories that appeal to children of all ages. We are looking for stories that inspire, inform, teach or entertain. A Purple Dragonfly seal on your book's cover tells parents, grandparents, educators and caregivers they are giving children the very best in reading excellence. Our judges are industry experts with specific knowledge about the categories over which they preside. Being honored with a Purple Dragonfly Award confers credibility upon the winner, as well as provides positive publicity to further their success. The goal of these awards is to give published authors the recognition they deserve and provide a helping hand to further their careers." The awards are open to books published in any calendar year and in any country that are available for purchase. Books entered must be printed in English. Traditionally published, partnership published and self-published books are permitted, as long as they fit the above criteria. E-books are not permitted; although, Five Star does have plans for an e-book contest in the future, so please check www.FiveStarBookAwards.com periodically for notification of contest launch. Final deadline for submissions is May 1, 2013; to be eligible, submissions must be postmarked May 1, 2013 or earlier. The deadline is the same each year. Submissions postmarked March 1, 2013 or earlier that meet all submission requirements are eligible for the Early Bird reward: A free copy of "The Economical Guide to Self-Publishing" or "Promote Like a Pro: Small Budget, Big Show." Prize: The grand prize winner will receive a $300 cash prize, 100 foil award seals (more can be ordered for an extra charge), 1 hour of marketing consultation from Five Star Publications, and $100 worth of Five Star Publications' titles, as well as publicity on Five Star Publications' websites and inclusion in a winners' news release sent to a comprehensive list of media outlets. The grand prize winner will also be placed in the Five Star Dragonfly Book Awards virtual bookstore with a thumbnail of the book's cover, price, 1-sentence description and link to Amazon.com for purchasing purposes, if applicable. 1st Place: All first-place winners of categories will be put into a drawing for a $100 prize. In addition, each first-place winner in each category receives a certificate commemorating their accomplishment, 25 foil award seals (more can be ordered for an extra charge) and mention on Five Star Publications' websites. "Our judges are industry experts with specific knowledge about the categories over which they preside. Being honored with a Purple Dragonfly Award confers credibility upon the winner, as well as provides positive publicity to further their success. The goal of these awards is to give published

authors the recognition they deserve and provide a helping hand to further their careers."

QUILL AND SCROLL INTERNATIONAL WRITING AND PHOTO CONTEST, AND BLOGGING COMPETITION

School of Journalism, Univ. of Iowa, 100 Adler Journalism Bldg., Iowa City IA 52242-2004. (319)335-3457. **Fax:** (319)335-3989. **E-mail:** quill-scroll@uiowa.edu. **E-mail:** vanessa-shelton@uiowa.edu. **Website:** quillandscroll.org. **Contact:** Vanessa Shelton, contest director. Entries must have been published in a high school or profesional newspaper or website during the previous year, and must be the work of a currently enrolled high school student. Open to students. Annual contest. Previously published submissions only. Submissions made by the author or school newspaper adviser. Deadline: February 5. Prize: Prize: Winners will receive *Quill and Scroll*'s National Award Gold Key and, if seniors, are eligible to apply for one of the scholarships offered by *Quill and Scroll*. All winning entries are automatically eligible for the International Writing and Photo Sweepstakes Awards. Engraved plaque awarded to sweepstakes winners.

⦿ RED HOUSE CHILDREN'S BOOK AWARD

2 Bridge Wood View, Norsforth, Leeds VI LS18 5PE United Kingdom . **E-mail:** marianneadey@aol.com. **Website:** www.redhousechildrensbookaward.co.uk. **Purpose of the award:** The R.H.C.B.A. is an annual prize for the best children's book of the year judged by the children themselves." Categories: (I) books for younger children, (II) books for younger readers, (III) books for older readers. Estab. 1980. Works must be published in the United Kingdom. Deadline for entries: December 31. SASE or e-mail for rules. Entries not returned. Awards "a magnificent silver and oak trophy worth over €6,000." Silver dishes to each category winner. Portfolios of children's work to all Top Ten authors and illustrators. Judging by children. Requirements for entrants: Work must be fiction and published in the UK during the current year (poetry is ineligible). Top 50 Books of the year will be published in current "Pick of the Year" publication.

⦿ THE RED HOUSE CHILDREN'S BOOK AWARD

Red House Children's Book Award, 123 Frederick Road, Cheam, Sutton, Surrey SM1 2HT United Kingdom. **E-mail:** info@rhcba.co.uk. **Website:** www.red

housechildrensbookaward.co.uk. **Contact:** Sinead Kromer, national co-ordinator. (formerly The Children's Book Award), Owned and co-ordinated by the Federation of Children's Book Groups (Reg. Charity No. 268289). Purpose of the award is to enable children choose the best works of fiction published in the UK. Prize: trophy and silver bookmarks, portfolio of children's letters and pictures. Categories: Books for Younger Children, Books for Younger Readers, Books for Older Readers. No entry fee. **Closing Date is December 31.** Either author or publisher may nominate title. Guidelines available on website. Accepts enquiries by email and phone. Shortlist announced in February and winners announced in May. Winners notified at award ceremony and dinner at the Birmingham Botanical Gardens and via the publisher. For contest results, visit the website.

☺ REGINA BOOK AWARD

P.O. Box 20025, Regina SK S4P 4J7 Canada. (306)569-1585. **E-mail:** director@bookawards.sk.ca. **Website:** www.bookawards.sk.ca. Offered annually. "In recognition of the vitality of the literary community in Regina, this award is presented to a Regina author for the best book, judged on the quality of writing." Books from the following categories will be considered: Children's; drama; fiction (short fiction by a single author, novellas, novels); nonfiction (all categories of nonfiction writing except cookbooks, directories, how-to books, or bibliographies of minimal critical content); poetry. Deadline: November 1. Prize: $2,000 (CAD).

TOMÁS RIVERA MEXICAN AMERICAN CHILDREN'S BOOK AWARD

Dr. Jesse Gainer, Texas State University, 601 University Drive, San Marcos TX 78666-4613. (512)245-2357. **Website:** http://www.education.txstate.edu/about/Map-Directions.html. **Contact:** Dr. Jesse Gainer, award director. Texas State University College of Education developed the Tomas Rivera Mexican American Children's Book Award to honor authors and illustrators who create literature that depicts the Mexican American experience. The award was established in 1995 and was named in honor of Dr. Tomas Rivera, a distinguished alumnus of Texas State University. The book will be written for children and young adults (0-16 years). The text and illustrations will be of highest quality. The portrayal/representations of Mexican Americans will be accurate and engaging, avoid stereotypes, and reflect rich characterization. The book may be fiction or non-fiction. See website for more details and directions. Deadline: November 1.

☺ ROCKY MOUNTAIN BOOK AWARD: ALBERTA CHILDREN'S CHOICE BOOK AWARD

Box 42, Lethbridge AB T1J 3Y3 Canada. (403)381-0855. **Website:** http://rmba.lethsd.ab.ca/. **Contact:** Michelle Dimnik, contest director. Submit entries to: Richard Chase, board member. **Open to students.** Annual contest. Purpose of contest: "Reading motivation for students, promotion of Canadian authors, illustrators and publishers." Previously unpublished submissions only. Submissions made by author's agent or nominated by a person or group. Must be published between 2010-2012. Register before January 15th to take part in the 2013 Rocky Mountain Book Award. SASE for contest rules and entry forms. No entry fee. Awards: Gold medal and author tour of selected Alberta schools. Judging by students. Requirements for entrants: Canadian authors and illustrators only.

ROYAL DRAGONFLY BOOK AWARDS

4696 W. Tyson St., Chandler AZ 85226. (480)940-8182. **Fax:** (480)940-8787. **E-mail:** info@fivestarpublications.com. **Website:** www.fivestarpublications.com; www.fivestarbookawards.com; www.royaldragonflybookawards.com. **Contact:** Lynda Exley. Offered annually for any previously published work to honor authors for writing excellence of all types of literature - fiction and nonfiction - in 50 categories, appealing to a wide range of ages and comprehensive list of genres. Open to any author published in English. Guidelines and entry forms available by request with SASE. Entry forms are also downloadable at www.royaldragonflybookawards.com. Entry fee is $50 for one title in one category, $45 per title when multiple books are entered or $45 per category when one book is entered in multiple categories. All entry fees are per title, per category. The Grand Prize winner receives $300, while another entrant will be the lucky winner of a $100 drawing. All first-place winners receive foil award seals and are included in a publicity campaign announcing winners. All first- and second-place winners and honorable mentions receive certificates.

☺ SASKATCHEWAN CHILDREN'S LITERATURE AWARD

Box 20025, Regina SK S4P 4J7 Canada. (306)569-1585. **Fax:** (306)569-4187. **E-mail:** director@bookawards.

sk.ca. **E-mail:** info@bookawards.sk.ca. **Website:** www.bookawards.sk.ca. **Contact:** Executive director, book submissions. Offered annually. "This award is presented to a Saskatchewan author or pair of authors, or to Saskatchewan author and a Saskatchewan illustrator, for the best book of children's literature, for ages 0-11, judged on the quality of the writing and illustration." Deadline: November 1. Prize: Prize: $2,000 (CAD).

✪ SASKATCHEWAN FIRST BOOK AWARD

P.O. Box 20025, Regina SK S4P 4J7 Canada. (306)569-1585. **E-mail:** director@bookawards.sk.ca. **Website:** www.bookawards.sk.ca. Offered annually. "This award is presented to a Saskatchewan author for the best first book, judged on the quality of writing." Books from the following categories will be considered: Children's; drama; fiction (short fiction by a single author, novellas, novels); nonfiction (all categories of nonfiction writing except cookbooks, directories, how-to books, or bibliographics of minimal critical content); and poetry. Deadline: November 1. Prize: Prize: $2,000 (CAD).

SCBWI MAGAZINE MERIT AWARDS

8271 Beverly Blvd., Los Angeles CA 90048. **Website:** www.scbwi.org. **Contact:** Stephanie Gordon, award coordinator. Purpose of the award: "to recognize outstanding original magazine work for young people published during that year and having been written or illustrated by members of SCBWI." Previously published submissions only. Entries must be submitted between January 1 and December 15 of the year of publication. For rules and procedures see website. No entry fee. Must be a SCBWI member. Awards plaques and honor certificates for each of 4 categories (fiction, nonfiction, illustration, poetry). Judging by a magazine editor and two "full" SCBWI members. "All magazine work for young people by an SCBWI member—writer, artist or photographer—is eligible during the year of original publication. In the case of co-authored work, both authors must be SCBWI members. Members must submit their own work." Requirements for entrants: 4 copies each of the published work and proof of publication (may be contents page) showing the name of the magazine and the date of issue. The SCBWI is a professional organization of writers and illustrators and others interested in chil-

dren's literature. Membership is open to the general public at large

SCBWI WORK-IN-PROGRESS GRANTS

Website: www.scbwi.org. "The SCBWI Work-in-Progress Grants have been established to assist children's book writers in the completion of a specific project." Four categories: (1) General Work-in-Progress Grant. (2) Grant for a Contemporary Novel for Young People. (3) Nonfiction Research Grant. (4) Grant for a Work Whose Author Has Never Had a Book Published. Requests for applications may be made beginning October 1. Completed applications accepted February 1-April 1 of each year. SASE for applications for grants. In any year, an applicant may apply for any of the grants except the one awarded for a work whose author has never had a book published. (The recipient of this grant will be chosen from entries in all categories.) Five grants of $1,500 will be awarded annually. Runner-up grants of $500 (one in each category) will also be awarded. "The grants are available to both full and associate members of the SCBWI. They are not available for projects on which there are already contracts." Previous recipients not eligible to apply.

✪ SHABO AWARD FOR CHILDREN'S PICTURE BOOK WRITERS

The Loft Literary Center, 1011 Washington Ave. S., Suite 200, Open Book Minneapolis MN 55415 . (612)215-2575. **Fax:** (612)215-2576. **E-mail:** loft@loft. org. **Website:** www.loft.org. "The Shabo Award is offered to children's picture book writers to develop 'nearly there' manuscripts into publishable pieces. Up to 8 advanced writers will be chosen annually. Participants should have few, or no, publications to date. Guidelines available online in April with an early June deadline." **Contact:** Jerod Santek. "The Shabo Award is offered to children's picture book writers to develop 'nearly there' manuscripts into publishable pieces. Up to 8 advanced writers will be chosen annually. Participants should have few, or no, publications to date. Guidelines available online in April." Deadline: June 25.

SKIPPING STONES BOOK AWARDS

Website: www.skippingstones.org. Open to published books, publications/magazines, educational videos, and DVDs. Annual awards. Purpose of contest: To recognize exceptional, literary and artistic contributions to juvenile/children's literature, as well as teaching resources and educational audio/video resources in the areas of multicultural awareness, nature and ecology, social issues, peace and nonviolence. Submissions made by the author or publishers and/or producers. Deadline for entries: February 1. Send request for contest rules and entry forms or visit website. Entry fee is $50; 50% discount for small nonprofit publishers. Each year, an honor roll of about 20 to 25 books and A/V with teaching resources are selected by a multicultural selection committee of editors, students, parents, teachers and librarians. Winners receive gold honor award seals, attractive honor certificates and publicity via multiple outlets. Many educational publications announce the winners of our book awards. "The reviews of winning books and educational videos/DVDs are published in the May-August issue of *Skipping Stones* and/or on our website."

SKIPPING STONES YOUTH HONOR AWARDS

P.O. Box 3939, Eugene OR 97403-0939. (541)342-4956. **E-mail:** editor@SkippingStones.org. **Website:** www.SkippingStones.org. **Open to students.** Annual awards. Purpose of contest: "to recognize youth, 7 to 17, for their contributions to multicultural awareness, nature and ecology, social issues, peace and nonviolence. Also to promote creativity, self-esteem and writing skills and to recognize important work being done by youth organizations." Submissions made by the author. Deadline for entries: June 25. SASE for contest rules or download from http://www.skipping-stones.org/youthhonor-02.htm. Entries must include certificate of originality by a parent and/or teacher and a cover letter that included cultural background information on the author. Submissions can either be mailed or e-mailed. Entry fee is $3 fee is waived for low-income students. Everyone who enters the contest receives the September-October issue featuring Youth Awards. Judging by *Skipping Stones* staff. "Up to ten awards are given in three categories: (1) Compositions (essays, poems, short stories, songs, travelogues, etc.)—Entries should be typed (double-spaced) or neatly handwritten. Fiction or nonfiction should be limited to 1,000 words; poems to 30 lines. Non-English writings are also welcome. (2) Artwork (drawings, cartoons, paintings or photo essays with captions)—Entries should have the artist's name, age and address on the back of each page. Send the originals with SASE. Black & white photos are especially welcome. Limit: 8 pieces. (3) Youth Organizations—Tell

us how your club or group works to: (a) preserve the nature and ecology in your area, (b) enhance the quality of life for low-income, minority or disabled or (c) improve racial or cultural harmony in your school or community. Use the same format as for compositions." The winners are published in the September-October issue of *Skipping Stones*. Now in its 23rd year, *Skipping Stones* is a winner of N.A.M.E.EDPRESS, Newsstand Resources and Parent's Choice Awards.

❶ KAY SNOW WRITING CONTEST

Willamette Writers, 2108 Buck St., West Linn OR 97068. (503)305-6729. **Fax:** (503)344-6174. **E-mail:** wilwrite@willamettewriters.com. **Website:** www.willamettewriters.com. **Contact:** Lizzy Shannon, contest director. "Willamette Writers is the largest writers' organization in Oregon and one of the largest writers' organizations in the United States. It is a nonprofit, tax-exempt Oregon corporation led by volunteers. Elected officials and directors administer an active program of monthly meetings, special seminars, workshops and annual writing conference. Continuing with established programs and starting new ones is only made possible by strong volunteer support." See website for specific details and rules. There are six different categories writers can enter: Adult Fiction, Adult Non-Fiction, Poetry, Juvenile Short Story, Screenwriting and Student Writer. "The purpose of this annual writing contest, named in honor of Willamette Writer's founder, Kay Snow, is to help writers reach professional goals in writing in a broad array of categories and to encourage student writers." Deadline: April 23. Prize: Prize: One first prize of $300, one second place prize of $150, and a third place prize of $50 per winning entry in each of the six categories.

SOUTHWEST WRITERS

3200 Carlisle Blvd., NE Suite #114, Albuquerque NM 87110. (505)830-6034. **E-mail:** swwriters@juno.com. **Website:** www.southwestwriters.com. The SouthWest Writers Writing Contest encourages and honors excellence in writing. In addition to competing for cash prizes and the coveted Storyteller Award, contest entrants may receive an optional written critique of their entry from a qualified contest critiquer. Non-profit organization dedicated to helping members of all levels in their writing. Members enjoy perks such as networking with professional and aspiring writers; substantial discounts on mini-conferences, workshops, writing classes, and annual and quarterly SWW writing contest; monthly newsletter; two writing programs per month; critique groups, critique service (also for nonmembers); discounts at bookstores and other businesses; and website linking. Submit first 20 pages and 1 page synopsis (using industry-standard formatting, Courier font, brad-bound). Deadline: May 1 (up to May 15 with a late fee). Submissions begin March 1. Prize: Prize: A 1st, 2nd, and 3rd place winner will be judged in each of the 12 categories. 1st place: $200; 2nd place: $150; 3rd place: $100. $1,500 for the Storyteller Award, the entry judged the best of all entries in all categories. All mss will be screened by a panel and the top 10 in each category will be sent to appropriate editors or literary agents to determine the final top 3 places.

SOUTHWEST WRITERS ANNUAL CONTEST

3721 Morris NE, Albuquerque NM 87111. (505)265-9485. **E-mail:** swwcontest@gmail.com. **Website:** www.southwestwriters.com; www.swwcontest.com. **Open to adults and students.** Annual contest. Estab. Purpose of contest: to encourage writers of all genres. Also offers mini-conferences, critique service—for $60/year, offers 2 monthly programs, monthly newsletter, annual writing and bi-monthly writing contests, other workshops, various discount perks, website linking, e-mail addresses, classes and critique service (open to nonmembers). See website for more information or call or write. Entries are open from March 1 to May 1 and may be submitted after May 1 until May 15 with payment of a late fee.

SYDNEY TAYLOR BOOK AWARD

P.O. Box 1118, Teaneck NJ 07666. (212)725-5359. **E-mail:** chair@sydneytaylorbookaward.org; heidi@cbiboca.org. **Website:** www.sydneytaylorbookaward.org. **Contact:** Barbara Bietz, chair. Offered annually for work published during the current year. "Given to distinguished contributions to Jewish literature for children. One award for younder readers, one for older readers, and one for teens." Publishers submit books. Guidelines on website. Awards certificate, cash award, and gold or silver seals for cover of winning book. December 31, "but we cannot guarantee that books received after December 1 will be considered.".

SYDNEY TAYLOR MANUSCRIPT COMPETITION

Sydney Taylor Manuscript Award Competition, 204 Park St., Montclair NJ 07042-2903. **E-mail:** stmaca jl@aol.com. **Website:** www.jewishlibraries.org/main/Awards/SydneyTaylorManuscriptAward.aspx. **Contact:** Aileen Grossberg. Download rules and forms from website. Must be an unpublished fiction writer or a student; also, books must range from 64-200 pages in length. "AJL assumes no responsibility for publication, but hopes this cash incentive will serve to encourage new writers of children's stories with Jewish themes for all children. This competition is for unpublished writers of fiction. Material should be for readers ages 8-11, with universal appeal that will serve to deepen the understanding of Judaism for all children, revealing positive aspects of Jewish life." Deadline: December 15. Prize: Prize: $1,000. Judging by qualified judges from within the Association of Jewish Libraries.

☼ TD CANADIAN CHILDREN'S LITERATURE AWARD

40 Orchard View Blvd., Suite 217, Toronto ON M4R 1B9 Canada. (416)975-0010, ext. 222. **Fax:** (416)975-8970. **Website:** www.bookcentre.ca. **Contact:** Meghan Howe. "All books, in any genre, written and illustrated by Canadians and for children ages 1-12 are eligible. Only books first published in Canada are eligible for submission. Books must be published between January 1 and December 31 of the previous calendar year. Open to Canadian citizens and/or permanent residents of Canada." To honour the most distinguished book of the year for young people in both English and French. Submission deadline: February 8. Prize: Prizes: Two prizes of $30,000, 1 for English, 1 for French. $10,000 will be divided among the Honour Book English titles and Honour Book French titles, to a maximum of 4; $2,500 shall go to each of the publishers of the English and French grand-prize winning books for promotion and publicity.

☼ TORONTO BOOK AWARDS

100 Queen St. W., City Clerk's Office, 2nd floor, West Tower, Toronto ON M5H 2N2 Canada. (416)392-7805. **Fax:** (416)392-1247. **E-mail:** bkurmey@toronto.ca. **E-mail:** protocol@toronto.ca. **Website:** www.toronto.ca/book_awards. **Contact:** Bev Kurmey, protocol officer. The Toronto Book Awards honour authors of books of literary or artistic merit that are evocative of Toronto. To be eligible, books must be published between January 1 and December 31 of previous year. Deadline: March 29. Prize: Prize: Each finalist receives $1,000 and the winning author receives the

remaining prize money ($15,000 total in prize money available).

VEGETARIAN ESSAY CONTEST

P.O. Box 1463, Baltimore MD 21203. (410)366-VEGE. **Fax:** (410)366-8804. **E-mail:** vrg@vrg.org. **Website:** www.vrg.org. A 2-3 page essay on any aspect of vegetarianism. Entrants should base their paper on interviewing, research, and/or personal opinon. You need not be a vegetarian to enter. Three different entry categories: age 14-18; age 9-13; and age 8 and under. Prize: Prize: $50 savings bond.

VFW VOICE OF DEMOCRACY

406 W. 34th St., Kansas City MO 64111. (816)968-1117. **E-mail:** kharmer@vfw.org. **Website:** www.vfw.org. The Voice of Democracy Program is open to students in grades 9-12 (on the Nov. 1 deadline), who are enrolled in a public, private or parochial high school or home study program in the United States and its territories. Contact your local VFW Post to enter. Purpose is to give high school students the opportunity to voice their opinions about their responsibility to our country and to convey those opinions via the broadcast media to all of America. Deadline: November 1. Prize: Prize: Winners receive awards ranging from $1,000-30,000.

WESTERN HERITAGE AWARDS

1700 NE 63rd St., Oklahoma City OK 73111-7997. (405)478-2250. **Fax:** (405)478-4714. **E-mail:** ssimpson@nationalcowboymuseum.org. **Website:** www.nationalcowboymuseum.org. **Contact:** Shayla Simpson, PR director. Previously published submissions only; must be published the calendar year before the awards are presented. Requirements for entrants: The material must pertain to the development or preservation of the West, either from a historical or contemporary viewpoint. Literary entries must have been published between December 1 and November 30 of calendar year. Film, music or television entries must have been released or aired between January 1 and December 31 of calendar year of entry. Works recognized during special awards ceremonies held annually at the museum. There is an autograph party preceding the awards. Awards ceremonies are sometimes broadcast. The WHA are presented annually to encourage the accurate and artistic telling of great stories of the West through 16 categories of western literature, television, film and music; including fiction, nonfiction, children's books and poetry. Deadline: December 31.

Prize: Prize: Awards a Wrangler bronze sculpture designed by famed western artist, John Free. Judged by a panel of judges selected each year with distinction in various fields of western art and heritage.

WESTERN WRITERS OF AMERICA

271CR 219, Encampment WY 82325. (307)329-8942. **Fax:** (307)327-5465 (call first). **E-mail:** wwa.moulton@gmail.com. **Website:** www.westernwriters.org. **Contact:** Candy Moulton, executive director. "17 Spur Award categories in various aspects of the American West." Send entry form with your published work. "The nonprofit Western Writers of America has promoted and honored the best in Western literature with the annual Spur Awards, selected by panels of judges. Awards, for material published last year, are given for works whose inspirations, image and literary excellence best represent the reality and spirit of the American West."

JACKIE WHITE MEMORIAL NATIONAL CHILDREN'S PLAY WRITING CONTEST

1800 Nelwood, Columbia MO 65202-1447. (573)874-5628. **E-mail:** bybetsy@yahoo.com. **Website:** www.cectheatre.org. **Contact:** Betsy Phillips, contest director. Send scripts to 309 Parkade Blvd., Columbia MO 65202. Annual contest. Purpose of contest: "To encourage writing of family-friendly scripts." SASE for contest rules and entry forms. Previously unpublished submissions only. Submissions made by author. Play may be performed during the following season. All submissions will be read by at least 3 readers. Author will receive a written evaluation of the script. Deadline: June 1, 2013. Prize: Awards $500 with production possible. "We reserve the right to award 1st place and prize monies without a production." Judging by current and past board members of CEC and by non-board members who direct plays at CEC.

LAURA INGALLS WILDER METAL

50 E. Huron, Chicago IL 60611. (800)545-2433. **E-mail:** alsc@ala.org. **Website:** www.ala.org/alsc. Award offered every 2 years. Purpose of the award: to recognize an author or illustrator whose books, published in the U.S. have over a period of years made a substantial and lasting contribution to children's literature. The candidates must be nominated by ALSC members. Medal presented at Newbery/Caldecott banquet during annual conference. Judging by Wilder Award Selection Committee.

WILLA LITERARY AWARD

E-mail: pamtartaglio@yahoo.com. **Website:** www.womenwritingthewest.org. **Contact:** Pam Tartaglio. The WILLA Literary Award honors the best in literature featuring women's or girls' stories set in the West published each year. Women Writing the West (WWW), a nonprofit association of writers and other professionals writing and promoting the Women's West, underwrites and presents the nationally recognized award annually (for work published between January 1 and December 31). The award is named in honor of Pulitzer Prize winner Willa Cather, one of the country's foremost novelists. The award is given in 7 categories: Historical fiction, contemporary fiction, original softcover fiction, creative nonfiction, scholarly nonfiction, poetry, and children's/young adult fiction/nonfiction. Deadline: February 1. Prize: Winner receives $100 and a trophy. Finalist receives a plaque. Award announcement is in early August, and awards are presented to the winners and finalists at the annual WWW Fall Conference. Judged by professional librarians not affiliated with WWW.

RITA WILLIAMS YOUNG ADULT PROSE PRIZE

E-mail: pennobhill@aol.com. **Website:** www.soulmakingcontest.us. **Contact:** Eileen Malone. The Soul Making Keats Literary Competition was started in 1992 by Eileen Malone as a poetry contest to further enhance the outreach of The Source Center for Spiritual Development and Wholeness which was founded by Janice Farrell, Regional Coordinator for Spiritual Directors International. All prose works must be typed, double-spaced, page numbered, and paper-clipped. Please indicate word count on title page Grades 9-12 or equivalent age. Up to 3,000 words in story, essay, journal entry, creative nonfiction or memoir. Deadline: November 30 (postmarked). Prize: Prize: $100 for first place; $50 for second place; $25 for third place. Judged by Rita Wiliams, an Emmy-award winning investigative reporter with KTVU-TV in Oakland, California.

PAUL A. WITTY OUTSTANDING LITERATURE AWARD

P.O. Box 10034, Lamar University, Beaumont TX 77710. (409)286-5941. **Fax:** (409)880-8384. **E-mail:** dorothy.sisk@lamar.edu. **Website:** www.reading.org. **Contact:** Dorothy Sisk, director. **Open to students.** Annual award. Categories of entries: poetry/prose at elementary, junior high and senior high levels. Unpublished submissions only. Deadline for entries: February 1. SASE for award rules and entry forms. SASE for return of entries. No entry fee. Awards $25 and plaque, also certificates of merit. Judging by 2 committees for screening and awarding. "The elementary students' entries must be legible and may not exceed 1,000 words. Secondary students' prose entries should be typed and may exceed 1,000 words if necessary. At both elementary and secondary levels, if poetry is entered, a set of five poems must be submitted. All entries and requests for applications must include a self-addressed, stamped envelope."

PAUL A. WITTY SHORT STORY AWARD

International Reading Association, 800 Barksdale Rd., PO Box 8139, Newark DE 19714-8139. (302)731-1600. **Fax:** (302)731-1057. **E-mail:** committees@reading.org. **Website:** www.reading.org. Offered to reward author of an original short story published for the first time in a periodical for children. Write for guidelines or download from website. Deadline: November 15. Prize: Prize: $1,000 stipend.

ALICE WOOD MEMORIAL OHIOANA AWARD FOR CHILDREN'S LITERATURE

274 E. First Ave., Suite 300, Columbus OH 43201. (614)466-3831. **Fax:** (614)728-6974. **E-mail:** ohioana@ohioana.org. **Website:** www.ohioana.org. **Contact:** Linda R. Hengst. Offered to an author whose body of work has made, and continues to make, a significant contribution to literature for children or young adults, and through their work as a writer, teacher, administrator, and community member, interest in children's literature has been encouraged and children have become involved with reading. Nomination forms for SASE. Recipient must have been born in Ohio or lived in Ohio at least 5 years. Guidelines for SASE. Accepts inquiries by phone and e-mail. Results announced in August or September. Winners notified by letter in May. For contest results, call or e-mail Ohioana Library: Linda Hengst, executive director. Deadline: December 31. Prize: $1,000.

WRITE A STORY FOR CHILDREN COMPETITION

Phone/Fax: (44)(148)783-2752. **E-mail:** enquiries@childrens-writers.co.uk. **Website:** www.childrens-writers.co.uk. **Contact:** Contest director. Annual contest for the best unpublished short story writer for children. Guidelines and entry forms online or send

CONTESTS, GRANTS & AWARDS

SAE/IRC. Open to any unpublished writer over the age of 18. Deadline:April 30. Prize: Prize: 1st Place: £2,000; 2nd Place: £300; 3rd Place: £200. Judged by a panel appointed by the Academy of Children's Writers.

WRITE NOW

Indiana Repertory Theatre, 140 W. Washington St., Indianapolis IN 46204. 480-921-5770. **E-mail:** info@writenow.co. **Website:** www.writenow.co. A national effort to advocate for playwrights and promote the development of new work for young audiences by: supporting the work of emerging and established playwrights through a biennial national competition and process-focused workshop; engaging a broad representation of the TYA field in an ongoing conversation about new play development; creating a stronger environment for new work by fostering connections and collaborations; cultivating a common language of shared values about new work from the perspectives of playwrights, producers, community stakeholders, and academia. The purpose of this biennial workshop is to encourage writers to create strikingly original scripts for young audiences. Playwrights from across the country are invited to submit scripts for review by a panel of peers. All submitted scripts will receive constructive feedback at the request of the playwright. At least four scripts will be selected as finalists to participate in the full workshop process, which includes a week on site at Childsplay with a development team, followed by a reading of the script at the Write Now gathering (transportation, housing, and a cash prize will be provided to the finalists). Semi-finalists will also be invited to read excerpts from their scripts at the Write Now gathering. Deadline: July 31.

WRITER'S DIGEST INTERNATIONAL SELF-PUBLISHED BOOK AWARDS

(715)445-4612, ext. 13430. **E-mail:** WritersDigestWritingCompetition@fwmedia.com. **Website:** www.writersdigest.com. **Contact:** Nicole Florence. Contest open to all English-language self-published books for which the authors have paid the full cost of publication, or the cost of printing has been paid for by a grant or as part of a prize. Categories include: Mainstream/Literary Fiction, Genre Fiction, Nonfiction, Inspirational (spiritual/new age), Life Stories (biographies/autobiographies/family histories/memoirs), Children's Books, Reference Books (directories/encyclopedias/guide books), Poetry, Middle-Grade/Young Adult Books. Deadline: May 1; Early bird deadline: April 1. Prize: Grand Prize: $3,000, promotion in *Writer's Digest* and *Publisher's Weekly*, and 10 copies of the book will be sent to major review houses with a guaranteed review in *Midwest Book Review*; 1st Place (9 winners): $1,000, promotion in *Writer's Digest*; Honorable Mentions: promotion in *Writer's Digest*, $50 of Writer's Digest Books, and a certificate.

WRITERS-EDITORS NETWORK ANNUAL INTERNATIONAL WRITING COMPETITION

E-mail: contest@writers-editors.com. **E-mail:** info@writers-editors.com. **Website:** www.writers-editors.com. **Contact:** Dana K. Cassell, executive director. Annual award to recognize publishable talent. Categories: Nonfiction (previously published article/essay/column/nonfiction book chapter; unpublished or self-published article/essay/column/nonfiction book chapter); fiction (unpublished or self-published short story or novel chapter); children's literature (unpublished or self-published short story/nonfiction article/book chapter/poem); poetry (unpublished or self-published free verse/traditional). Guidelines available online. Open to any writer. Accepts inquiries by e-mail, phone and mail. Entry form online. Results announced May 31. Winners notified by mail and posted on website. Results available for SASE or visit website. Deadline: March 15. Prize: Prize: 1st Place: $100; 2nd Place: $75; 3rd Place: $50. All winners and Honorable Mentions will receive certificates as warranted. Judged by editors, librarians, and writers.

☯ WRITERS GUILD OF ALBERTA AWARDS

Percy Page Centre, 11759 Groat Rd., Edmonton AB T5M 3K6 Canada. (780)422-8174. **Fax:** (780)422-2663. **E-mail:** mail@writersguild.ab.ca. **Website:** www.writersguild.ab.ca. **Contact:** Executive Director. Offers the following awards: Wilfrid Eggleston Award for Nonfiction; Georges Bugnet Award for Fiction; Howard O'Hagan Award for Short Story; Stephan G. Stephansson Award for Poetry; R. Ross Annett Award for Children's Literature; Gwen Pharis Ringwood Award for Drama; Jon Whyte Memorial Essay Prize; James H. Gray Award for Short Nonfiction; Amber Bowerman Memorial Travel Writing Award. Eligible entries will have been published anywhere in the world between January 1 and December 31 of the current year. The authors must have been residents of Alberta for at least 12 of the 18 months prior to December 31. Unpublished mss, except in the drama, essay, and short nonfiction categories, are not eligible. Anthologies are not eligible. Works may be submitted by authors, publishers, or any interested parties. Deadline: December 31. Prize: Prize: Winning authors receive $1,500; essay prize winners receive $700.

WRITERS' LEAGUE OF TEXAS BOOK AWARDS

611 S. Congress Ave., Suite 505, Austin TX 78704. (512)499-8914. **Fax:** (512)499-0441. **E-mail:** wlt@writersleague.org. **E-mail:** sara@writersleague.org. **Website:** www.writersleague.org. Open to Texas authors of books published the previous two years. Authors are required to show proof of Texas residency, but are not required to be members of the Writers' League of Texas. Deadline: Open to submissions from January 1 to April 30. Prize: Prize: $750, a commemorative award, and an appearance at a WLT Third Thursday panel at BookPeople in Austin, TX.

WRITING CONFERENCE WRITING CONTESTS

P.O. Box 664, Ottawa KS 66067-0664. (785)242-1995. **Fax:** (785)242-1995. **E-mail:** jbushman@writingconference.com. **E-mail:** support@studentq.com. **Website:** www.writingconference.com. **Contact:** John H. Bushman, contest director. Unpublished submissions only. Submissions made by the author or teacher. Purpose of contest: to further writing by students with awards for narration, exposition and poetry at the elementary, middle school and high school levels. Deadline: January 8. Prize: Prize: Awards plaque and publication of winning entry in The Writers' Slate online, April issue. Judged by a panel of teachers.

YEARBOOK EXCELLENCE CONTEST

100 Adler Journalism Building, Iowa City IA 52242-2004. (319)335-3457. **Fax:** (319)335-3989. **E-mail:** quill-scroll@uiowa.edu. **Website:** www.uiowa.edu/~quill-sc. **Contact:** Vanessa Shelton, executive director. High school students who are contributors to or staff members of a student yearbook at any public or private high school are invited to enter the competition. Awards will be made in each of the 18 divisions. There are two enrollment categories: Class A: more than 750 students; Class B: 749 or less. Winners will receive Quill and Scroll's National Award Gold Key and, if seniors, are eligible to apply for one of the Edward J. Nell Memorial or George and Ophelia

Gallup scholarships. Open to students whose schools have Quill and Scroll charters.Previously published submissions only. Submissions made by the author or school yearbook adviser. Must be published in the 12-month span prior to contest deadline. Visit website for list of current and previous winners. To recognize and reward student journalists for their work in yearbooks and to provide student winners an opportunity to apply for a scholarship to be used freshman year in college for students planning to major in journalism. Deadline: November 1.

☁ YOUNG ADULT CANADIAN BOOK AWARD

1150 Morrison Dr., Suite 400, Ottawa ON K2H 8S9 Canada. (613)232-9625. **Fax:** (613)563-9895. **Website:** www.cla.ca. **Contact:** Barb Janicek. This award recognizes an author of an outstanding English language Canadian book which appeals to young adults between the ages of 13 and 18. To be eligible for consideration, the following must apply; it must be a work of fiction (novel, collection of short stories, or graphic novel), the title must be a Canadian publication in either hardcover or paperback, and the author must be a Canadian citizen or landed immigrant. The award is given annually, when merited, at the Canadian Library Association's annual conference. Established in 1980 by the Young Adult Caucus of the Saskatchewan Library Association. Deadline: December 1. Prize: Prize: $1,000.

YOUNG READER'S CHOICE AWARD

E-mail: jwilson@yrl.ab.ca. **Website:** www.pnla.org. **Contact:** Jocie Wilson. "Nominated titles are those published 3 years prior to the award year (for example, for the 2011 list nominees must have a copyright date of 2008), printed in the U.S. or Canada, and are already favorites with readers. All nominations will be reviewed and voted on by a committee assigned to a particular division (Junior/Middle/Senior) and consisting of at least four (4) people (two YRCA state/provincial representatives and at least two persons of their choosing)." Deadline: February 1. "Books will be judged on popularity with readers. Age appropriateness will be considered when choosing which of the three divisions a book is placed. Other considerations may include reading enjoyment; reading level; interest level; genre representation; gender representation; racial diversity; diversity of social, political, economic, or religions viewpoints; regional consideration; effectiveness of expression; and imagination. The Pacific Northwest Library Association is committed to intellectual freedom and diversity of ideas. No title will be excluded because of race, nationality, religion, gender, sexual orientation, political or social view of either the author or the material."

THE YOUTH HONOR AWARD PROGRAM

Skipping Stones Magazine, P.O. Box 3939, Eugene OR 97403. (541)342-4956. **E-mail:** info@skippingstones.org. **E-mail:** editor@skippingstones.org. **Website:** www.skippingstones.org. **Contact:** Arun N. Toke, Editor and Publisher. "Original writing and art from youth, ages 7 to 17, should be typed or neatly handwritten. The entries should be appropriate for ages 7 to 17. Prose under 1,000 words; poems under 30 lines. Non-English and bilingual writings are welcome." To promote multicultural, international and nature awareness. Deadline: June 25. Prize: Prize: An Honor Award Certificate, a subscription to Skipping Stones and five nature and/or multicultural books. They are also invited to join the Student Review Board.

ANNA ZORNIO MEMORIAL CHILDREN'S THEATRE PLAYWRITING COMPETITION

Department of Theatre and Dance, PCAC, 30 Academic Way, Durham NH 03824. (603)862-3044. **Fax:** (603)862-0298. **E-mail:** mike.wood@unh.edu. **Website:** www.unh.edu/theatre-dance/zornio. **Contact:** Michael Wood. Offered every 4 years for unpublished well-written plays or musicals appropriate for young audiences with a maximum length of 60 minutes. May submit more than 1 play, but not more than 3. Purpose of the award: "to honor the late Anna Zornio, an alumna of The University of New Hampshire, for dedication to and inspiration of playwriting for young people, K-12th grade." Deadline: March of 2016. Prize: Prize: $500.

SUBJECT INDEX

ANIMAL

BIOGRAPHY

HISTORY (NONFICTION)

HOBBIES

HOLIDAY

HUMOR (NONFICTION)

INTERVIEW/PEOPLE

MULTICULTURAL (NONFICTION)

MUSIC/DANCE/DRAMA

PROBLEM-SOLVING

PROBLEM-SOLVING (NONFICTION)

TEXTBOOKS

TRAVEL

EDITOR AND AGENT NAMES INDEX

AGE-LEVEL INDEX

PHOTOGRAPHY INDEX

MAGAZINES

ILLUSTRATION INDEX

POETRY INDEX

GENERAL INDEX

WRITER'S DIGEST

Is Your Manuscript Ready?

Trust 2nd Draft Critique Service to prepare your writing to catch the eye of agents and editors. You can expect:

- Expert evaluation from a hand-selected, professional critiquer
- Know-how on reaching your target audience
- Red flags for consistency, mechanics, and grammar
- Tips on revising your manuscript and query to increase your odds of publication

Visit **WritersDigestShop.com/2nd-draft** for more information.

THE PERFECT COMPANION TO *GUIDE TO LITERARY AGENTS*

The Writer's Market Guide to Getting Published

Learn exactly what it takes to get your work into the marketplace, get it published, and get paid for it!

Available from **WritersDigestShop.com** and your favorite book retailers.

To get started, join our mailing list: **WritersDigest.com/enews**

FOLLOW US ON:

 Find more gre   ps, networking and advice by foll   ng **@writersdigest**

 And become a fan of our Facebook page: **facebook.com/writersdigest**